YOWAMUSHI PEDAL

WATARU WATANABE

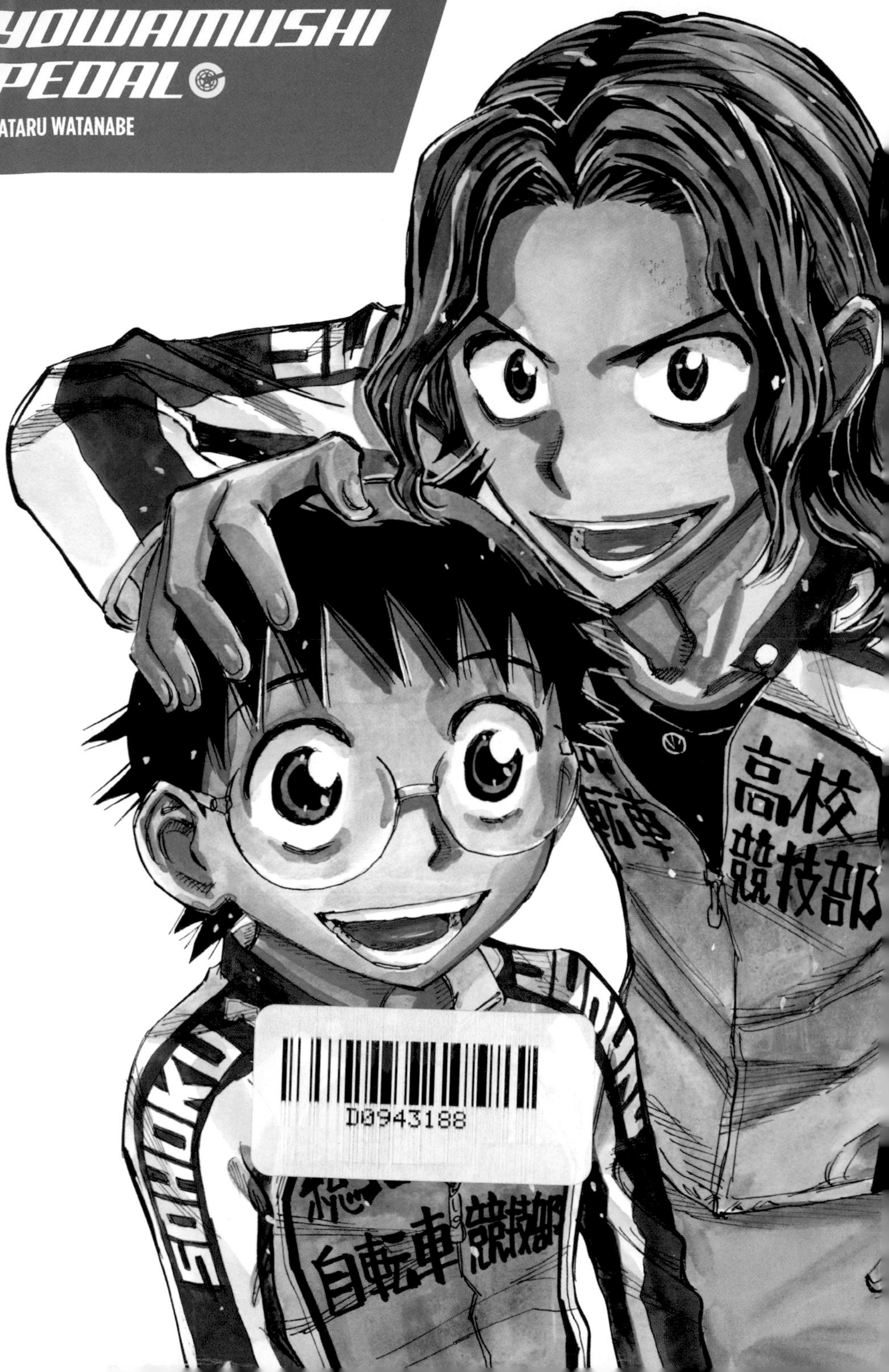
高校
競技部
SOHOKU
自転車

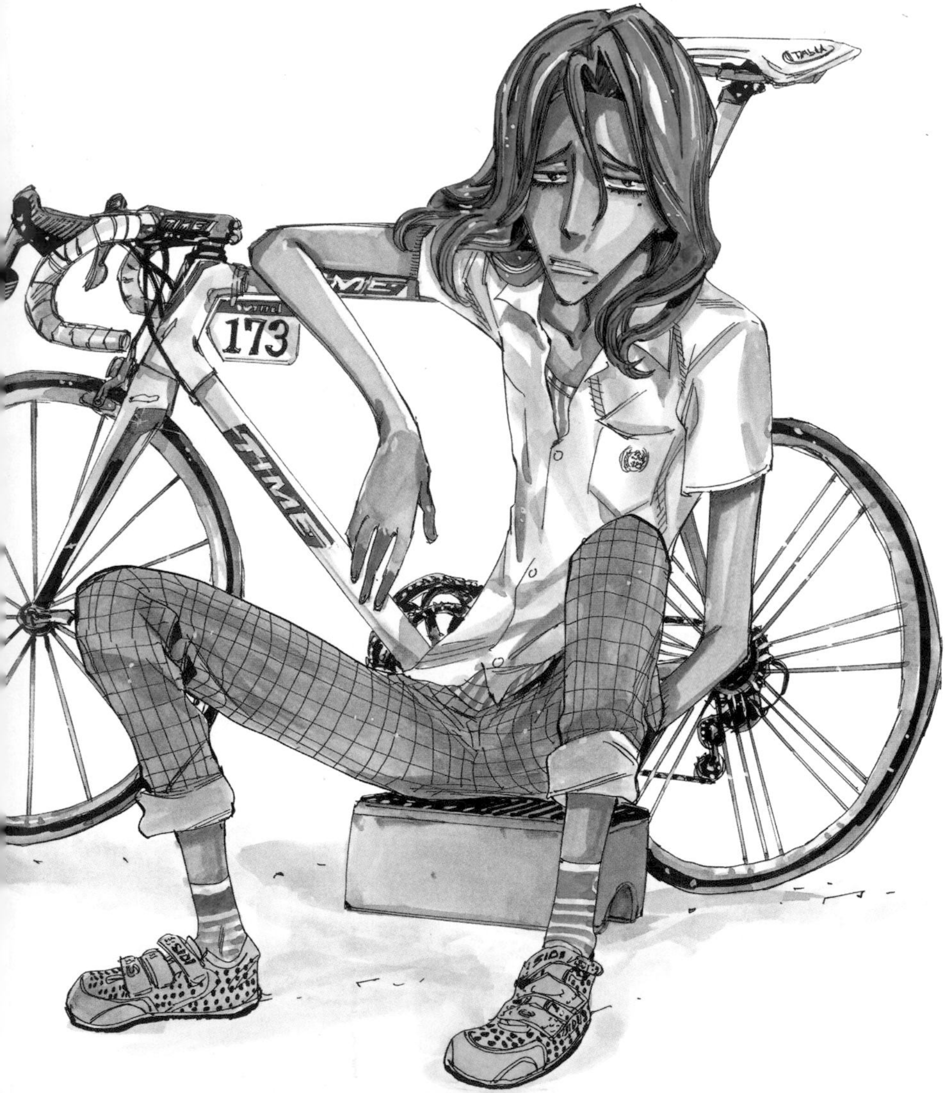
173

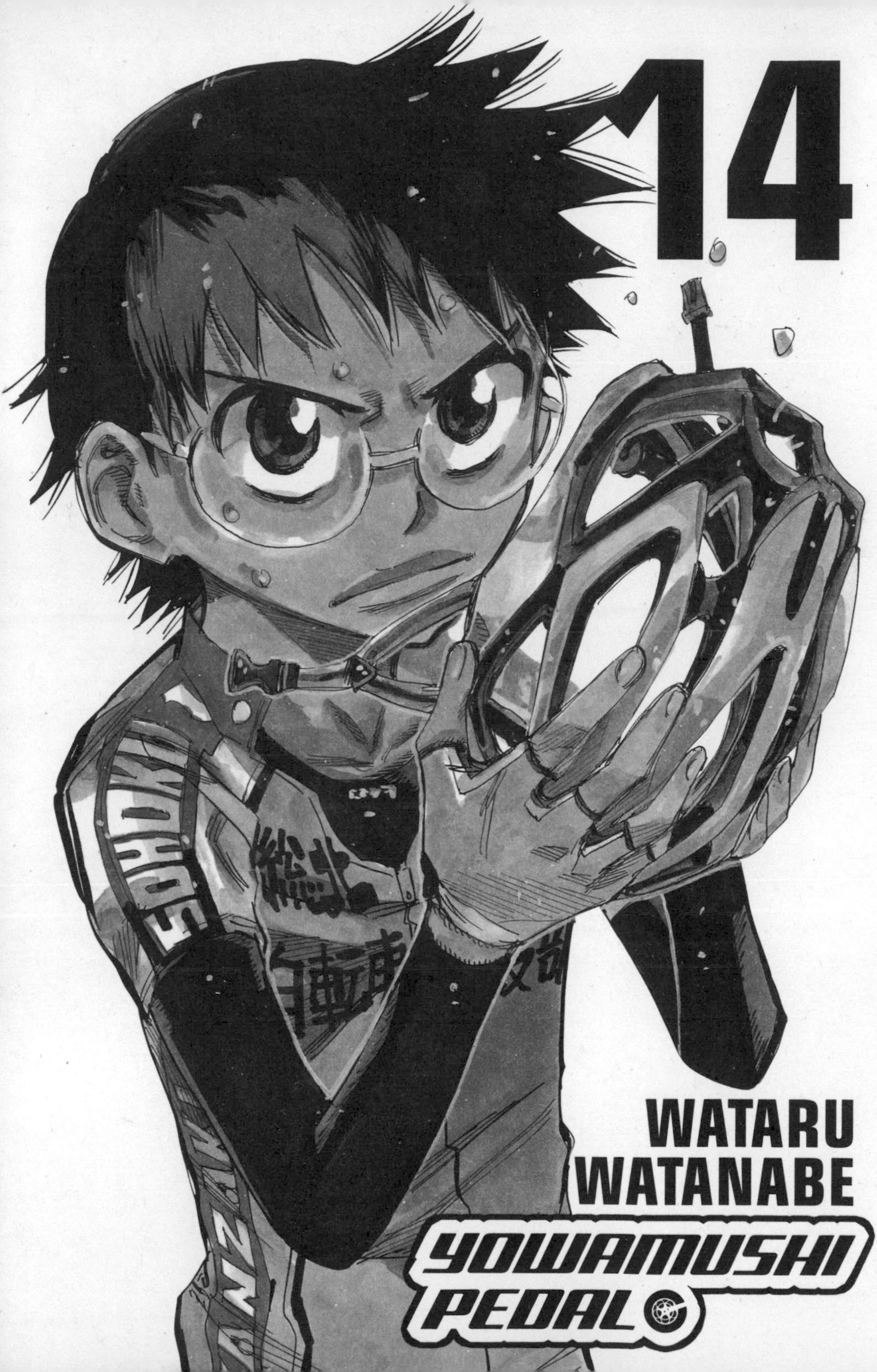

14

WATARU WATANABE

YOWAMUSHI PEDAL

YOWAMUSHI PEDAL

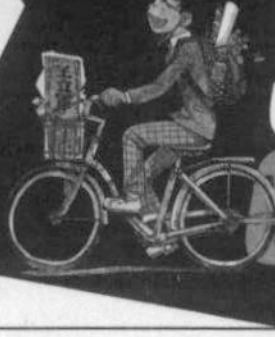

STORY & CHARACTER

INTRODUCTION

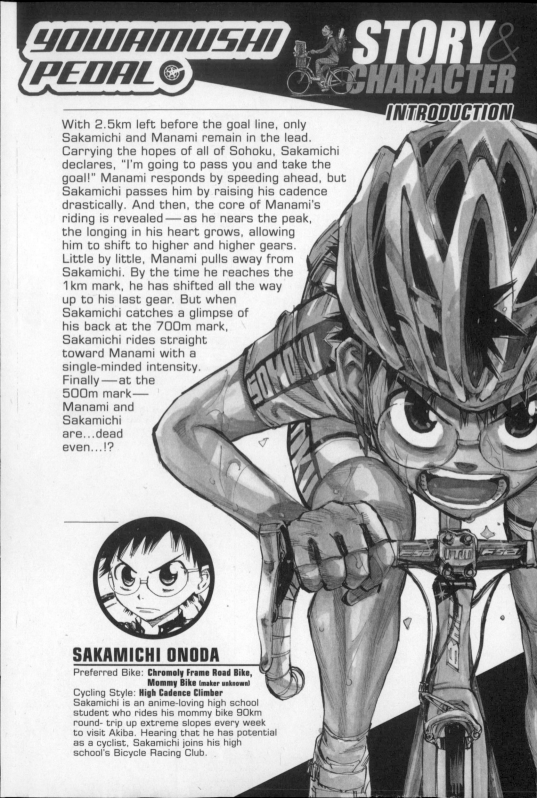

With 2.5km left before the goal line, only Sakamichi and Manami remain in the lead. Carrying the hopes of all of Sohoku, Sakamichi declares, “I’m going to pass you and take the goal!” Manami responds by speeding ahead, but Sakamichi passes him by raising his cadence drastically. And then, the core of Manami’s riding is revealed—as he nears the peak, the longing in his heart grows, allowing him to shift to higher and higher gears. Little by little, Manami pulls away from Sakamichi. By the time he reaches the 1km mark, he has shifted all the way up to his last gear. But when Sakamichi catches a glimpse of his back at the 700m mark, Sakamichi rides straight toward Manami with a single-minded intensity. Finally—at the 500m mark—Manami and Sakamichi are...dead even...!?

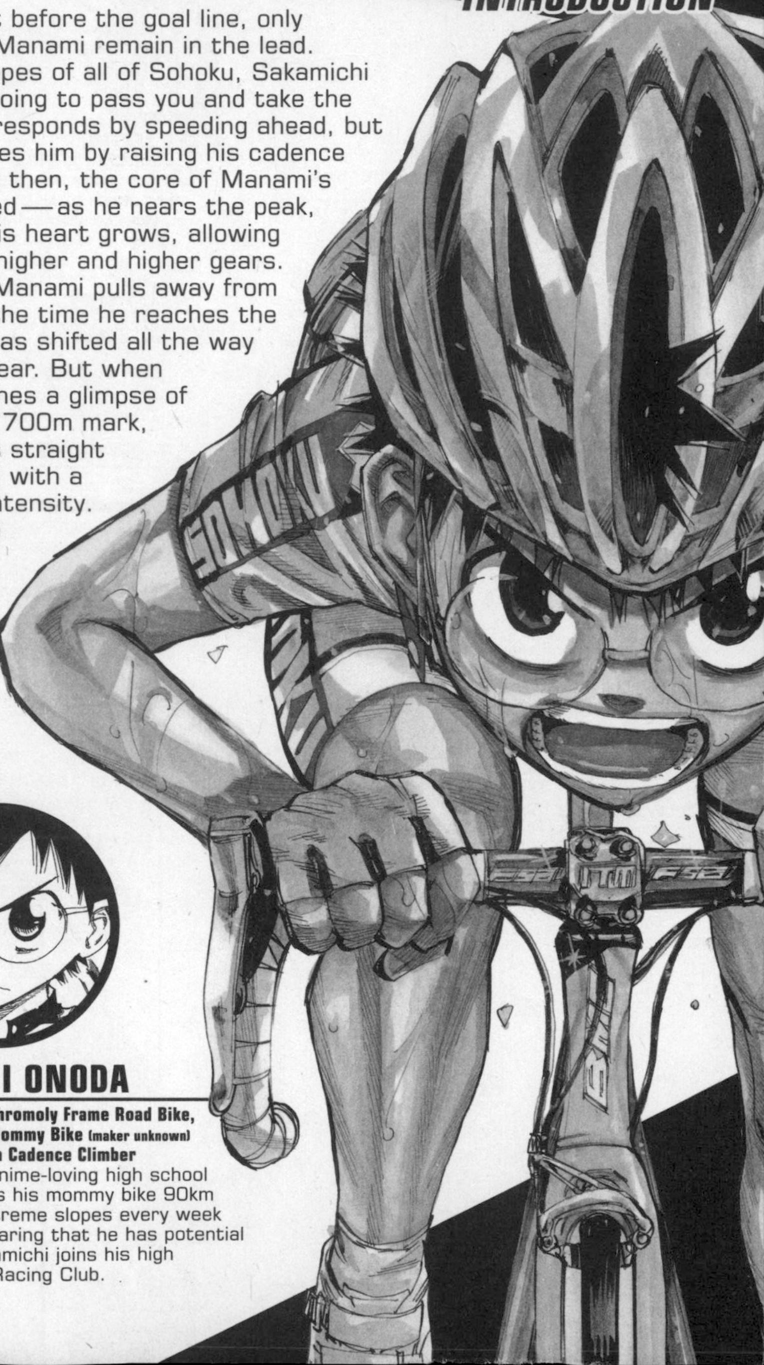

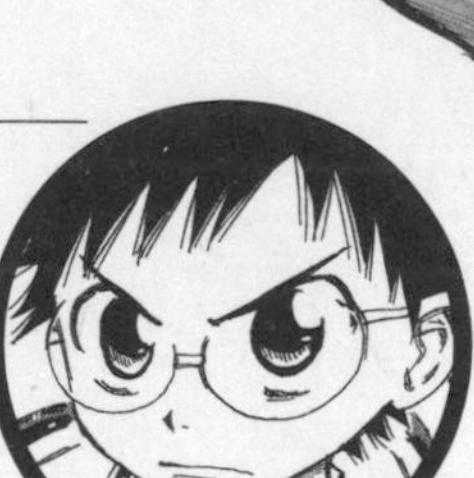

SAKAMICHI ONODA

Preferred Bike: **Chromoly Frame Road Bike, Mommy Bike** (maker unknown)
Cycling Style: **High Cadence Climber**
Sakamichi is an anime-loving high school student who rides his mommy bike 90km round- trip up extreme slopes every week to visit Akiba. Hearing that he has potential as a cyclist, Sakamichi joins his high school’s Bicycle Racing Club.

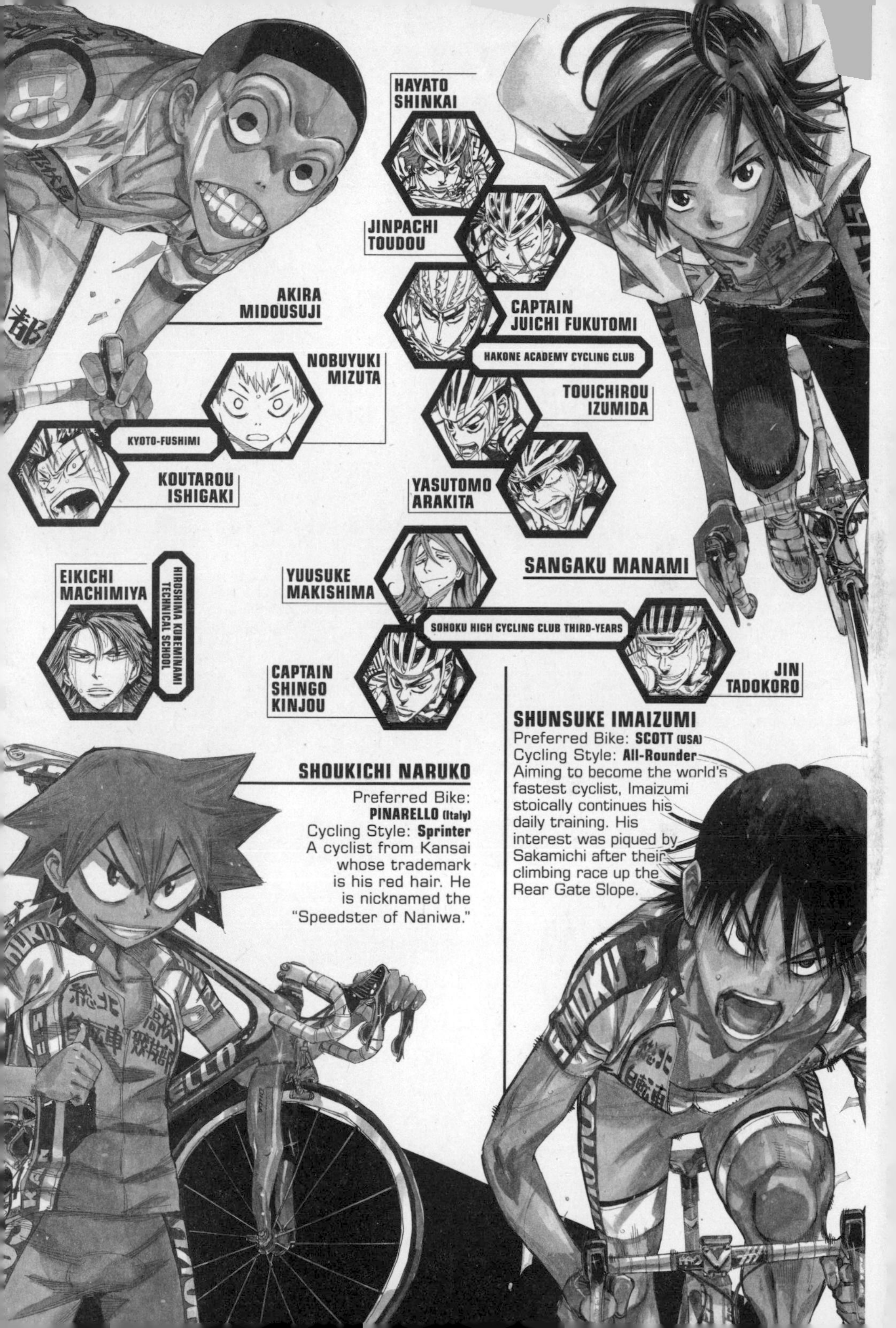
HAYATO SHINKAI
JINPACHI TOUDOU
AKIRA MIDOUSUJI
CAPTAIN JUICHI FUKUTOMI
HAKONE ACADEMY CYCLING CLUB
NOBUYUKI MIZUTA
KYOTO-FUSHIMI
KOUTAROU ISHIGAKI
TOUICHIROU IZUMIDA
YASUTOMO ARAKITA
SANGAKU MANAMI
EIKICHI MACHIMIYA
HIROSHIMA KUREMINAMI TECHNICAL SCHOOL
YUUSUKE MAKISHIMA
SOHOKU HIGH CYCLING CLUB THIRD-YEARS
CAPTAIN SHINGO KINJOU
JIN TADOKORO
SHUNSUKE IMAIZUMI
Preferred Bike: SCOTT (USA)
Cycling Style: All-Rounder
Aiming to become the world's fastest cyclist, Imaizumi stoically continues his daily training. His interest was piqued by Sakamichi after their climbing race up the Rear Gate Slope.
SHOUKICHI NARUKO
Preferred Bike: PINARELLO (Italy)
Cycling Style: Sprinter
A cyclist from Kansai whose trademark is his red hair. He is nicknamed the "Speedster of Naniwa."

VOL.14 *YOWAMUSHI PEDAL* CONTENTS

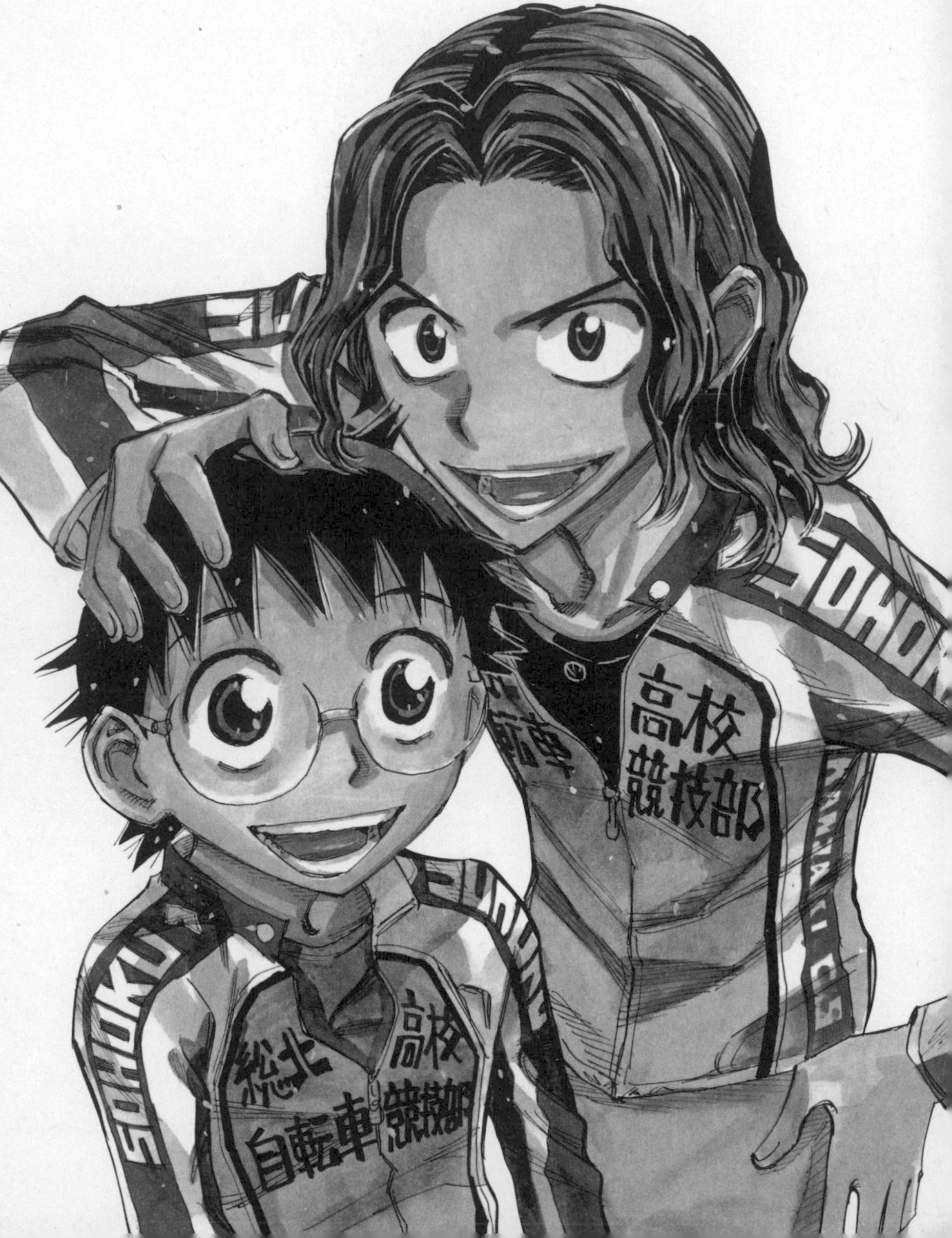
SOHOKU
総北高校
自転車競技部
高校
競技部

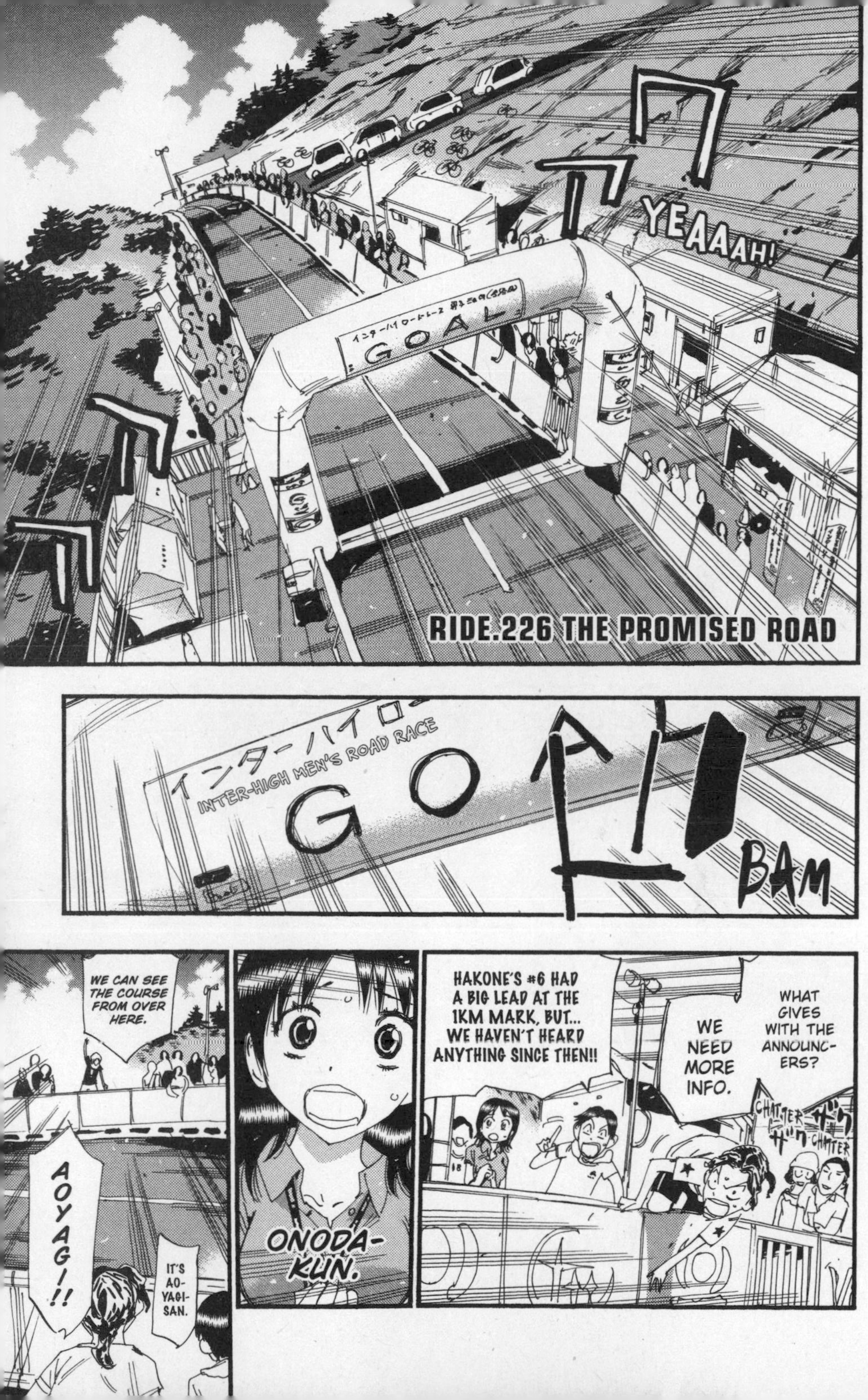
YEAAAAH!
RIDE.226 THE PROMISED ROAD
INTER-HIGH MEN'S ROAD RACE
GOAL
BAM
WHAT GIVES WITH THE ANNOUNCERS?
WE NEED MORE INFO.
HAKONE'S #6 HAD A BIG LEAD AT THE 1KM MARK, BUT... WE HAVEN'T HEARD ANYTHING SINCE THEN!!
CHATTER CHATTER
ONODA-KUN.
WE CAN SEE THE COURSE FROM OVER HERE.
AOYAGI!!
IT'S AOYAGI-SAN.

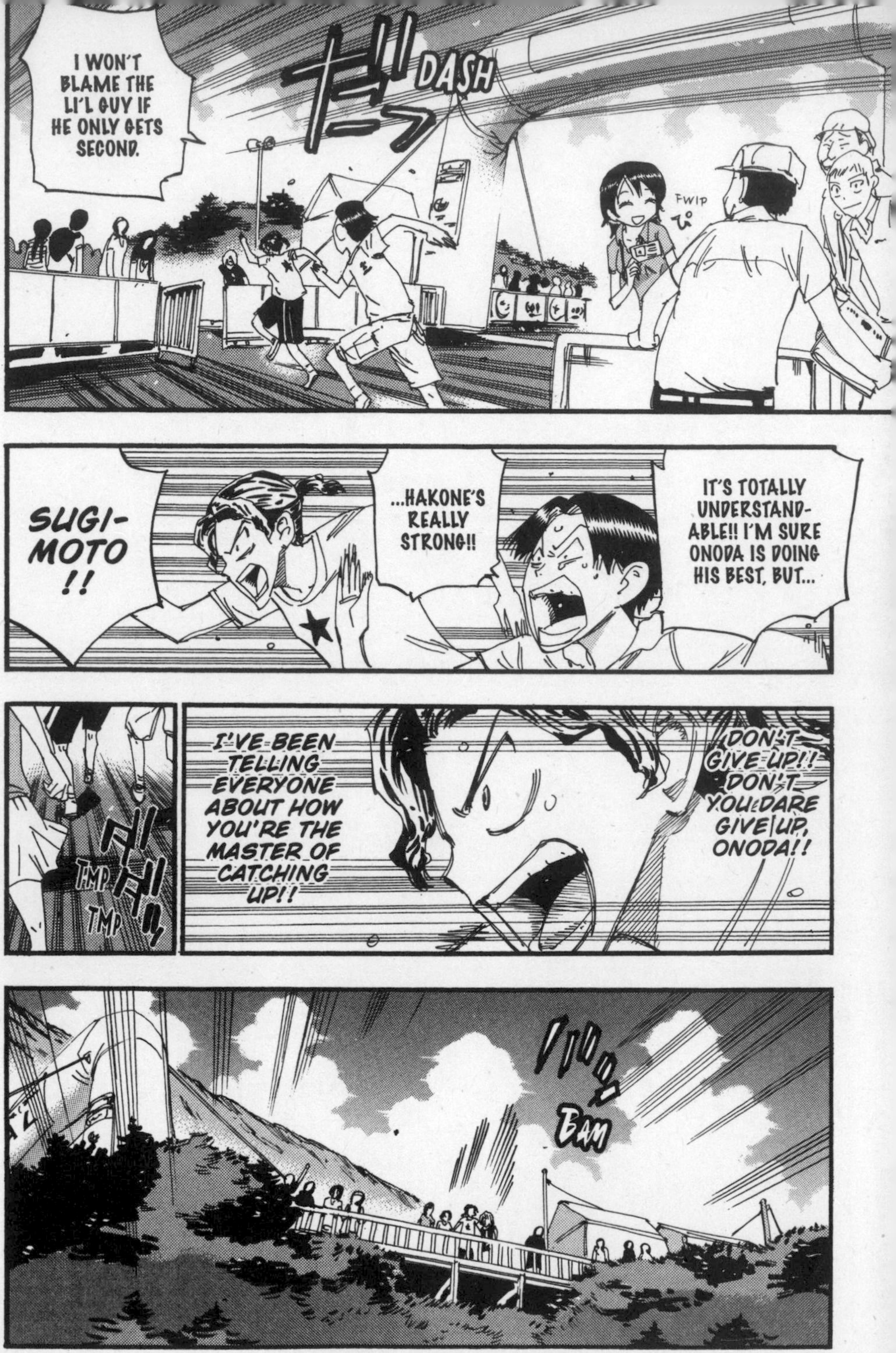
I WON'T BLAME THE LI'L GUY IF HE ONLY GETS SECOND.
DASH
FWIP
IT'S TOTALLY UNDERSTANDABLE!! I'M SURE ONODA IS DOING HIS BEST, BUT...
...HAKONE'S REALLY STRONG!!
SUGIMOTO!!
DON'T GIVE UP!! DON'T YOU DARE GIVE UP, ONODA!!
I'VE BEEN TELLING EVERYONE ABOUT HOW YOU'RE THE MASTER OF CATCHING UP!!
TMP TMP
BAM

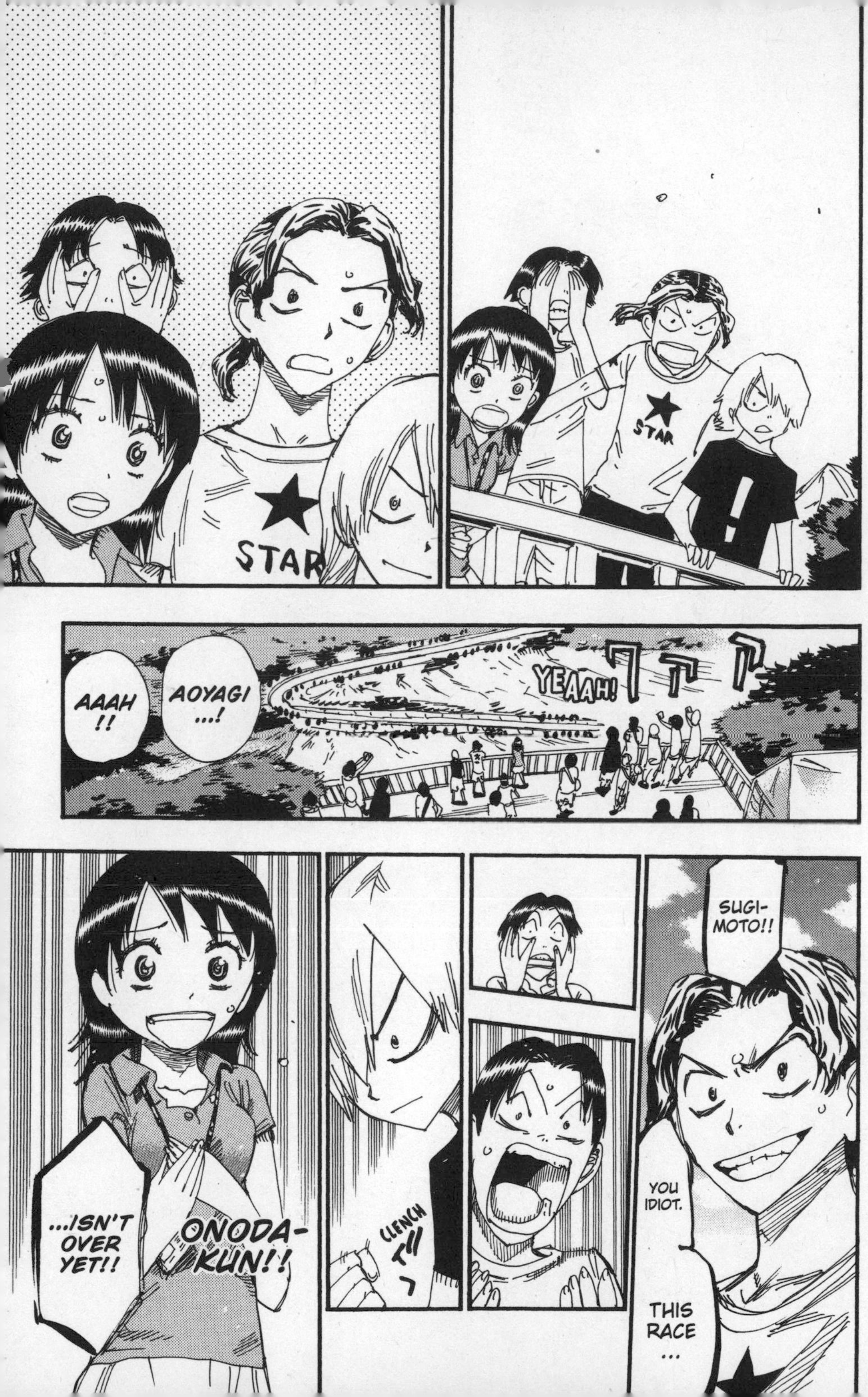
YEAAAH!
AOYAGI ...!
AAAH !!
SUGI-MOTO!!
YOU IDIOT.
THIS RACE ...
CLENCH
ONODA-KUN!!
...ISN'T OVER YET!!

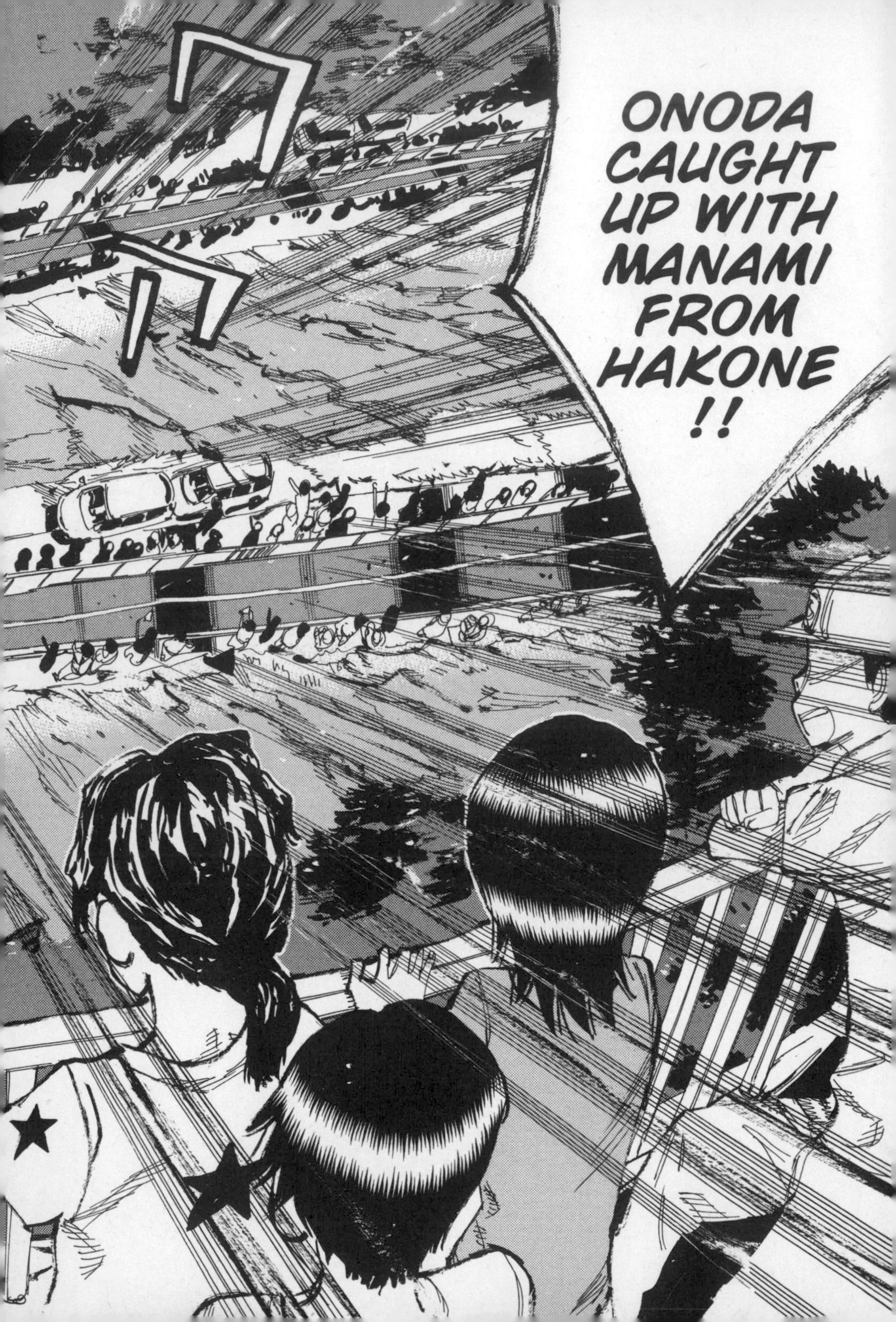
ONODA CAUGHT UP WITH MANAMI FROM HAKONE !!

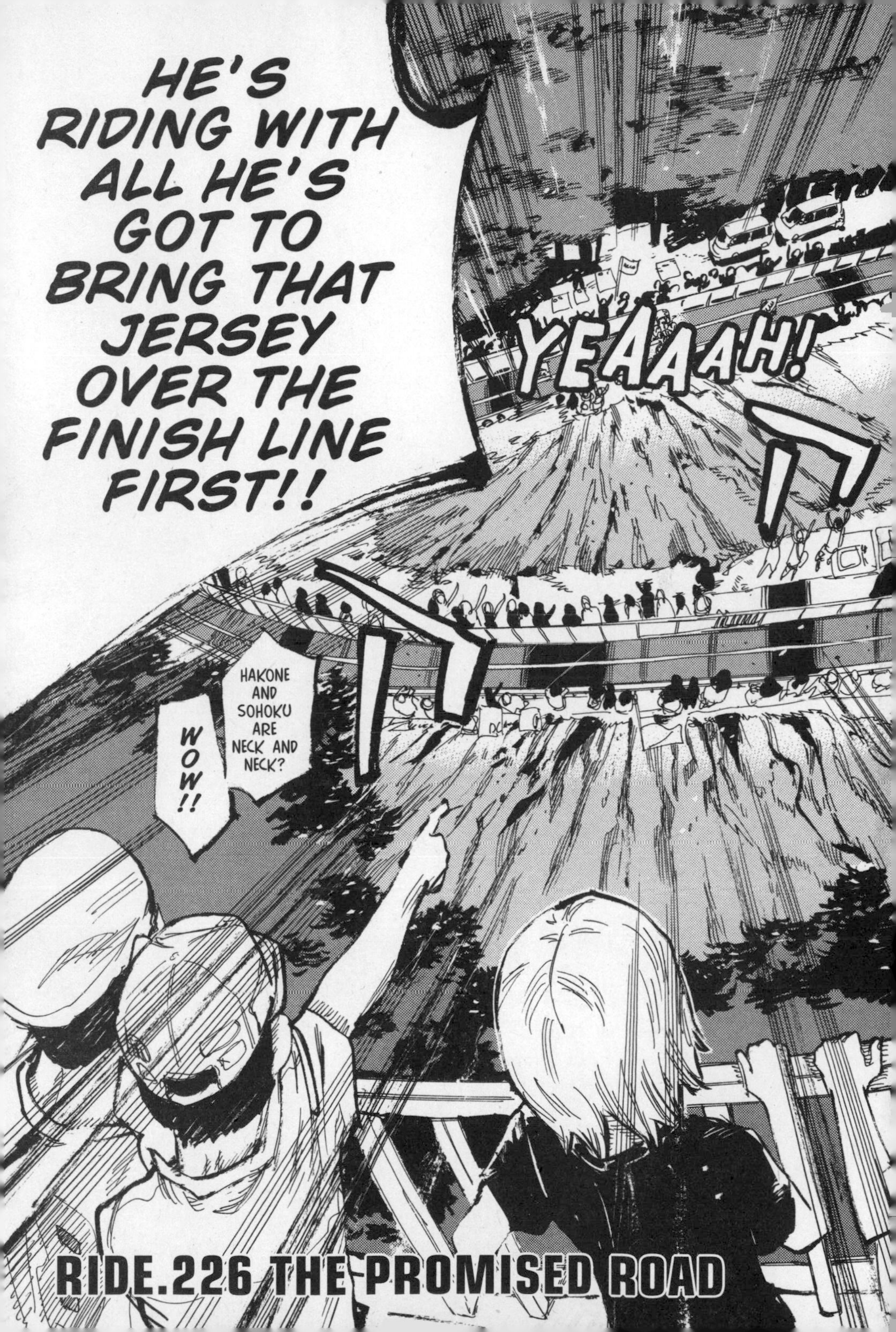
HE'S RIDING WITH ALL HE'S GOT TO BRING THAT JERSEY OVER THE FINISH LINE FIRST!!
YEAAAAH!
HAKONE AND SOHOKU ARE NECK AND NECK?
WOW!!
RIDE.226 THE PROMISED ROAD

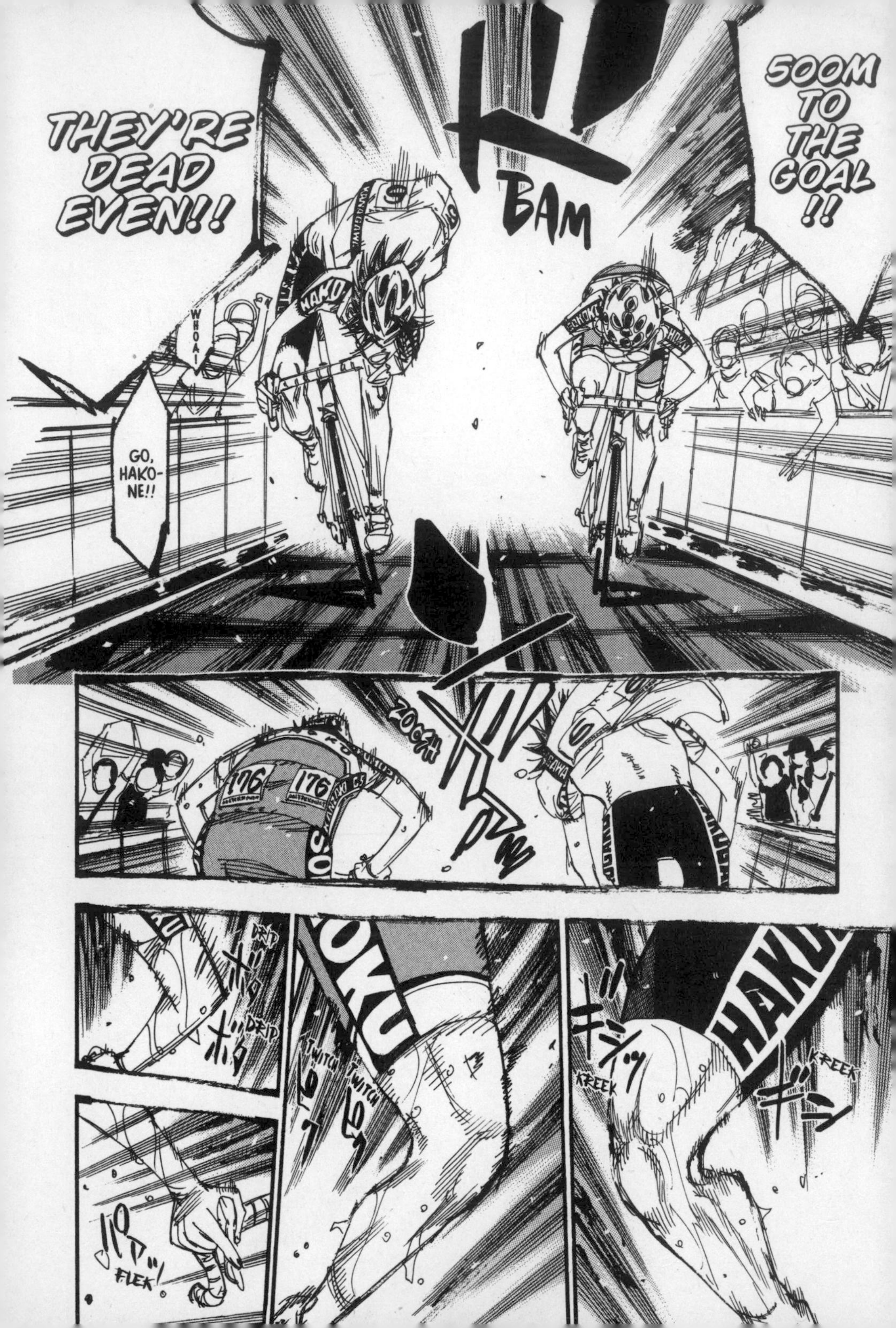
500M TO THE GOAL!!
BAM
THEY'RE DEAD EVEN!!
WHOA!
GO, HAKONE!!
ZOOM
KREEK
KREEK
TWITCH TWITCH
DRIP DRIP
FLEK!

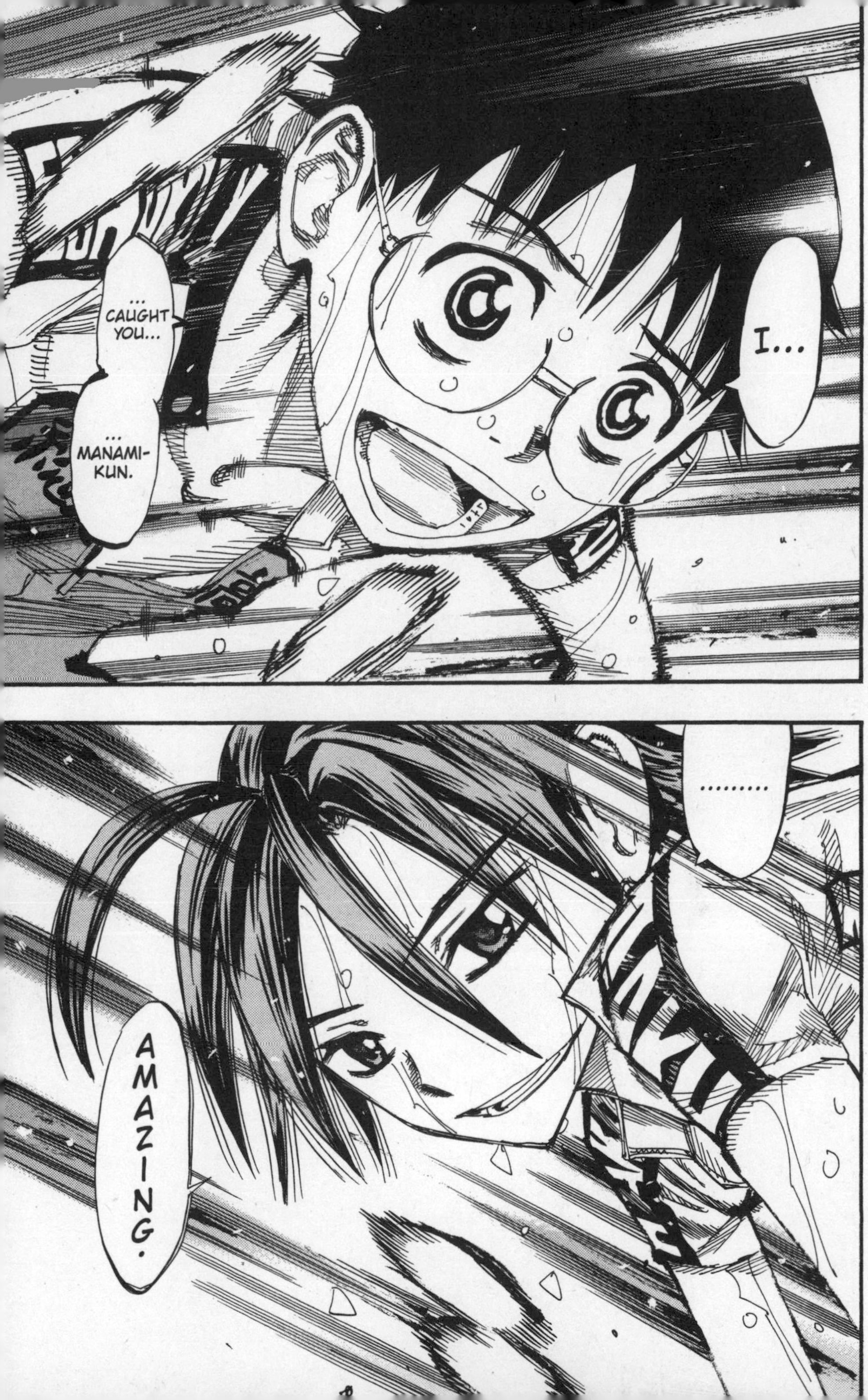
I...
...CAUGHT YOU...
...MANAMI-KUN.
....
AMAZING.

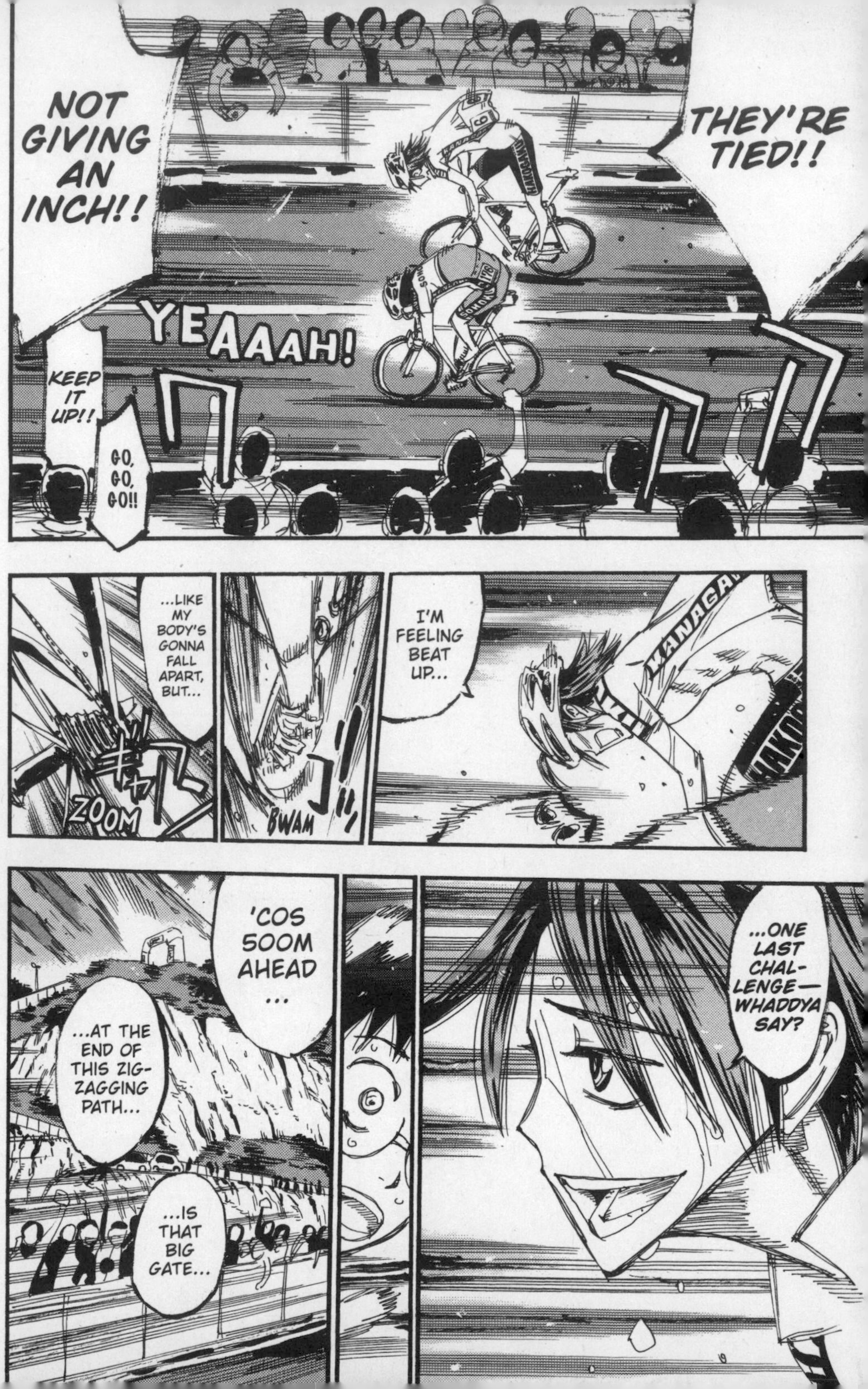
THEY'RE TIED!!
NOT GIVING AN INCH!!
YEAAAH!
KEEP IT UP!!
GO, GO, GO!!
I'M FEELING BEAT UP...
BWAM
...LIKE MY BODY'S GONNA FALL APART, BUT...
ZOOM
...ONE LAST CHAL-LENGE—WHADDYA SAY?
'COS 500M AHEAD ...
...AT THE END OF THIS ZIG-ZAGGING PATH...
...IS THAT BIG GATE...

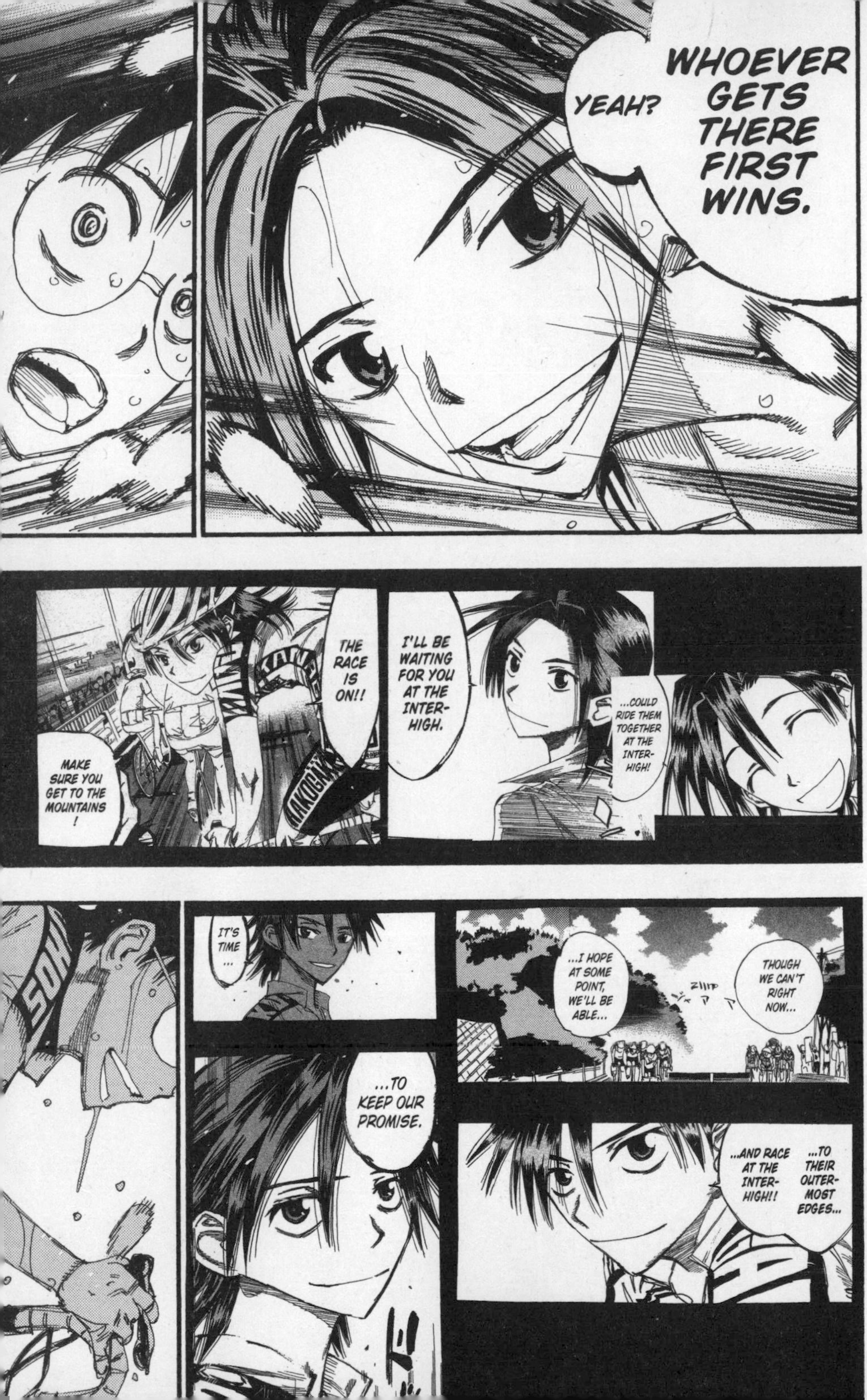
WHOEVER GETS THERE FIRST WINS.
YEAH?
...COULD RIDE THEM TOGETHER AT THE INTER-HIGH!
I'LL BE WAITING FOR YOU AT THE INTER-HIGH.
THE RACE IS ON!!
MAKE SURE YOU GET TO THE MOUNTAINS!
THOUGH WE CAN'T RIGHT NOW...
ZIIIP
...I HOPE AT SOME POINT, WE'LL BE ABLE...
IT'S TIME...
...TO THEIR OUTER-MOST EDGES...
...AND RACE AT THE INTER-HIGH!!
...TO KEEP OUR PROMISE.

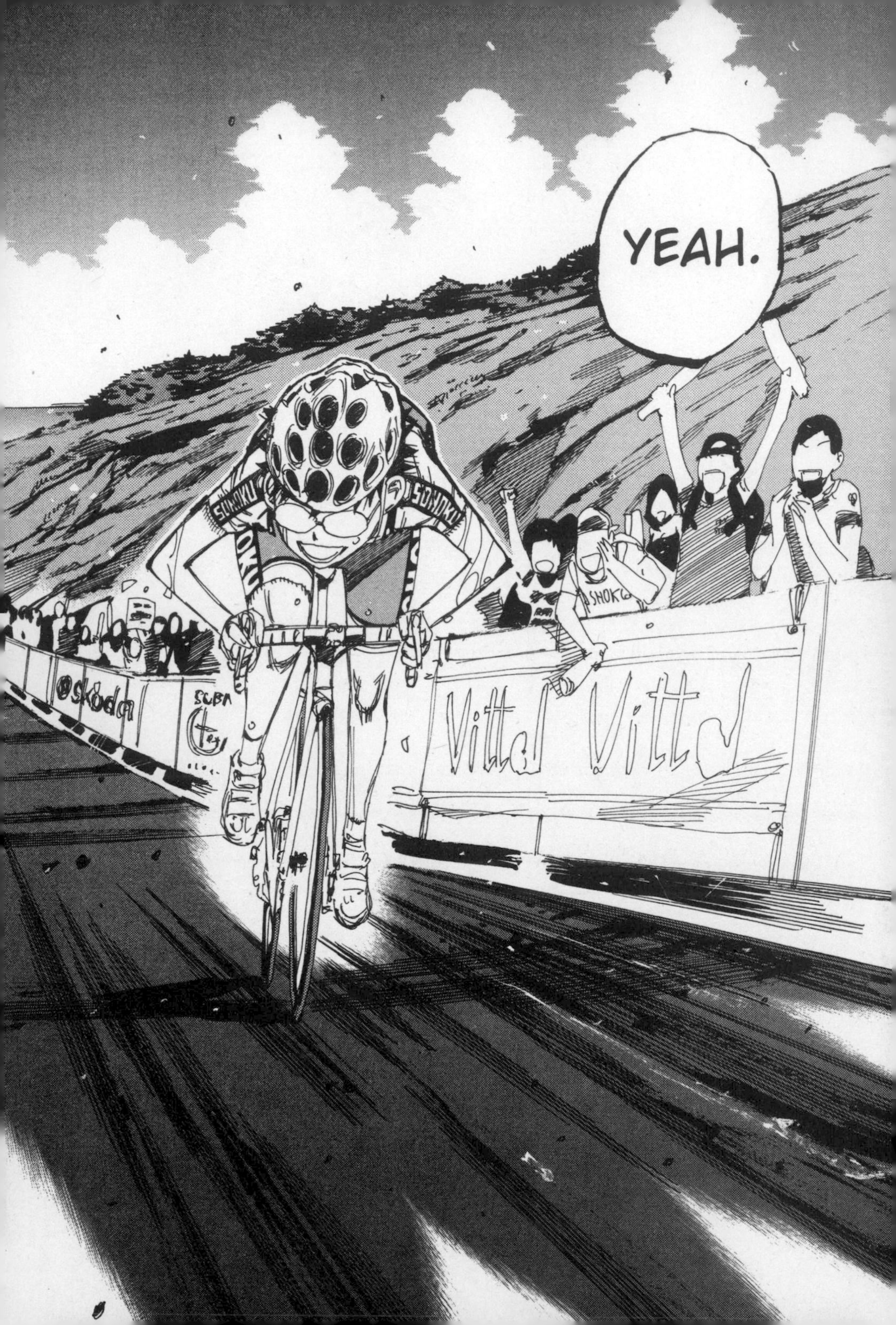
YEAH.

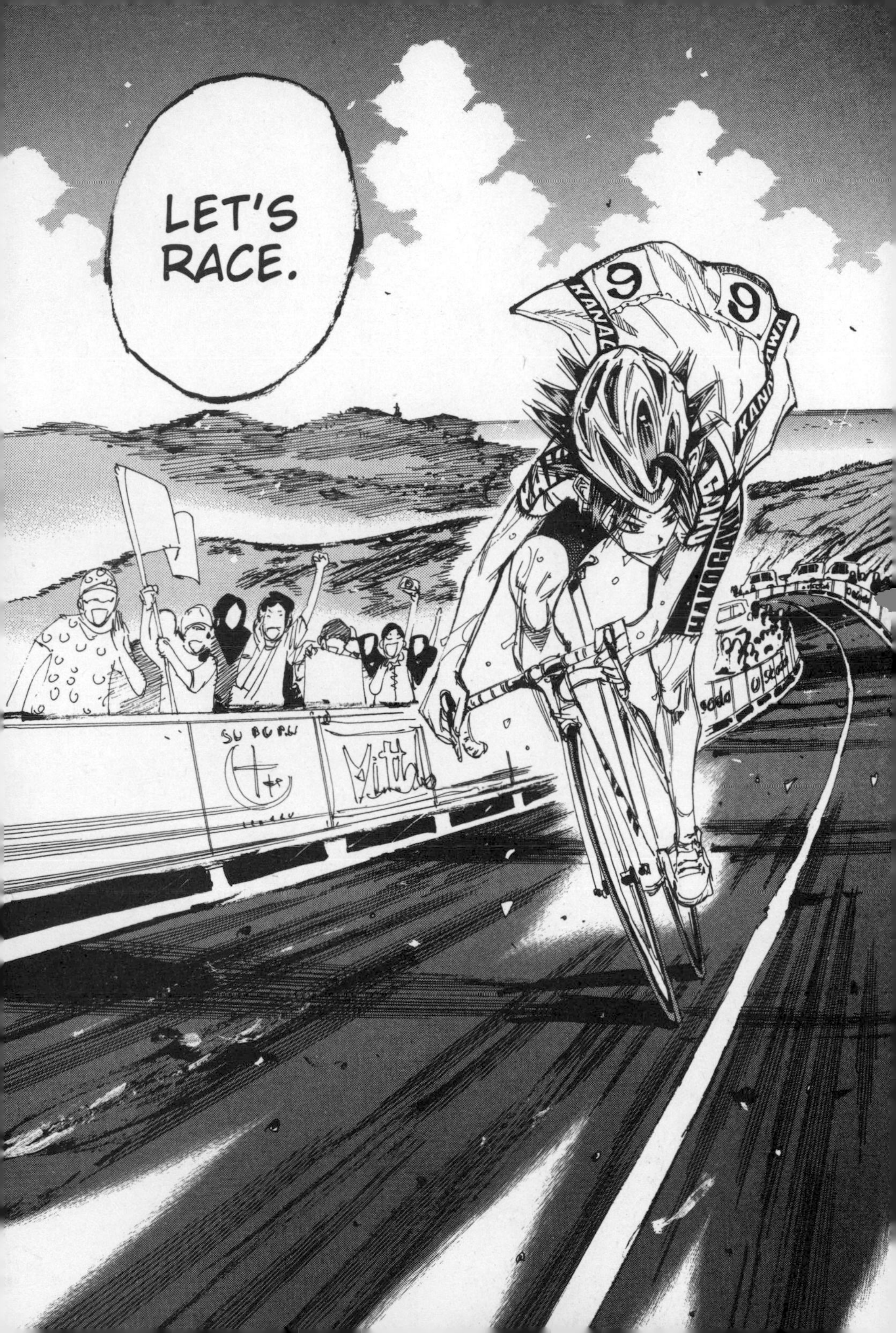
LET'S RACE.
HAKOGAKU

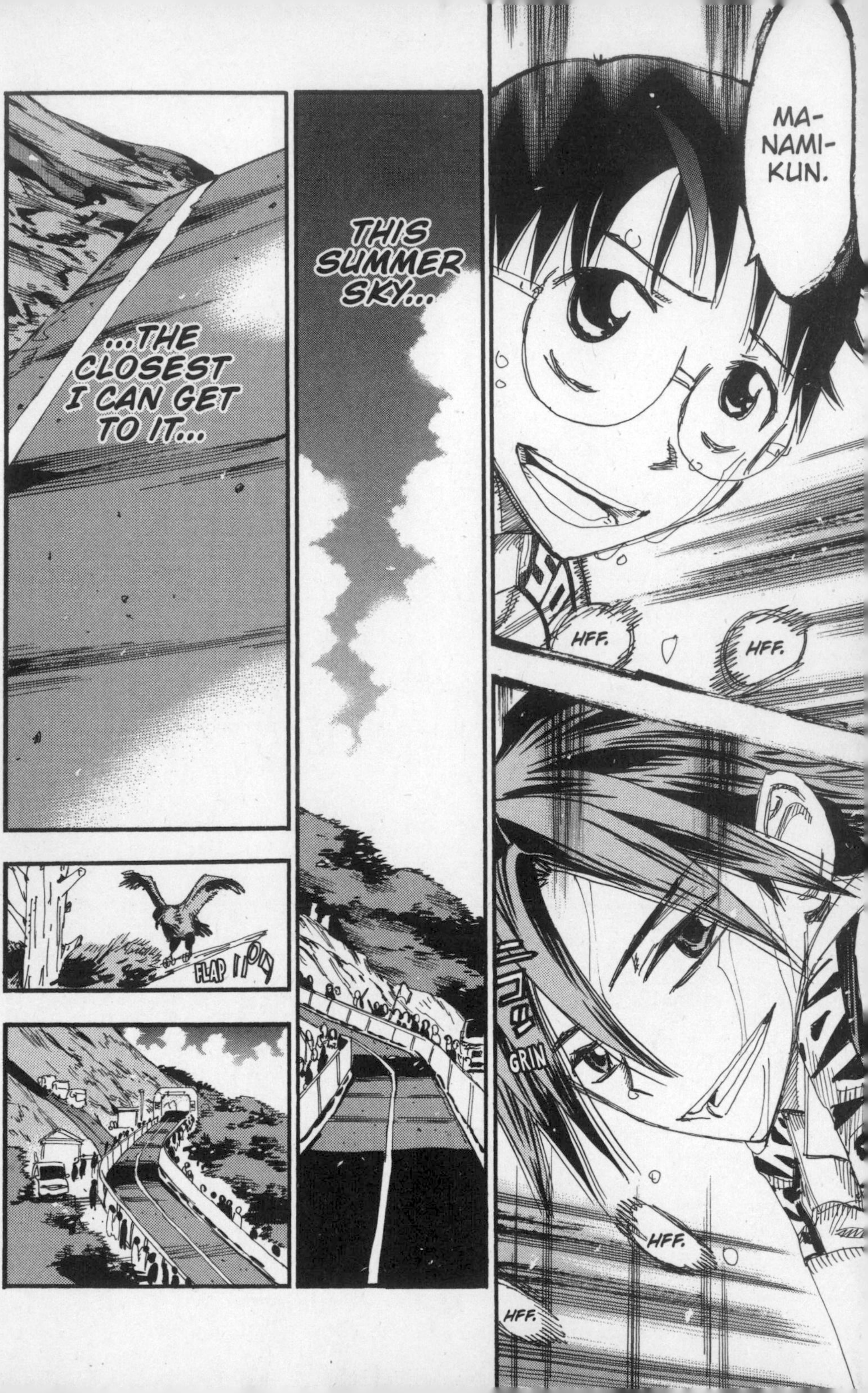

MA-NAMI-KUN.
HFF.
HFF.
GRIN
HFF.
HFF.
THIS SUMMER SKY...
...THE CLOSEST I CAN GET TO IT...
FLAP

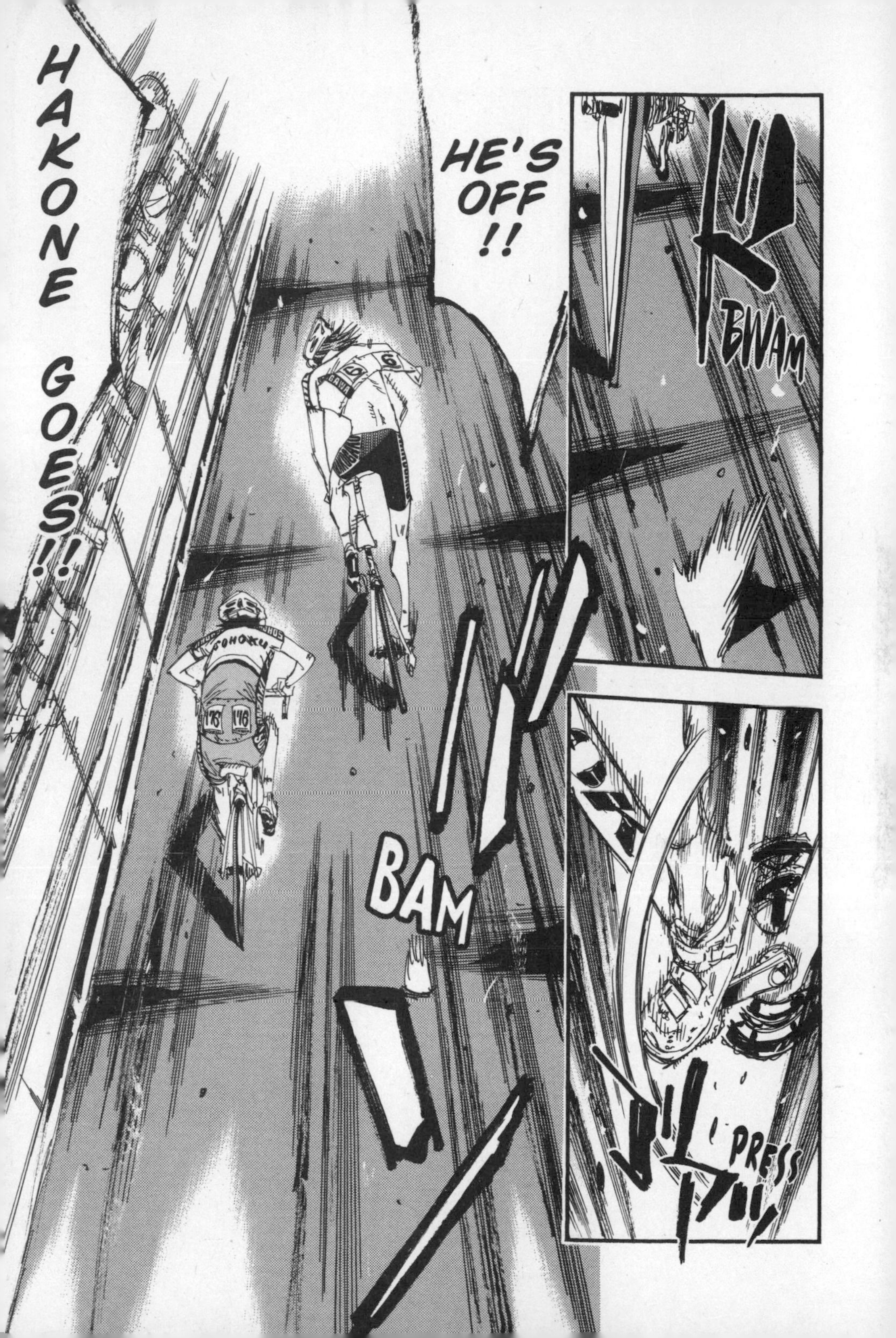
BWAM
PRESS
HE'S OFF!!
BAM
HAKONE GOES!!

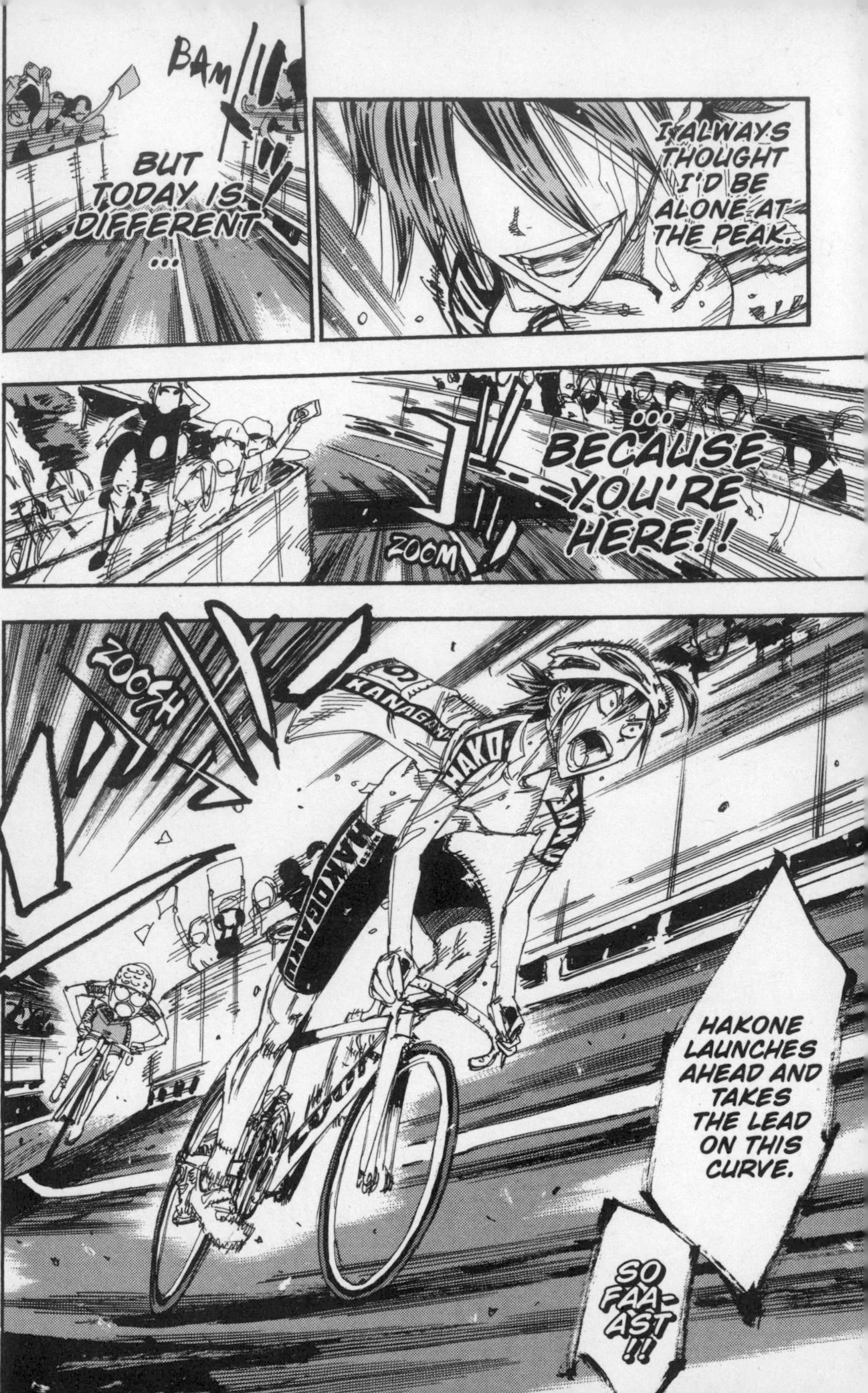
I ALWAYS THOUGHT I'D BE ALONE AT THE PEAK.
BAM!!
BUT TODAY IS DIFFERENT...
...BECAUSE YOU'RE HERE!!
ZOOM
ZOOSH
HAKONE LAUNCHES AHEAD AND TAKES THE LEAD ON THIS CURVE.
SO FAA-AST!!

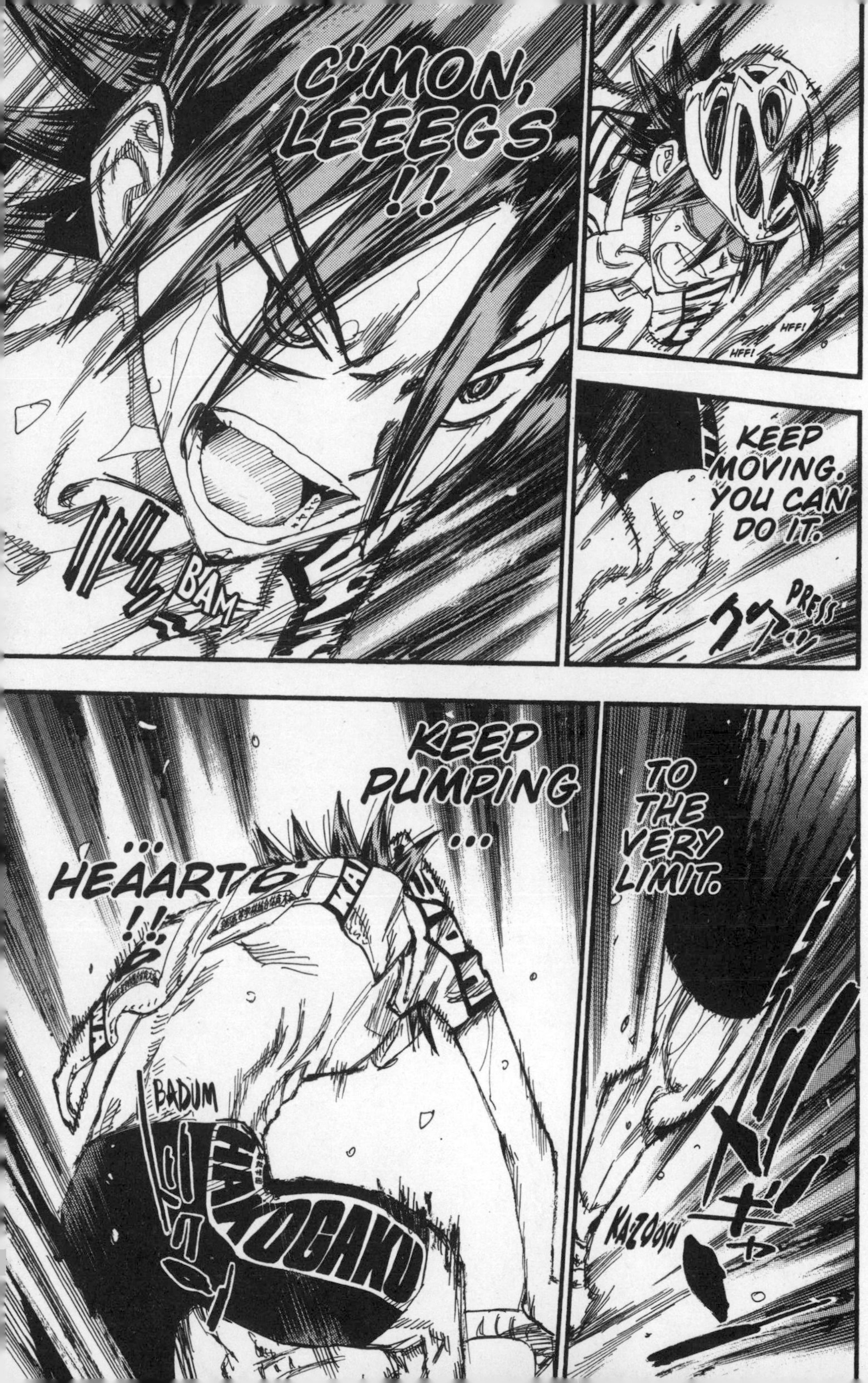
HFF!
HFF!
KEEP MOVING. YOU CAN DO IT.
PRESS
C'MON, LEEEGS!!
BAM
TO THE VERY LIMIT.
KAZOOSH
KEEP PUMPING...
...HEÄART O!!
BADUM
HAKOGAKU

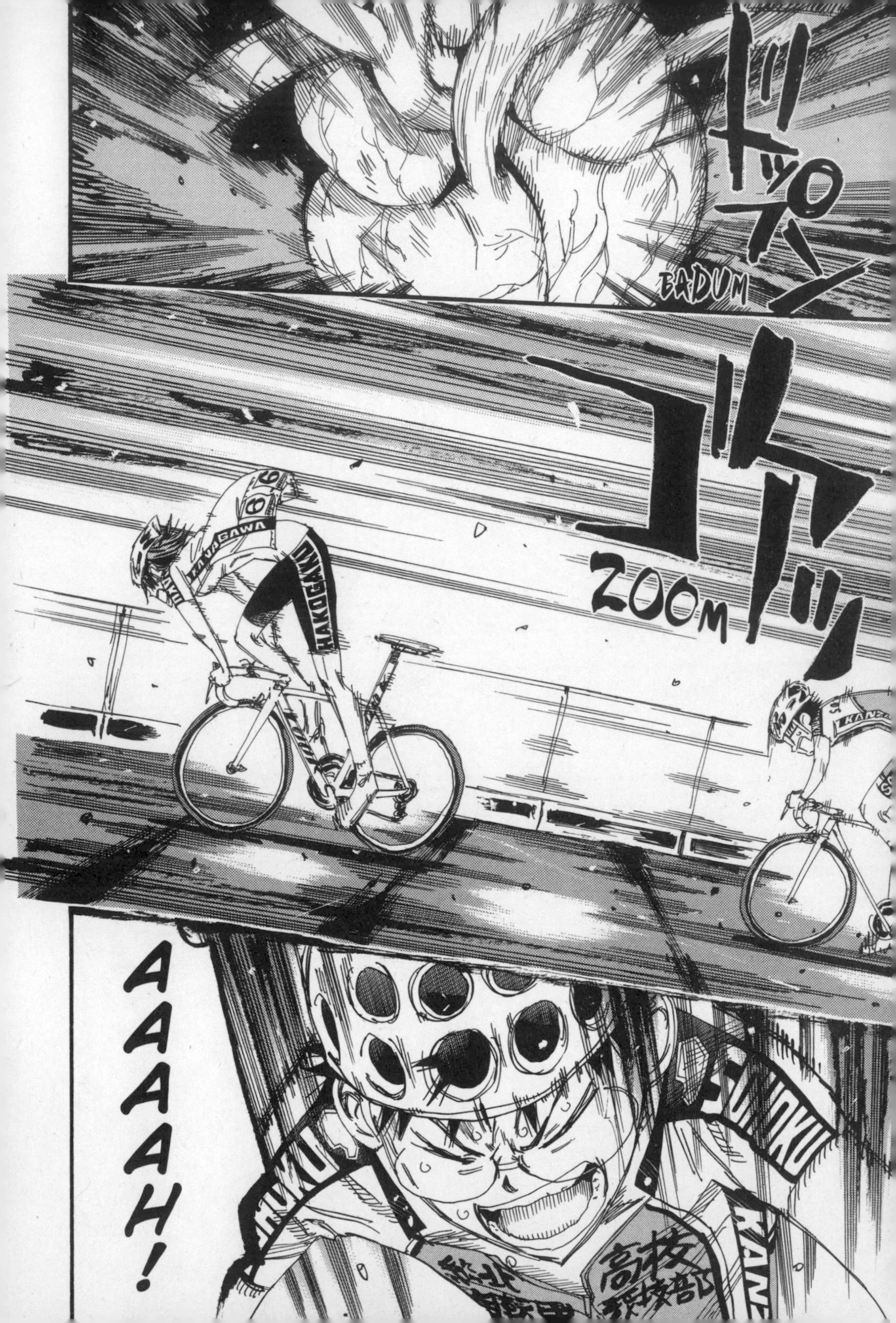
ドッパン
BADUM
ゴウッ
ZOOM
高校
総北
AAAAAH!

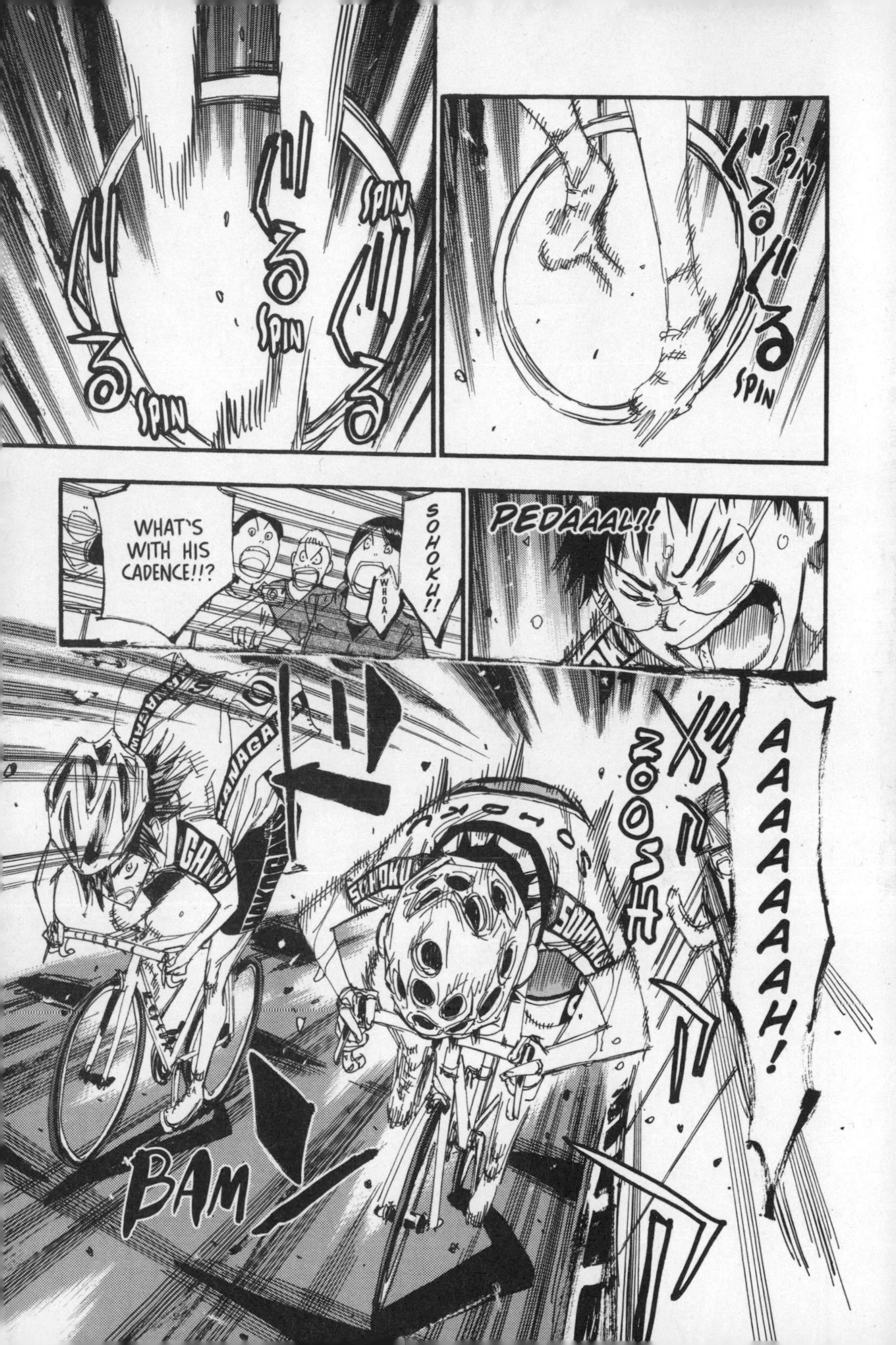
SPIN
SPIN
SPIN
SPIN
SPIN
PEDAAAL!!
SOHOKU!!
WHOA!
WHAT'S WITH HIS CADENCE!!?
AAAAAAAAAH!
ZOOOSH
BAM

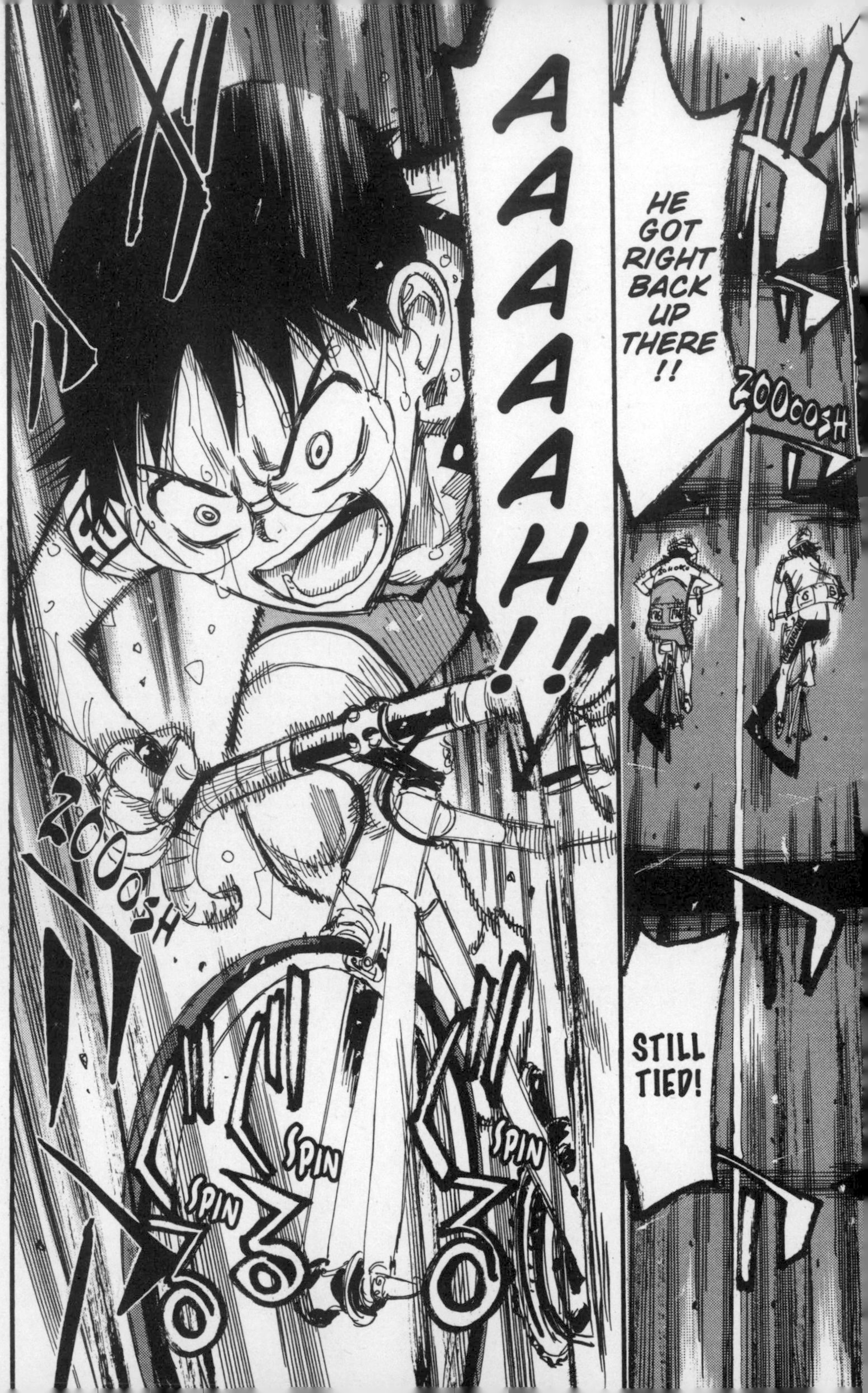
HE GOT RIGHT BACK UP THERE!!
ZOOOOSH
STILL TIED!
AAAAAH!!!
ZOOOOSH
SPIN
SPIN
SPIN

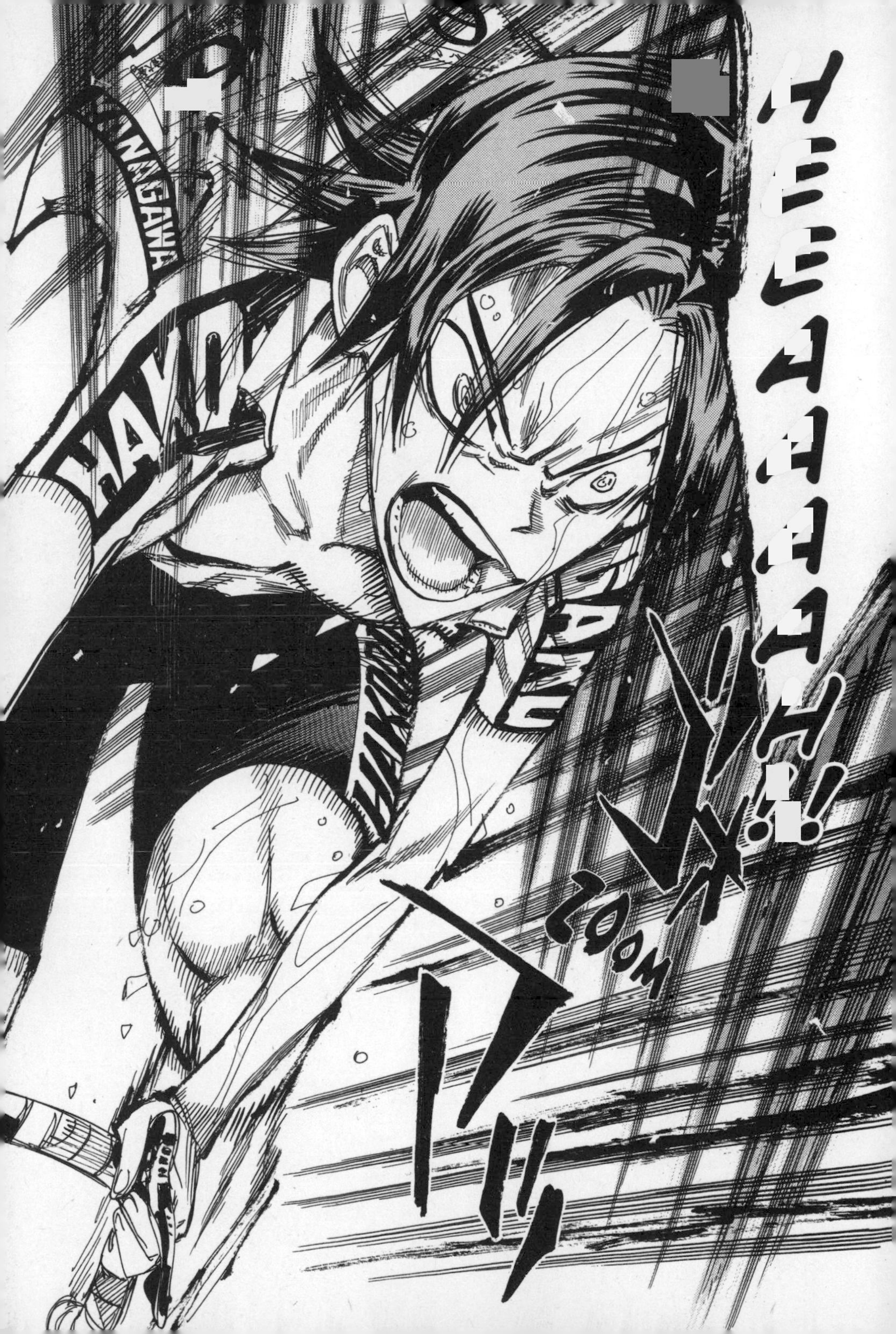
HEEAAAAH!!
ZOOM

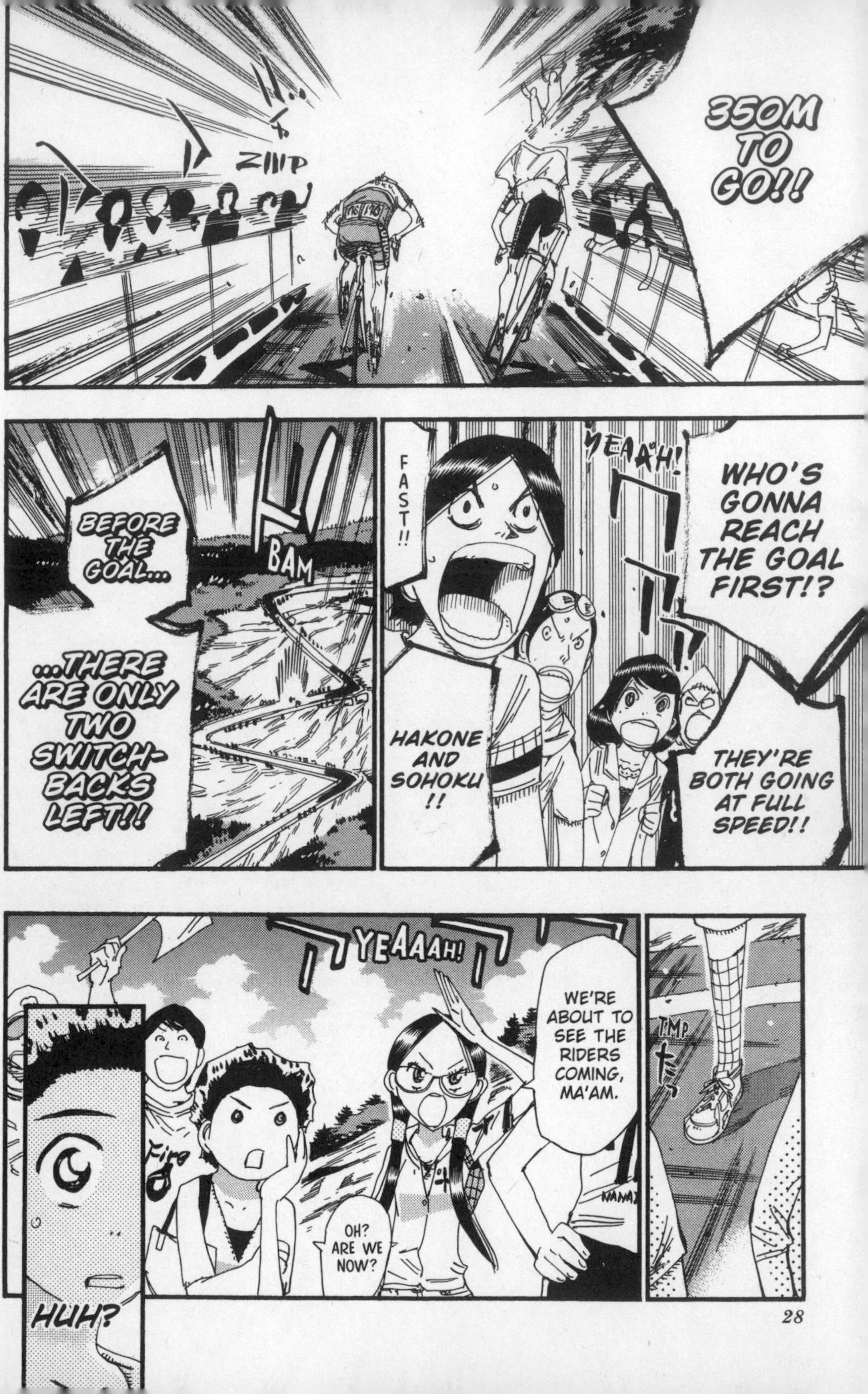
350M TO GO!!
ZIIIP
WHO'S GONNA REACH THE GOAL FIRST!?
YEAAAH!
FAST!!
THEY'RE BOTH GOING AT FULL SPEED!!
HAKONE AND SOHOKU!!
BAM
BEFORE THE GOAL...
...THERE ARE ONLY TWO SWITCH-BACKS LEFT!!
TMP
WE'RE ABOUT TO SEE THE RIDERS COMING, MA'AM.
YEAAAH!
OH? ARE WE NOW?
HUH?

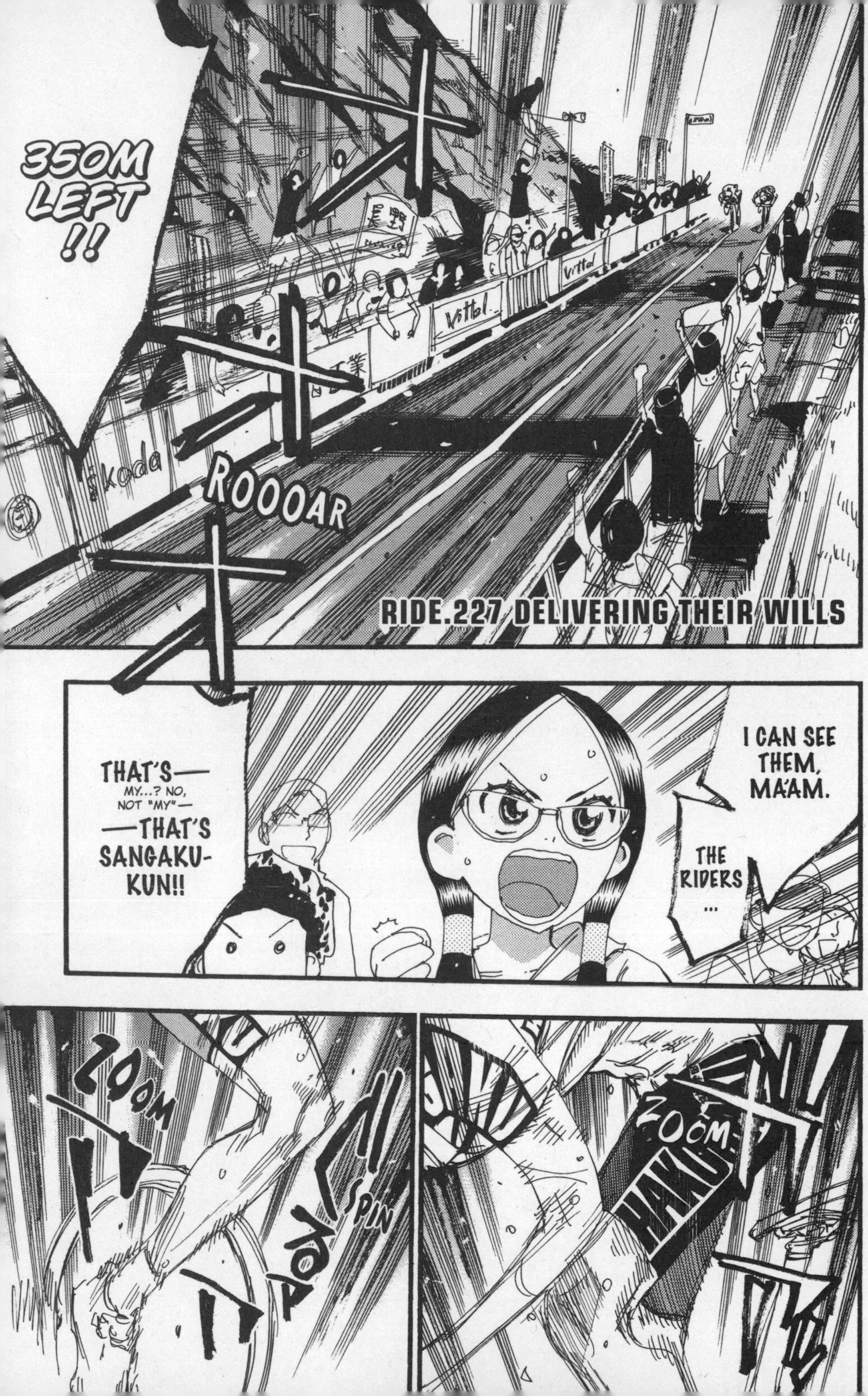
350M LEFT!!
ROOOAR
RIDE.227 DELIVERING THEIR WILLS
I CAN SEE THEM, MA'AM.
THE RIDERS...
THAT'S—
MY...? NO, NOT "MY"—
—THAT'S SANGAKU-KUN!!
ZOOM
ZOOM
SPIN

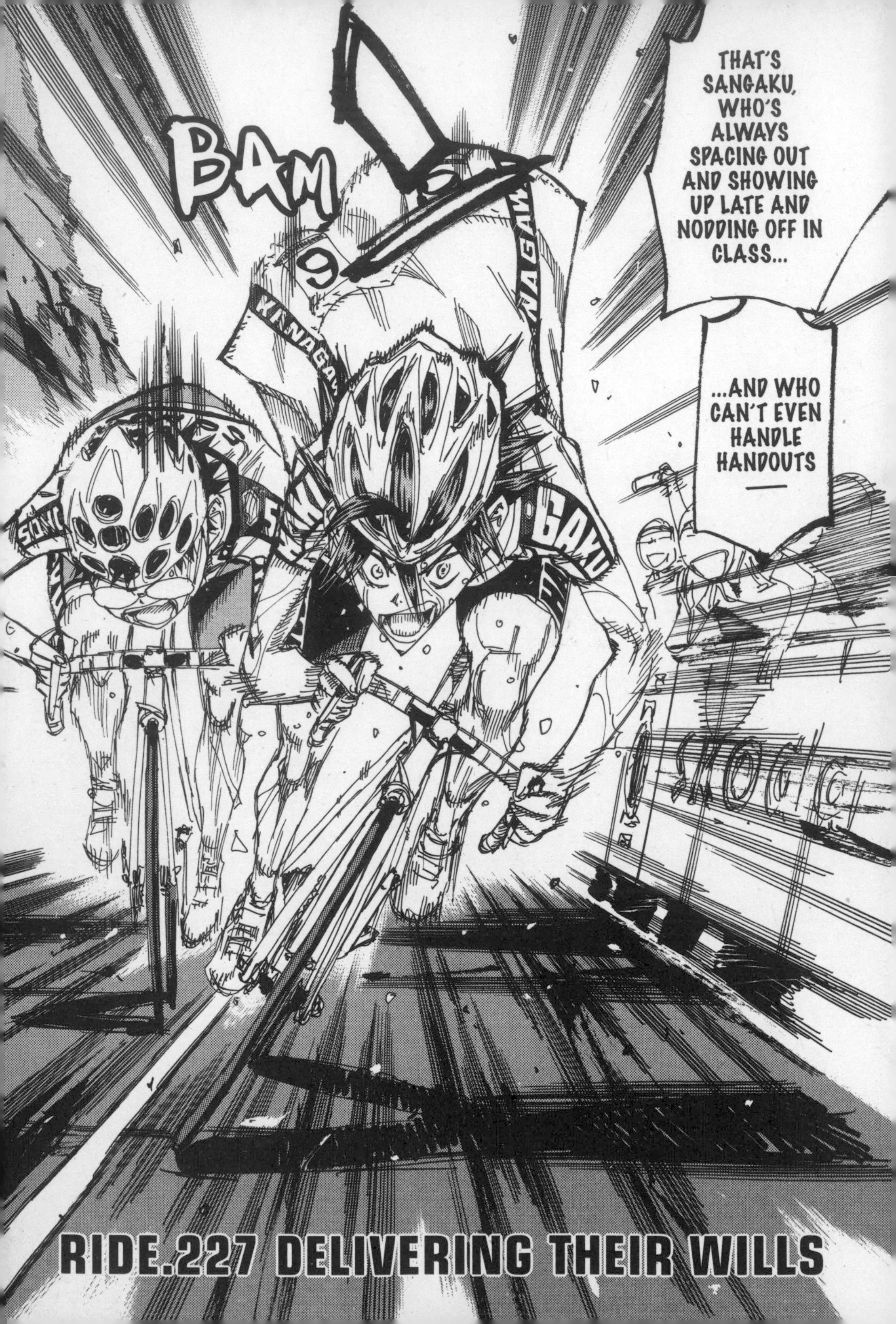
THAT'S SANGAKU, WHO'S ALWAYS SPACING OUT AND SHOWING UP LATE AND NODDING OFF IN CLASS...
...AND WHO CAN'T EVEN HANDLE HANDOUTS —
BAM

RIDE.227 DELIVERING THEIR WILLS

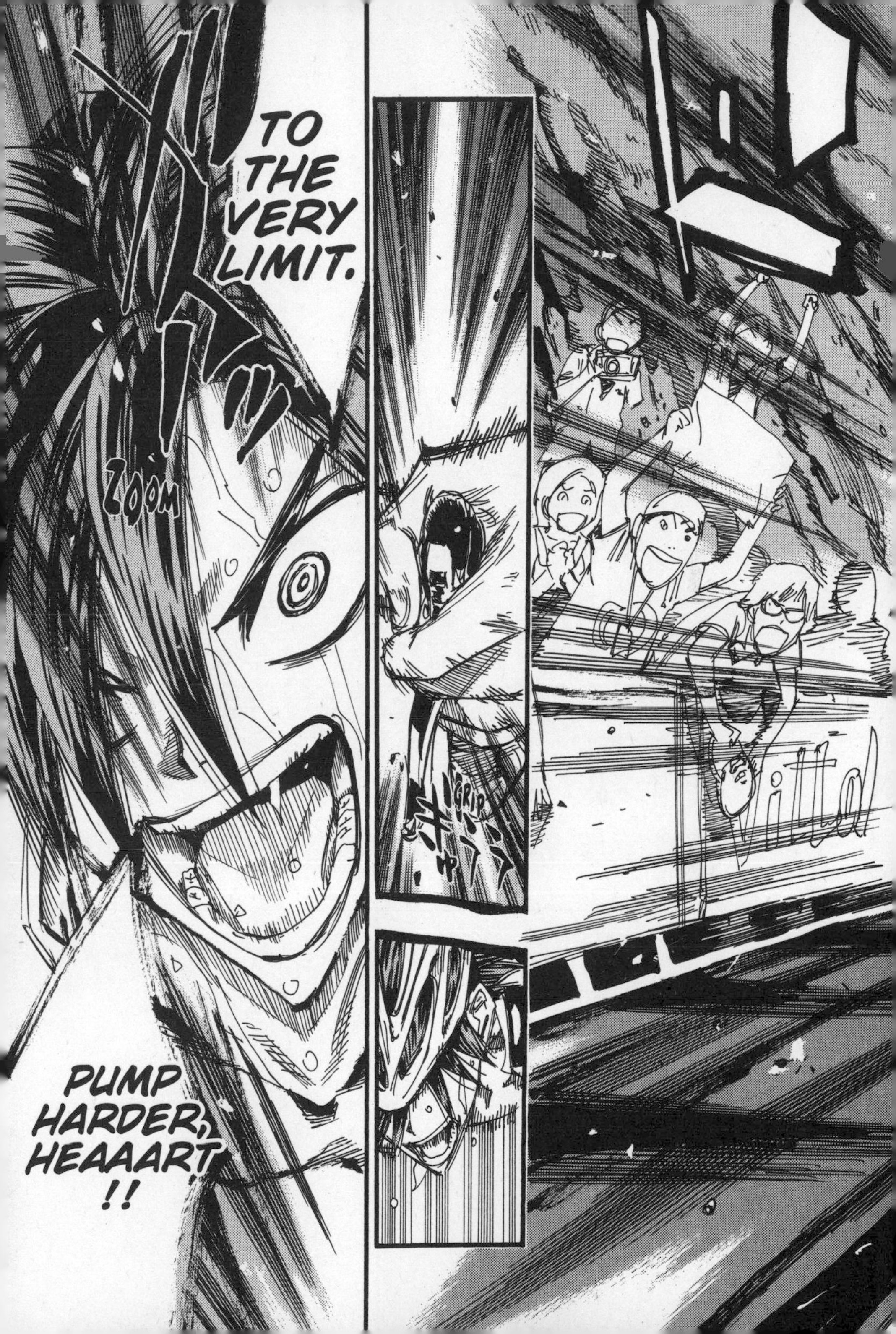
GRIP
TO THE VERY LIMIT.
ZOOM
PUMP HARDER, HEAAART!!

I CAN REALLY FEEL IT—

THE BEATING OF YOUR HEART.

CHATTER

CHATTER

BADUM

SANGAKU!!

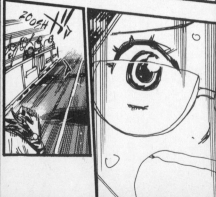

ZOOSH

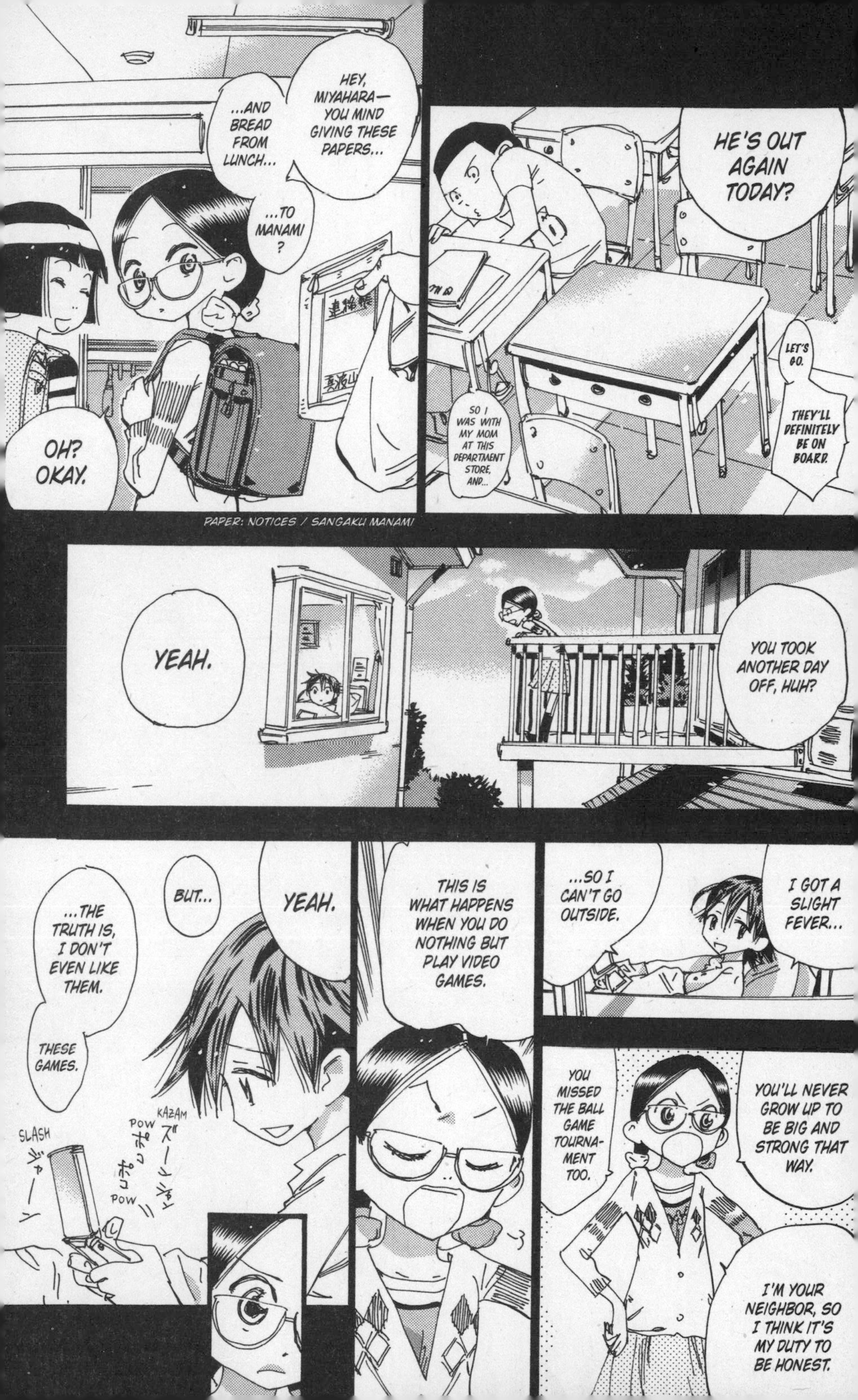
HE'S OUT AGAIN TODAY?
LET'S GO.
THEY'LL DEFINITELY BE ON BOARD.
SO I WAS WITH MY MOM AT THIS DEPARTMENT STORE, AND...
HEY, MIYAHARA— YOU MIND GIVING THESE PAPERS...
...AND BREAD FROM LUNCH...
...TO MANAMI?
OH? OKAY.
PAPER: NOTICES / SANGAKU MANAMI
YOU TOOK ANOTHER DAY OFF, HUH?
YEAH.
I GOT A SLIGHT FEVER...
...SO I CAN'T GO OUTSIDE.
YOU'LL NEVER GROW UP TO BE BIG AND STRONG THAT WAY.
YOU MISSED THE BALL GAME TOURNAMENT TOO.
I'M YOUR NEIGHBOR, SO I THINK IT'S MY DUTY TO BE HONEST.
THIS IS WHAT HAPPENS WHEN YOU DO NOTHING BUT PLAY VIDEO GAMES.
YEAH.
BUT...
...THE TRUTH IS, I DON'T EVEN LIKE THEM.
THESE GAMES.
KAZAM
POW
POW
SLASH

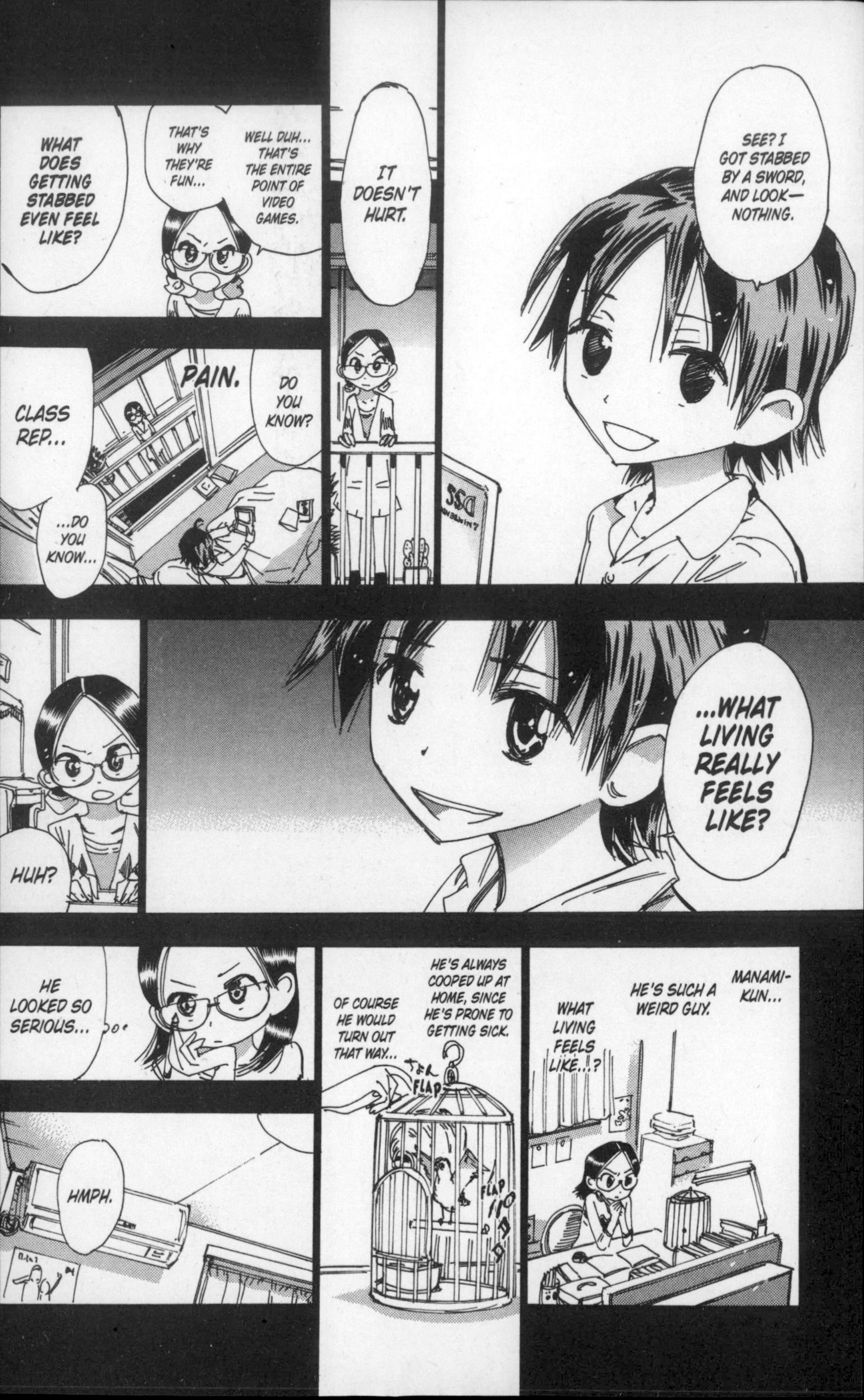

SEE? I GOT STABBED BY A SWORD, AND LOOK— NOTHING.
IT DOESN'T HURT.
WELL DUH... THAT'S THE ENTIRE POINT OF VIDEO GAMES.
THAT'S WHY THEY'RE FUN...
WHAT DOES GETTING STABBED EVEN FEEL LIKE?
DO YOU KNOW?
PAIN.
CLASS REP...
...DO YOU KNOW...
...WHAT LIVING REALLY FEELS LIKE?
HUH?
MANAMI-KUN...
HE'S SUCH A WEIRD GUY.
WHAT LIVING FEELS LIKE...?
HE'S ALWAYS COOPED UP AT HOME, SINCE HE'S PRONE TO GETTING SICK.
OF COURSE HE WOULD TURN OUT THAT WAY...
FLAP
FLAP
HE LOOKED SO SERIOUS...
HMPH.

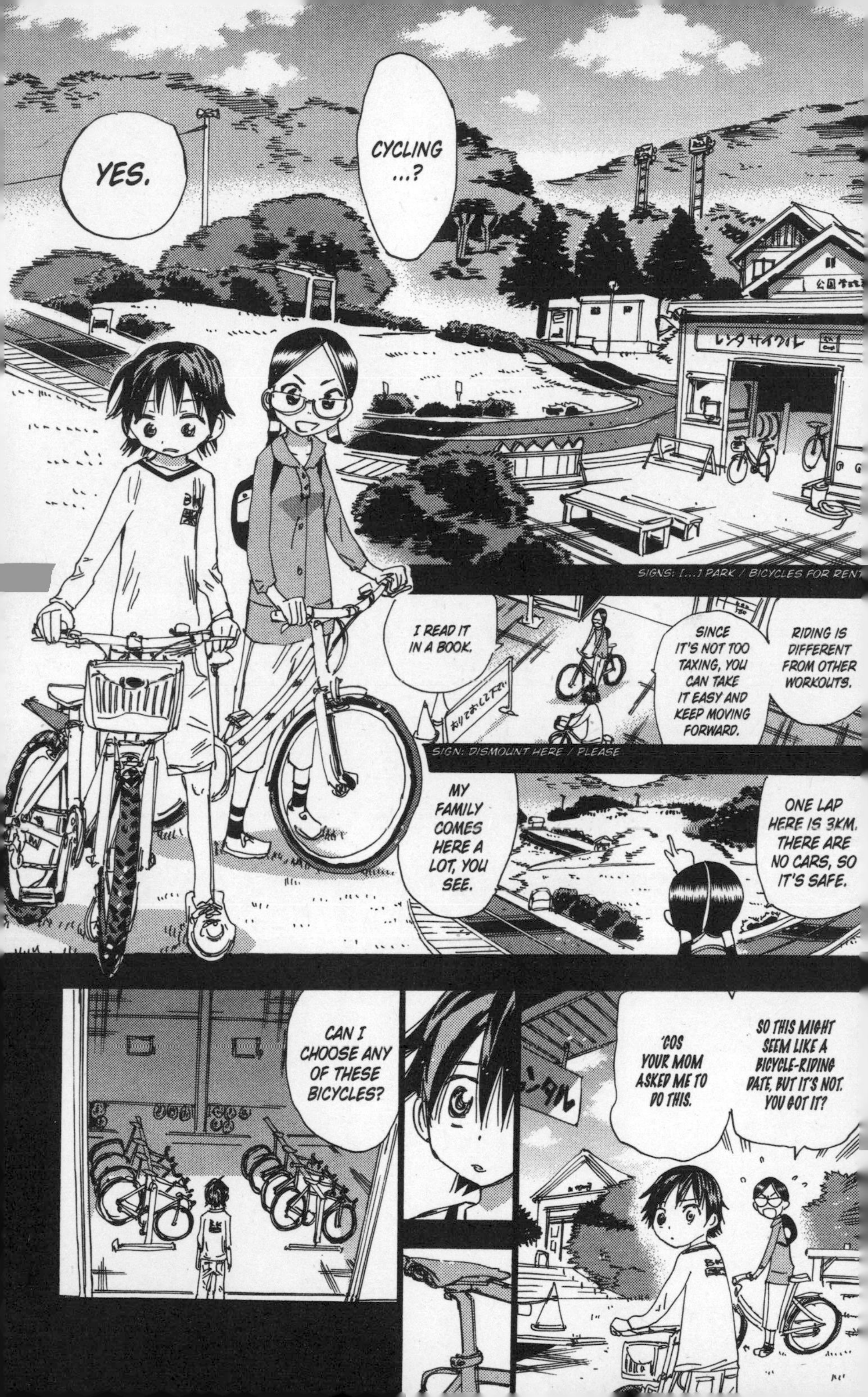
CYCLING ...?
YES.
SIGNS: [...] PARK / BICYCLES FOR RENT
RIDING IS DIFFERENT FROM OTHER WORKOUTS.
SINCE IT'S NOT TOO TAXING, YOU CAN TAKE IT EASY AND KEEP MOVING FORWARD.
I READ IT IN A BOOK.
SIGN: DISMOUNT HERE / PLEASE
ONE LAP HERE IS 3KM. THERE ARE NO CARS, SO IT'S SAFE.
MY FAMILY COMES HERE A LOT, YOU SEE.
SO THIS MIGHT SEEM LIKE A BICYCLE-RIDING DATE, BUT IT'S NOT. YOU GOT IT?
'COS YOUR MOM ASKED ME TO DO THIS.
CAN I CHOOSE ANY OF THESE BICYCLES?

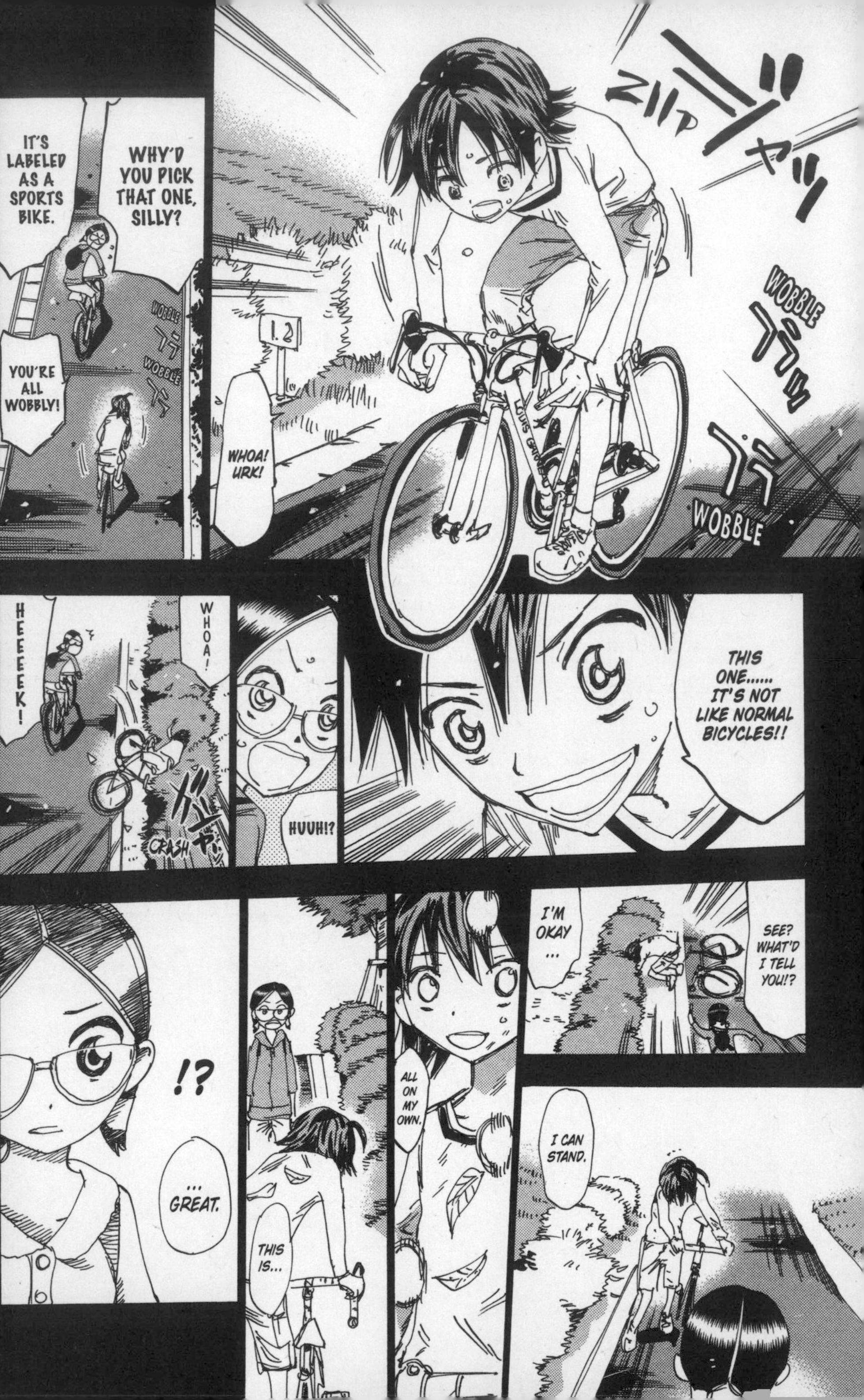
ZIIP
WOBBLE
WOBBLE
WHOA! URK!
WHY'D YOU PICK THAT ONE, SILLY?
IT'S LABELED AS A SPORTS BIKE.
WOBBLE
WOBBLE
YOU'RE ALL WOBBLY!
THIS ONE...... IT'S NOT LIKE NORMAL BICYCLES!!
HUUH!?
WHOA!
CRASH
HEEEEEK!
SEE? WHAT'D I TELL YOU!?
I'M OKAY ...
I CAN STAND.
ALL ON MY OWN.
THIS IS...
!?
... GREAT.

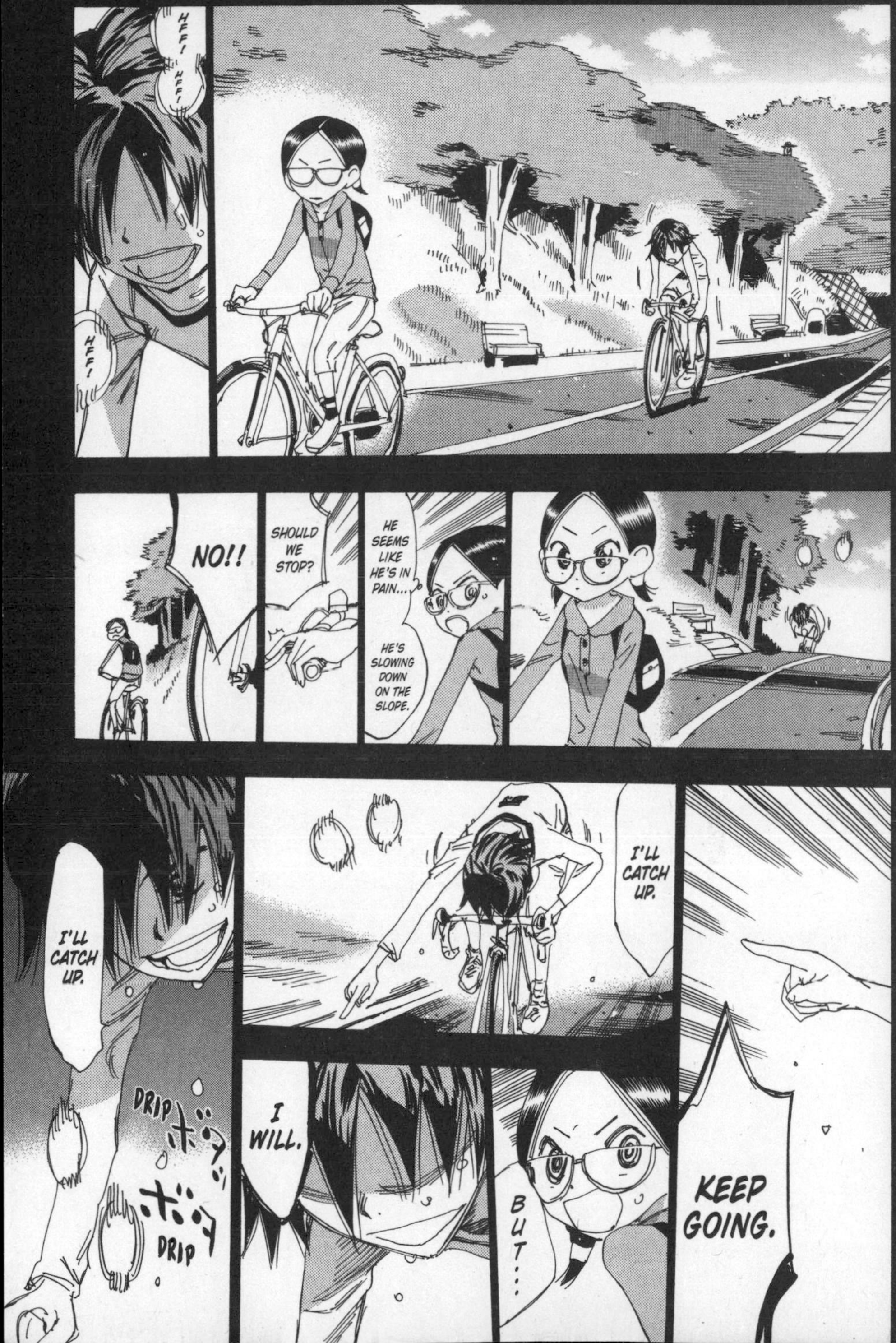
HFF! HFF!
HFF!
HE SEEMS LIKE HE'S IN PAIN...
HE'S SLOWING DOWN ON THE SLOPE.
SHOULD WE STOP?
NO!!
I'LL CATCH UP.
KEEP GOING.
BUT...
I WILL.
I'LL CATCH UP.
DRIP
DRIP

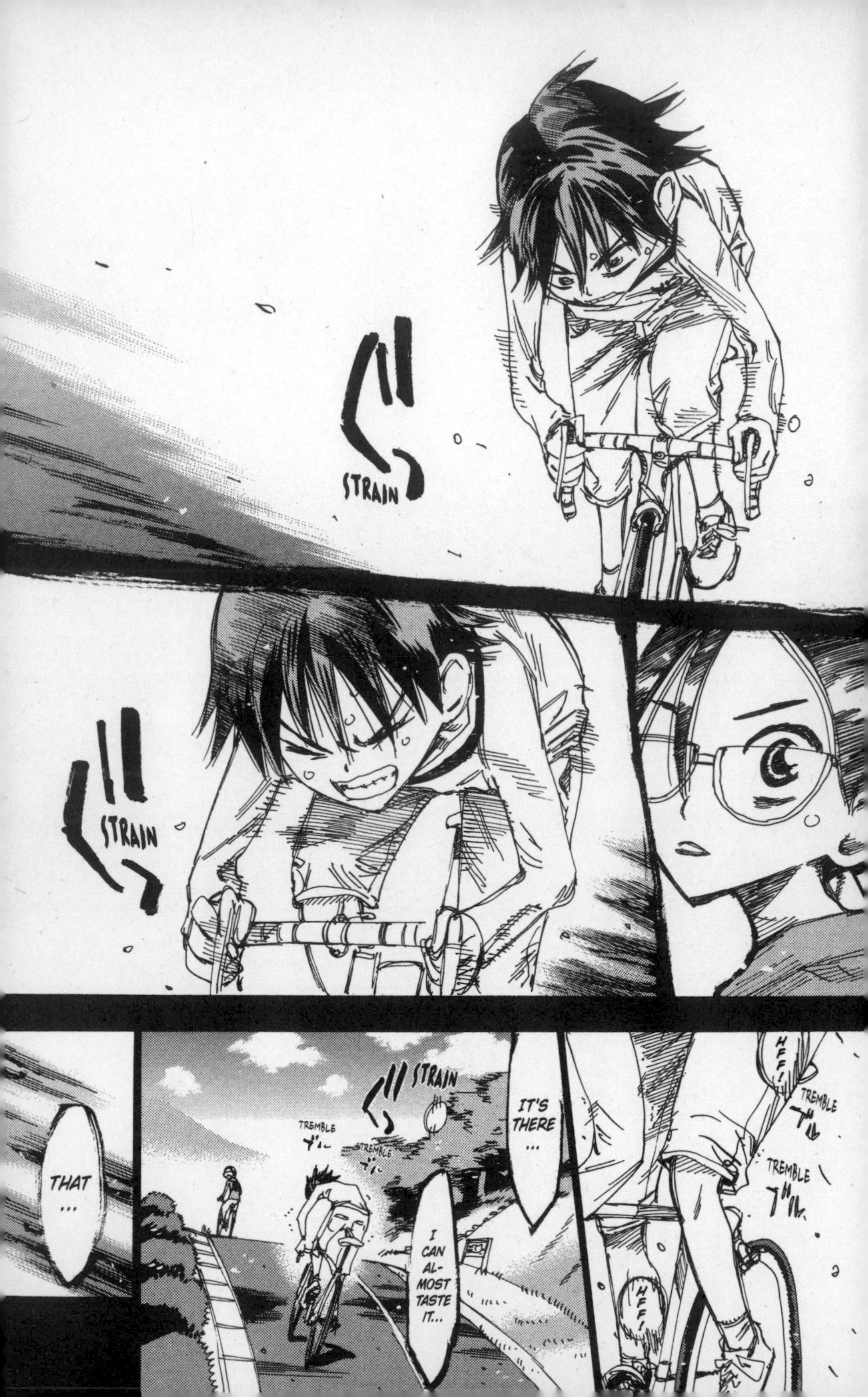
STRAIN
STRAIN
HFF!
TREMBLE
TREMBLE
HFF!
IT'S THERE ...
I CAN AL-MOST TASTE IT...
STRAIN
TREMBLE
TREMBLE
THAT ...

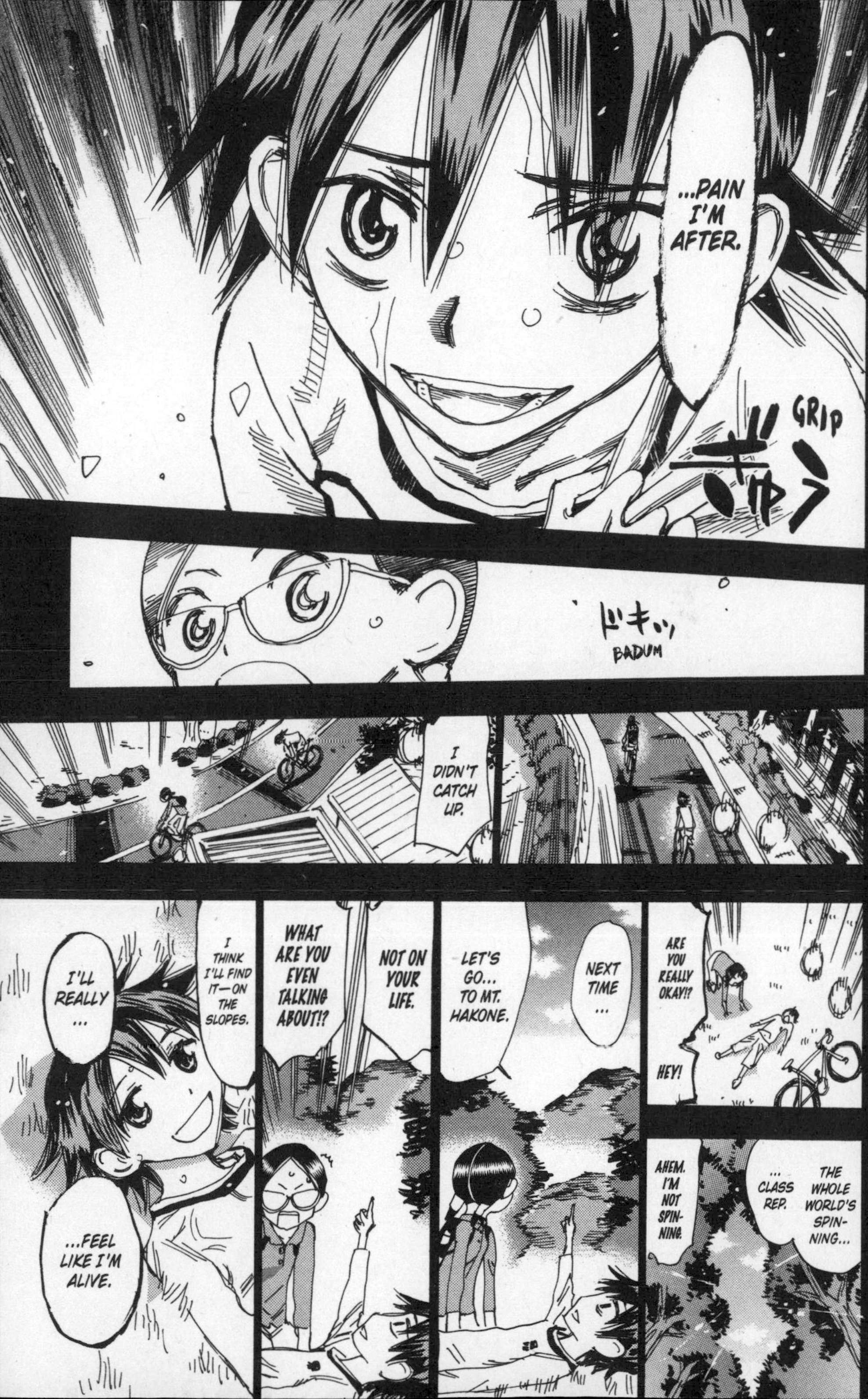
...PAIN I'M AFTER.
GRIP
ギュう
ドキッ
BADUM
I DIDN'T CATCH UP.
ARE YOU REALLY OKAY!?
HEY!
THE WHOLE WORLD'S SPIN-NING...
...CLASS REP.
AHEM. I'M NOT SPIN-NING.
NEXT TIME...
LET'S GO... TO MT. HAKONE.
NOT ON YOUR LIFE.
WHAT ARE YOU EVEN TALKING ABOUT!?
I THINK I'LL FIND IT—ON THE SLOPES.
I'LL REALLY...
...FEEL LIKE I'M ALIVE.

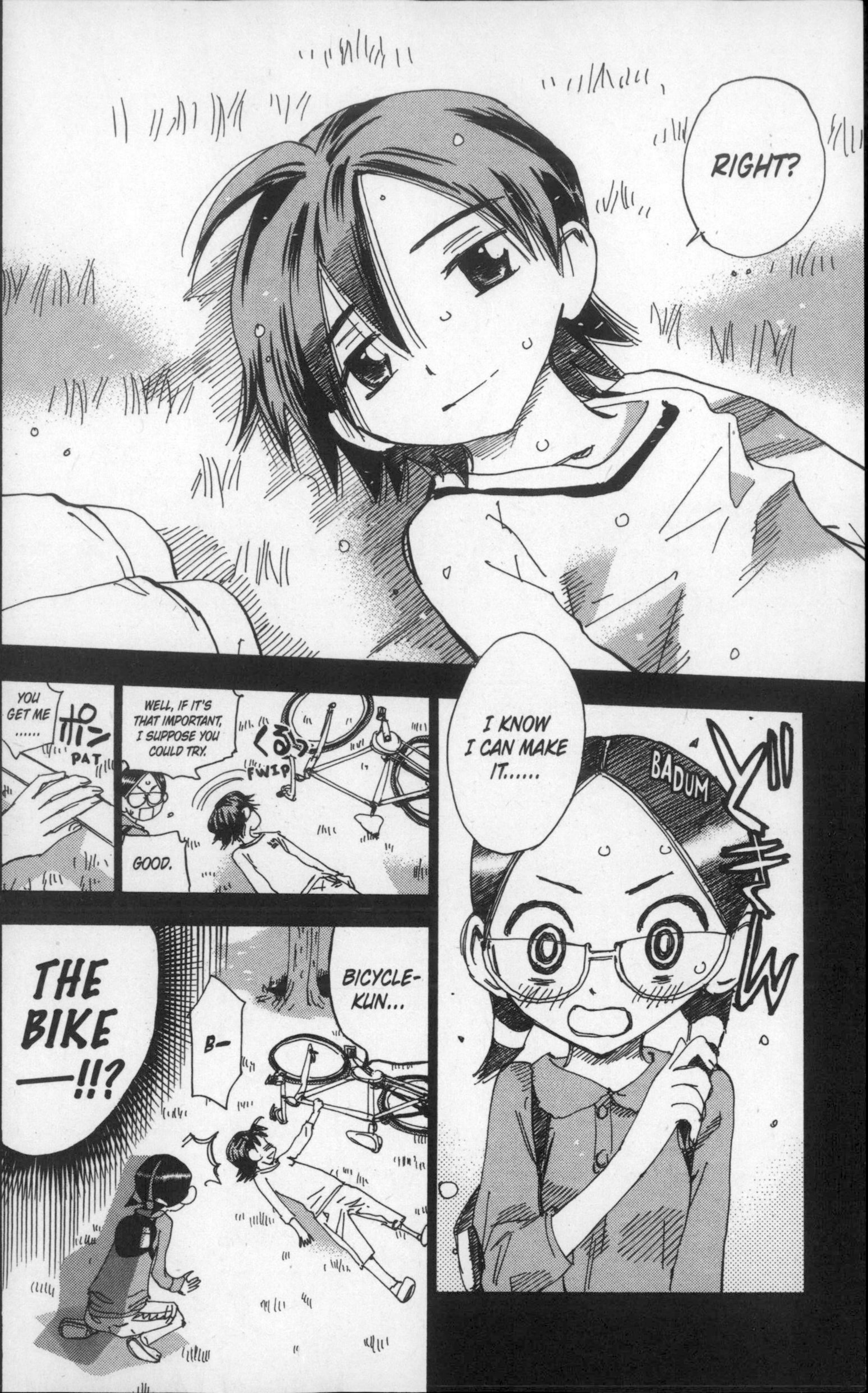
RIGHT?
I KNOW I CAN MAKE IT......
BADUM
WELL, IF IT'S THAT IMPORTANT, I SUPPOSE YOU COULD TRY.
FWIP
GOOD.
YOU GET ME ......
PAT
BICYCLE-KUN...
B—
THE BIKE—!!?

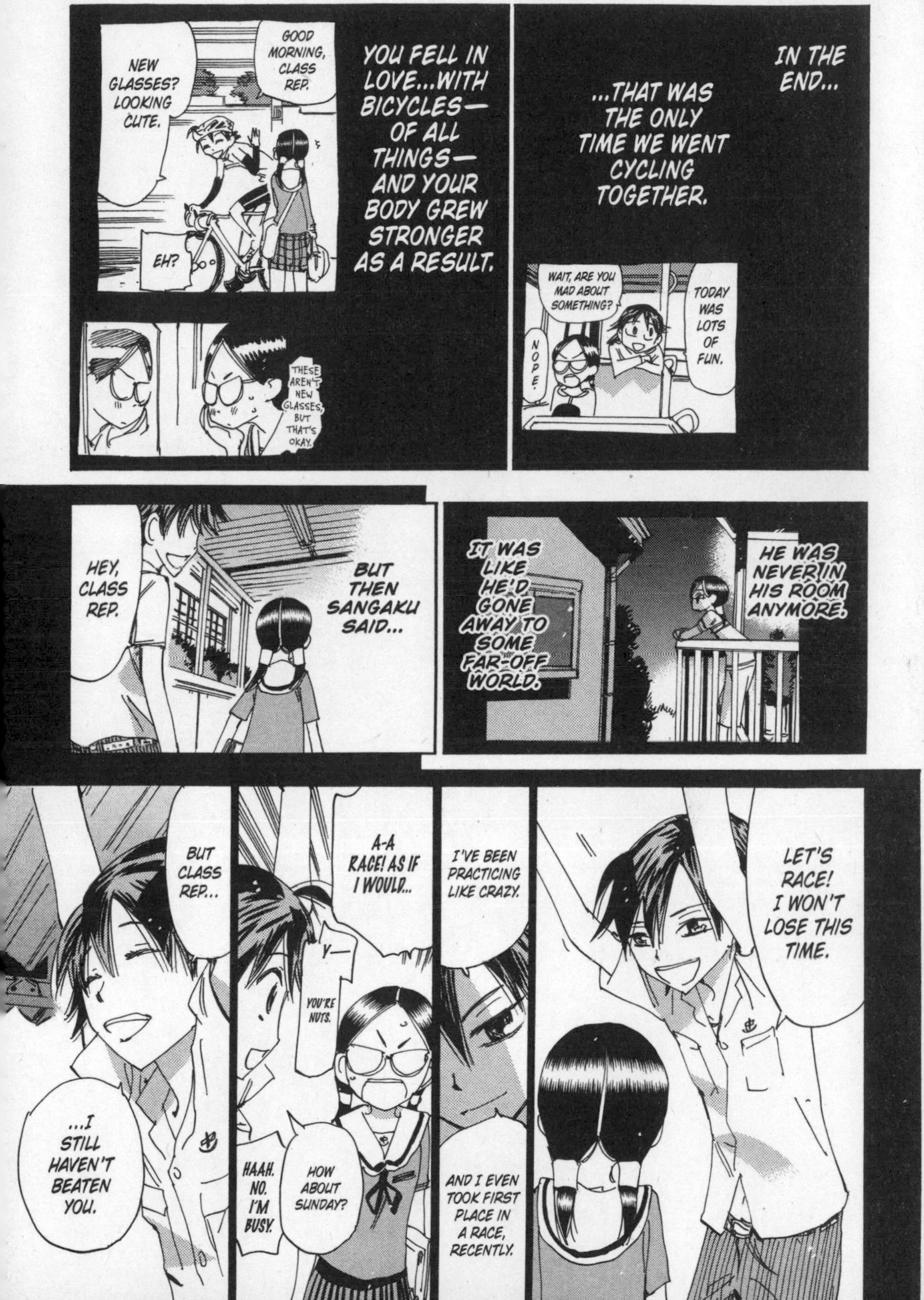
IN THE END...
...THAT WAS THE ONLY TIME WE WENT CYCLING TOGETHER.
TODAY WAS LOTS OF FUN.
WAIT, ARE YOU MAD ABOUT SOMETHING?
NOPE.
YOU FELL IN LOVE...WITH BICYCLES—OF ALL THINGS—AND YOUR BODY GREW STRONGER AS A RESULT.
GOOD MORNING, CLASS REP.
NEW GLASSES? LOOKING CUTE.
EH?
THESE AREN'T NEW GLASSES, BUT THAT'S OKAY.
HE WAS NEVER IN HIS ROOM ANYMORE.
IT WAS LIKE HE'D GONE AWAY TO SOME FAR-OFF WORLD.
BUT THEN SANGAKU SAID...
HEY, CLASS REP.
LET'S RACE! I WON'T LOSE THIS TIME.
I'VE BEEN PRACTICING LIKE CRAZY.
AND I EVEN TOOK FIRST PLACE IN A RACE, RECENTLY.
A-A RACE! AS IF I WOULD...
Y—
YOU'RE NUTS.
HOW ABOUT SUNDAY?
HAAH. NO. I'M BUSY.
BUT CLASS REP...
...I STILL HAVEN'T BEATEN YOU.

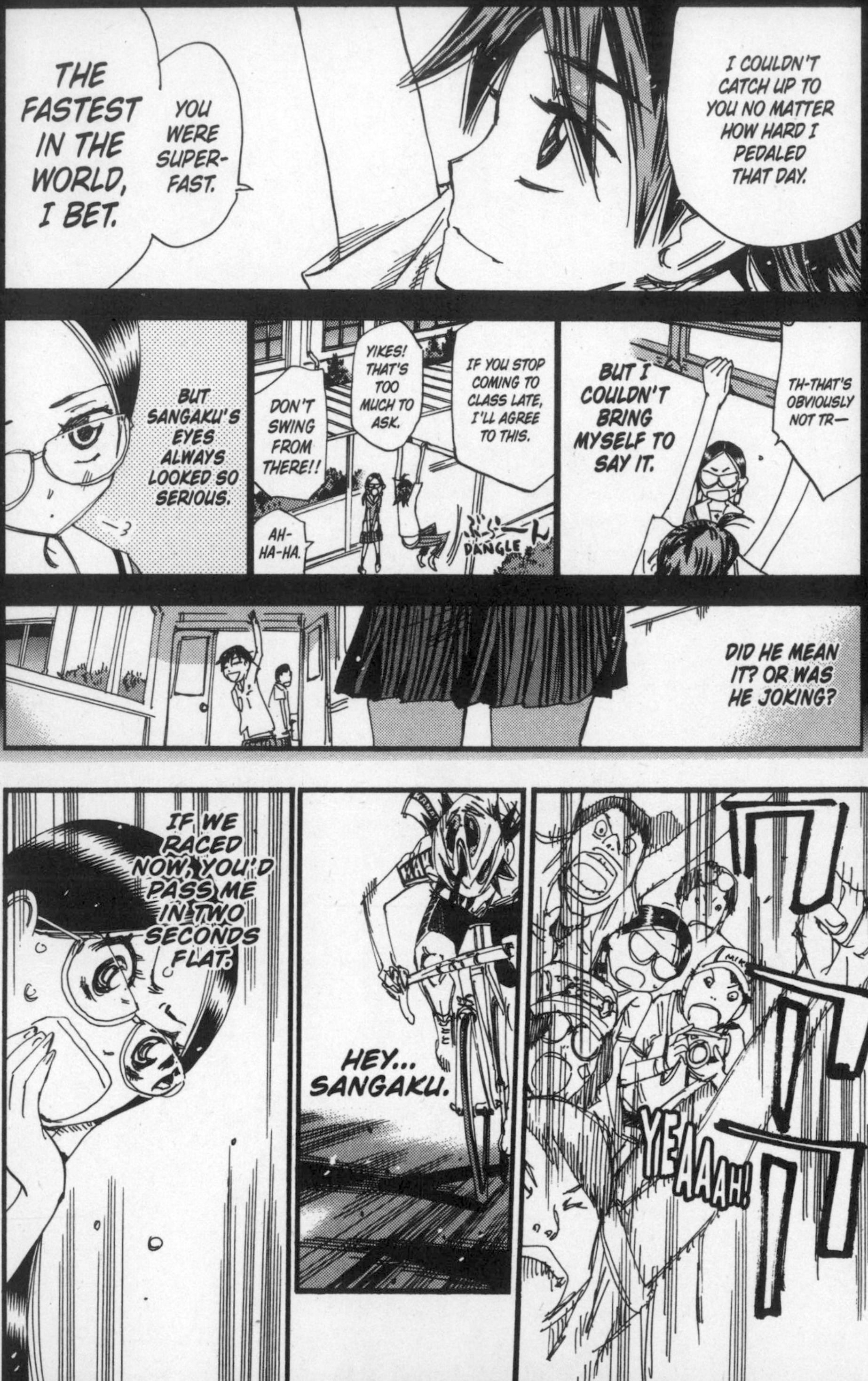
I COULDN'T CATCH UP TO YOU NO MATTER HOW HARD I PEDALED THAT DAY.
YOU WERE SUPER-FAST.
THE FASTEST IN THE WORLD, I BET.
TH-THAT'S OBVIOUSLY NOT TR—
BUT I COULDN'T BRING MYSELF TO SAY IT.
IF YOU STOP COMING TO CLASS LATE, I'LL AGREE TO THIS.
YIKES! THAT'S TOO MUCH TO ASK.
DON'T SWING FROM THERE!!
AH-HA-HA.
DANGLE
BUT SANGAKU'S EYES ALWAYS LOOKED SO SERIOUS.
DID HE MEAN IT? OR WAS HE JOKING?
YEAAAAH!
HEY... SANGAKU.
IF WE RACED NOW, YOU'D PASS ME IN TWO SECONDS FLAT.

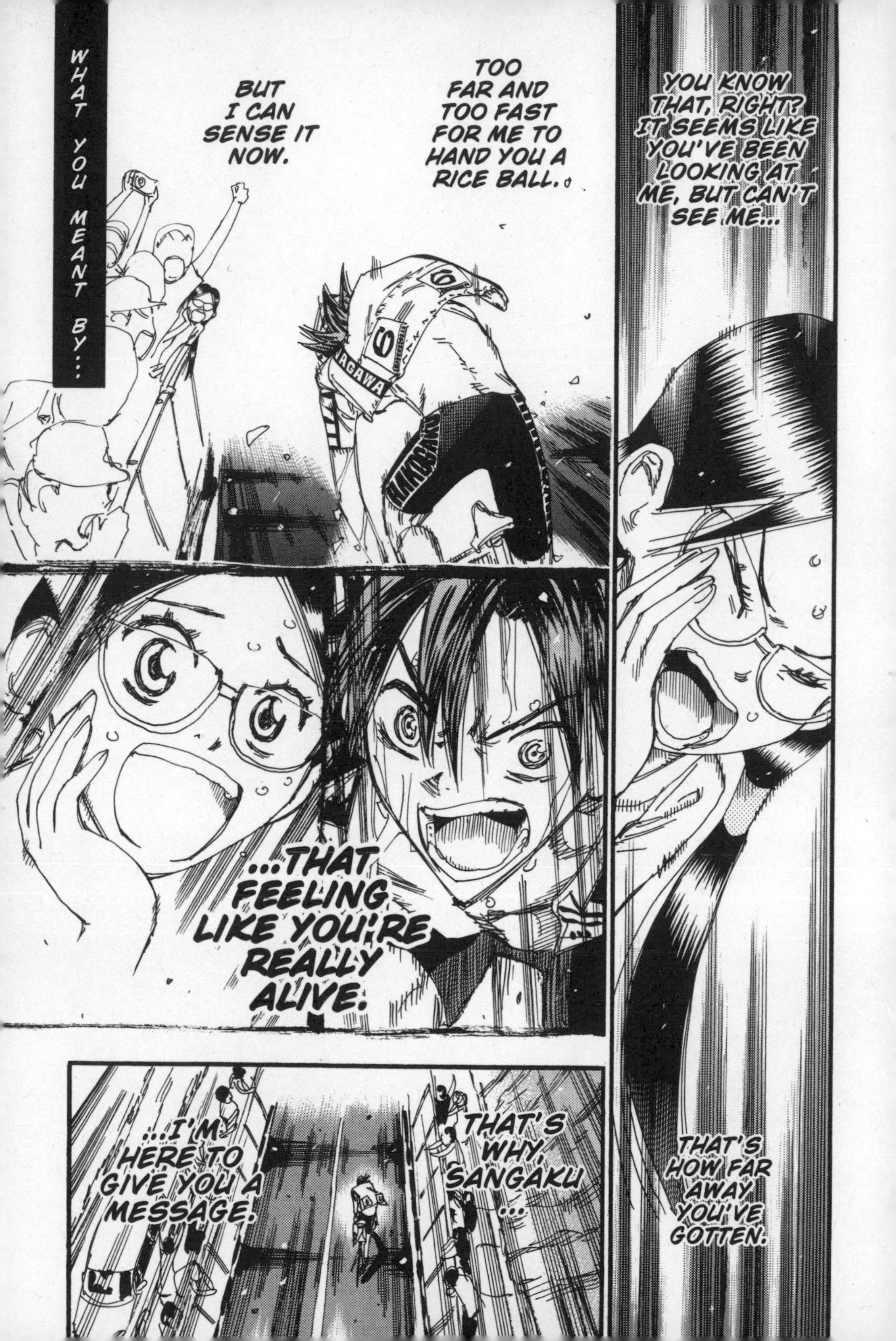
YOU KNOW THAT, RIGHT? IT SEEMS LIKE YOU'VE BEEN LOOKING AT ME, BUT CAN'T SEE ME...
THAT'S HOW FAR AWAY YOU'VE GOTTEN.
TOO FAR AND TOO FAST FOR ME TO HAND YOU A RICE BALL.
BUT I CAN SENSE IT NOW.
WHAT YOU MEANT BY...
...THAT FEELING LIKE YOU'RE REALLY ALIVE.
THAT'S WHY, SANGAKU...
...I'M HERE TO GIVE YOU A MESSAGE.

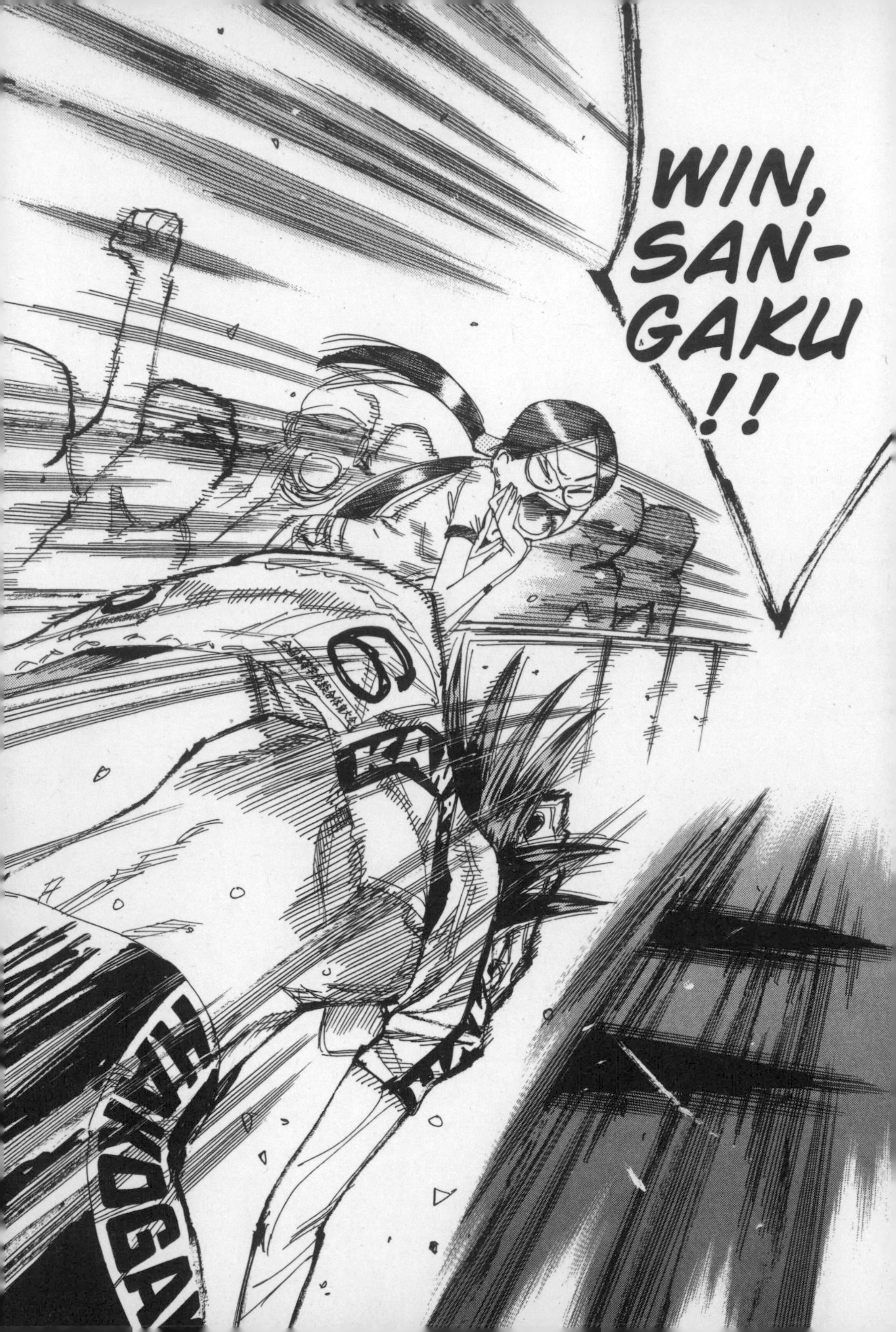
WIN, SAN-GAKU!!

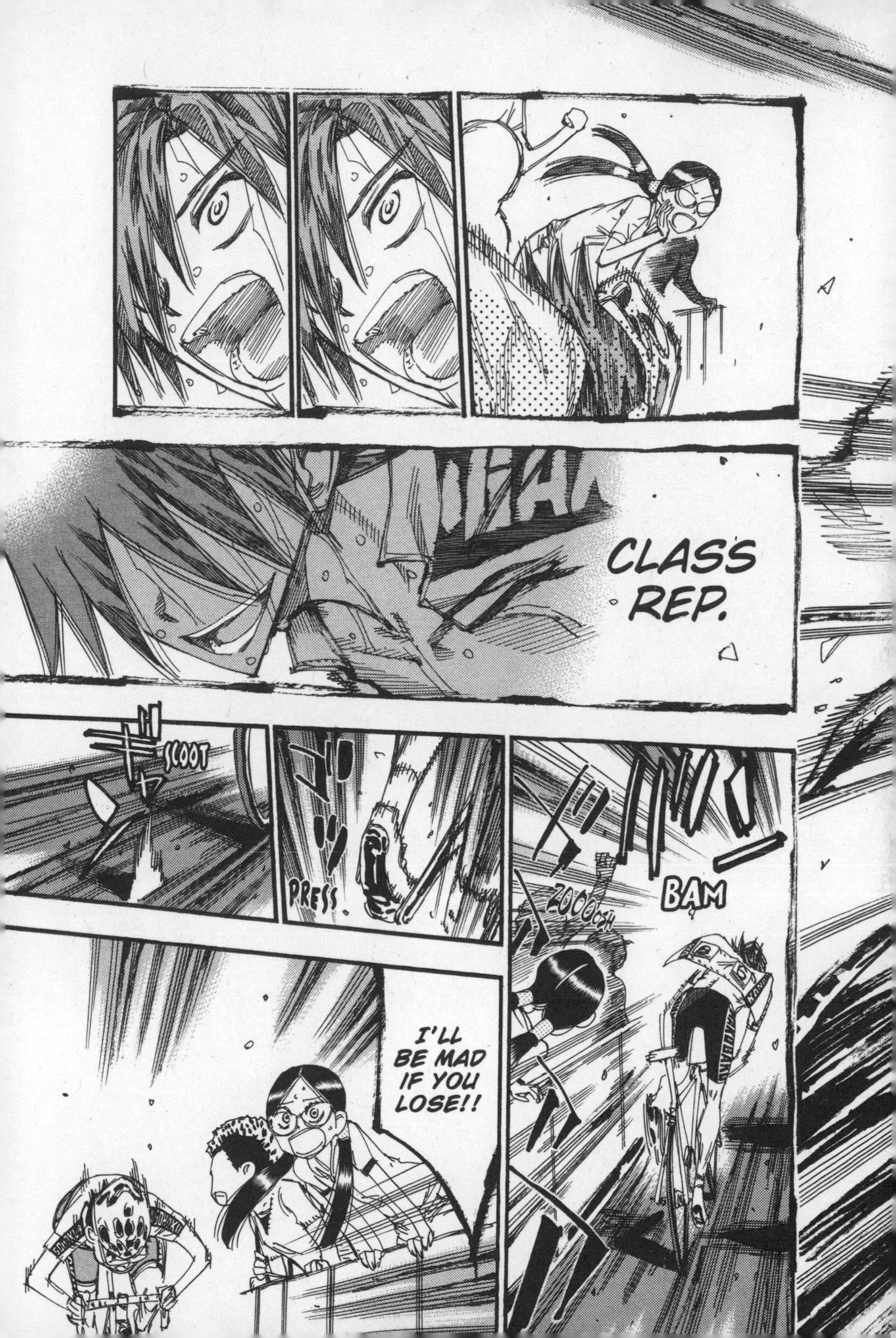
CLASS REP.
BAM
ZOOOOSH
PRESS
SCOOT
I'LL BE MAD IF YOU LOSE!!

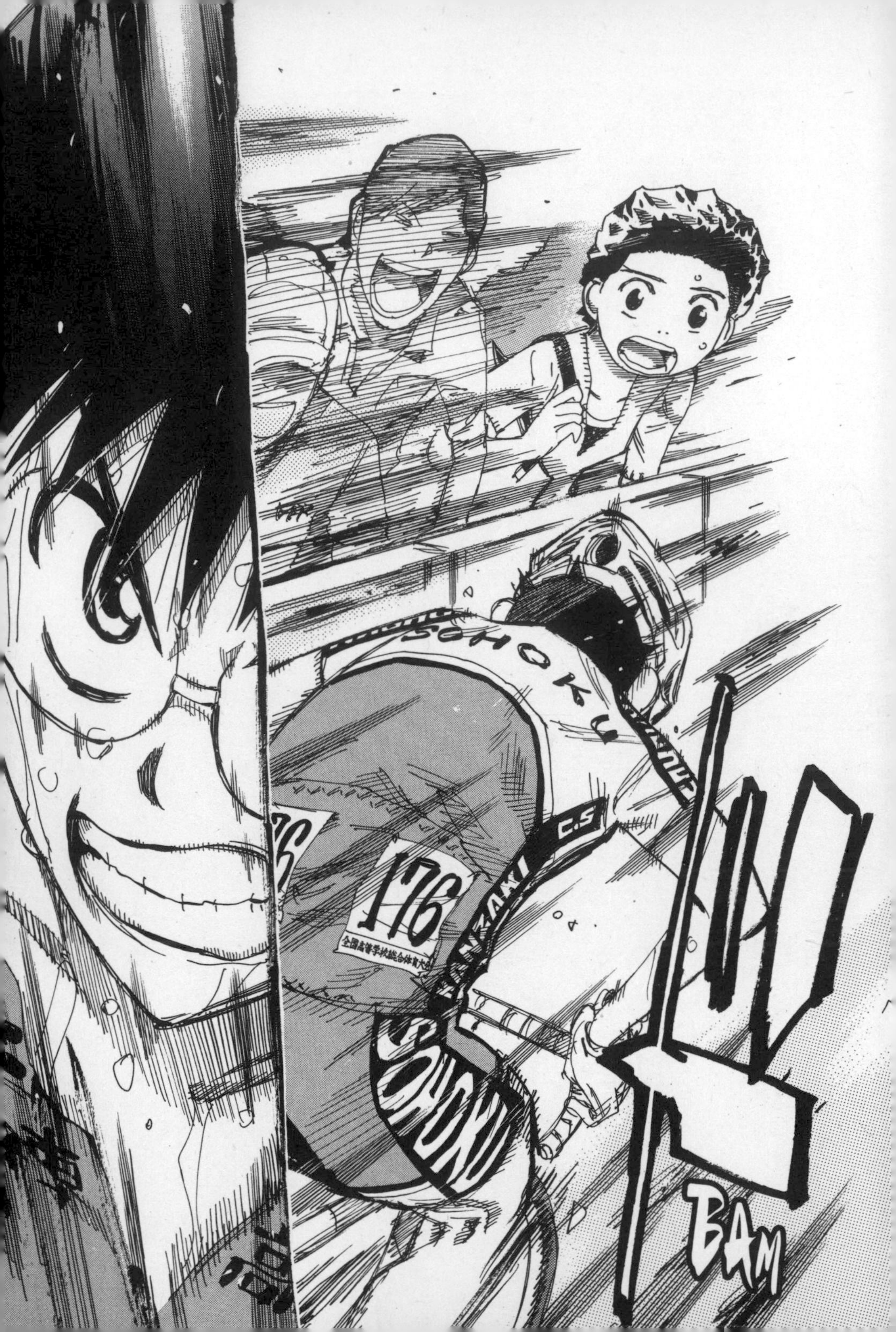
SOHOKU
176
全国高等学校総合体育大会
BAM

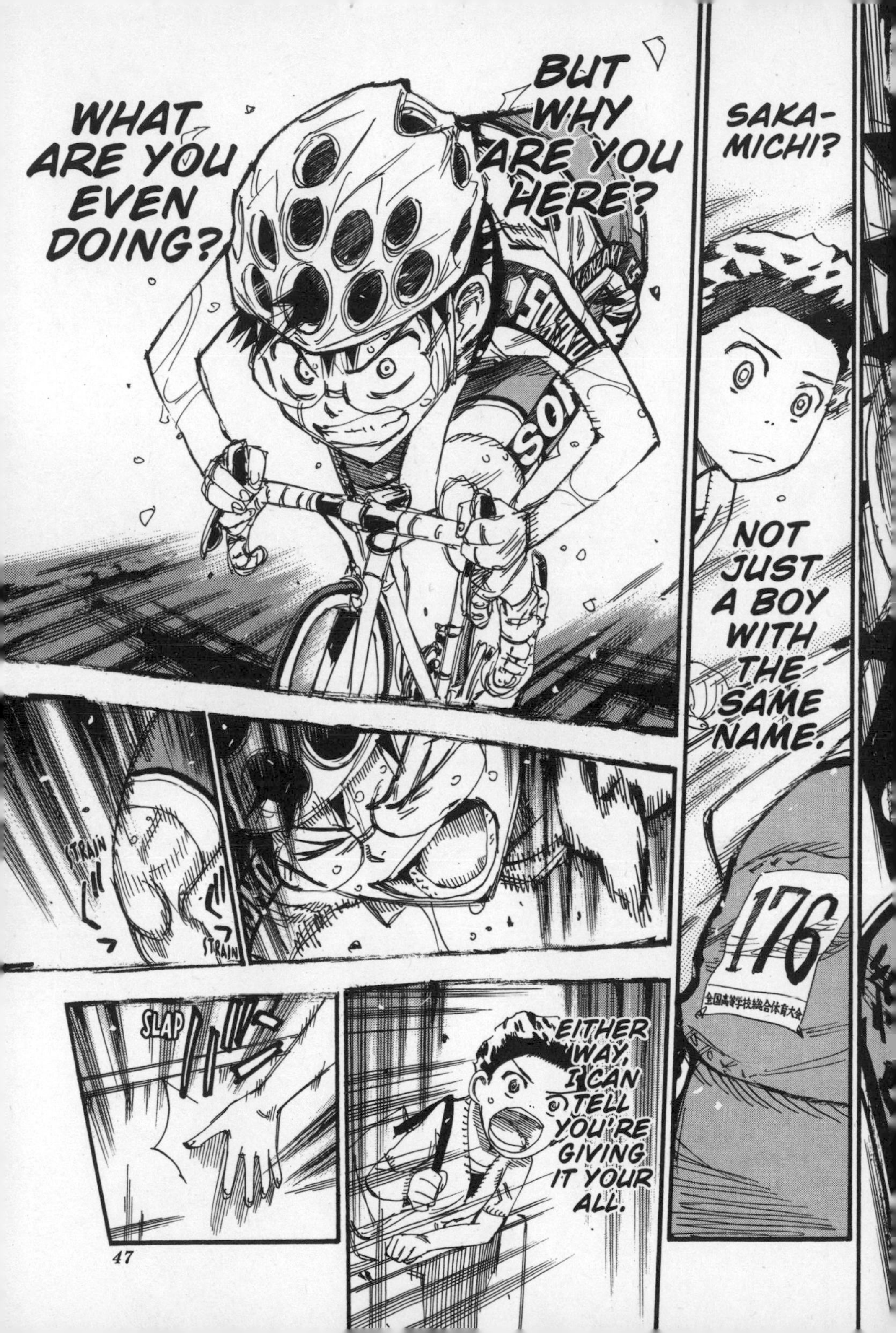
SAKA-MICHI?
NOT JUST A BOY WITH THE SAME NAME.
176
全国高等学校総合体育大会
BUT WHY ARE YOU HERE?
WHAT ARE YOU EVEN DOING?
STRAIN
STRAIN
EITHER WAY, I CAN TELL YOU'RE GIVING IT YOUR ALL.
SLAP

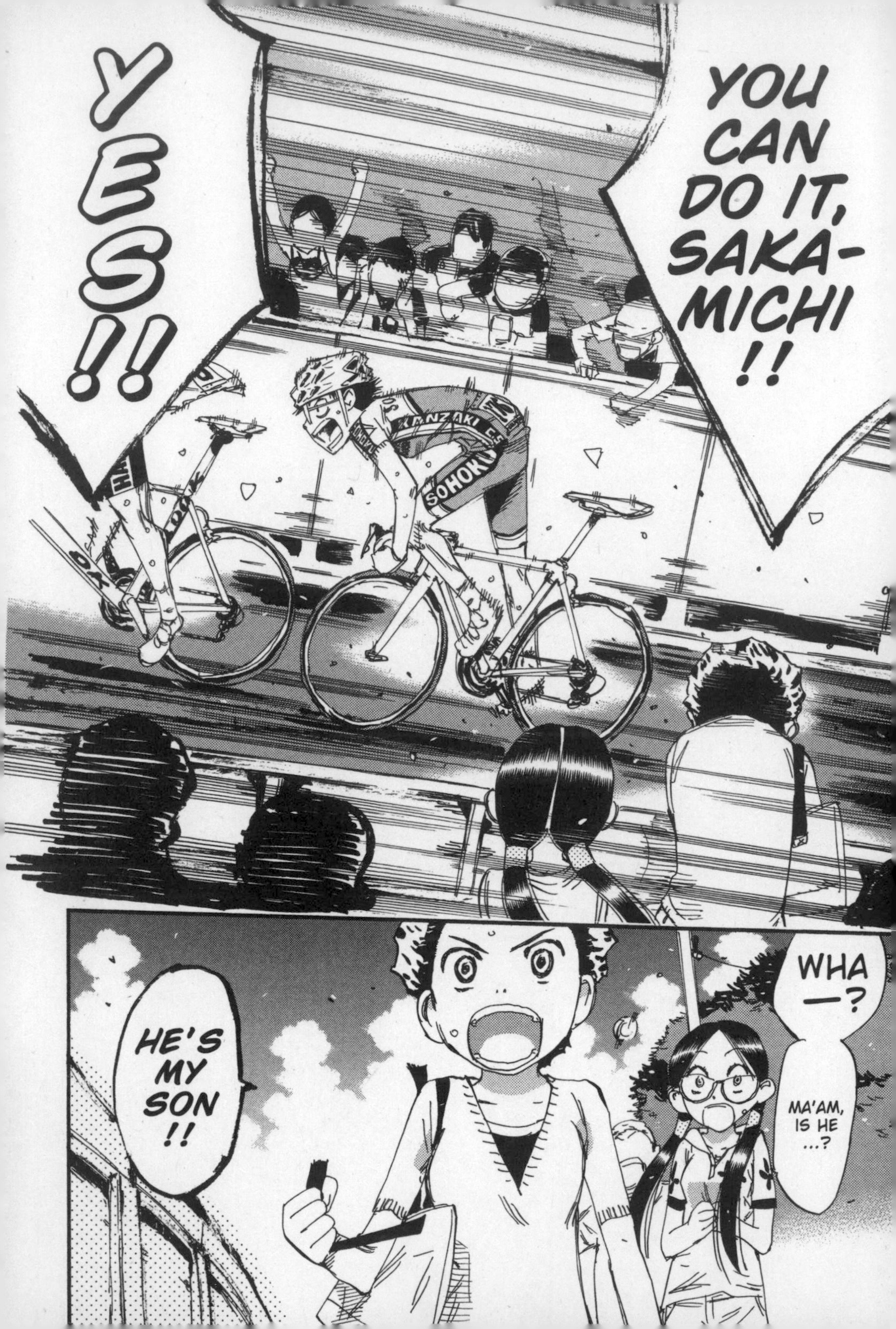
YOU CAN DO IT, SAKAMICHI!!
YES!!
WHA—?
MA'AM, IS HE ...?
HE'S MY SON!!

RIDE.228 ALL THAT'S LEFT IS THE GOAL

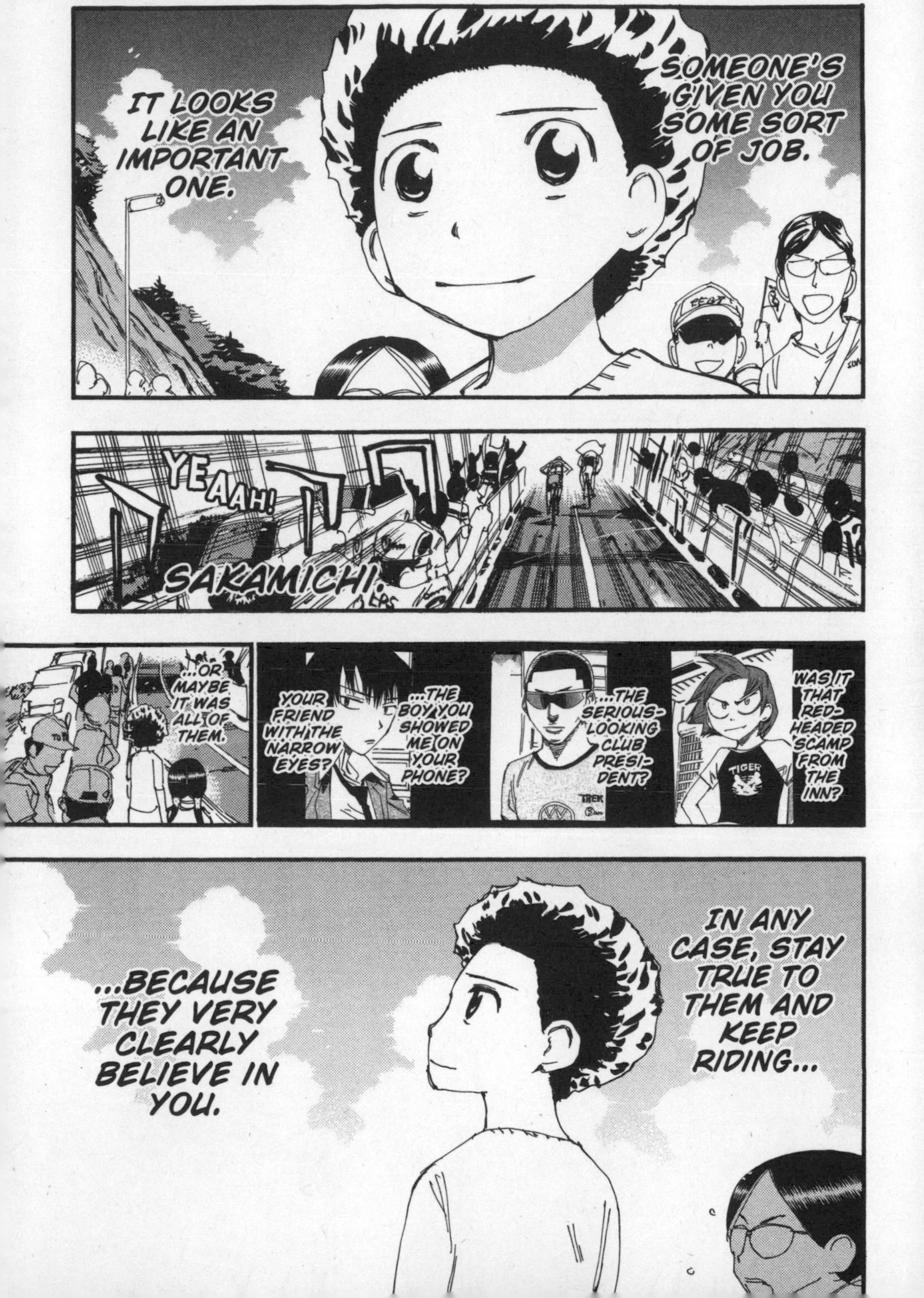
SOMEONE'S GIVEN YOU SOME SORT OF JOB.
IT LOOKS LIKE AN IMPORTANT ONE.
YEAAAH!
SAKAMICHI.
WAS IT THAT RED-HEADED SCAMP FROM THE INN?
...THE SERIOUS-LOOKING CLUB PRESIDENT?
...THE BOY YOU SHOWED ME ON YOUR PHONE?
YOUR FRIEND WITH THE NARROW EYES?
...OR MAYBE IT WAS ALL OF THEM.
IN ANY CASE, STAY TRUE TO THEM AND KEEP RIDING...
...BECAUSE THEY VERY CLEARLY BELIEVE IN YOU.

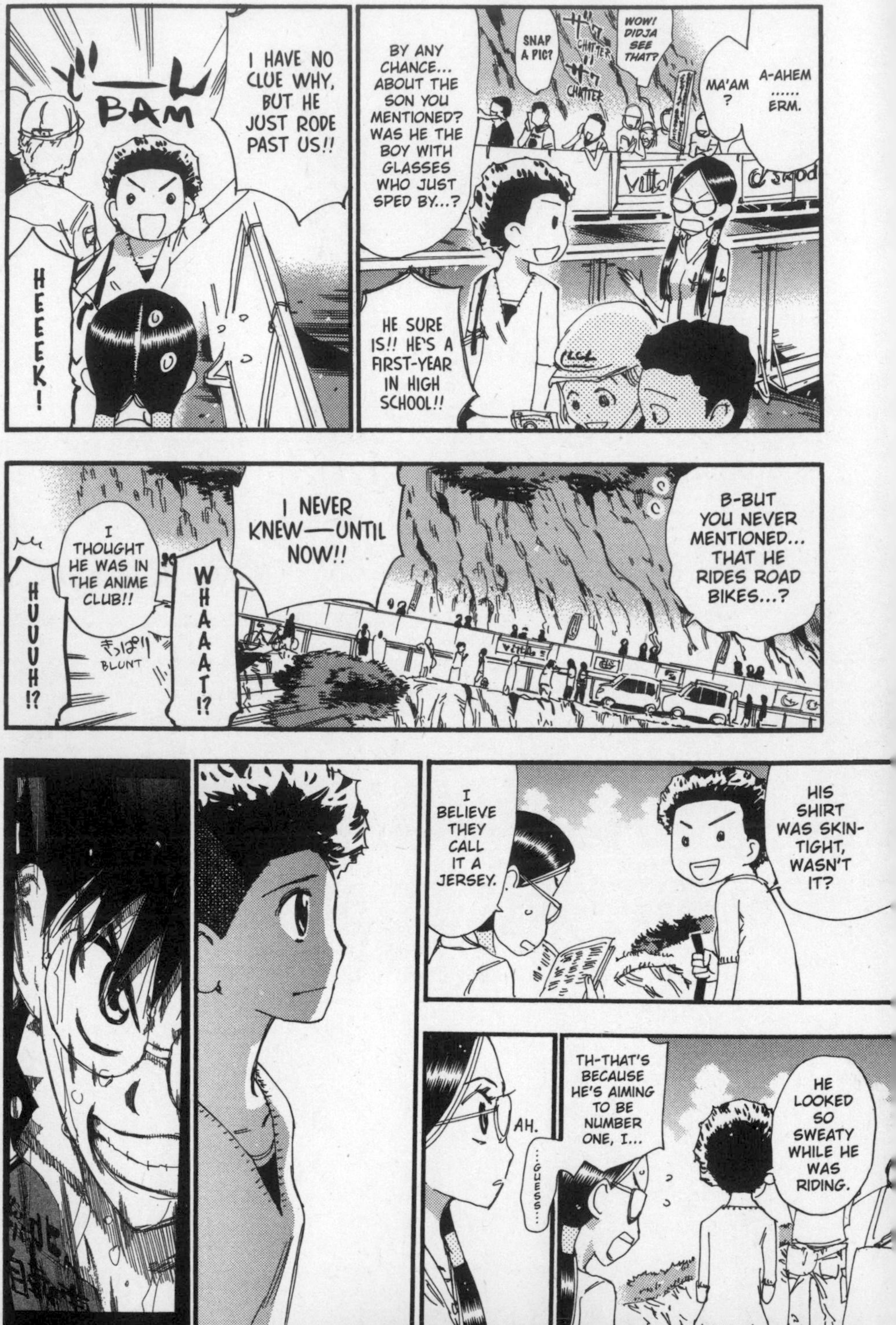
A-AHEM ...... ERM.
MA'AM ?
WOW! DIDJA SEE THAT?
ザワ CHATTER
ザワ CHATTER
SNAP A PIC?
BY ANY CHANCE... ABOUT THE SON YOU MENTIONED? WAS HE THE BOY WITH GLASSES WHO JUST SPED BY...?
HE SURE IS!! HE'S A FIRST-YEAR IN HIGH SCHOOL!!
I HAVE NO CLUE WHY, BUT HE JUST RODE PAST US!!
ど—ん BAM
HEEEEK!
B-BUT YOU NEVER MENTIONED... THAT HE RIDES ROAD BIKES...?
I NEVER KNEW—UNTIL NOW!!
WHAAAT!?
I THOUGHT HE WAS IN THE ANIME CLUB!!
きっぱり BLUNT
HUUUUH!?
HIS SHIRT WAS SKIN-TIGHT, WASN'T IT?
I BELIEVE THEY CALL IT A JERSEY.
HE LOOKED SO SWEATY WHILE HE WAS RIDING.
TH-THAT'S BECAUSE HE'S AIMING TO BE NUMBER ONE, I...
...GUESS...
AH.

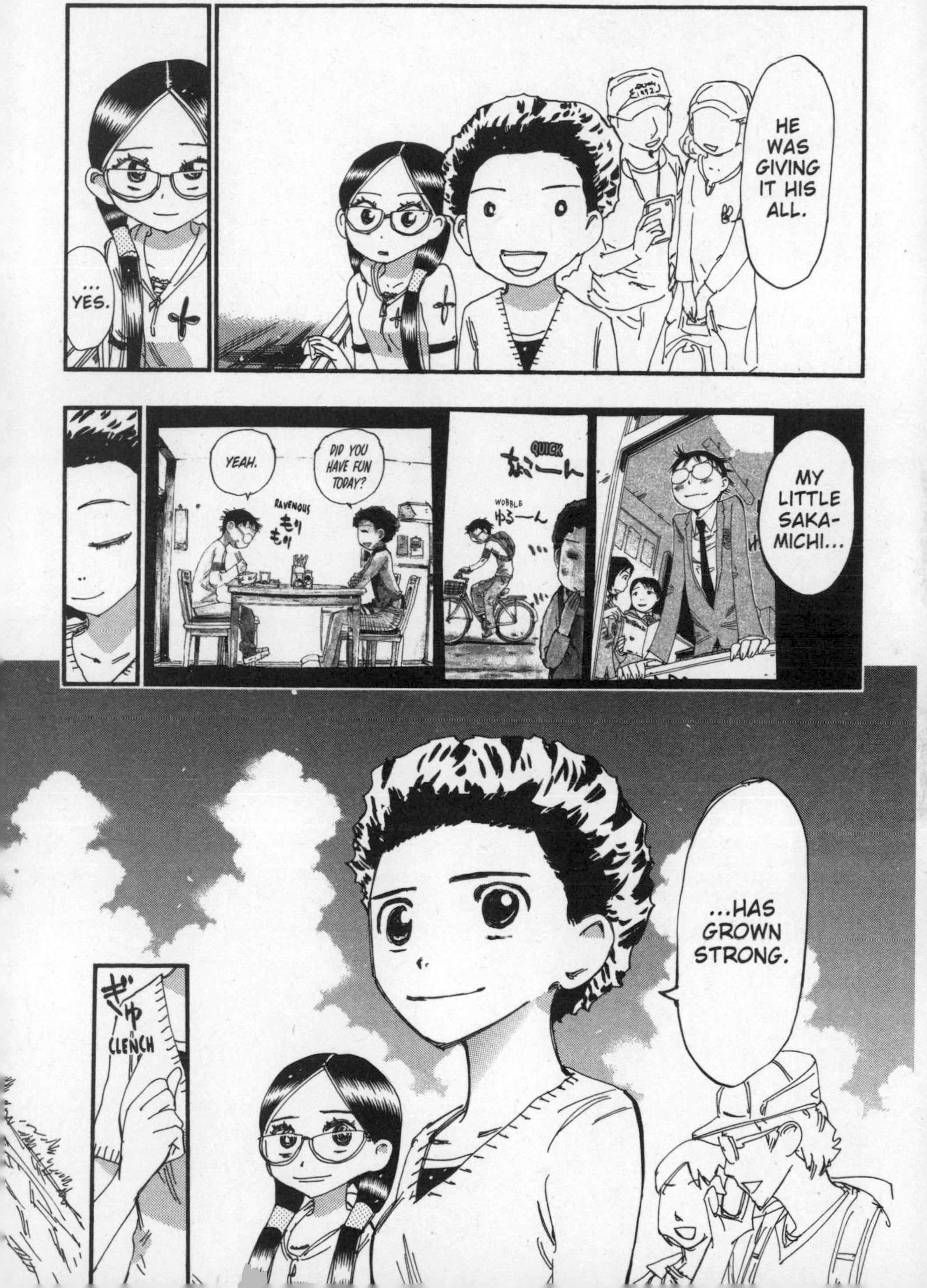
HE WAS GIVING IT HIS ALL.
...YES.
MY LITTLE SAKA-MICHI...
QUICK
WOBBLE
DID YOU HAVE FUN TODAY?
YEAH.
RAVENOUS
...HAS GROWN STRONG.
CLENCH

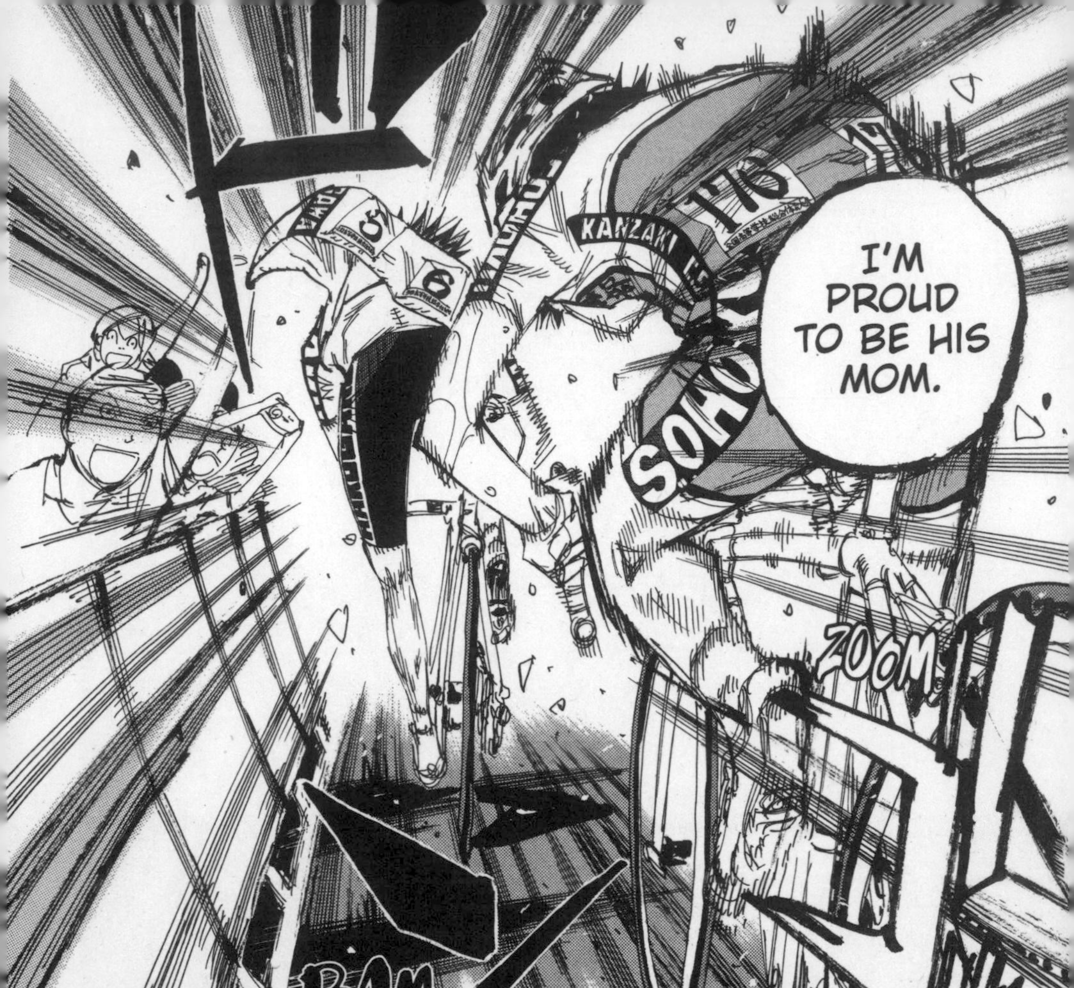
I'M PROUD TO BE HIS MOM.
ZOOM
BAM
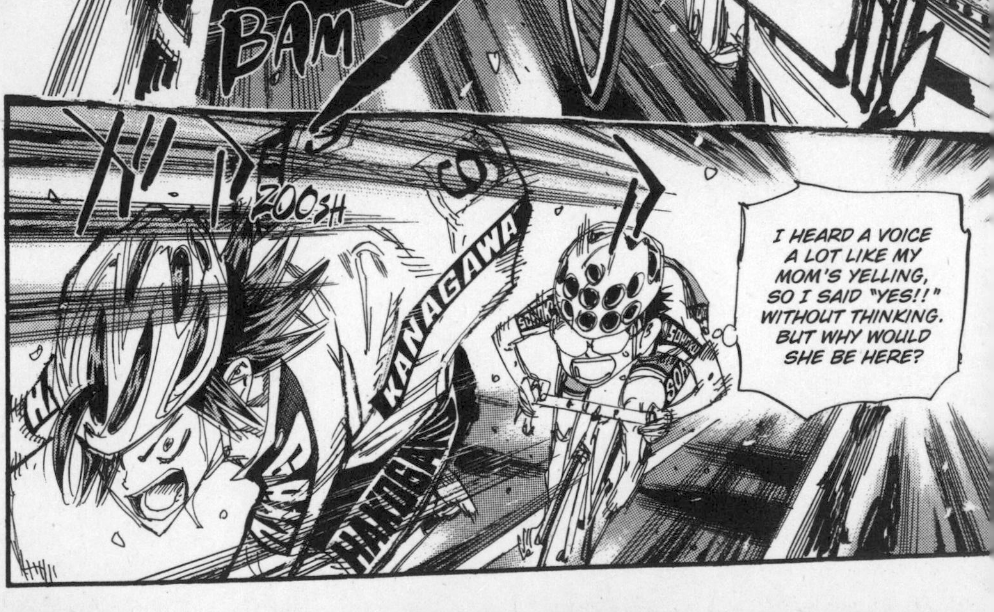
ZOOSH
I HEARD A VOICE A LOT LIKE MY MOM'S YELLING, SO I SAID "YES!!" WITHOUT THINKING. BUT WHY WOULD SHE BE HERE?

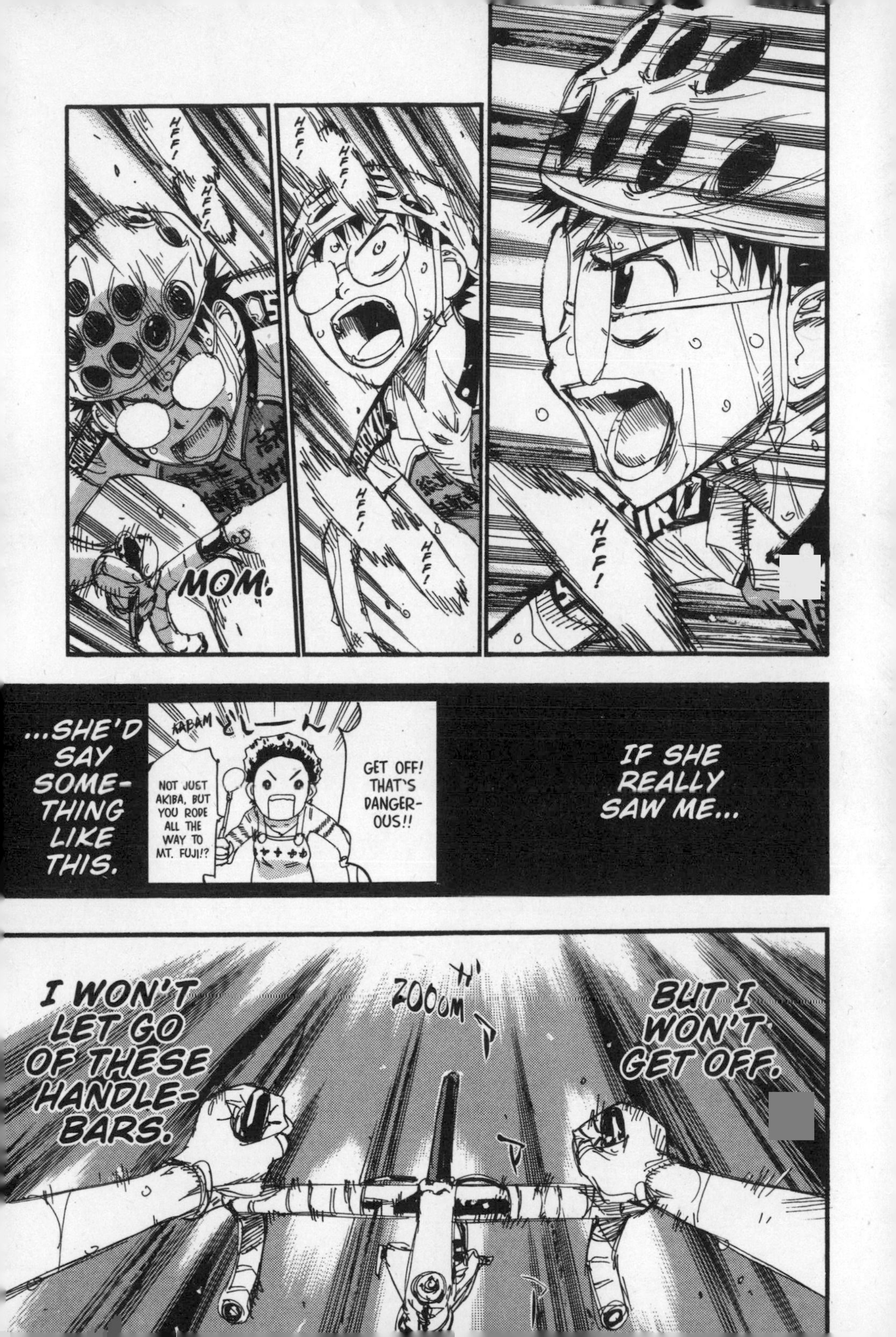
HFF!
HFF!
HFF!
HFF!
HFF!
HFF!
HFF!
HFF!
MOM.
IF SHE REALLY SAW ME...
KABAM どしーん
GET OFF! THAT'S DANGER-OUS!!
NOT JUST AKIBA, BUT YOU RODE ALL THE WAY TO MT. FUJI!?
...SHE'D SAY SOME-THING LIKE THIS.
BUT I WON'T GET OFF.
ZOOOM
I WON'T LET GO OF THESE HANDLE-BARS.

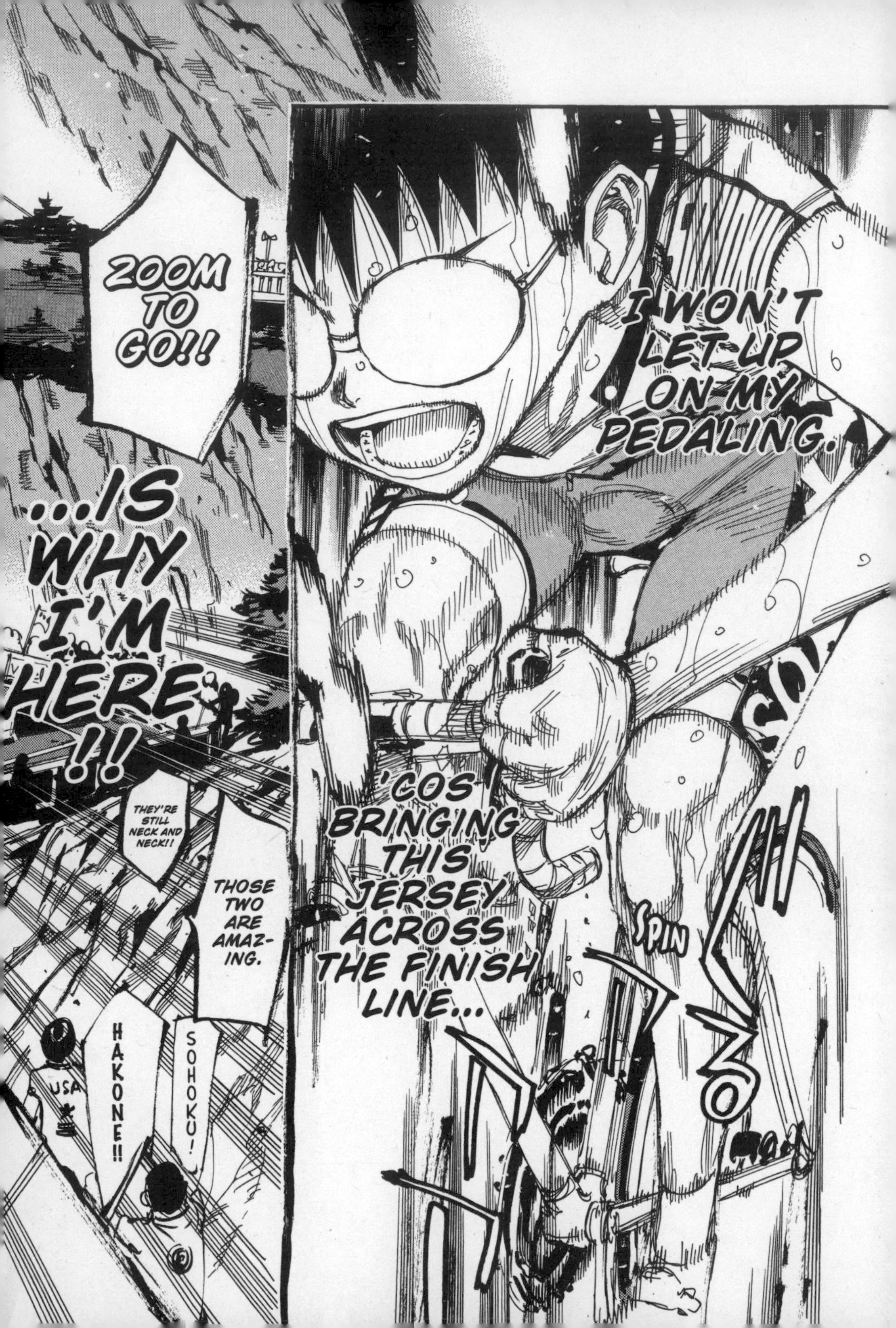
I WON'T LET UP ON MY PEDALING.
'COS BRINGING THIS JERSEY ACROSS THE FINISH LINE...
SPIN
ZOOM TO GO!!
...IS WHY I'M HERE!!
THEY'RE STILL NECK AND NECK!!
THOSE TWO ARE AMAZ-ING.
SOHOKU!
HAKONE!!
USA

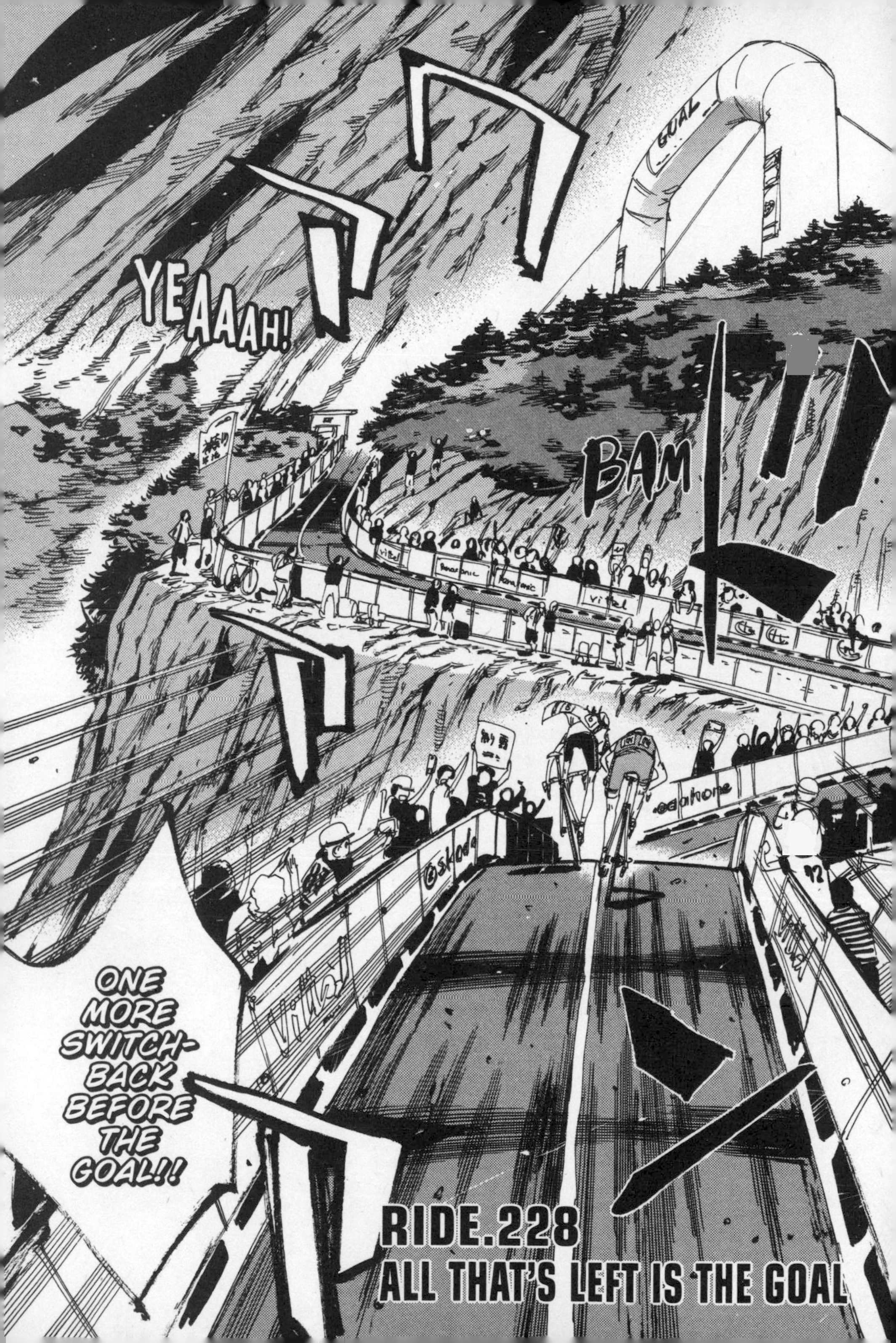
BAM
YEAAAH!
ONE MORE SWITCH-BACK BEFORE THE GOAL!!
RIDE.228
ALL THAT'S LEFT IS THE GOAL

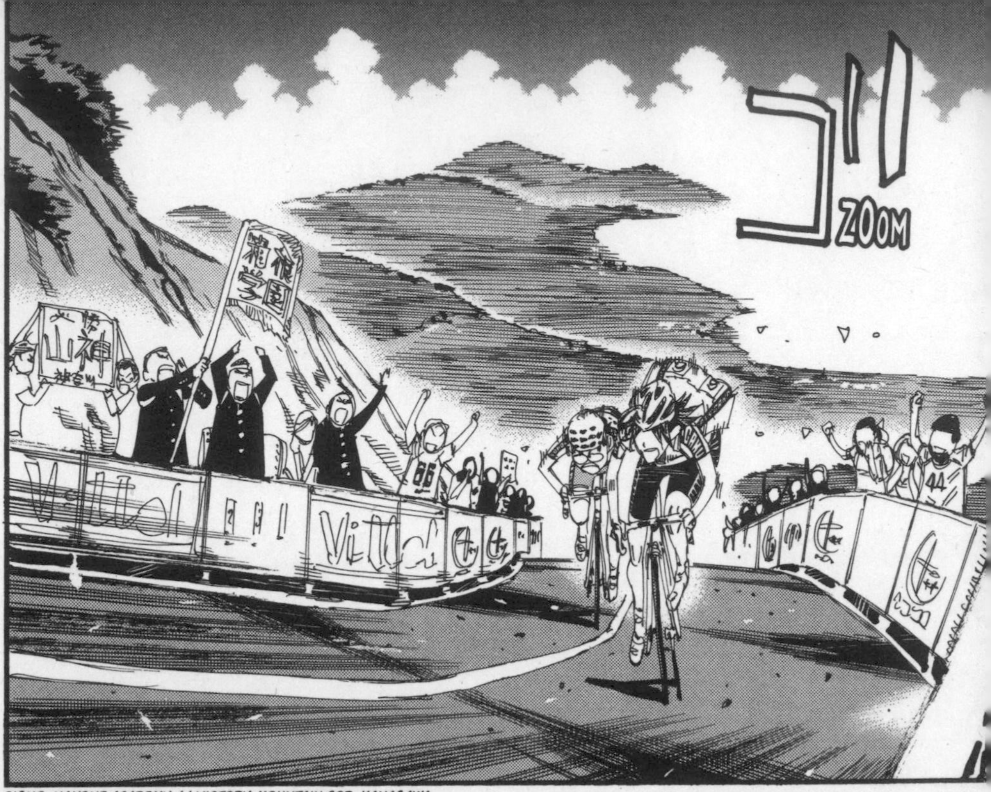
ZOOM

SIGNS: HAKONE ACADEMY // VICTORY, MOUNTAIN GOD, KANAGAWA

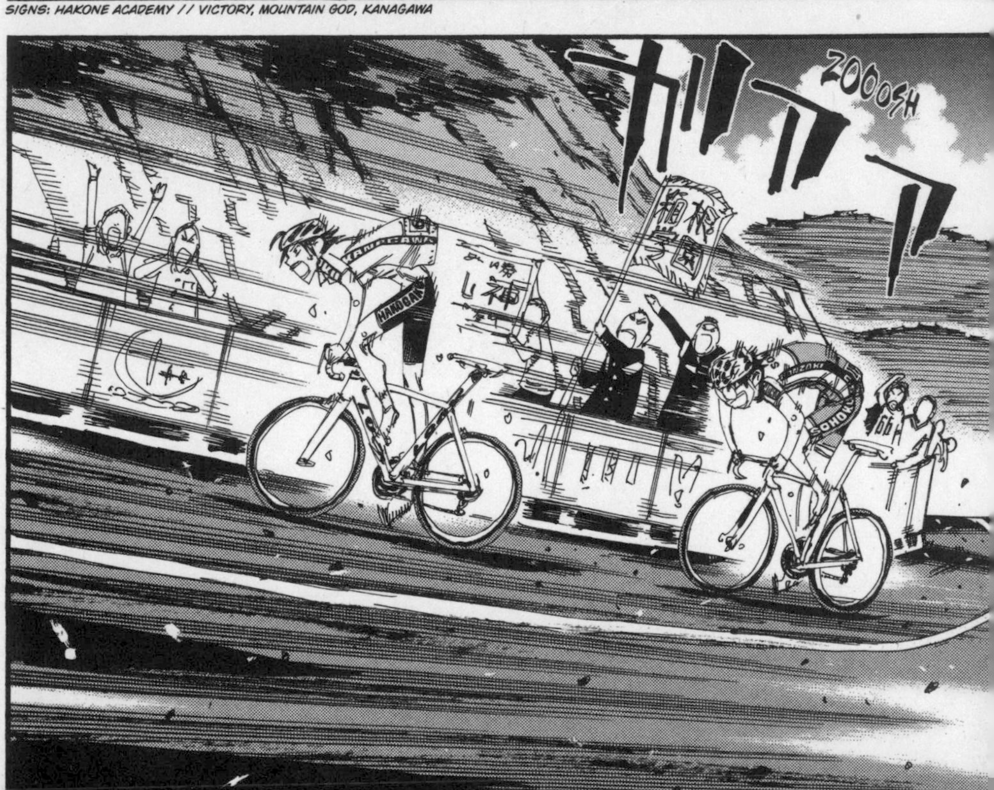
ZOOOSH

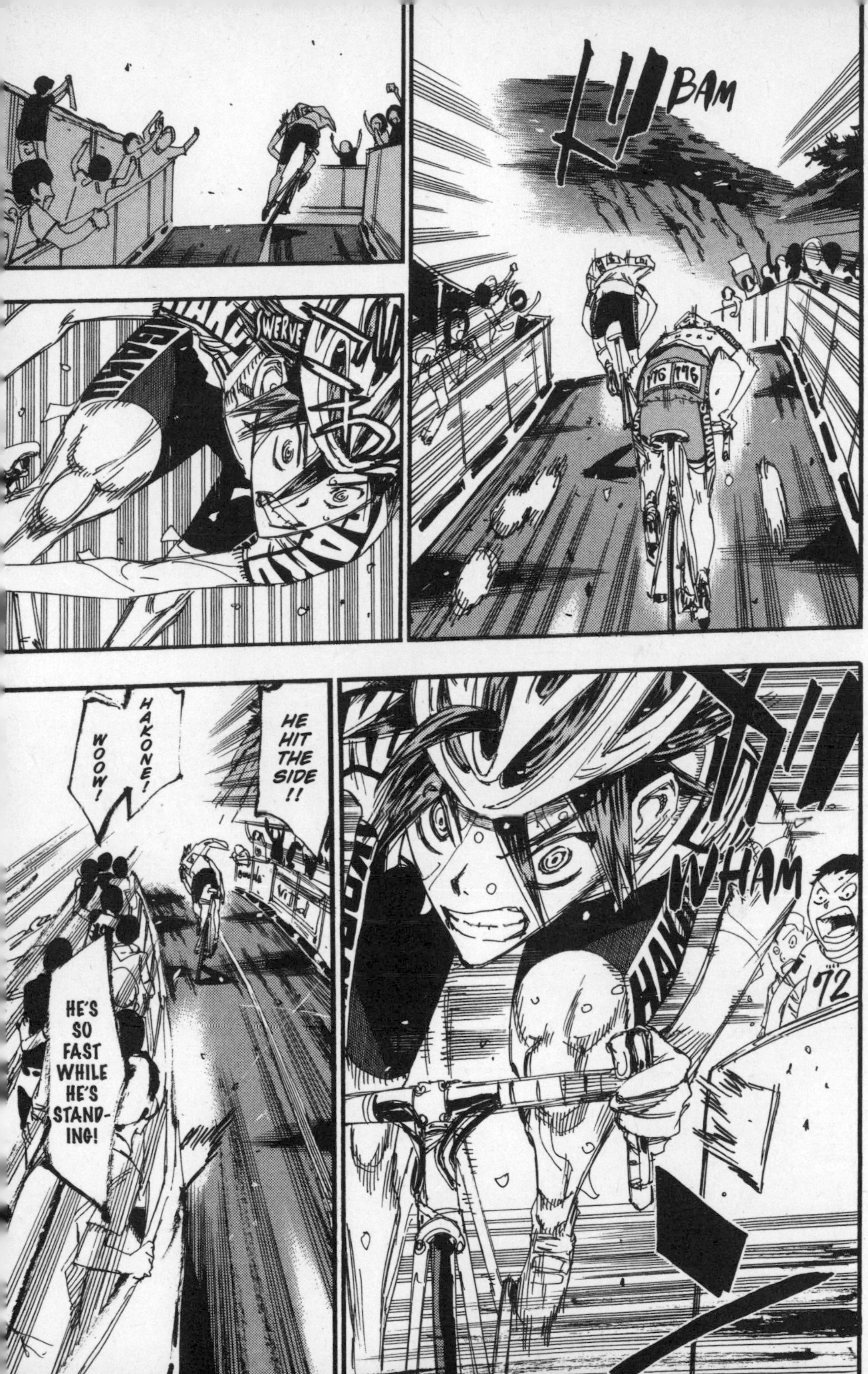
BAM
SWERVE
WHAM
HE HIT THE SIDE!!
HAKONE! WOOOW!
HE'S SO FAST WHILE HE'S STANDING!

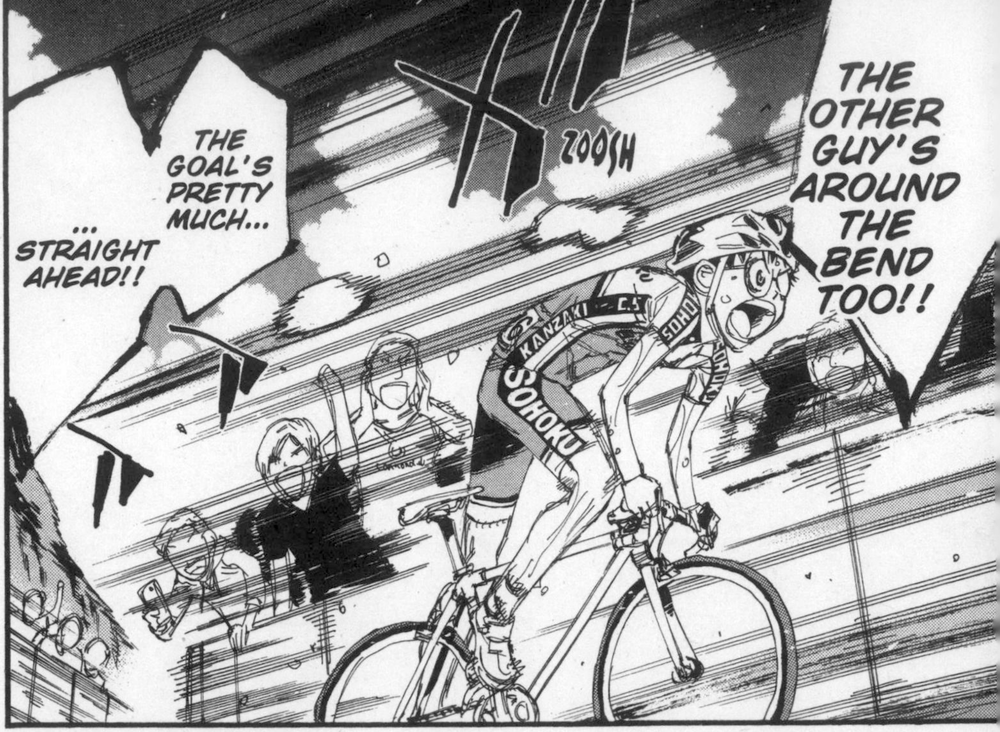
THE OTHER GUY'S AROUND THE BEND TOO!!
ZOOSH
THE GOAL'S PRETTY MUCH...
...STRAIGHT AHEAD!!
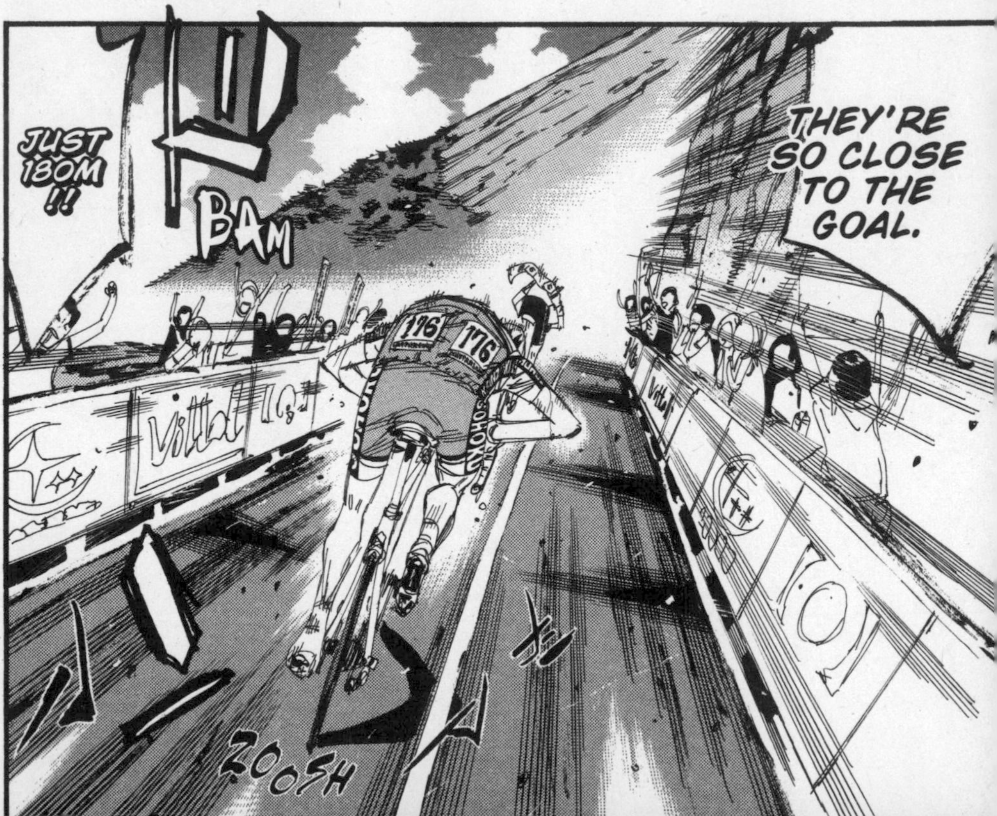
THEY'RE SO CLOSE TO THE GOAL.
BAM
JUST 180M!!
ZOOSH

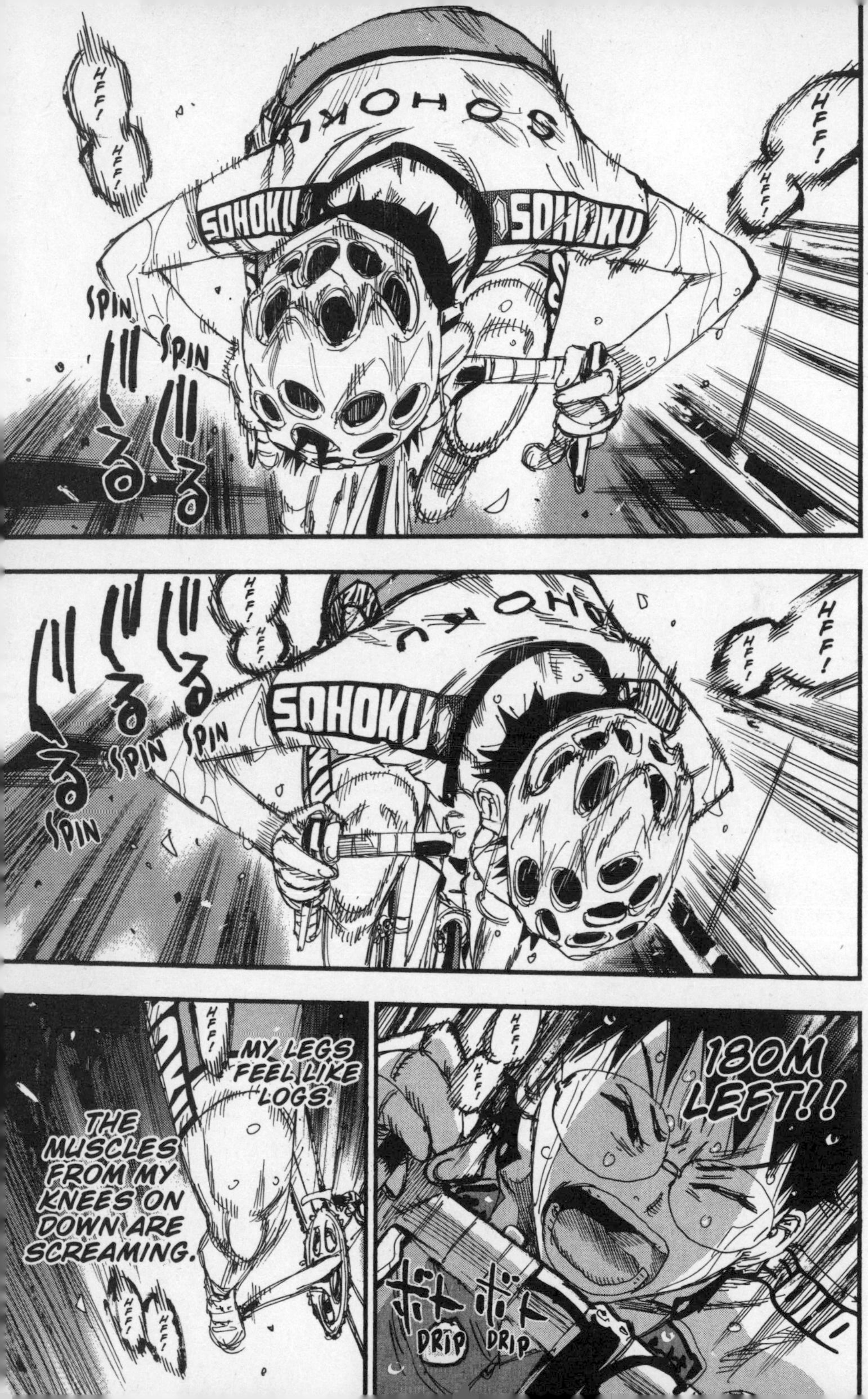
HFF! HFF!
SOHOKU
SOHOKU SOHOKU
HFF! HFF!
SPIN
SPIN
HFF! HFF!
SOHOKU
SOHOKU
HFF! HFF!
SPIN
SPIN
SPIN
180M LEFT!!
HFF! HFF!
DRIP DRIP
MY LEGS FEEL LIKE LOGS.
THE MUSCLES FROM MY KNEES ON DOWN ARE SCREAMING.
HFF! HFF!
HFF!
HFF! HFF!

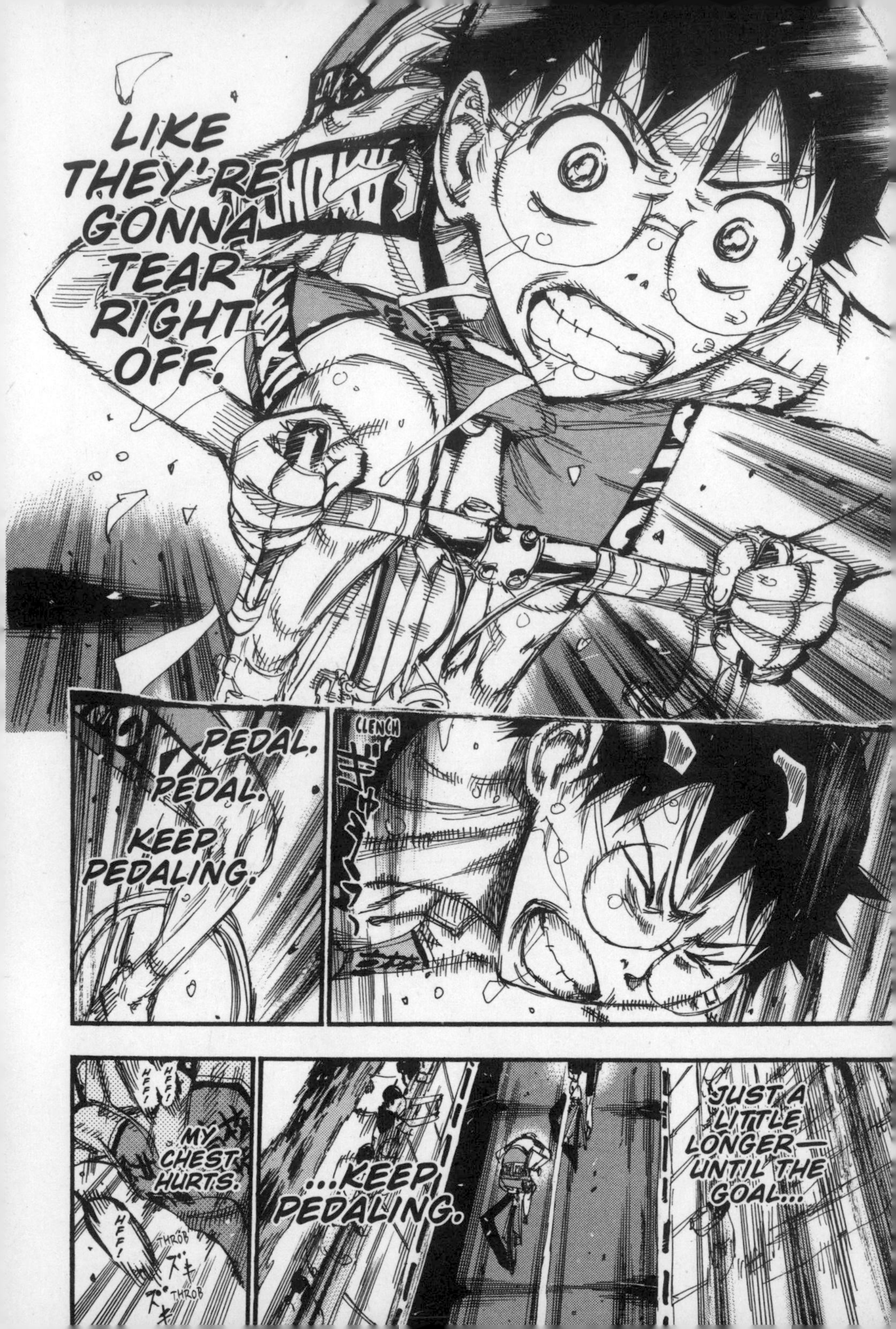
LIKE THEY'RE GONNA TEAR RIGHT OFF.
CLENCH
PEDAL. PEDAL.
KEEP PEDALING.
HFF! HFF!
MY CHEST HURTS.
HFF!
THROB
THROB
JUST A LITTLE LONGER— UNTIL THE GOAL...
...KEEP PEDALING.

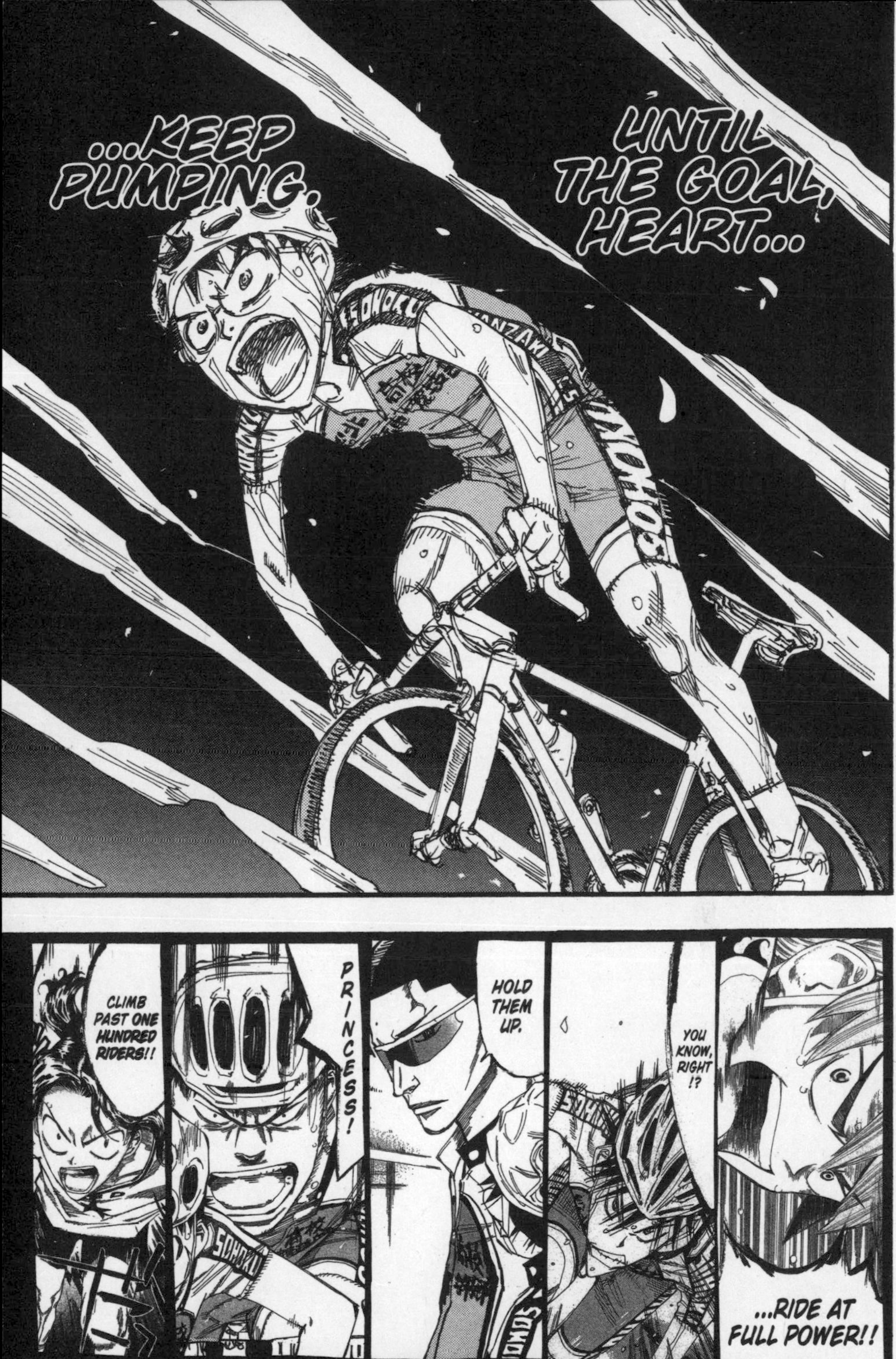
UNTIL THE GOAL, HEART...
...KEEP PUMPING.
YOU KNOW, RIGHT!?
...RIDE AT FULL POWER!!
HOLD THEM UP.
PRINCESS!
CLIMB PAST ONE HUNDRED RIDERS!!

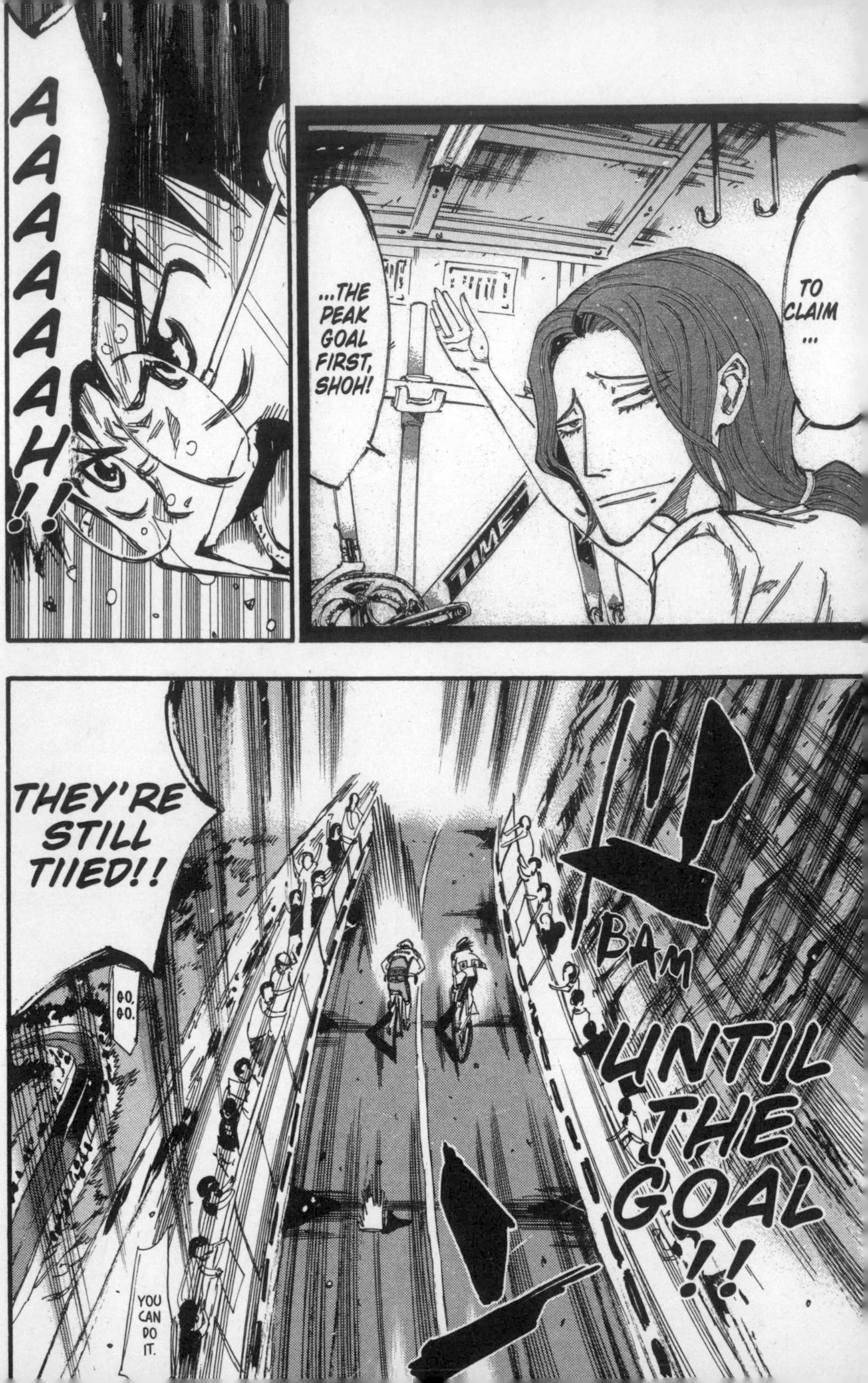
TO CLAIM ...
...THE PEAK GOAL FIRST, SHOH!
AAAAAAAH!!
THEY'RE STILL TIIED!!
BAM
UNTIL THE GOAL!!
GO, GO.
YOU CAN DO IT.

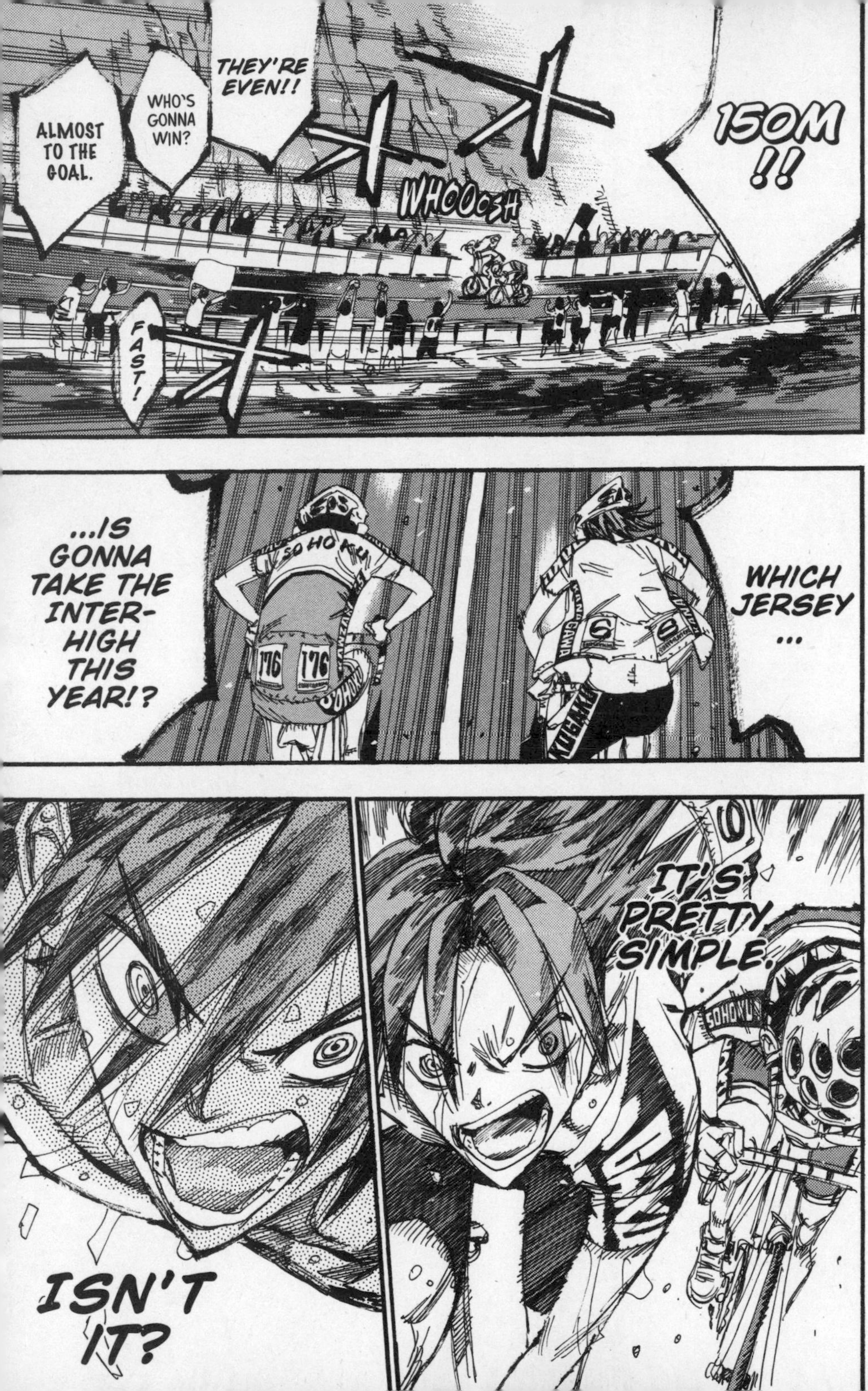
150M !!
THEY'RE EVEN!!
WHO'S GONNA WIN?
ALMOST TO THE GOAL.
WHOOOSH
FAST!
WHICH JERSEY ...
...IS GONNA TAKE THE INTER-HIGH THIS YEAR!?
IT'S PRETTY SIMPLE.
ISN'T IT?

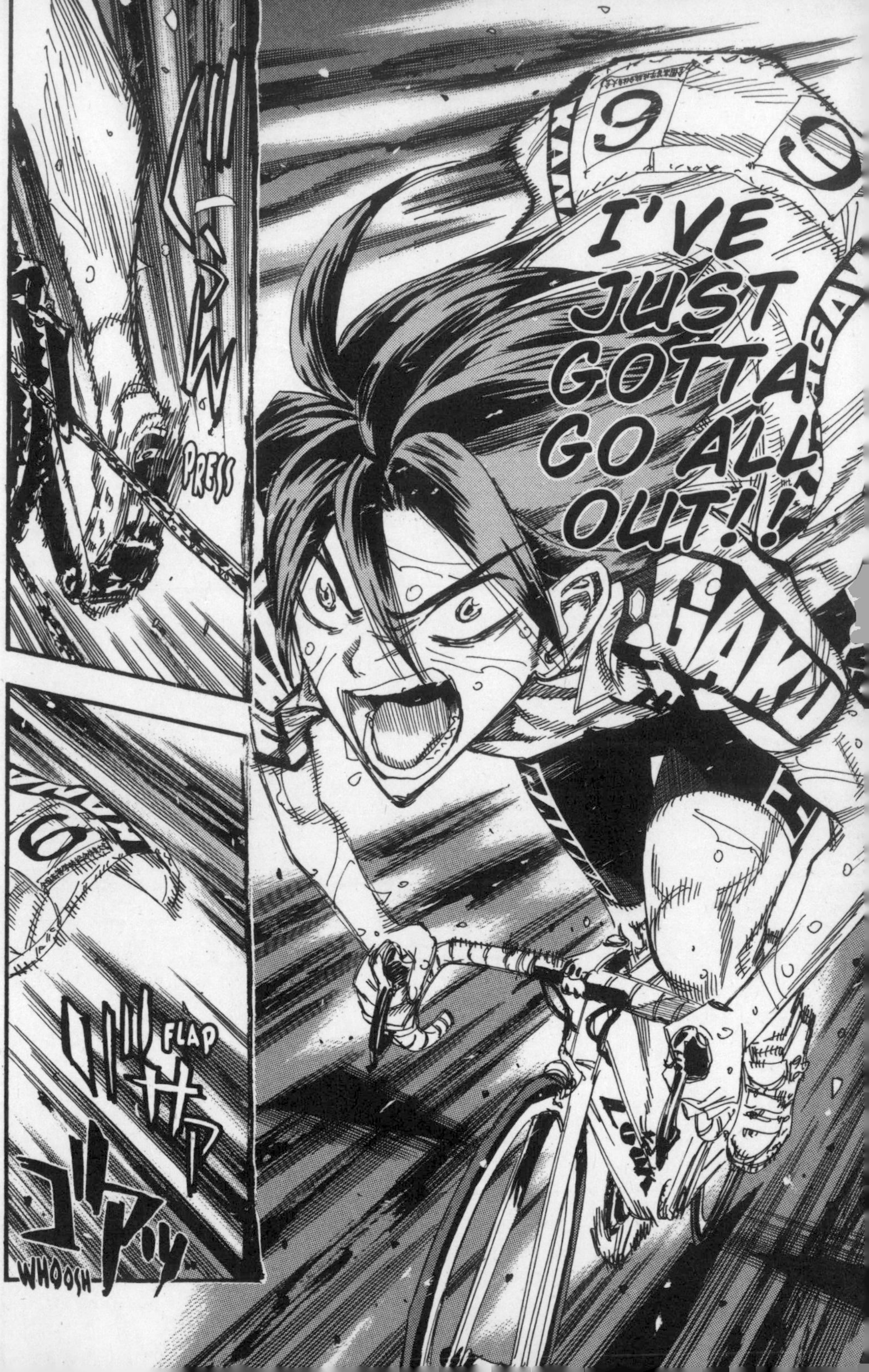
I'VE JUST GOTTA GO ALL OUT!!
PRESS
FLAP
WHOOSH

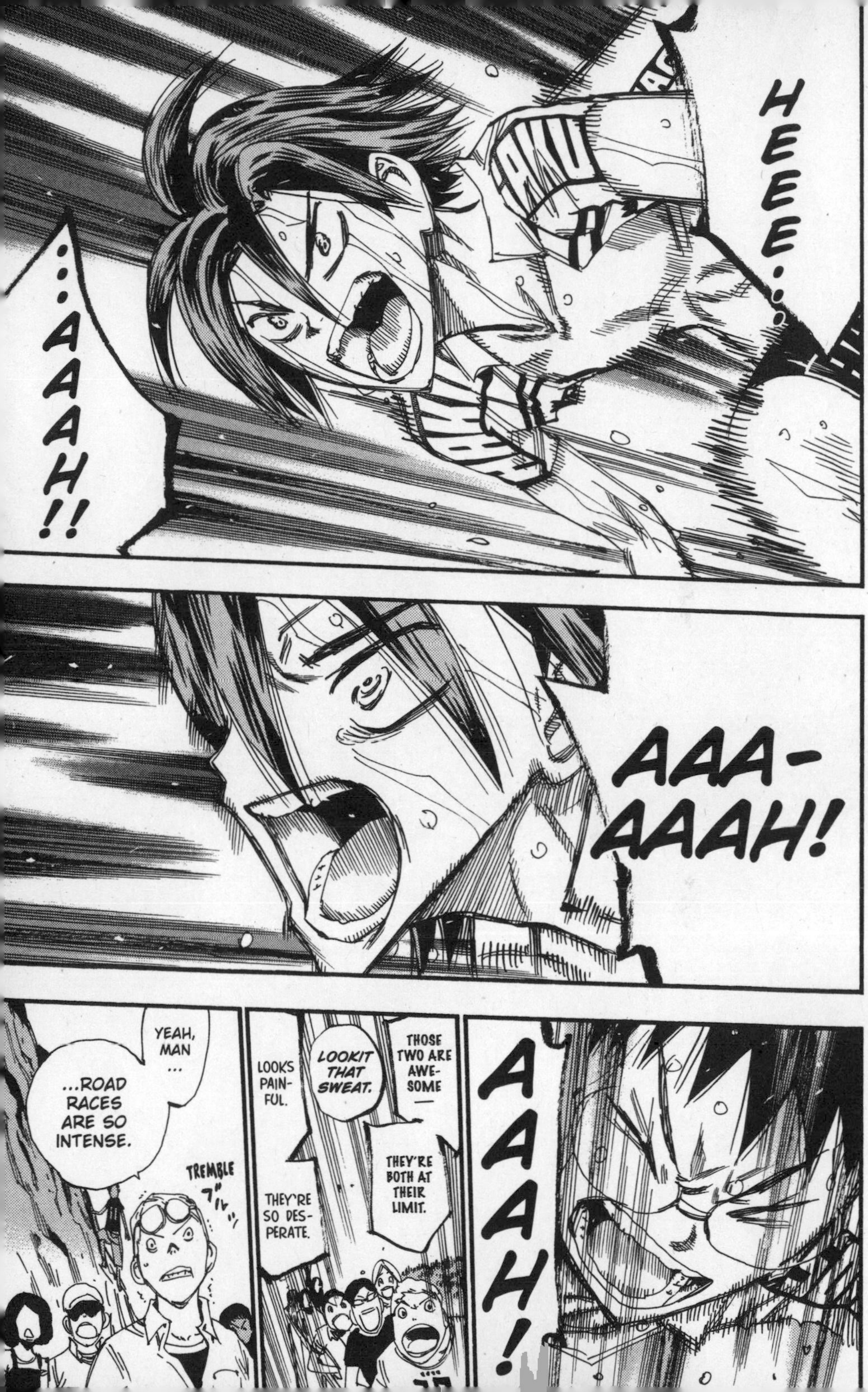
HEEEE...
...AAAAH!!
AAA-AAAH!
AAAAH!
THOSE TWO ARE AWE-SOME —
LOOKIT THAT SWEAT.
LOOKS PAIN-FUL.
THEY'RE BOTH AT THEIR LIMIT.
THEY'RE SO DES-PERATE.
YEAH, MAN ...
...ROAD RACES ARE SO INTENSE.
TREMBLE

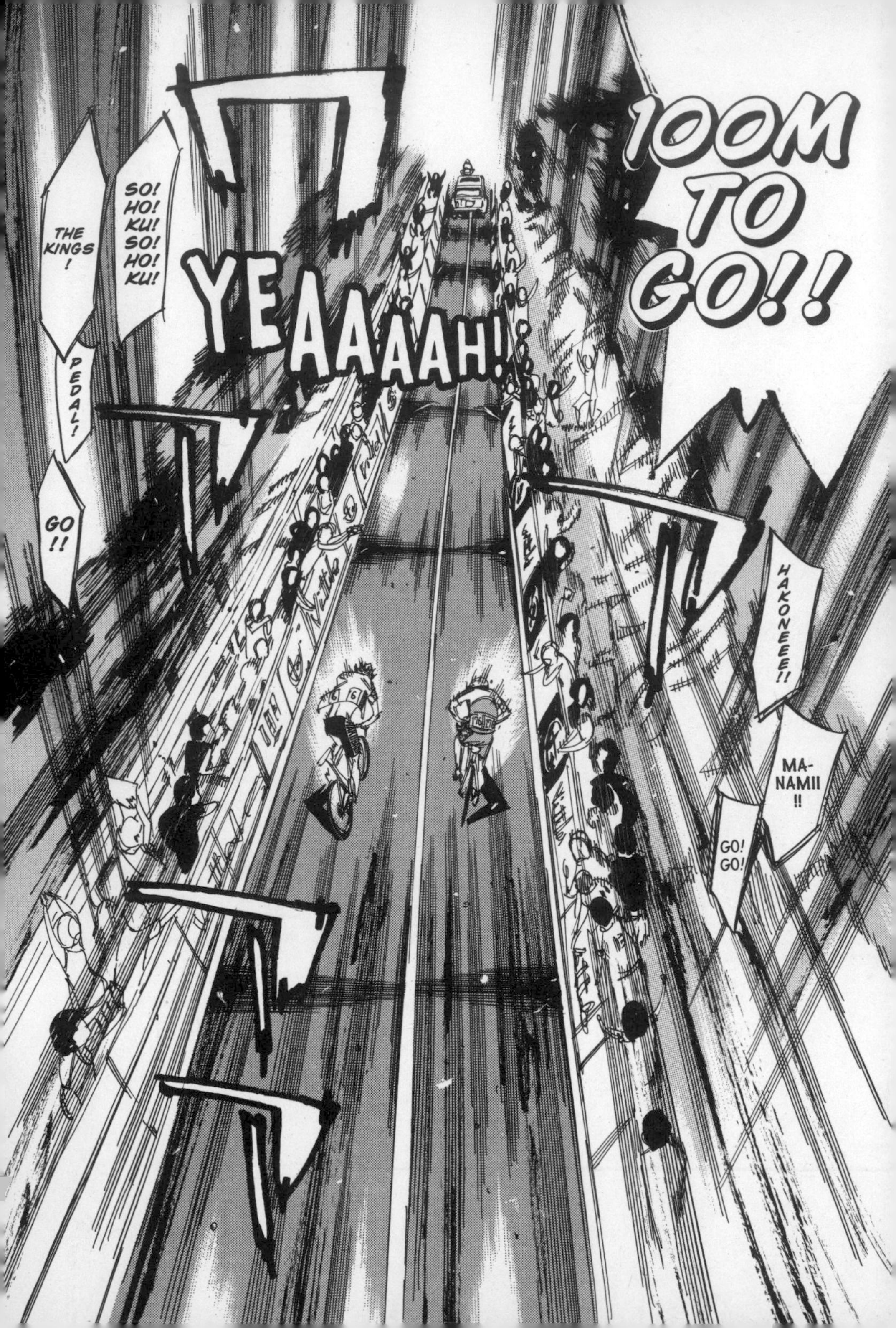
100M TO GO!!
YEAAAAAH!
SO! HO! KU! SO! HO! KU!
THE KINGS!
PEDAL!
GO!!
HAKONEEE!!
MA-NAMII!!
GO! GO!

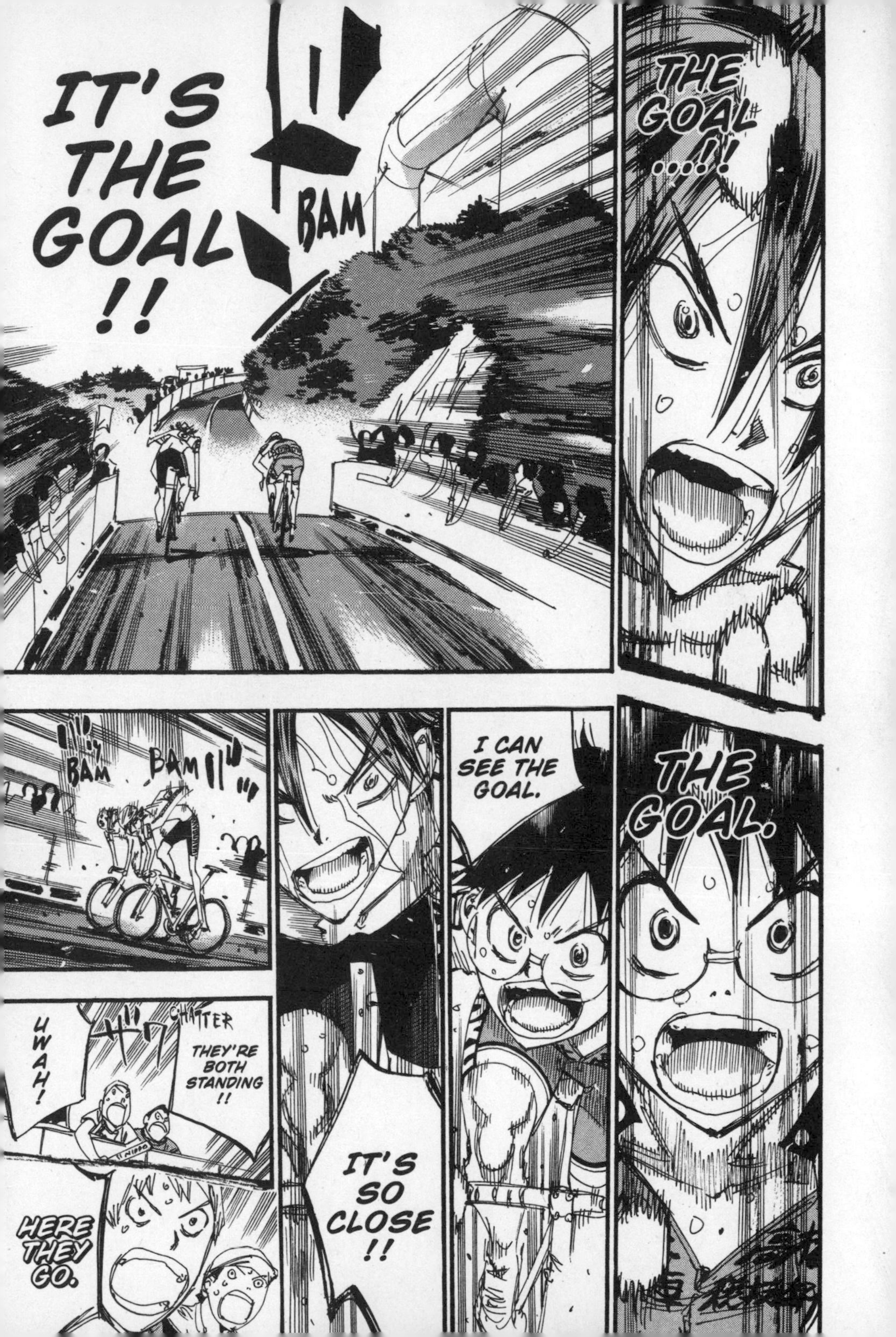
THE GOAL ...!!
IT'S THE GOAL !!
BAM
THE GOAL.
I CAN SEE THE GOAL.
IT'S SO CLOSE !!
BAM
BAM
CHATTER
THEY'RE BOTH STANDING !!
UWAH!
HERE THEY GO.

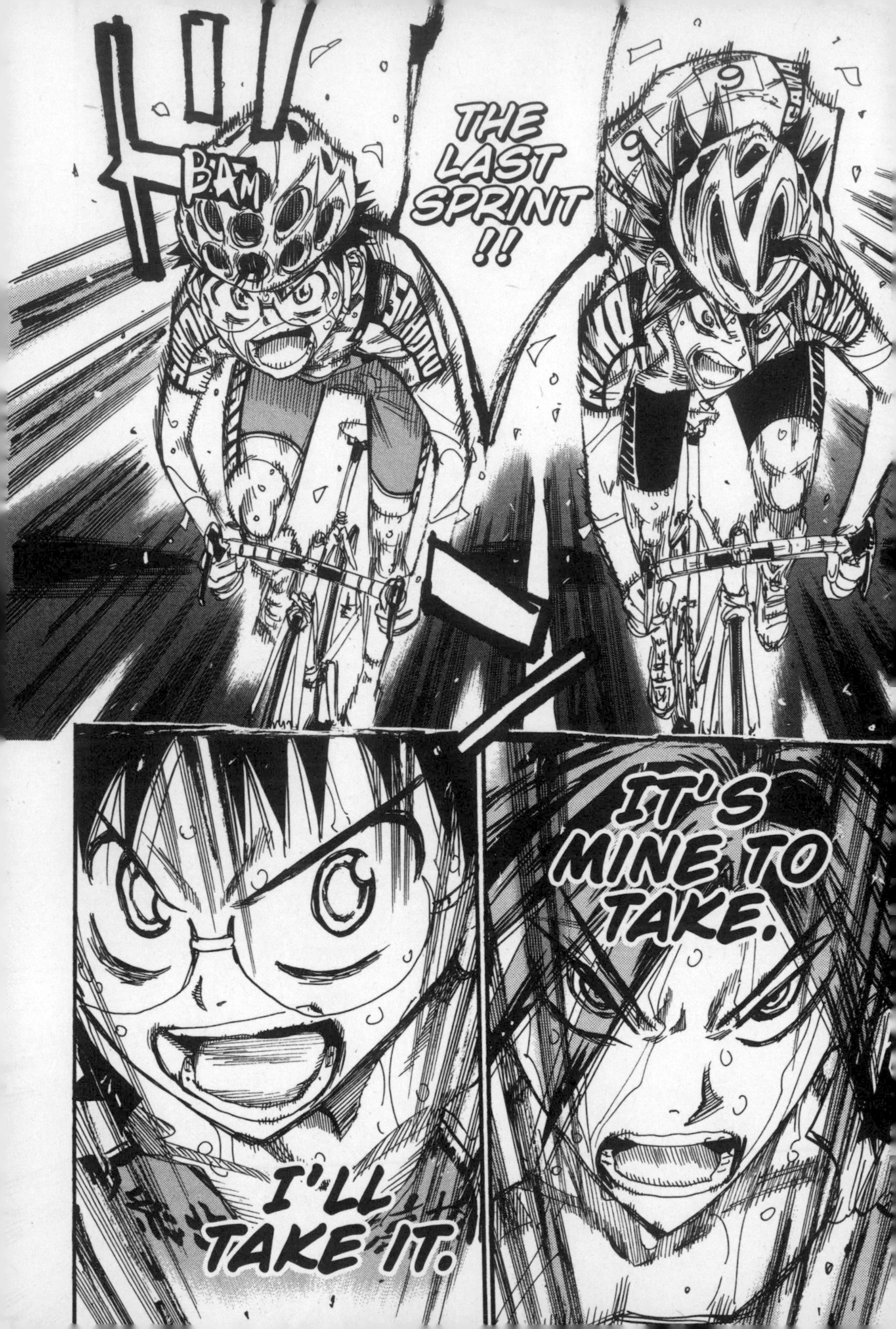
THE LAST SPRINT !!
BAM
IT'S MINE TO TAKE.
I'LL TAKE IT.

RIDE.229 THE LAST SPRINT

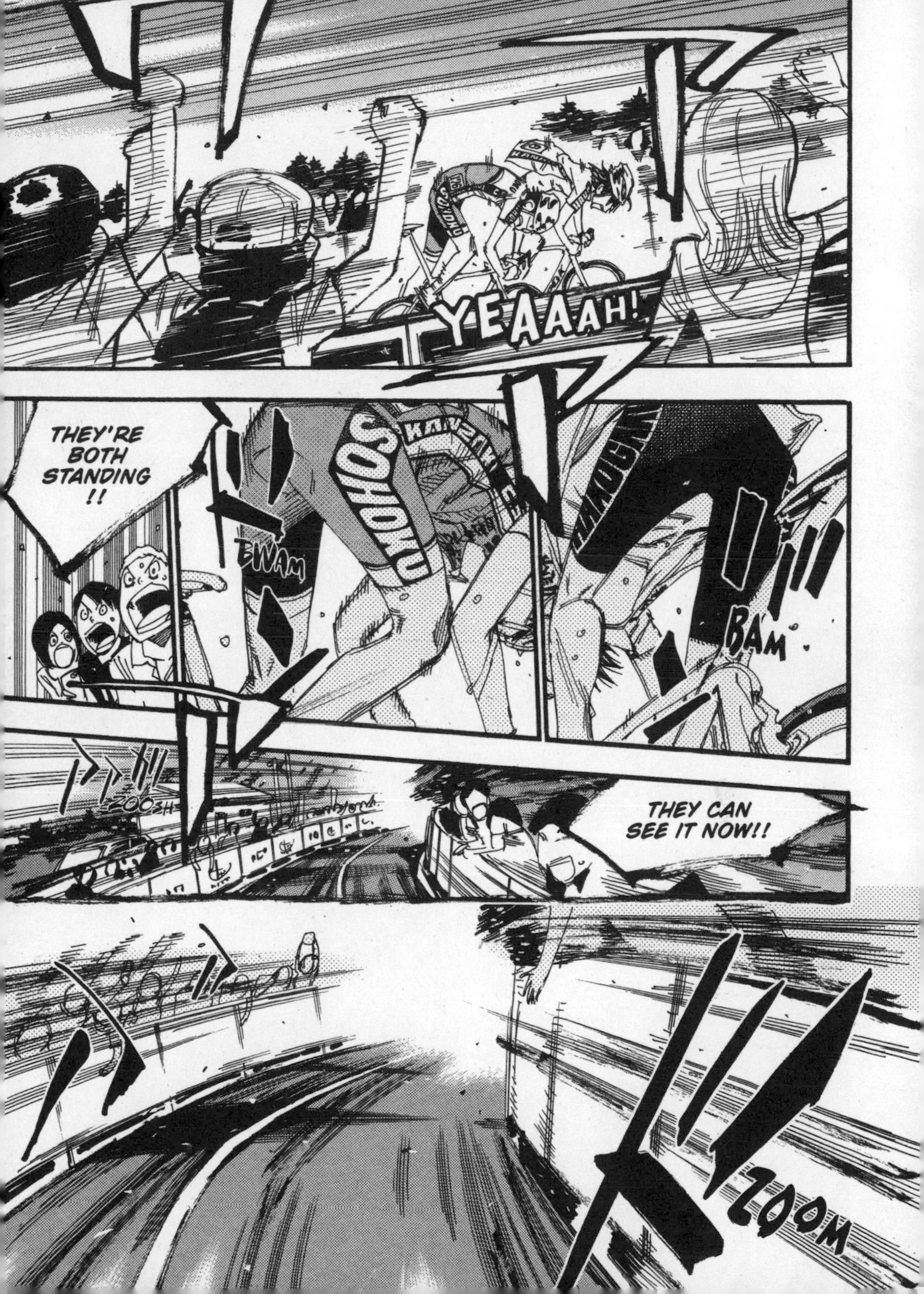
YEAAAAH!
THEY'RE BOTH STANDING !!
BAM
BWAM
THEY CAN SEE IT NOW!!
ZOOSH
ZOOM

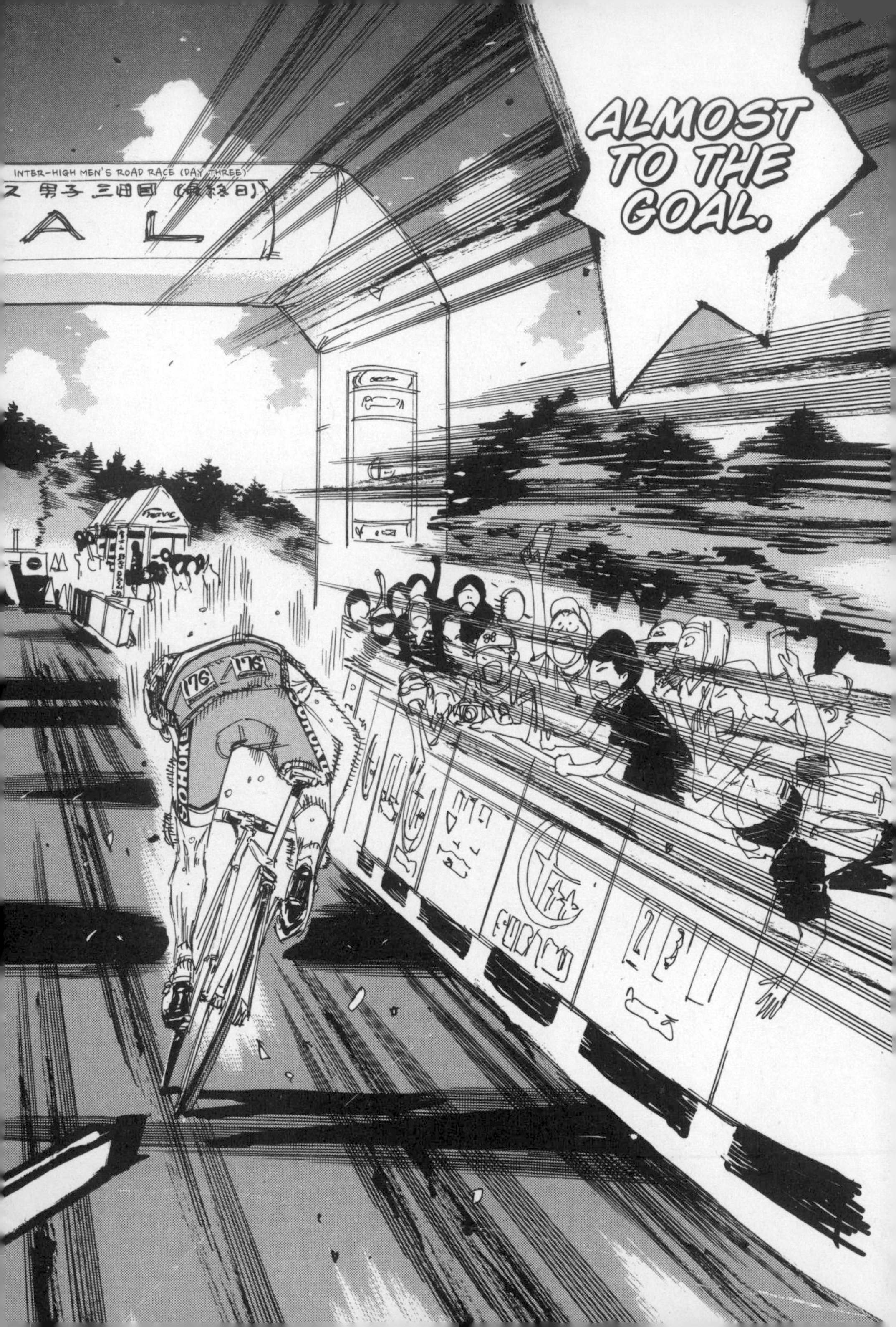
ALMOST TO THE GOAL.
INTER-HIGH MEN'S ROAD RACE (DAY THREE)

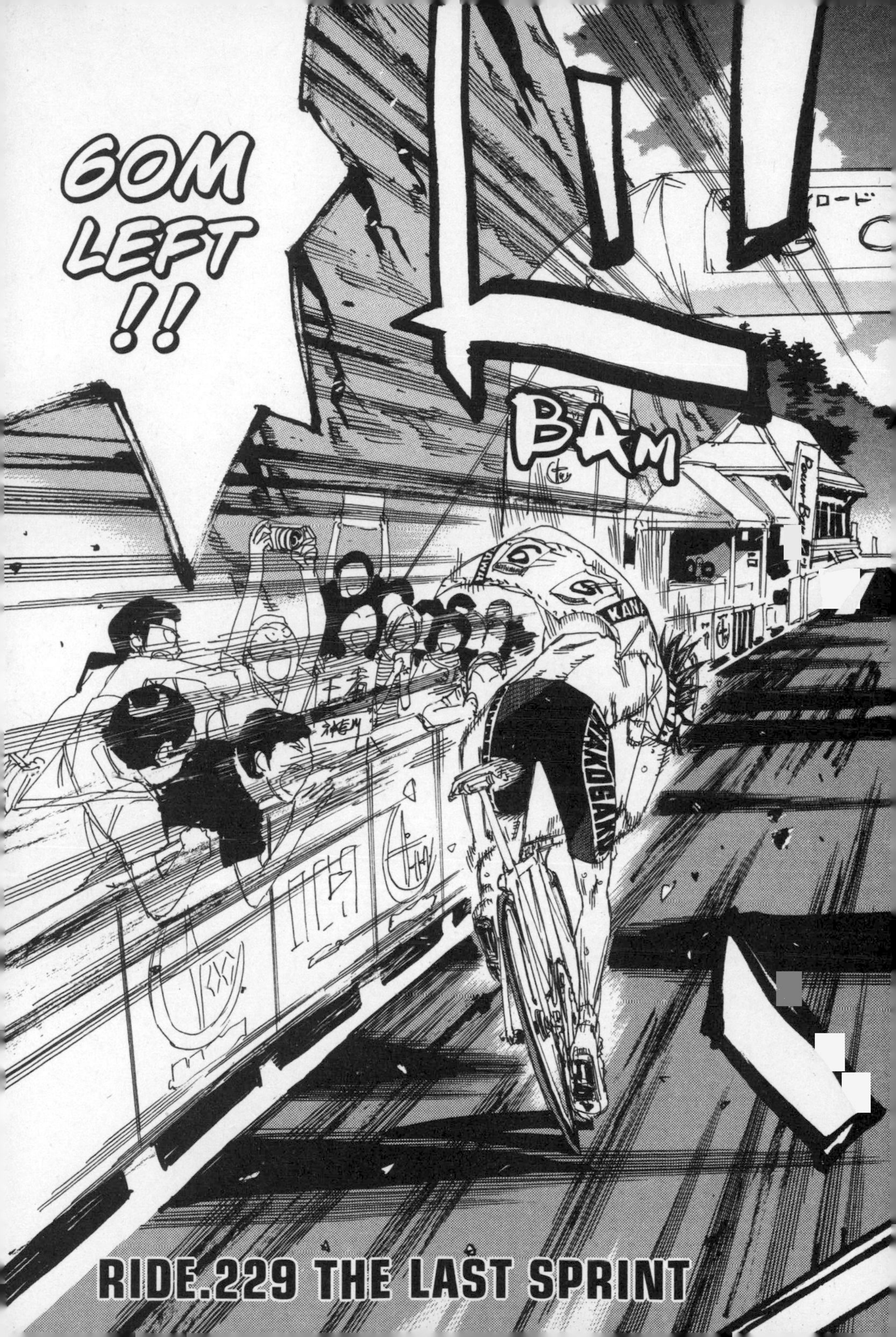
60M LEFT!!
BAM

RIDE.229 THE LAST SPRINT

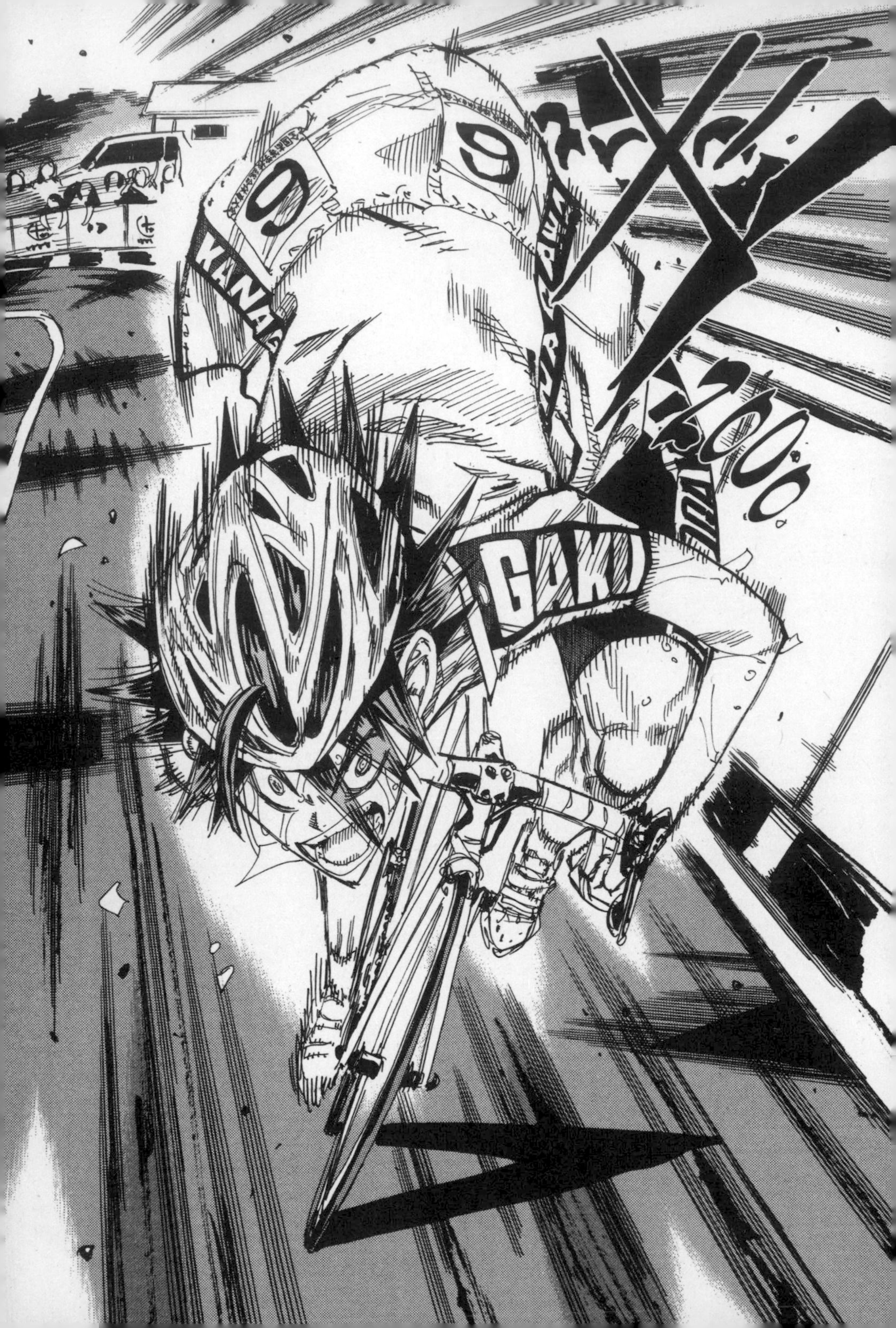
KANA
GAKU

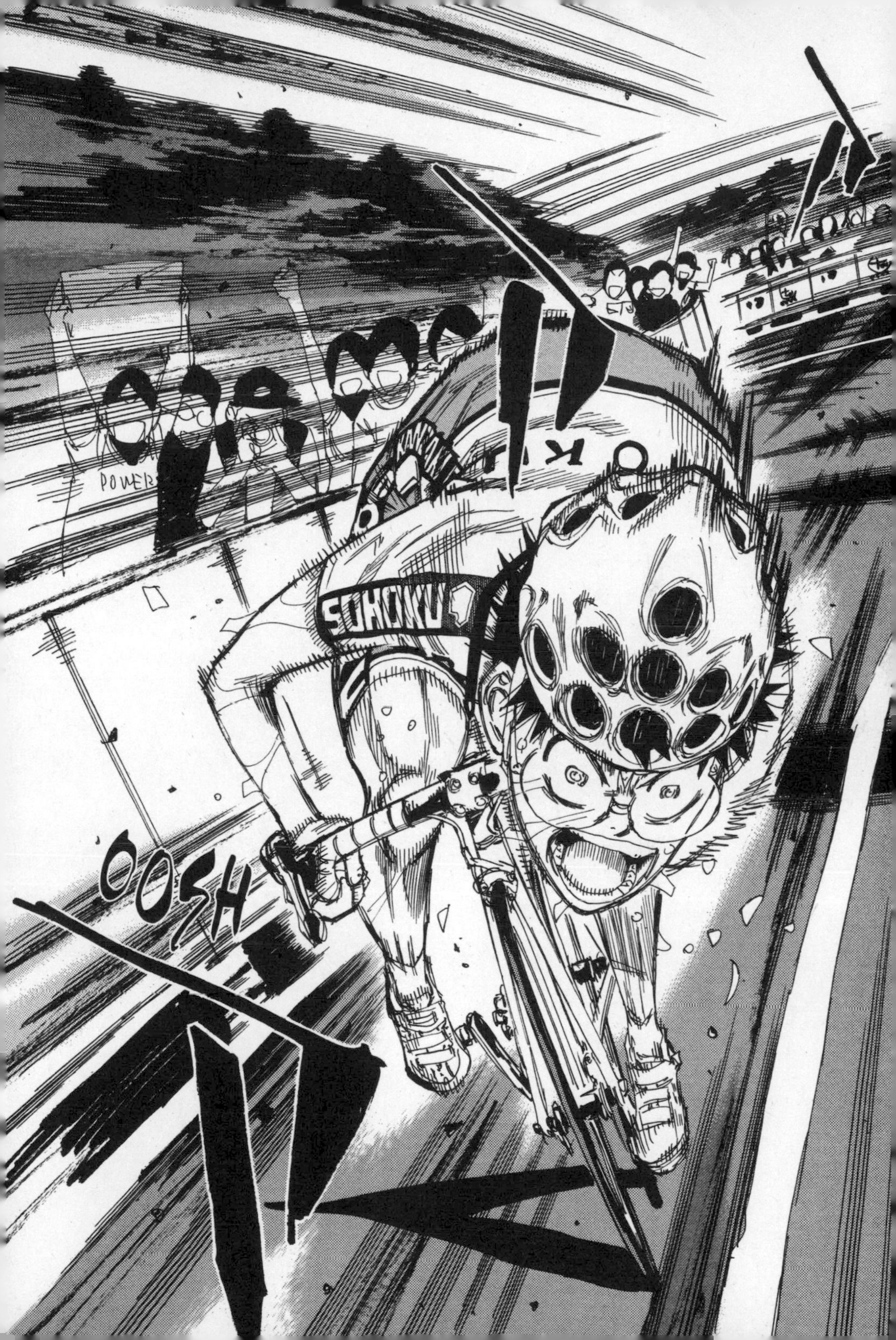
POWER
SOHOKU
OOSH

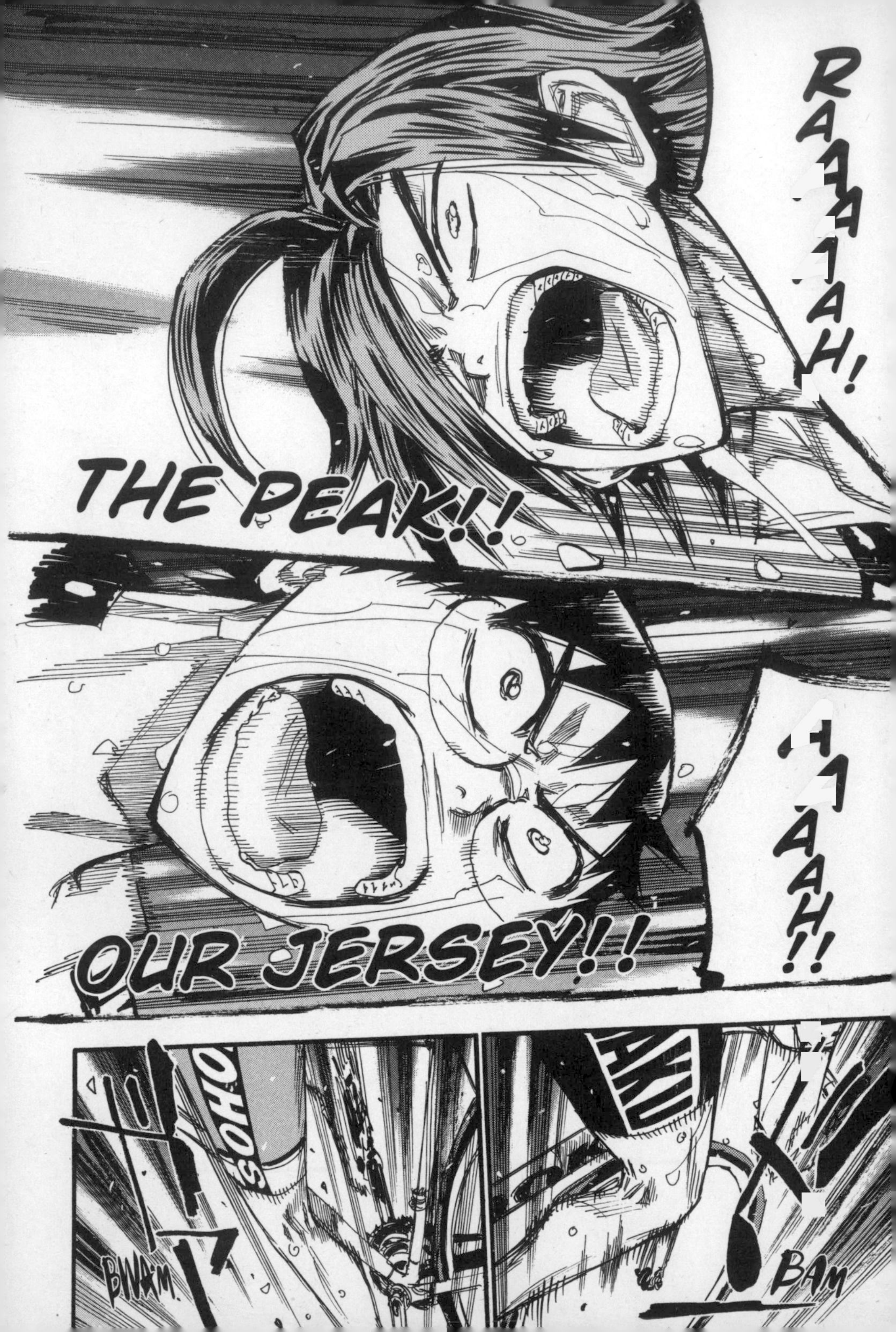
RAAAAAH!
THE PEAK!!
AAAAAH!!
OUR JERSEY!!
BAM
BWAM

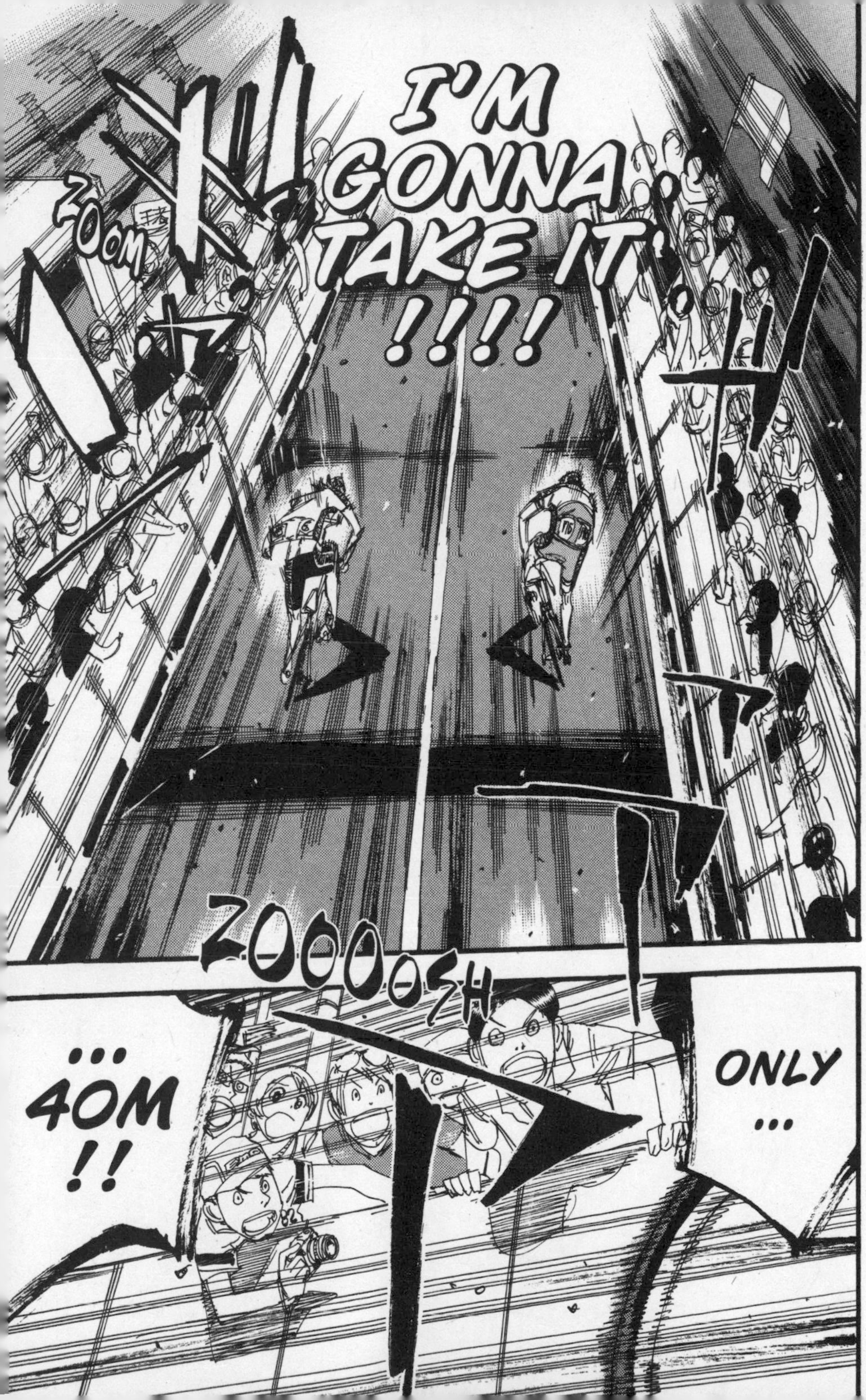
I'M GONNA TAKE IT !!!!
ZOOM
ZOOOOOSH
ONLY ...
... 40M !!

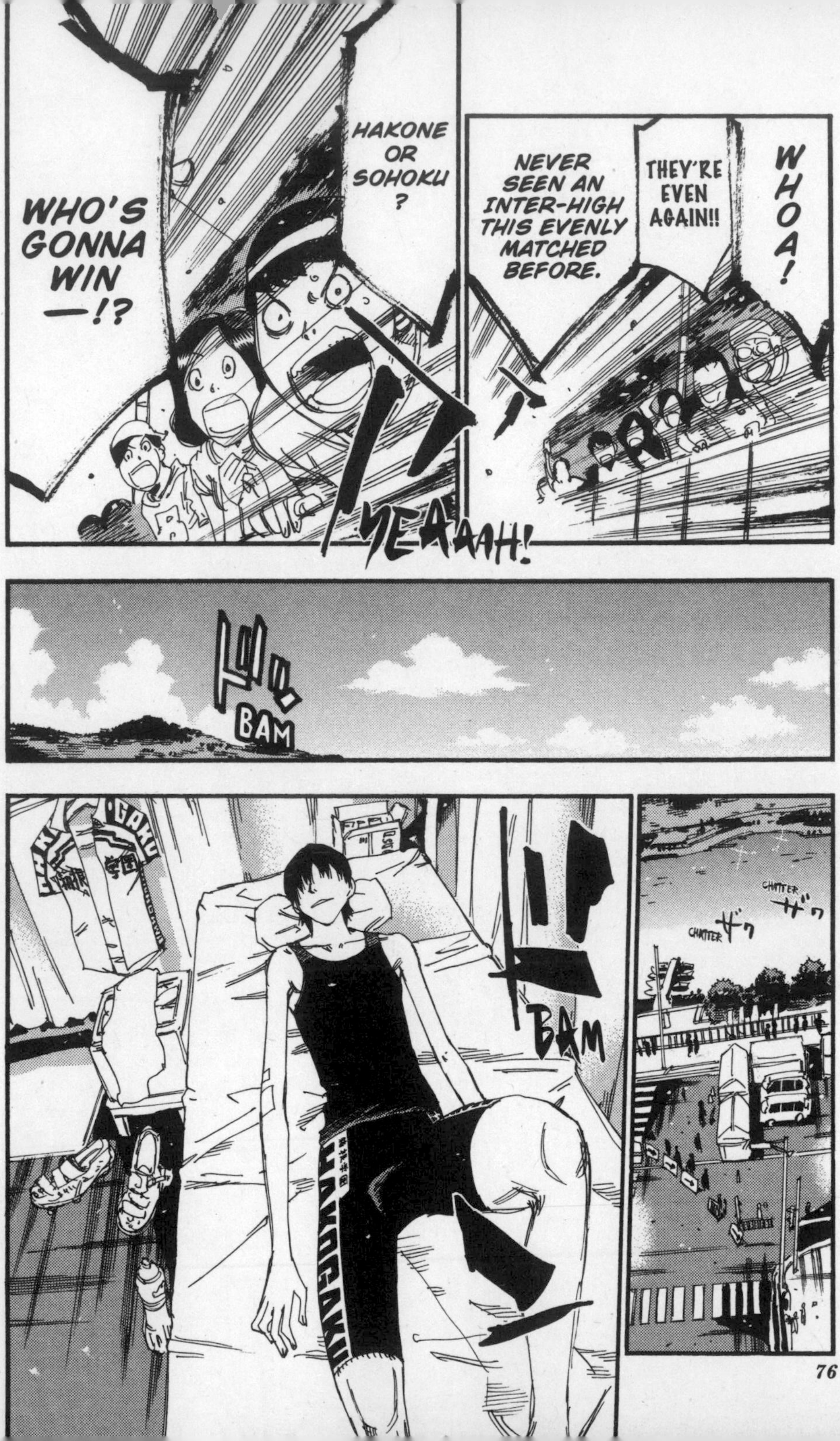
WHOA!
THEY'RE EVEN AGAIN!!
NEVER SEEN AN INTER-HIGH THIS EVENLY MATCHED BEFORE.
HAKONE OR SOHOKU?
WHO'S GONNA WIN—!?
YEAAAH!
BAM
CHATTER
CHATTER
BAM

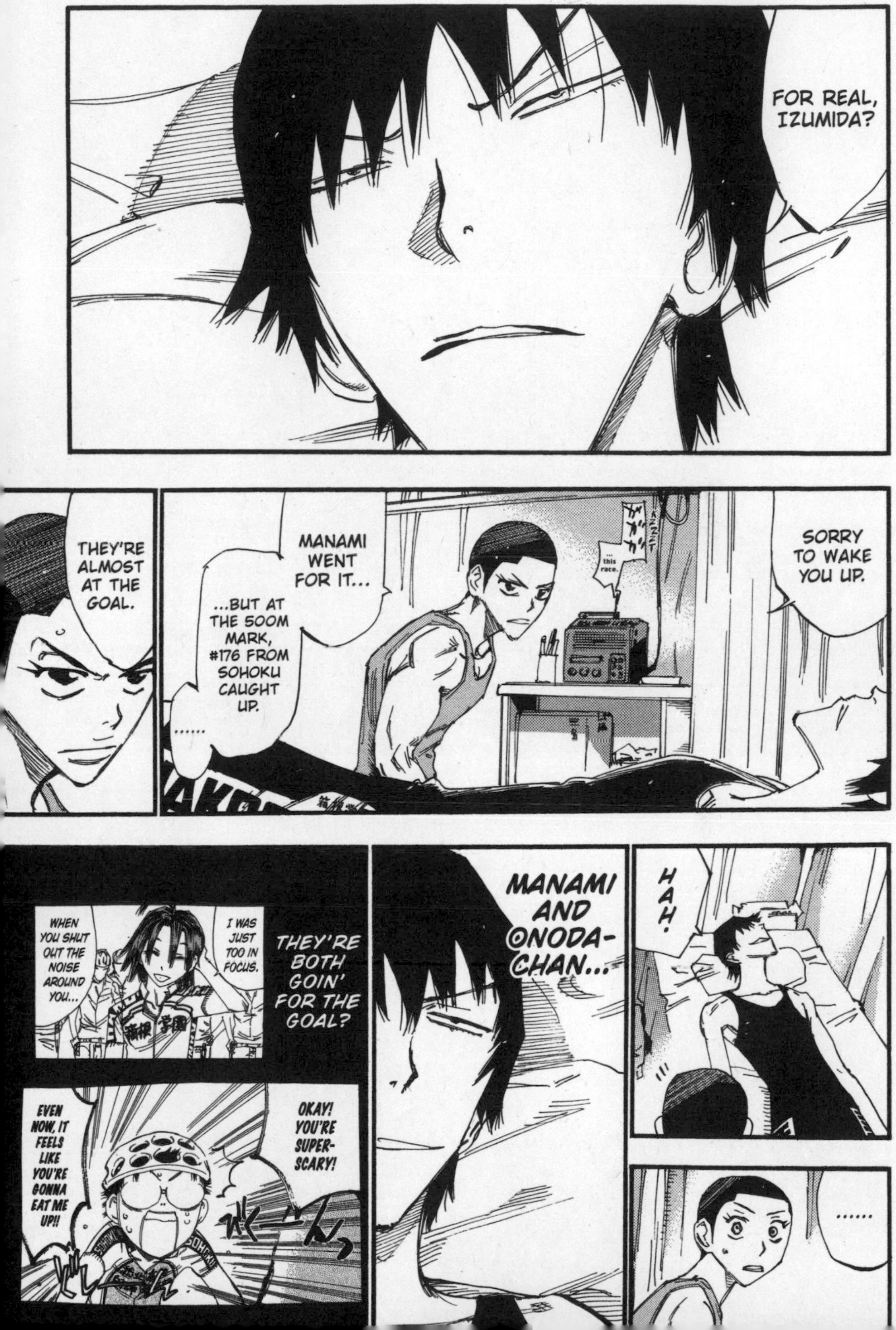
FOR REAL, IZUMIDA?
SORRY TO WAKE YOU UP.
... this race.
MANAMI WENT FOR IT...
...BUT AT THE 500M MARK, #176 FROM SOHOKU CAUGHT UP.
......
THEY'RE ALMOST AT THE GOAL.
HAH!
......
MANAMI AND ONODA-CHAN...
THEY'RE BOTH GOIN' FOR THE GOAL?
I WAS JUST TOO IN FOCUS.
WHEN YOU SHUT OUT THE NOISE AROUND YOU...
OKAY! YOU'RE SUPER-SCARY!
EVEN NOW, IT FEELS LIKE YOU'RE GONNA EAT ME UP!!

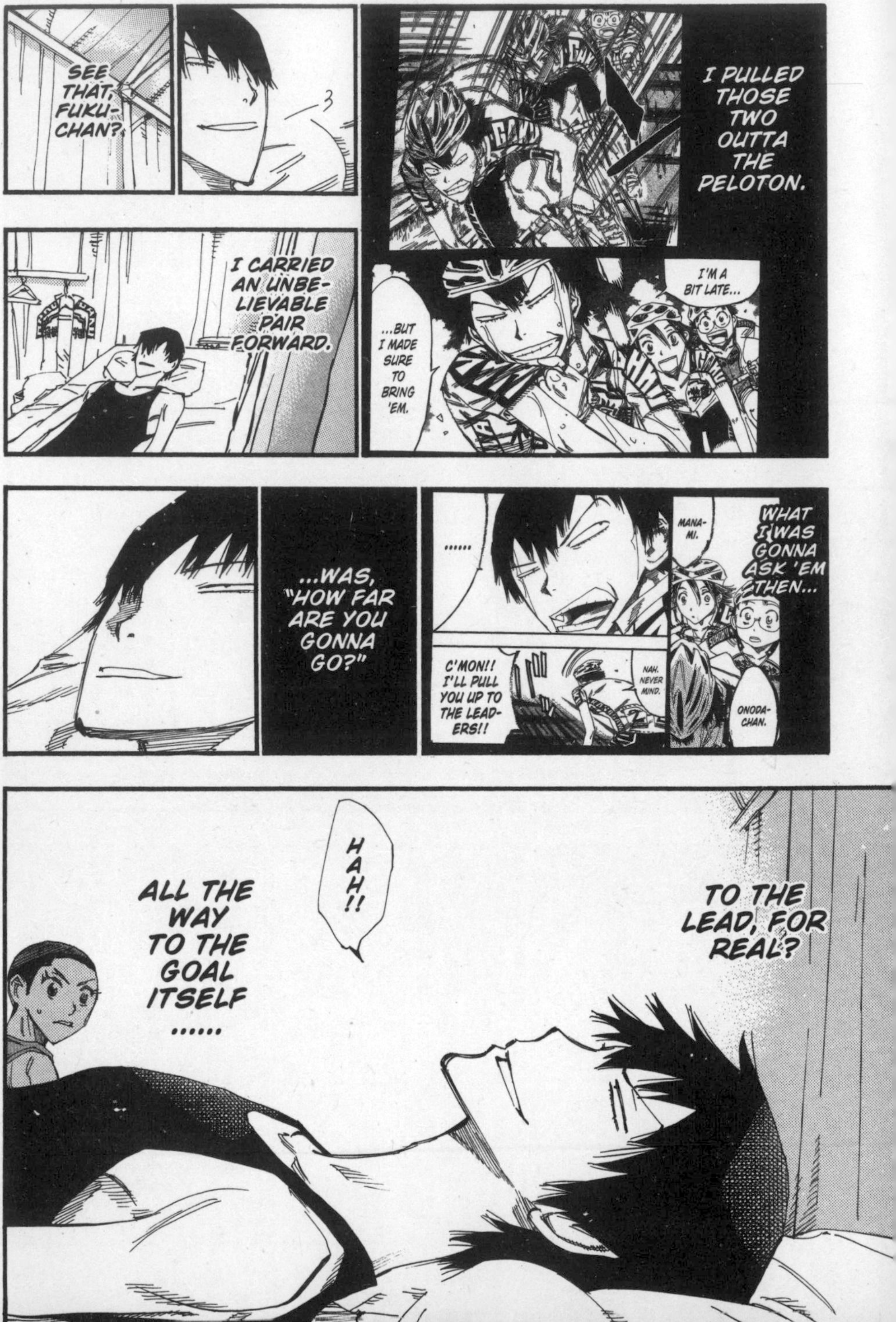
I PULLED THOSE TWO OUTTA THE PELOTON.
SEE THAT, FUKU-CHAN?
I'M A BIT LATE...
...BUT I MADE SURE TO BRING 'EM.
I CARRIED AN UNBE-LIEVABLE PAIR FORWARD.
WHAT I WAS GONNA ASK 'EM THEN...
MANA-MI.
ONODA-CHAN.
......
NAH, NEVER MIND.
C'MON!! I'LL PULL YOU UP TO THE LEAD-ERS!!
...WAS, "HOW FAR ARE YOU GONNA GO?"
TO THE LEAD, FOR REAL?
HAH!!
ALL THE WAY TO THE GOAL ITSELF
......

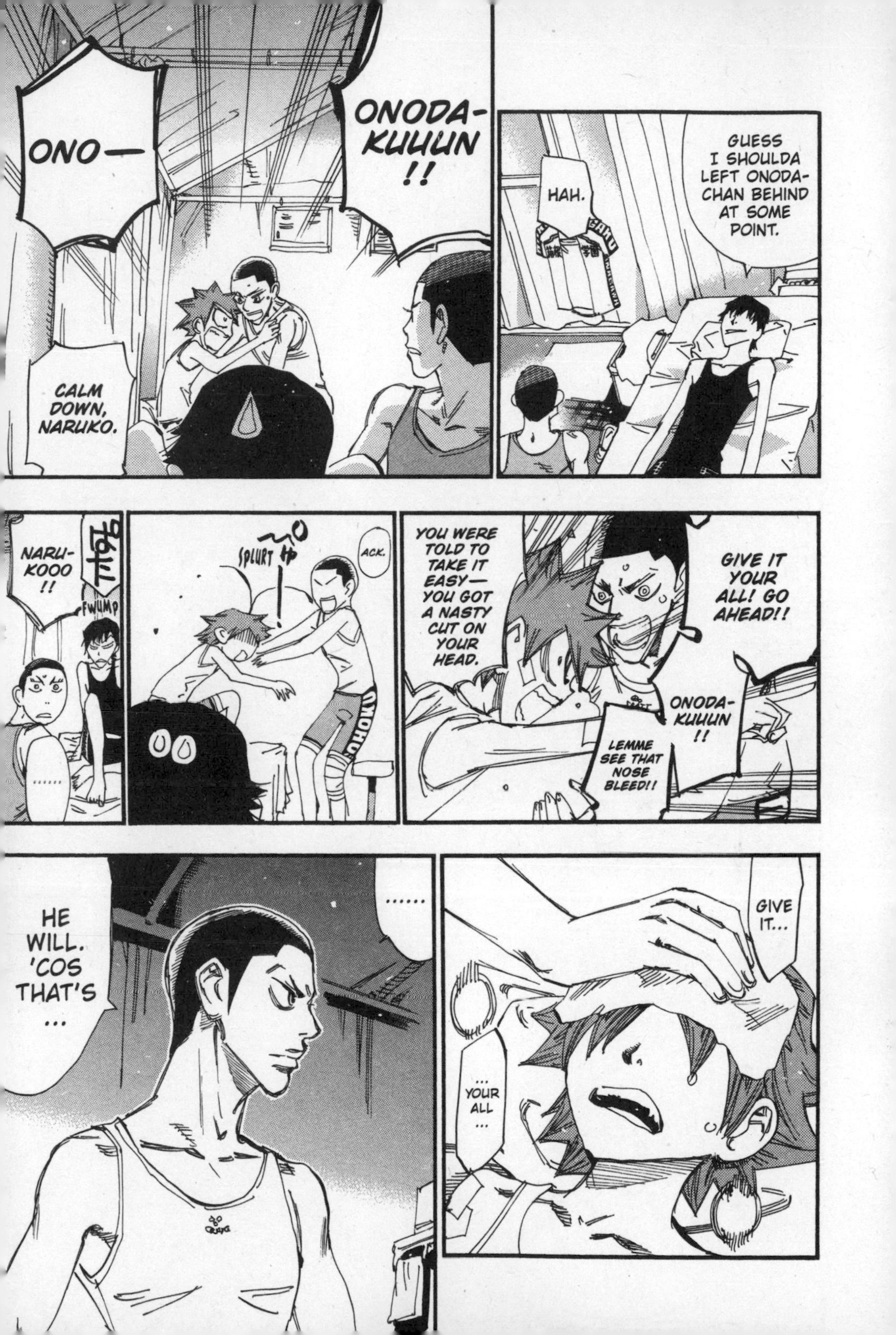

GUESS I SHOULDA LEFT ONODA-CHAN BEHIND AT SOME POINT.
HAH.
ONODA-KUUUN!!
ONO—
CALM DOWN, NARUKO.
GIVE IT YOUR ALL! GO AHEAD!!
YOU WERE TOLD TO TAKE IT EASY—YOU GOT A NASTY CUT ON YOUR HEAD.
ONODA-KUUUN!!
LEMME SEE THAT NOSE BLEED!!
ACK.
SPLURT
NARU-KOOO!!
FWUMP
......
GIVE IT...
...YOUR ALL...
......
HE WILL. 'COS THAT'S...

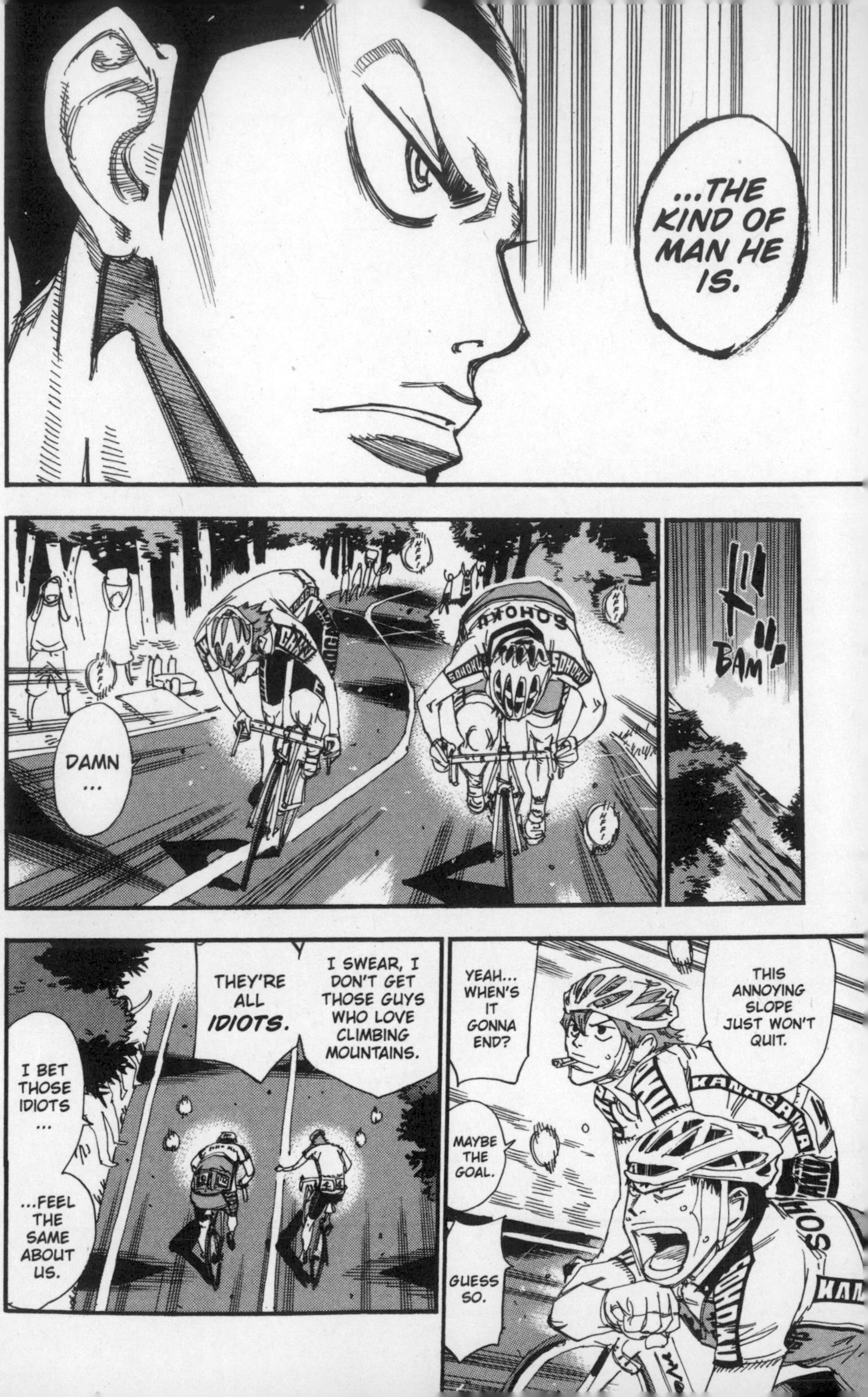
...THE KIND OF MAN HE IS.
BAM
DAMN ...
THIS ANNOYING SLOPE JUST WON'T QUIT.
YEAH... WHEN'S IT GONNA END?
MAYBE THE GOAL.
GUESS SO.
I SWEAR, I DON'T GET THOSE GUYS WHO LOVE CLIMBING MOUNTAINS.
THEY'RE ALL IDIOTS.
I BET THOSE IDIOTS ...
...FEEL THE SAME ABOUT US.

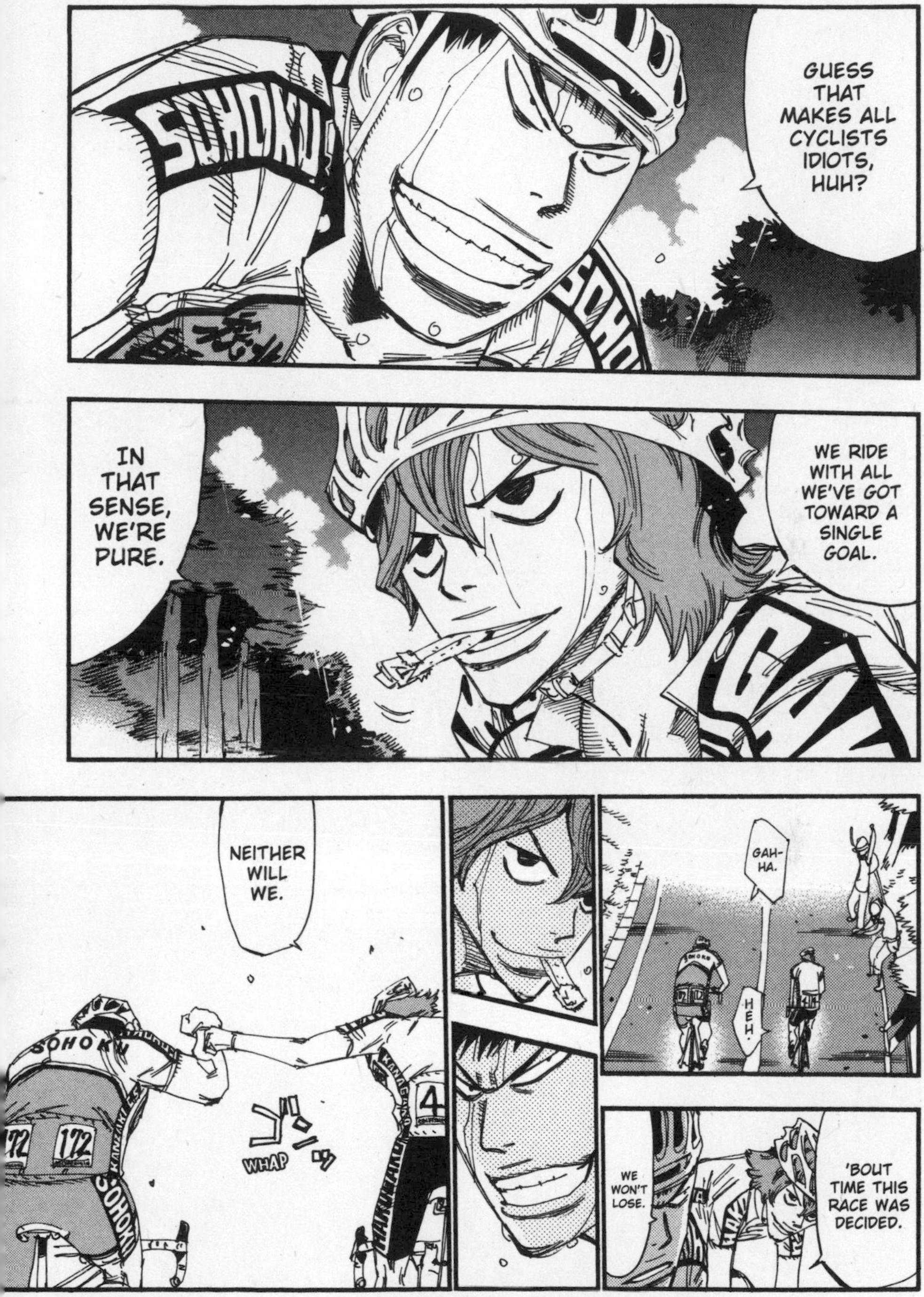
GUESS THAT MAKES ALL CYCLISTS IDIOTS, HUH?
WE RIDE WITH ALL WE'VE GOT TOWARD A SINGLE GOAL.
IN THAT SENSE, WE'RE PURE.
GAH-HA.
HEH.
'BOUT TIME THIS RACE WAS DECIDED.
WE WON'T LOSE.
NEITHER WILL WE.
WHAP

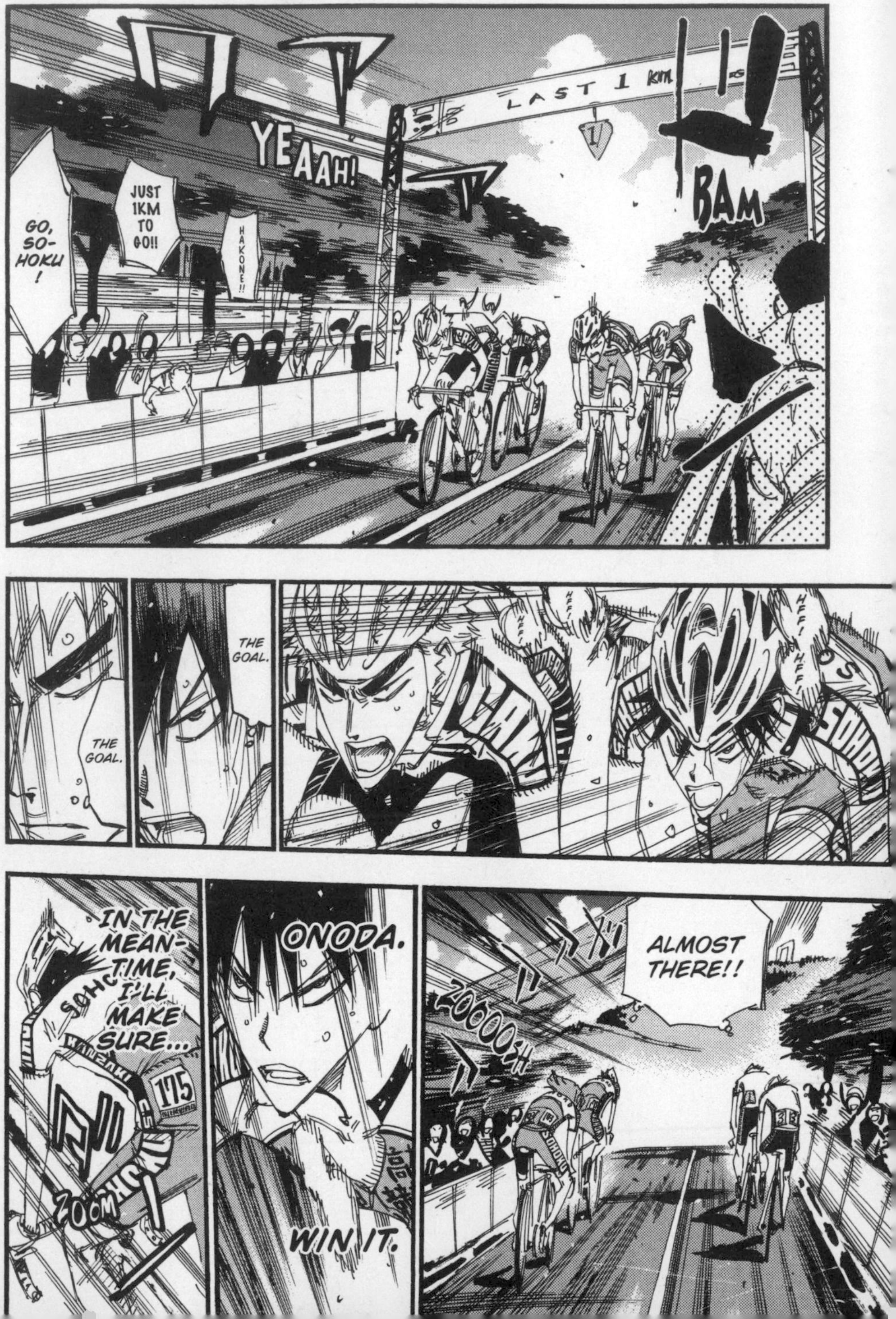
BAM
LAST 1 km
YEAAH!
HAKONE!!
JUST 1KM TO GO!!
GO, SO-HOKU!
HFF! HFF!
HFF!
THE GOAL.
THE GOAL.
ALMOST THERE!!
ZOOOOSH
ONODA.
WIN IT.
IN THE MEAN-TIME, I'LL MAKE SURE...
ZOOM

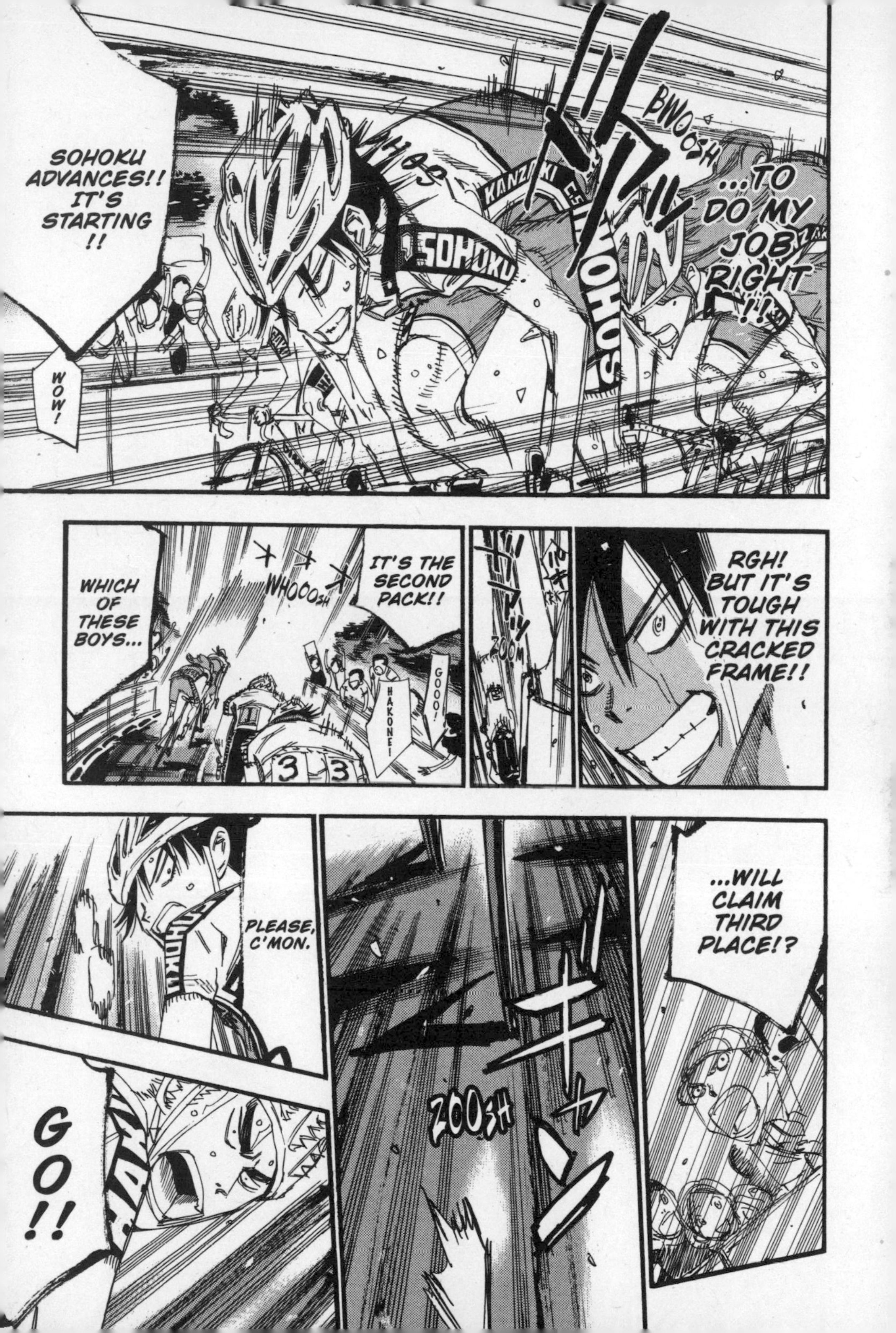
BWOOSH
...TO DO MY JOB RIGHT!!
SOHOKU ADVANCES!! IT'S STARTING!!
WOW!
RGH! BUT IT'S TOUGH WITH THIS CRACKED FRAME!!
KRK
ZOOM
IT'S THE SECOND PACK!!
WHOOOSH
WHICH OF THESE BOYS...
GOOO!
HAKONE!
...WILL CLAIM THIRD PLACE!?
ZOOSH
PLEASE, C'MON.
GO!!

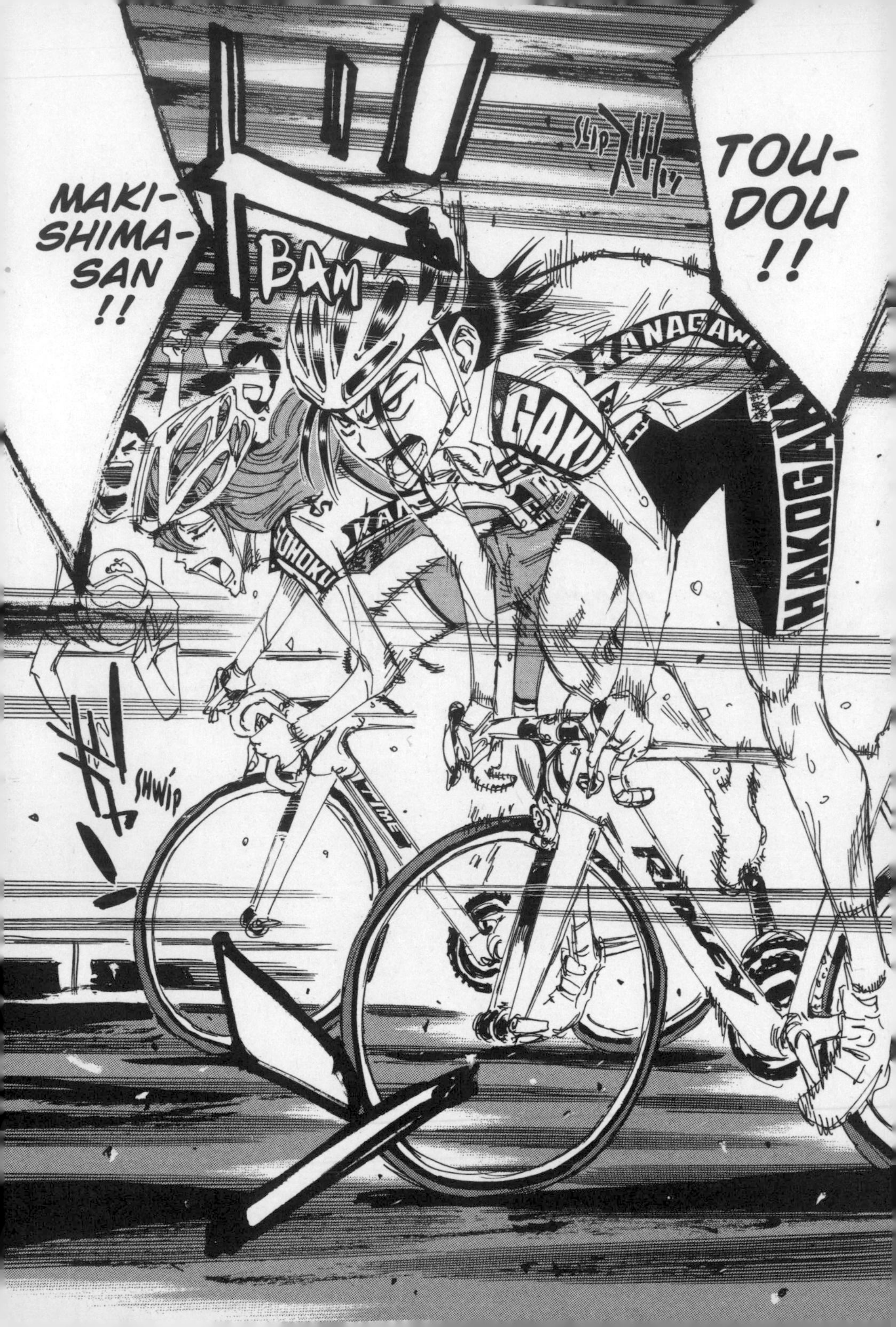
TOU-DOU!!
SLIP
BAM
MAKI-SHIMA-SAN!!
SHWIP

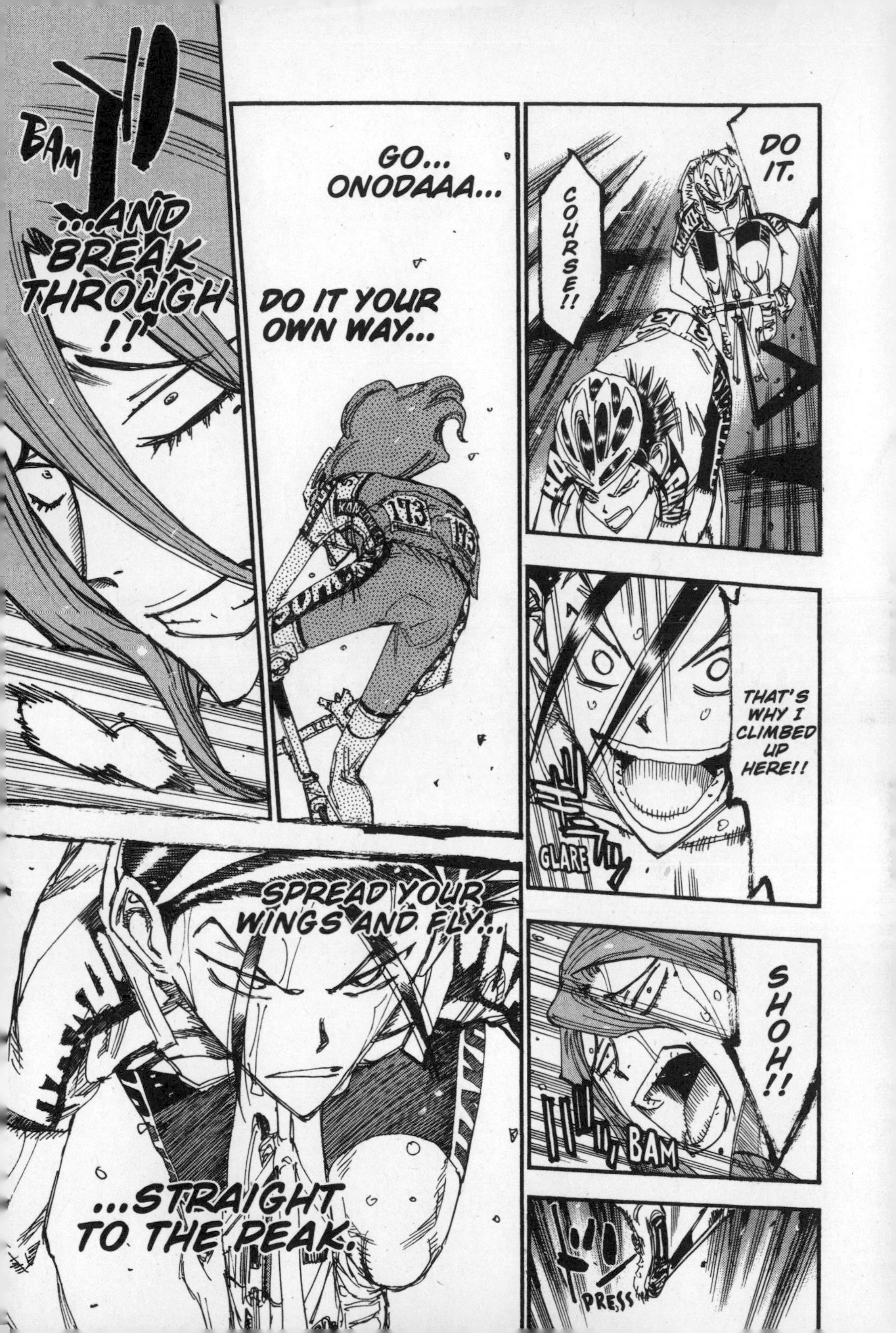
DO IT.
COURSE!!
GO... ONODAAA...
DO IT YOUR OWN WAY...
BAM
...AND BREAK THROUGH!!
THAT'S WHY I CLIMBED UP HERE!!
GLARE
SHOH!!
BAM
PRESS
SPREAD YOUR WINGS AND FLY...
...STRAIGHT TO THE PEAK.

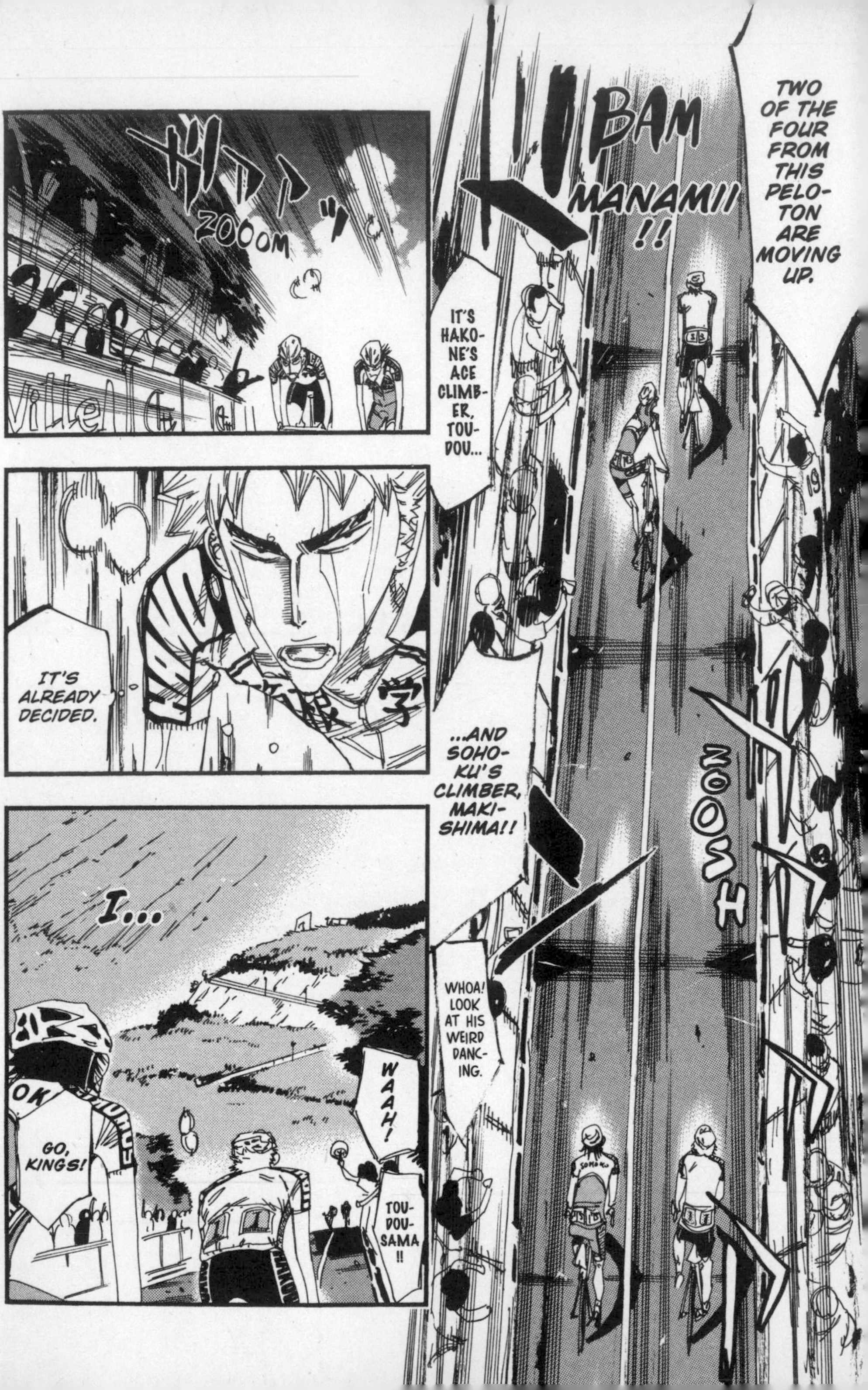
TWO OF THE FOUR FROM THIS PELOTON ARE MOVING UP.
BAM
MANAMI!!
IT'S HAKONE'S ACE CLIMBER, TOUDOU...
...AND SOHOKU'S CLIMBER, MAKISHIMA!!
WHOA! LOOK AT HIS WEIRD DANCING.
ZOOOM
IT'S ALREADY DECIDED.
I...
WAAAH!
TOUDOU-SAMA!!
GO, KINGS!

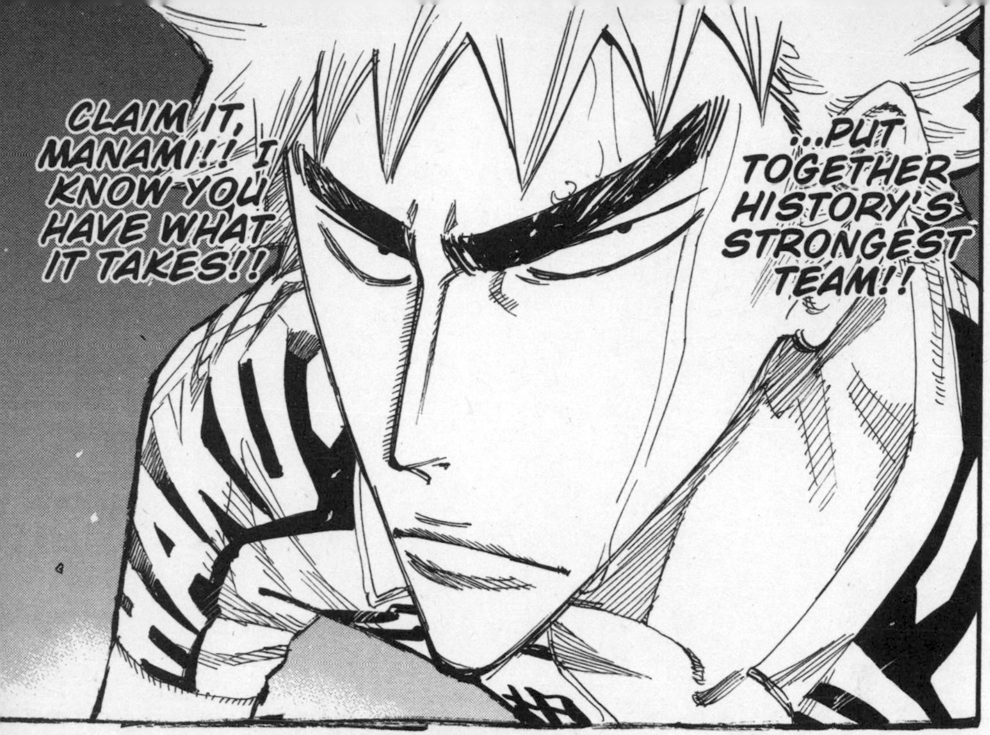
...PUT TOGETHER HISTORY'S STRONGEST TEAM!!
CLAIM IT, MANAMI!! I KNOW YOU HAVE WHAT IT TAKES!!

FLAG: KANAGAWA HAKONE ACADEMY
SIGN: SPIRIT OF KINGS / SHIRTS: HAKONE ACADEMY CYCLING CLUB

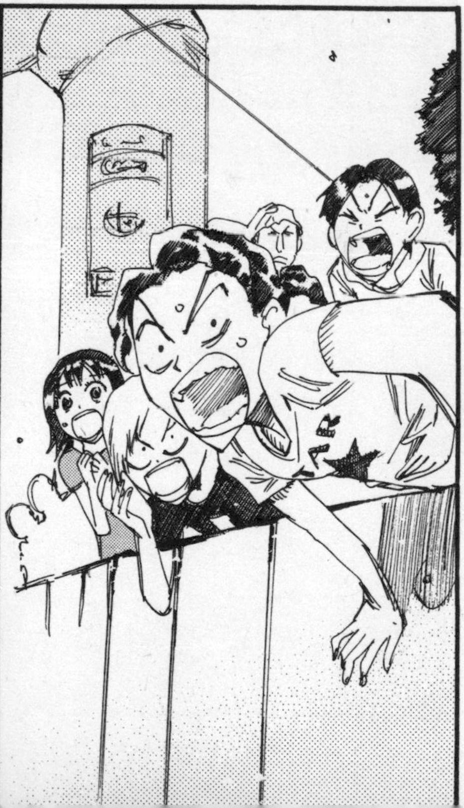

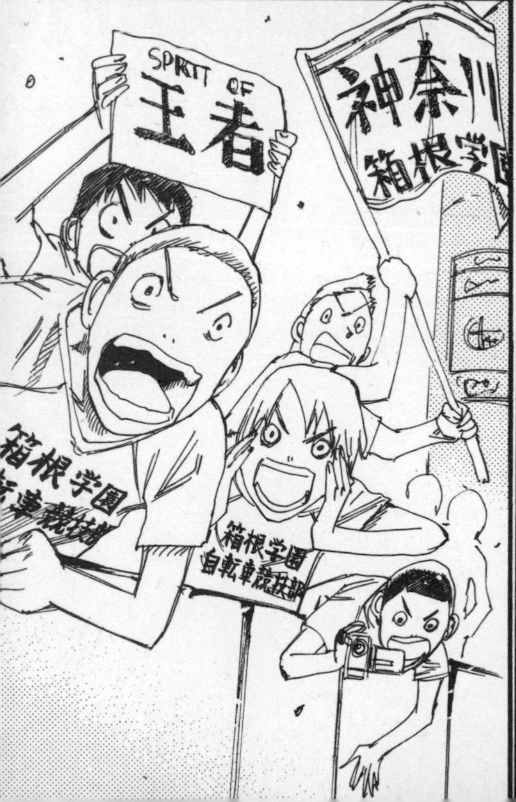
神奈川
箱根学園
SPIRIT OF
王者
箱根学園
自転車競技部

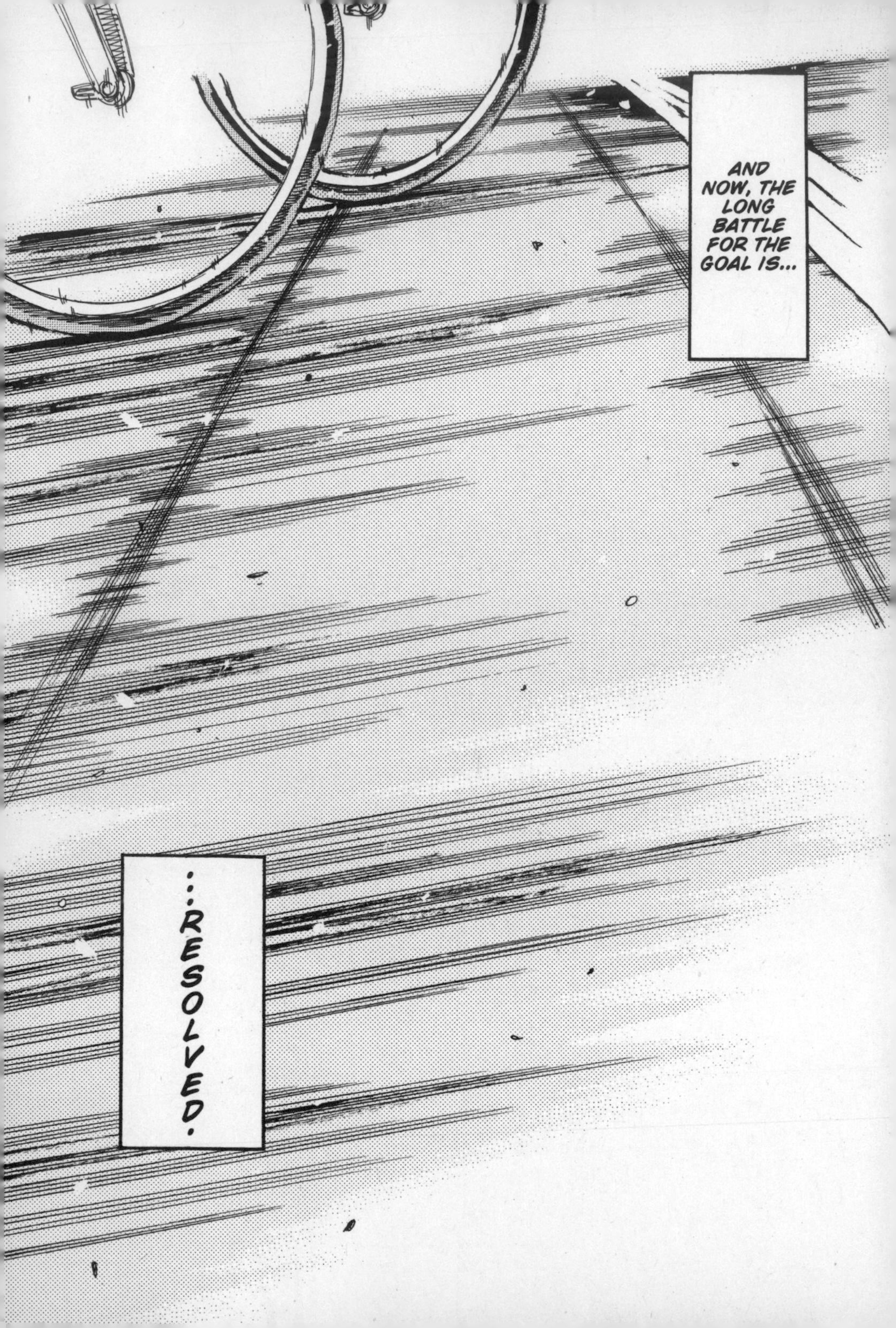
AND NOW, THE LONG BATTLE FOR THE GOAL IS...
...RESOLVED.

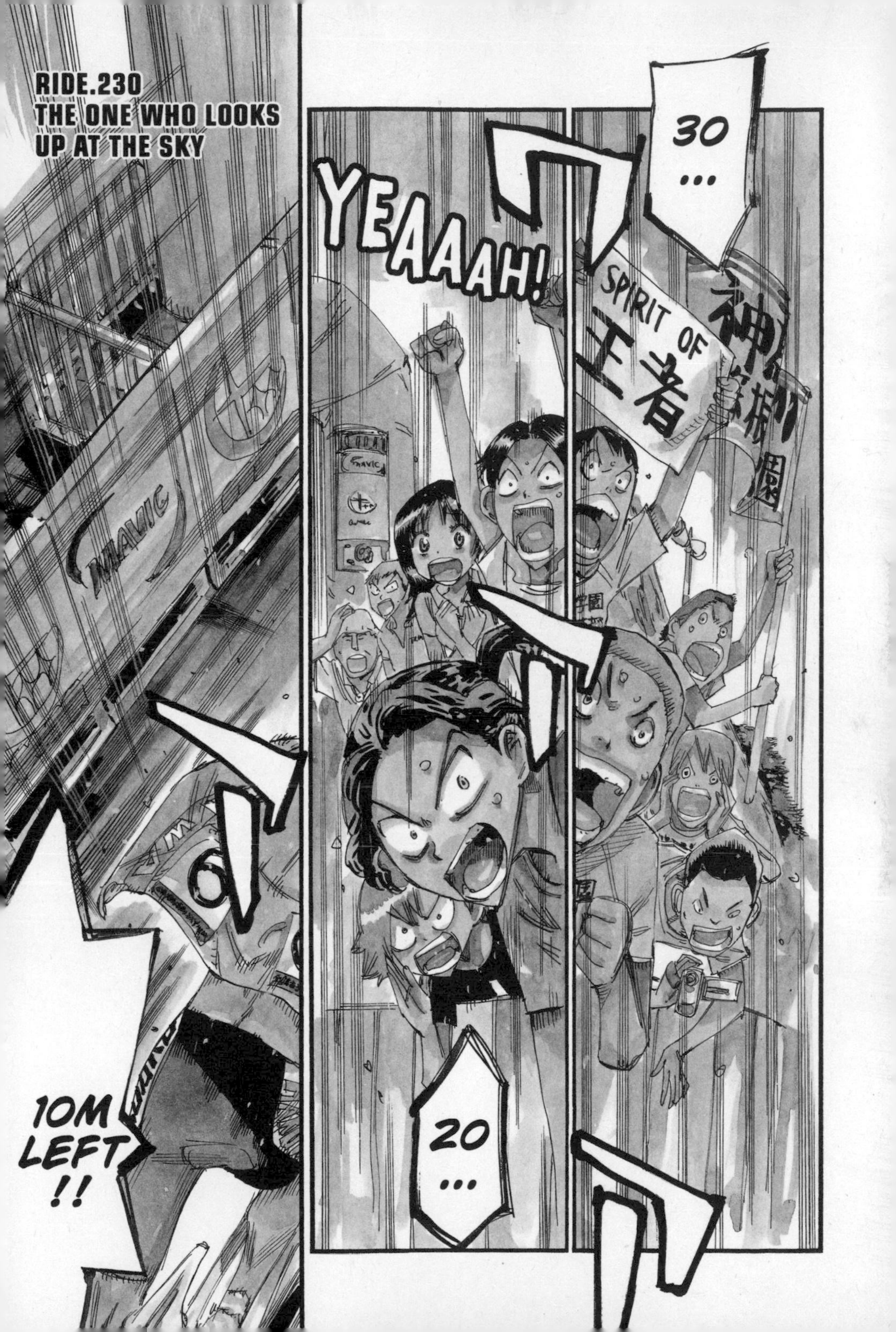
30 ...
SPIRIT OF 王者
YEAAAH!
20 ...
RIDE.230
THE ONE WHO LOOKS UP AT THE SKY
10M LEFT !!

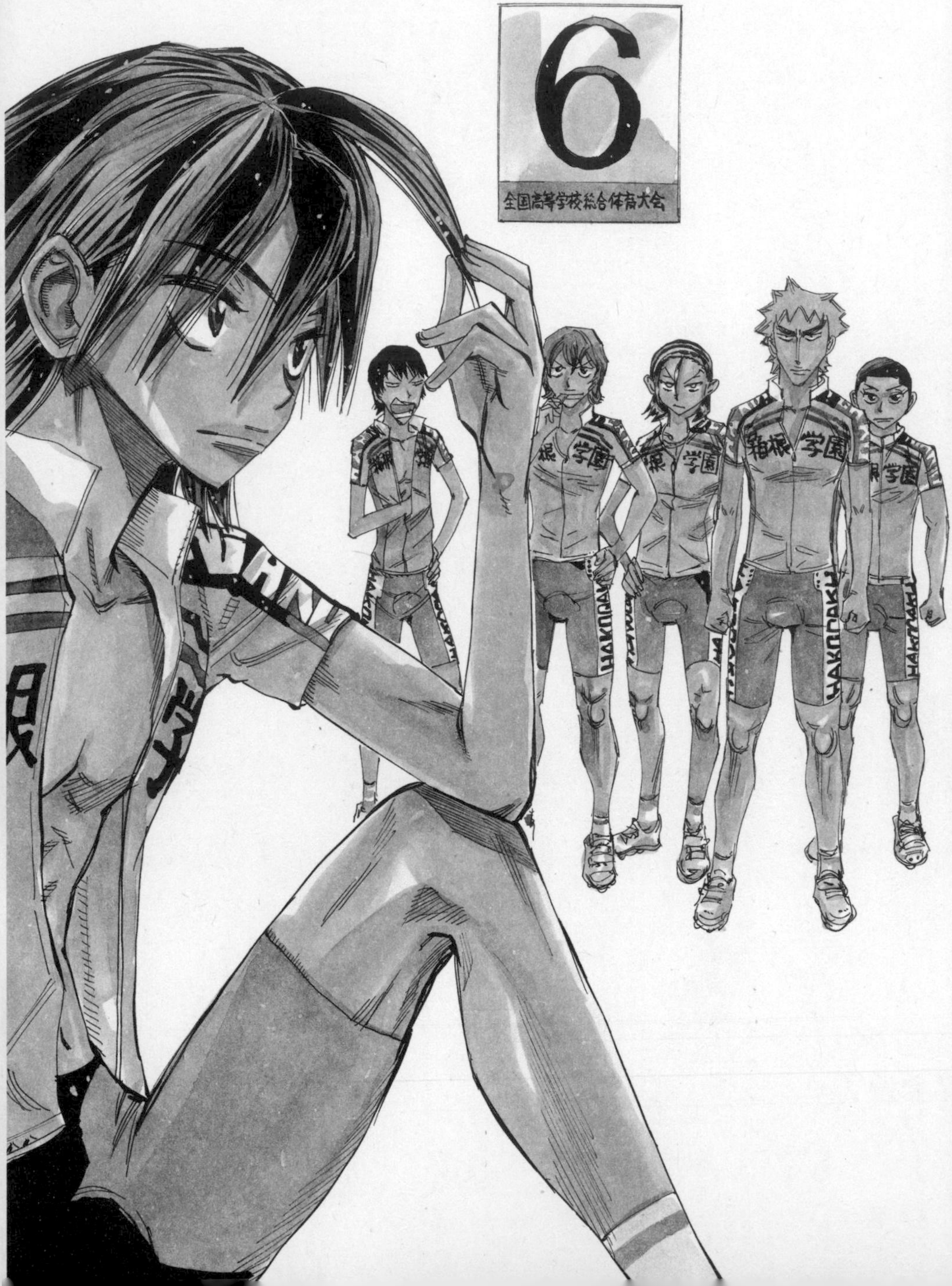
6
全国高等学校総合体育大会
箱根学園
HAKOGAKU

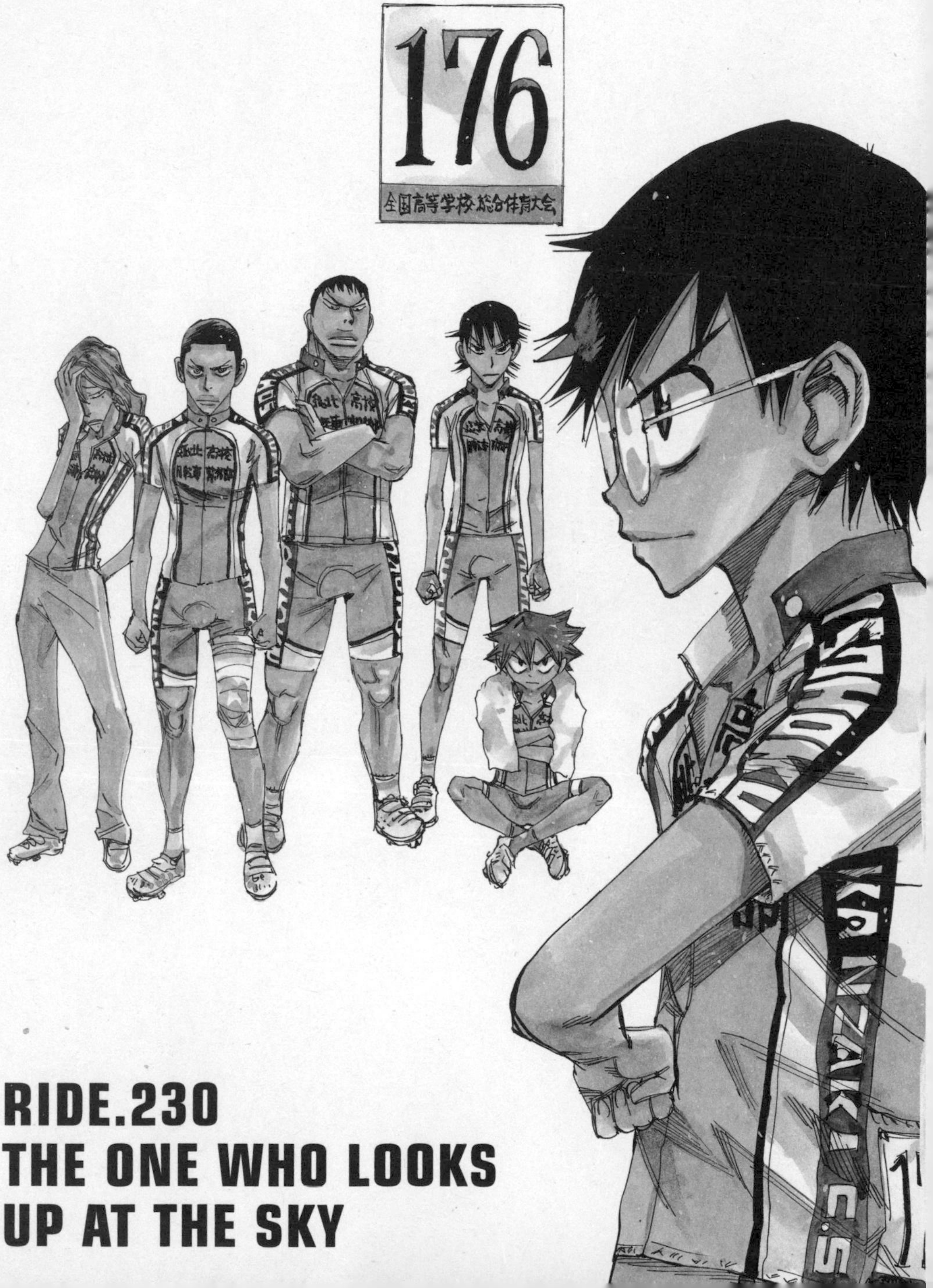
176
全国高等学校総合体育大会

RIDE.230
THE ONE WHO LOOKS UP AT THE SKY

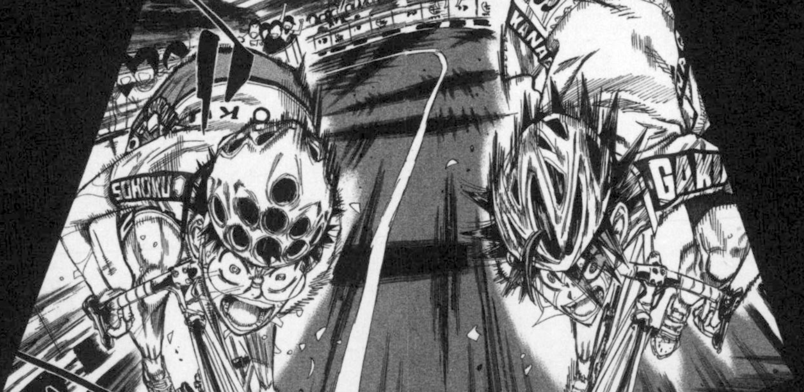
SAKAMICHI & SANGAKU

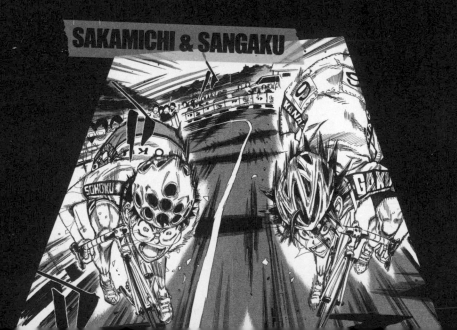

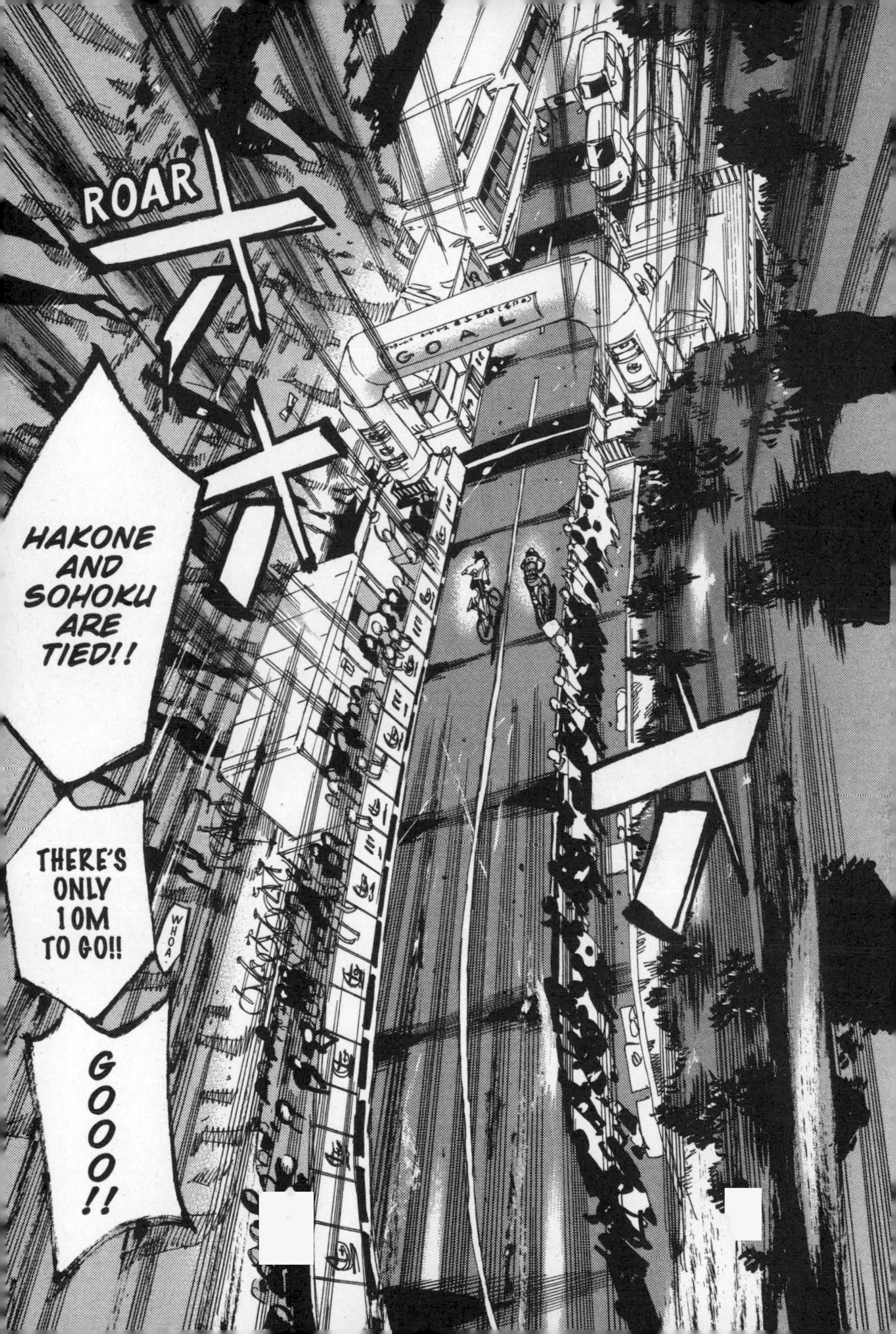
ROAR
HAKONE AND SOHOKU ARE TIED!!
THERE'S ONLY 10M TO GO!!
WHOA
GOOOOO!!
GOAL

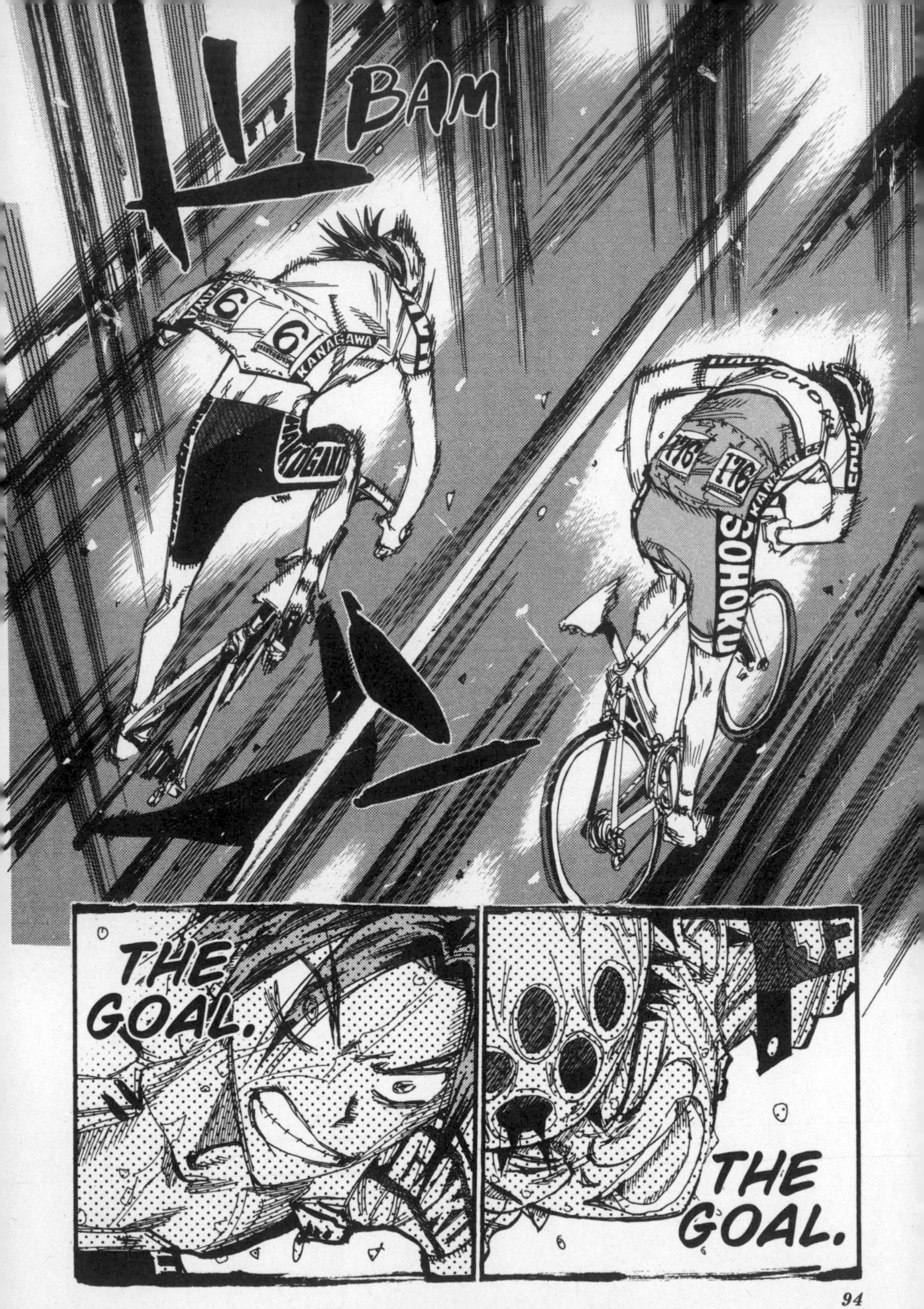
BAM
THE GOAL.
THE GOAL.

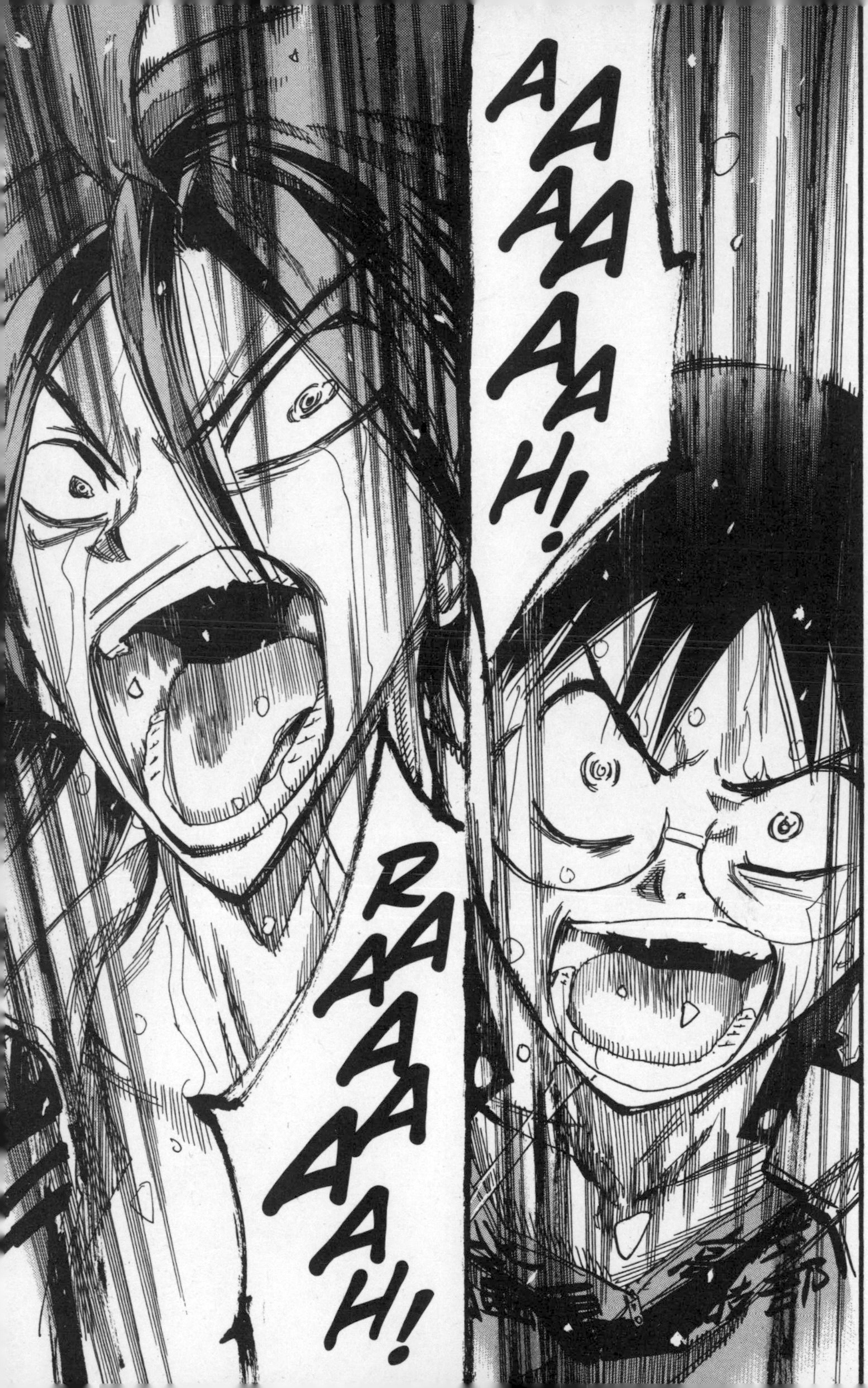
AAAAAAH!
RAAAAAH!

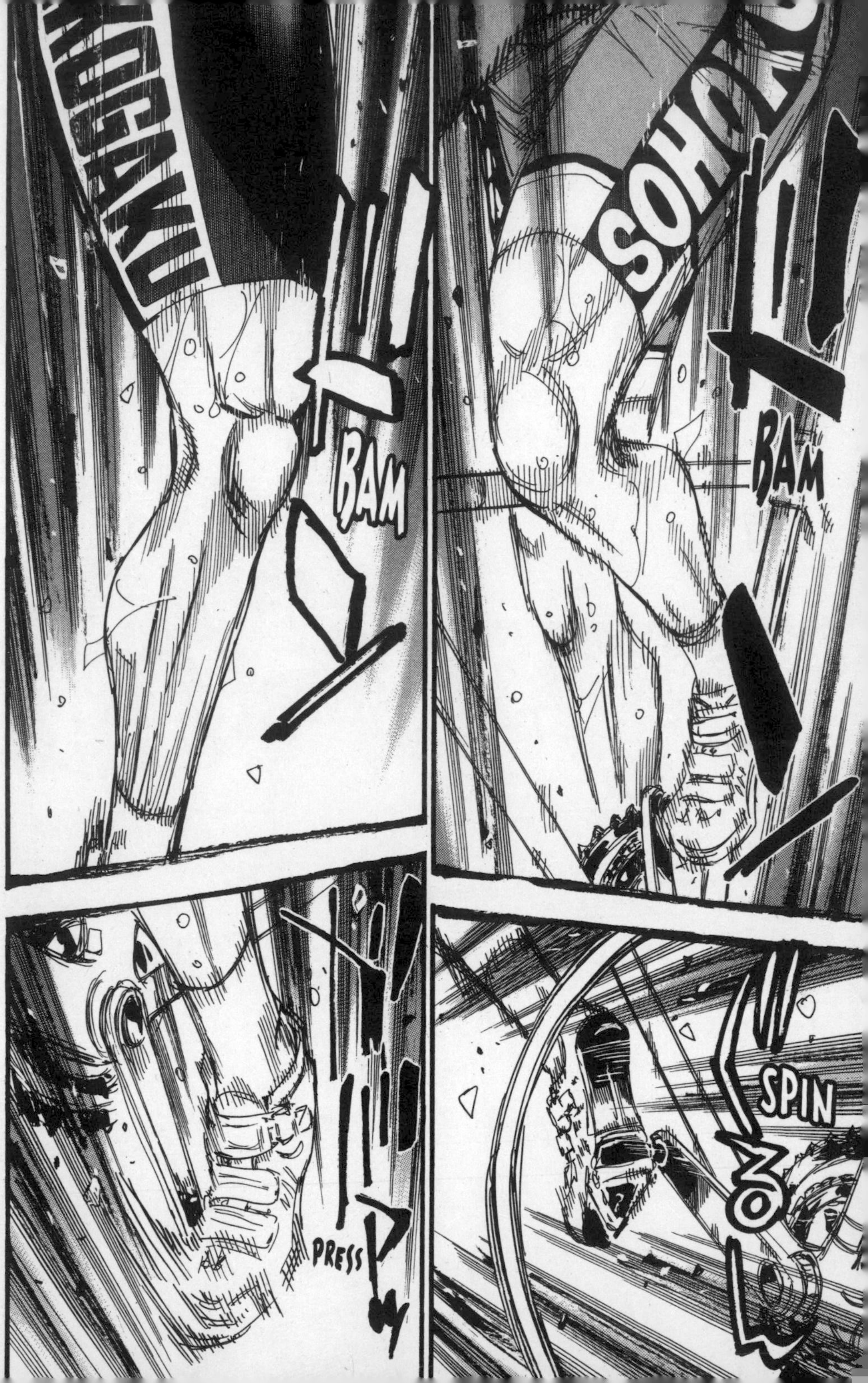
SOHO
BAM
OGAKU
BAM
SPIN
PRESS

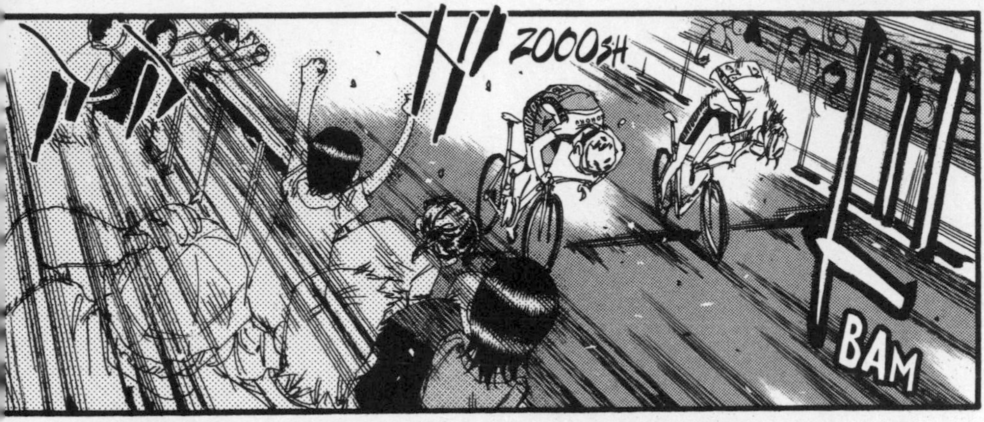
ZOOOSH
BAM

BANNER: KANAGAWA HAKONE ACADEMY

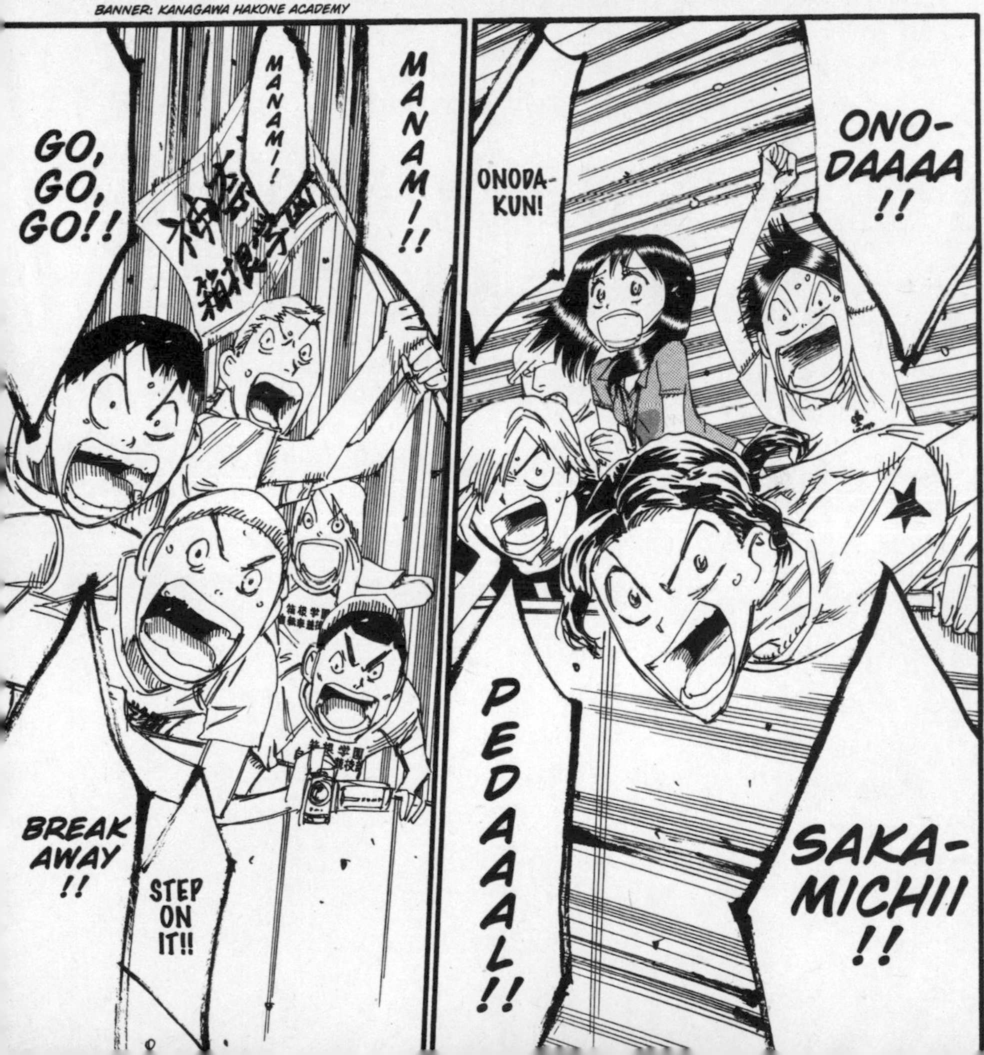
ONO-DAAAA!!
ONODA-KUN!
SAKA-MICHI!!
PEDAAAAL!!
MANAMI!!
MANAMI!
GO, GO, GO!!
BREAK AWAY!!
STEP ON IT!!

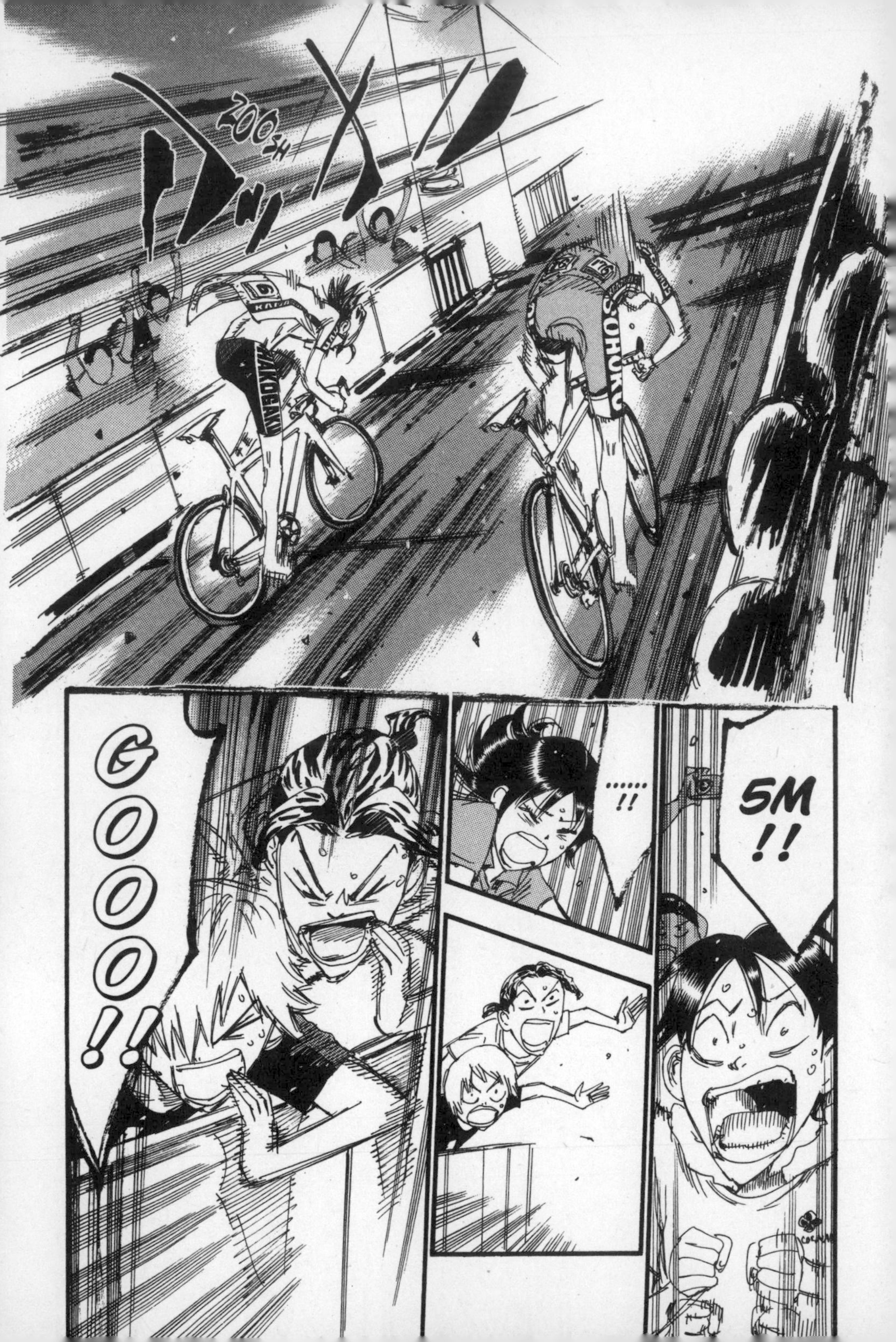
ZOOSH
......!!
SM !!
GOOOOO!!

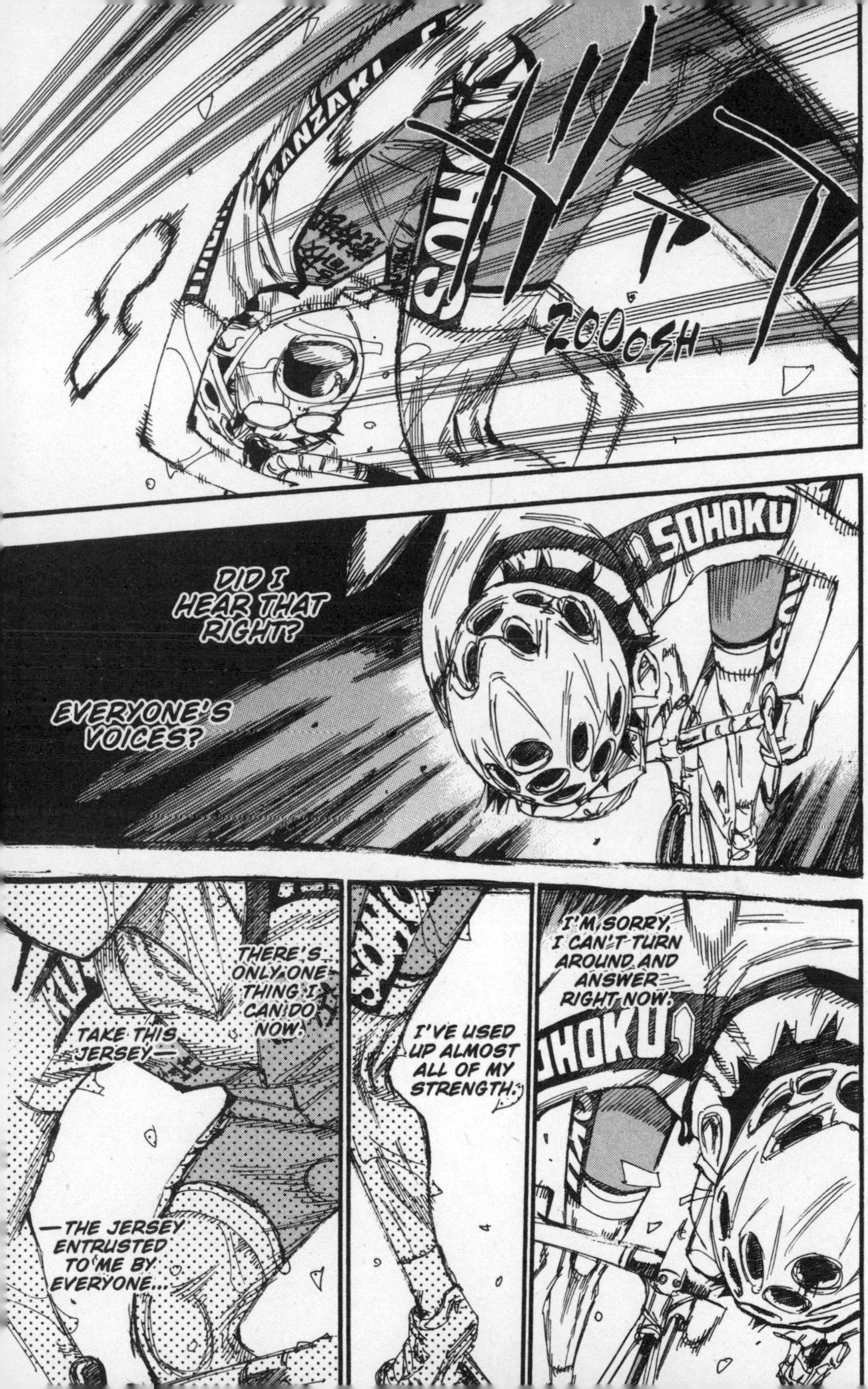
ZOOOSH
DID I HEAR THAT RIGHT?
EVERYONE'S VOICES?
I'M SORRY, I CAN'T TURN AROUND AND ANSWER RIGHT NOW.
I'VE USED UP ALMOST ALL OF MY STRENGTH.
THERE'S ONLY ONE THING I CAN DO NOW.
TAKE THIS JERSEY—
—THE JERSEY ENTRUSTED TO ME BY EVERYONE...

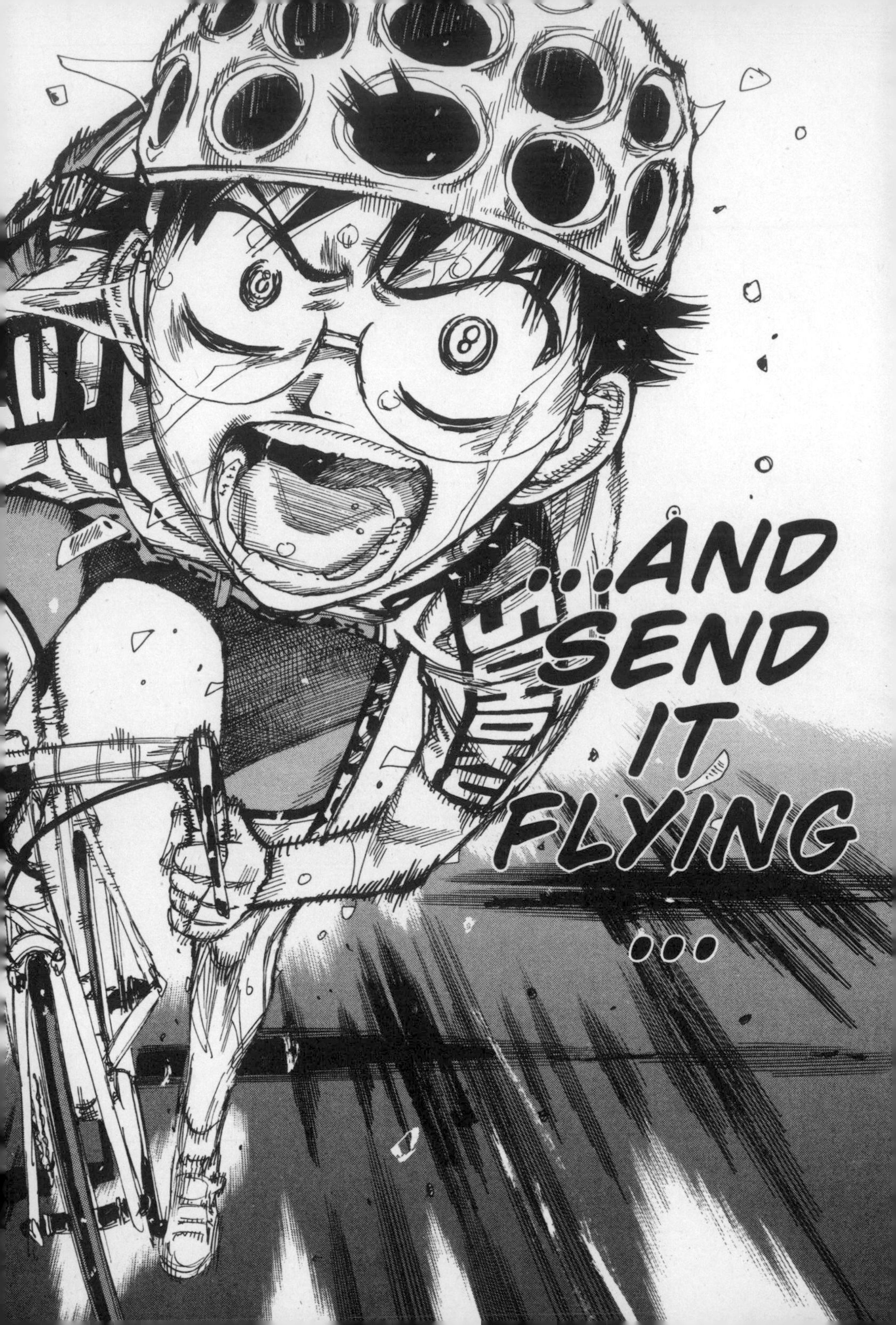
...AND SEND IT FLYING...

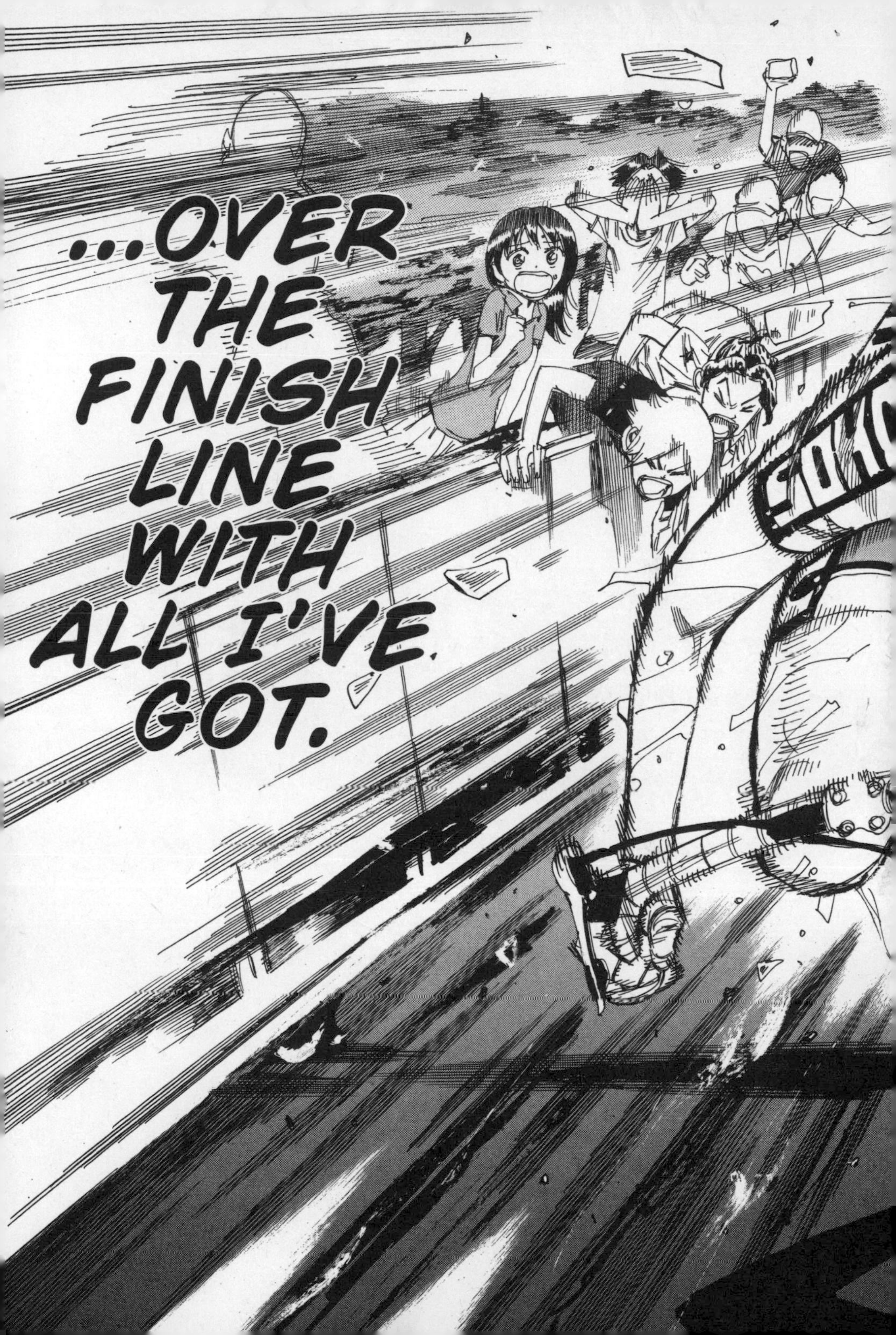
...OVER THE FINISH LINE WITH ALL I'VE GOT.

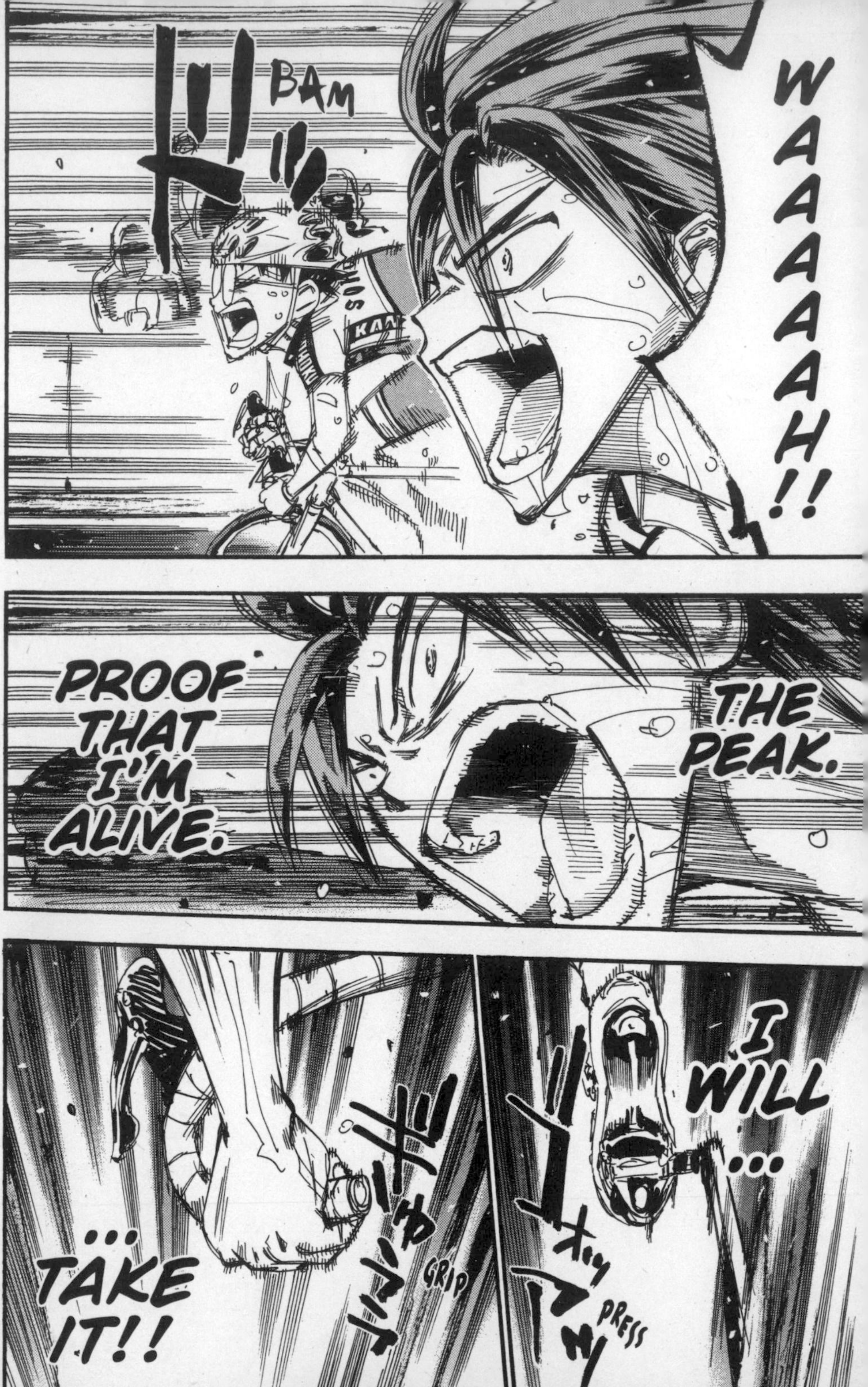
WAAAAAAAH!!
BAM
THE PEAK.
PROOF THAT I'M ALIVE.
I WILL...
PRESS
GRIP
...TAKE IT!!

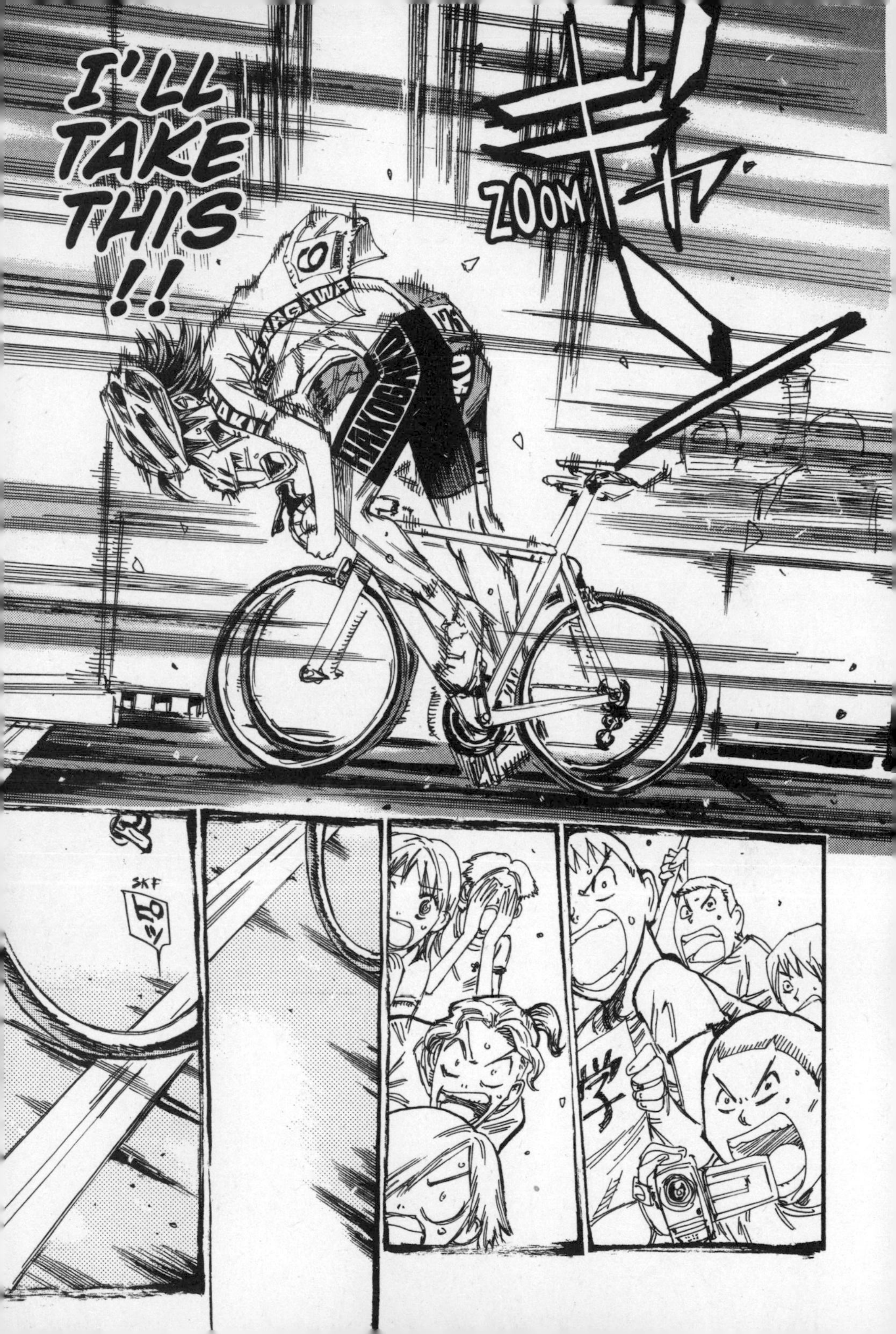
ZOOM
I'LL TAKE THIS!!
SKF

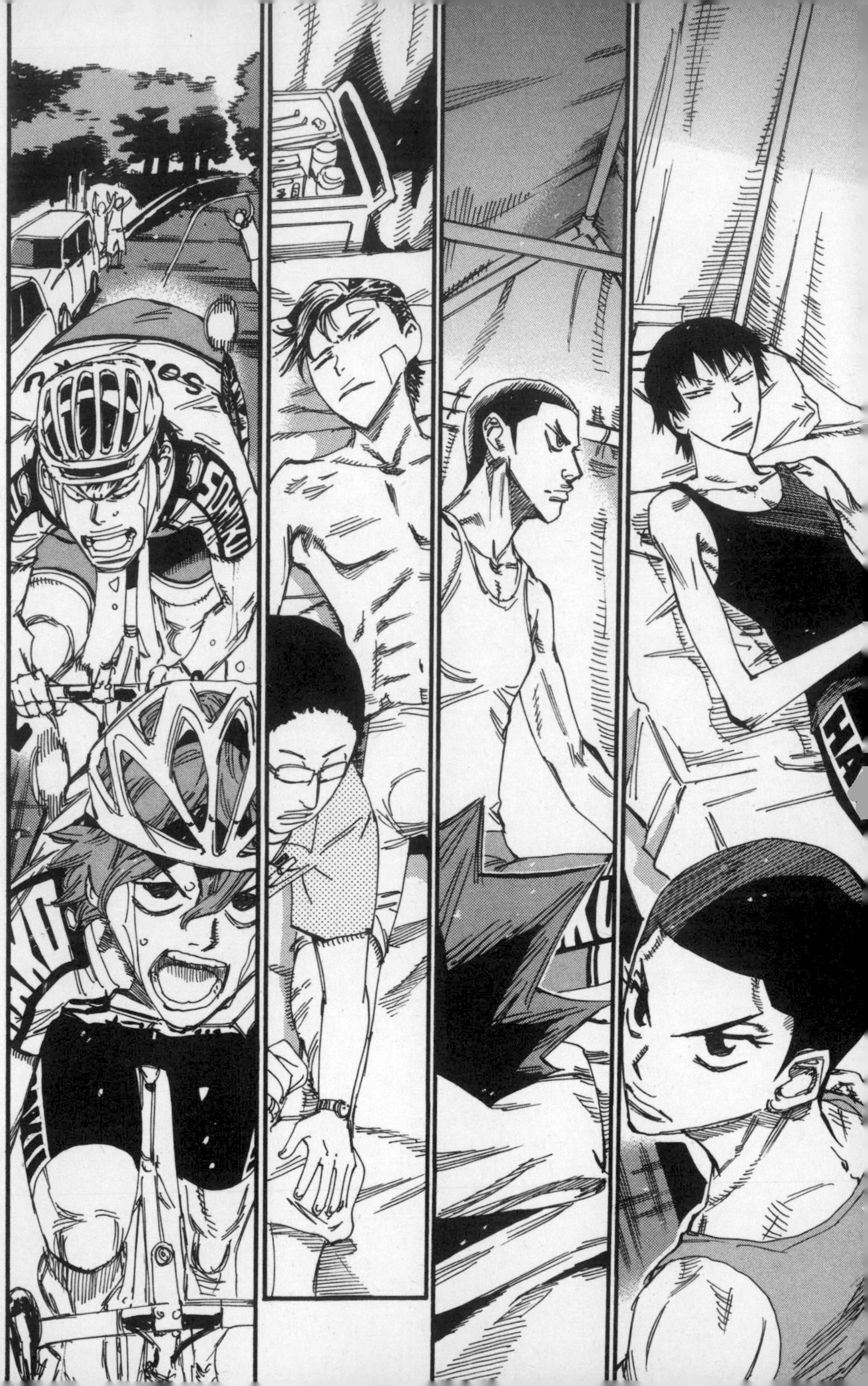

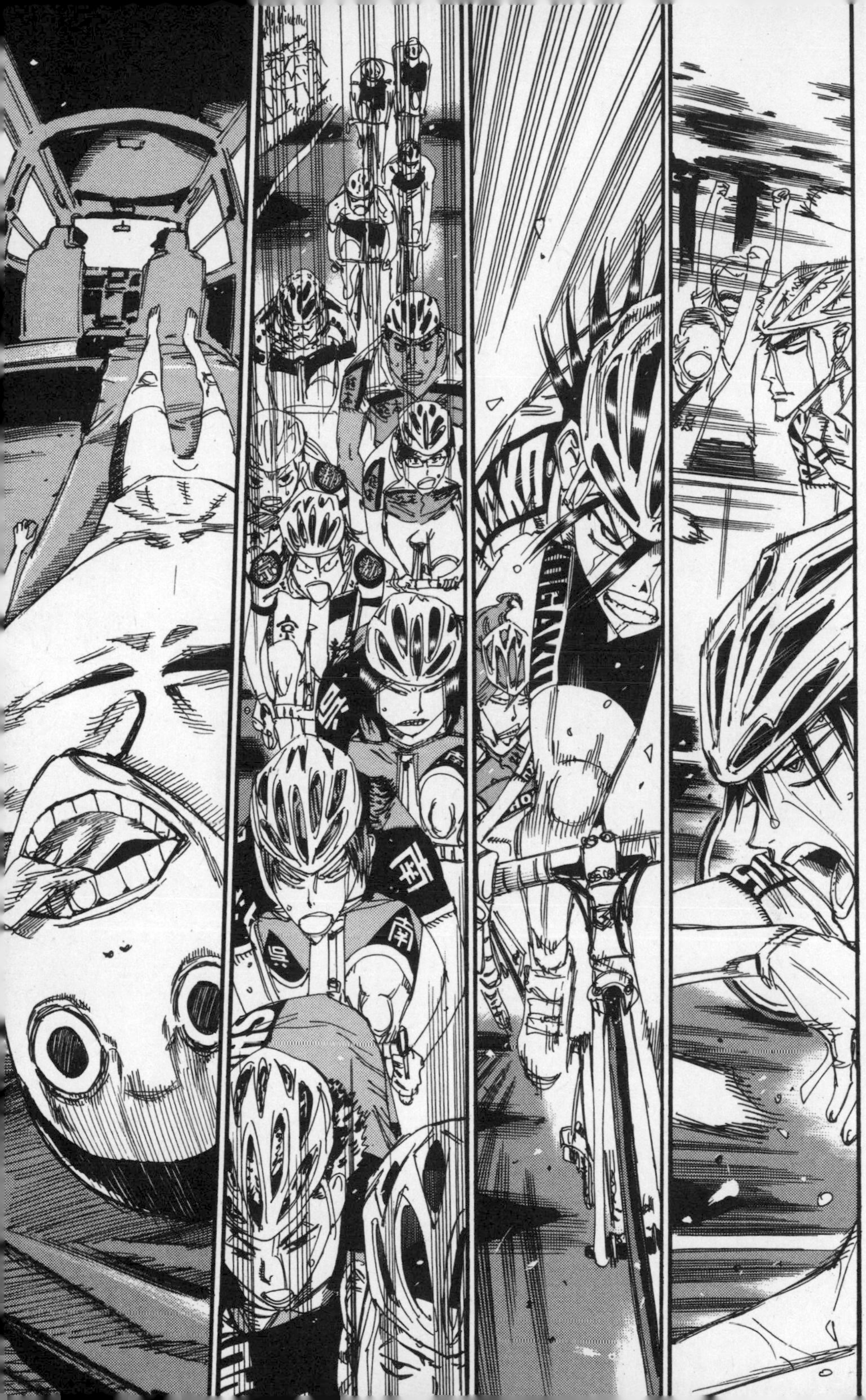

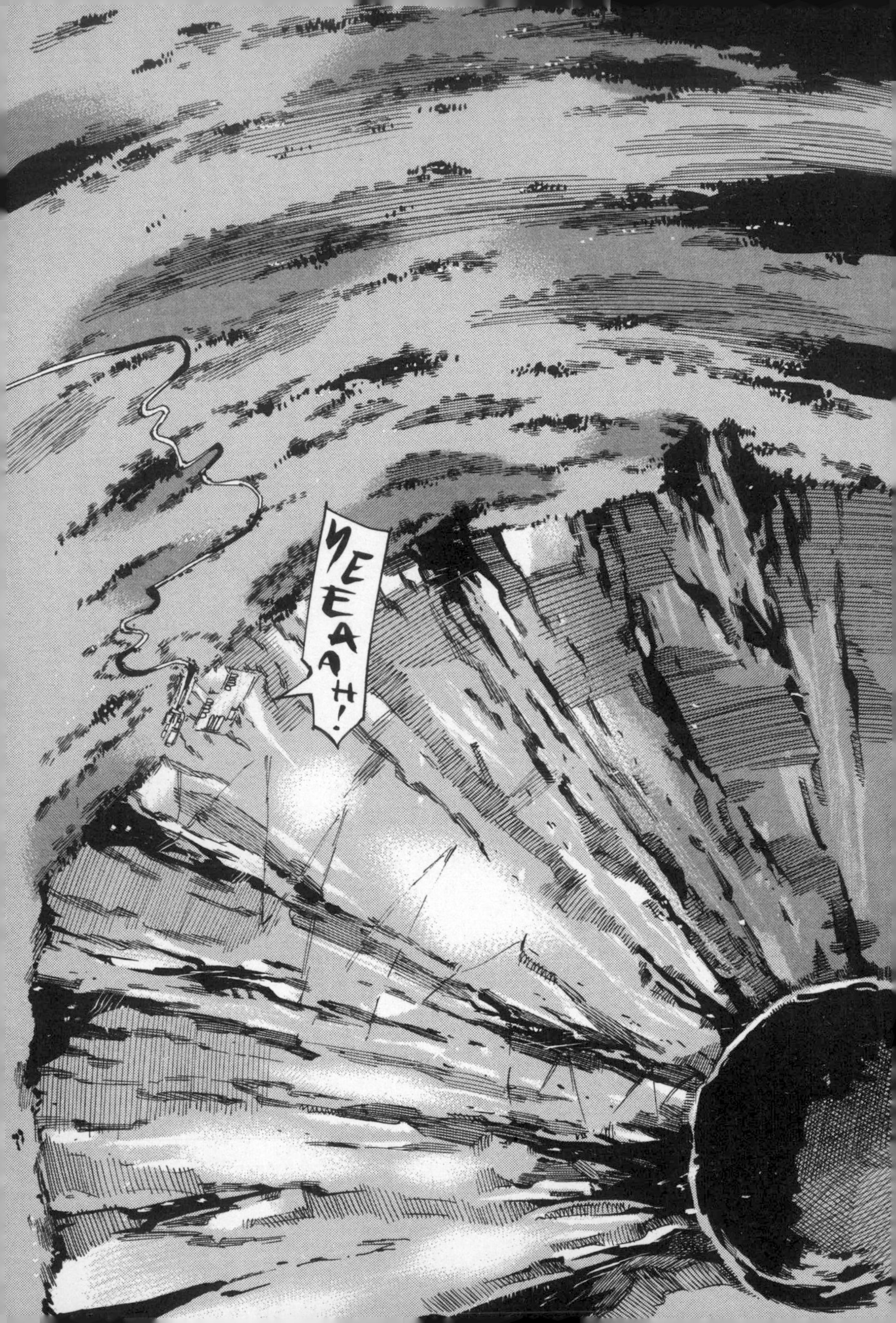
NYEEAAH!

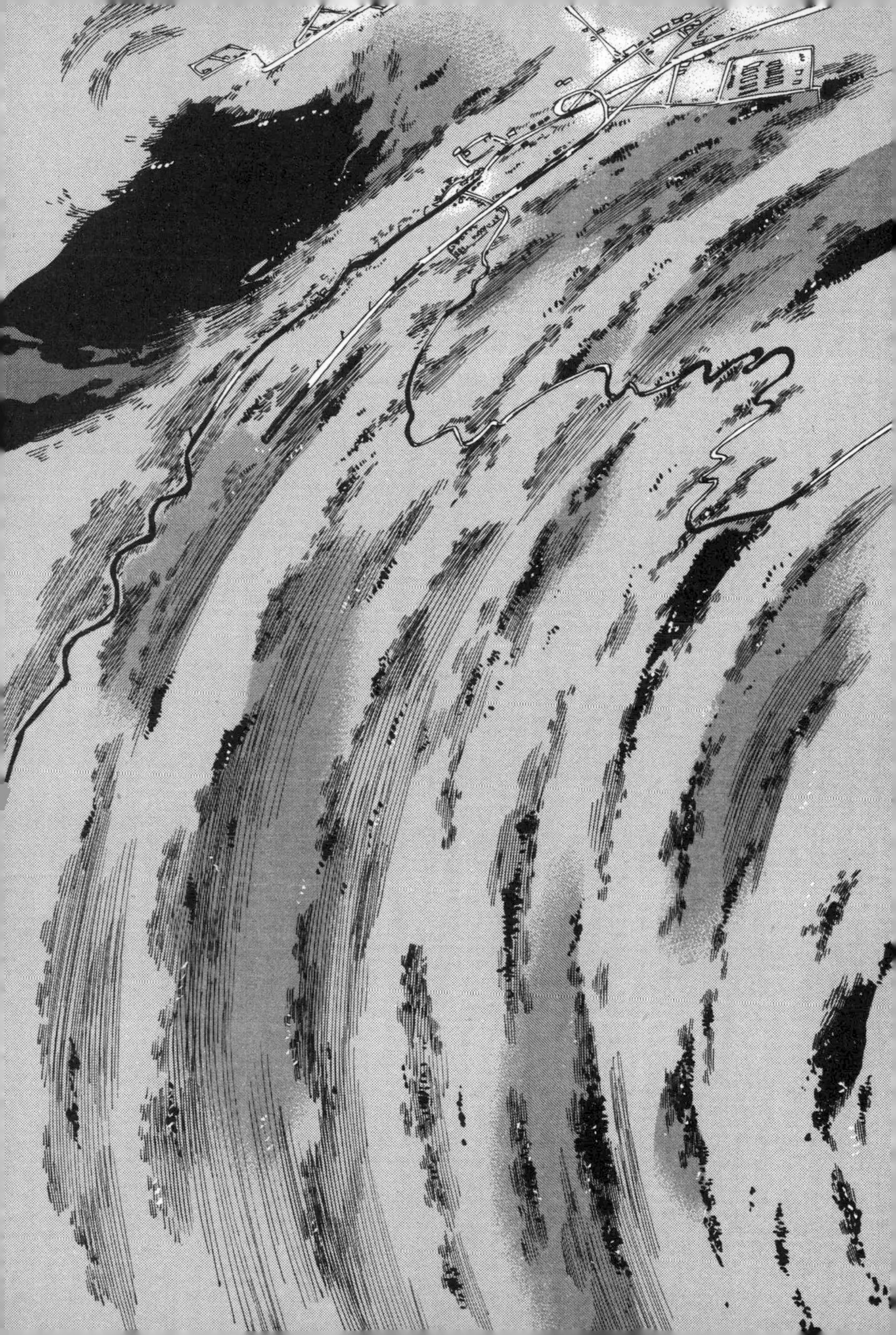

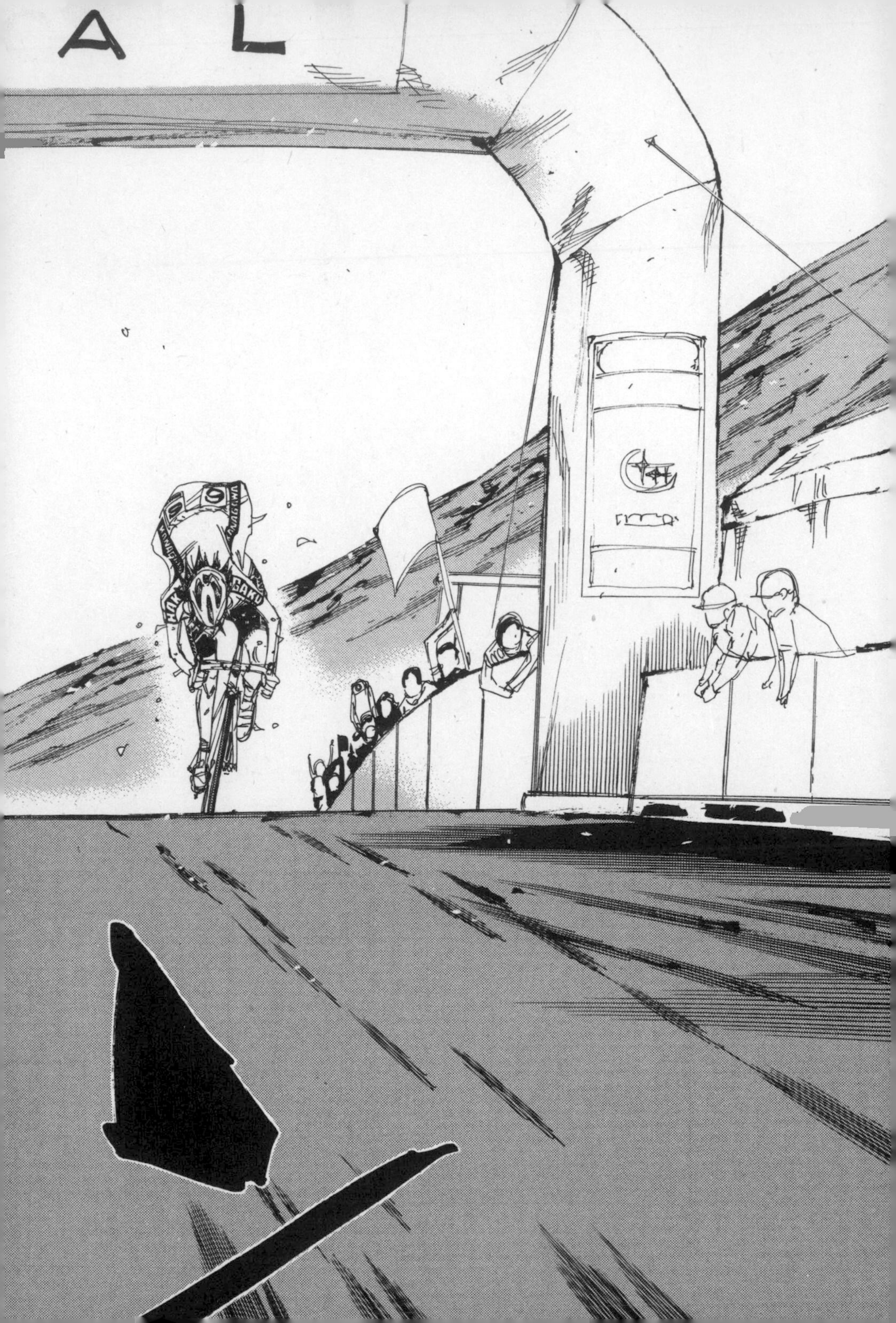
A L

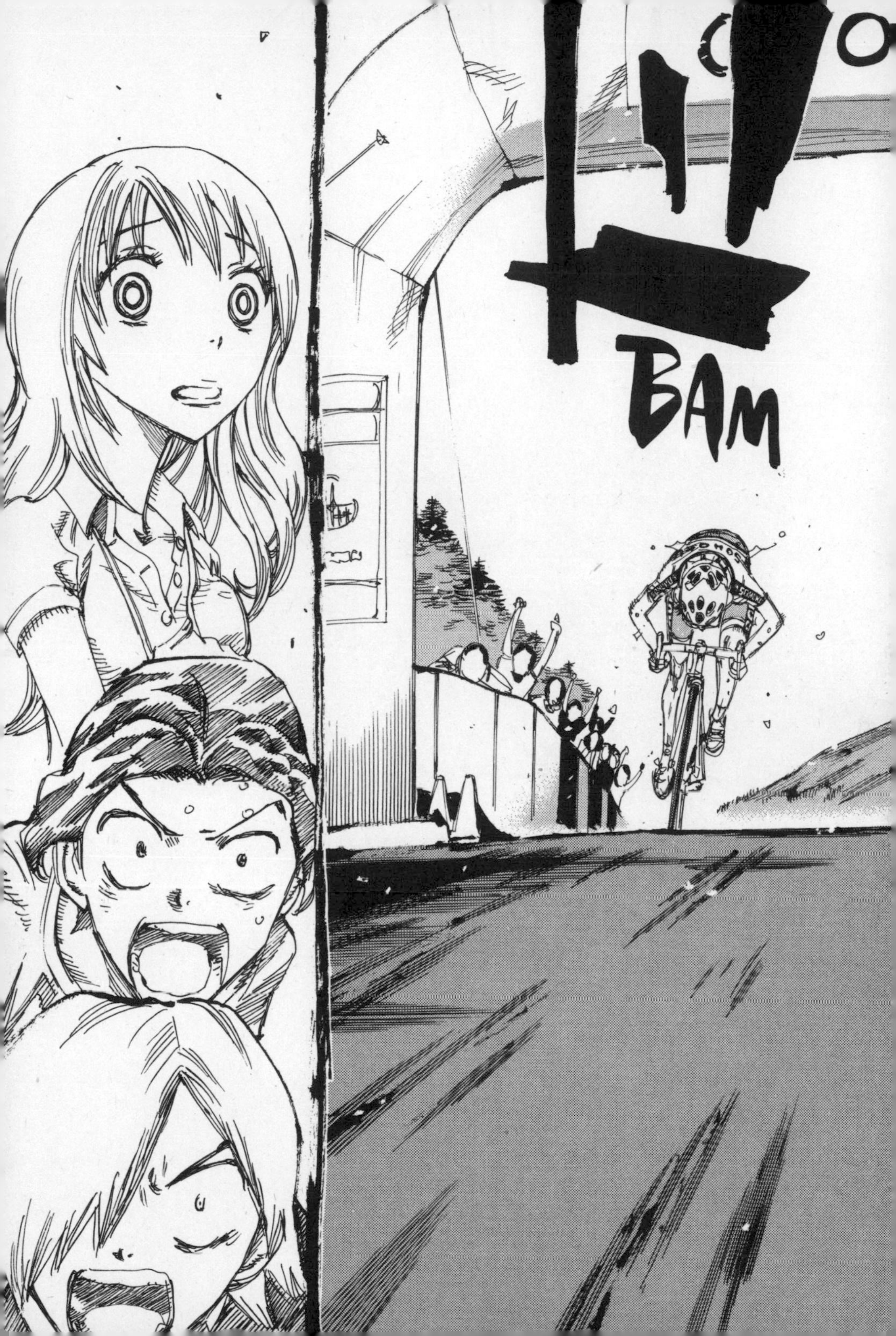
BAM

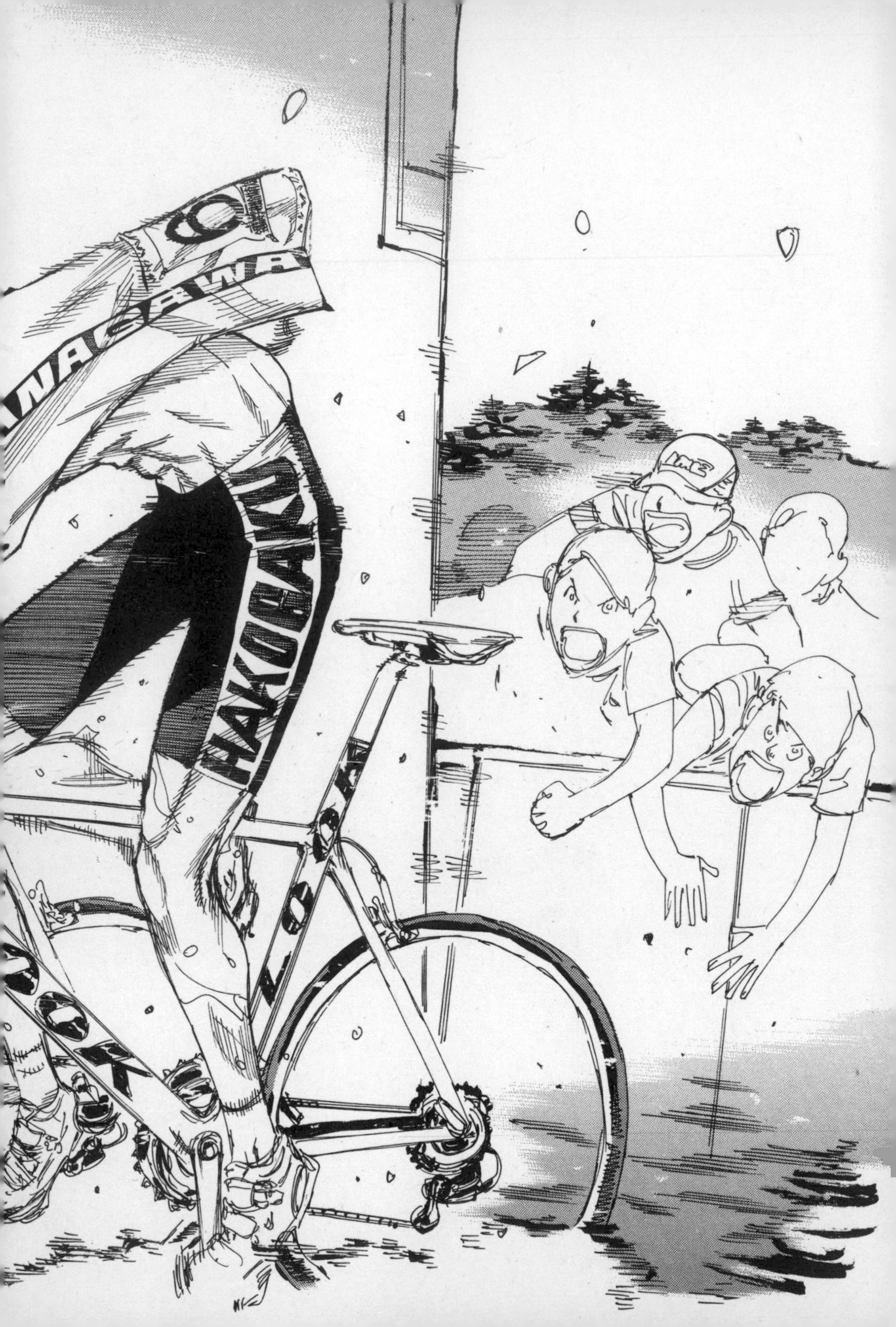
HAKOGAKU

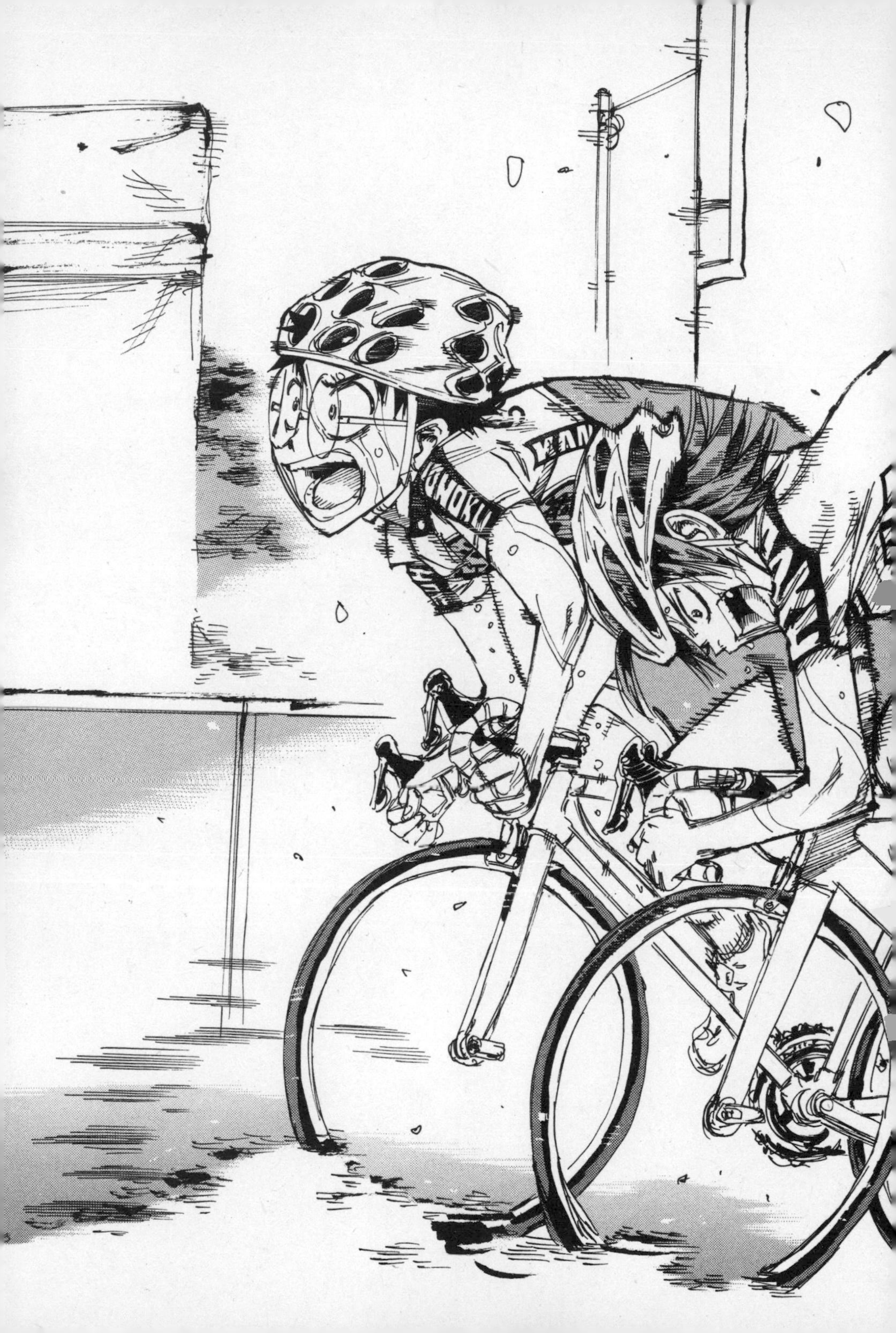

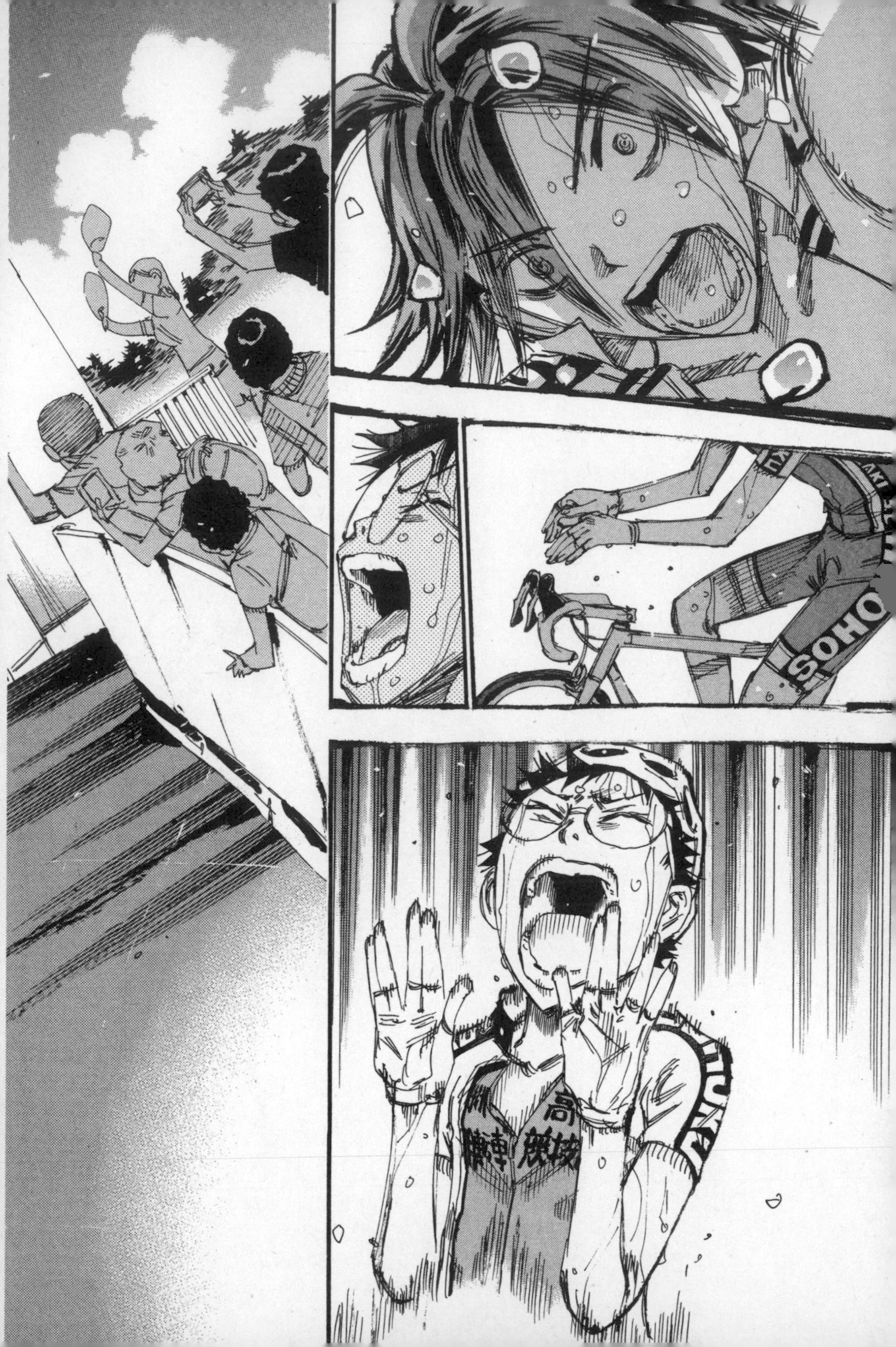
SOHO

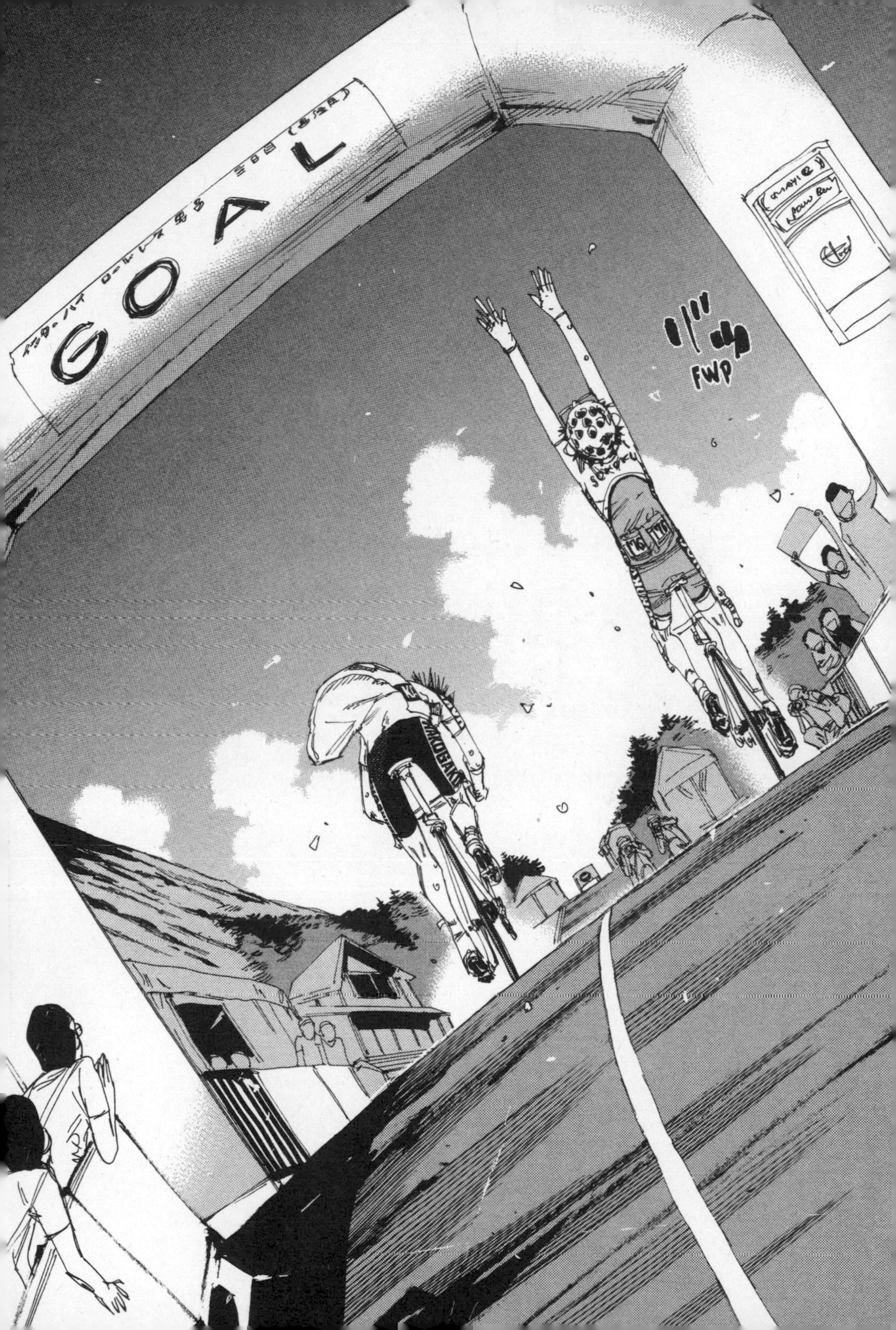
GOAL
FWP

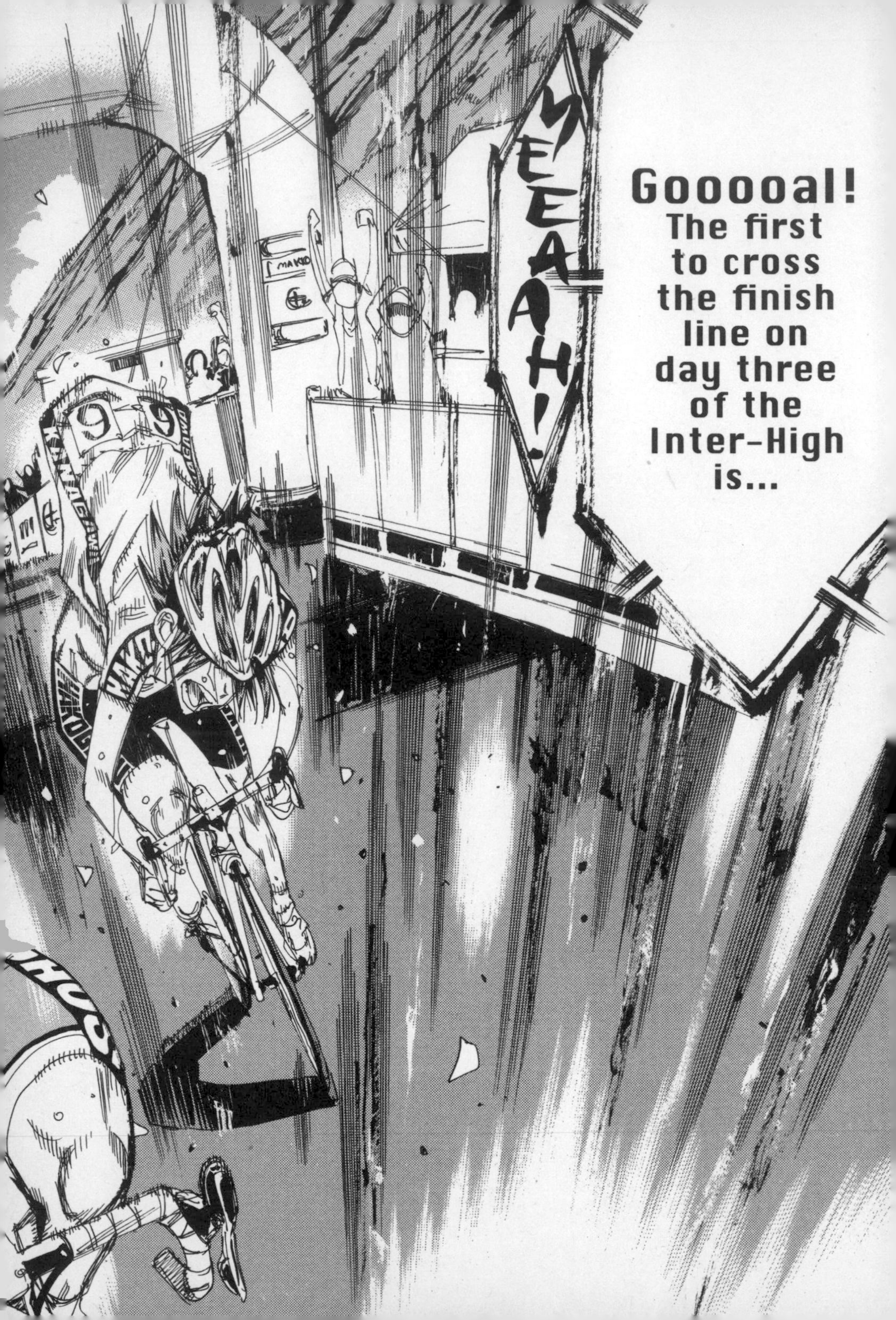
YEEAAAH!
Goooooal! The first to cross the finish line on day three of the Inter-High is...

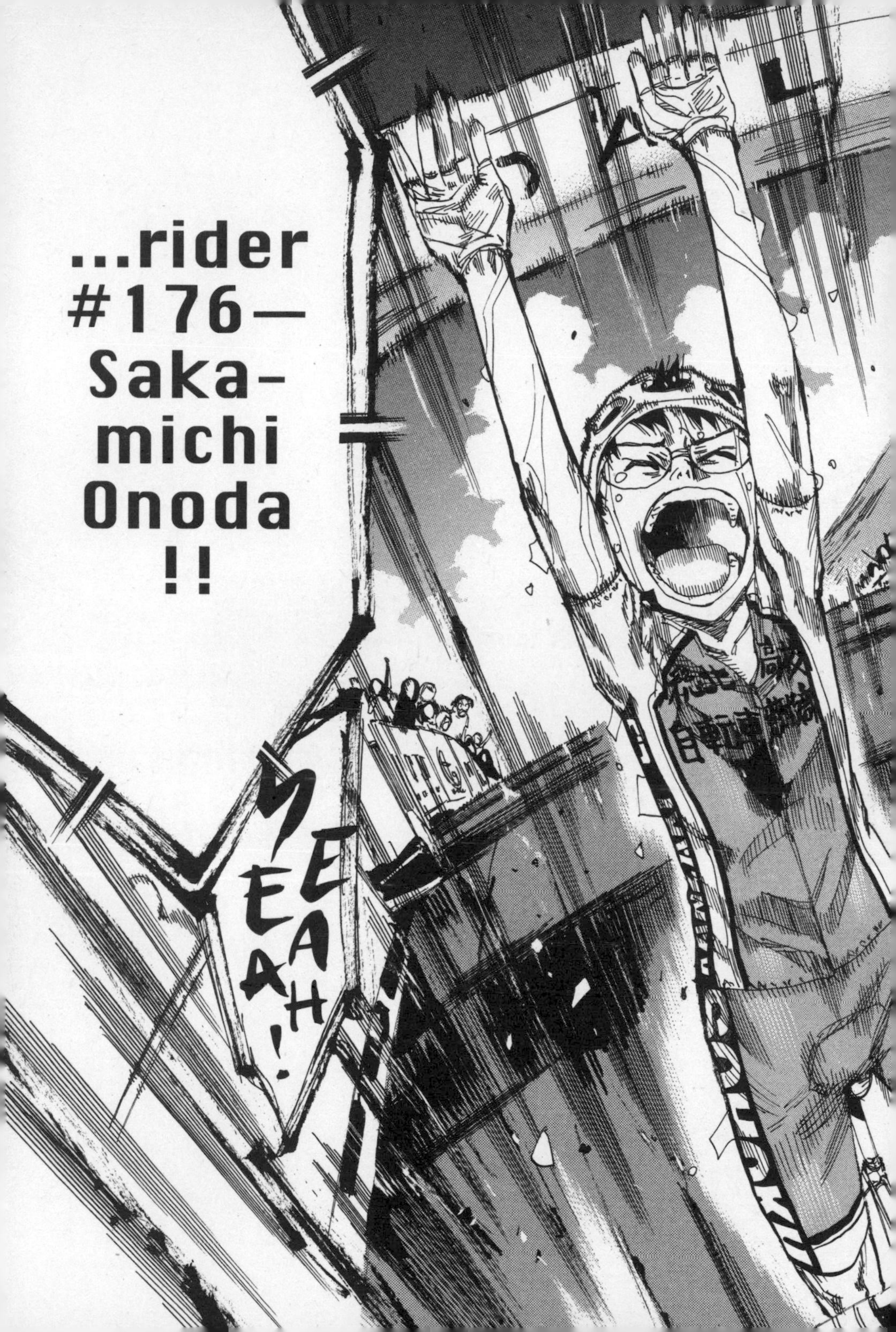
...rider #176—Saka-michi Onoda !!
MEEEAAAH!

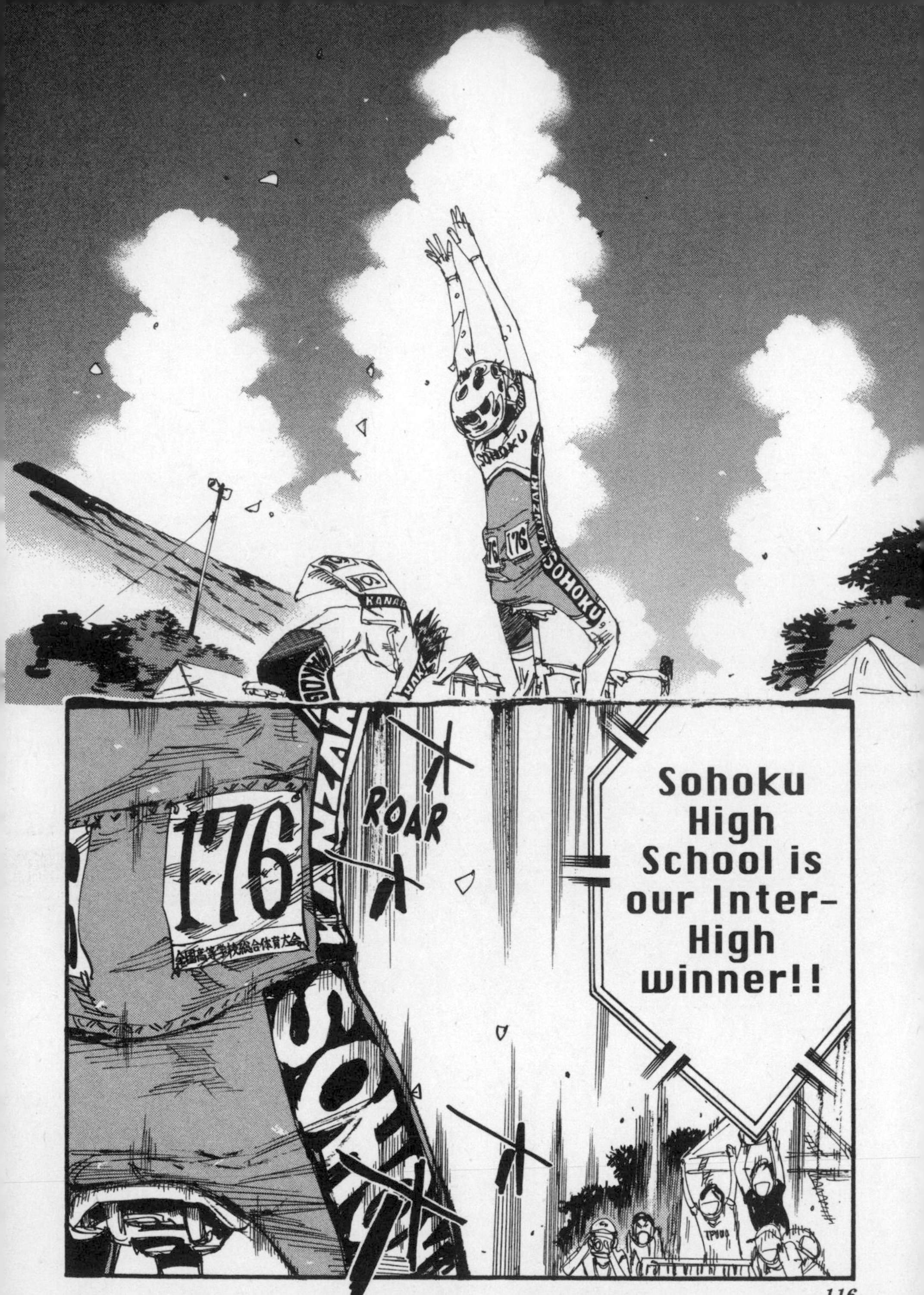
Sohoku High School is our Inter-High winner!!
ROAR
176
全国高等学校総合体育大会

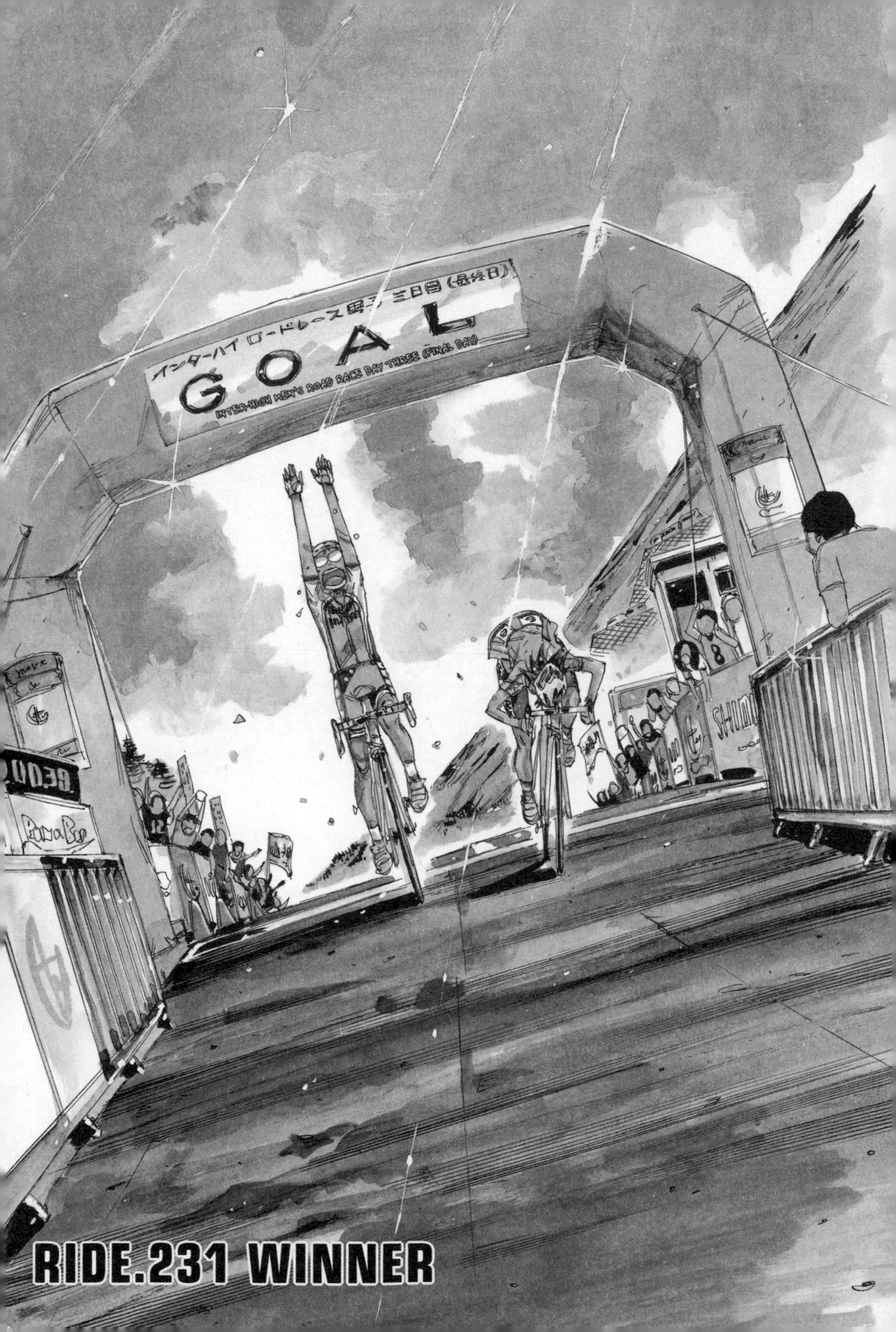
インターハイ ロードレース男子 三日目(最終日)
GOAL
INTER-HIGH MEN'S ROAD RACE DAY THREE (FINAL DAY)

RIDE.231 WINNER

SAKAMICHI
SOHOKU

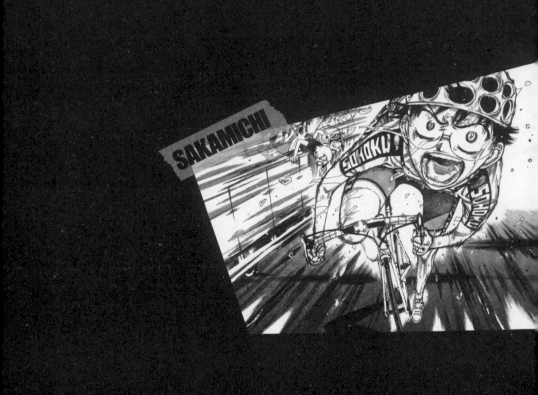

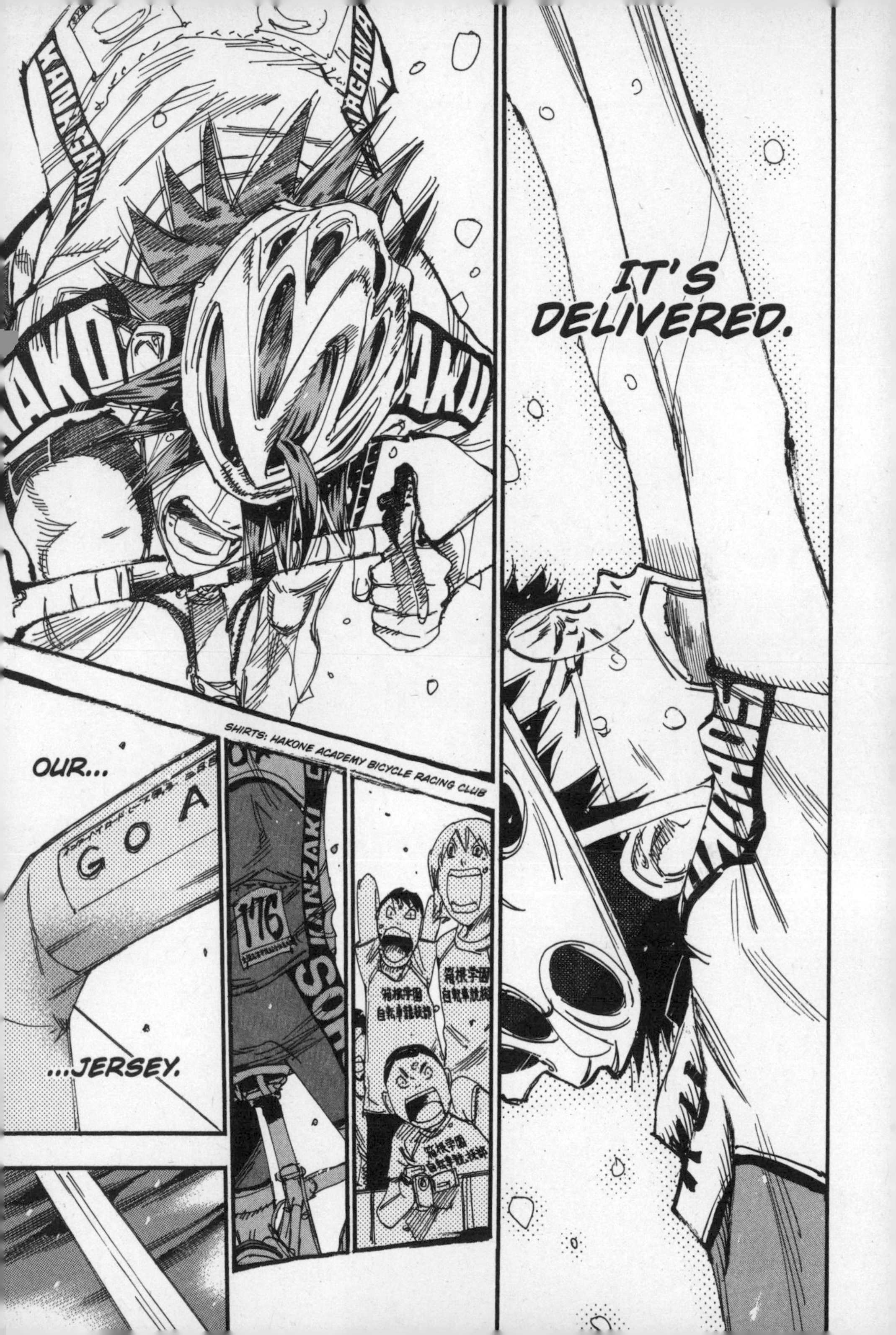
IT'S DELIVERED.
SHIRTS: HAKONE ACADEMY BICYCLE RACING CLUB
OUR...
...JERSEY.

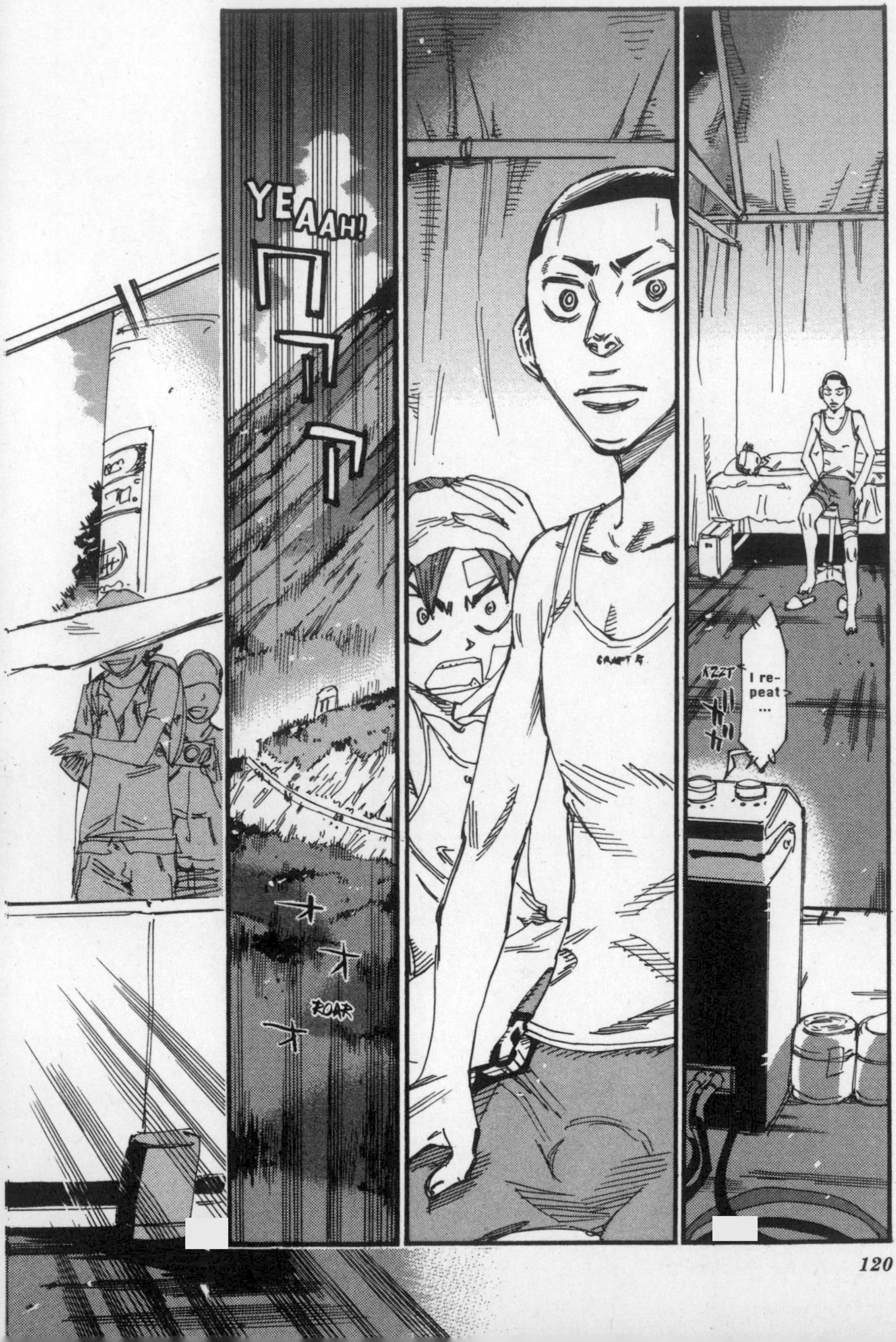
KZZT
I re-
peat
...
YEAAAH!
ROAR

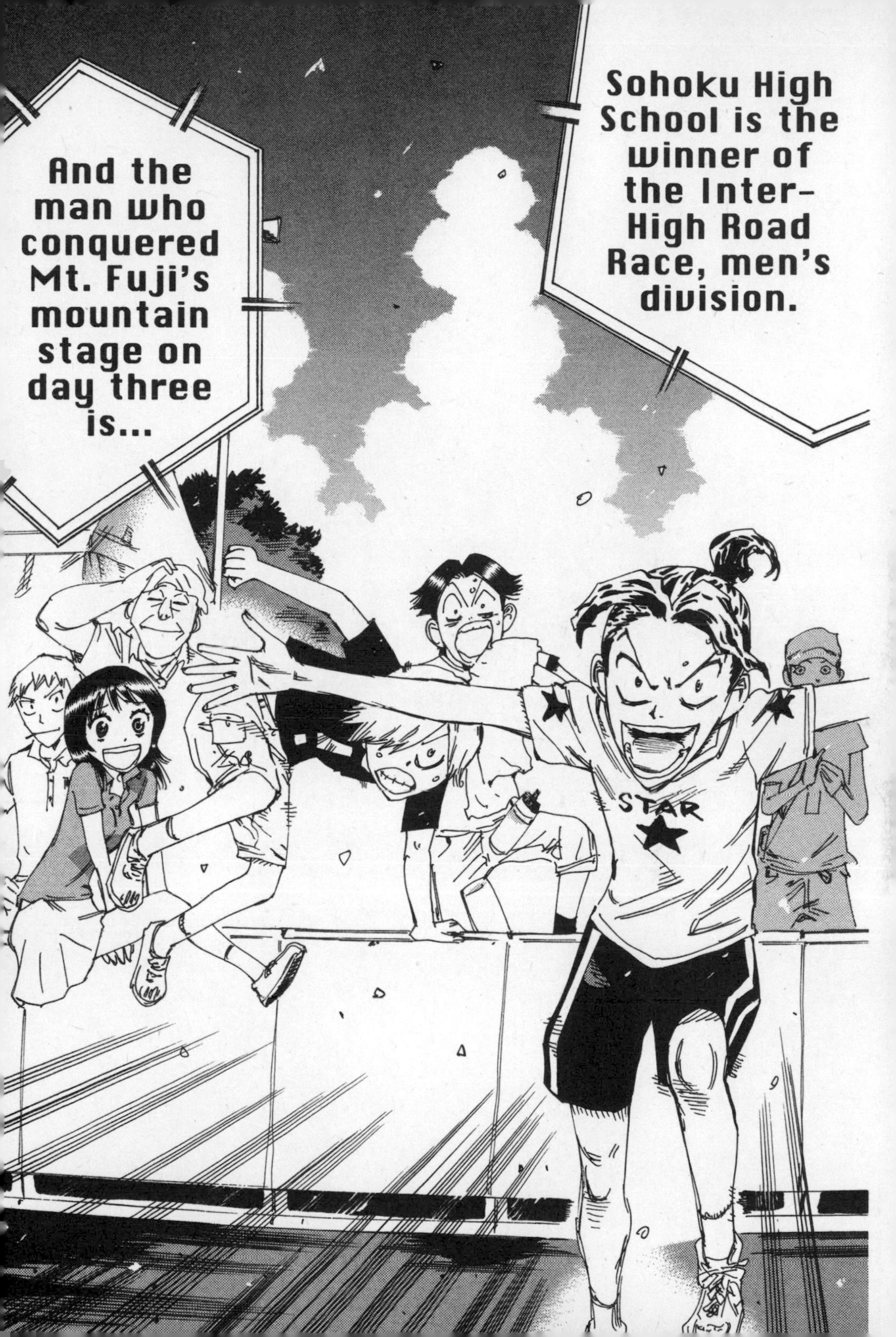
Sohoku High School is the winner of the Inter-High Road Race, men's division.
And the man who conquered Mt. Fuji's mountain stage on day three is...

#176—Saka-michi Onoda!!

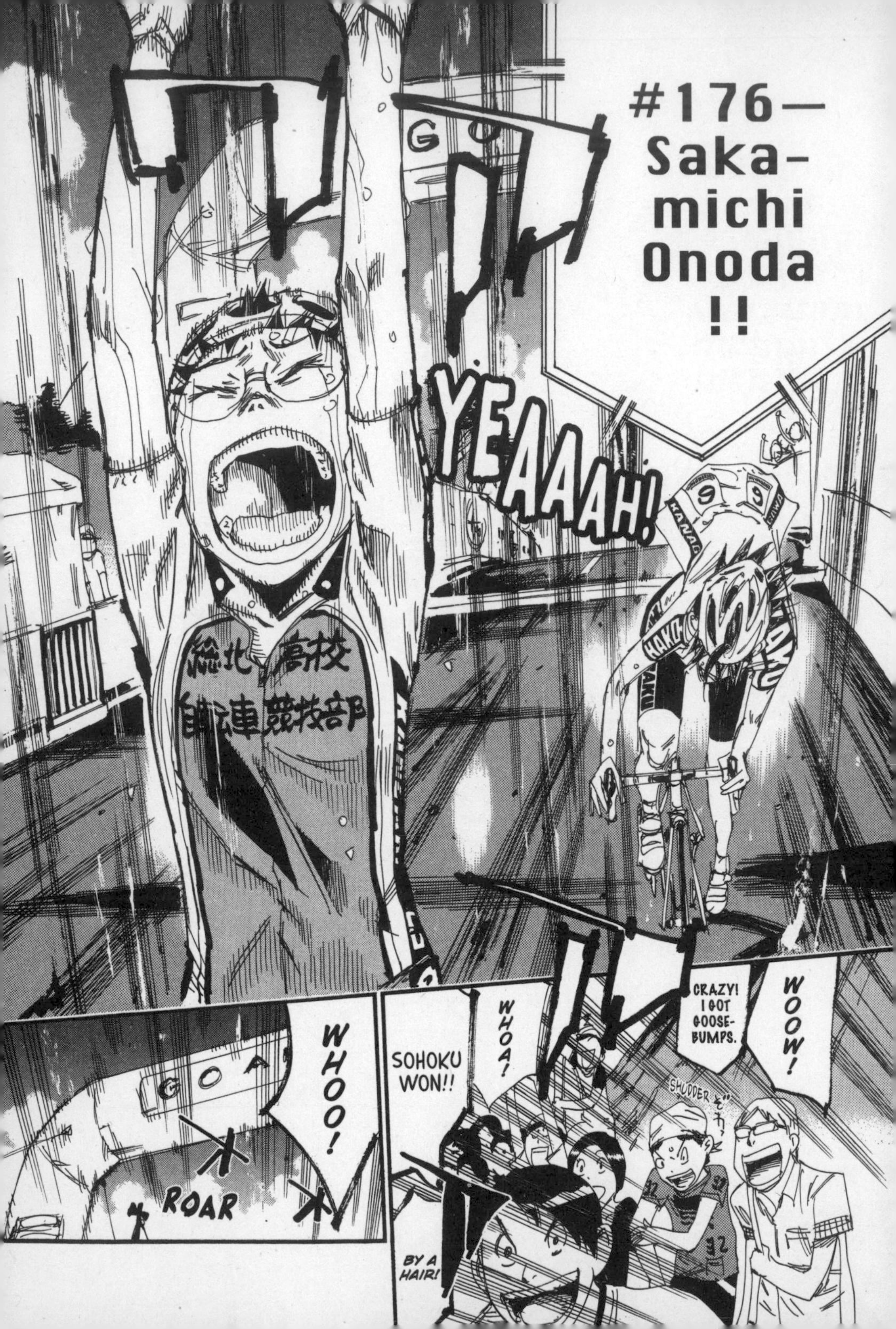
YEAAAAH!
総北高校
自転車競技部
WOOOW!
CRAZY! I GOT GOOSE-BUMPS.
SHUDDER
WHOA!
SOHOKU WON!!
BY A HAIR!
WHOOO!
ROAR

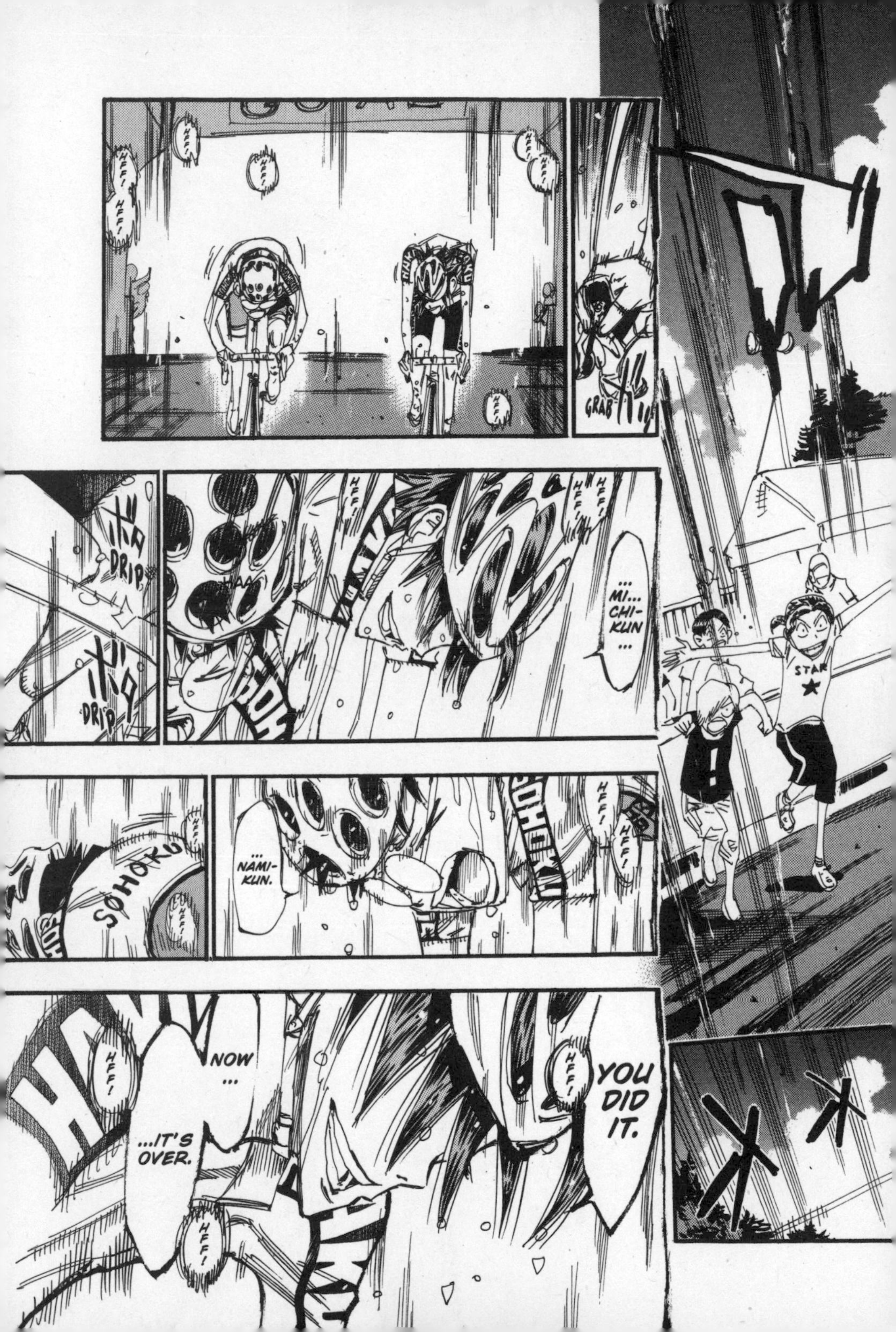
STAR
GRAB
HFF!
HFF!
HFF!
HFF!
HFF!
HFF!
HFF!
HFF!
...MI... CHI-KUN...
DRIP
DRIP
HFF!
HFF!
...NAMI-KUN.
HFF!
HFF!
SOHOKU
YOU DID IT.
HFF!
NOW...
...IT'S OVER.
HFF!
HFF!

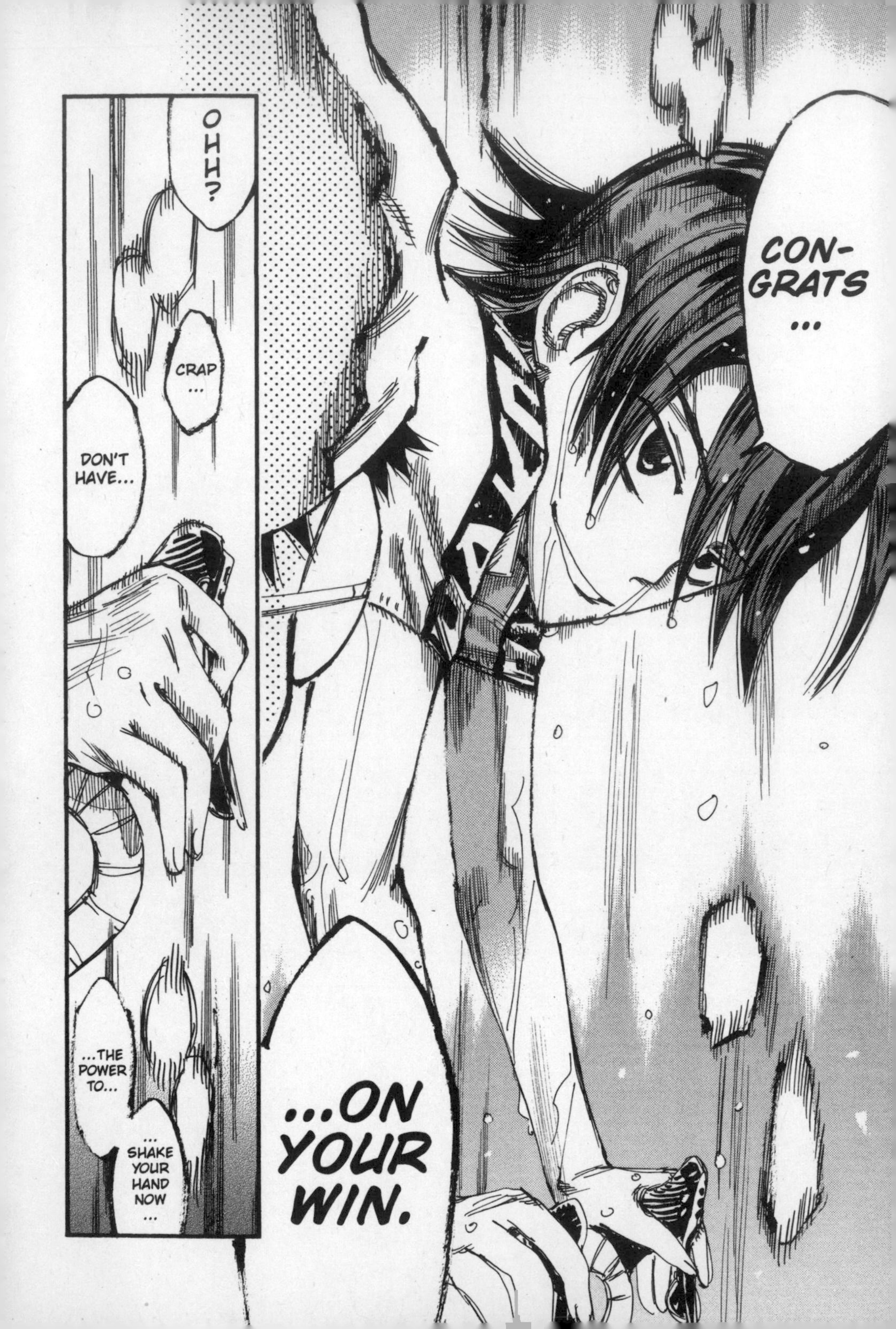
CON-GRATS...
...ON YOUR WIN.
OHH?
CRAP...
DON'T HAVE...
...THE POWER TO...
...SHAKE YOUR HAND NOW...

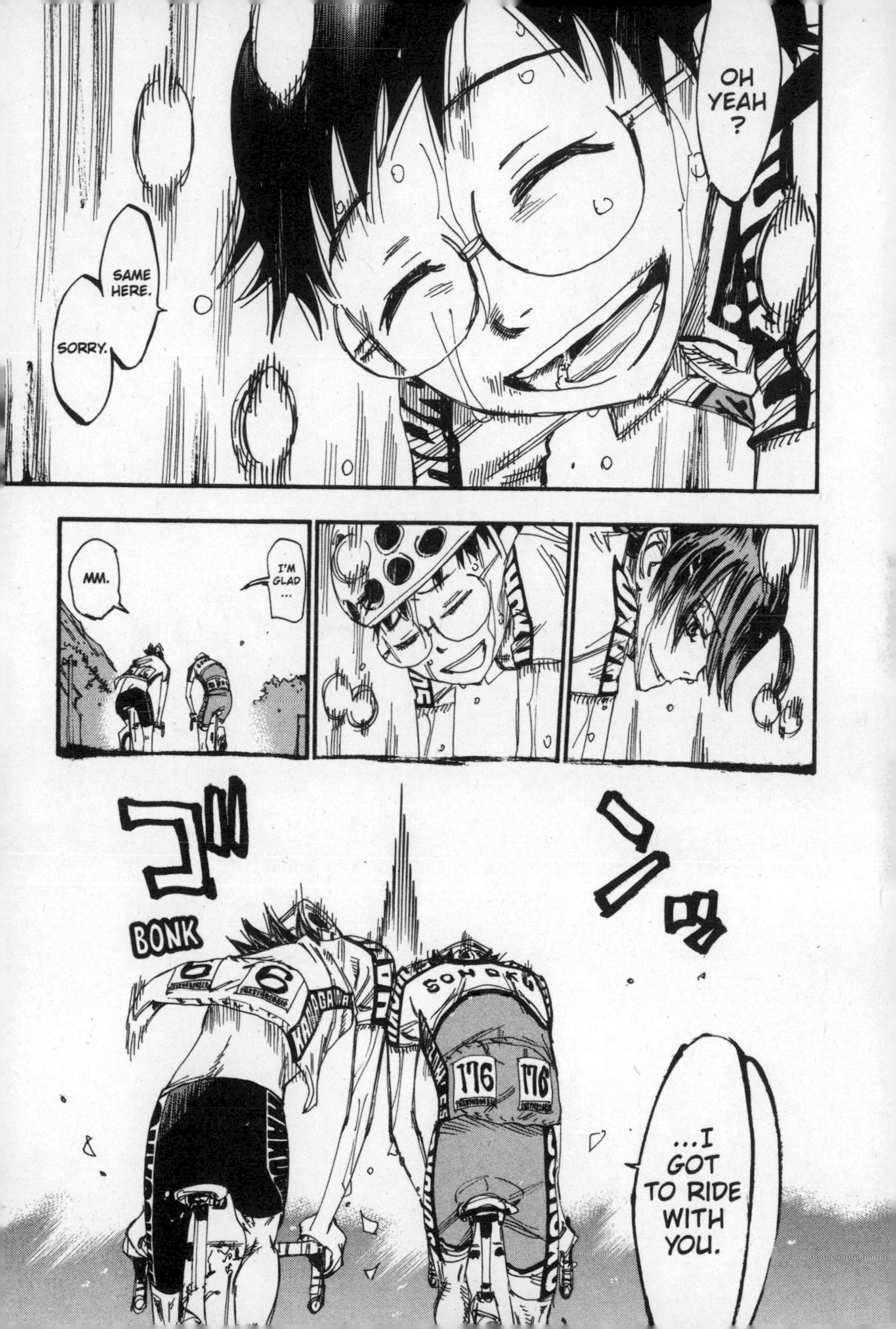
OH YEAH?
SAME HERE.
SORRY.
I'M GLAD...
MM.
BONK
...I GOT TO RIDE WITH YOU.

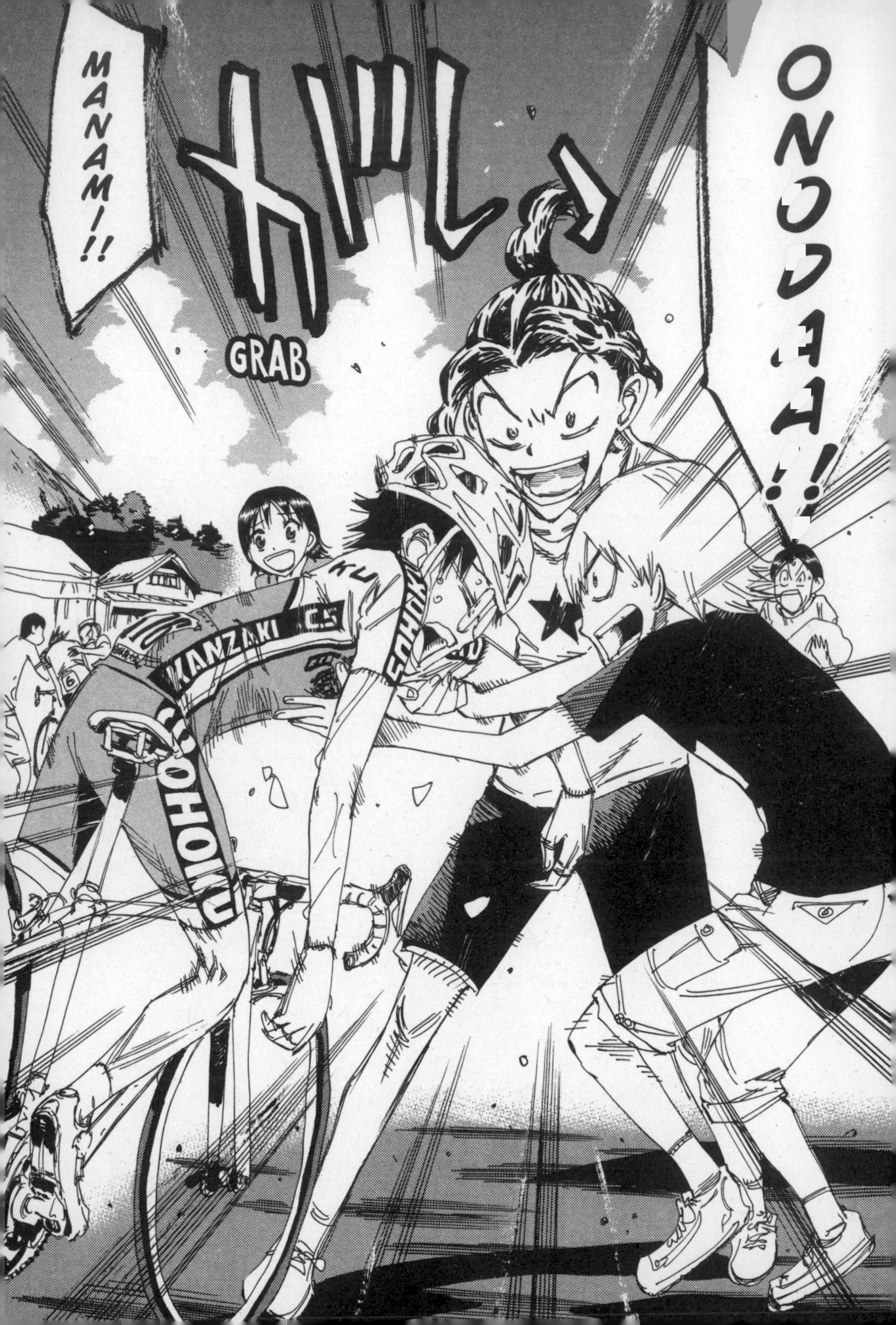
ONODAAA!!
GRAB
MANAMI!!

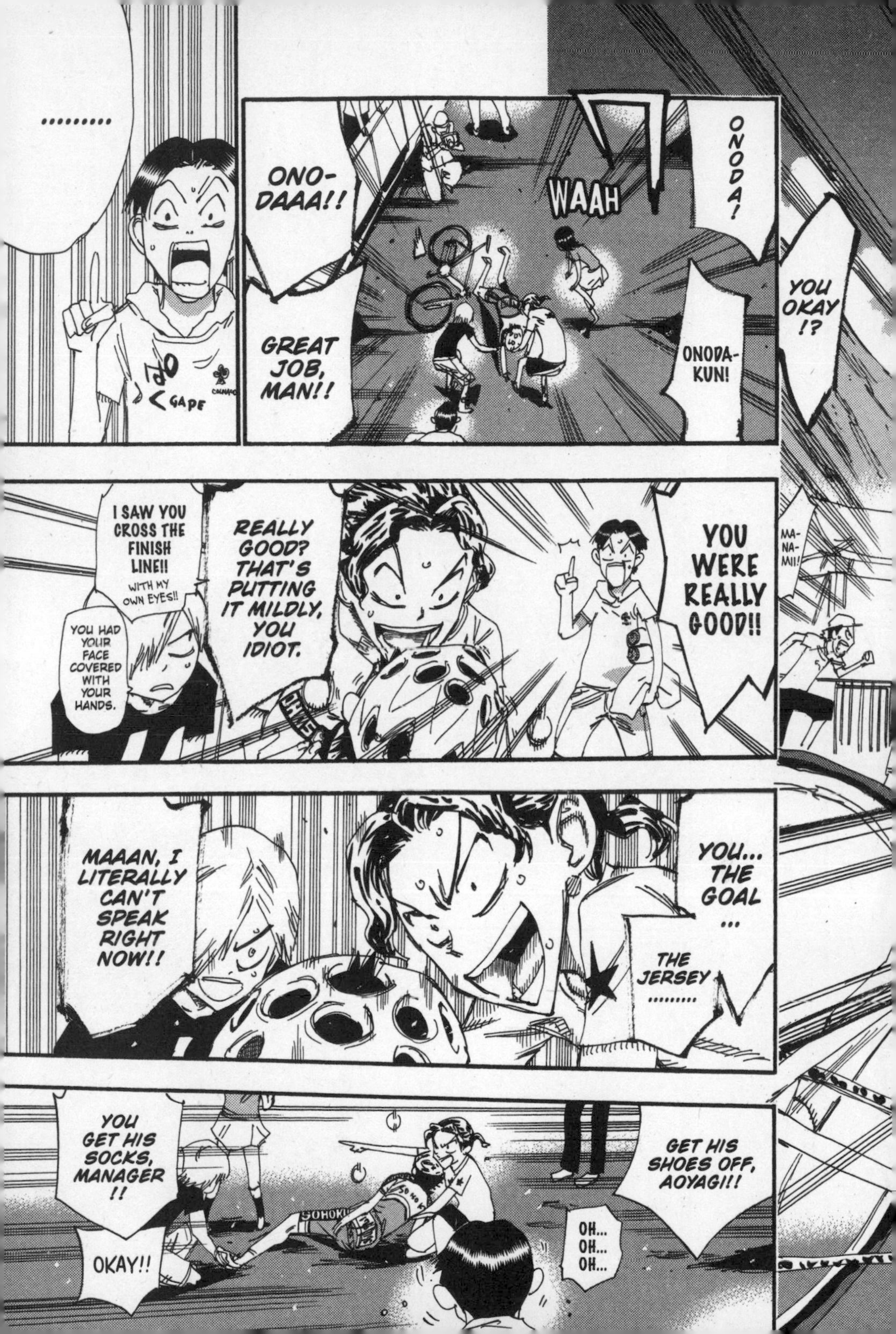
YOU OKAY !?
ONODA!
WAAH
ONODA-KUN!
ONO-DAAA!!
GREAT JOB, MAN!!
....
MA-NA-MI!!
YOU WERE REALLY GOOD!!
REALLY GOOD? THAT'S PUTTING IT MILDLY, YOU IDIOT.
I SAW YOU CROSS THE FINISH LINE!! WITH MY OWN EYES!!
YOU HAD YOUR FACE COVERED WITH YOUR HANDS.
YOU... THE GOAL ...
THE JERSEY ....
MAAAN, I LITERALLY CAN'T SPEAK RIGHT NOW!!
GET HIS SHOES OFF, AOYAGI!!
OH... OH... OH...
YOU GET HIS SOCKS, MANAGER !!
OKAY!!

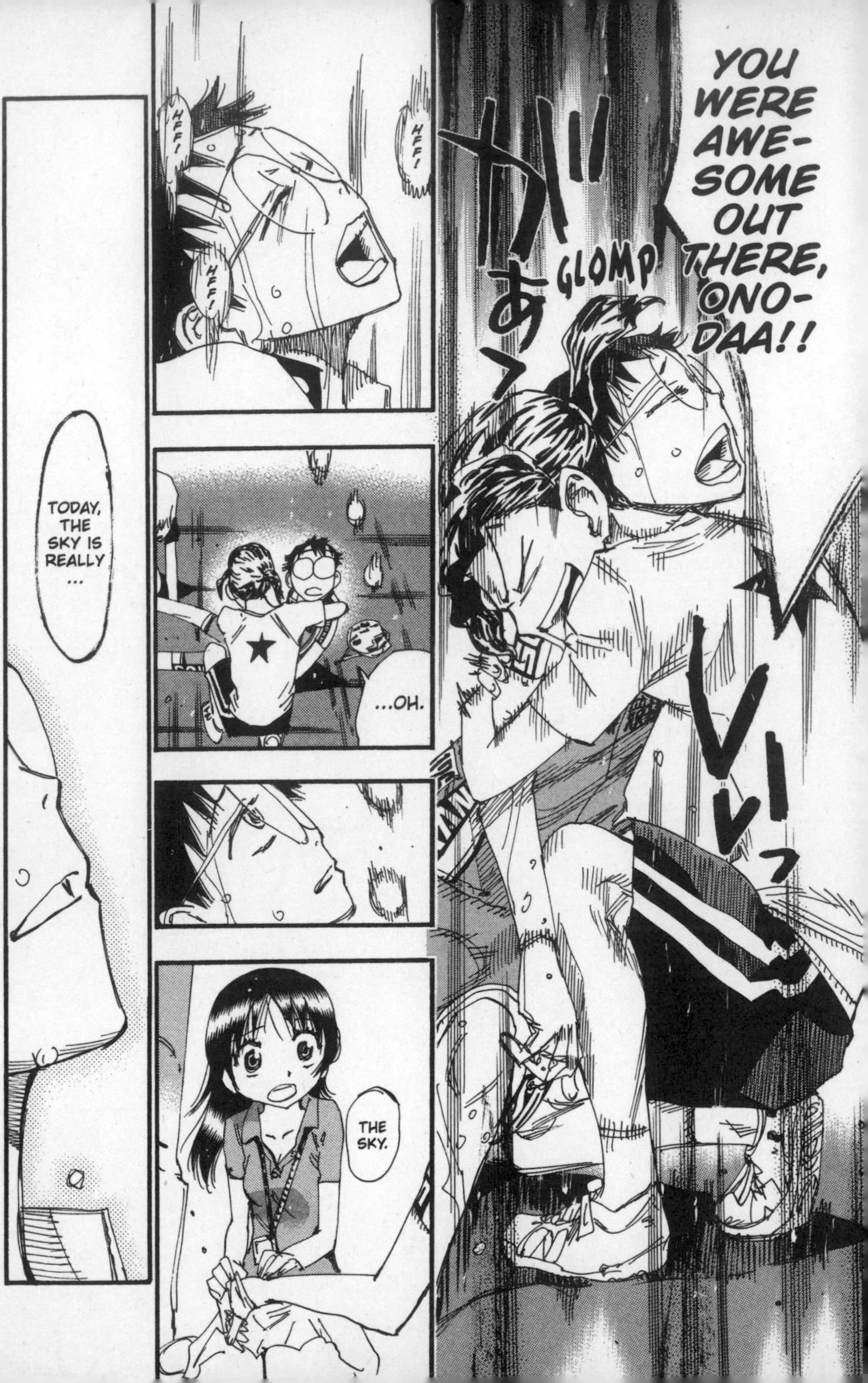
YOU WERE AWE-SOME OUT THERE, ONO-DAA!!
GLOMP
HFF!
HFF!
HFF!
...OH.
THE SKY.
TODAY, THE SKY IS REALLY ...

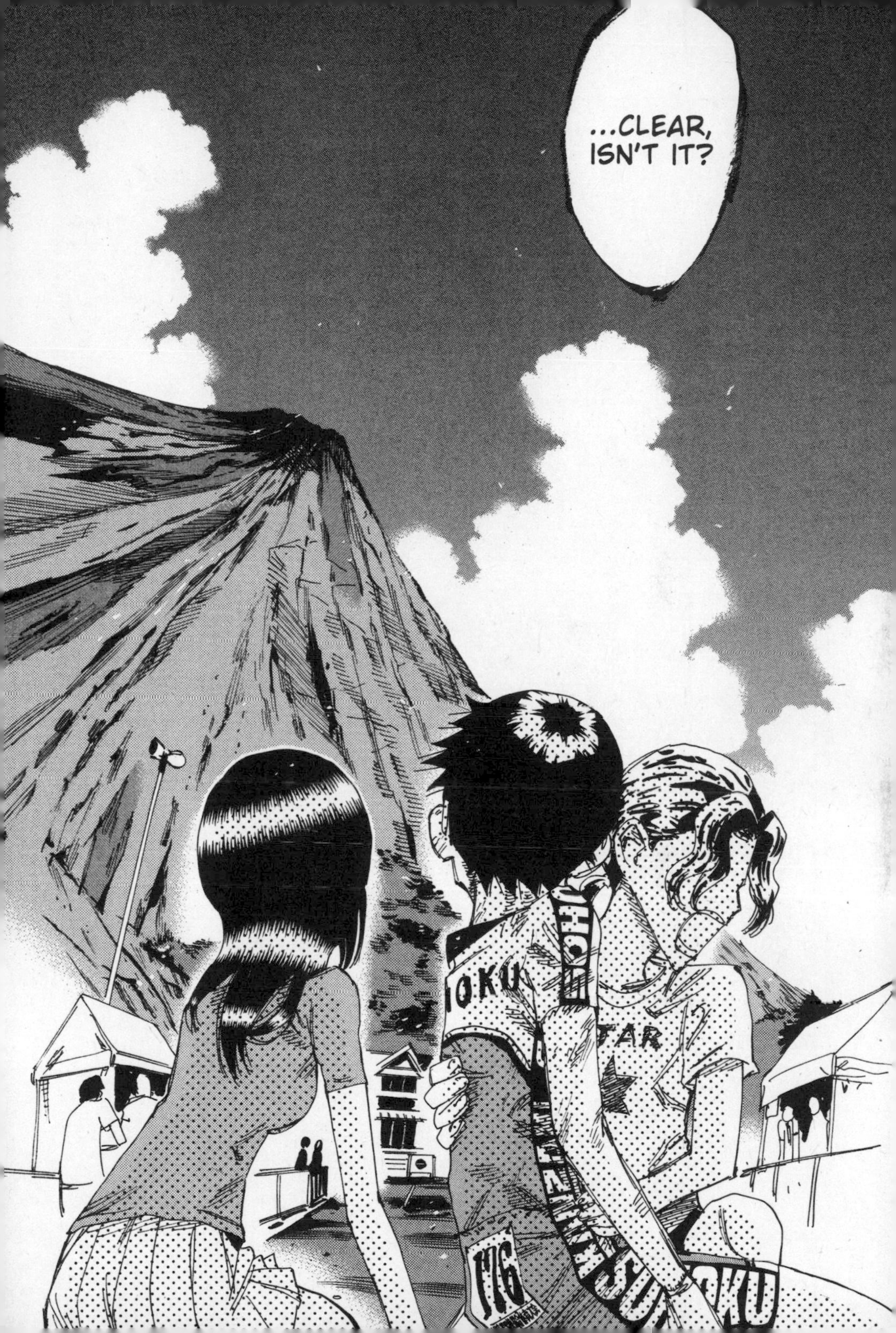
...CLEAR, ISN'T IT?

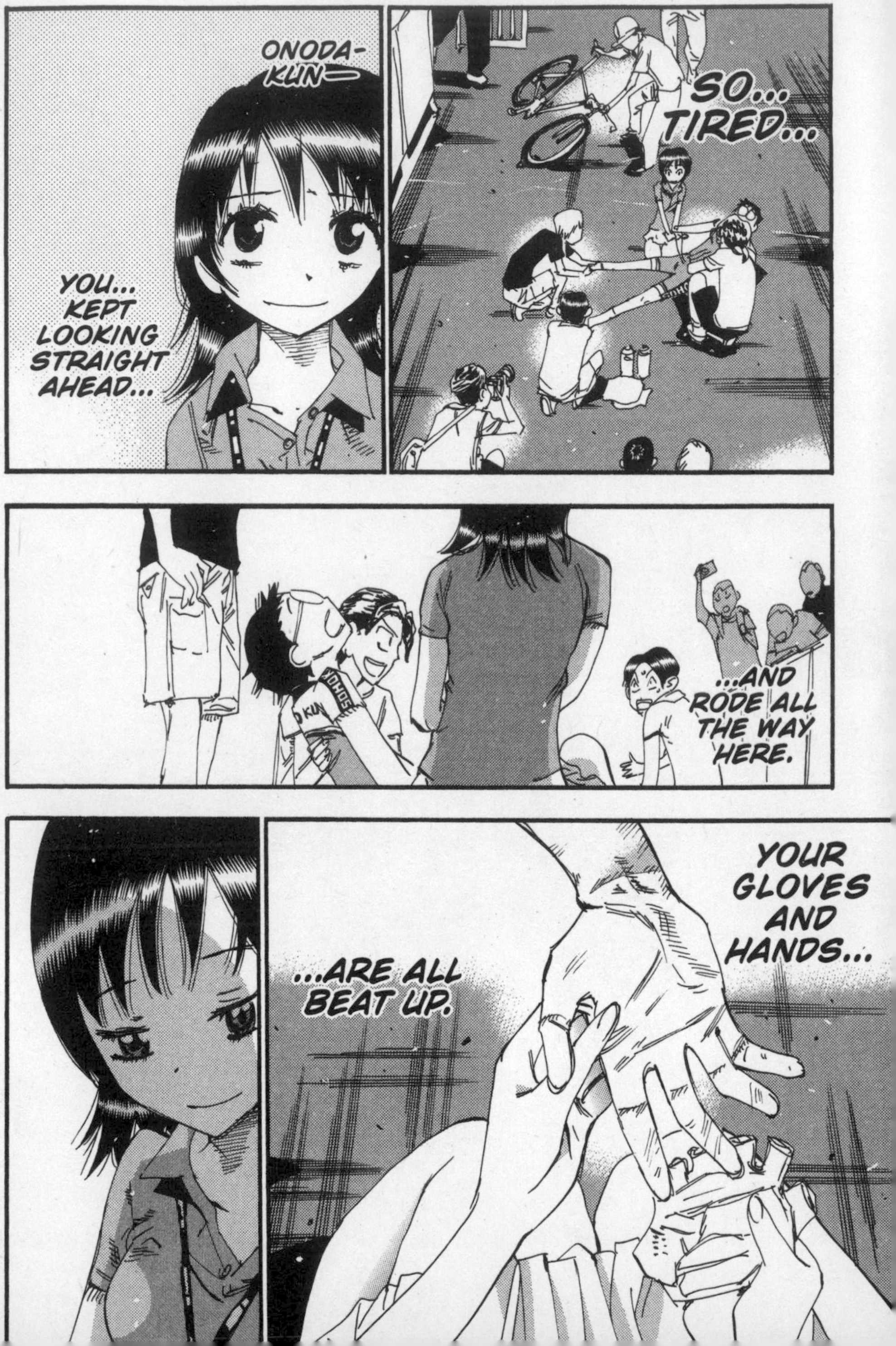
SO... TIRED...
ONODA-KUN—
YOU... KEPT LOOKING STRAIGHT AHEAD...
...AND RODE ALL THE WAY HERE.
YOUR GLOVES AND HANDS...
...ARE ALL BEAT UP.

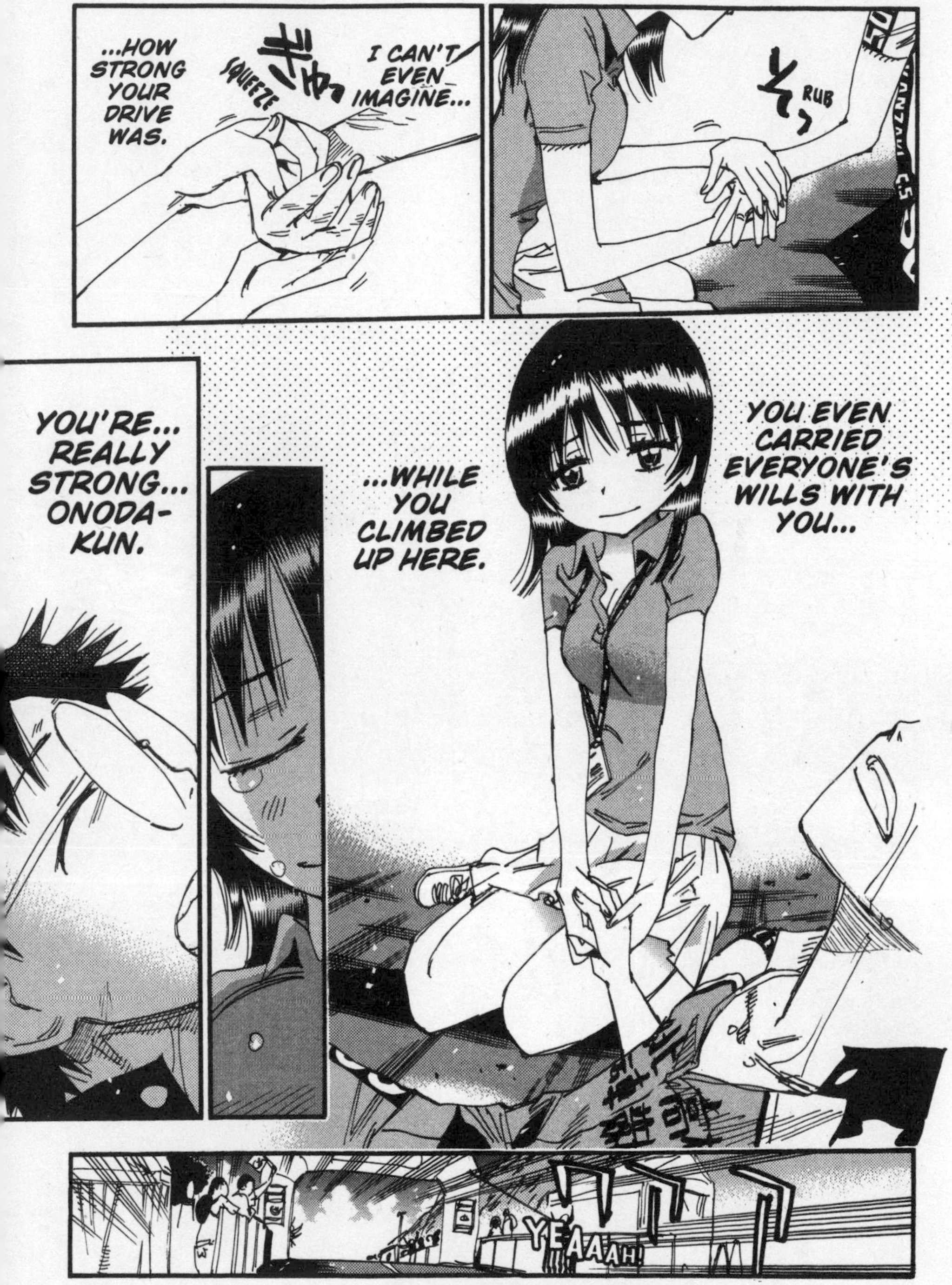
そっ
RUB
I CAN'T EVEN IMAGINE...
ぎゅっ
SQUEEZE
...HOW STRONG YOUR DRIVE WAS.
YOU EVEN CARRIED EVERYONE'S WILLS WITH YOU...
...WHILE YOU CLIMBED UP HERE.
YOU'RE... REALLY STRONG... ONODA-KUN.
YEAAAH!

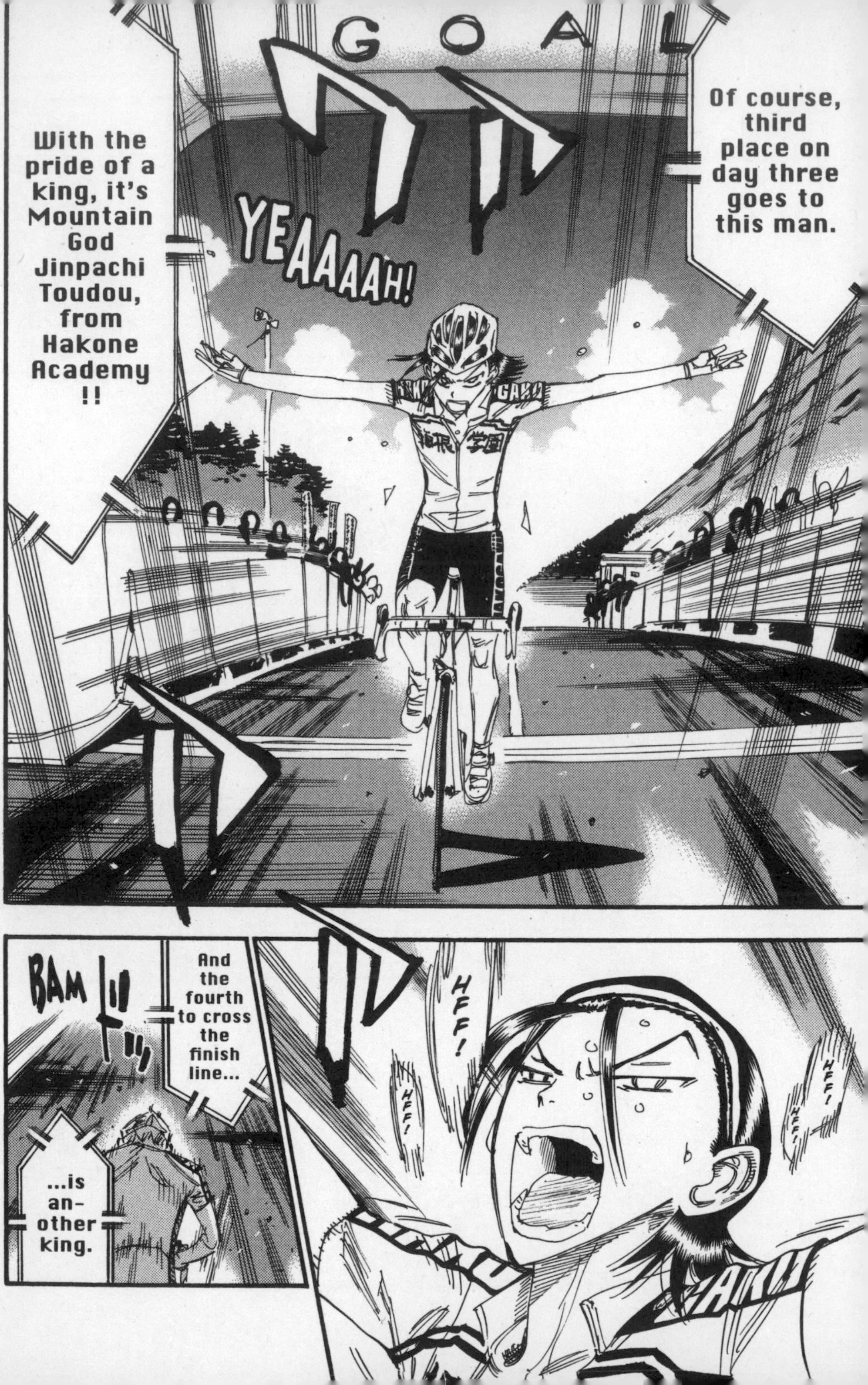
GOAL
Of course, third place on day three goes to this man.
YEAAAAH!
With the pride of a king, it's Mountain God Jinpachi Toudou, from Hakone Academy!!
HFF!
HFF!
HFF!
HFF!
And the fourth to cross the finish line...
BAM
...is an-other king.

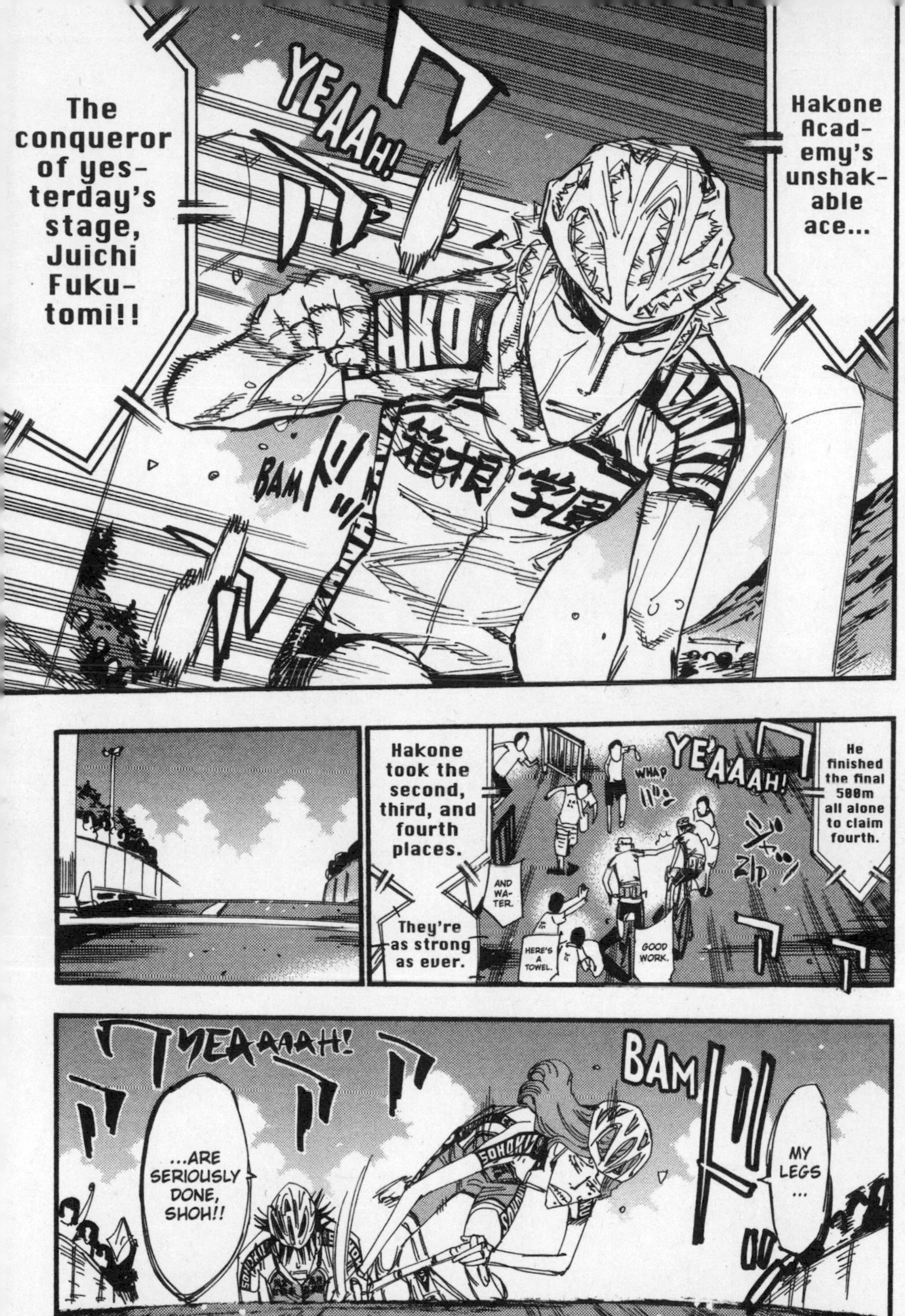
Hakone Academy's unshakable ace...
YEAAAH!
The conqueror of yesterday's stage, Juichi Fukutomi!!
BAM
He finished the final 500m all alone to claim fourth.
YE'AAAAH!
WHAP
ZIP
Hakone took the second, third, and fourth places.
AND WATER.
GOOD WORK.
HERE'S A TOWEL.
They're as strong as ever.
MY LEGS...
BAM
YEAAAAH!
...ARE SERIOUSLY DONE, SHOH!!

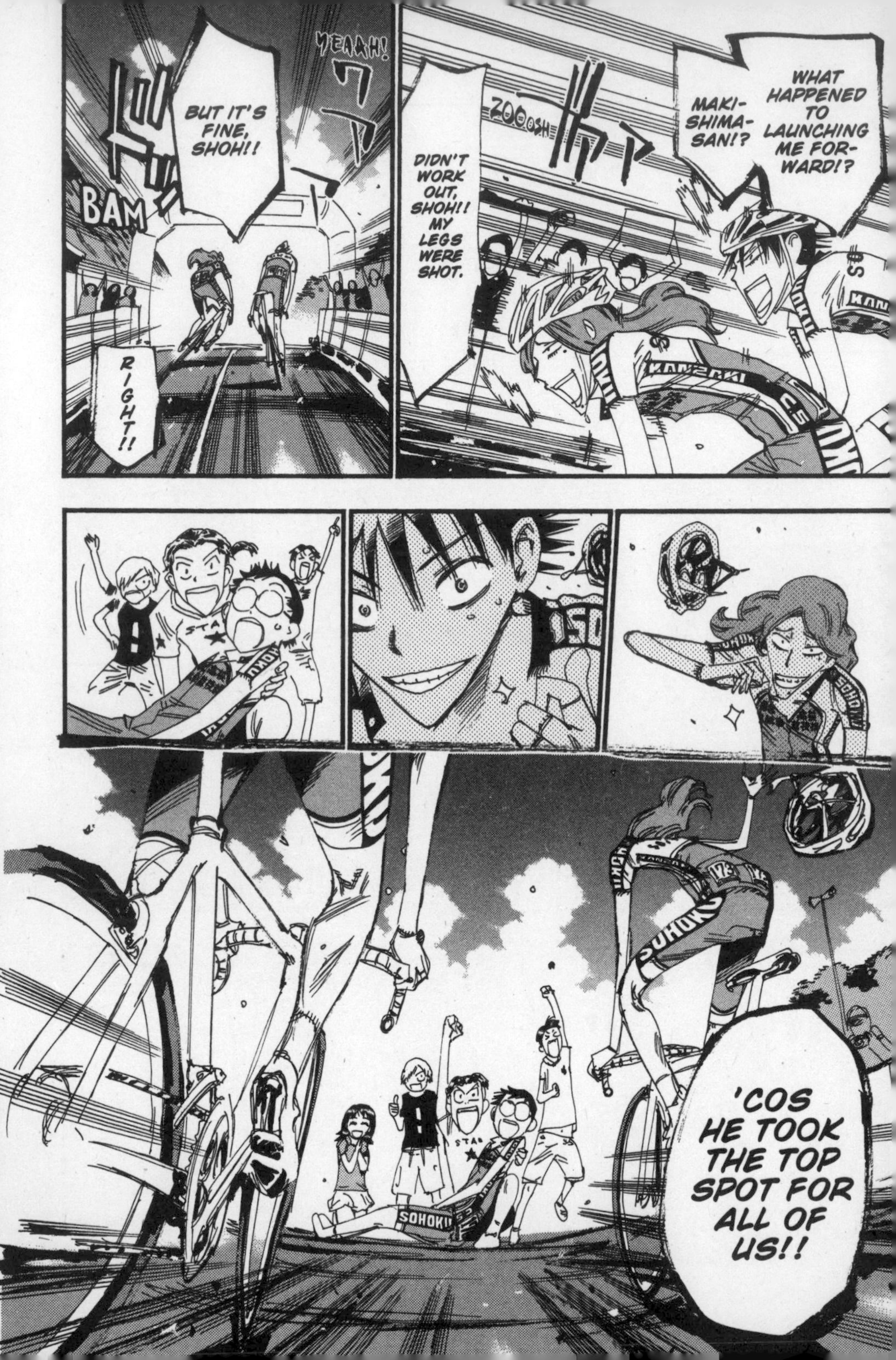
WHAT HAPPENED TO LAUNCHING ME FORWARD!? MAKI-SHIMA-SAN!?
ZOOOSH
DIDN'T WORK OUT, SHOH!! MY LEGS WERE SHOT.
YEAAH!
BUT IT'S FINE, SHOH!!
BAM
RIGHT!!
'COS HE TOOK THE TOP SPOT FOR ALL OF US!!

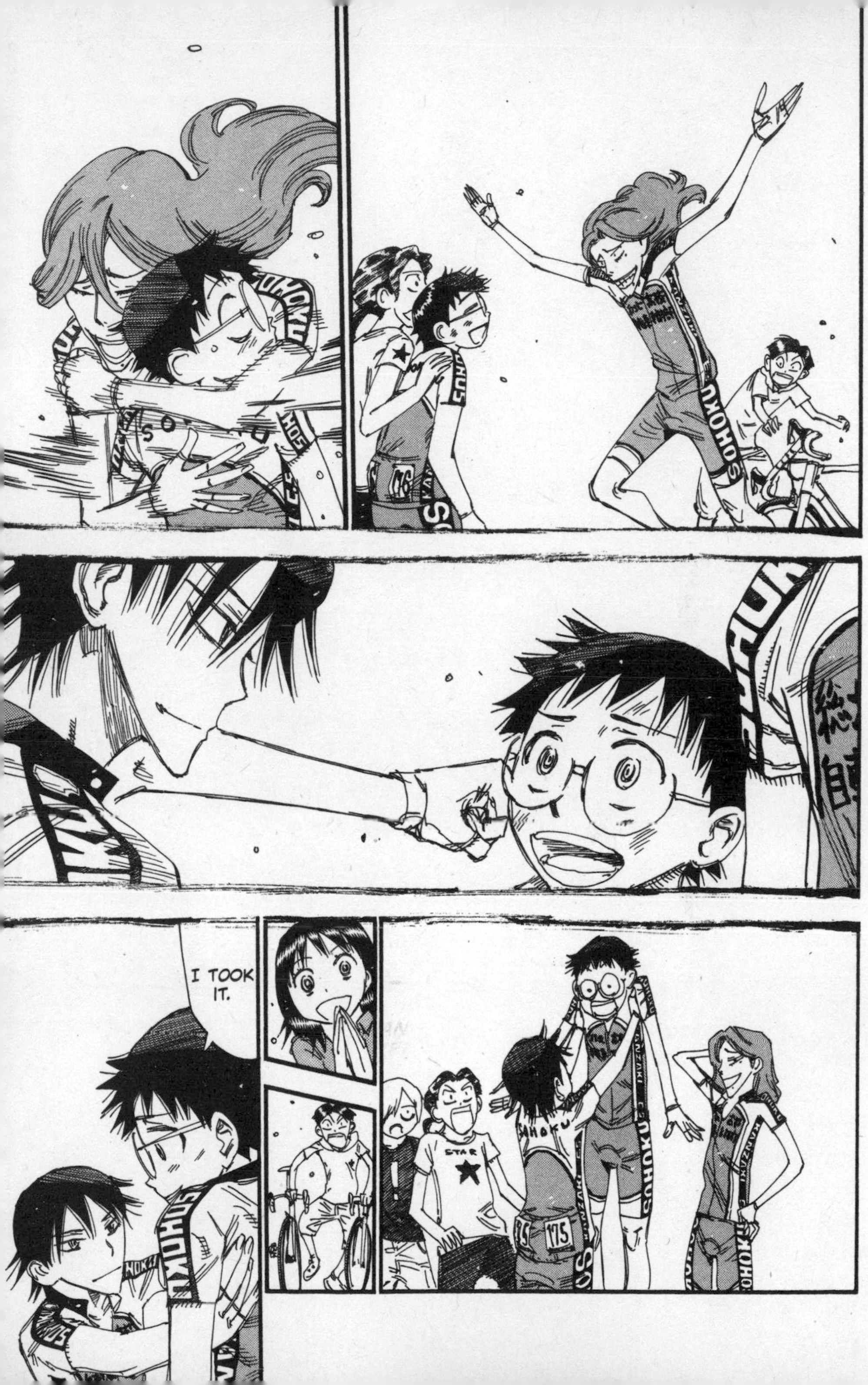
I TOOK IT.

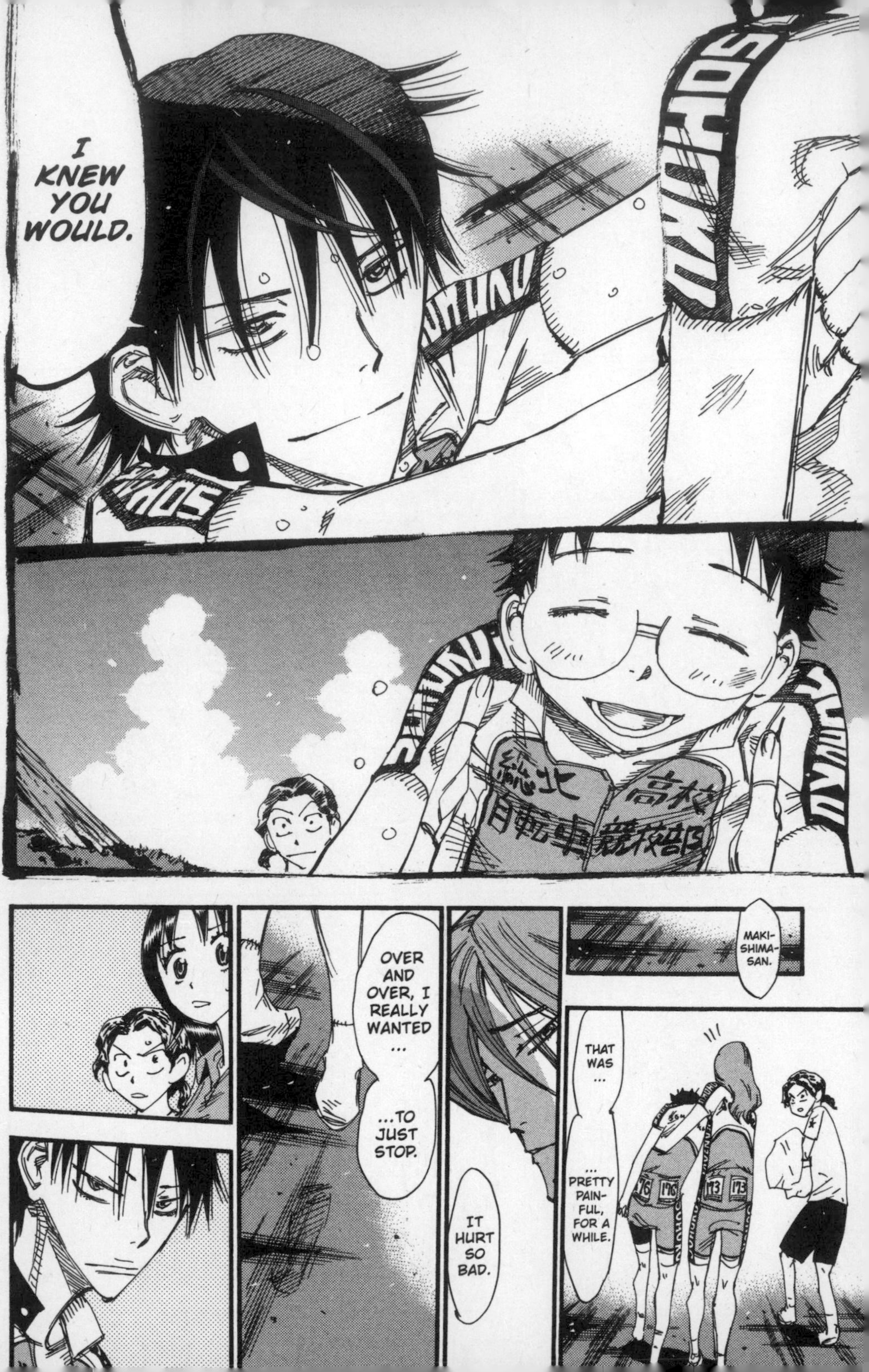
I KNEW YOU WOULD.
MAKI-SHIMA-SAN.
THAT WAS ...
... PRETTY PAIN-FUL, FOR A WHILE.
IT HURT SO BAD.
OVER AND OVER, I REALLY WANTED ...
...TO JUST STOP.

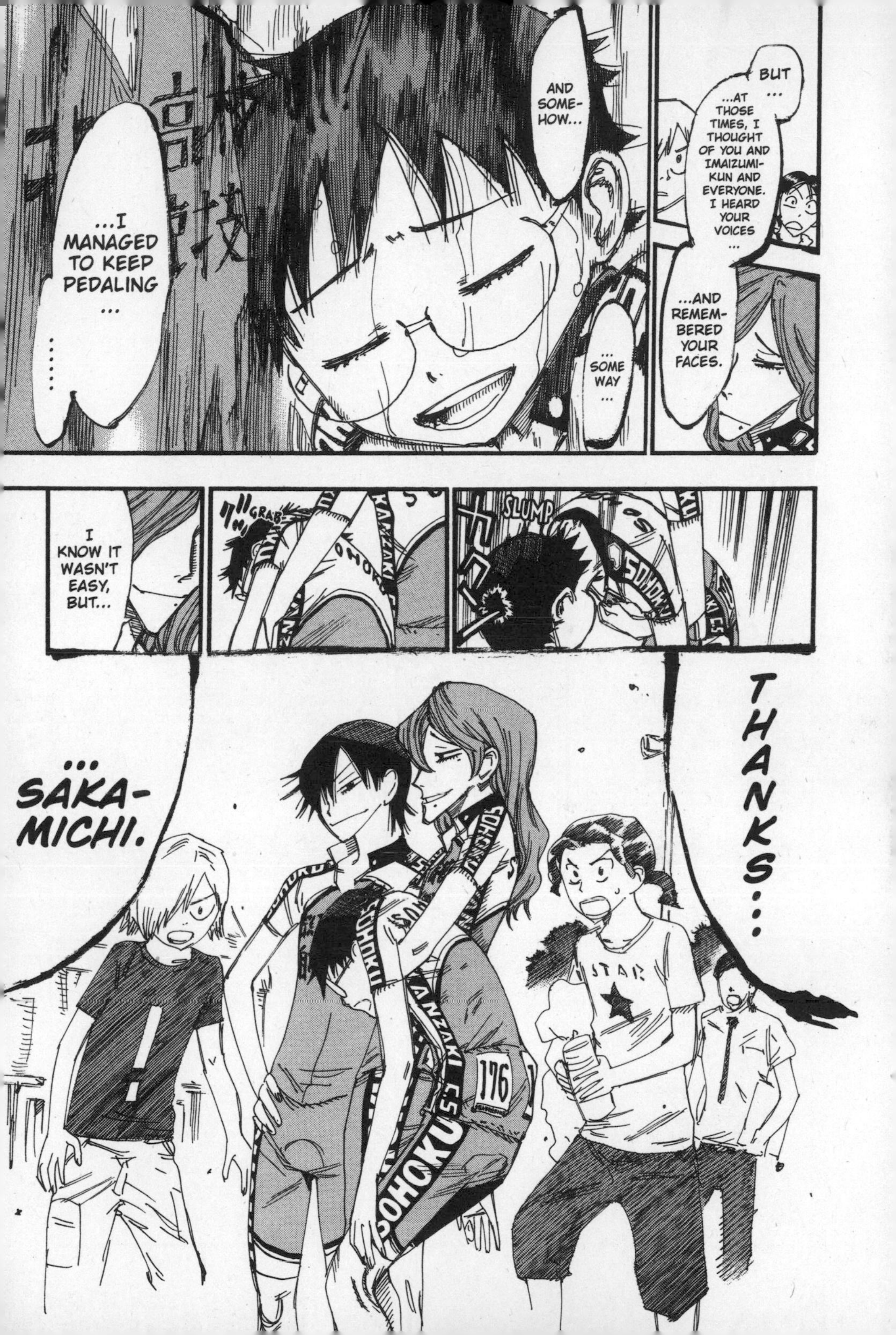
BUT ...
...AT THOSE TIMES, I THOUGHT OF YOU AND IMAIZUMI-KUN AND EVERYONE. I HEARD YOUR VOICES ...
...AND REMEMBERED YOUR FACES.
AND SOMEHOW...
...SOME WAY...
...I MANAGED TO KEEP PEDALING ...
......
SLUMP
GRAB
I KNOW IT WASN'T EASY, BUT...
THANKS...
...SÄKA-MICHI.

YOU REALLY PULLED IT OFF, ONODA-KUUUN!!

RAAAAH !!

SPLURT

ACK! STUPID BLOOD—TRYIN' TO ESCAPE MY BODY.

DAAAMN, ONODA-KUUUN !!

FOR REAL? REALLY FOR REAL?

ONO-DA!!

ONODA!!

YOU'VE JUST BEEN SAYING "ONODA" THIS WHOLE TIME!!

PLIP

PLIP

ONO-DA!!

SIGN: FIRST-AID TENT

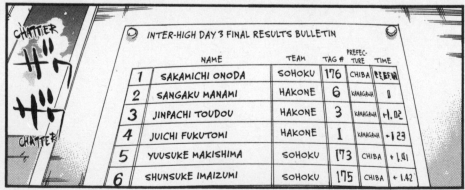

CHATTER

CHATTER

INTER-HIGH DAY 3 FINAL RESULTS BULLETIN

	NAME	TEAM	TAG #	PREFEC-TURE	TIME
1	SAKAMICHI ONODA	SOHOKU	176	CHIBA	
2	SANGAKU MANAMI	HAKONE	6	KANAGAWA	0
3	JINPACHI TOUDOU	HAKONE	3	KANAGAWA	+1.02
4	JUICHI FUKUTOMI	HAKONE	1	KANAGAWA	+1.23
5	YUUSUKE MAKISHIMA	SOHOKU	173	CHIBA	+1.41
6	SHUNSUKE IMAIZUMI	SOHOKU	175	CHIBA	+1.42

RIDE.232 15CM HIGH

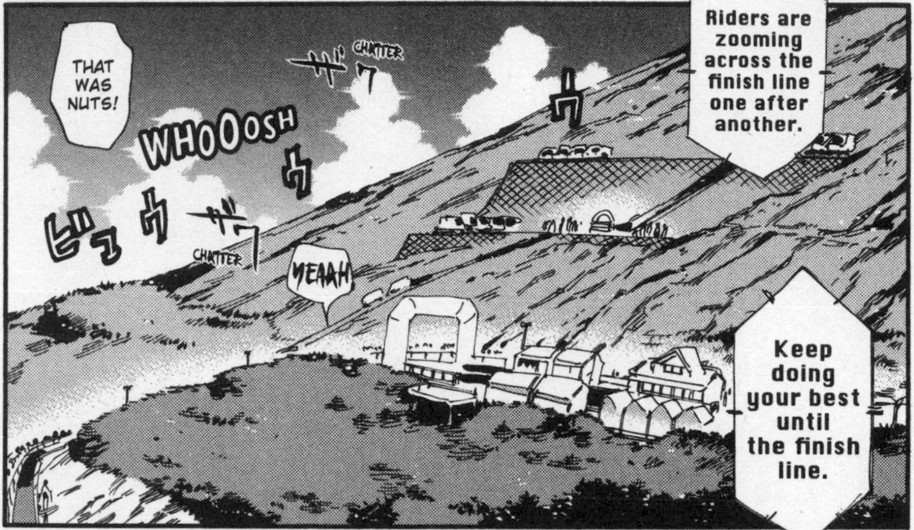
Riders are zooming across the finish line one after another.
CHATTER
YEAAH
THAT WAS NUTS!
WHOOOSH
CHATTER
Keep doing your best until the finish line.

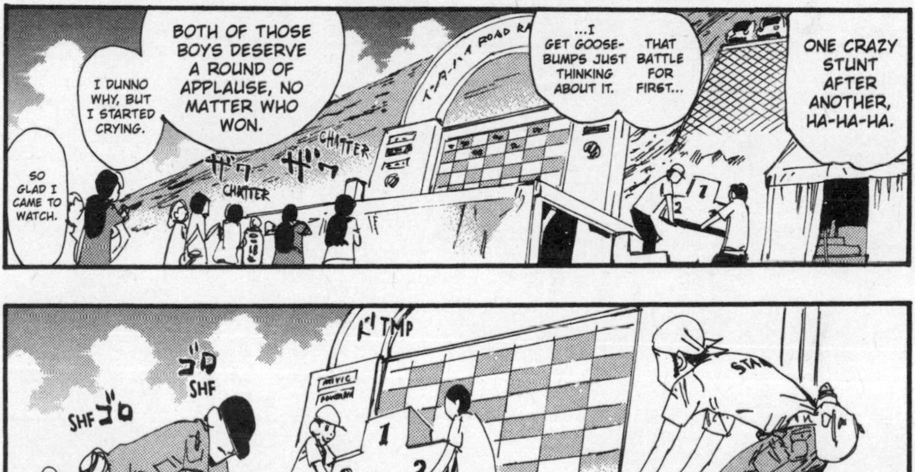
ONE CRAZY STUNT AFTER ANOTHER, HA-HA-HA.
THAT BATTLE FOR FIRST...
...I GET GOOSE-BUMPS JUST THINKING ABOUT IT.
BOTH OF THOSE BOYS DESERVE A ROUND OF APPLAUSE, NO MATTER WHO WON.
I DUNNO WHY, BUT I STARTED CRYING.
CHATTER
CHATTER
SO GLAD I CAME TO WATCH.

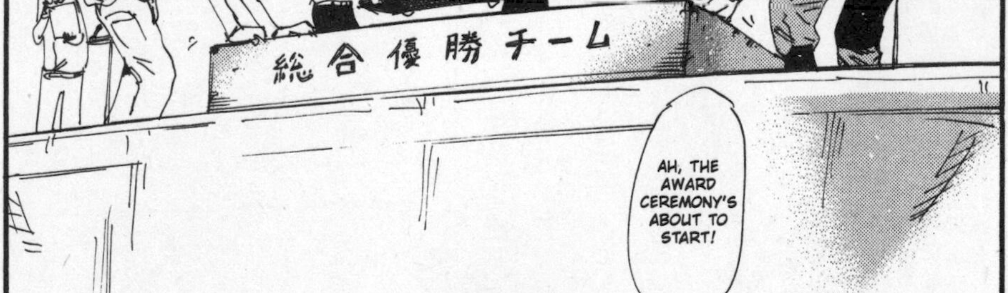
SHF
SHF
総合優勝チーム
AH, THE AWARD CEREMONY'S ABOUT TO START!

PLATFORM: OVERALL WINNING TEAM

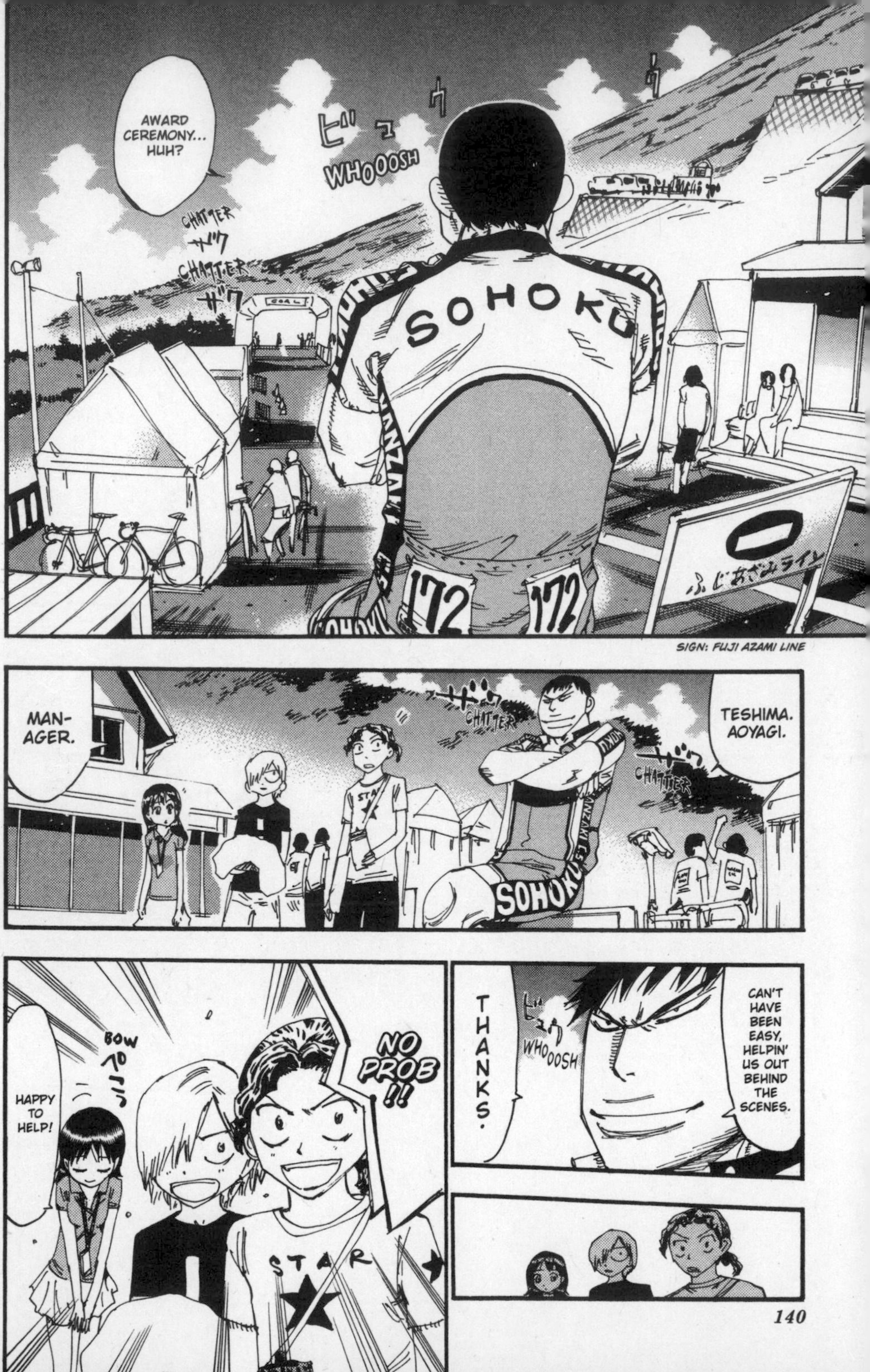
AWARD CEREMONY... HUH?
WHOOOSH
CHATTER
CHATTER
SIGN: FUJI AZAMI LINE
TESHIMA. AOYAGI.
CHATTER
CHATTER
MAN-AGER.
CAN'T HAVE BEEN EASY, HELPIN' US OUT BEHIND THE SCENES.
WHOOOSH
THANKS.
NO PROB!!
BOW
HAPPY TO HELP!

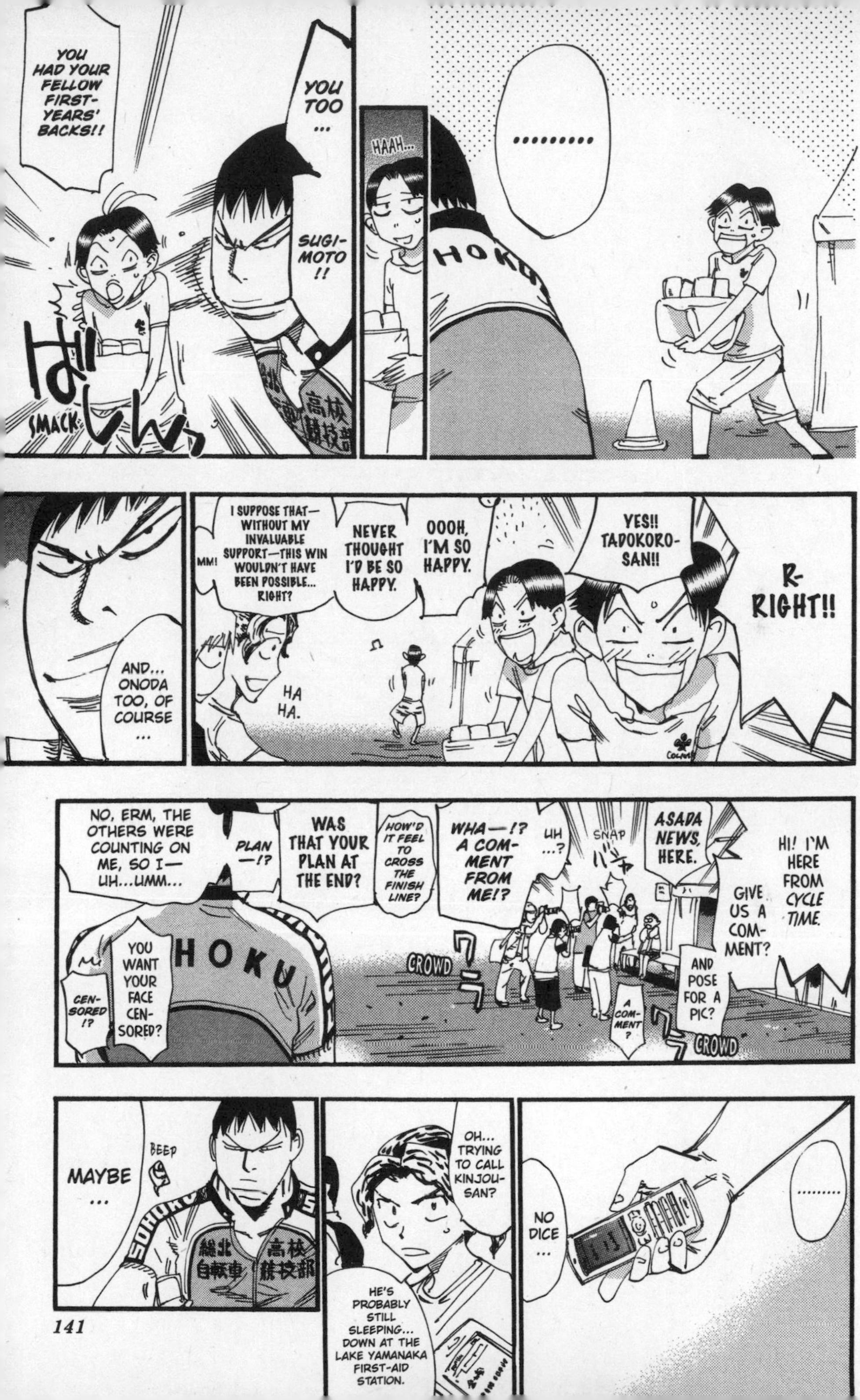
....
HAAH...
YOU TOO ...
SUGI-MOTO !!
YOU HAD YOUR FELLOW FIRST-YEARS' BACKS!!
SMACK
R-RIGHT!!
YES!! TADOKORO-SAN!!
OOOH, I'M SO HAPPY.
NEVER THOUGHT I'D BE SO HAPPY.
MM!
I SUPPOSE THAT—WITHOUT MY INVALUABLE SUPPORT—THIS WIN WOULDN'T HAVE BEEN POSSIBLE... RIGHT?
HA HA.
AND... ONODA TOO, OF COURSE ...
HI! I'M HERE FROM CYCLE TIME.
GIVE US A COM-MENT?
AND POSE FOR A PIC?
ASADA NEWS, HERE.
SNAP
UH ...?
WHA—!? A COM-MENT FROM ME!?
A COM-MENT ?
CROWD
CROWD
HOW'D IT FEEL TO CROSS THE FINISH LINE?
WAS THAT YOUR PLAN AT THE END?
PLAN —!?
NO, ERM, THE OTHERS WERE COUNTING ON ME, SO I—UH...UMM...
YOU WANT YOUR FACE CEN-SORED?
CEN-SORED !?
....
NO DICE ...
OH... TRYING TO CALL KINJOU-SAN?
HE'S PROBABLY STILL SLEEPING... DOWN AT THE LAKE YAMANAKA FIRST-AID STATION.
BEEP
MAYBE ...

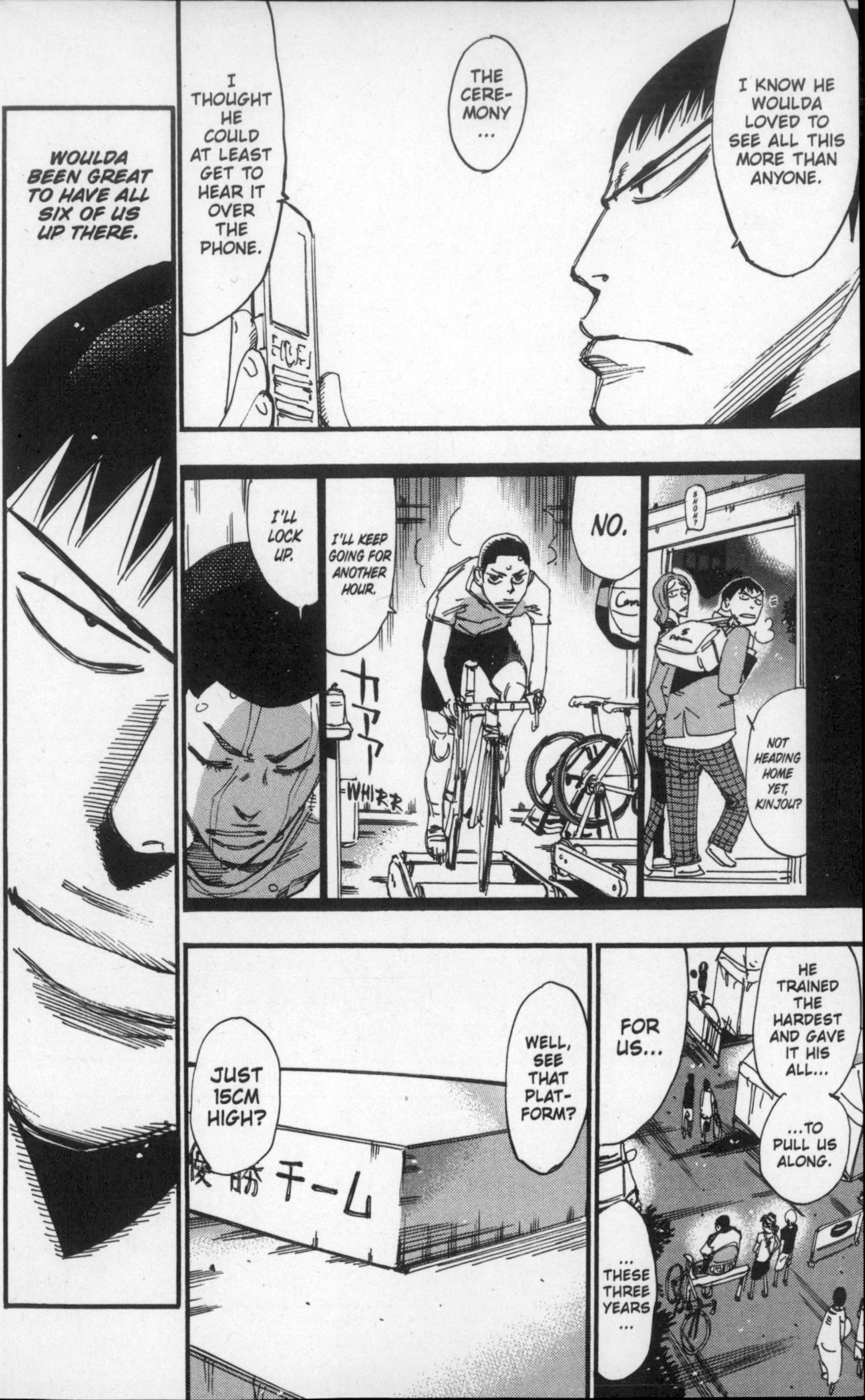
I KNOW HE WOULDA LOVED TO SEE ALL THIS MORE THAN ANYONE.
THE CEREMONY...
I THOUGHT HE COULD AT LEAST GET TO HEAR IT OVER THE PHONE.
SHOH?
NOT HEADING HOME YET, KINJOU?
NO.
I'LL KEEP GOING FOR ANOTHER HOUR.
WHIRR
I'LL LOCK UP.
HE TRAINED THE HARDEST AND GAVE IT HIS ALL...
...TO PULL US ALONG.
FOR US...
...THESE THREE YEARS...
WELL, SEE THAT PLATFORM?
JUST 15CM HIGH?
WOULDA BEEN GREAT TO HAVE ALL SIX OF US UP THERE.

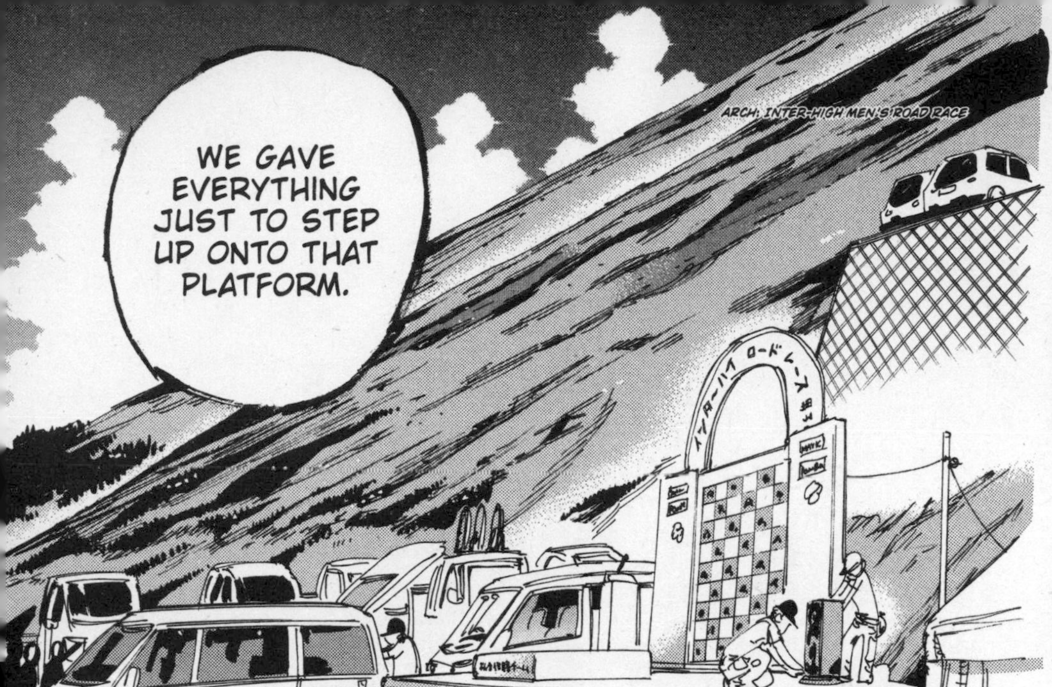
WE GAVE EVERYTHING JUST TO STEP UP ONTO THAT PLATFORM.
ARCH: INTER-HIGH MEN'S ROAD RACE
RIDE.232
15CM HIGH

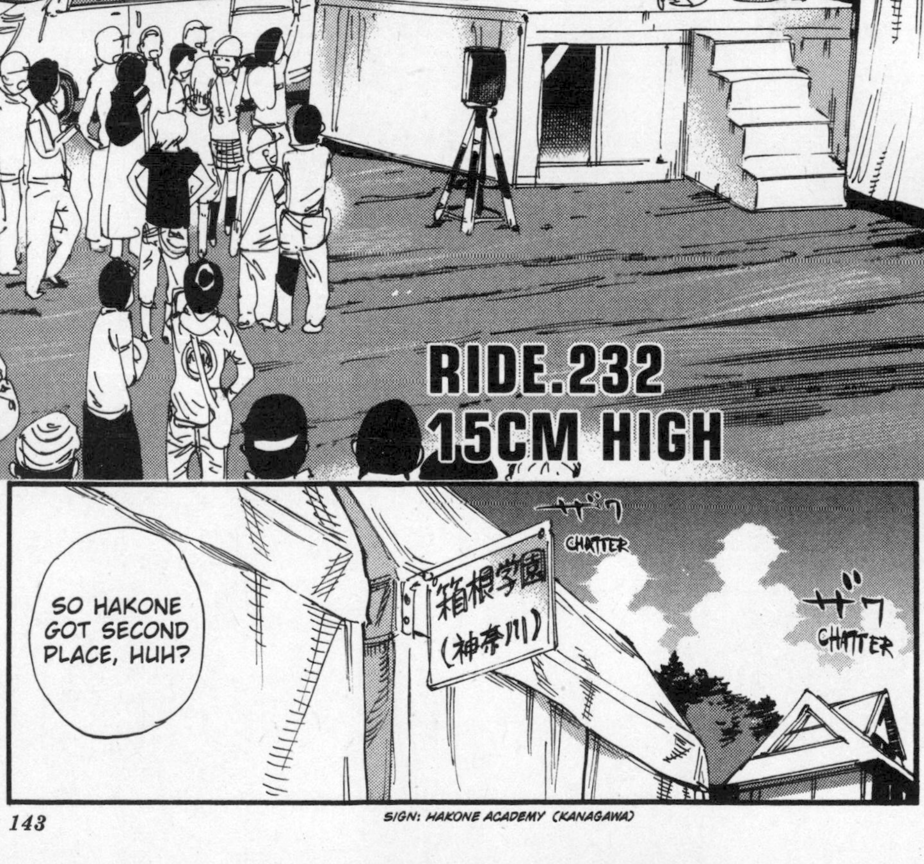
CHATTER
CHATTER
箱根学園
(神奈川)
SO HAKONE GOT SECOND PLACE, HUH?

SIGN: HAKONE ACADEMY (KANAGAWA)

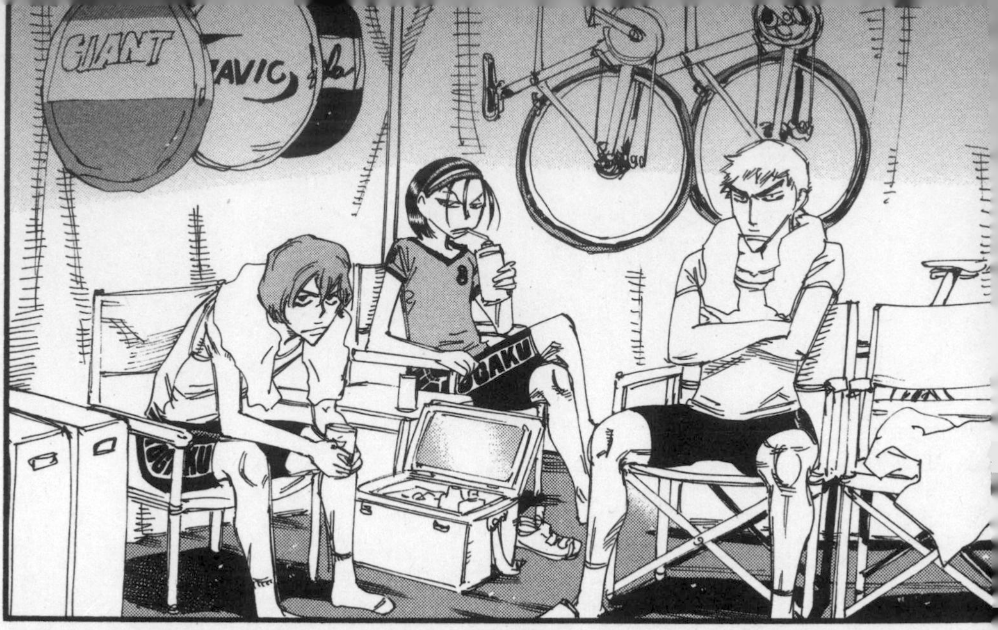
GIANT
MAVIC
OGAKU
OGAKU

SHIRT: HAKONE ACADEMY BICYCLE RACING CLUB

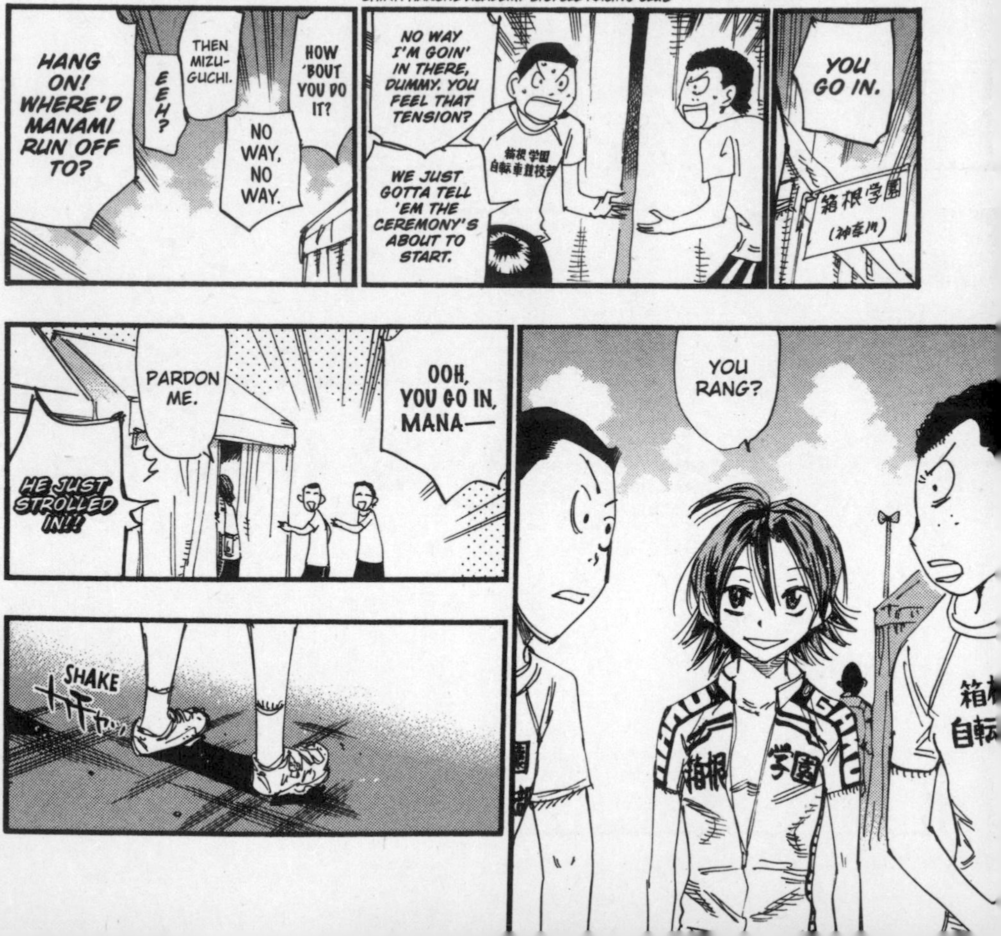
YOU GO IN.
箱根学園
(神奈川)
NO WAY I'M GOIN' IN THERE, DUMMY. YOU FEEL THAT TENSION?
箱根 学園
自転車競技部
WE JUST GOTTA TELL 'EM THE CEREMONY'S ABOUT TO START.
THEN MIZU-GUCHI.
HOW 'BOUT YOU DO IT?
NO WAY, NO WAY.
EEH?
HANG ON! WHERE'D MANAMI RUN OFF TO?
YOU RANG?
箱根 学園
箱根
自転
OOH, YOU GO IN, MANA—
PARDON ME.
HE JUST STROLLED IN!!
SHAKE

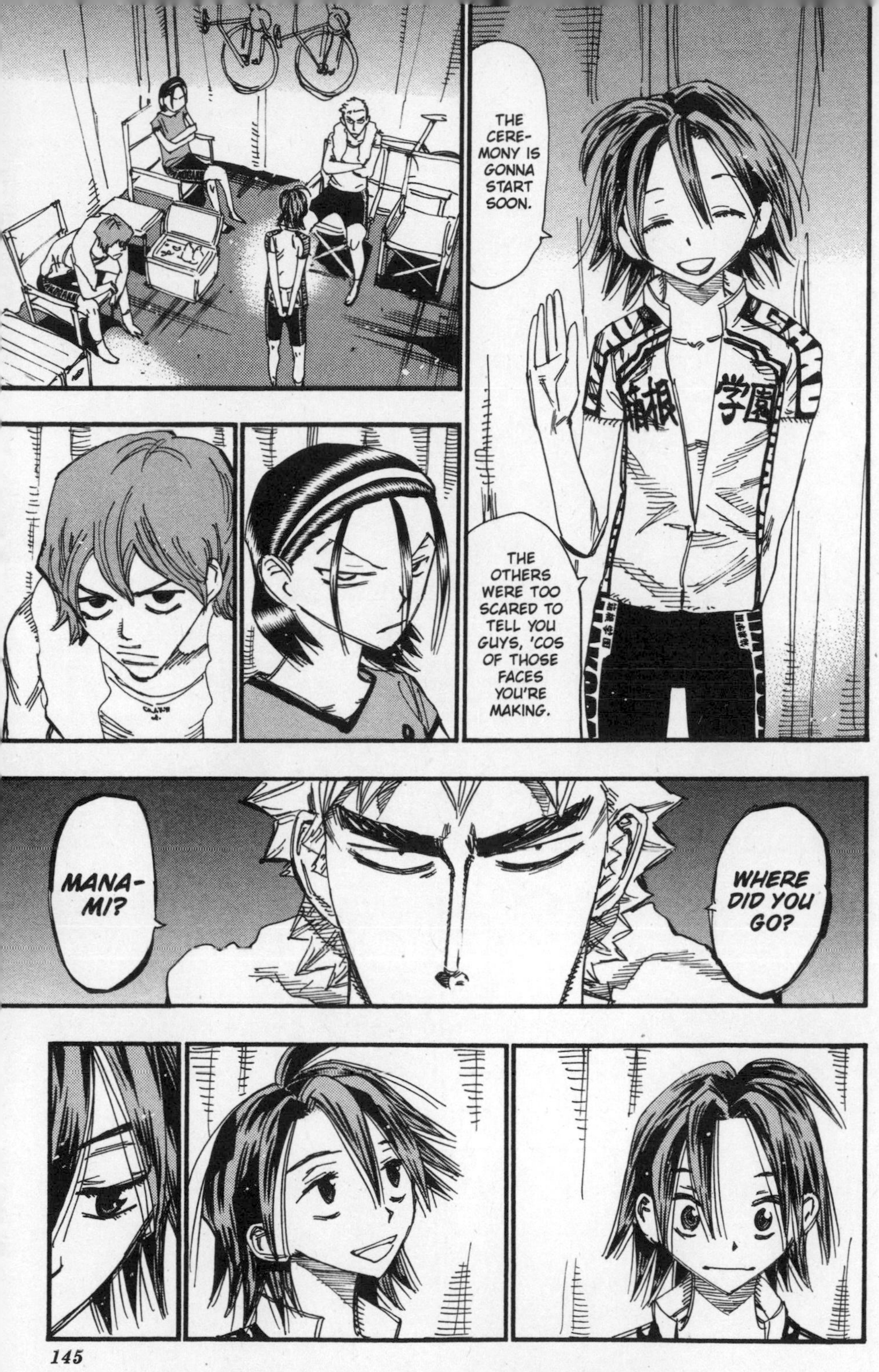
THE CEREMONY IS GONNA START SOON.
THE OTHERS WERE TOO SCARED TO TELL YOU GUYS, 'COS OF THOSE FACES YOU'RE MAKING.
WHERE DID YOU GO?
MANAMI?

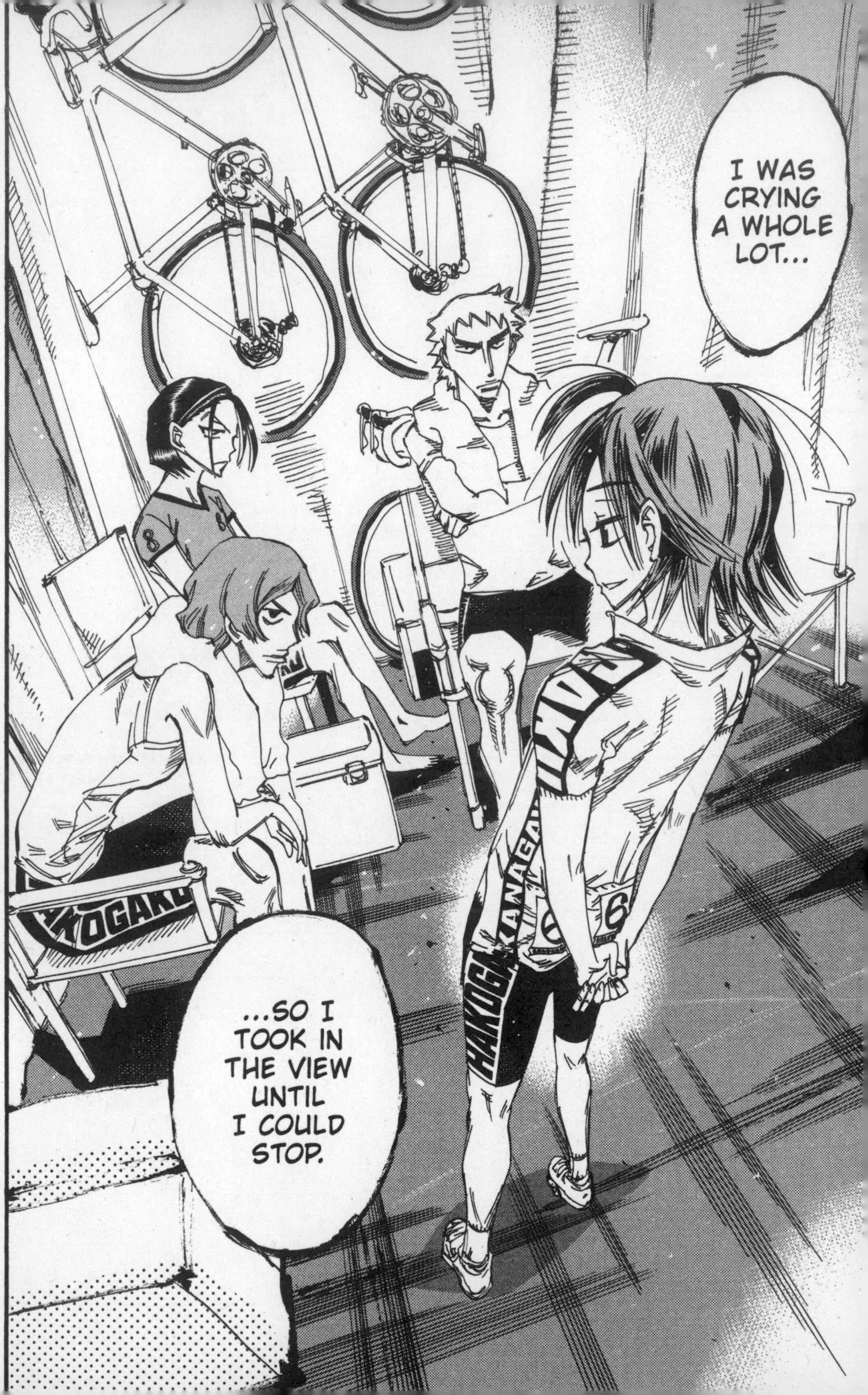
I WAS CRYING A WHOLE LOT...
...SO I TOOK IN THE VIEW UNTIL I COULD STOP.
HAKOGAKU

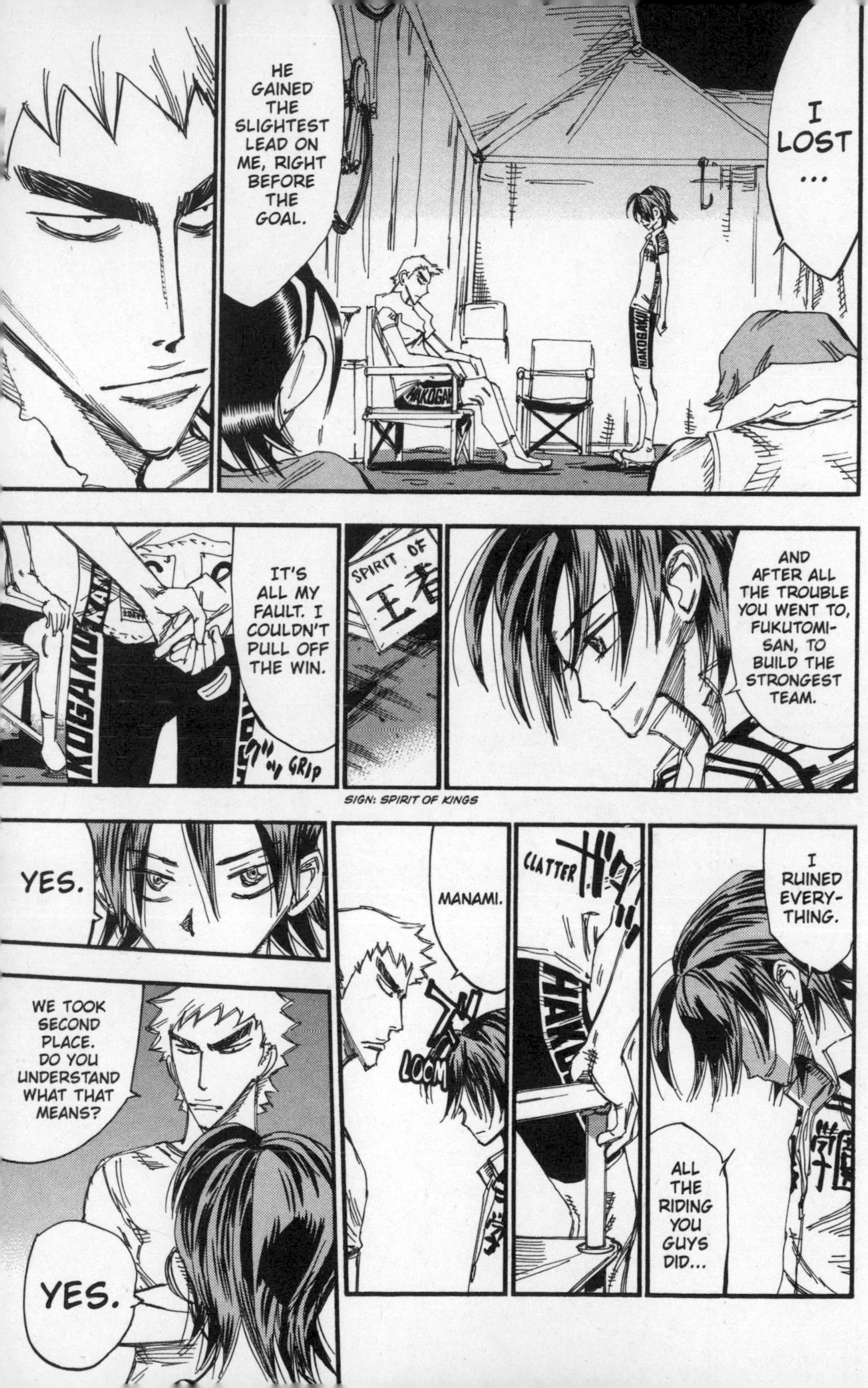
I LOST...
HE GAINED THE SLIGHTEST LEAD ON ME, RIGHT BEFORE THE GOAL.
AND AFTER ALL THE TROUBLE YOU WENT TO, FUKUTOMI-SAN, TO BUILD THE STRONGEST TEAM.
SPIRIT OF 王者
IT'S ALL MY FAULT. I COULDN'T PULL OFF THE WIN.
GRIP
I RUINED EVERYTHING.
ALL THE RIDING YOU GUYS DID...
CLATTER
MANAMI.
LOOM
YES.
WE TOOK SECOND PLACE. DO YOU UNDERSTAND WHAT THAT MEANS?
YES.
SIGN: SPIRIT OF KINGS

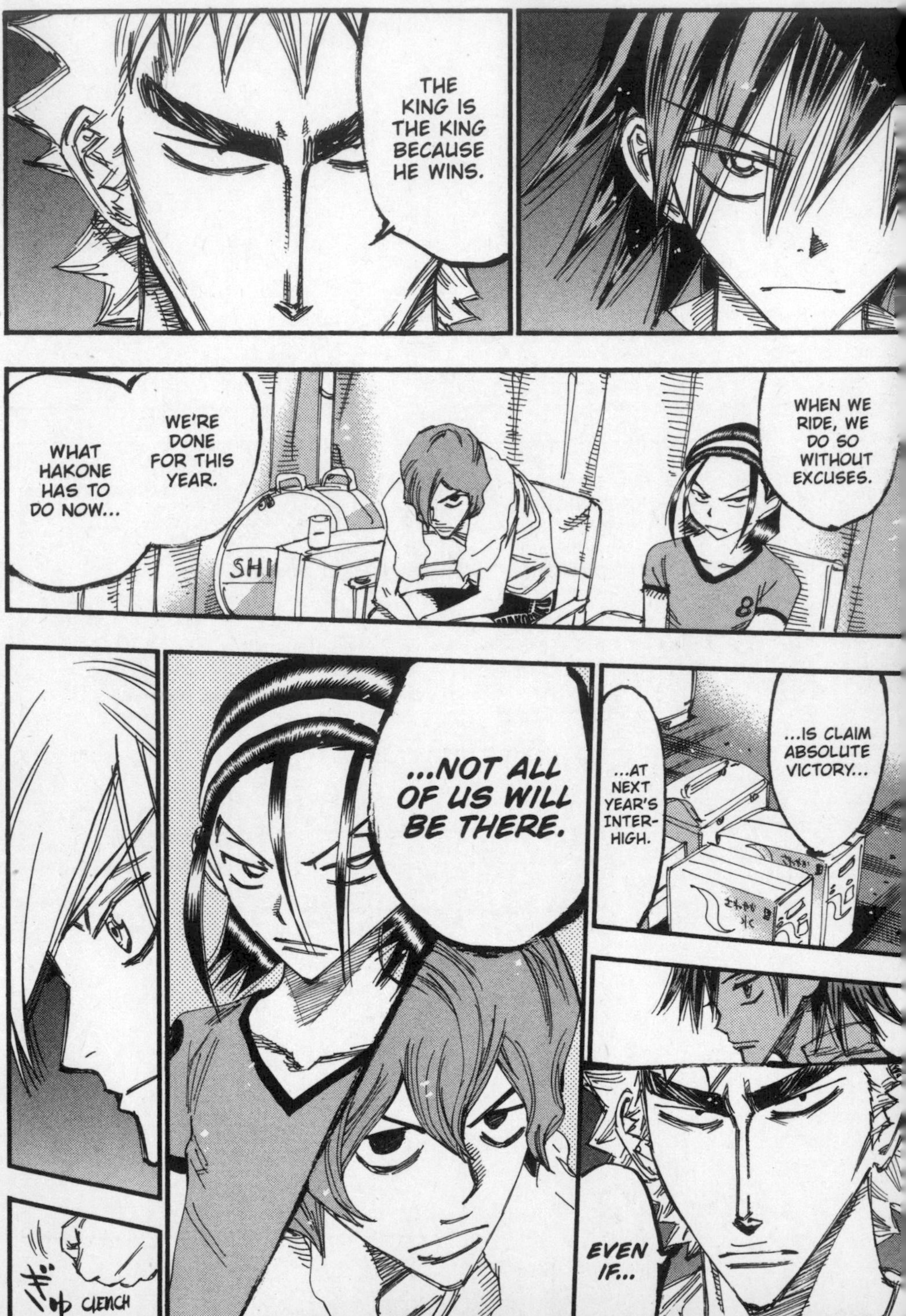
THE KING IS THE KING BECAUSE HE WINS.
WHEN WE RIDE, WE DO SO WITHOUT EXCUSES.
WE'RE DONE FOR THIS YEAR.
WHAT HAKONE HAS TO DO NOW...
...IS CLAIM ABSOLUTE VICTORY...
...AT NEXT YEAR'S INTER-HIGH.
EVEN IF...
...NOT ALL OF US WILL BE THERE.
CLENCH

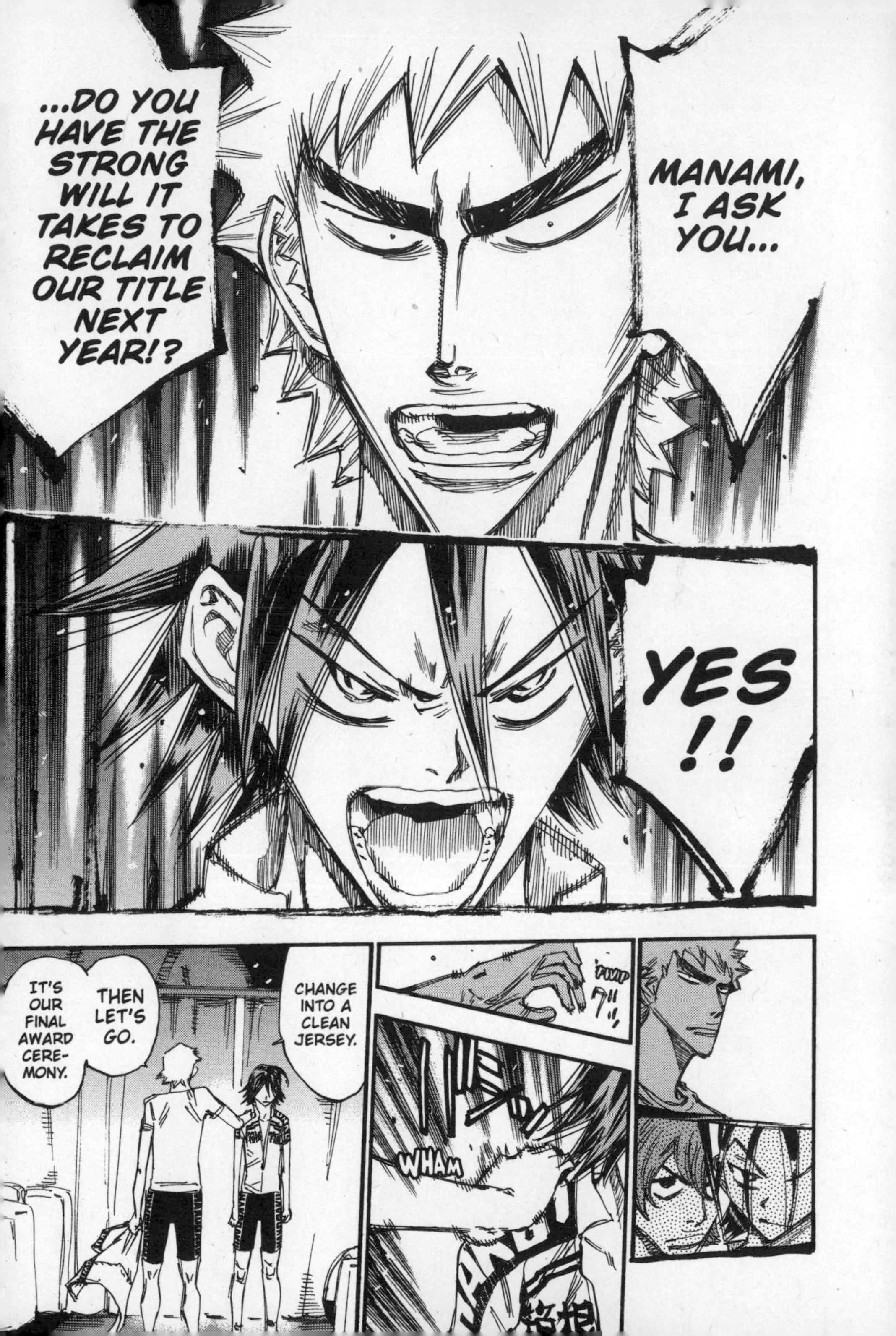
MANAMI, I ASK YOU...
...DO YOU HAVE THE STRONG WILL IT TAKES TO RECLAIM OUR TITLE NEXT YEAR!?
YES!!
FWIP
WHAM
CHANGE INTO A CLEAN JERSEY.
THEN LET'S GO.
IT'S OUR FINAL AWARD CEREMONY.

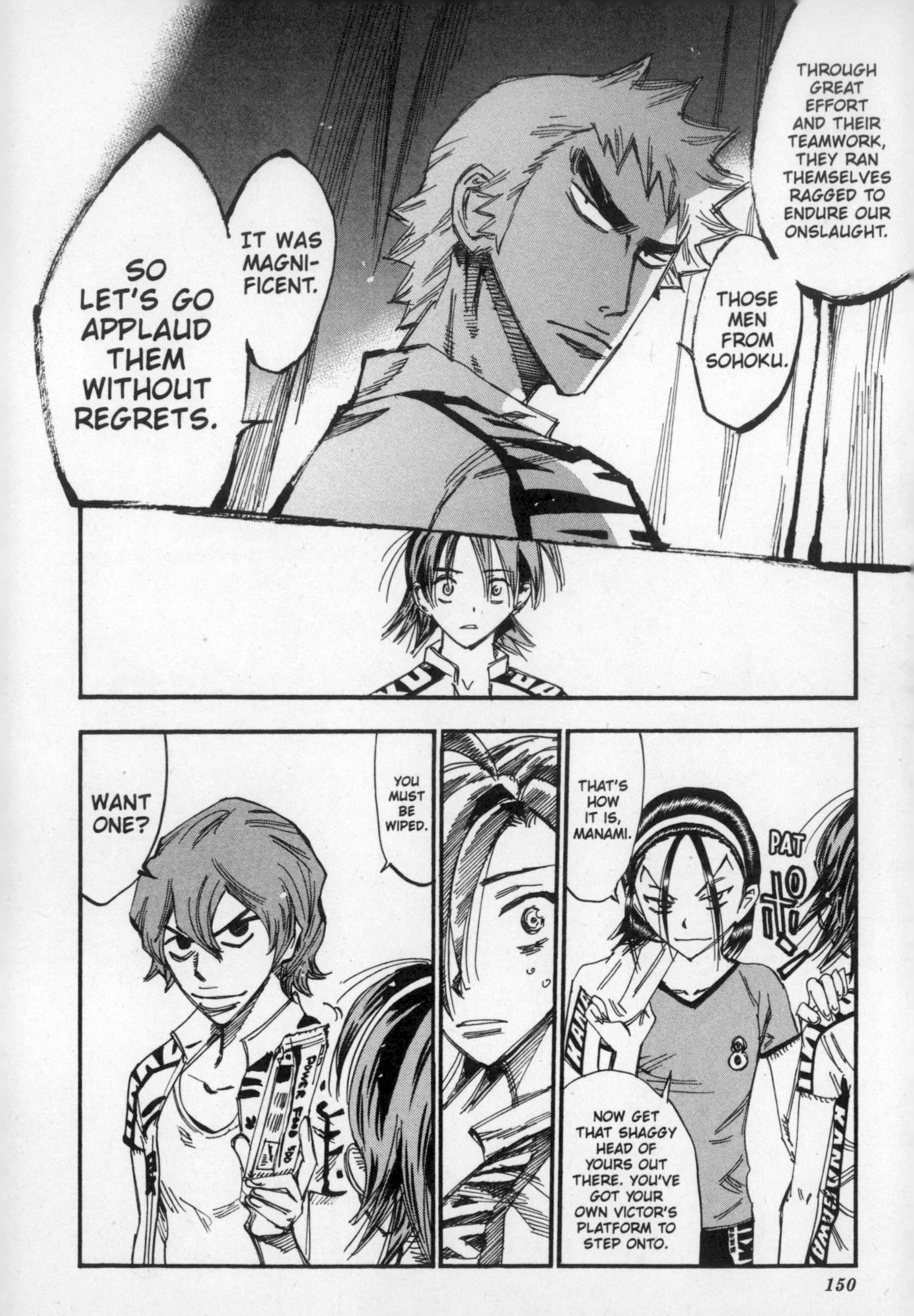
THROUGH GREAT EFFORT AND THEIR TEAMWORK, THEY RAN THEMSELVES RAGGED TO ENDURE OUR ONSLAUGHT.
THOSE MEN FROM SOHOKU.
IT WAS MAGNIFI-FICENT.
SO LET'S GO APPLAUD THEM WITHOUT REGRETS.
THAT'S HOW IT IS, MANAMI.
PAT
NOW GET THAT SHAGGY HEAD OF YOURS OUT THERE. YOU'VE GOT YOUR OWN VICTOR'S PLATFORM TO STEP ONTO.
YOU MUST BE WIPED.
WANT ONE?
POWER FOOD 500

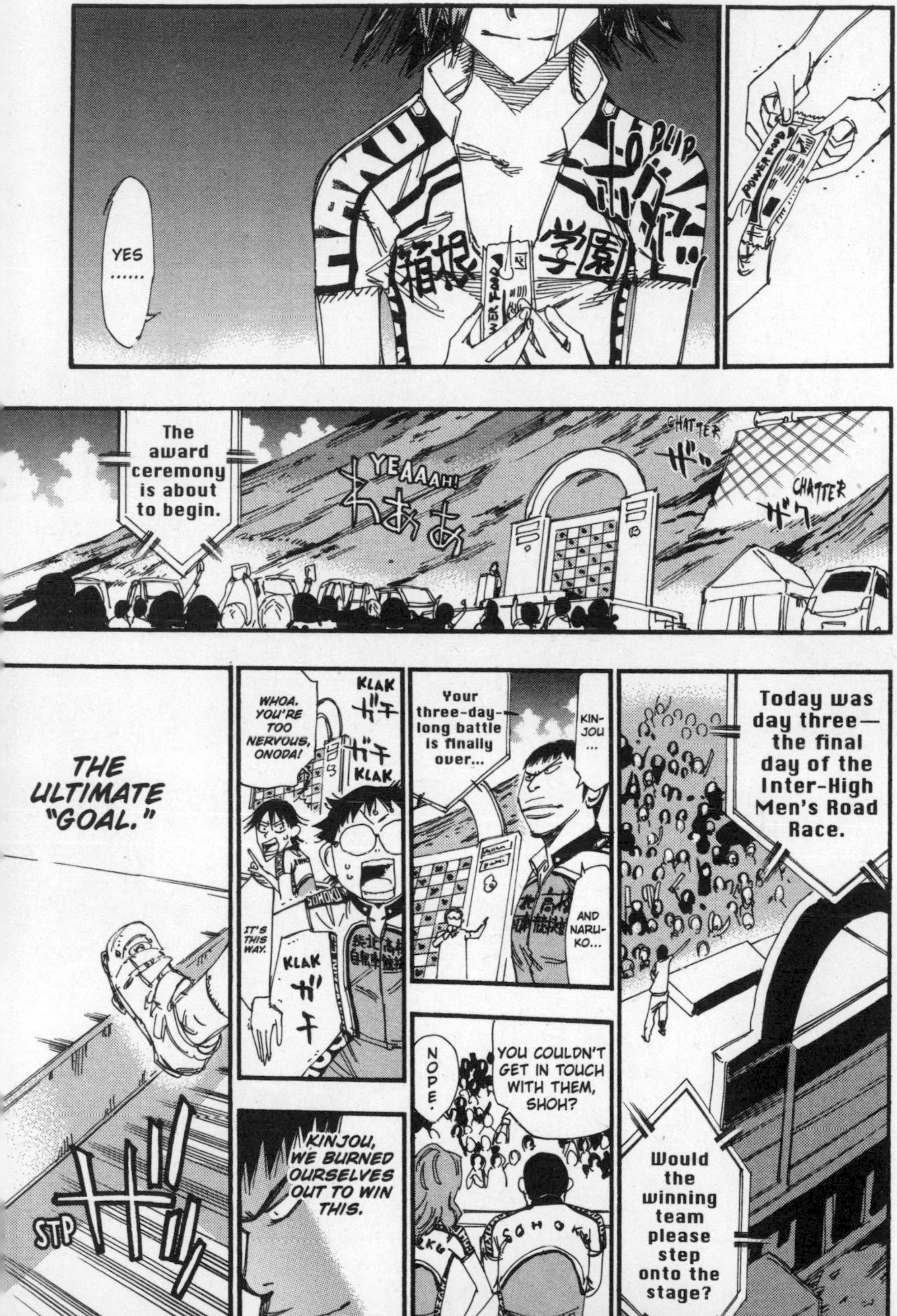
POWER FOOD
PLIP
YES ......
The award ceremony is about to begin.
CHATTER
CHATTER
YEAAAH!
Today was day three—the final day of the Inter-High Men's Road Race.
Would the winning team please step onto the stage?
KIN-JOU ...
Your three-day-long battle is finally over...
AND NARUKO...
YOU COULDN'T GET IN TOUCH WITH THEM, SHOH?
NOPE.
KLAK
WHOA. YOU'RE TOO NERVOUS, ONODA!
KLAK
IT'S THIS WAY.
KLAK
KINJOU, WE BURNED OURSELVES OUT TO WIN THIS.
THE ULTIMATE "GOAL."
STP

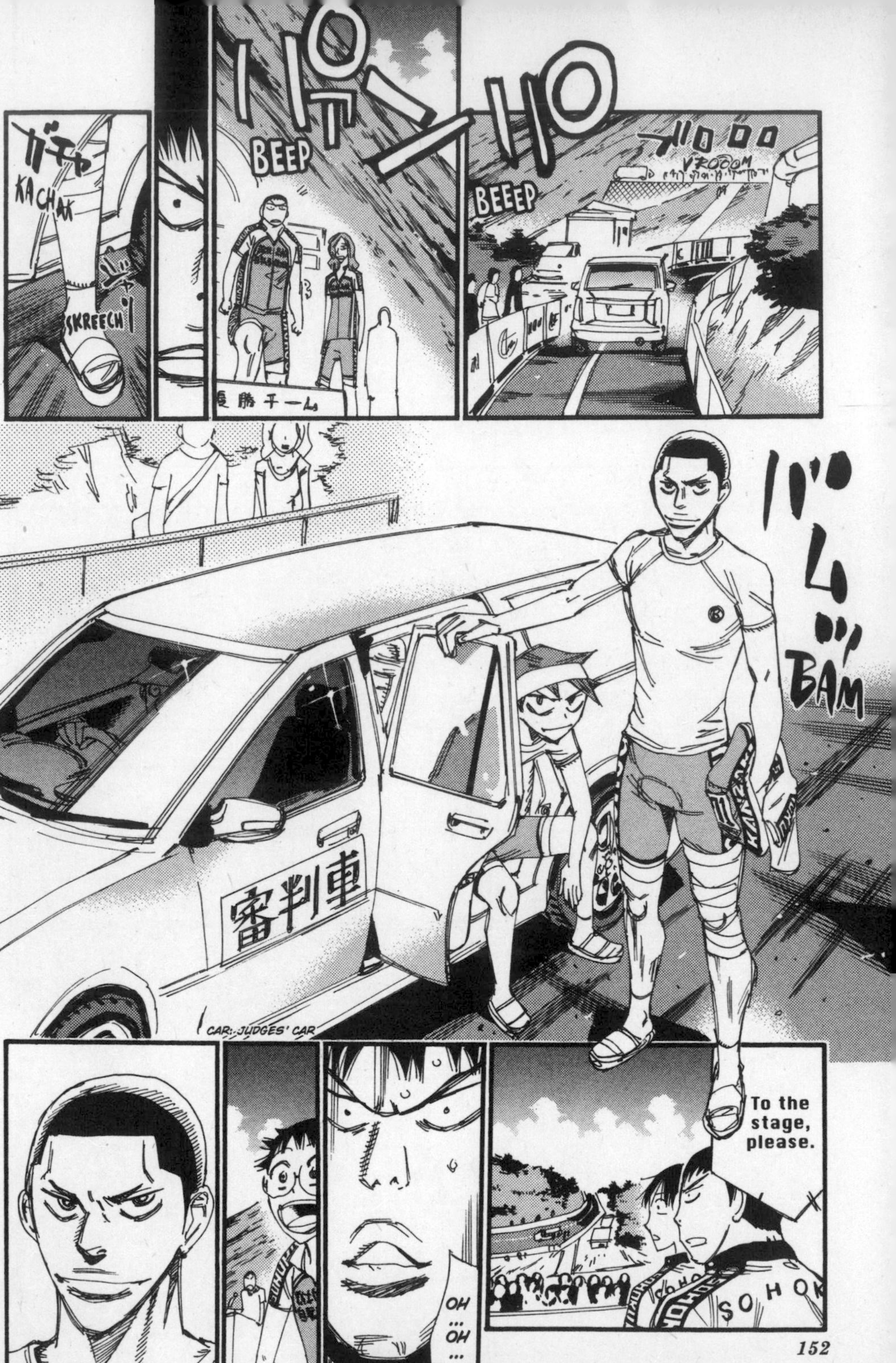
BEEEP
VROOOM
BEEP
ガチャ
KACHAK
SKREECH
バムッ
BAM
審判車
CAR: JUDGES' CAR
To the stage, please.
SOHOK
OH... OH...

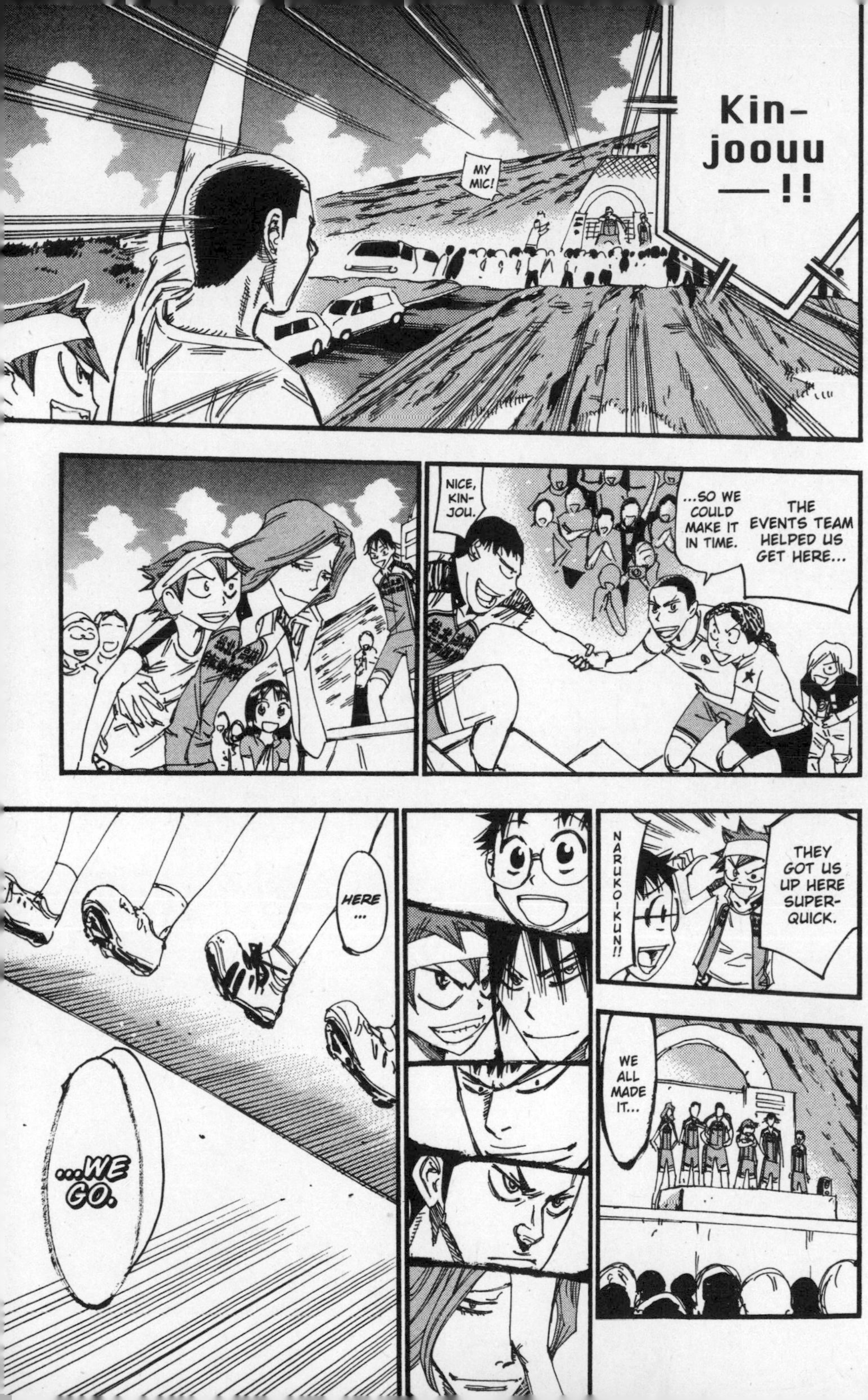
Kin-joouu—!!
MY MIC!
THE EVENTS TEAM HELPED US GET HERE...
...SO WE COULD MAKE IT IN TIME.
NICE, KINJOU.
THEY GOT US UP HERE SUPER-QUICK.
NARUKOI-KUN!!
WE ALL MADE IT...
HERE...
...WE GO.

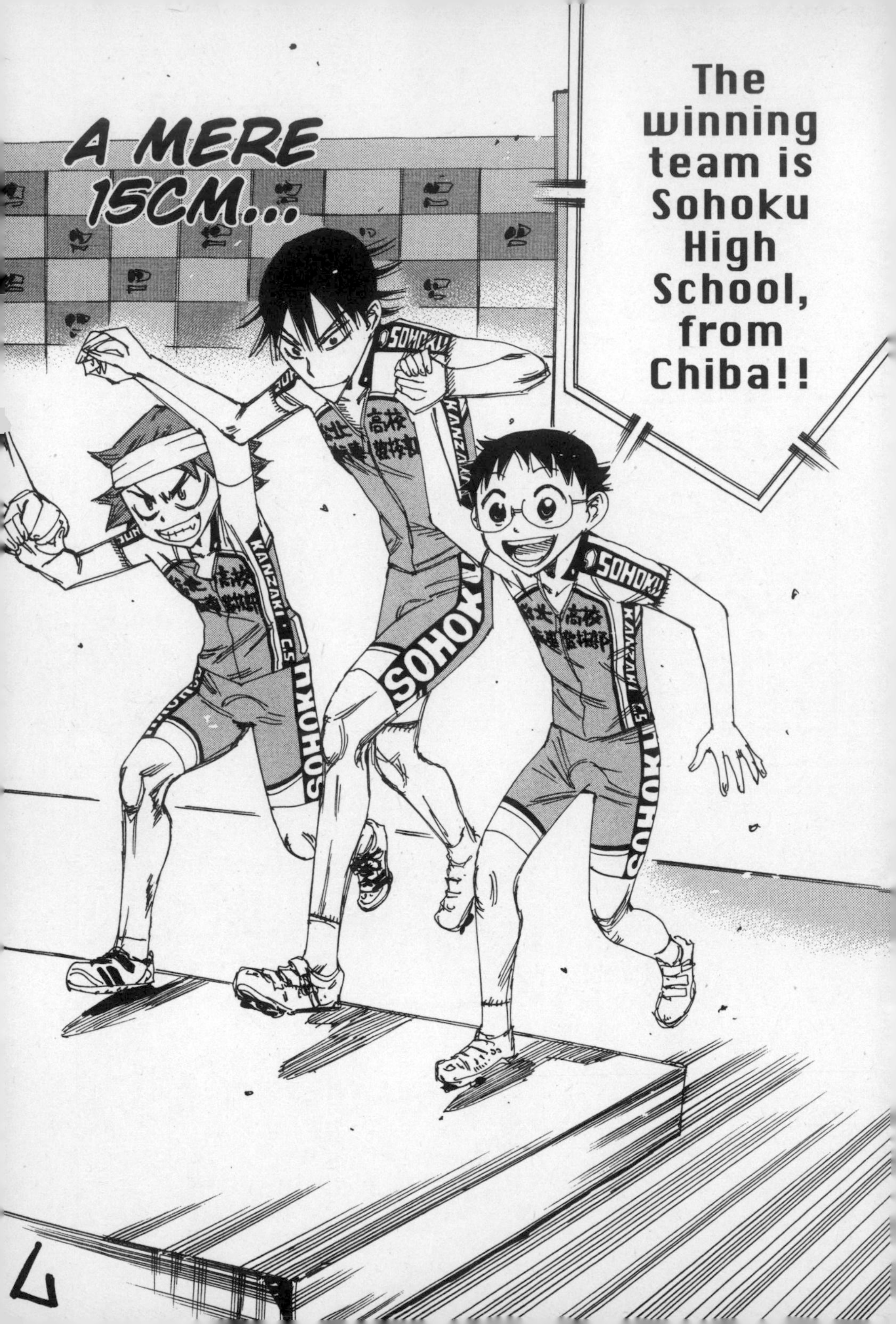
The winning team is Sohoku High School, from Chiba!!
A MERE 15CM...
SOHOKU
SOHOKU
SOHOKU

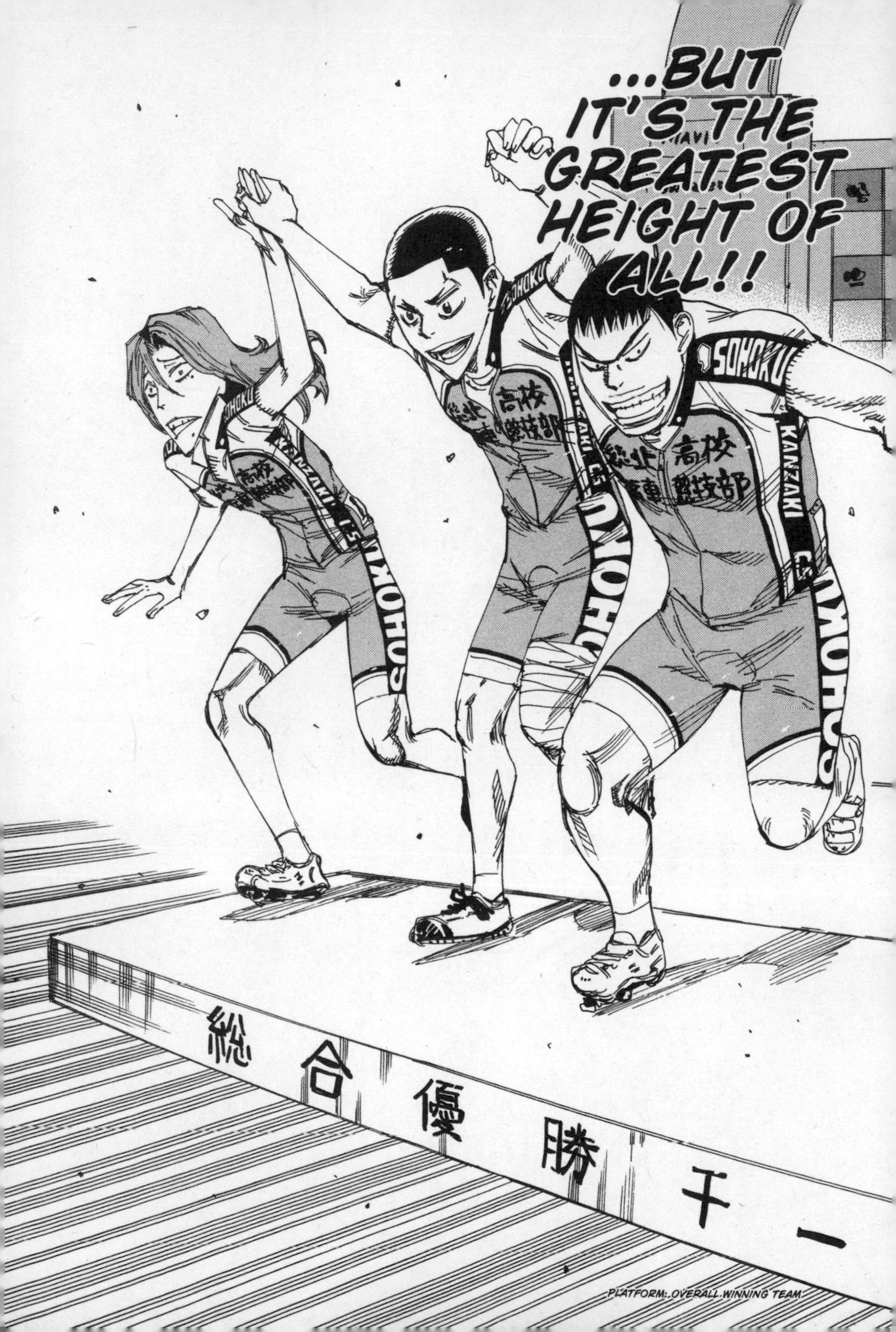
...BUT IT'S THE GREATEST HEIGHT OF ALL!!
総合優勝チーム
PLATFORM: OVERALL WINNING TEAM

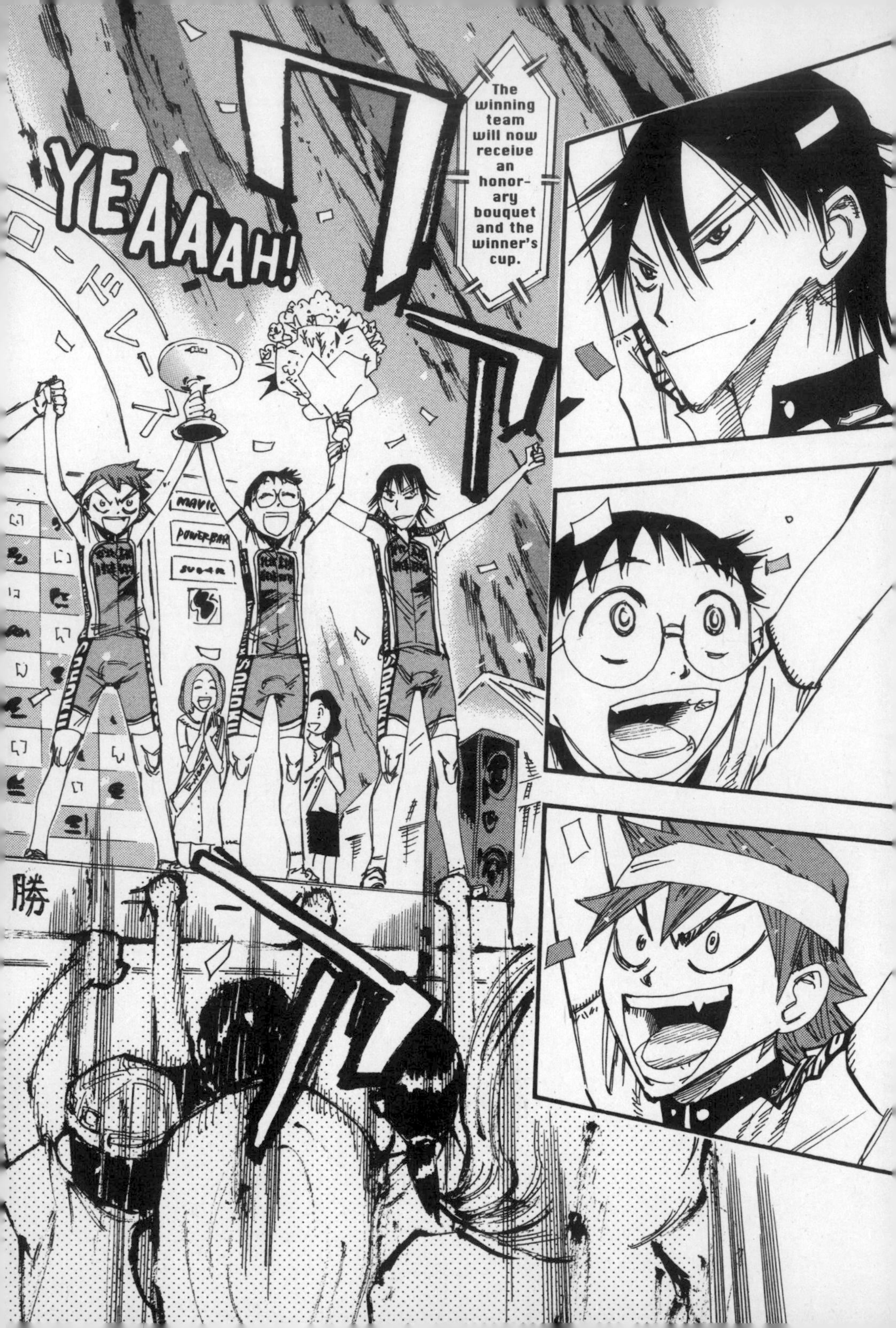
The winning team will now receive an honorary bouquet and the winner's cup.
YEAAAAH!
MAVIC
POWERBAR
SUGAR
勝

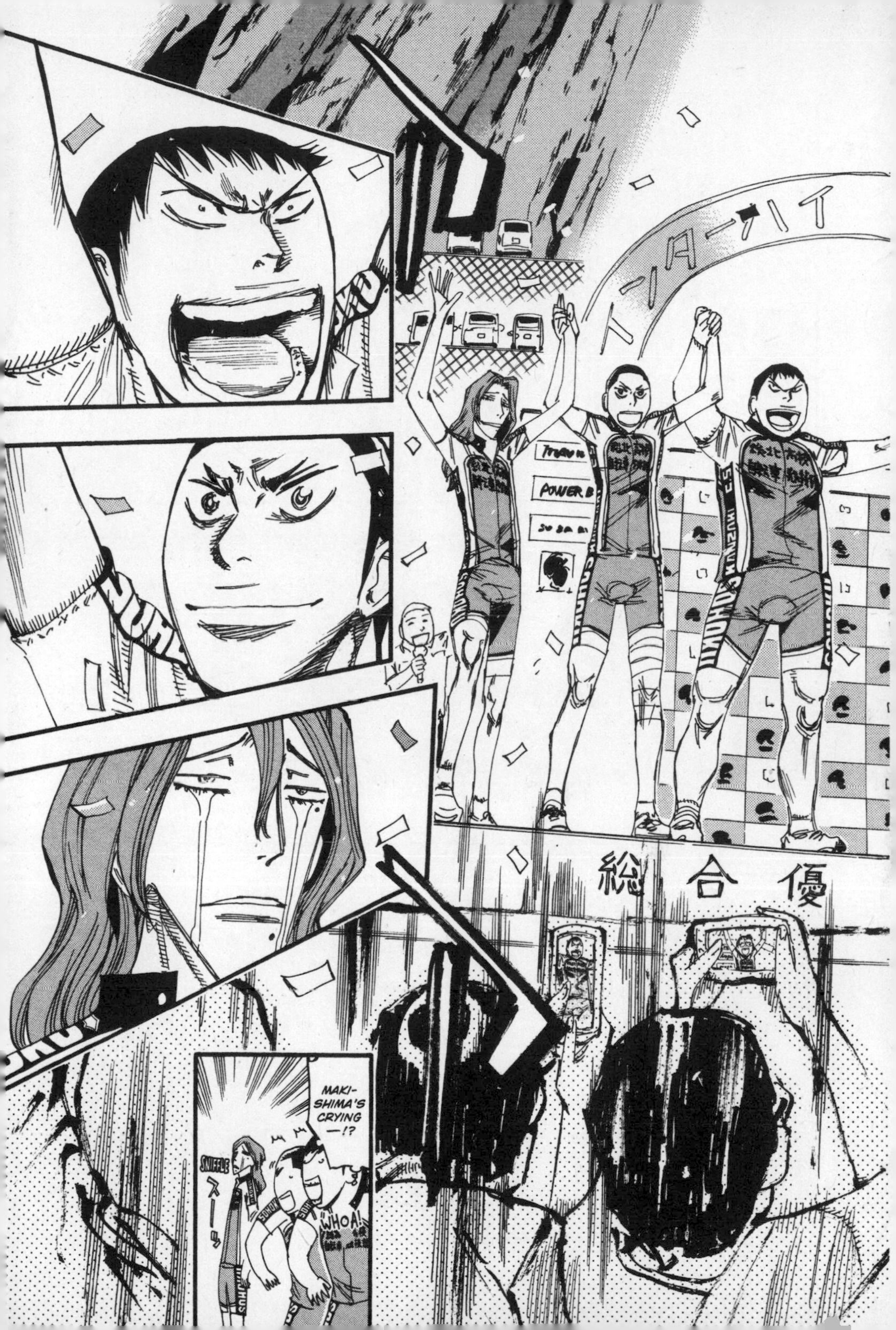

インターハイ
POWER B
総合優
MAKI-SHIMA'S CRYING —!?
WHOA!
SNIFFLE
スーッ

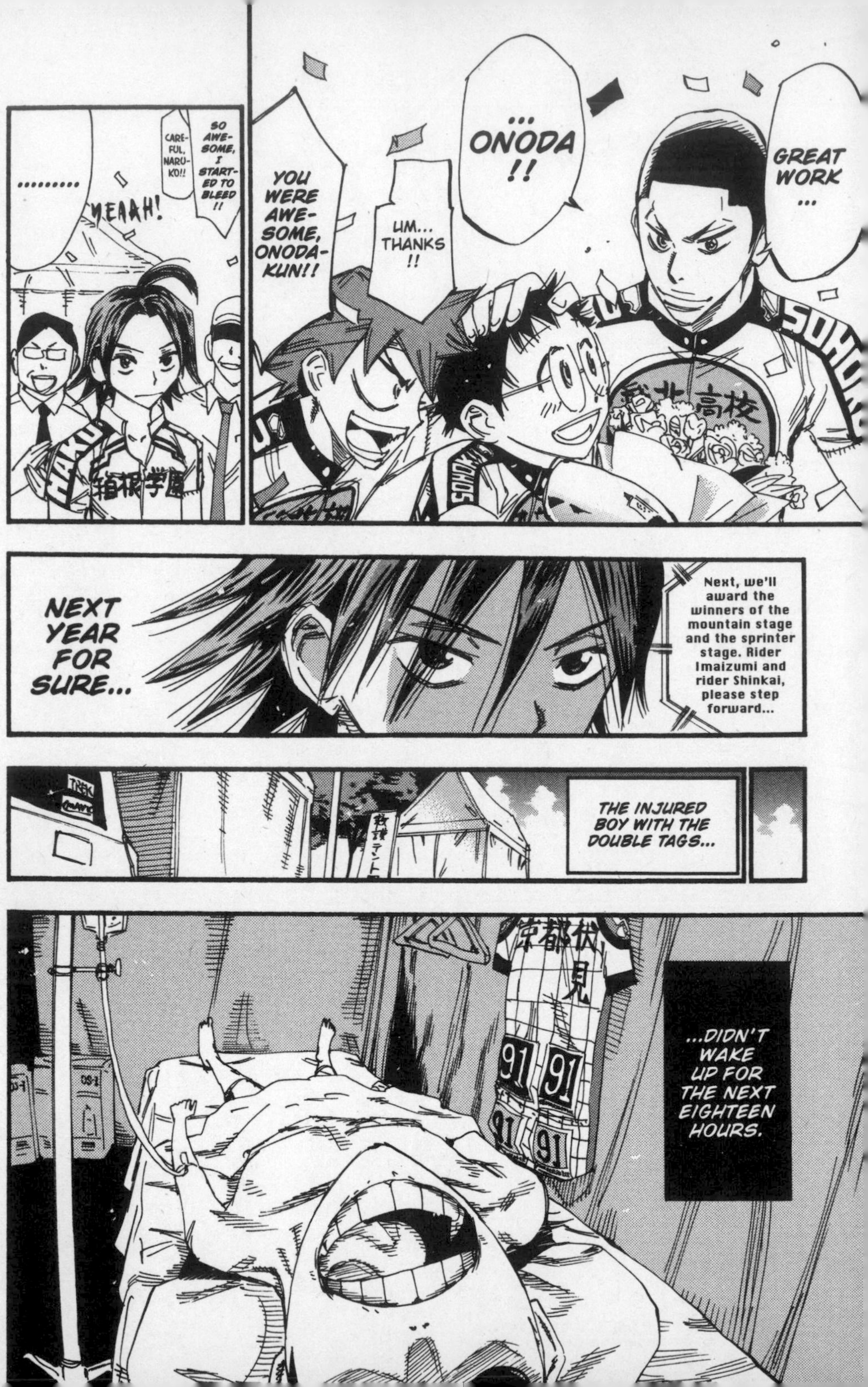
GREAT WORK...
...ONODA!!
UM... THANKS!!
YOU WERE AWESOME, ONODA-KUN!!
SO AWESOME, I STARTED TO BLEED!!
CAREFUL, NARUKO!!
YEAAH!
....
Next, we'll award the winners of the mountain stage and the sprinter stage. Rider Imaizumi and rider Shinkai, please step forward...
NEXT YEAR FOR SURE...
THE INJURED BOY WITH THE DOUBLE TAGS...
...DIDN'T WAKE UP FOR THE NEXT EIGHTEEN HOURS.

RIDE.233 INTER-HIGH SPECIAL STAGE

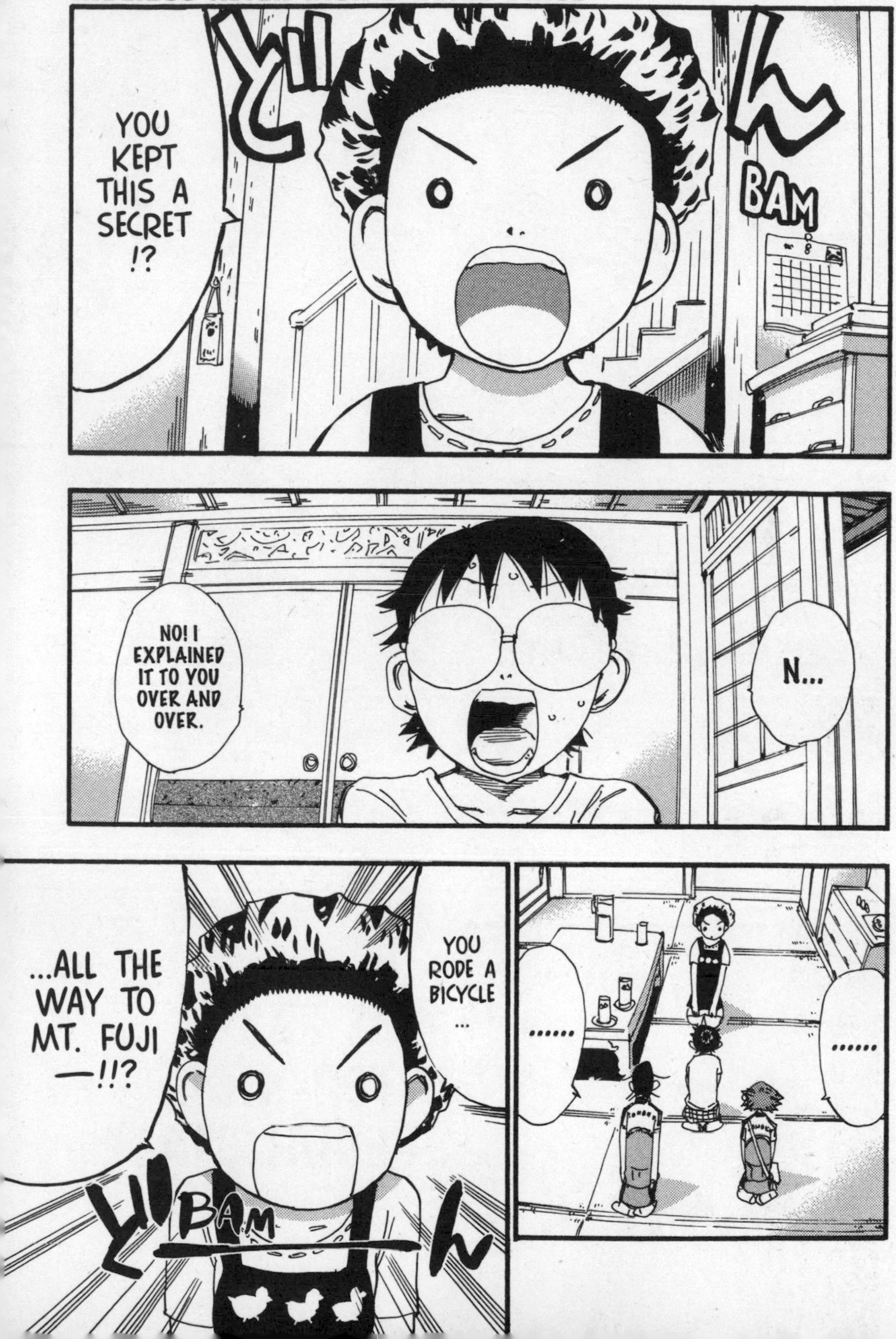
YOU KEPT THIS A SECRET !?
BAM
N...
NO! I EXPLAINED IT TO YOU OVER AND OVER.
......
......
YOU RODE A BICYCLE ...
...ALL THE WAY TO MT. FUJI —!!?
BAM

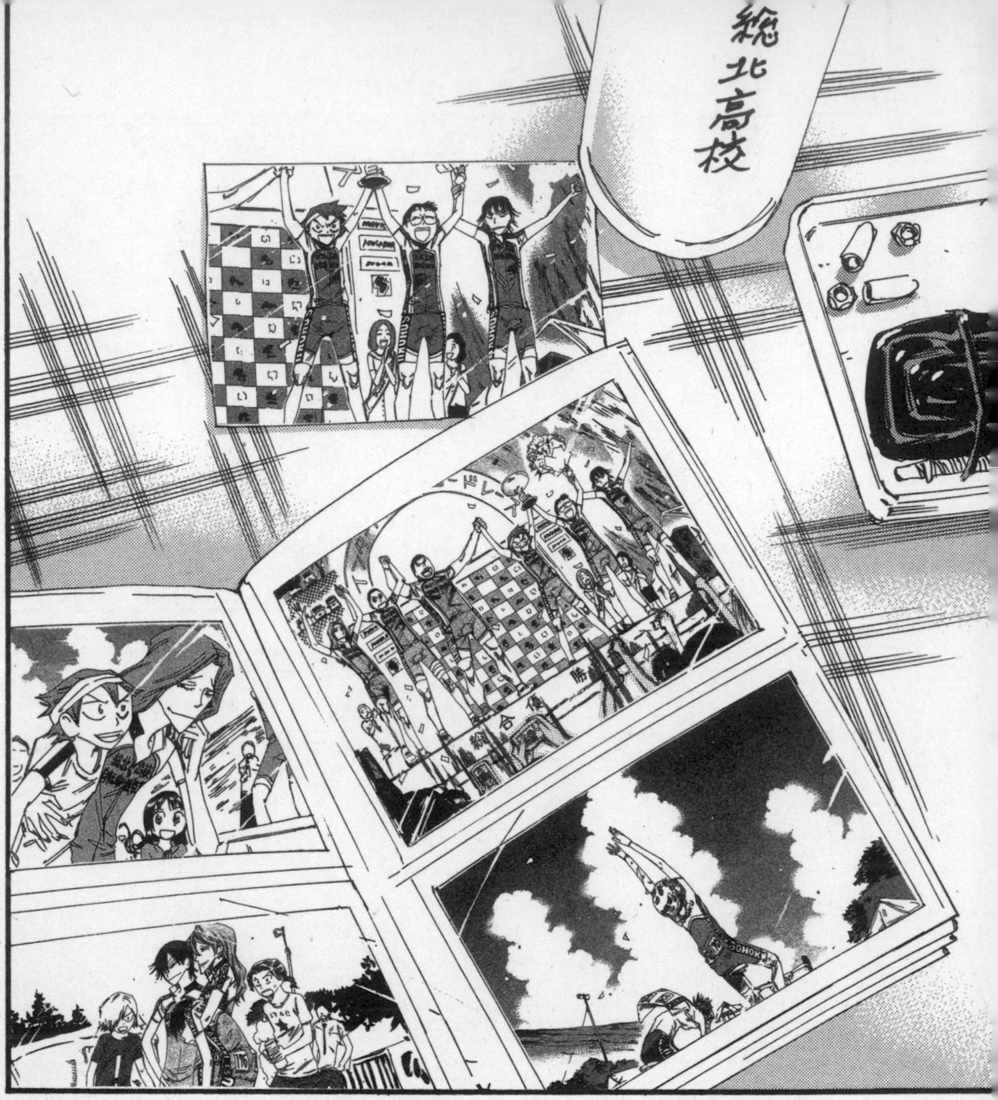
総北高校

BOTTLE: SOHOKU HIGH

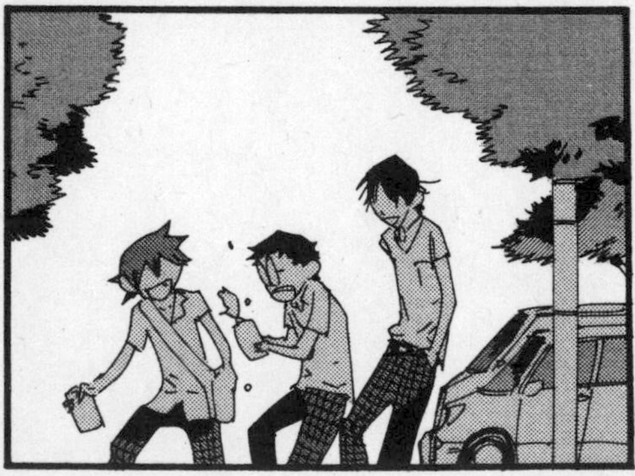

RIDE.233 INTER-HIGH SPECIAL STAGE

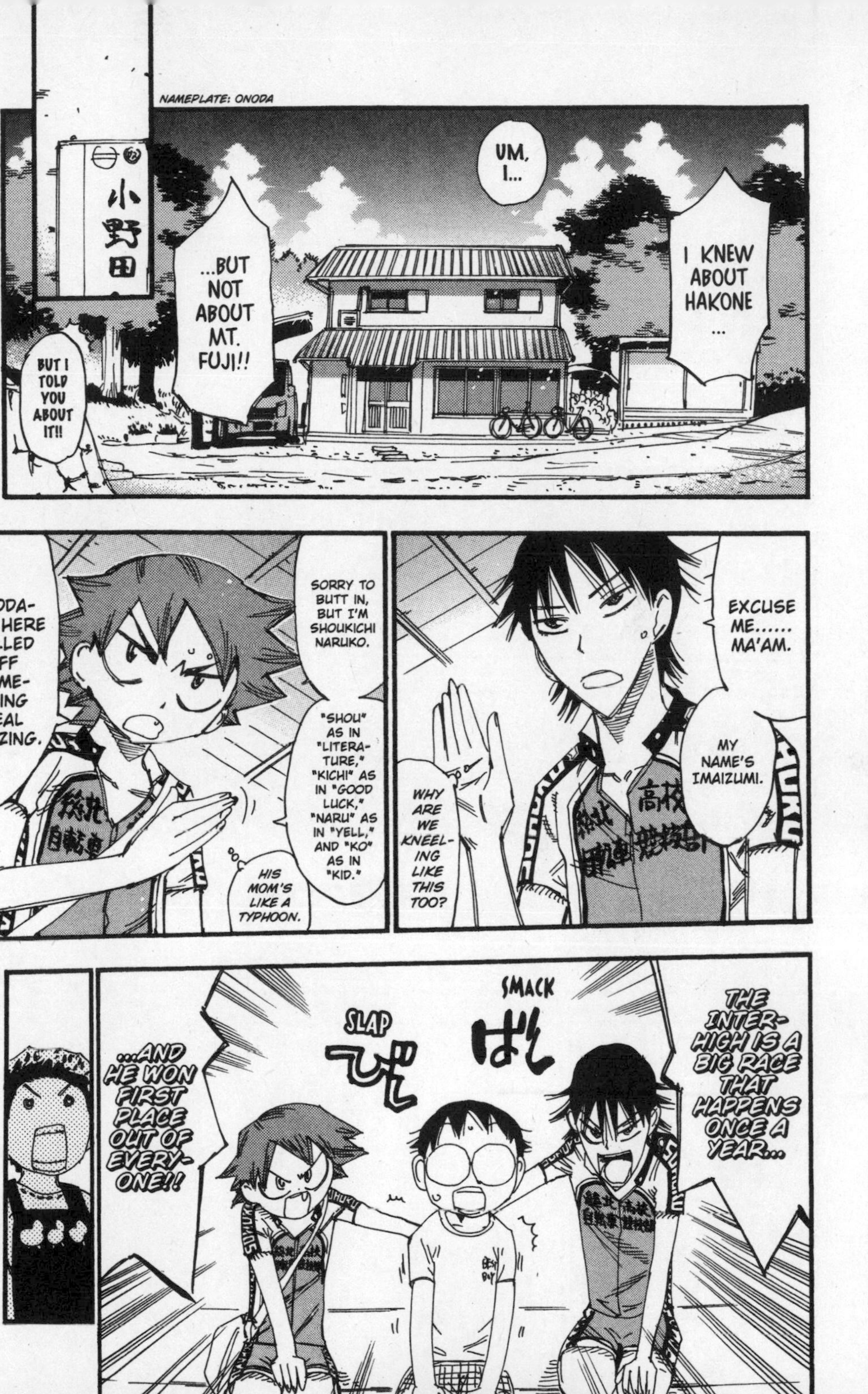
NAMEPLATE: ONODA
小野田
I KNEW ABOUT HAKONE ...
UM, I...
...BUT NOT ABOUT MT. FUJI!!
BUT I TOLD YOU ABOUT IT!!
EXCUSE ME...... MA'AM.
MY NAME'S IMAIZUMI.
WHY ARE WE KNEELING LIKE THIS TOO?
SORRY TO BUTT IN, BUT I'M SHOUKICHI NARUKO.
"SHOU" AS IN "LITERATURE," "KICHI" AS IN "GOOD LUCK," "NARU" AS IN "YELL," AND "KO" AS IN "KID."
ONODA-KUN HERE PULLED OFF SOMETHING REAL AMAZING.
HIS MOM'S LIKE A TYPHOON.
THE INTER-HIGH IS A BIG RACE THAT HAPPENS ONCE A YEAR...
SMACK
SLAP
...AND HE WON FIRST PLACE OUT OF EVERY-ONE!!

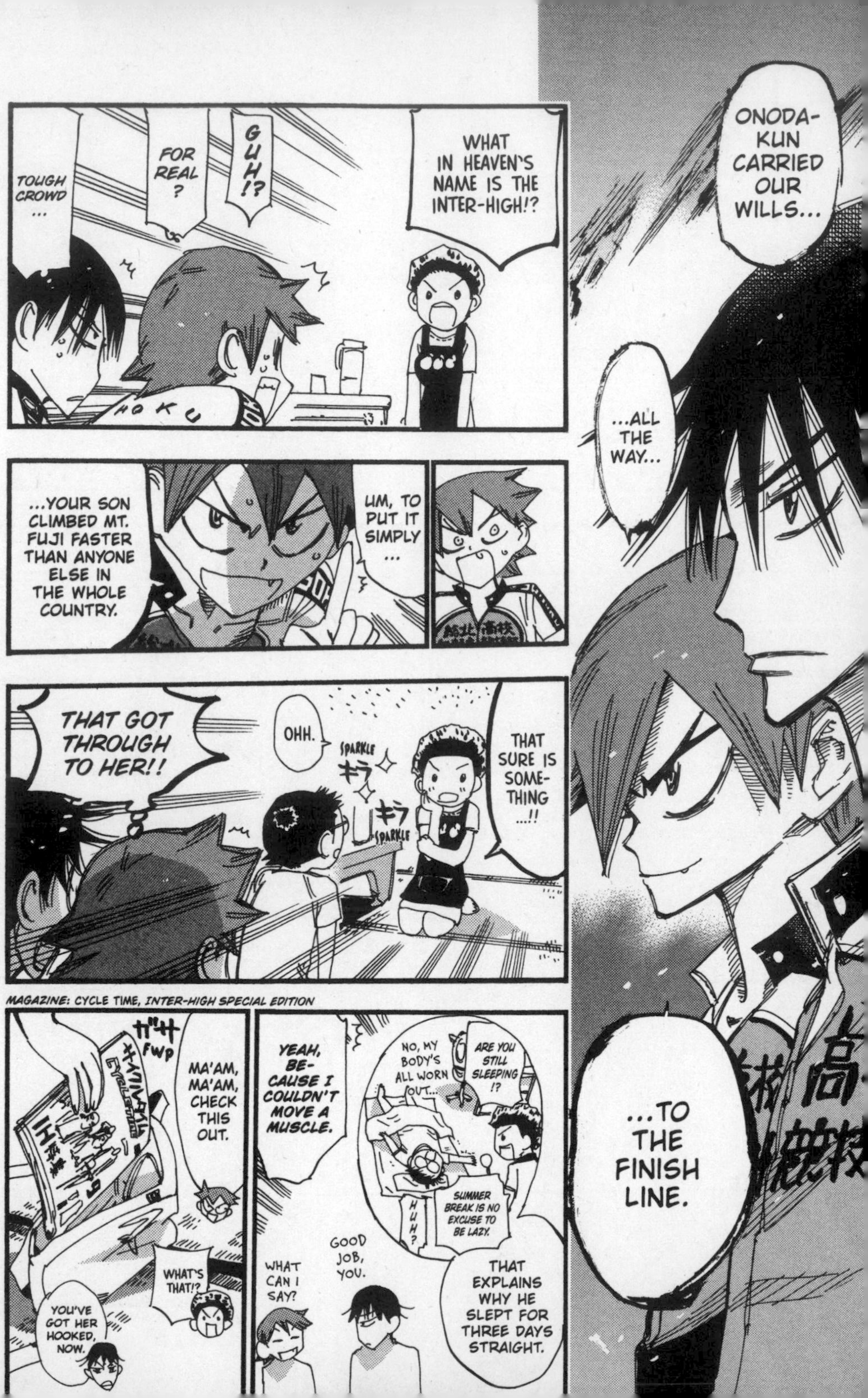
ONODA-KUN CARRIED OUR WILLS...
...ALL THE WAY...
...TO THE FINISH LINE.
WHAT IN HEAVEN'S NAME IS THE INTER-HIGH!?
GUH!?
FOR REAL?
TOUGH CROWD...
HOKU
UM, TO PUT IT SIMPLY...
...YOUR SON CLIMBED MT. FUJI FASTER THAN ANYONE ELSE IN THE WHOLE COUNTRY.
THAT SURE IS SOMETHING...!!
キラ SPARKLE
キラ SPARKLE
OHH.
THAT GOT THROUGH TO HER!!
MAGAZINE: CYCLE TIME, INTER-HIGH SPECIAL EDITION
ARE YOU STILL SLEEPING!?
NO, MY BODY'S ALL WORN OUT...
SUMMER BREAK IS NO EXCUSE TO BE LAZY.
HUH?
THAT EXPLAINS WHY HE SLEPT FOR THREE DAYS STRAIGHT.
YEAH, BE-CAUSE I COULDN'T MOVE A MUSCLE.
GOOD JOB, YOU.
WHAT CAN I SAY?
ガサ FWP
MA'AM, MA'AM, CHECK THIS OUT.
WHAT'S THAT!?
YOU'VE GOT HER HOOKED, NOW.

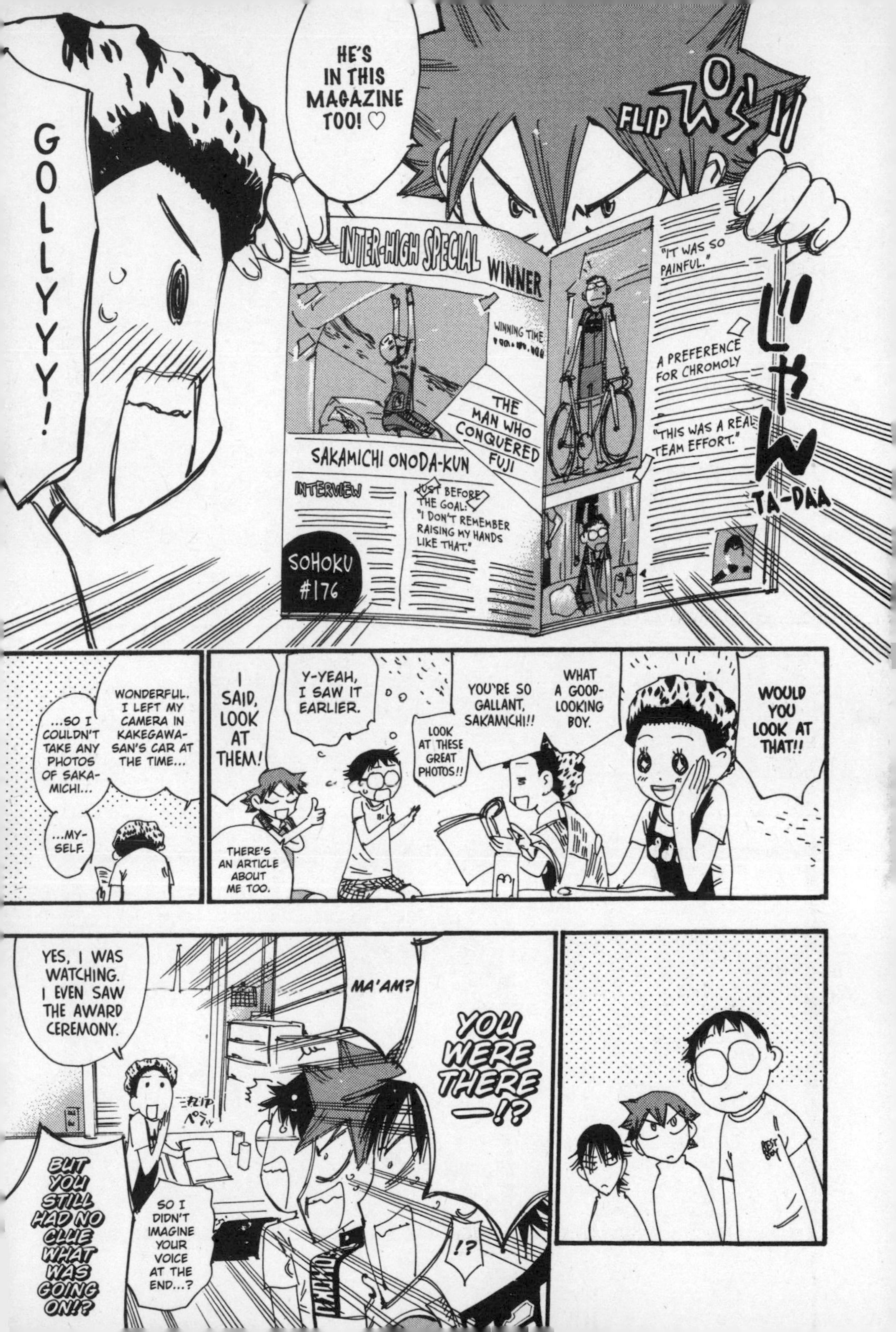
FLIP
HE'S IN THIS MAGAZINE TOO! ♡
INTER-HIGH SPECIAL
WINNER
WINNING TIME
THE MAN WHO CONQUERED FUJI
SAKAMICHI ONODA-KUN
INTERVIEW
JUST BEFORE THE GOAL: "I DON'T REMEMBER RAISING MY HANDS LIKE THAT."
SOHOKU #176
"IT WAS SO PAINFUL."
A PREFERENCE FOR CHROMOLY
"THIS WAS A REAL TEAM EFFORT."
TA-DAA
GOLLYYY!
WOULD YOU LOOK AT THAT!!
WHAT A GOOD-LOOKING BOY.
YOU'RE SO GALLANT, SAKAMICHI!!
LOOK AT THESE GREAT PHOTOS!!
Y-YEAH, I SAW IT EARLIER.
I SAID, LOOK AT THEM!
THERE'S AN ARTICLE ABOUT ME TOO.
WONDERFUL. I LEFT MY CAMERA IN KAKEGAWA-SAN'S CAR AT THE TIME...
...SO I COULDN'T TAKE ANY PHOTOS OF SAKAMICHI...
...MYSELF.
MA'AM?
YES, I WAS WATCHING. I EVEN SAW THE AWARD CEREMONY.
YOU WERE THERE—!?
FLIP
!?
SO I DIDN'T IMAGINE YOUR VOICE AT THE END...?
BUT YOU STILL HAD NO CLUE WHAT WAS GOING ON!?

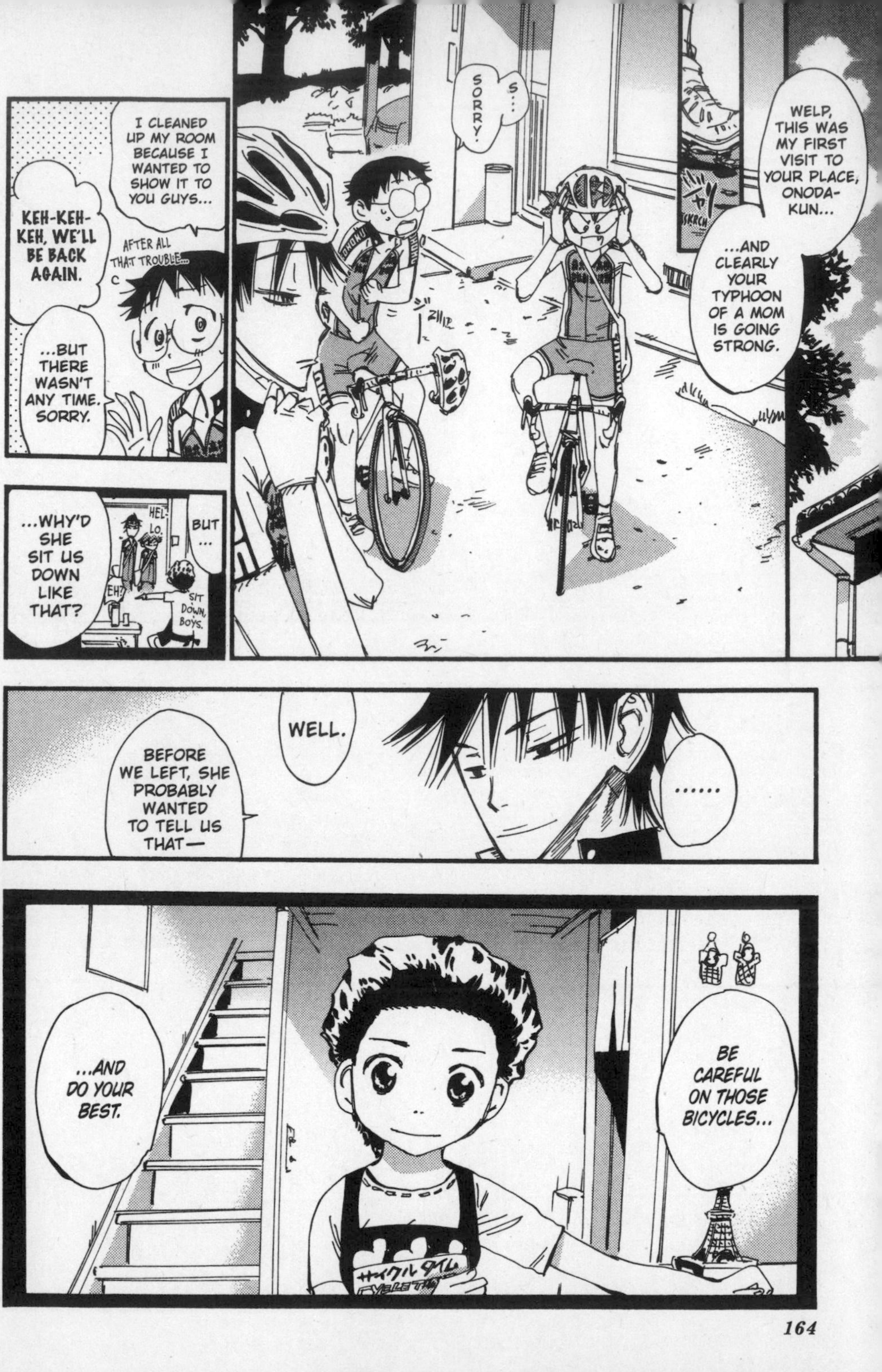
WELP, THIS WAS MY FIRST VISIT TO YOUR PLACE, ONODA-KUN...
...AND CLEARLY YOUR TYPHOON OF A MOM IS GOING STRONG.
SKRCH
S... SORRY.
ZZIP
I CLEANED UP MY ROOM BECAUSE I WANTED TO SHOW IT TO YOU GUYS...
AFTER ALL THAT TROUBLE...
...BUT THERE WASN'T ANY TIME. SORRY.
KEH-KEH-KEH, WE'LL BE BACK AGAIN.
BUT...
...WHY'D SHE SIT US DOWN LIKE THAT?
HEL-LO.
SIT DOWN, BOYS.
EH?
......
WELL.
BEFORE WE LEFT, SHE PROBABLY WANTED TO TELL US THAT—
BE CAREFUL ON THOSE BICYCLES...
...AND DO YOUR BEST.

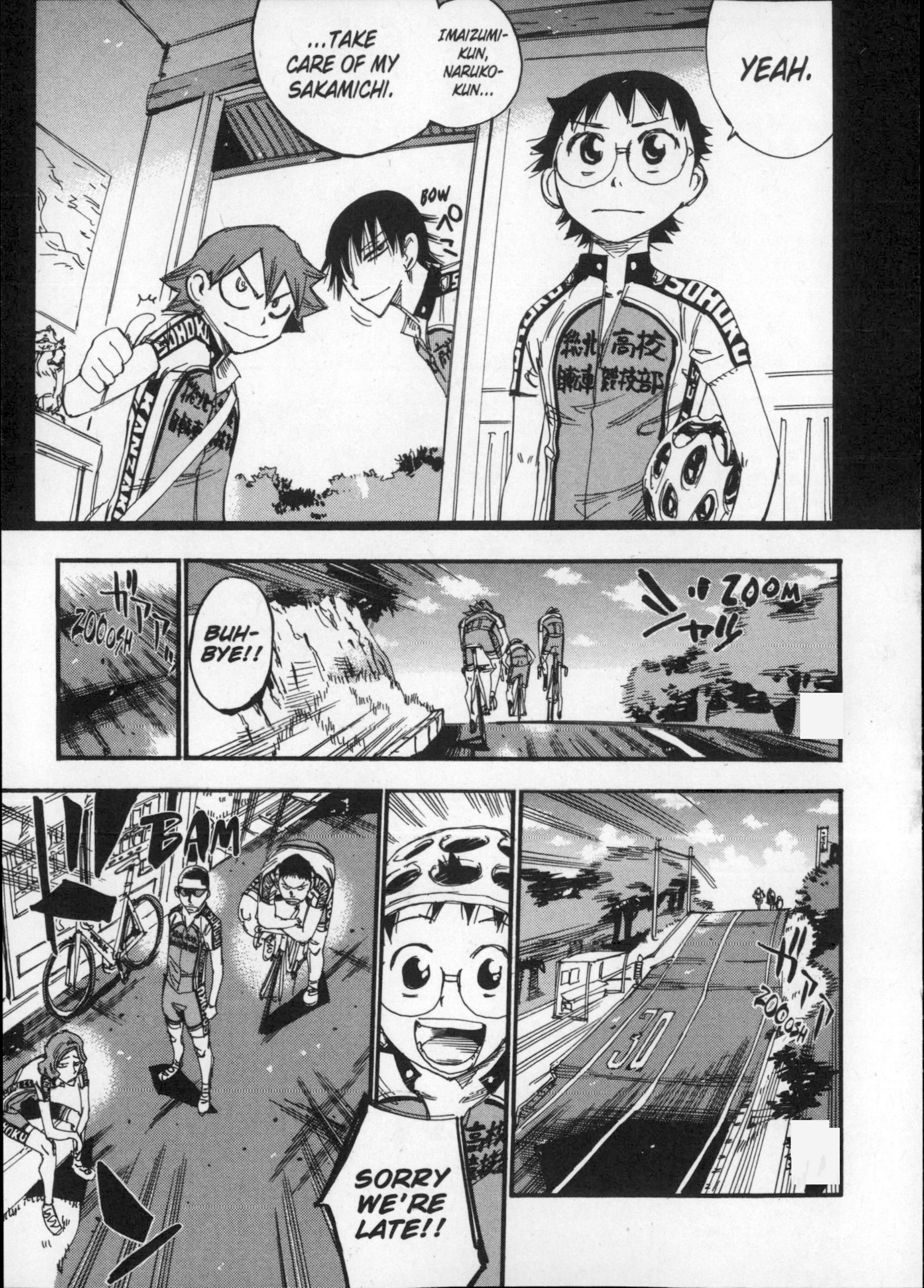
IMAIZUMI-KUN, NARUKO-KUN...
...TAKE CARE OF MY SAKAMICHI.
BOW
YEAH.
ZOOM
BUH-BYE!!
ZOOOSH
ZOOOSH
SORRY WE'RE LATE!!
BAM

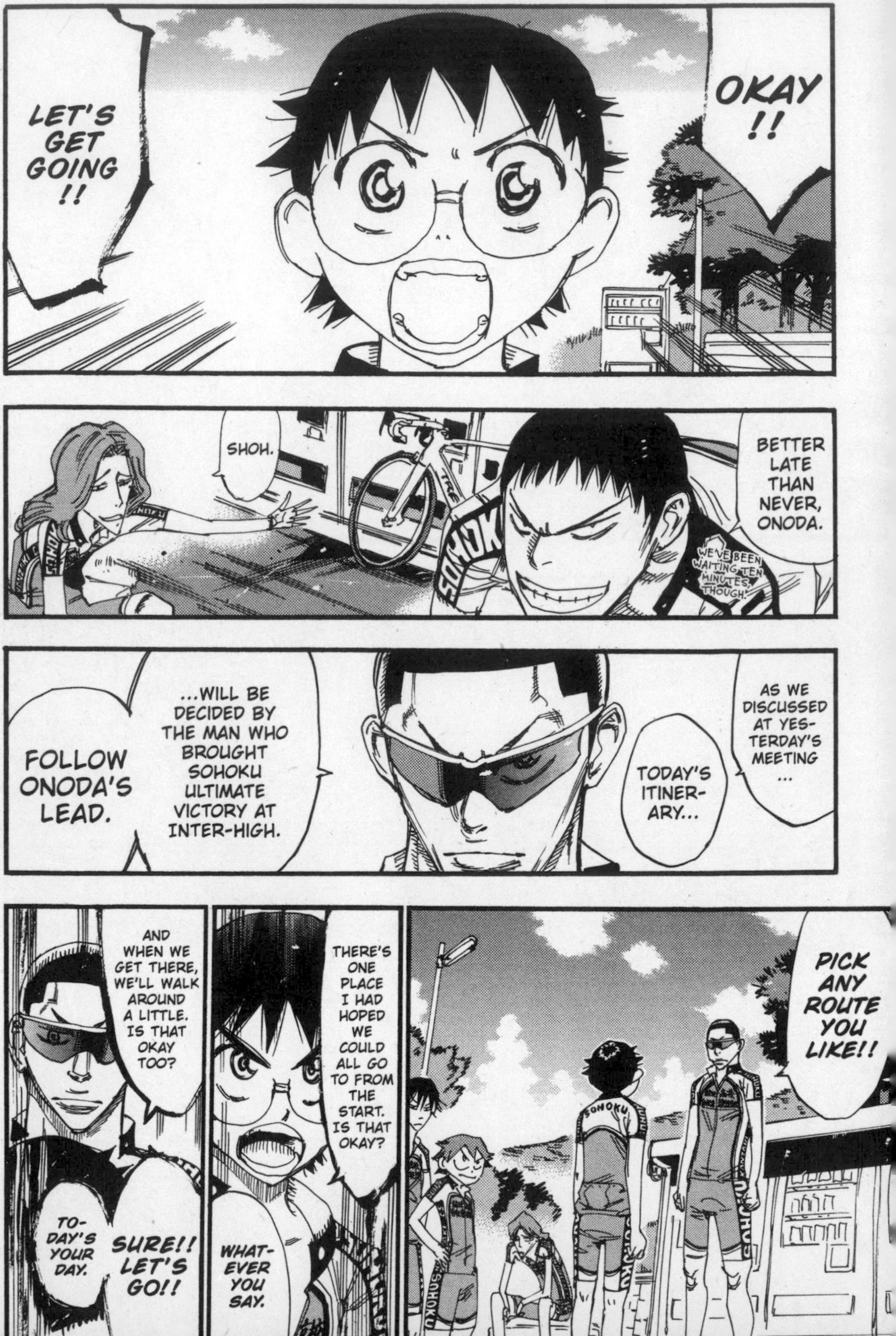

OKAY !!
LET'S GET GOING !!
BETTER LATE THAN NEVER, ONODA.
WE'VE BEEN WAITING TEN MINUTES, THOUGH!
SHOH.
AS WE DISCUSSED AT YES-TERDAY'S MEETING ...
TODAY'S ITINER-ARY...
...WILL BE DECIDED BY THE MAN WHO BROUGHT SOHOKU ULTIMATE VICTORY AT INTER-HIGH.
FOLLOW ONODA'S LEAD.
PICK ANY ROUTE YOU LIKE!!
THERE'S ONE PLACE I HAD HOPED WE COULD ALL GO TO FROM THE START. IS THAT OKAY?
WHAT-EVER YOU SAY.
AND WHEN WE GET THERE, WE'LL WALK AROUND A LITTLE. IS THAT OKAY TOO?
SURE!! LET'S GO!!
TO-DAY'S YOUR DAY.

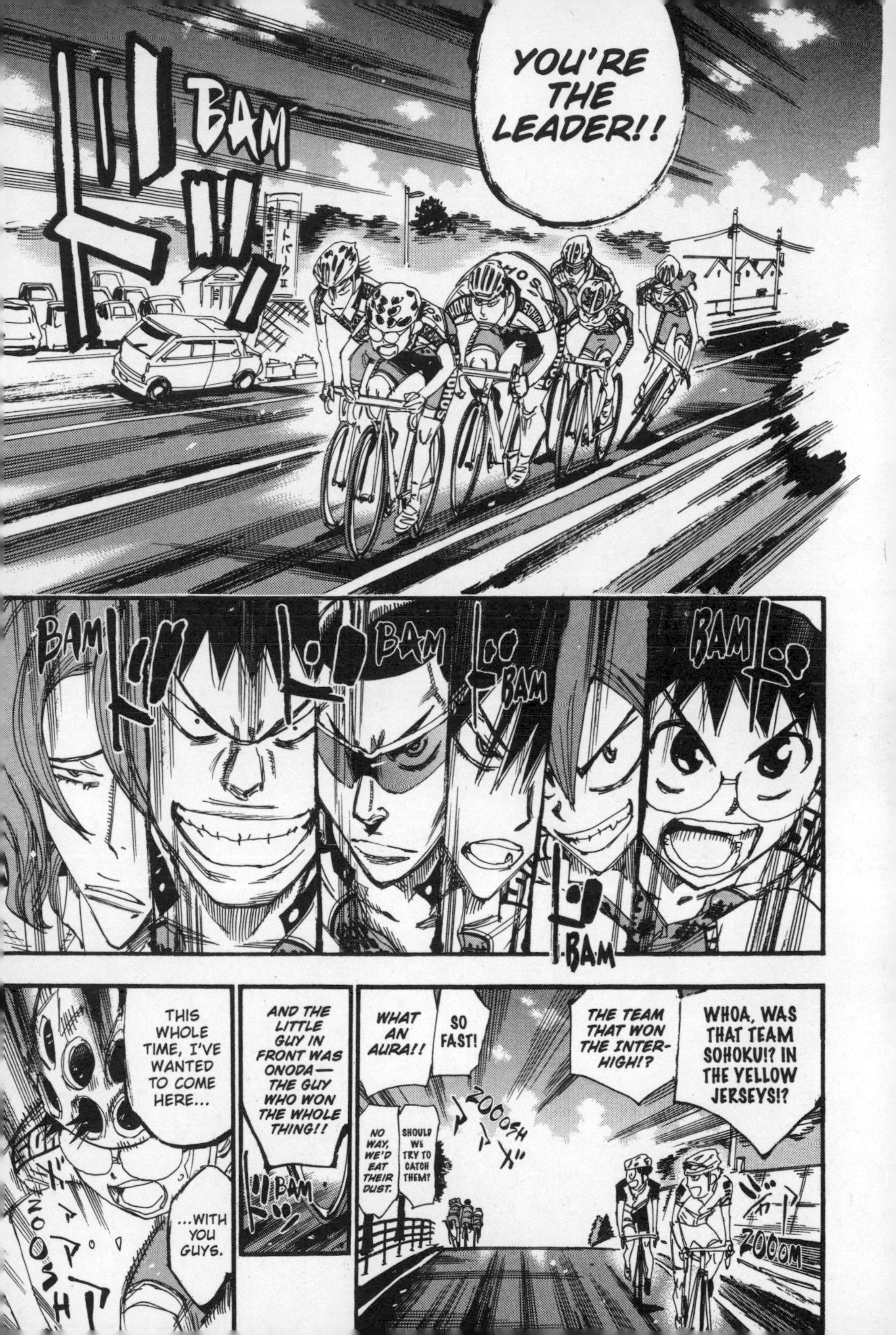
YOU'RE THE LEADER!!
BAM
BAM
BAM
BAM
BAM
BAM
WHOA, WAS THAT TEAM SOHOKU!? IN THE YELLOW JERSEYS!?
THE TEAM THAT WON THE INTER-HIGH!?
SO FAST!
WHAT AN AURA!!
ZOOOM
ZOOOSH
SHOULD WE TRY TO CATCH THEM?
NO WAY, WE'D EAT THEIR DUST.
AND THE LITTLE GUY IN FRONT WAS ONODA— THE GUY WHO WON THE WHOLE THING!!
BAM
THIS WHOLE TIME, I'VE WANTED TO COME HERE...
...WITH YOU GUYS.
ZOOOSH

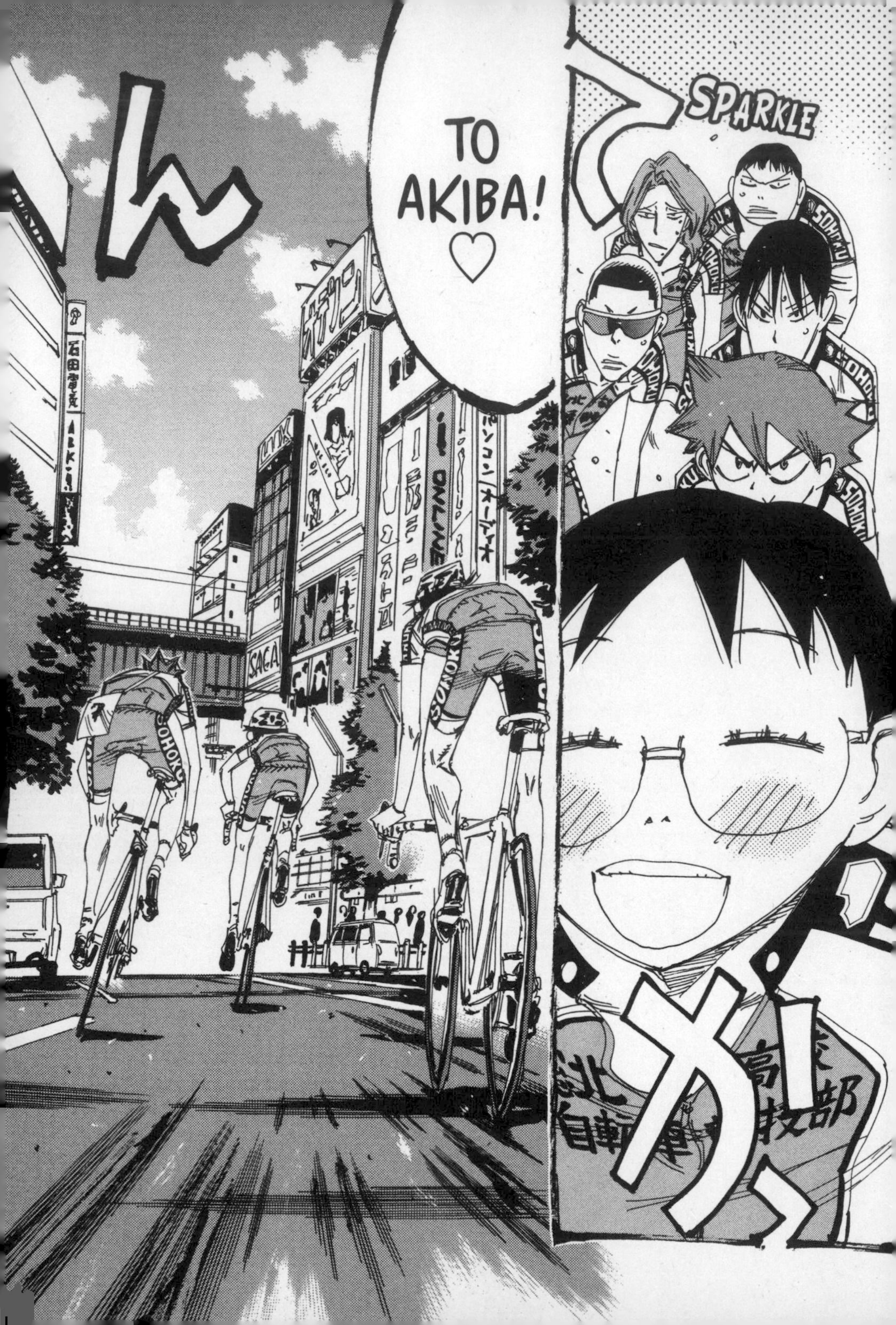
SPARKLE
TO AKIBA! ♡

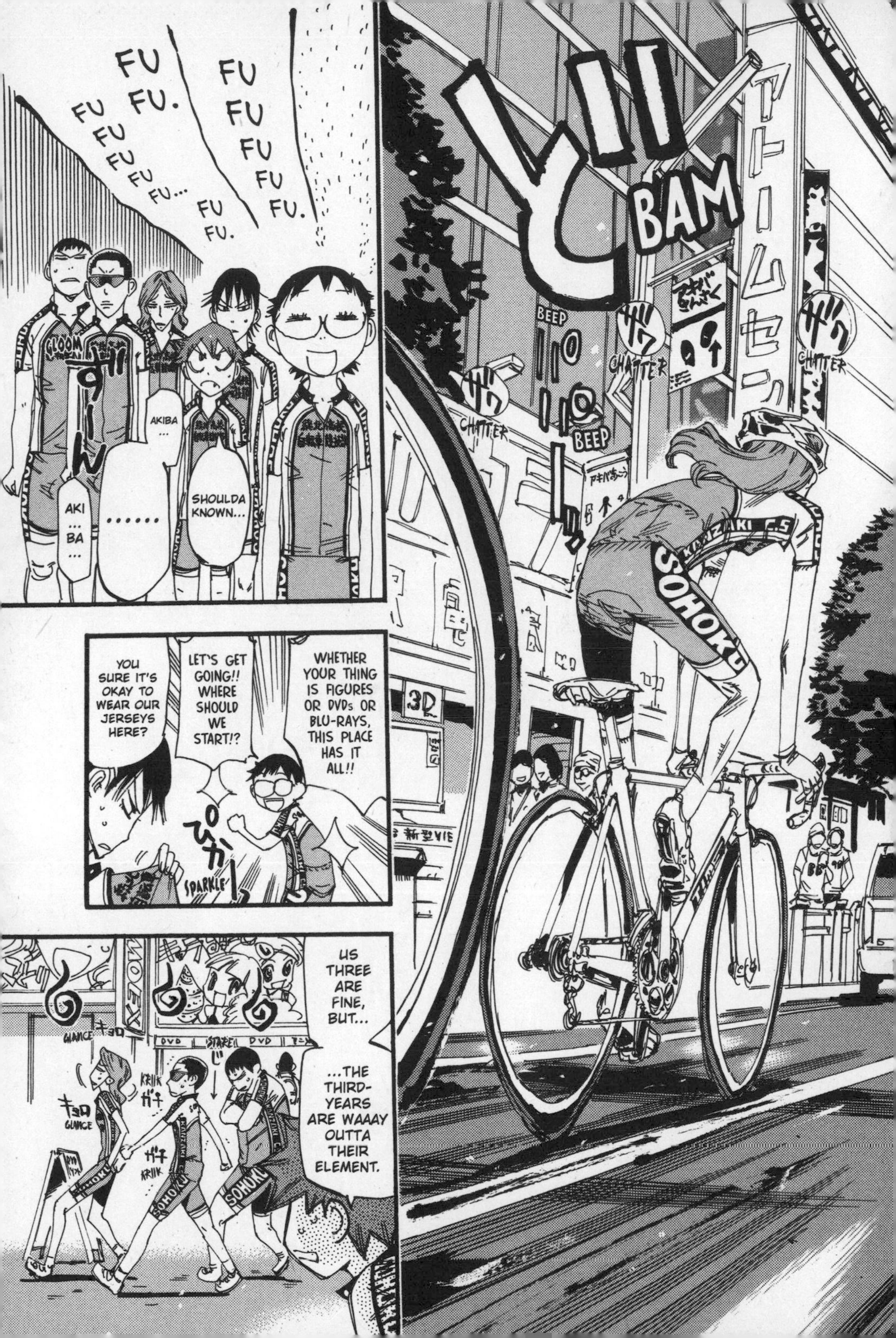
BAM
BEEP
BEEP
CHATTER
CHATTER
CHATTER
FU FU FU FU FU FU. FU FU.
FU FU. FU FU FU FU FU...
SHOULDA KNOWN...
AKIBA ...
......
AKI ... BA ...
WHETHER YOUR THING IS FIGURES OR DVDs OR BLU-RAYS, THIS PLACE HAS IT ALL!!
LET'S GET GOING!! WHERE SHOULD WE START!?
YOU SURE IT'S OKAY TO WEAR OUR JERSEYS HERE?
SPARKLE
US THREE ARE FINE, BUT...
...THE THIRD-YEARS ARE WAAAY OUTTA THEIR ELEMENT.
GLANCE
STARE
KRIIK
KRIIK
GLANCE

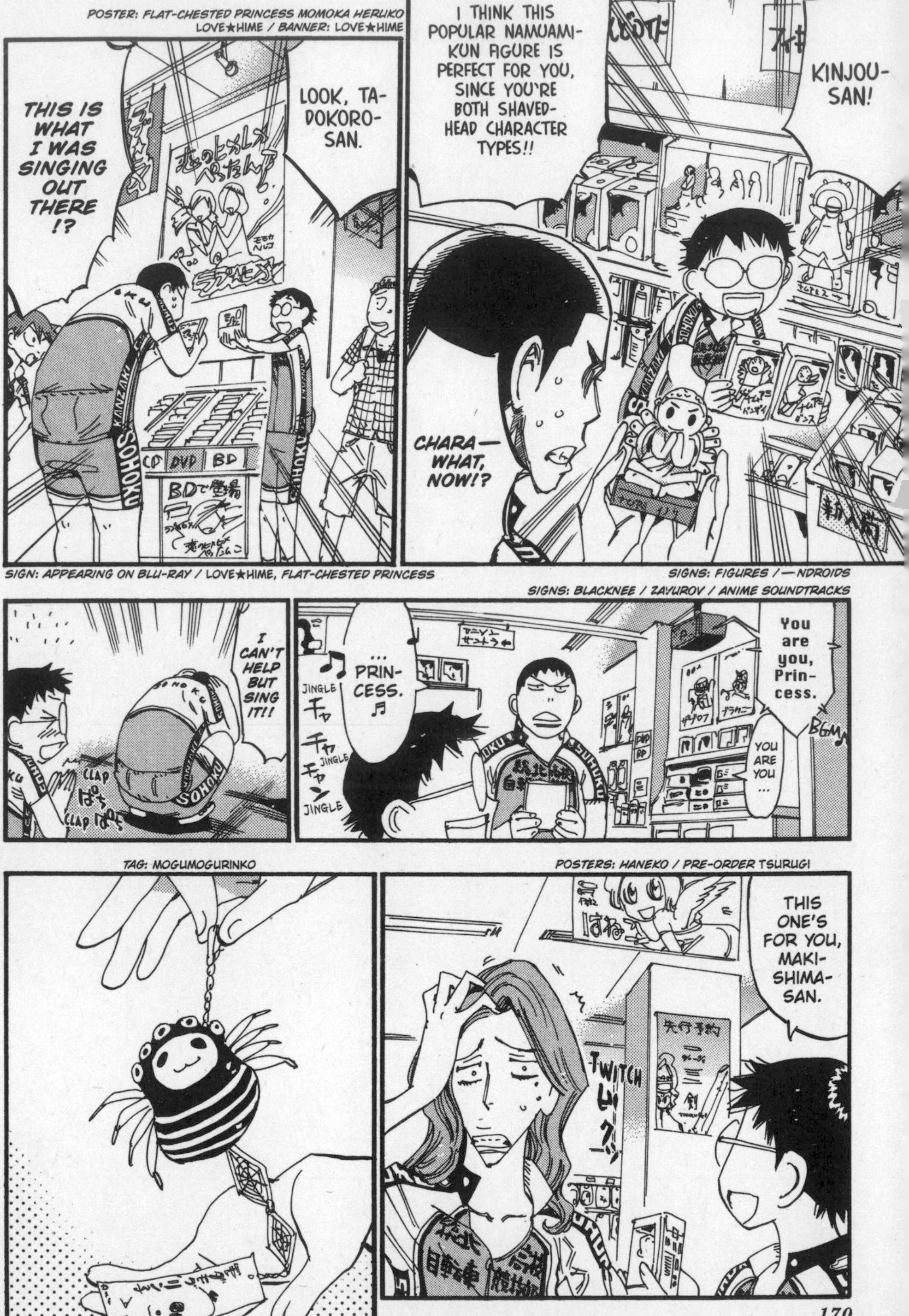
KINJOU-SAN!
I THINK THIS POPULAR NAMUAMI-KUN FIGURE IS PERFECT FOR YOU, SINCE YOU'RE BOTH SHAVED-HEAD CHARACTER TYPES!!
CHARA—WHAT, NOW!?
SIGNS: FIGURES / —NDROIDS
LOOK, TA-DOKORO-SAN.
THIS IS WHAT I WAS SINGING OUT THERE!?
POSTER: FLAT-CHESTED PRINCESS MOMOKA HERUKO
LOVE★HIME / BANNER: LOVE★HIME
CD DVD BD
SIGN: APPEARING ON BLU-RAY / LOVE★HIME, FLAT-CHESTED PRINCESS
SIGNS: BLACKNEE / ZAVUROV / ANIME SOUNDTRACKS
You are you, Prin-cess.
BGM
YOU ARE YOU ...
... PRINCESS.
JINGLE
JINGLE
JINGLE
I CAN'T HELP BUT SING IT!!
CLAP
CLAP
POSTERS: HANEKO / PRE-ORDER TSURUGI
THIS ONE'S FOR YOU, MAKI-SHIMA-SAN.
TWITCH
TAG: MOGUMOGURINKO

SIGN: MIZUNA KOTORI BGM SINGLE PRE-ORDER NOW

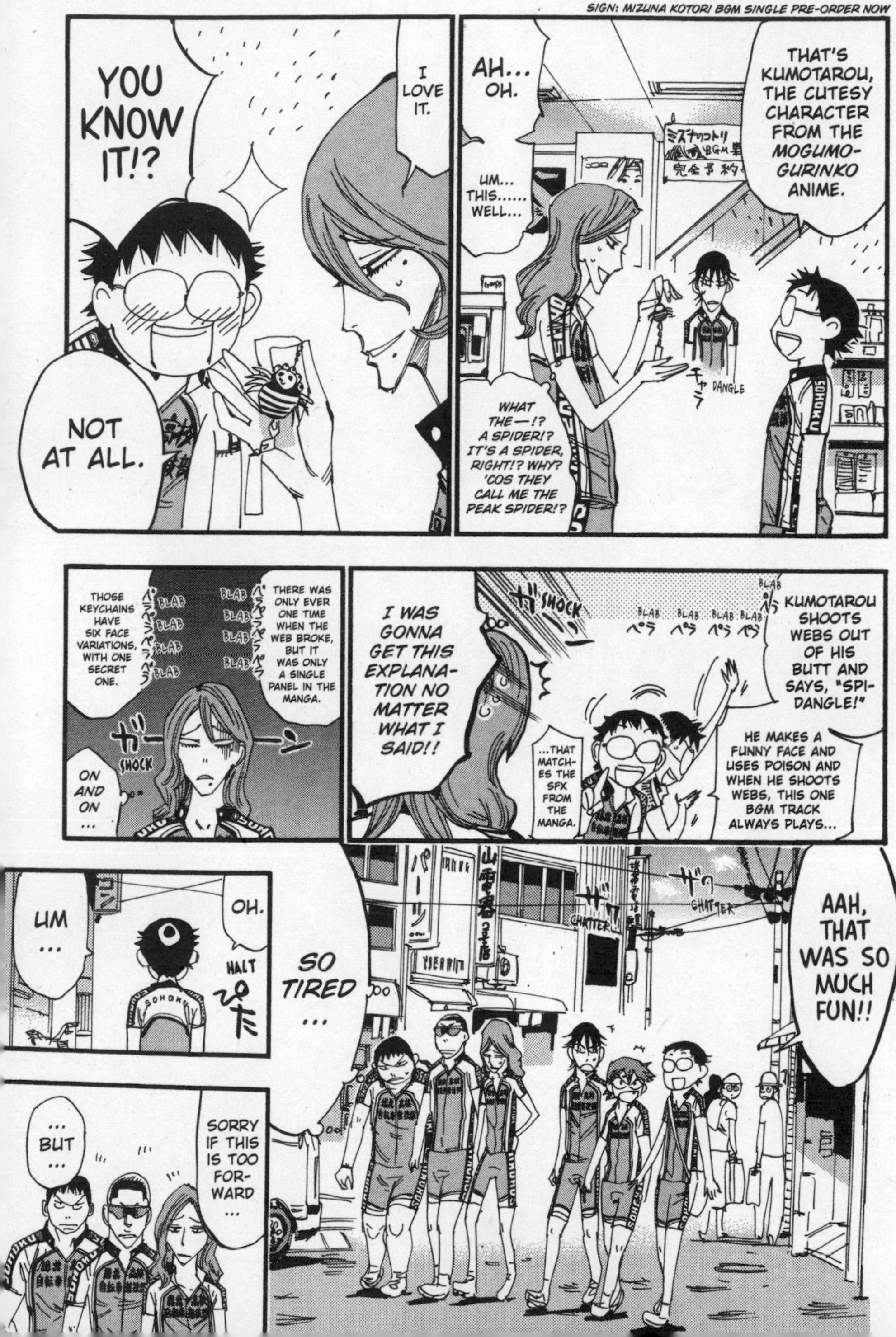
THAT'S KUMOTAROU, THE CUTESY CHARACTER FROM THE MOGUMO-GURINKO ANIME.
AH... OH.
UM... THIS...... WELL...
DANGLE
WHAT THE—!? A SPIDER!? IT'S A SPIDER, RIGHT!? WHY? 'COS THEY CALL ME THE PEAK SPIDER!?
I LOVE IT.
YOU KNOW IT!?
NOT AT ALL.
KUMOTAROU SHOOTS WEBS OUT OF HIS BUTT AND SAYS, "SPI-DANGLE!"
BLAB BLAB BLAB BLAB BLAB
HE MAKES A FUNNY FACE AND USES POISON AND WHEN HE SHOOTS WEBS, THIS ONE BGM TRACK ALWAYS PLAYS...
SHOCK
I WAS GONNA GET THIS EXPLANATION NO MATTER WHAT I SAID!!
...THAT MATCHES THE SFX FROM THE MANGA.
THERE WAS ONLY EVER ONE TIME WHEN THE WEB BROKE, BUT IT WAS ONLY A SINGLE PANEL IN THE MANGA.
BLAB BLAB BLAB BLAB
THOSE KEYCHAINS HAVE SIX FACE VARIATIONS, WITH ONE SECRET ONE.
BLAB BLAB BLAB BLAB
SHOCK
ON AND ON ...
AAH, THAT WAS SO MUCH FUN!!
CHATTER
CHATTER
SO TIRED ...
OH.
HALT
UM ...
SORRY IF THIS IS TOO FOR-WARD ...
... BUT ...

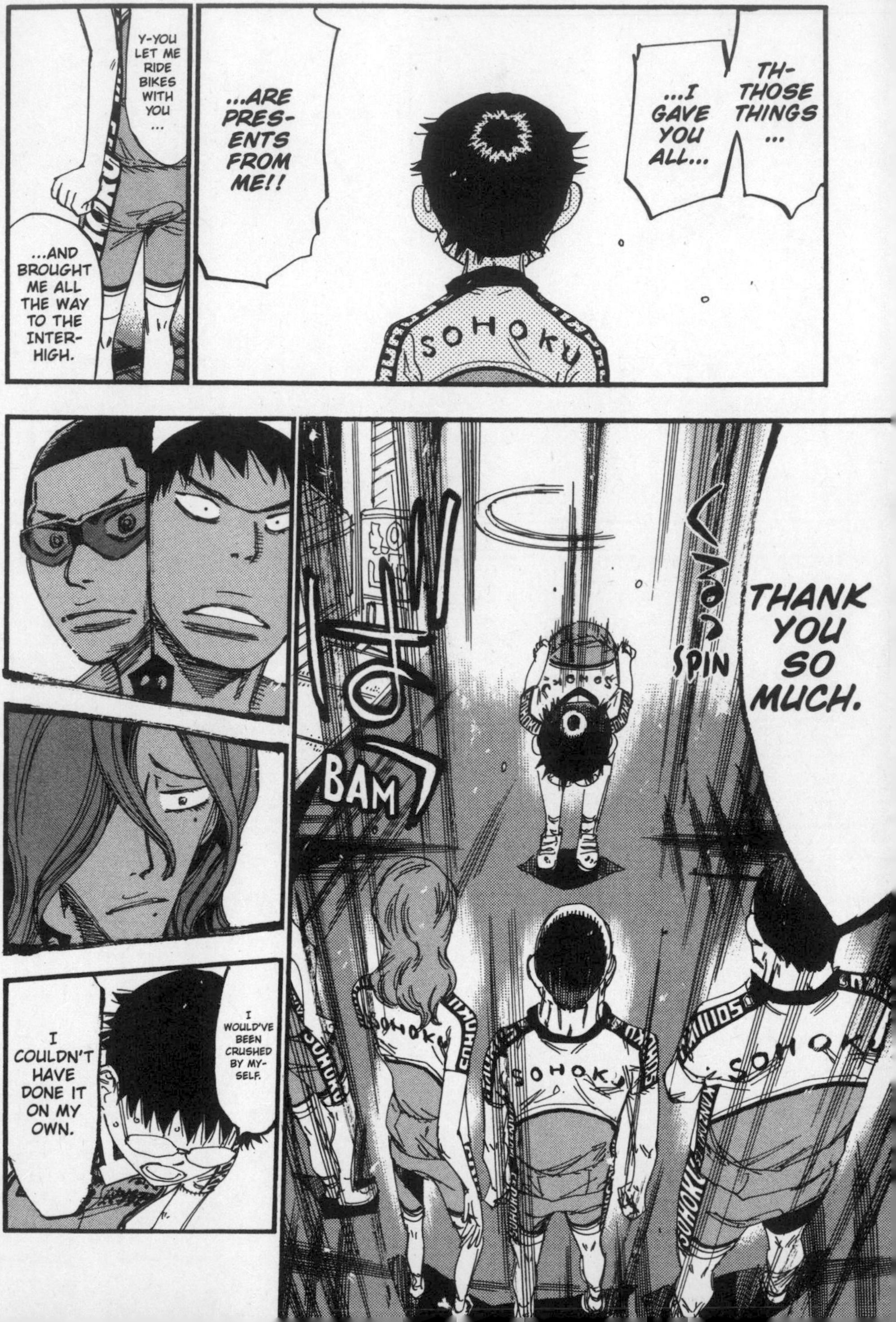
TH- THOSE THINGS ...
...I GAVE YOU ALL...
...ARE PRESENTS FROM ME!!
Y-YOU LET ME RIDE BIKES WITH YOU ...
...AND BROUGHT ME ALL THE WAY TO THE INTER-HIGH.
THANK YOU SO MUCH.
SPIN
BAM
I WOULD'VE BEEN CRUSHED BY MY-SELF.
I COULDN'T HAVE DONE IT ON MY OWN.

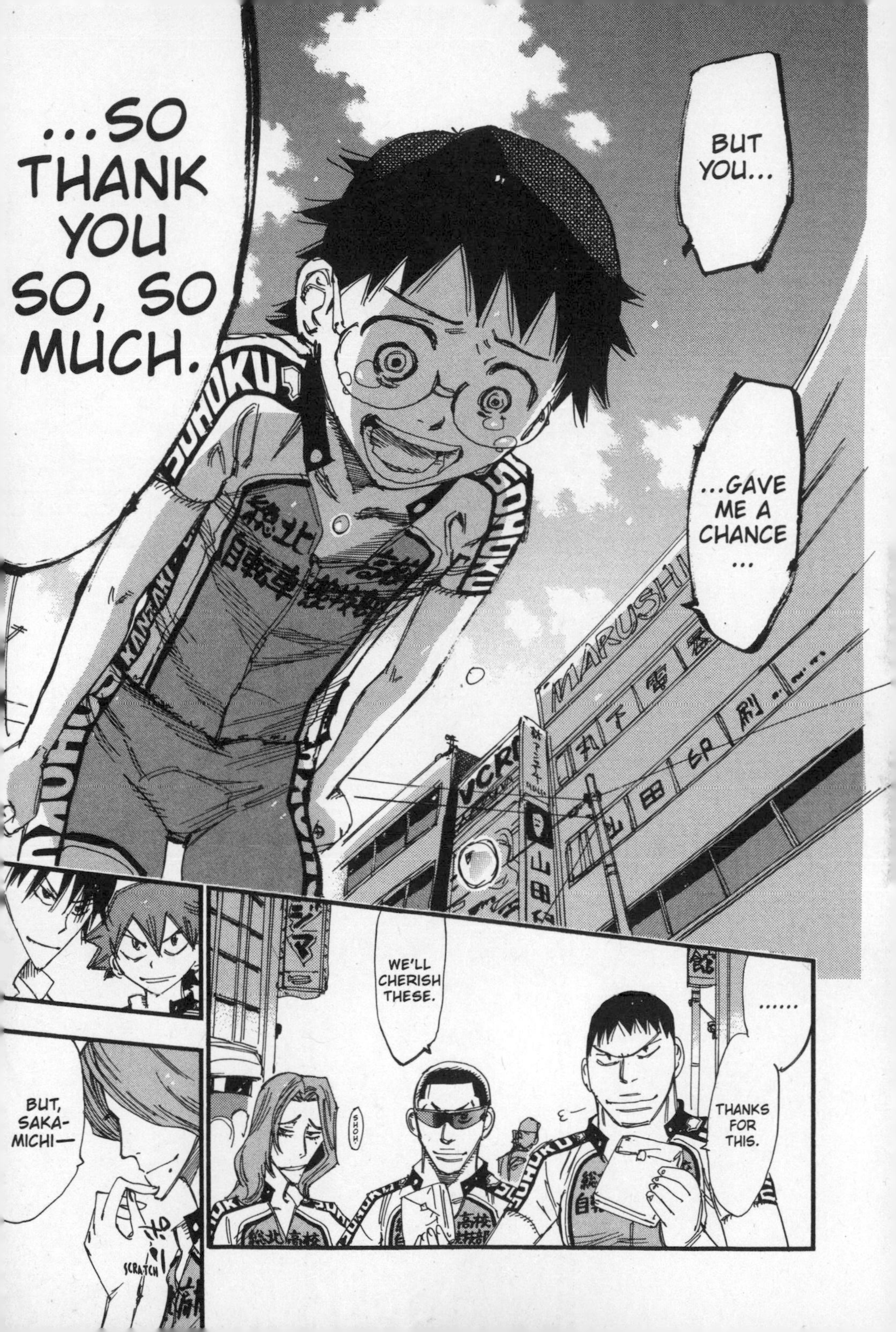
BUT YOU...
...GAVE ME A CHANCE...
...SO THANK YOU SO, SO MUCH.
......
THANKS FOR THIS.
WE'LL CHERISH THESE.
BUT, SAKA-MICHI—
SCRATCH

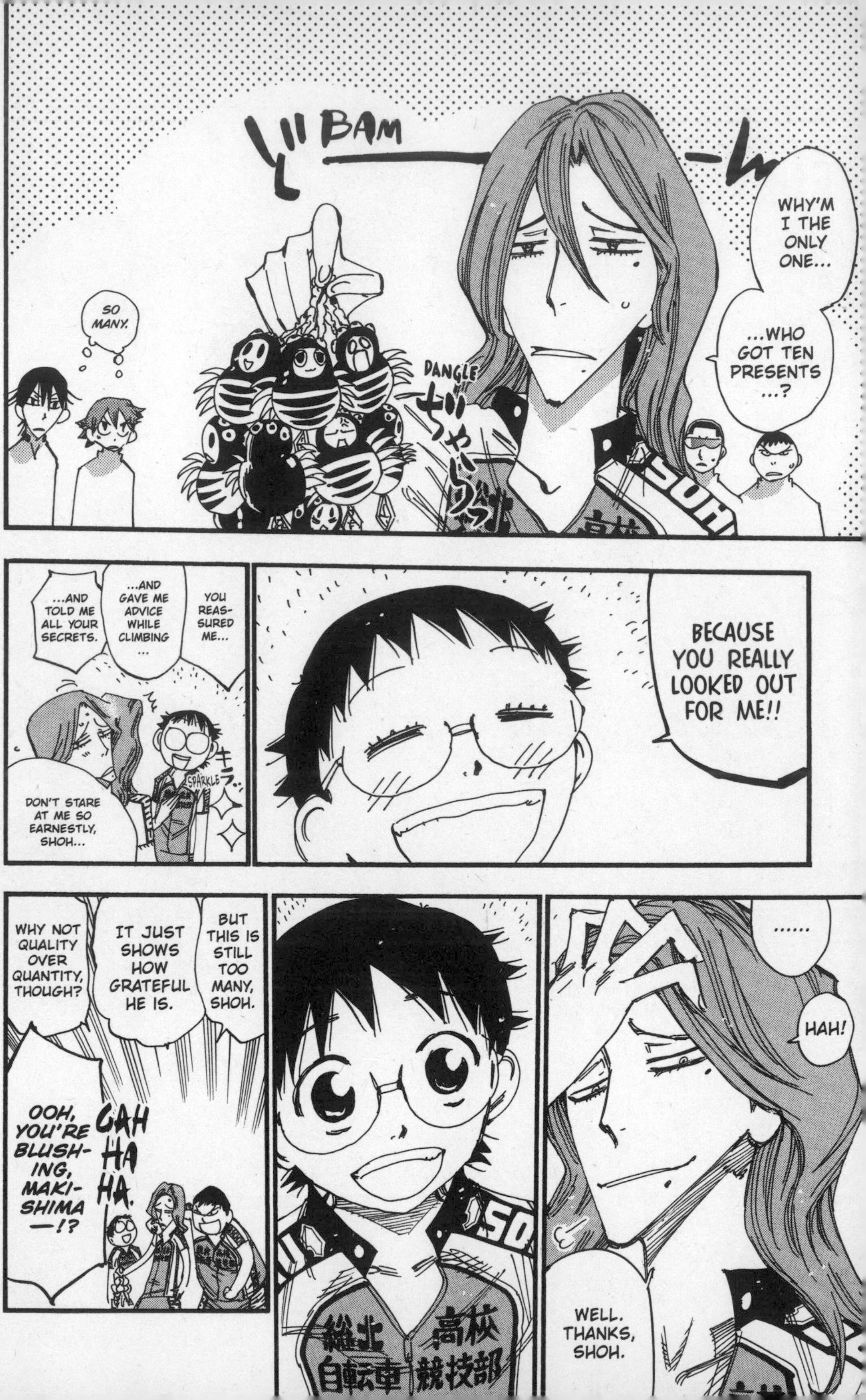
BAM
WHY'M I THE ONLY ONE...
...WHO GOT TEN PRESENTS ...?
DANGLE
SO MANY.
BECAUSE YOU REALLY LOOKED OUT FOR ME!!
YOU REASSURED ME...
...AND GAVE ME ADVICE WHILE CLIMBING ...
...AND TOLD ME ALL YOUR SECRETS.
SPARKLE
DON'T STARE AT ME SO EARNESTLY, SHOH...
......
HAH!
WELL. THANKS, SHOH.
総北高校
自転車競技部
BUT THIS IS STILL TOO MANY, SHOH.
IT JUST SHOWS HOW GRATEFUL HE IS.
WHY NOT QUALITY OVER QUANTITY, THOUGH?
GAH HA HA.
OOH, YOU'RE BLUSH-ING, MAKI-SHIMA—!?

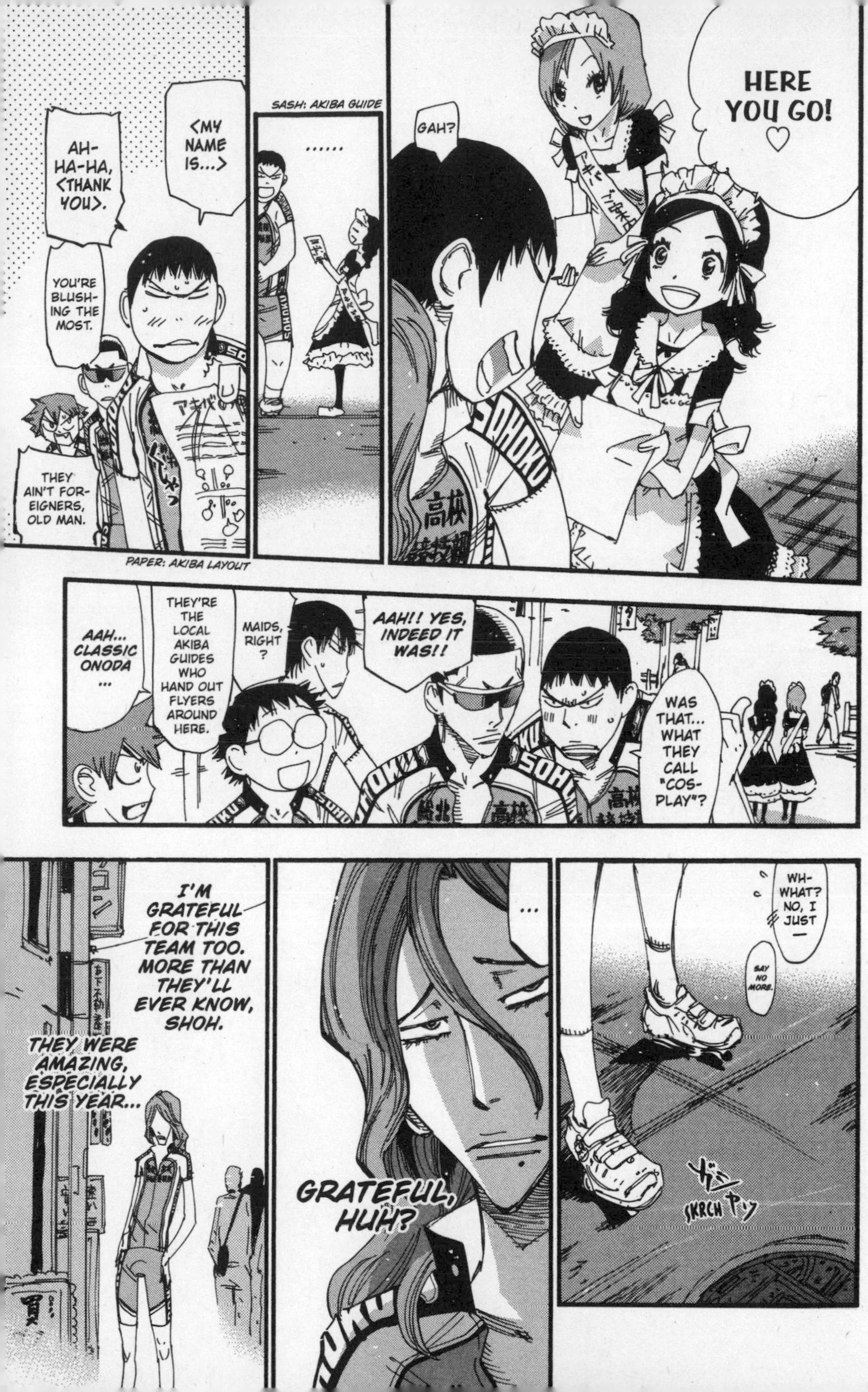
HERE YOU GO! ♡
GAH?
......
SASH: AKIBA GUIDE
<MY NAME IS...>
AH-HA-HA, <THANK YOU>.
YOU'RE BLUSHING THE MOST.
THEY AIN'T FOREIGNERS, OLD MAN.
PAPER: AKIBA LAYOUT
WAS THAT... WHAT THEY CALL "COS-PLAY"?
AAH!! YES, INDEED IT WAS!!
MAIDS, RIGHT?
THEY'RE THE LOCAL AKIBA GUIDES WHO HAND OUT FLYERS AROUND HERE.
AAH... CLASSIC ONODA ...
WH-WHAT? NO, I JUST—
SAY NO MORE.
SKRCH
...
GRATEFUL, HUH?
I'M GRATEFUL FOR THIS TEAM TOO. MORE THAN THEY'LL EVER KNOW, SHOH.
THEY WERE AMAZING, ESPECIALLY THIS YEAR...

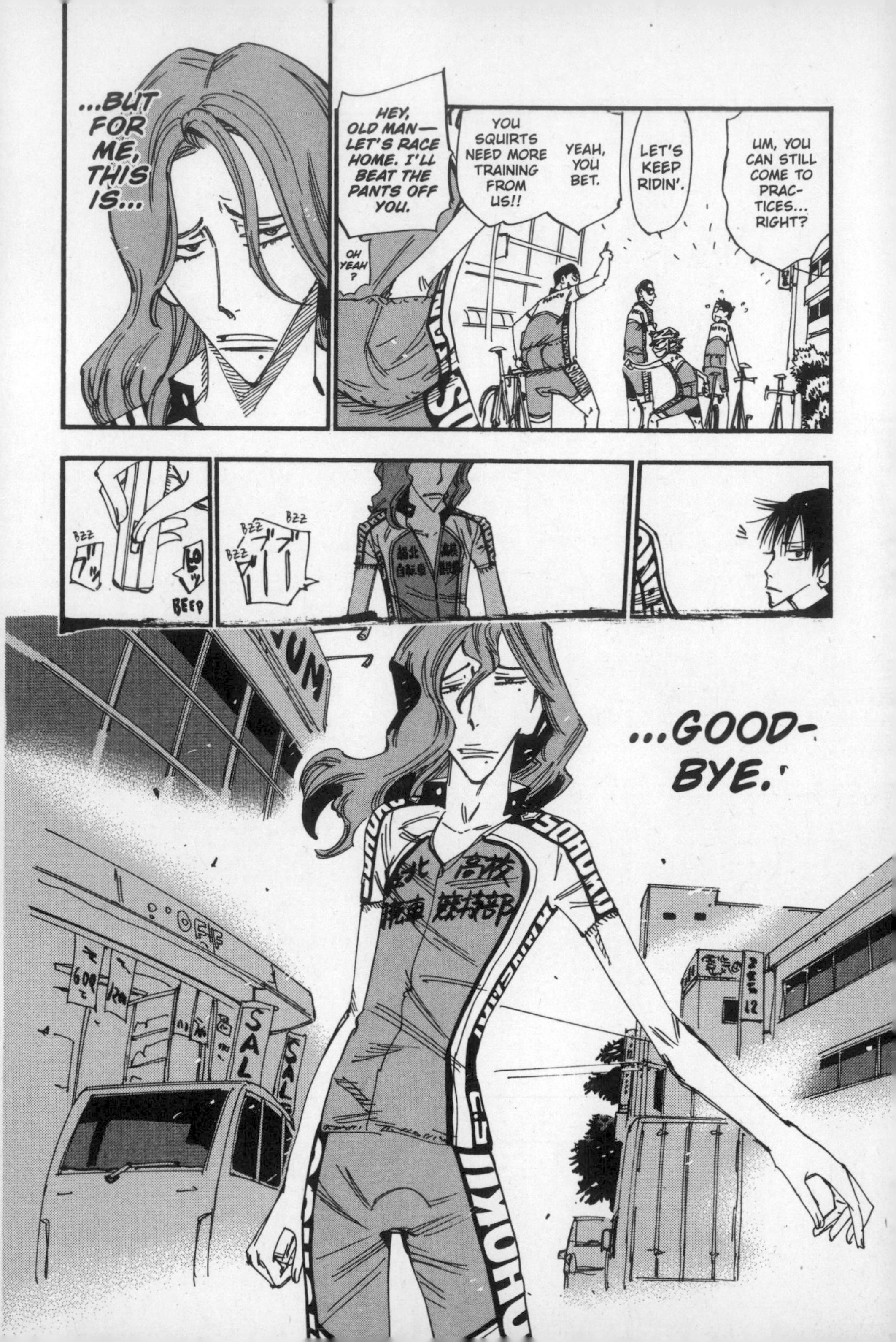
UM, YOU CAN STILL COME TO PRAC-TICES... RIGHT?
LET'S KEEP RIDIN'.
YEAH, YOU BET.
YOU SQUIRTS NEED MORE TRAINING FROM US!!
HEY, OLD MAN— LET'S RACE HOME. I'LL BEAT THE PANTS OFF YOU.
OH YEAH?
...BUT FOR ME, THIS IS...
BZZ
BZZ
BZZ
BZZ
BEEP
...GOOD-BYE.

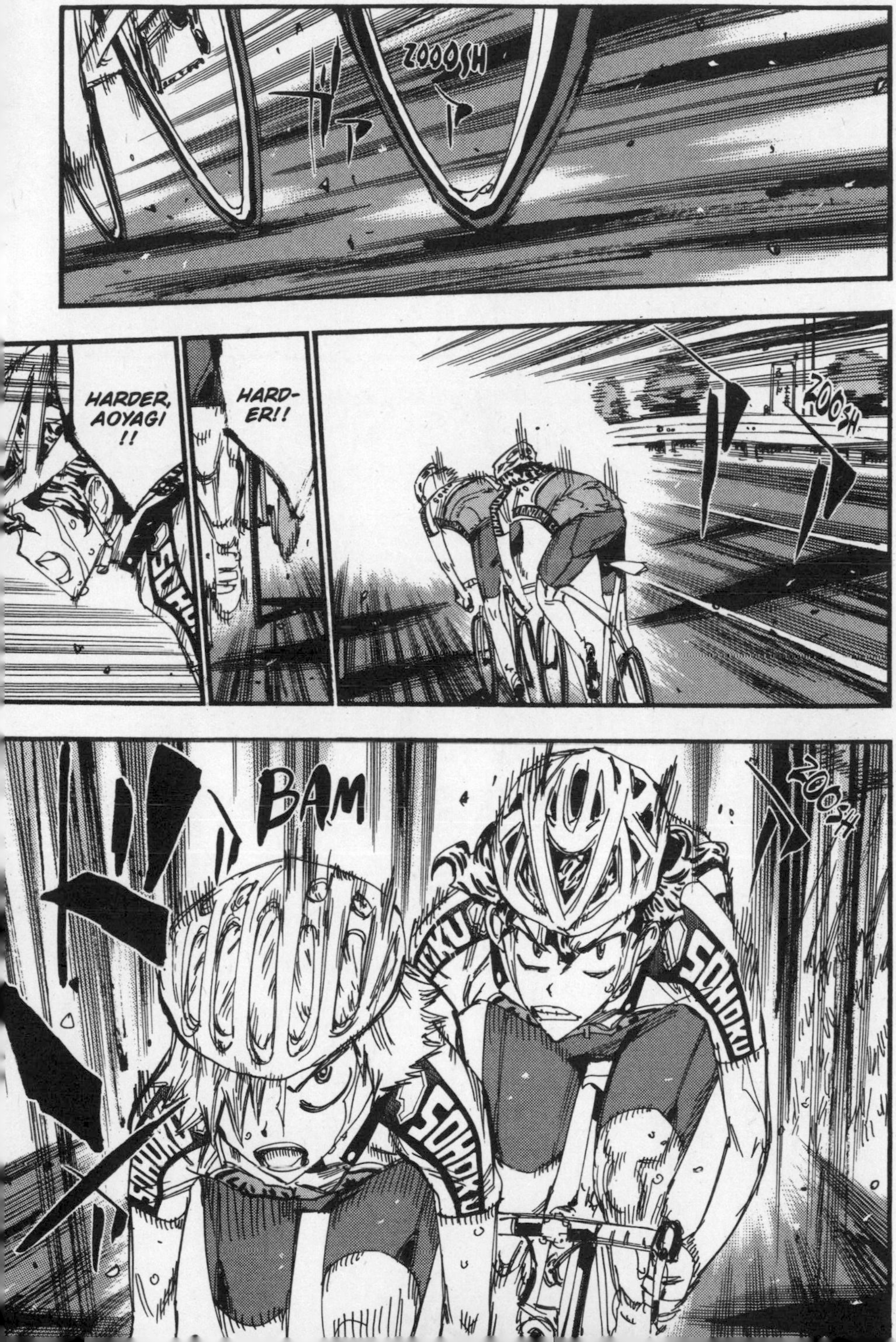
ZOOOSH
ZOOSH
HARDER!!
HARDER, AOYAGI!!
ZOOSH
BAM

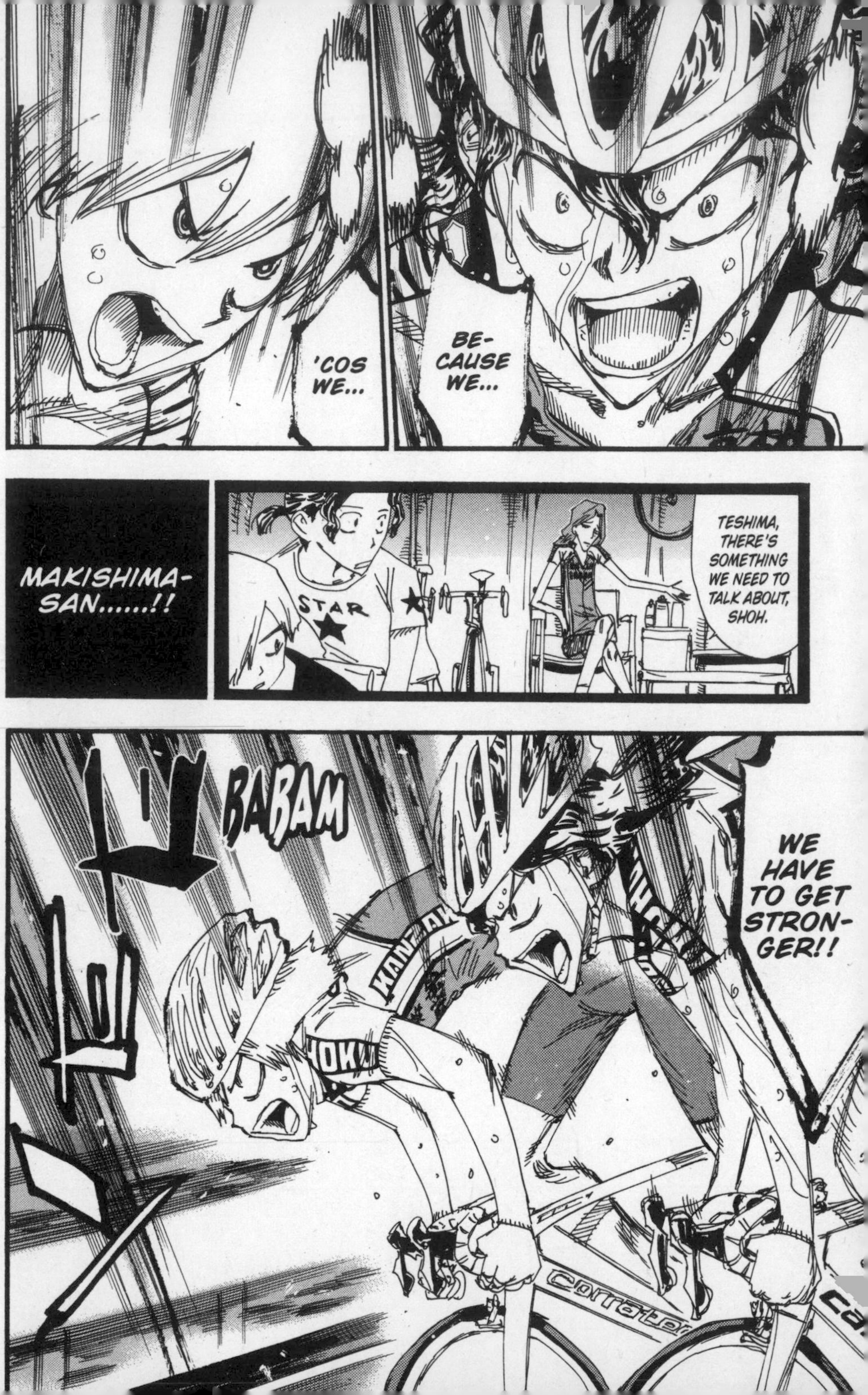
BE-
CAUSE
WE...
'COS
WE...
TESHIMA, THERE'S SOMETHING WE NEED TO TALK ABOUT, SHOH.
MAKISHIMA-SAN......!!
BABAM
WE HAVE TO GET STRONGER!!

RIDE.234 NEW MACHINE

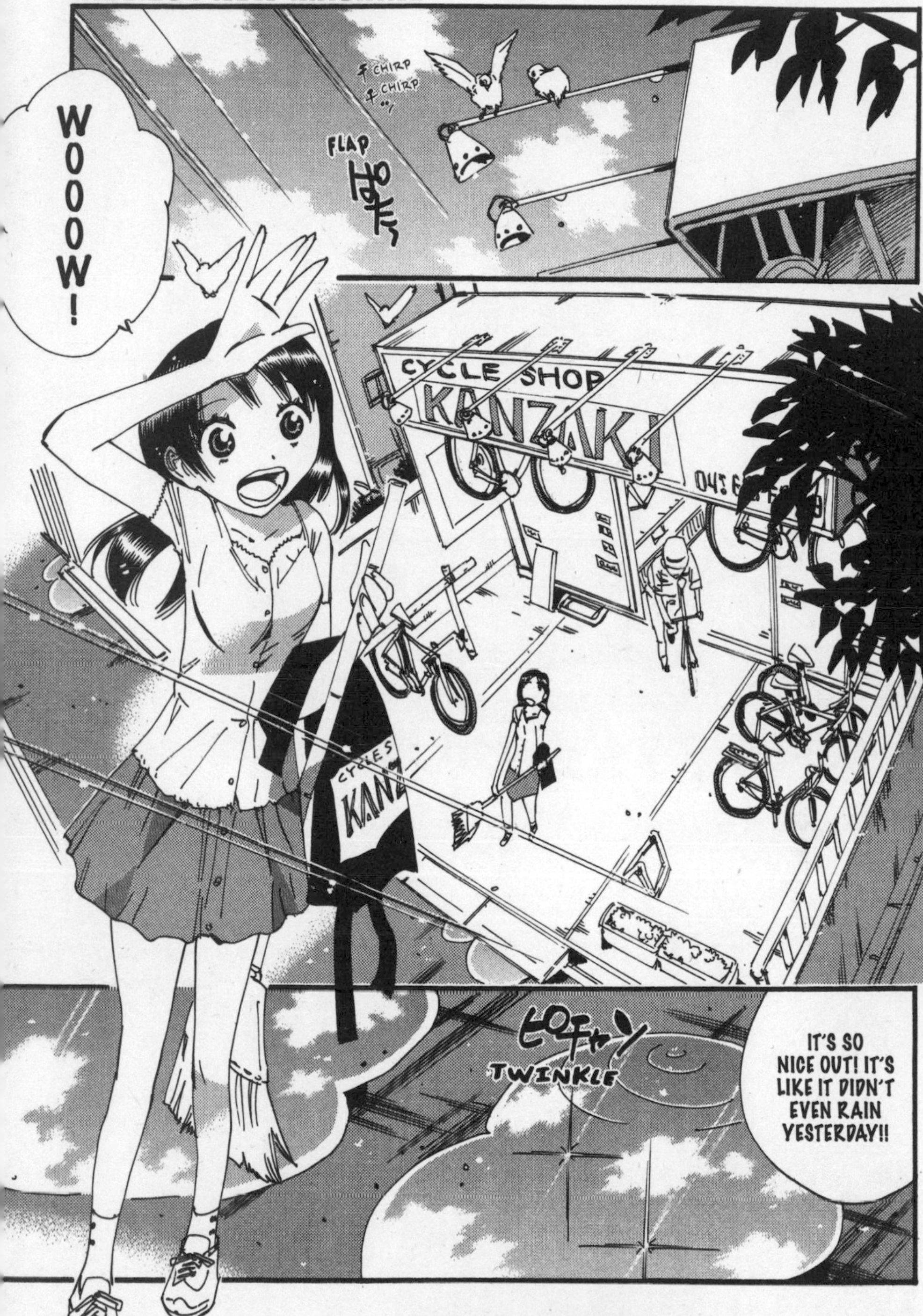
CHIRP
CHIRP
FLAP
WOOOOW!
CYCLE SHOP KANZAKI
CYCLES KANZ
TWINKLE
IT'S SO NICE OUT! IT'S LIKE IT DIDN'T EVEN RAIN YESTERDAY!!

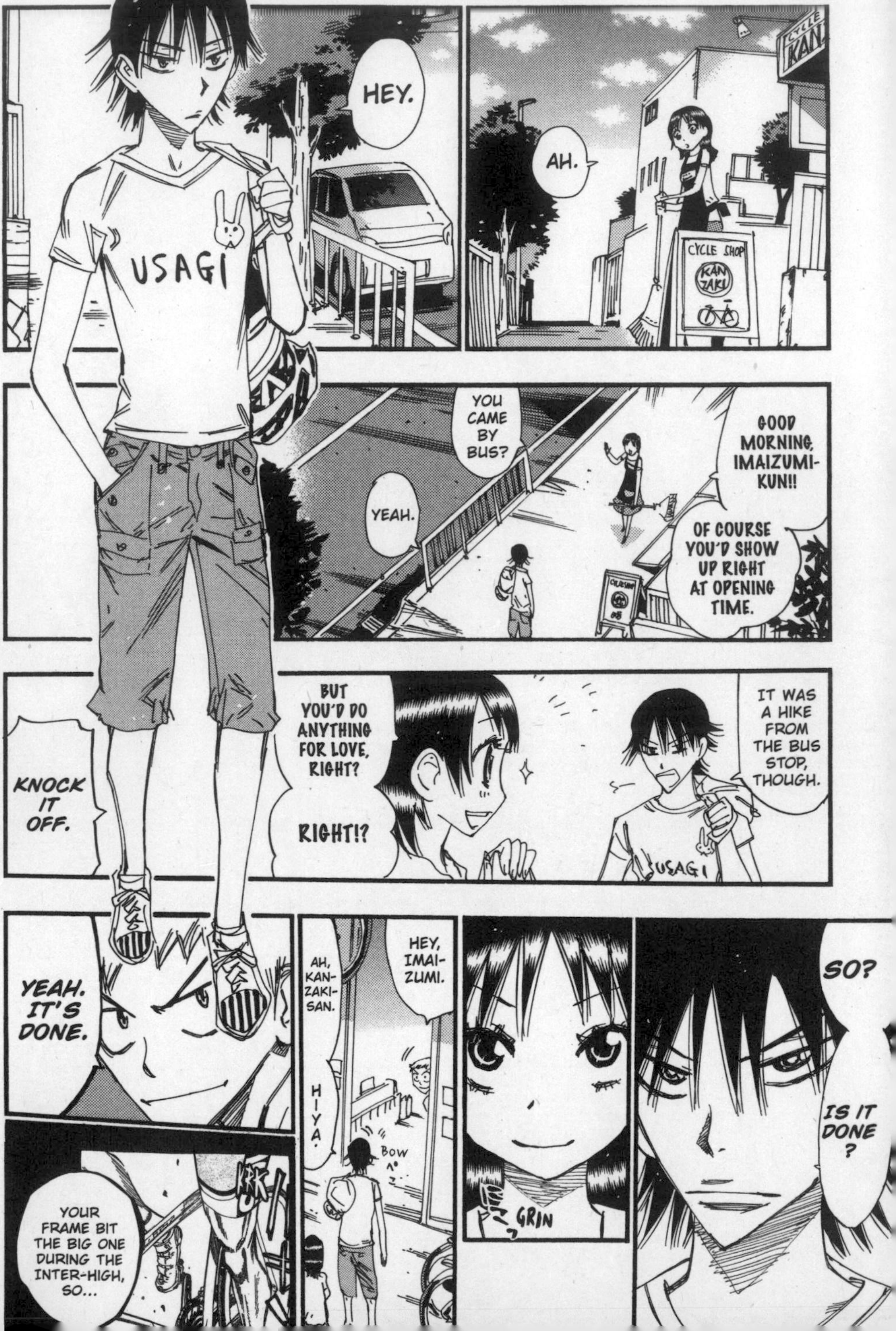
AH.
HEY.
GOOD MORNING, IMAIZUMI-KUN!!
OF COURSE YOU'D SHOW UP RIGHT AT OPENING TIME.
YOU CAME BY BUS?
YEAH.
IT WAS A HIKE FROM THE BUS STOP, THOUGH.
BUT YOU'D DO ANYTHING FOR LOVE, RIGHT?
RIGHT!?
KNOCK IT OFF.
SO?
IS IT DONE?
GRIN
HEY, IMAIZUMI.
AH, KANZAKI-SAN.
HIYA.
BOW
YEAH. IT'S DONE.
YOUR FRAME BIT THE BIG ONE DURING THE INTER-HIGH, SO...

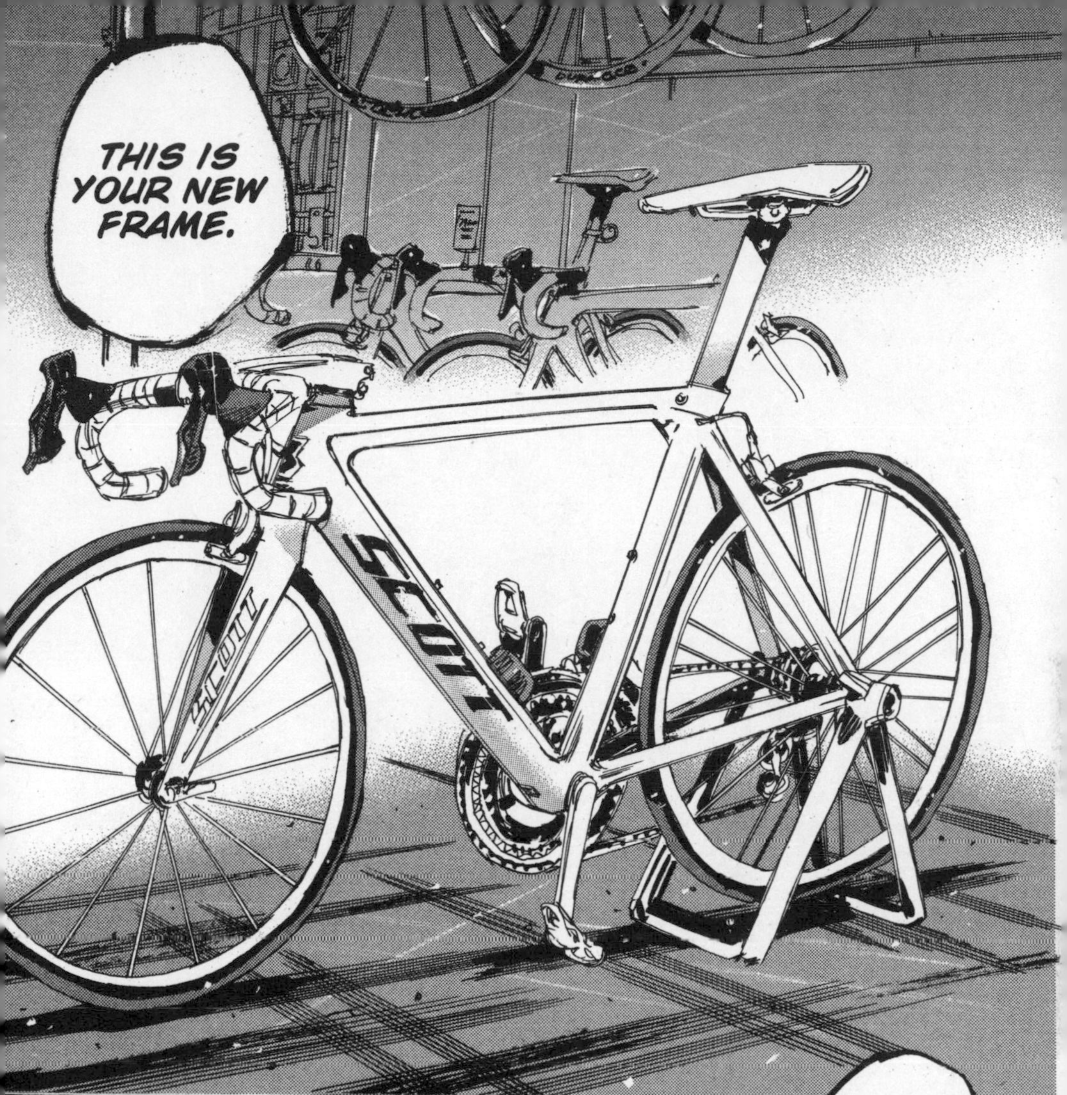
THIS IS YOUR NEW FRAME.
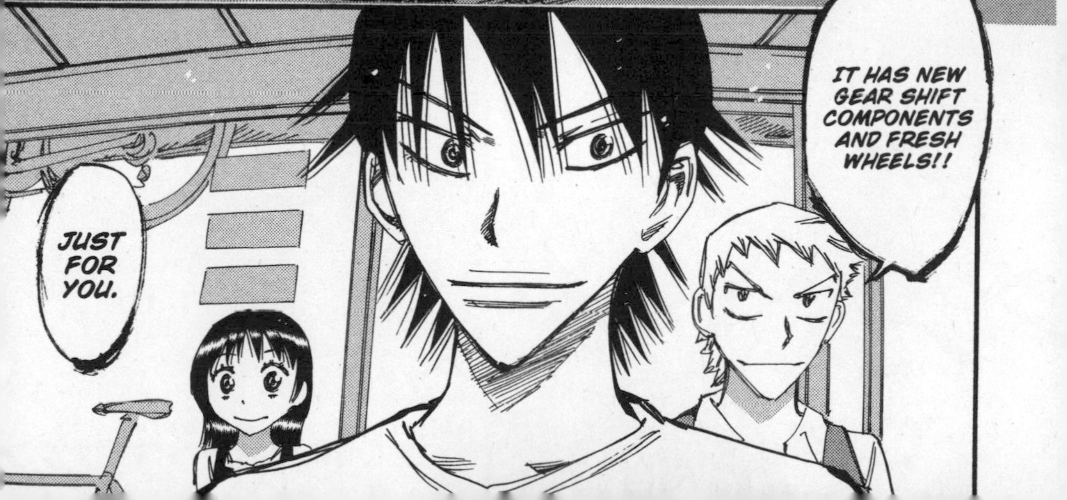
IT HAS NEW GEAR SHIFT COMPONENTS AND FRESH WHEELS!!
JUST FOR YOU.

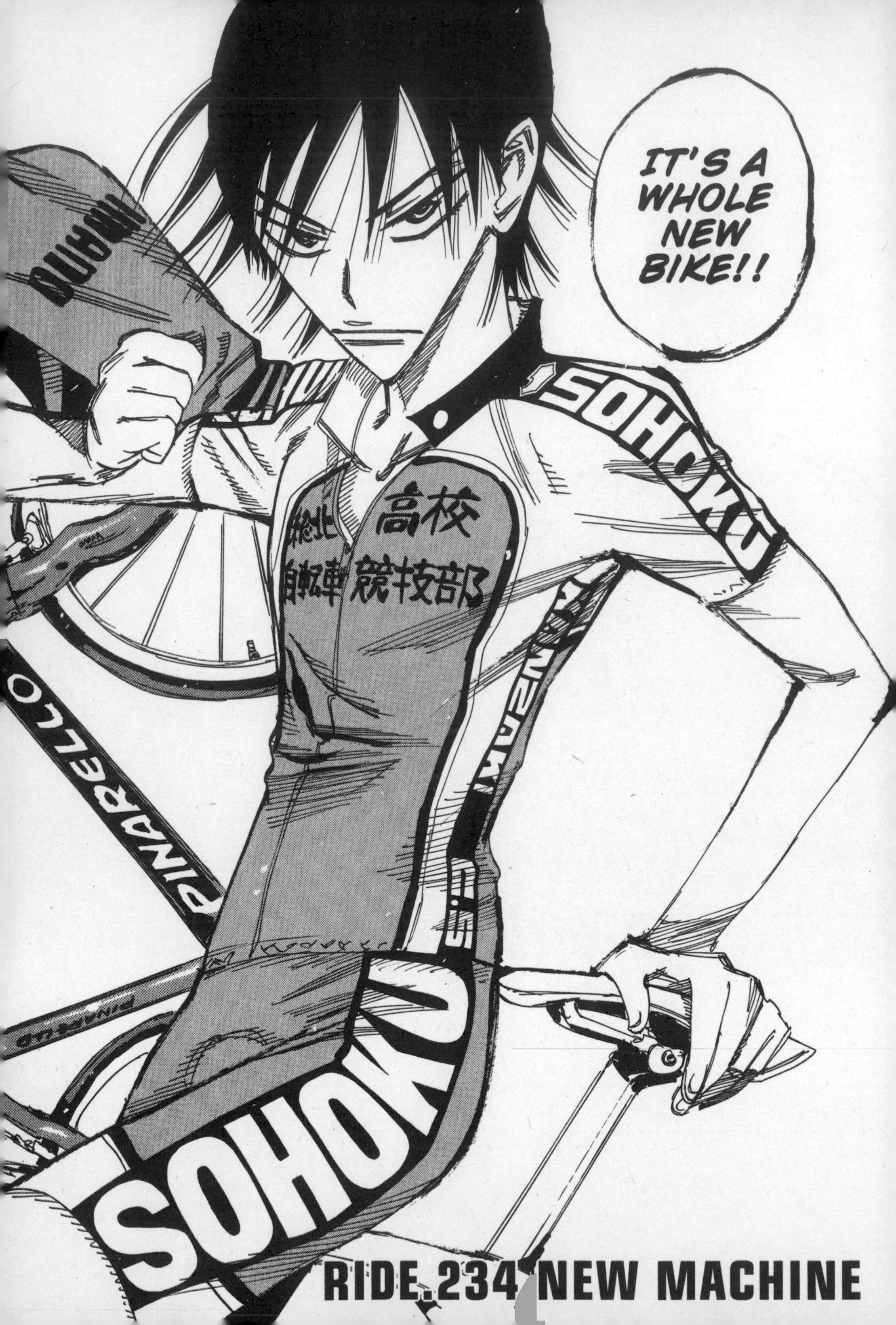
IT'S A WHOLE NEW BIKE!!
SOHOKU
総北高校
自転車競技部
PINARELLO
SOHOKU

RIDE.234 NEW MACHINE

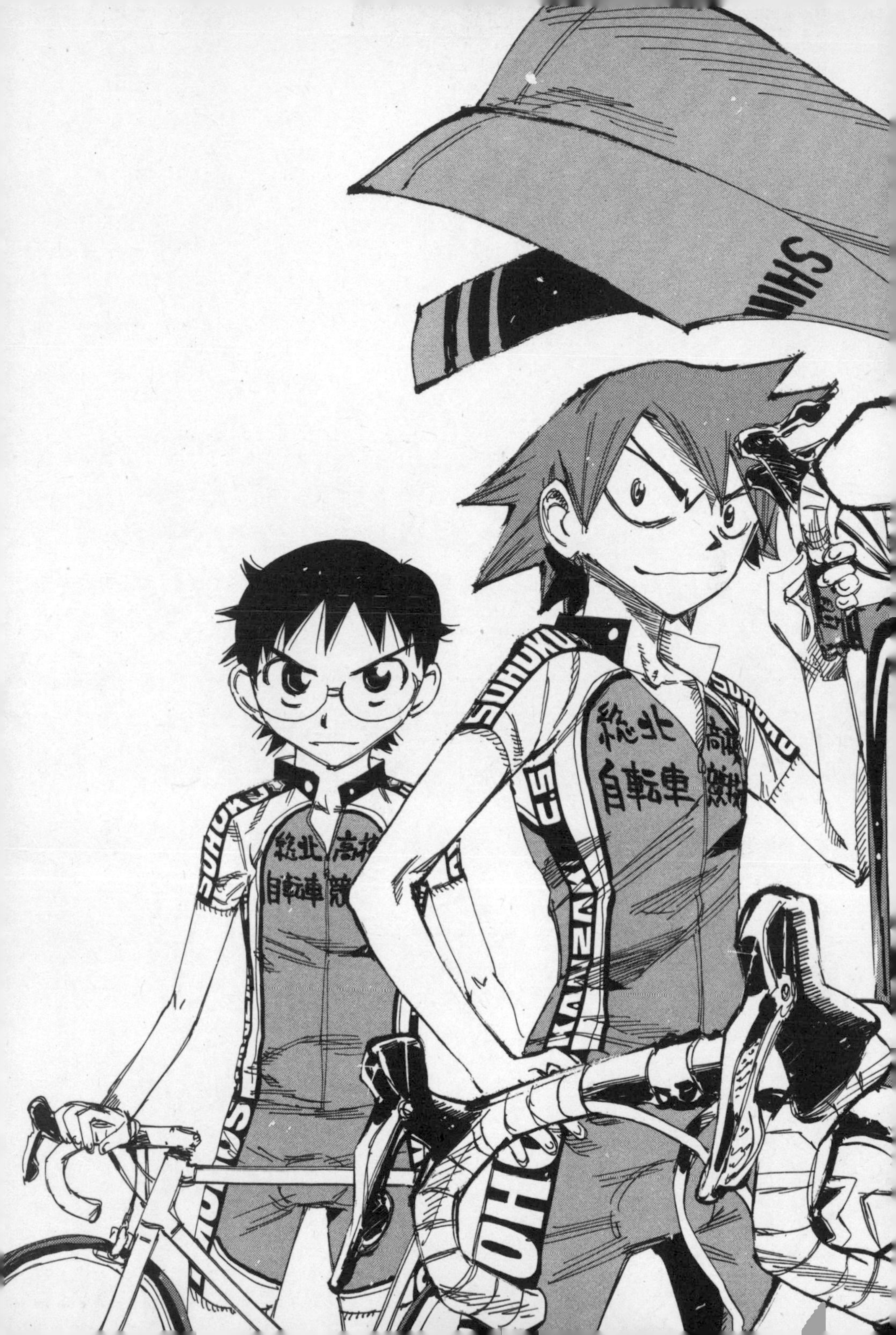
総北
自転車

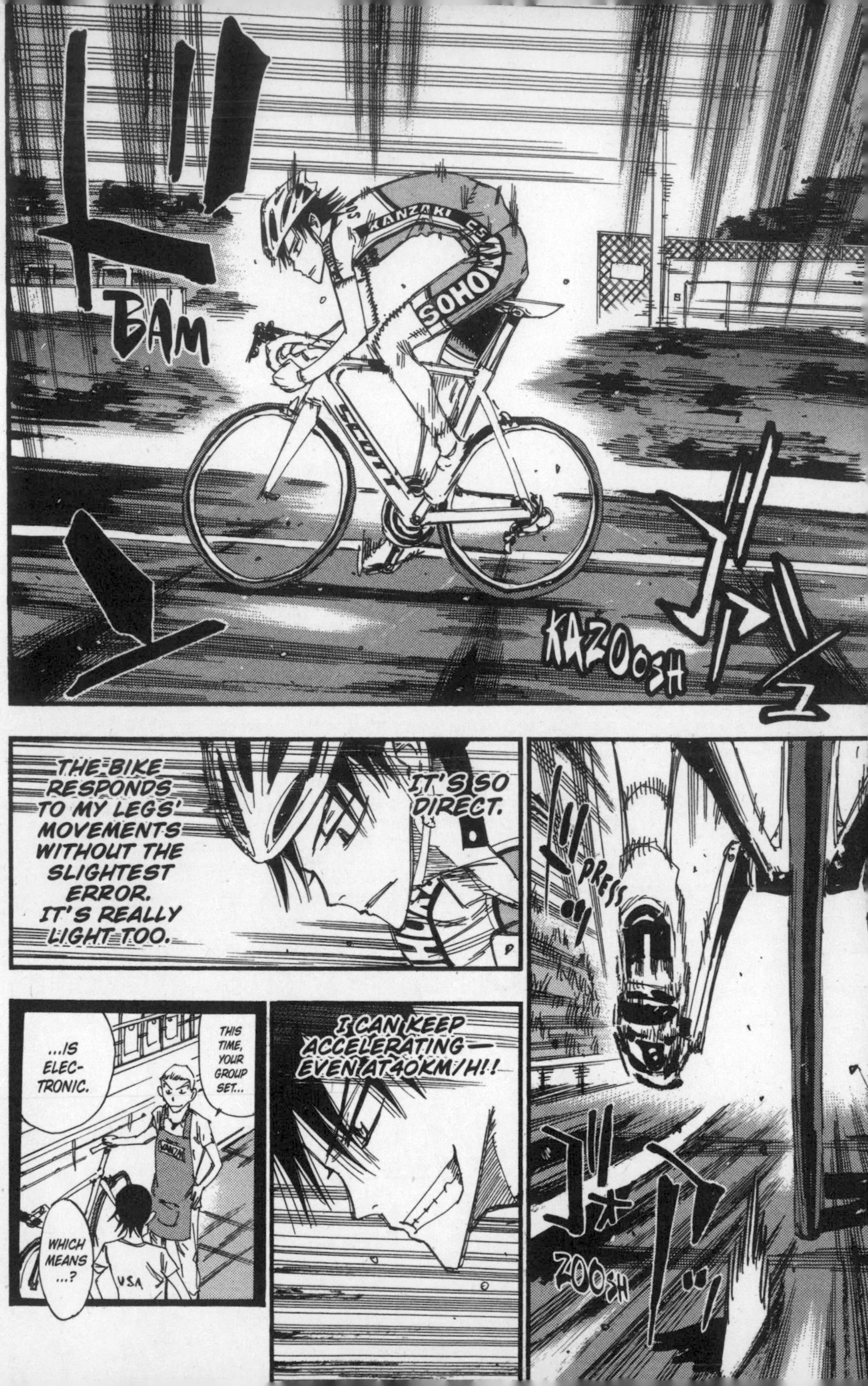
BAM
KAZOOSH
PRESS
ZOOSH
THE BIKE RESPONDS TO MY LEGS' MOVEMENTS WITHOUT THE SLIGHTEST ERROR. IT'S REALLY LIGHT TOO.
IT'S SO DIRECT.
I CAN KEEP ACCELERATING—EVEN AT 40KM/H!!
THIS TIME, YOUR GROUP SET...
...IS ELECTRONIC.
WHICH MEANS ...?

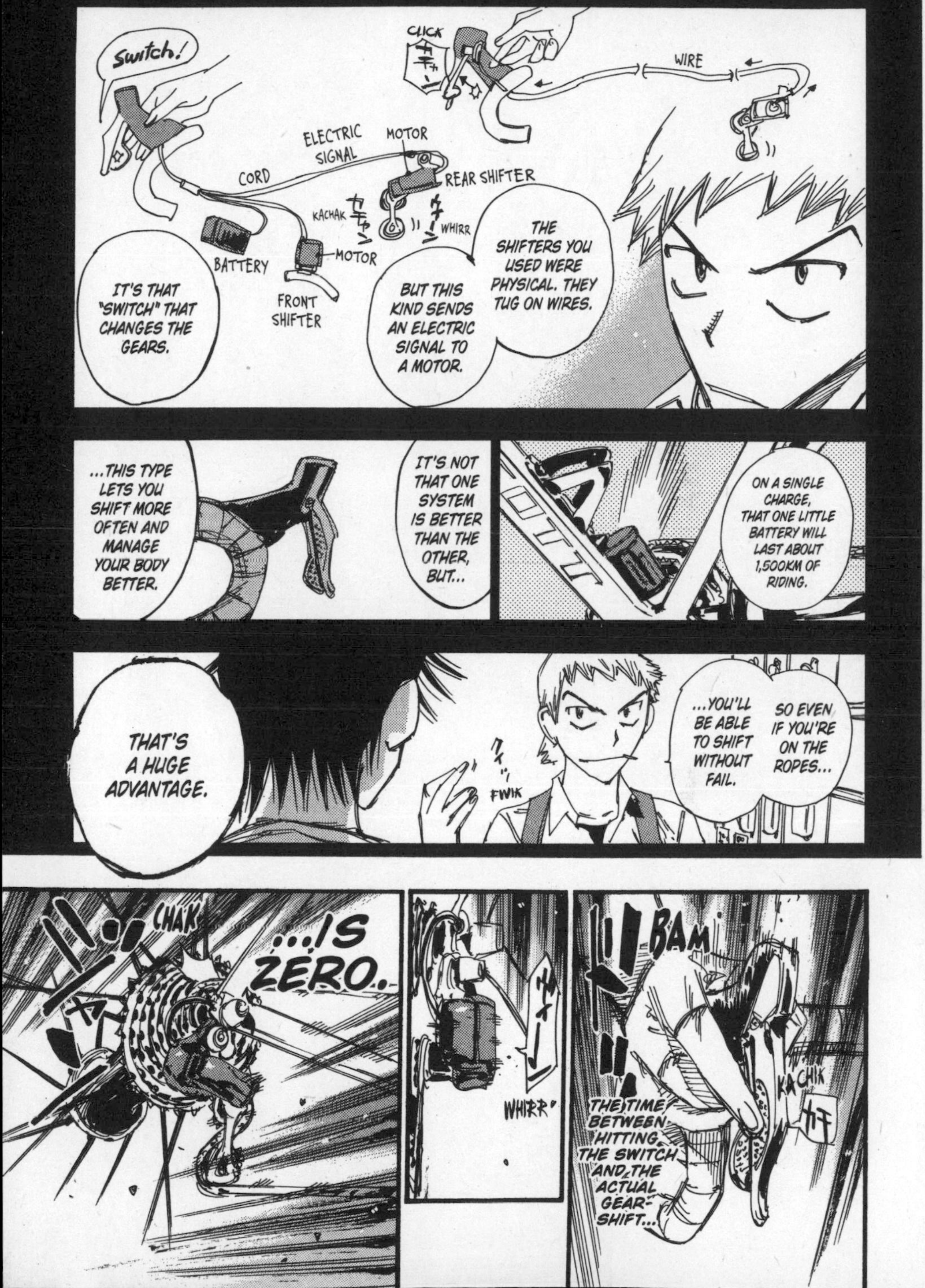
CLICK
WIRE
Switch!
ELECTRIC SIGNAL
MOTOR
REAR SHIFTER
CORD
KACHAK
WHIRR
BATTERY
MOTOR
FRONT SHIFTER
THE SHIFTERS YOU USED WERE PHYSICAL. THEY TUG ON WIRES.
BUT THIS KIND SENDS AN ELECTRIC SIGNAL TO A MOTOR.
IT'S THAT "SWITCH" THAT CHANGES THE GEARS.
ON A SINGLE CHARGE, THAT ONE LITTLE BATTERY WILL LAST ABOUT 1,500KM OF RIDING.
IT'S NOT THAT ONE SYSTEM IS BETTER THAN THE OTHER, BUT...
...THIS TYPE LETS YOU SHIFT MORE OFTEN AND MANAGE YOUR BODY BETTER.
SO EVEN IF YOU'RE ON THE ROPES...
...YOU'LL BE ABLE TO SHIFT WITHOUT FAIL.
FWIK
THAT'S A HUGE ADVANTAGE.
BAM
KACHIK
THE TIME BETWEEN HITTING THE SWITCH AND THE ACTUAL GEAR-SHIFT...
WHIRR
CHAK
...IS ZERO.

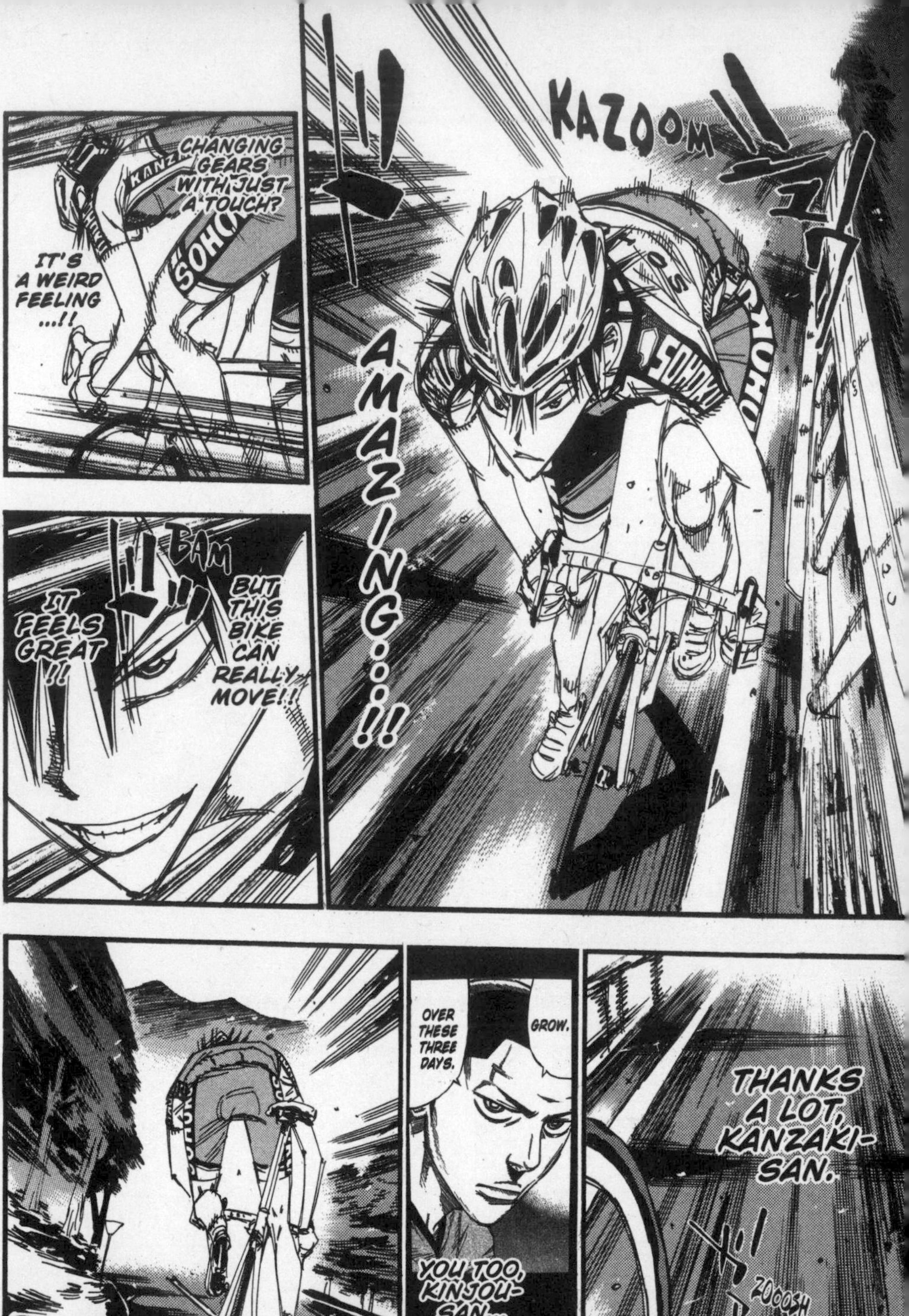
KAZOOM
AMAZING...!!
CHANGING GEARS WITH JUST A TOUCH?
IT'S A WEIRD FEELING...!!
BAM
BUT THIS BIKE CAN REALLY MOVE!!
IT FEELS GREAT!!
THANKS A LOT, KANZAKI-SAN.
ZOOOSH
GROW.
OVER THESE THREE DAYS.
YOU TOO, KINJOU-SAN...

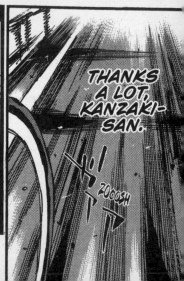

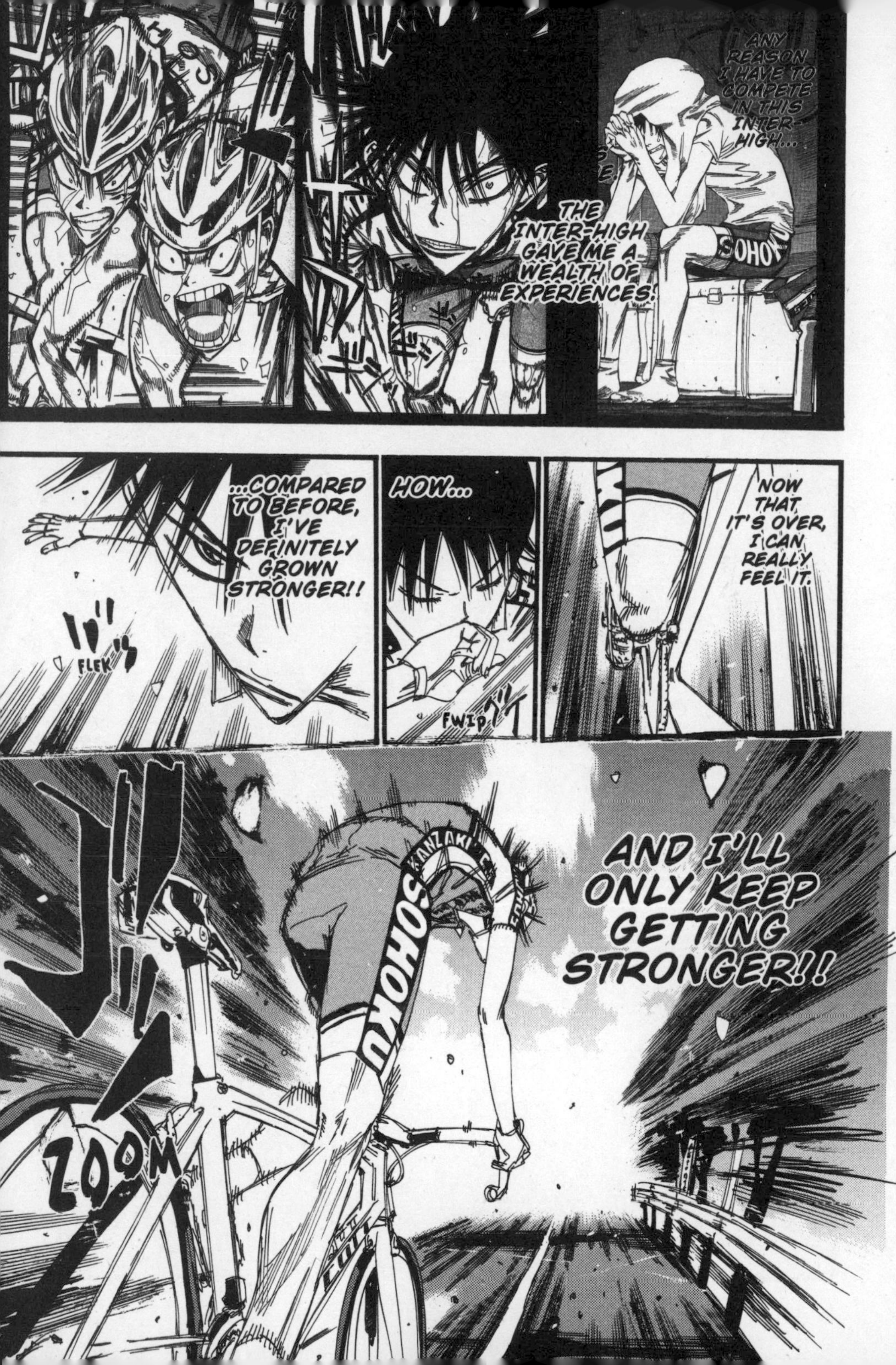
ANY REASON I HAVE TO COMPETE IN THIS INTER-HIGH...
THE INTER-HIGH GAVE ME A WEALTH OF EXPERIENCES!
NOW THAT IT'S OVER, I CAN REALLY FEEL IT.
HOW...
FWIP
...COMPARED TO BEFORE, I'VE DEFINITELY GROWN STRONGER!!
FLEK
AND I'LL ONLY KEEP GETTING STRONGER!!
ZOOM

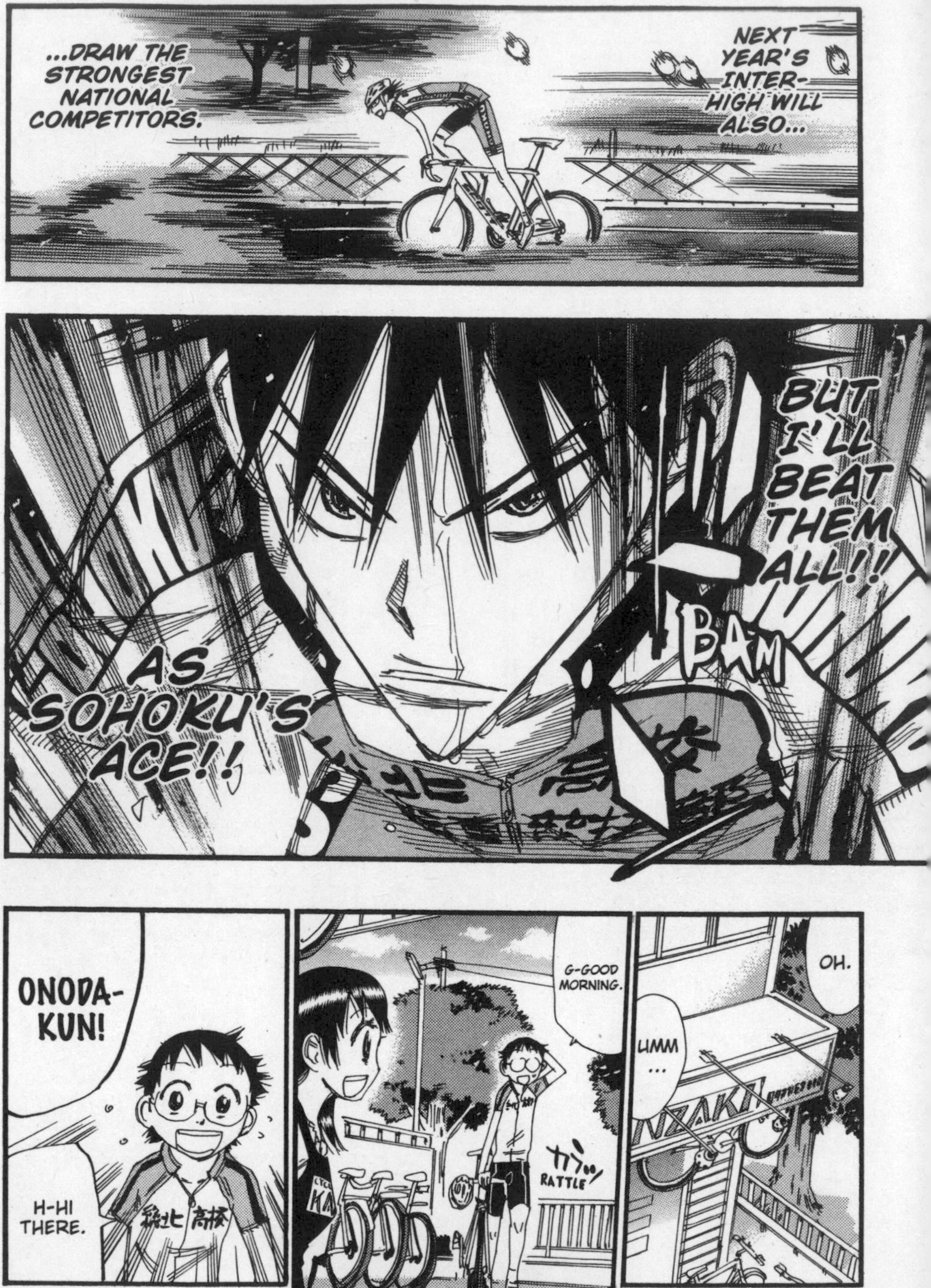
NEXT YEAR'S INTER-HIGH WILL ALSO...
...DRAW THE STRONGEST NATIONAL COMPETITORS.
BUT I'LL BEAT THEM ALL!!
BAM
AS SOHOKU'S ACE!!
OH.
UMM ...
G-GOOD MORNING.
RATTLE
ONODA-KUN!
H-HI THERE.

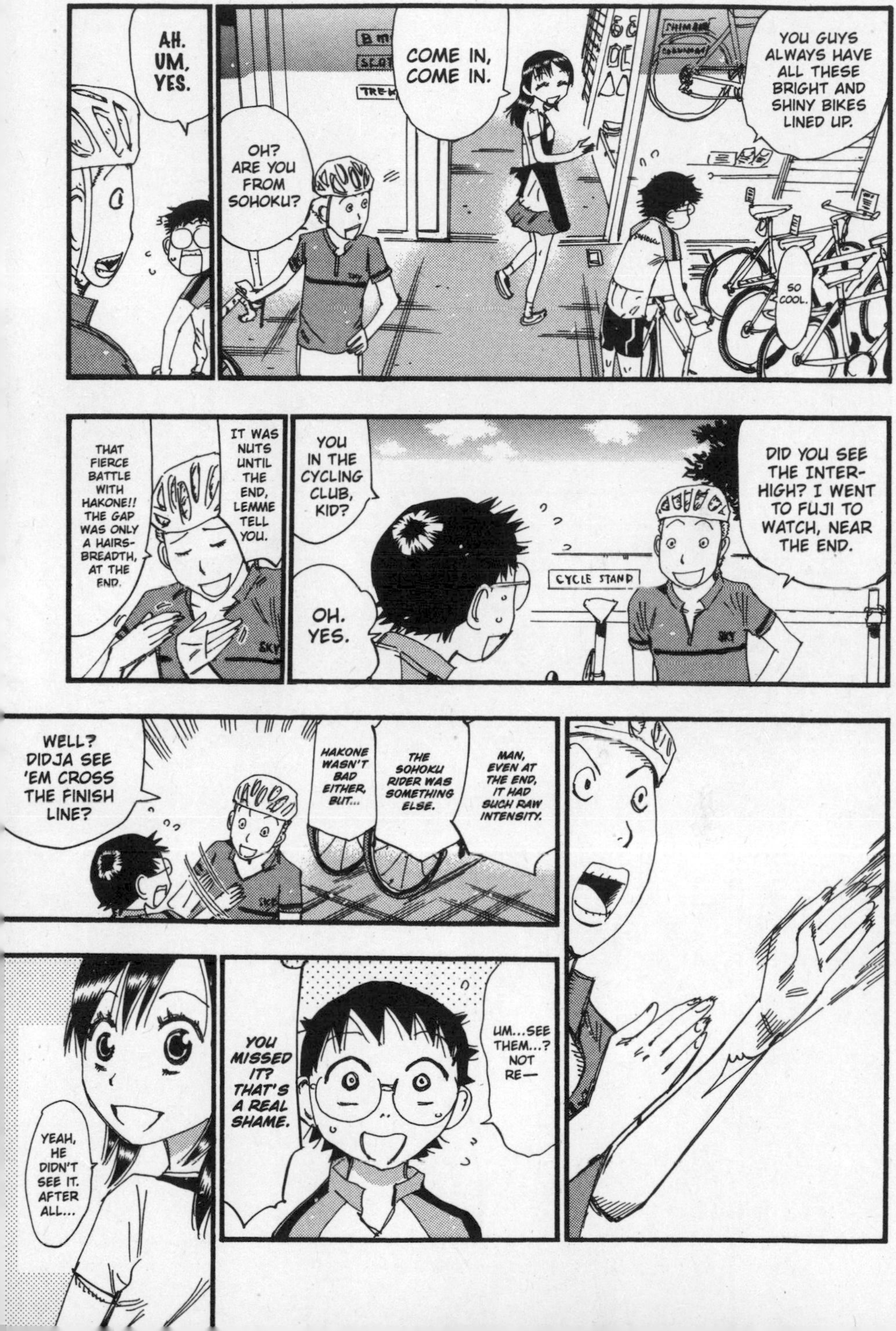
YOU GUYS ALWAYS HAVE ALL THESE BRIGHT AND SHINY BIKES LINED UP.
SO COOL.
COME IN, COME IN.
OH? ARE YOU FROM SOHOKU?
AH. UM, YES.
YOU IN THE CYCLING CLUB, KID?
OH. YES.
DID YOU SEE THE INTER-HIGH? I WENT TO FUJI TO WATCH, NEAR THE END.
CYCLE STAND
IT WAS NUTS UNTIL THE END, LEMME TELL YOU.
THAT FIERCE BATTLE WITH HAKONE!! THE GAP WAS ONLY A HAIRS-BREADTH, AT THE END.
MAN, EVEN AT THE END, IT HAD SUCH RAW INTENSITY.
THE SOHOKU RIDER WAS SOMETHING ELSE.
HAKONE WASN'T BAD EITHER, BUT...
WELL? DIDJA SEE 'EM CROSS THE FINISH LINE?
UM...SEE THEM...? NOT RE—
YOU MISSED IT? THAT'S A REAL SHAME.
YEAH, HE DIDN'T SEE IT. AFTER ALL...

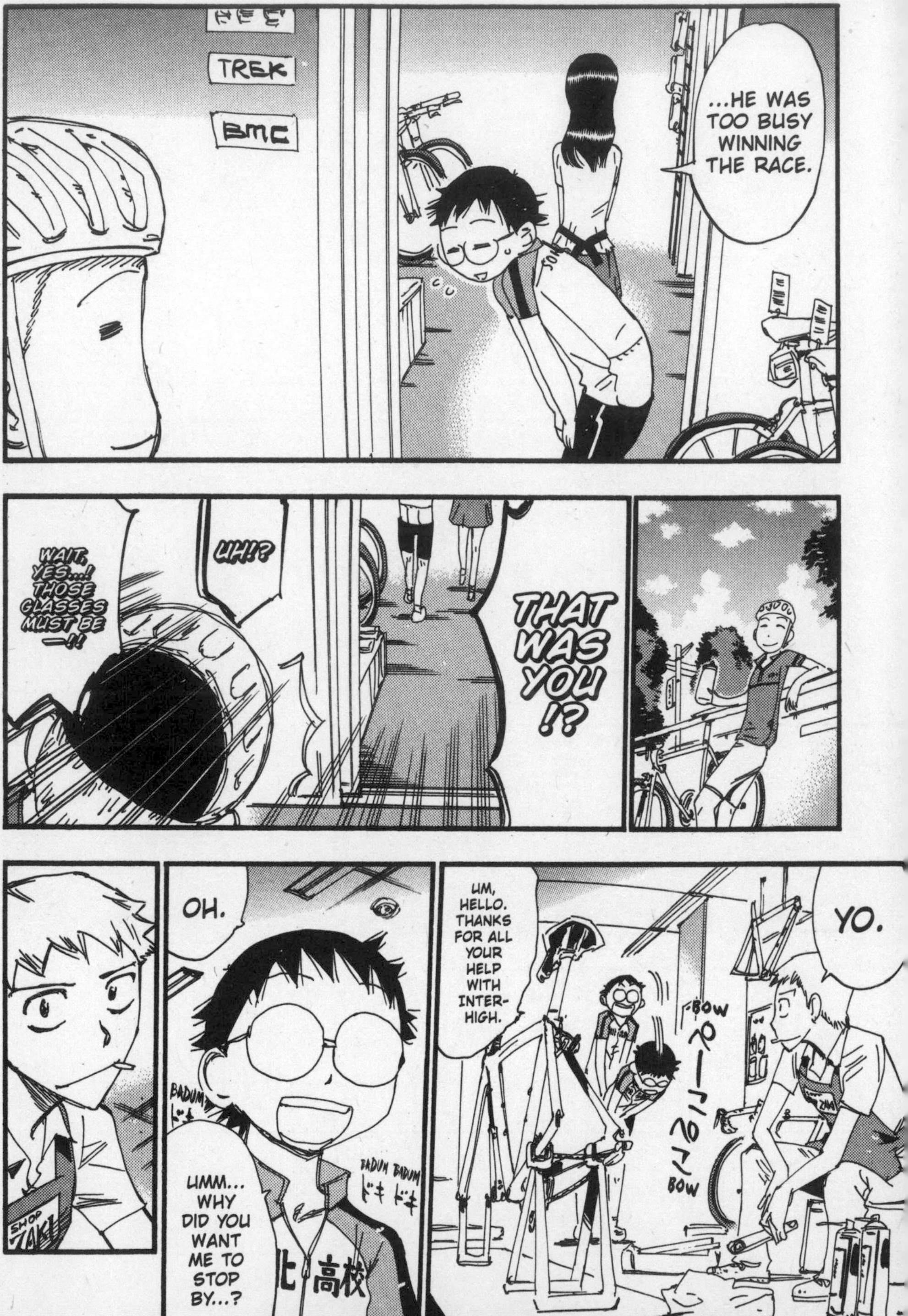
TREK
BMC
...HE WAS TOO BUSY WINNING THE RACE.
THAT WAS YOU!?
UH!?
WAIT, YES...! THOSE GLASSES MUST BE—!!
YO.
UM, HELLO. THANKS FOR ALL YOUR HELP WITH INTER-HIGH.
BOW
ペーコペコ
BOW
OH.
BADUM
ドキ
BADUM BADUM
ドキドキ
UMM... WHY DID YOU WANT ME TO STOP BY...?
北高校
SHOP

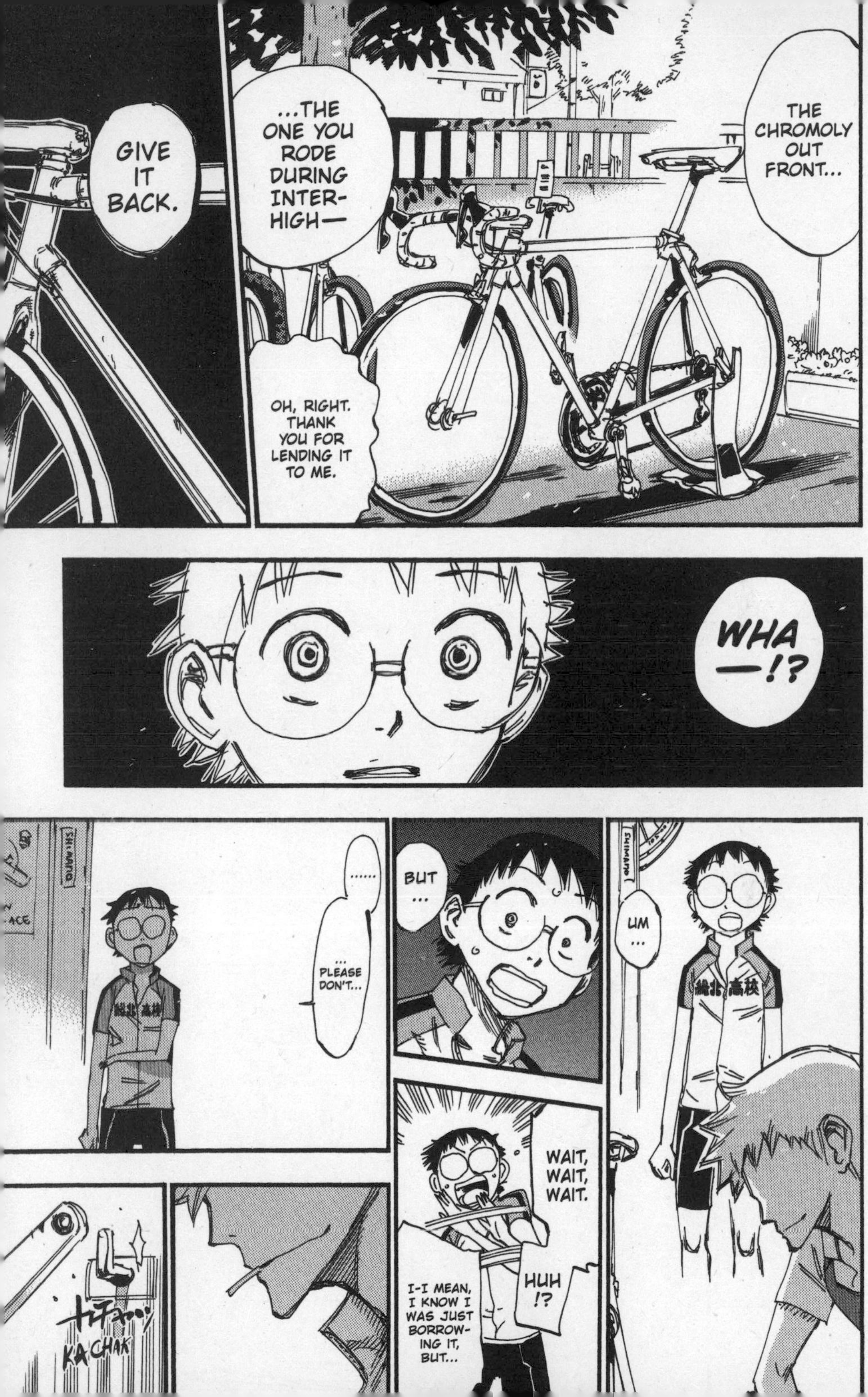
THE CHROMOLY OUT FRONT...
...THE ONE YOU RODE DURING INTER-HIGH—
OH, RIGHT. THANK YOU FOR LENDING IT TO ME.
GIVE IT BACK.
WHA—!?
UM ...
BUT ...
......
... PLEASE DON'T...
WAIT, WAIT, WAIT.
HUH !?
I-I MEAN, I KNOW I WAS JUST BORROWING IT, BUT...
KACHAK

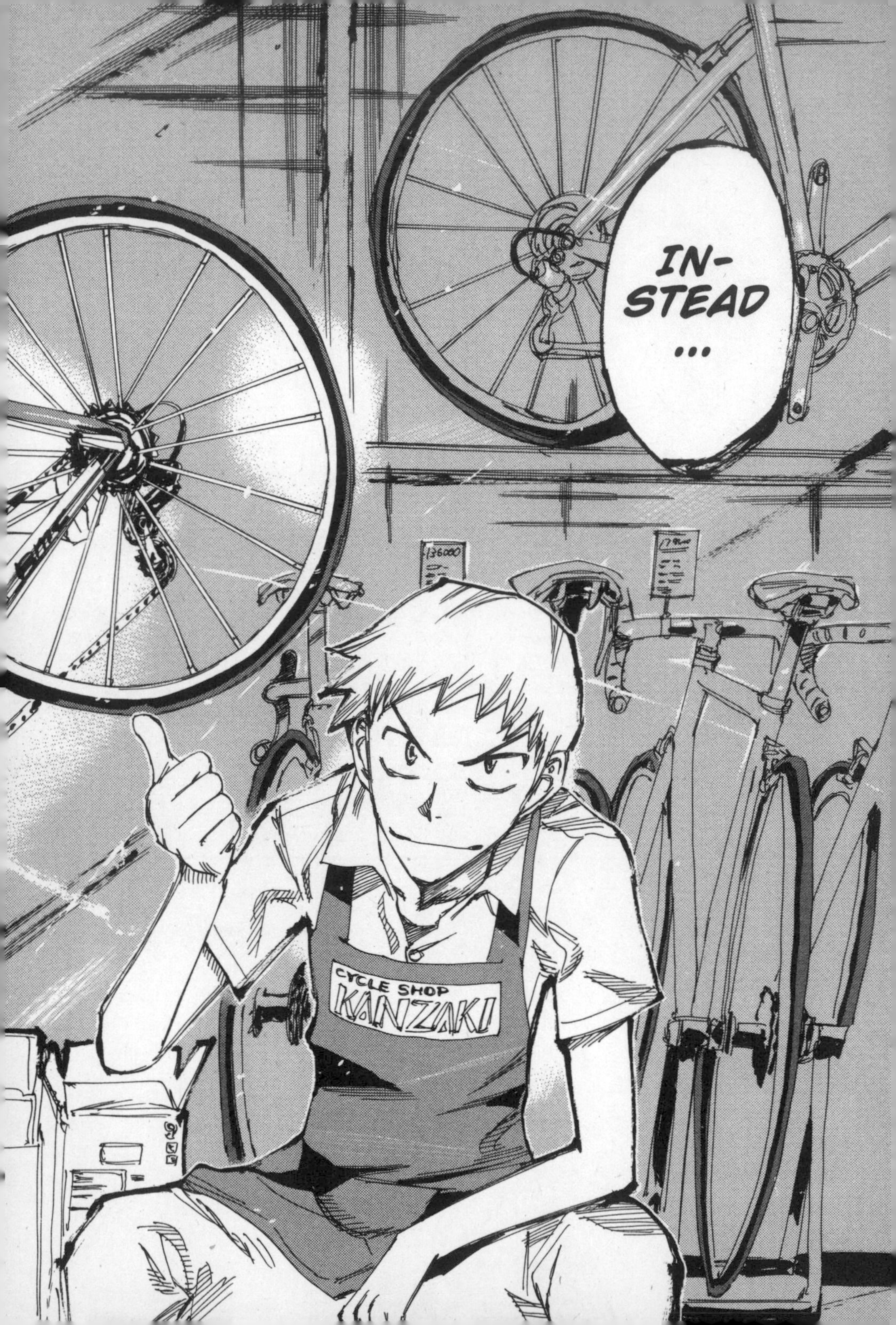
IN-STEAD ...
CYCLE SHOP KANZAKI

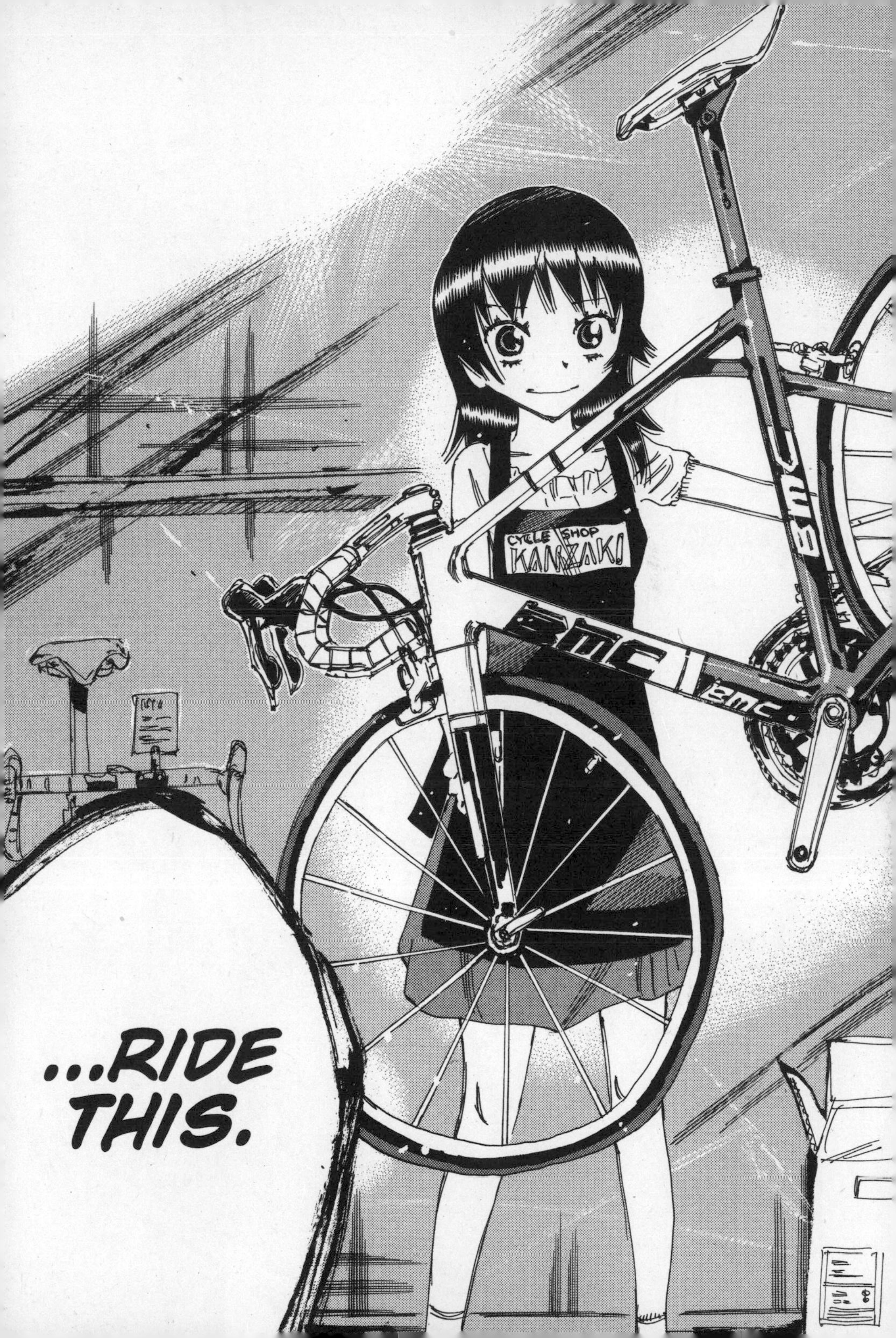
...RIDE THIS.
CYCLE SHOP KANZAKI
BMC

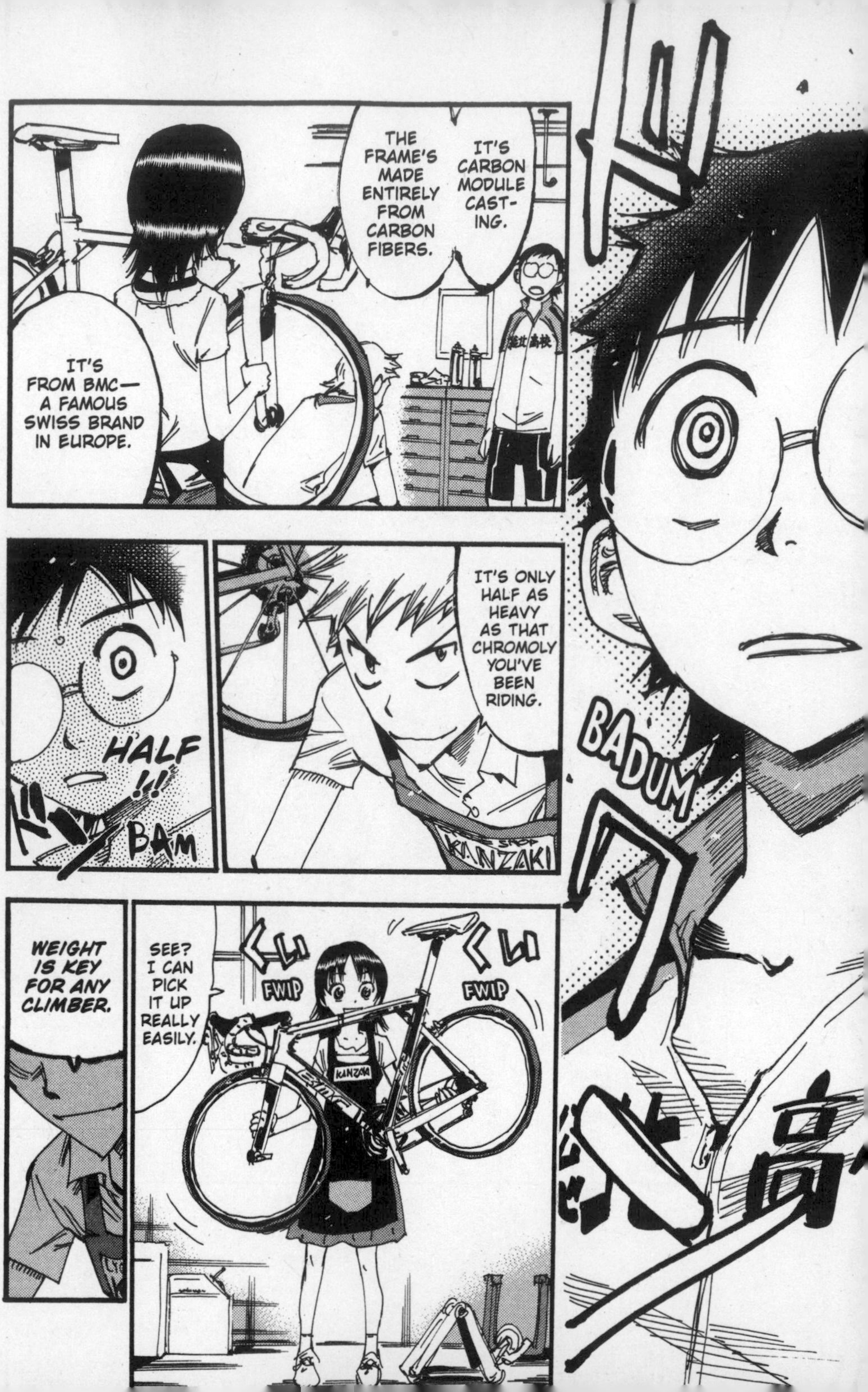
IT'S FROM BMC— A FAMOUS SWISS BRAND IN EUROPE.
THE FRAME'S MADE ENTIRELY FROM CARBON FIBERS.
IT'S CARBON MODULE CAST-ING.
IT'S ONLY HALF AS HEAVY AS THAT CHROMOLY YOU'VE BEEN RIDING.
HALF!!
BAM
BADUM
SEE? I CAN PICK IT UP REALLY EASILY.
FWIP
FWIP
WEIGHT IS KEY FOR ANY CLIMBER.

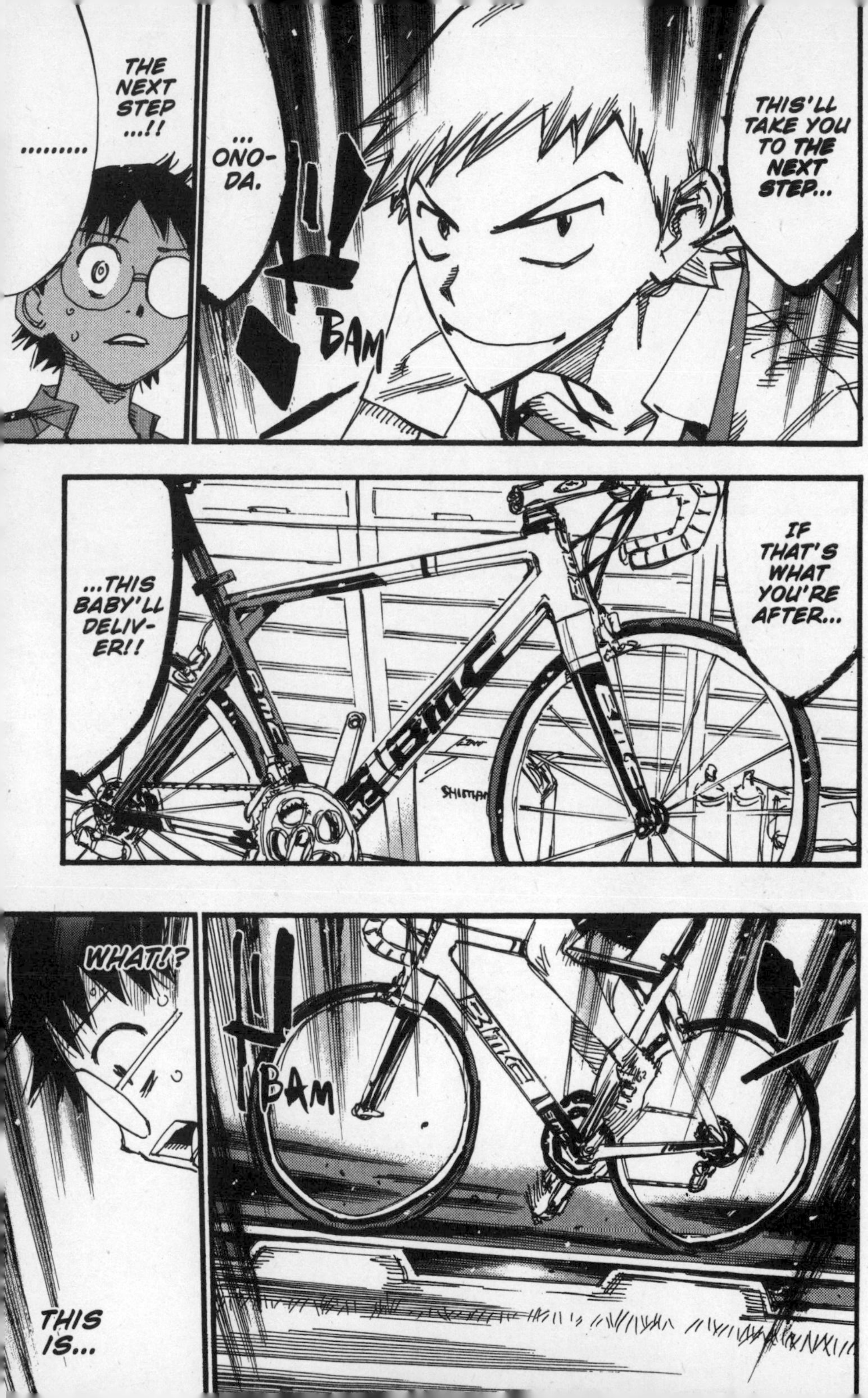
THIS'LL TAKE YOU TO THE NEXT STEP...
...ONO-DA.
BAM
THE NEXT STEP ...!!
....
IF THAT'S WHAT YOU'RE AFTER...
...THIS BABY'LL DELIVER!!
BAM
WHAT!?
THIS IS...

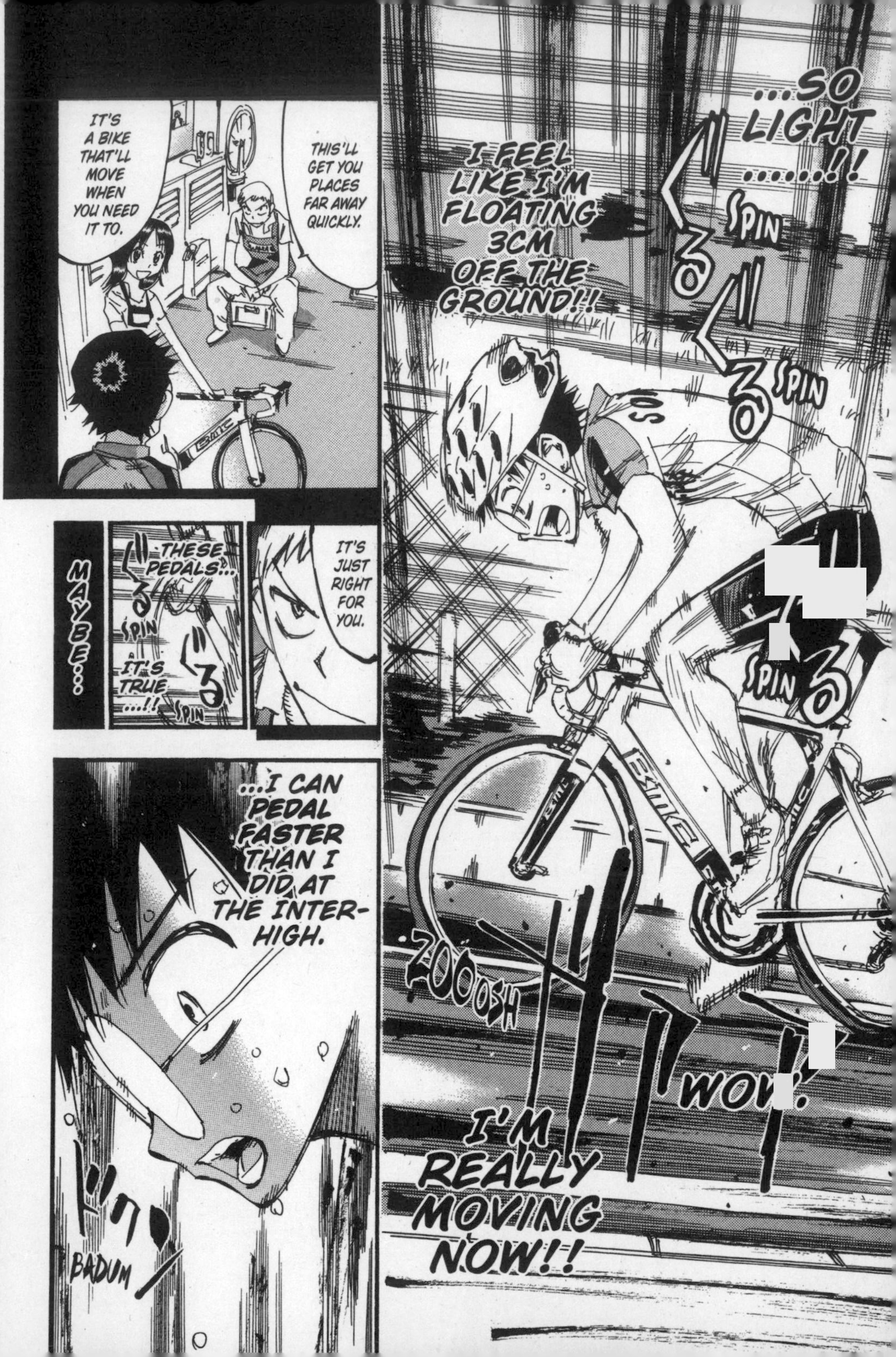
...SO LIGHT ......!!
I FEEL LIKE I'M FLOATING 3CM OFF THE GROUND!!
SPIN
SPIN
SPIN
ZOOOSH
WOW!
I'M REALLY MOVING NOW!!
THIS'LL GET YOU PLACES FAR AWAY QUICKLY.
IT'S A BIKE THAT'LL MOVE WHEN YOU NEED IT TO.
IT'S JUST RIGHT FOR YOU.
THESE PEDALS...
SPIN
IT'S TRUE ...!!
SPIN
MAYBE...
...I CAN PEDAL FASTER THAN I DID AT THE INTER-HIGH.
BADUM

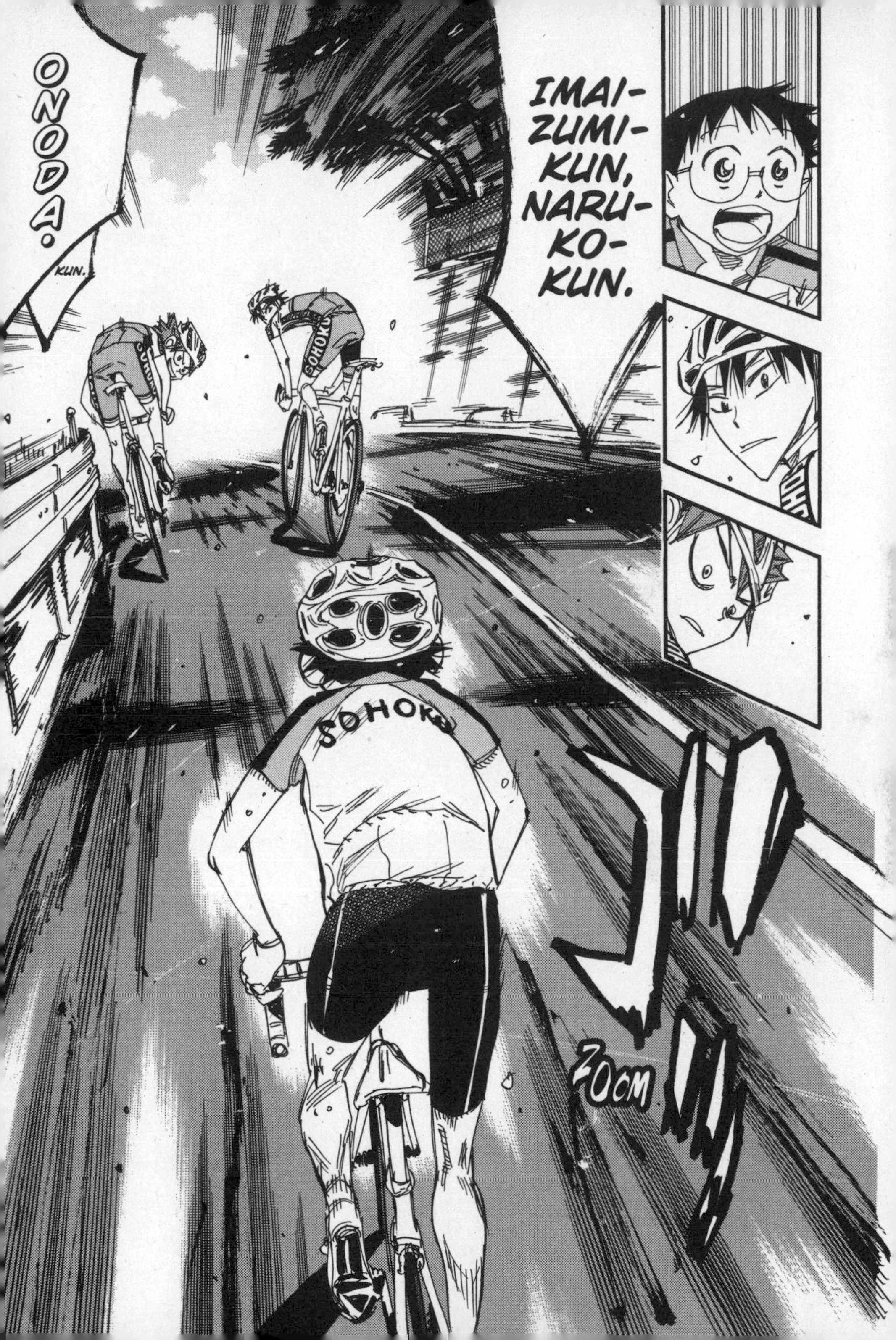
IMAI-
ZUMI-
KUN,
NARU-
KO-
KUN.
ONODA.
KUN.
ZOOM

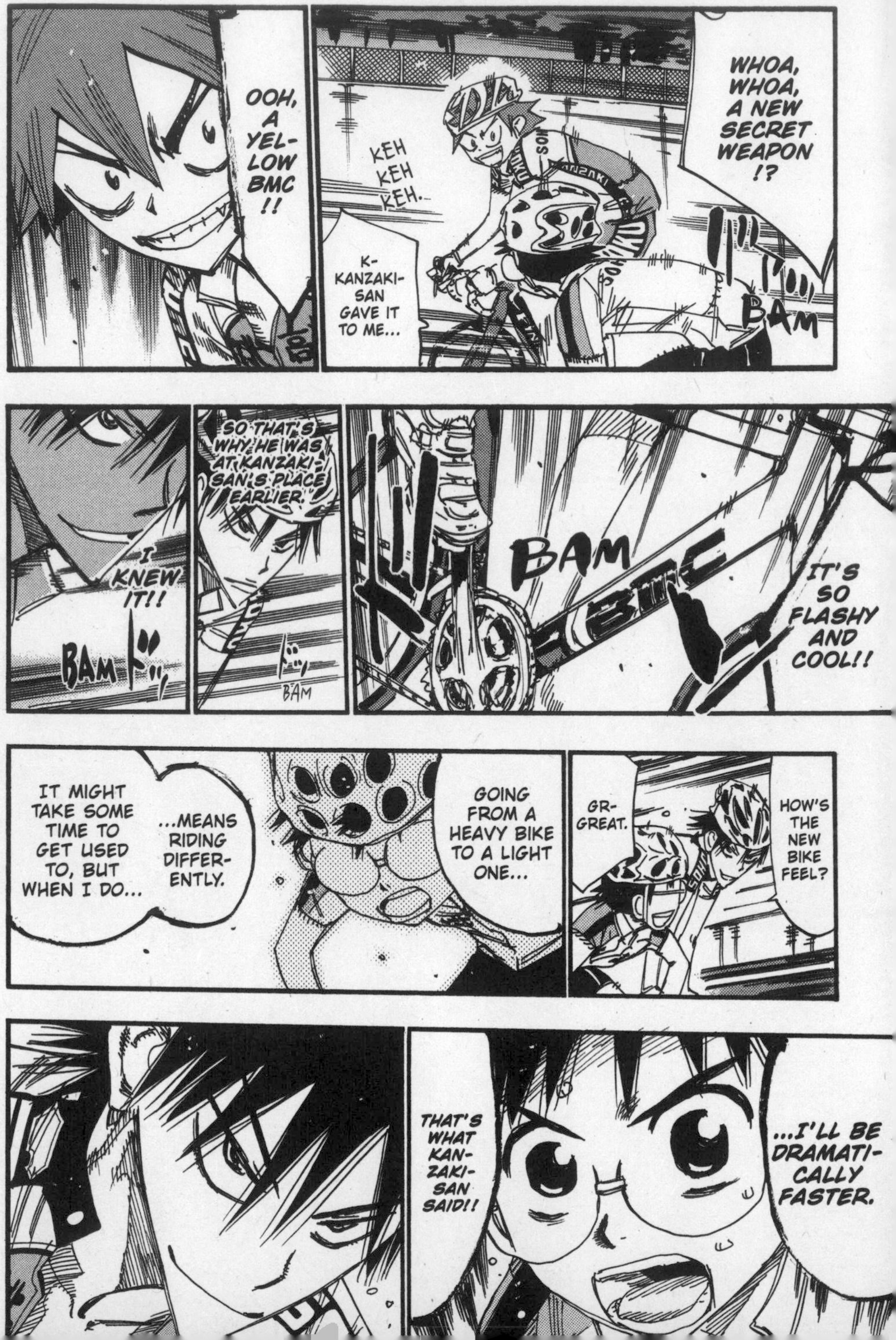
WHOA, WHOA, A NEW SECRET WEAPON !?
BAM
KEH KEH KEH.
K-KANZAKI-SAN GAVE IT TO ME...
OOH, A YEL-LOW BMC !!
IT'S SO FLASHY AND COOL!!
BAM
SO THAT'S WHY HE WAS AT KANZAKI-SAN'S PLACE EARLIER.
BAM
I KNEW IT!!
BAM
HOW'S THE NEW BIKE FEEL?
GR-GREAT.
GOING FROM A HEAVY BIKE TO A LIGHT ONE...
...MEANS RIDING DIFFER-ENTLY.
IT MIGHT TAKE SOME TIME TO GET USED TO, BUT WHEN I DO...
...I'LL BE DRAMATI-CALLY FASTER.
THAT'S WHAT KAN-ZAKI-SAN SAID!!

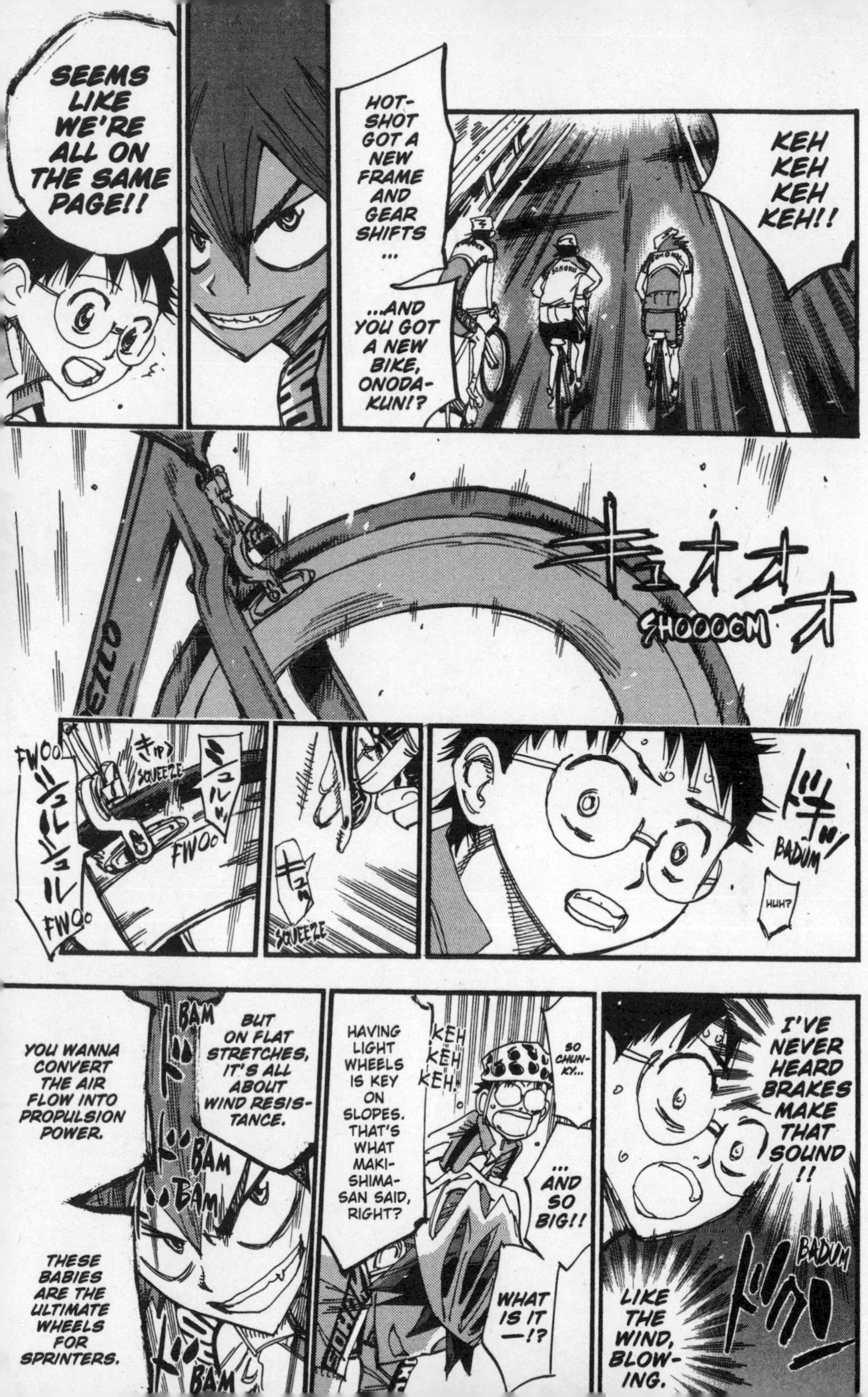
KEH KEH KEH KEH!!
HOT-SHOT GOT A NEW FRAME AND GEAR SHIFTS...
...AND YOU GOT A NEW BIKE, ONODA-KUN!?
SEEMS LIKE WE'RE ALL ON THE SAME PAGE!!
SHOOOOM
BADUM
HUH?
SQUEEZE
SQUEEZE
FWOO
FWOO
FWOO
I'VE NEVER HEARD BRAKES MAKE THAT SOUND!!
BADUM
LIKE THE WIND, BLOWING.
SO CHUNKY...
...AND SO BIG!!
KEH KEH KEH
HAVING LIGHT WHEELS IS KEY ON SLOPES. THAT'S WHAT MAKISHIMA-SAN SAID, RIGHT?
WHAT IS IT—!?
BAM
BUT ON FLAT STRETCHES, IT'S ALL ABOUT WIND RESISTANCE.
YOU WANNA CONVERT THE AIR FLOW INTO PROPULSION POWER.
BAM
BAM
THESE BABIES ARE THE ULTIMATE WHEELS FOR SPRINTERS.
BAM

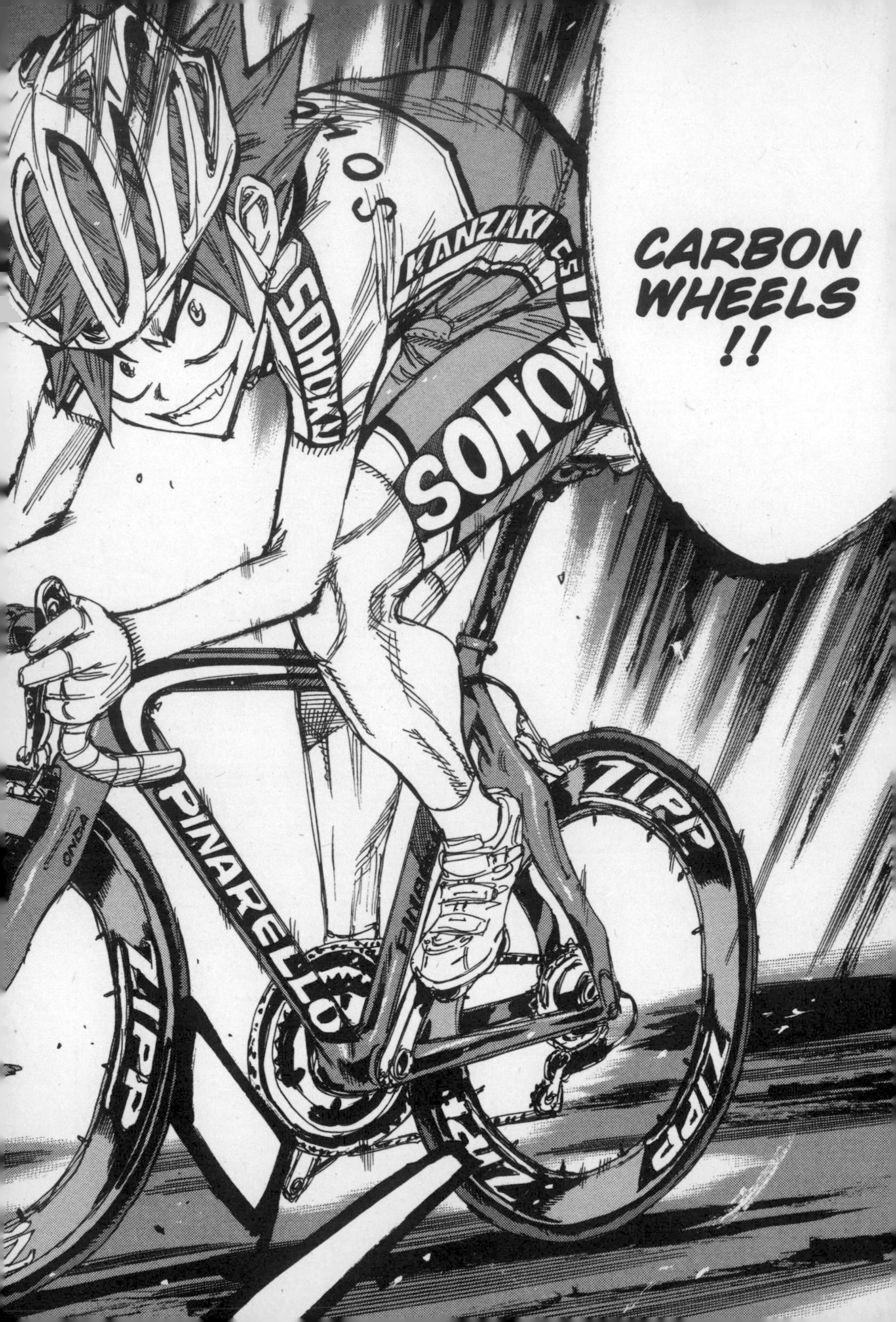
CARBON WHEELS !!

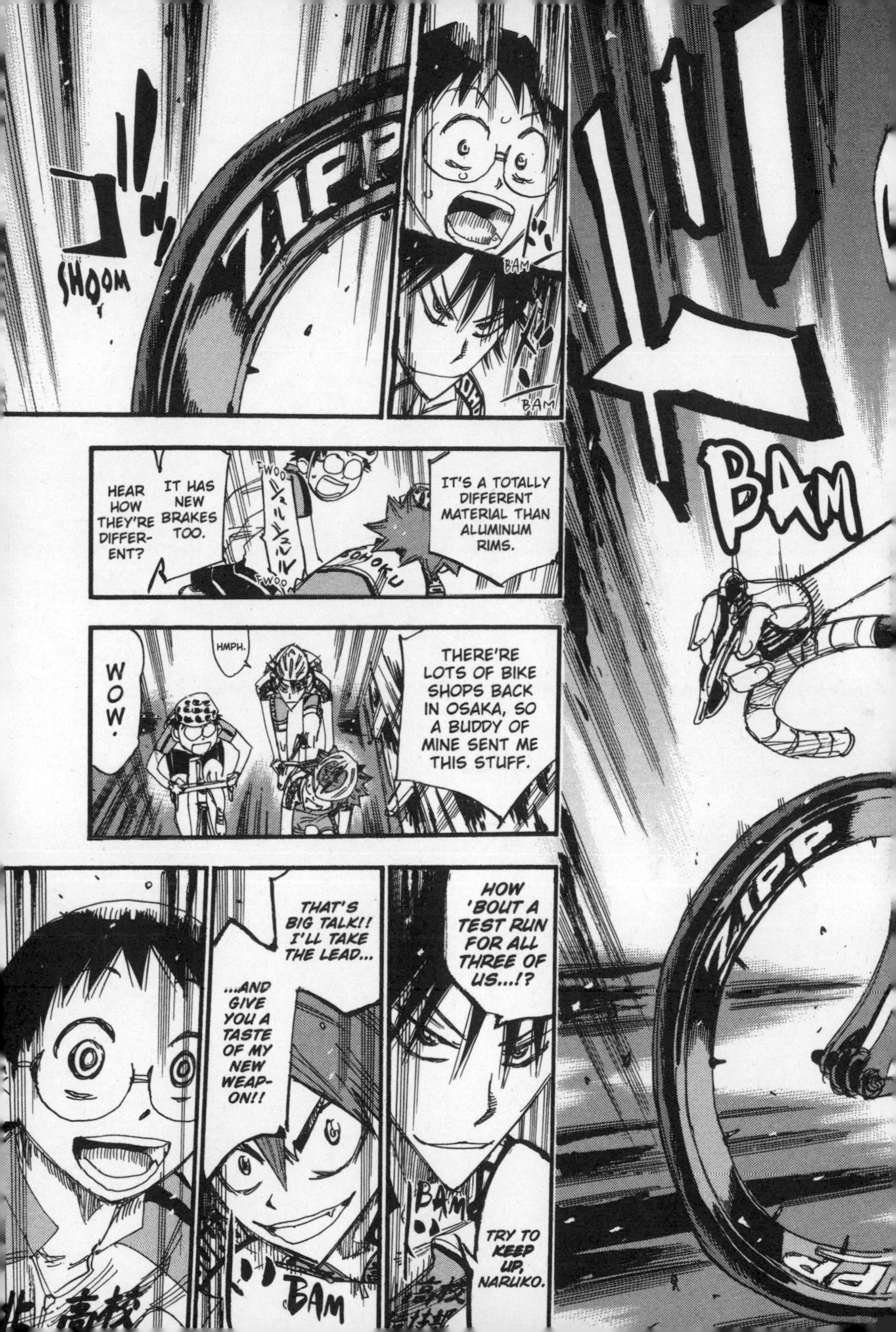
BAM
BAM
BAM
SHOOM
IT'S A TOTALLY DIFFERENT MATERIAL THAN ALUMINUM RIMS.
FWOO
FWOO
IT HAS NEW BRAKES TOO.
HEAR HOW THEY'RE DIFFER-ENT?
THERE'RE LOTS OF BIKE SHOPS BACK IN OSAKA, SO A BUDDY OF MINE SENT ME THIS STUFF.
HMPH.
WOW.
HOW 'BOUT A TEST RUN FOR ALL THREE OF US...!?
TRY TO KEEP UP, NARUKO.
BAM
THAT'S BIG TALK!! I'LL TAKE THE LEAD...
...AND GIVE YOU A TASTE OF MY NEW WEAP-ON!!
BAM

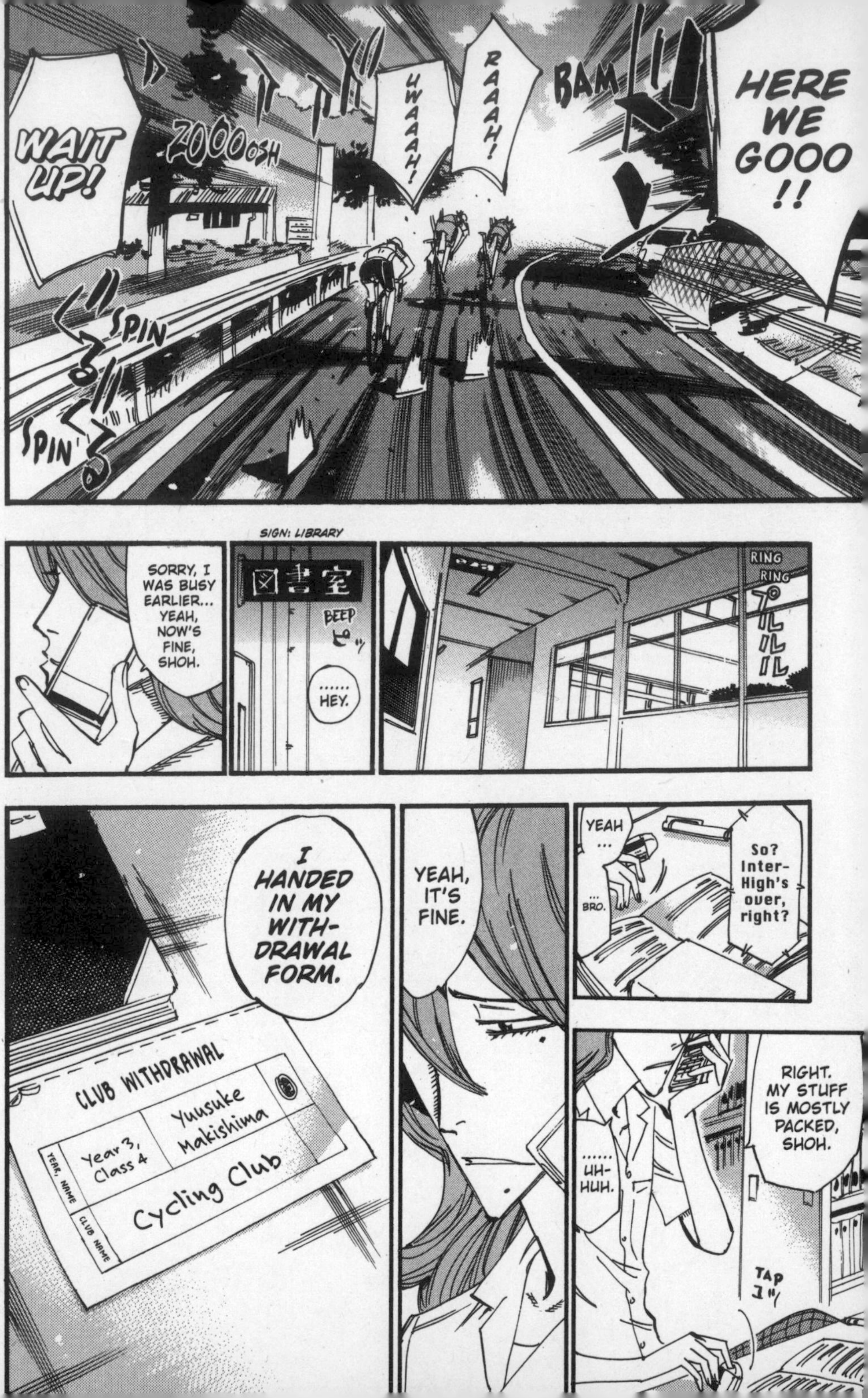
HERE WE GOOO!!
BAM
RAAAAH!
UWAAAAH!
ZOOOOSH
WAIT UP!
SPIN
SPIN
RING RING
プルルル
SIGN: LIBRARY
図書室
BEEP
ピッ
......HEY.
SORRY, I WAS BUSY EARLIER... YEAH, NOW'S FINE, SHOH.
So? Inter-High's over, right?
YEAH...
...BRO.
RIGHT. MY STUFF IS MOSTLY PACKED, SHOH.
......UH-HUH.
TAP
YEAH, IT'S FINE.
I HANDED IN MY WITHDRAWAL FORM.
CLUB WITHDRAWAL
YEAR, NAME
Year 3, Class 4
Yuusuke Makishima
CLUB NAME
Cycling Club

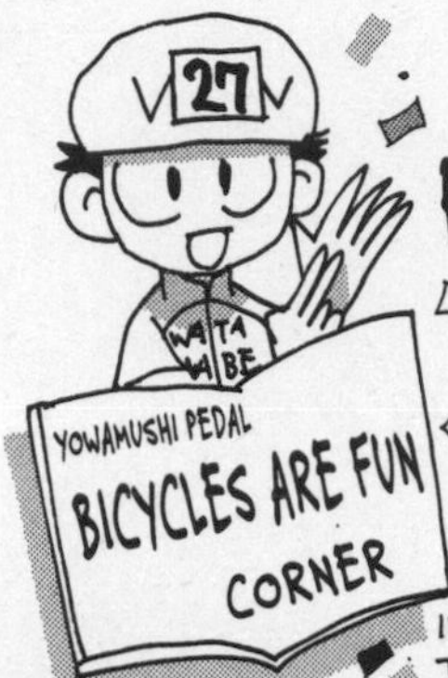
27
WATANABE
YOWAMUSHI PEDAL
BICYCLES ARE FUN
CORNER

LET'S TALK: FINALLY, THE INTER-HIGH GOAL!!!

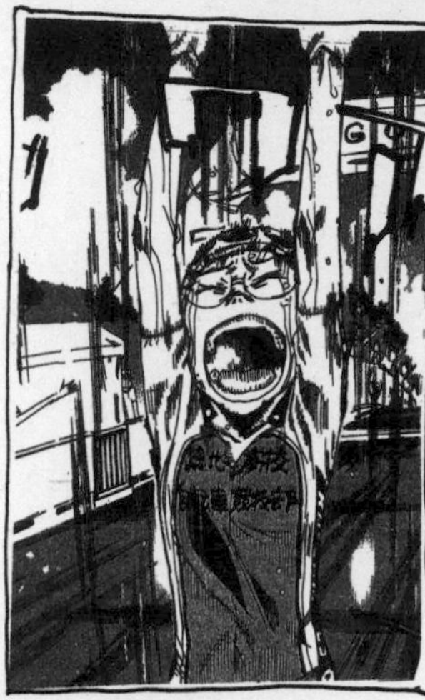

IN THIS VOLUME, WE FINALLY REACHED THE END OF THE LONG, LONG BATTLE THAT WAS INTER-HIGH!! IT STARTED IN OMNIBUS 5 (RIDE.71)—AND THIS IS OMNIBUS 14—SO THAT MEANS...............

THE RACE SPANNED **TEN WHOLE OMNIBUSES!!** THEY DID A LOT OF RIDING (LOL). SPENDING TEN OMNIBUSES ON IT MIGHT MAKE IT "MANGA HISTORY'S LONGEST-EVER SINGLE SPORTING EVENT" (LOL). FOR THIS STORY, I HAD ALWAYS MAPPED OUT THE LITTLE DETAILS IN ADVANCE, BUT WHEN IT CAME TIME TO DRAW THEM, THINGS OFTEN ENDED UP DIFFERENT THAN THE ORIGINAL PLAN (LOL).

(THINKING IT UP IN MY HEAD AND DRAWING IT OUT ARE TWO VERY DIFFERENT THINGS)

FOR INSTANCE, I HAD INTENDED TO HAVE MANAMI HELP ONODA AFTER THE LATTER FELL OVER ON DAY 1, BUT...ONODA GOT BACK UP AND KEPT RIDING ALL ON HIS OWN!! THAT ALLOWED MAKISHIMA-SAN TO JUMP AHEAD, WHICH WORKED OUT (IT WOULD'VE ALL BEEN FOR NOTHING IF ONODA HAD GOTTEN HELP (LOL)). AND WHEN TADOKORO SLOWED DOWN ON DAY 2—THAT WAS ANOTHER THING I HAD PLANNED FOR THE MIDDLE SECTION, BUT I NEVER IMAGINED HE'D COME TO A GRINDING HALT LIKE HE DID (LOL). I ALSO THOUGHT ABOUT HAVING MIDOUSUJI-KUN DROP OUT ON DAY 2, BUT HE ENDED UP SURVIVING ALL THE WAY TO THE FINAL 3KM ON DAY 3. FINALLY, THE PLAN WAS TO HAVE MANAMI AND ONODA EXPEND ALL THEIR STRENGTH AND JUST SORT OF LIMP ACROSS THE FINISH LINE, BUT......AFTER I STARTED DRAWING, IT HAD TO BE ALL "FULL-POWER GOAL"! THIS SERIES IS SUCH A DELIGHT TO DRAW, SINCE EVEN I CAN'T ALWAYS SEE WHAT'S COMING NEXT. THE ONE THING I ALWAYS STRIVE FOR IS SCENES THAT ARE FUN AND INTERESTING BECAUSE THE CHARACTERS ARE GIVING IT THEIR ALL.

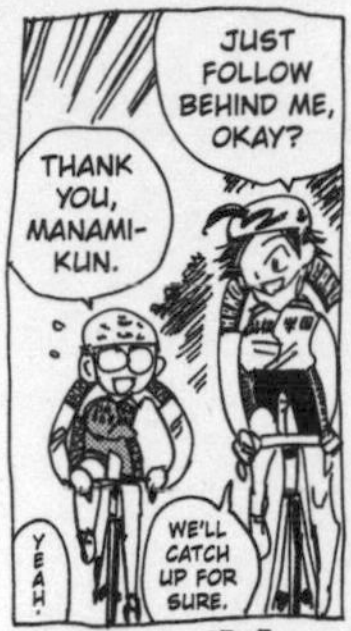
JUST FOLLOW BEHIND ME, OKAY?
THANK YOU, MANAMI-KUN.
WE'LL CATCH UP FOR SURE.
YEAH.
RIDE.89—A SCENE THAT MIGHT'VE BEEN

HOWEVER...

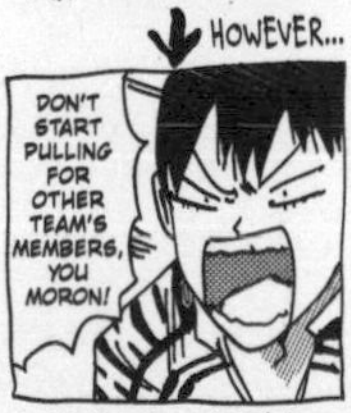
DON'T START PULLING FOR OTHER TEAM'S MEMBERS, YOU MORON!
...ARAKITA WOULD'VE BEEN MAD AS HELL (LOL)

THANKS FOR YOUR CONTINUED SUPPORT OF *YOWAMUSHI PEDAL!!*

THIS STORY'S NOT OVER YET!!

WE GOT THROUGH THE INTER-HIGH IN ONE PIECE! THANK YOU TO MY EDITOR, STAFF, EVERYONE INVOLVED, AND OF COURSE, TO YOU—THE READERS!!

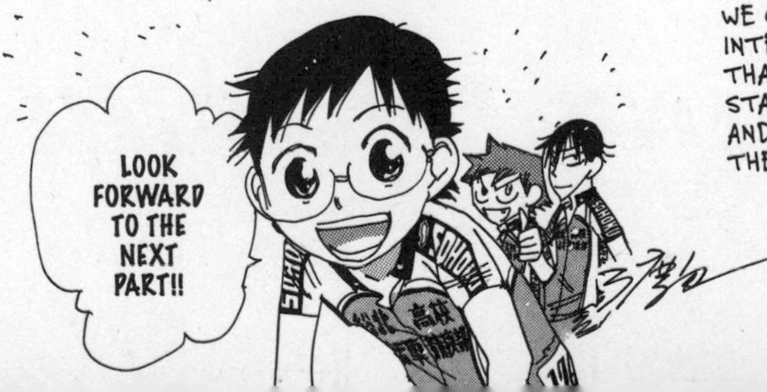
LOOK FORWARD TO THE NEXT PART!!

2013. 3

YOWAMUSHI
PEDAL

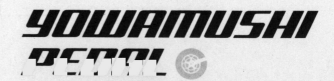

RIDE.235 FINAL RIDE ON MT. MINEGAYAMA

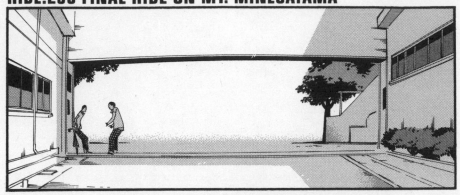

CLUB WITHDRAWAL

| Year 3, Class 4 | Yuusuke Makishima |

Cycling Club

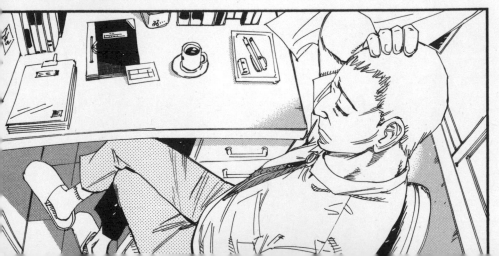

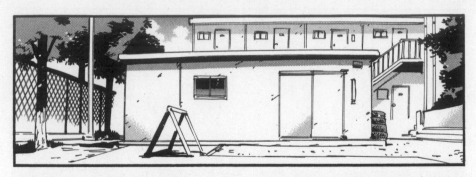

WHY THE LONG FACE, ME? SHOH...

AT THE INTER-HIGH...

...I FUL-FILLED MY DREAM.

I TOOK THE PEAK, SHOH.

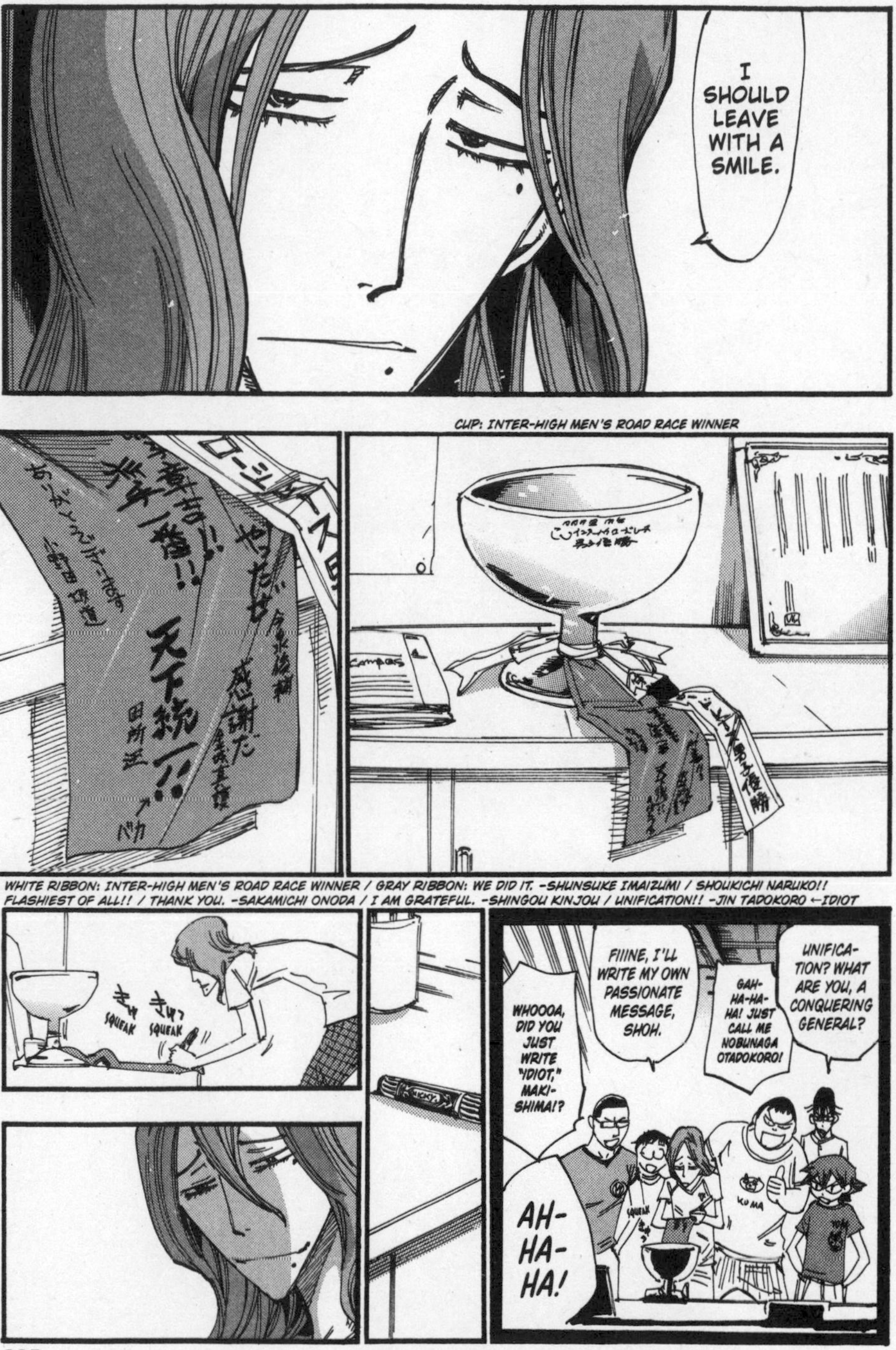
I SHOULD LEAVE WITH A SMILE.
CUP: INTER-HIGH MEN'S ROAD RACE WINNER
WHITE RIBBON: INTER-HIGH MEN'S ROAD RACE WINNER / GRAY RIBBON: WE DID IT. -SHUNSUKE IMAIZUMI / SHOUKICHI NARUKO!! FLASHIEST OF ALL!! / THANK YOU. -SAKAMICHI ONODA / I AM GRATEFUL. -SHINGOU KINJOU / UNIFICATION!! -JIN TADOKORO ←IDIOT
UNIFICATION? WHAT ARE YOU, A CONQUERING GENERAL?
GAH-HA-HA! JUST CALL ME NOBUNAGA OTADOKORO!
FIIINE, I'LL WRITE MY OWN PASSIONATE MESSAGE, SHOH.
WHOOOA, DID YOU JUST WRITE "IDIOT," MAKI-SHIMA!?
AH-HA-HA!
SQUEAK
SQUEAK
SQUEAK

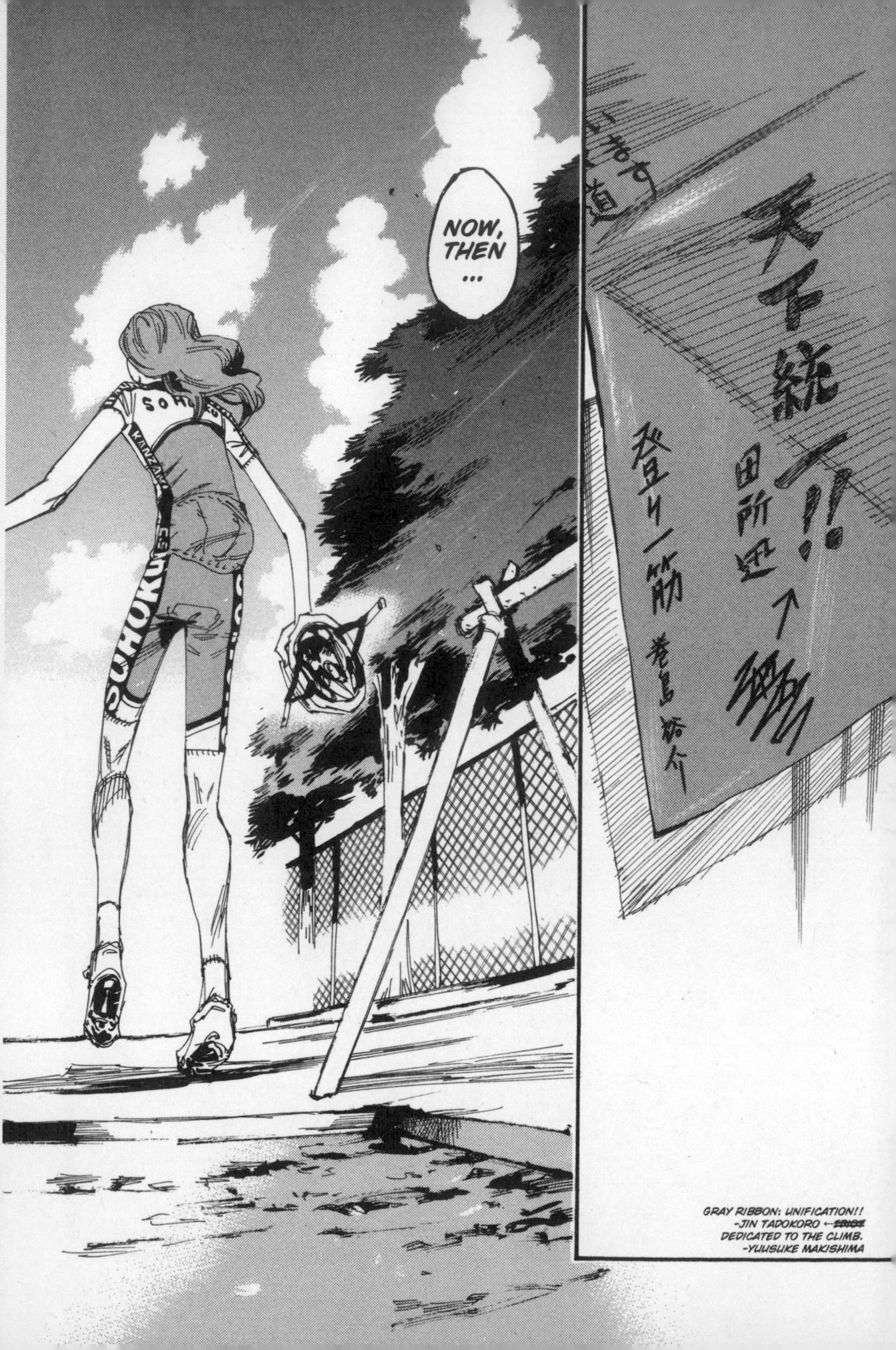
GRAY RIBBON: UNIFICATION!!
-JIN TADOKORO ←
DEDICATED TO THE CLIMB.
-YUUSUKE MAKISHIMA
NOW, THEN ...

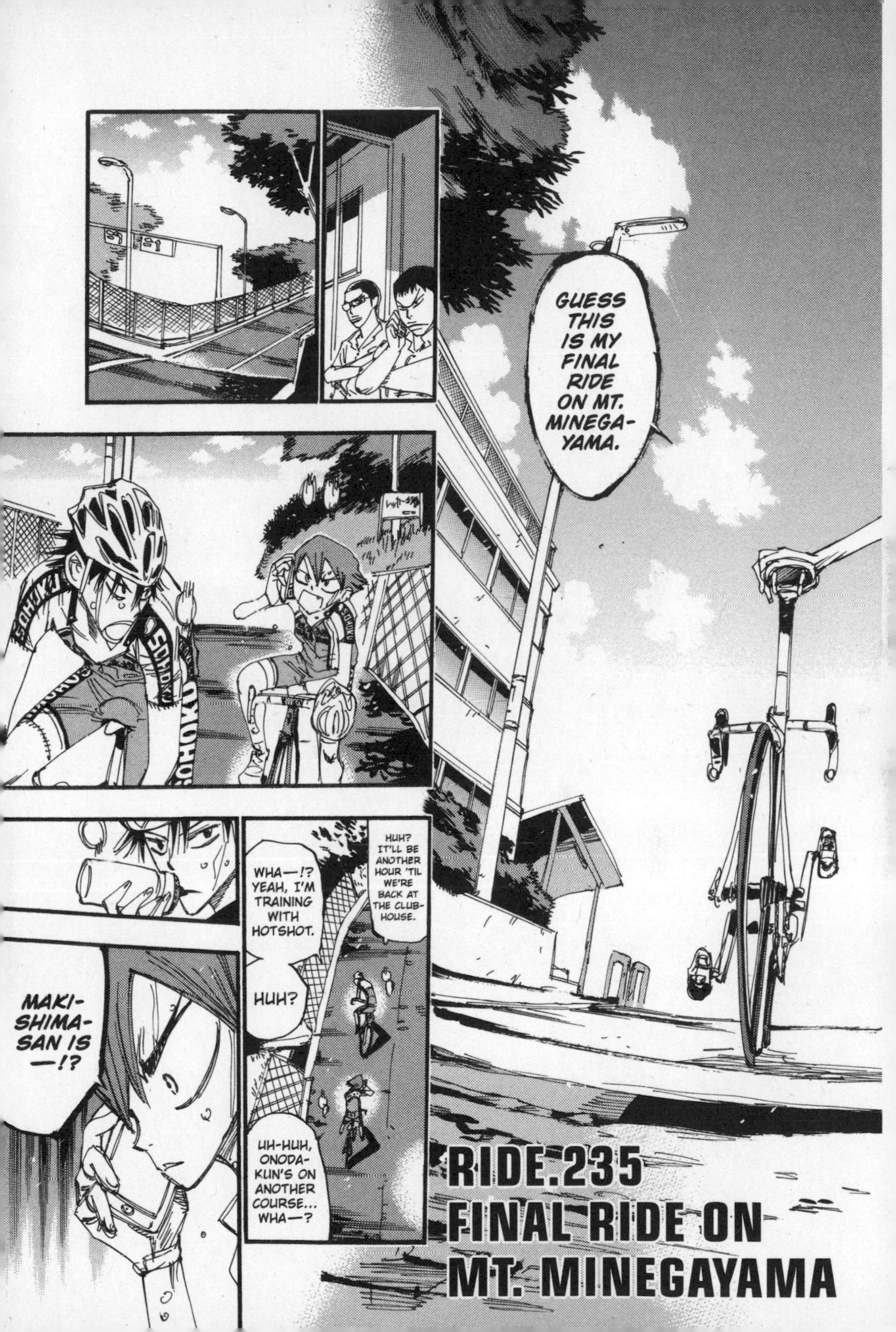
GUESS THIS IS MY FINAL RIDE ON MT. MINEGAYAMA.
RIDE.235 FINAL RIDE ON MT. MINEGAYAMA
HUH? IT'LL BE ANOTHER HOUR 'TIL WE'RE BACK AT THE CLUB-HOUSE.
WHA—!? YEAH, I'M TRAINING WITH HOTSHOT.
HUH?
UH-HUH, ONODA-KUN'S ON ANOTHER COURSE... WHA—?
MAKI-SHIMA-SAN IS —!?

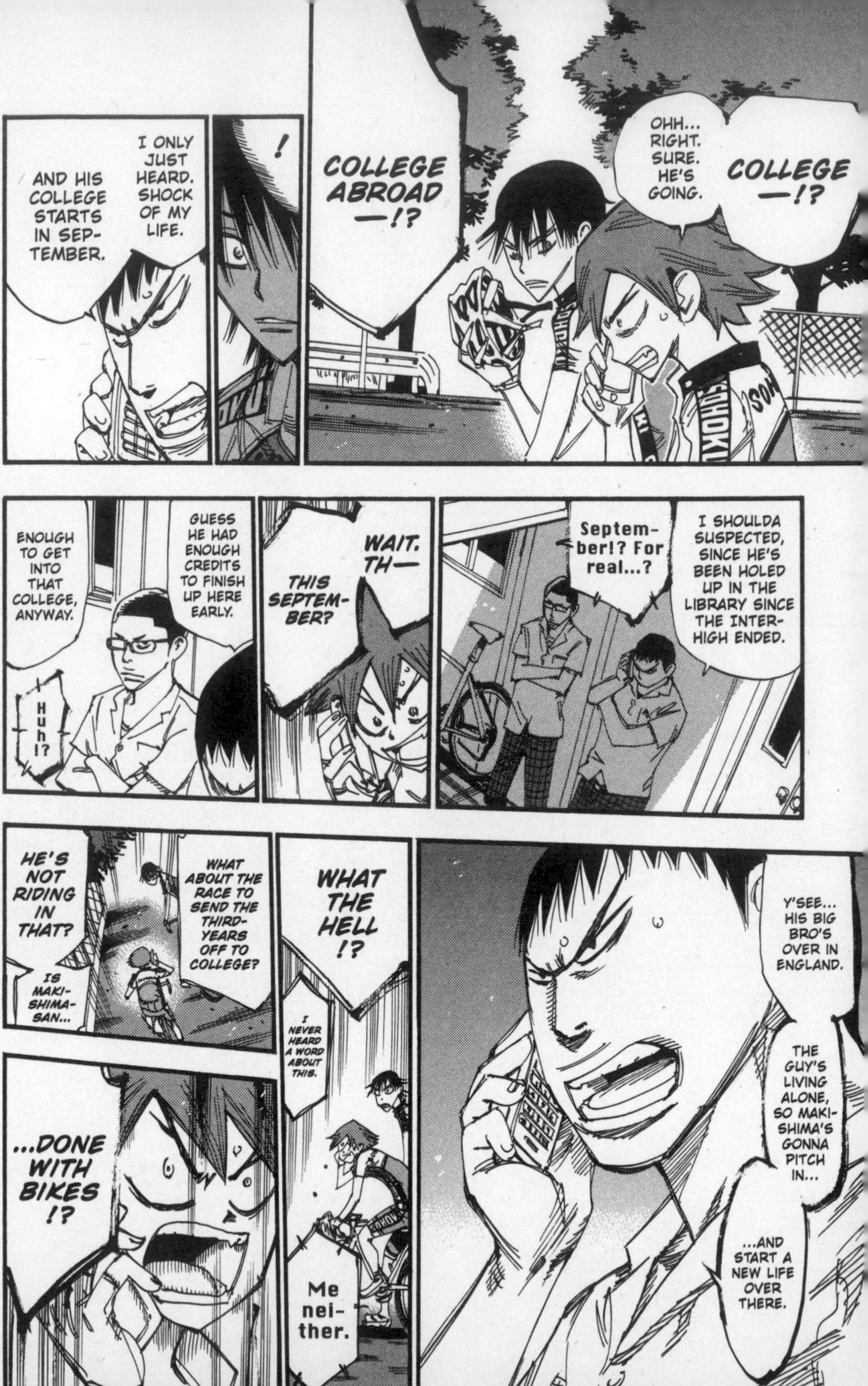
COLLEGE —!?
OHH... RIGHT. SURE. HE'S GOING.
COLLEGE ABROAD —!?
!
I ONLY JUST HEARD. SHOCK OF MY LIFE.
AND HIS COLLEGE STARTS IN SEPTEMBER.
I SHOULDA SUSPECTED, SINCE HE'S BEEN HOLED UP IN THE LIBRARY SINCE THE INTER-HIGH ENDED.
September!? For real...?
WAIT. TH—
THIS SEPTEMBER?
GUESS HE HAD ENOUGH CREDITS TO FINISH UP HERE EARLY.
ENOUGH TO GET INTO THAT COLLEGE, ANYWAY.
Huh!?
Y'SEE... HIS BIG BRO'S OVER IN ENGLAND.
THE GUY'S LIVING ALONE, SO MAKISHIMA'S GONNA PITCH IN...
...AND START A NEW LIFE OVER THERE.
WHAT THE HELL!?
I NEVER HEARD A WORD ABOUT THIS.
Me neither.
WHAT ABOUT THE RACE TO SEND THE THIRD-YEARS OFF TO COLLEGE?
HE'S NOT RIDING IN THAT?
IS MAKISHIMA-SAN...
...DONE WITH BIKES!?

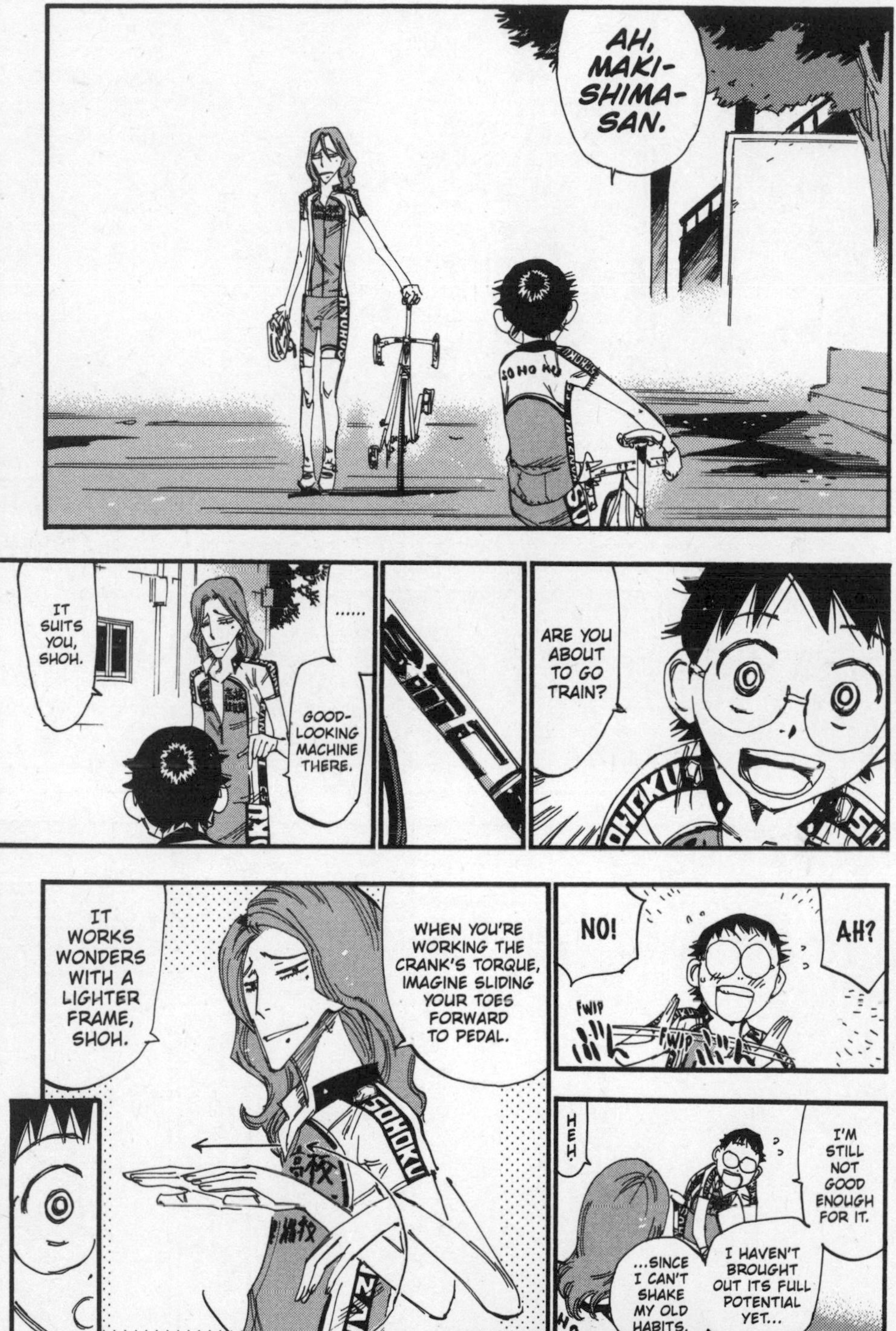
AH, MAKI-SHIMA-SAN.
ARE YOU ABOUT TO GO TRAIN?
......
GOOD-LOOKING MACHINE THERE.
IT SUITS YOU, SHOH.
AH?
NO!
FWIP ぶん
FWIP ぶん
I'M STILL NOT GOOD ENOUGH FOR IT.
I HAVEN'T BROUGHT OUT ITS FULL POTENTIAL YET...
...SINCE I CAN'T SHAKE MY OLD HABITS.
HEH.
WHEN YOU'RE WORKING THE CRANK'S TORQUE, IMAGINE SLIDING YOUR TOES FORWARD TO PEDAL.
IT WORKS WONDERS WITH A LIGHTER FRAME, SHOH.

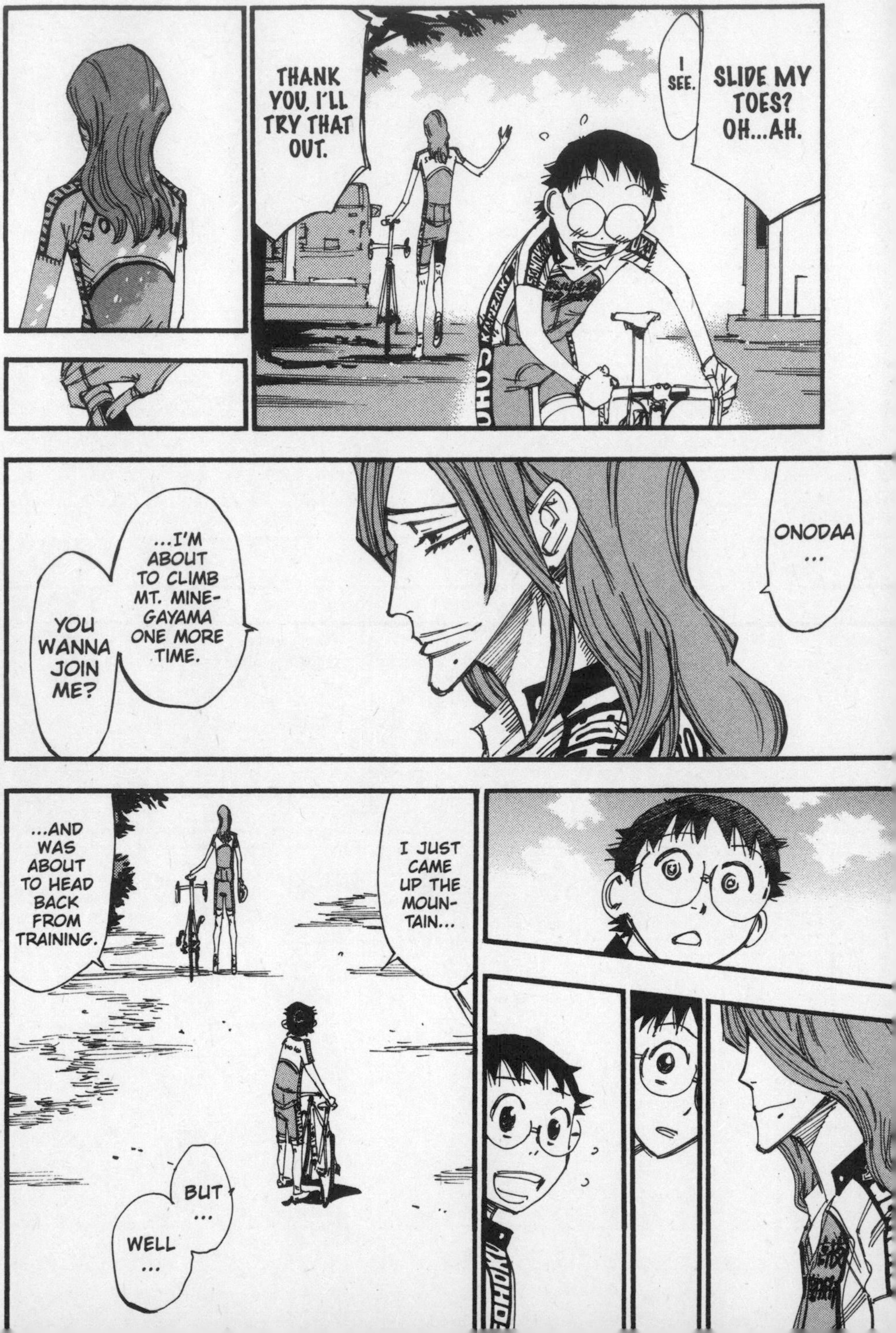
SLIDE MY TOES? OH...AH.
I SEE.
THANK YOU, I'LL TRY THAT OUT.
ONODAA ...
...I'M ABOUT TO CLIMB MT. MINE-GAYAMA ONE MORE TIME.
YOU WANNA JOIN ME?
I JUST CAME UP THE MOUN-TAIN...
...AND WAS ABOUT TO HEAD BACK FROM TRAINING.
BUT ...
WELL ...

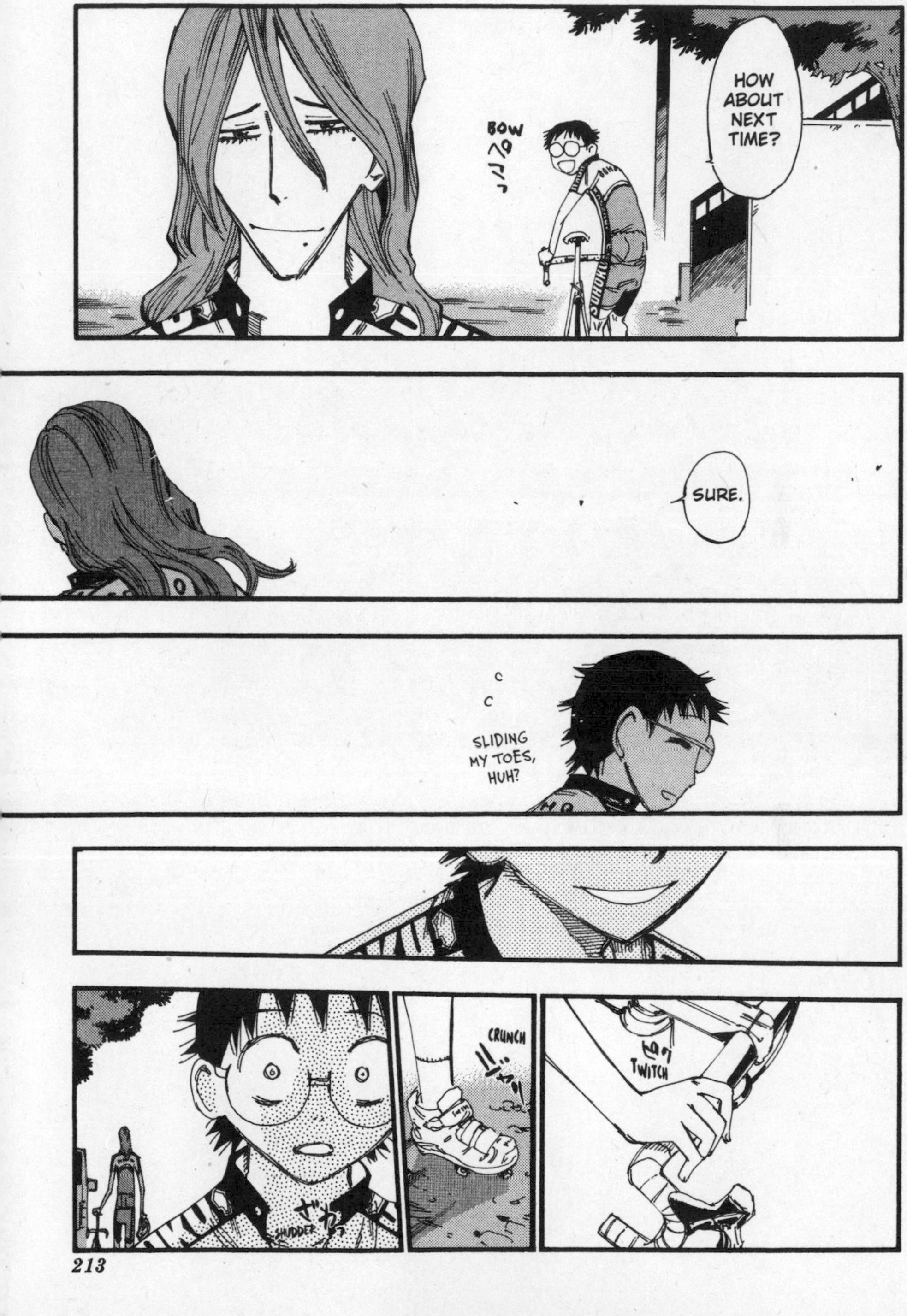
HOW ABOUT NEXT TIME?
BOW
SURE.
SLIDING MY TOES, HUH?
TWITCH
CRUNCH
SHUDDER

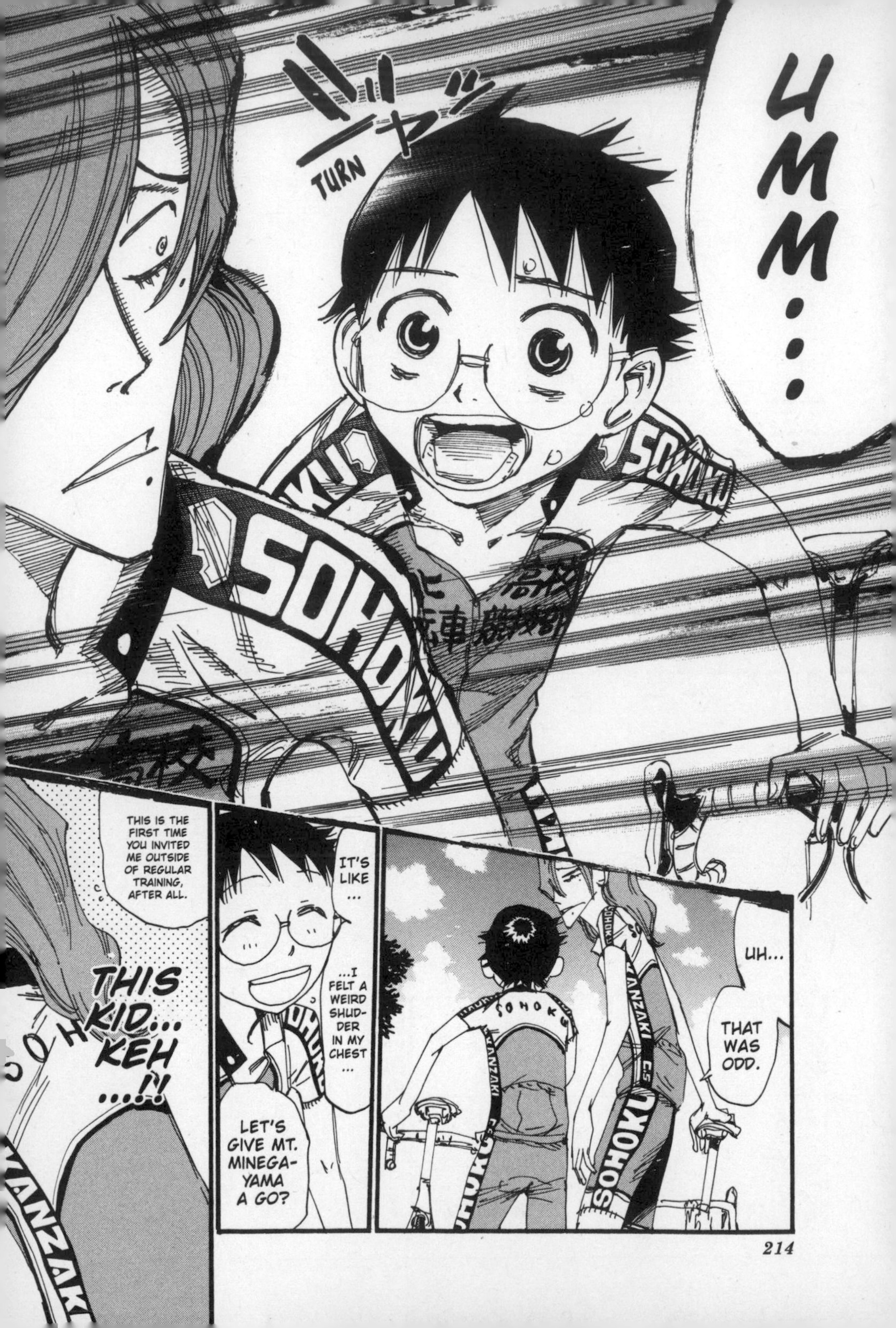
UMM...
TURN
UH...
THAT WAS ODD.
IT'S LIKE ...
...I FELT A WEIRD SHUDDER IN MY CHEST ...
LET'S GIVE MT. MINEGAYAMA A GO?
THIS IS THE FIRST TIME YOU INVITED ME OUTSIDE OF REGULAR TRAINING, AFTER ALL.
THIS KID... KEH ...!!

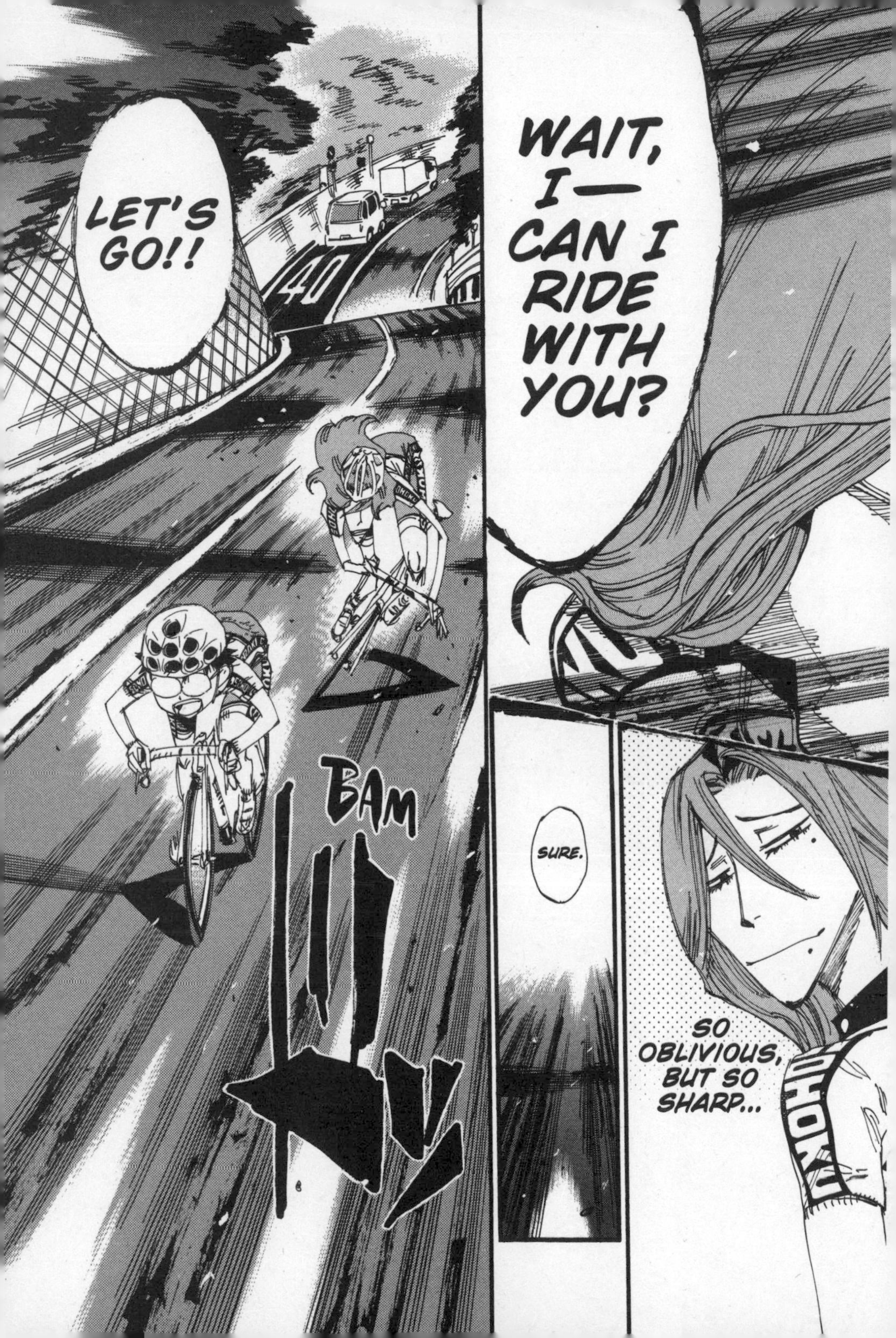
WAIT, I— CAN I RIDE WITH YOU?
SURE.
SO OBLIVIOUS, BUT SO SHARP...
LET'S GO!!
BAM

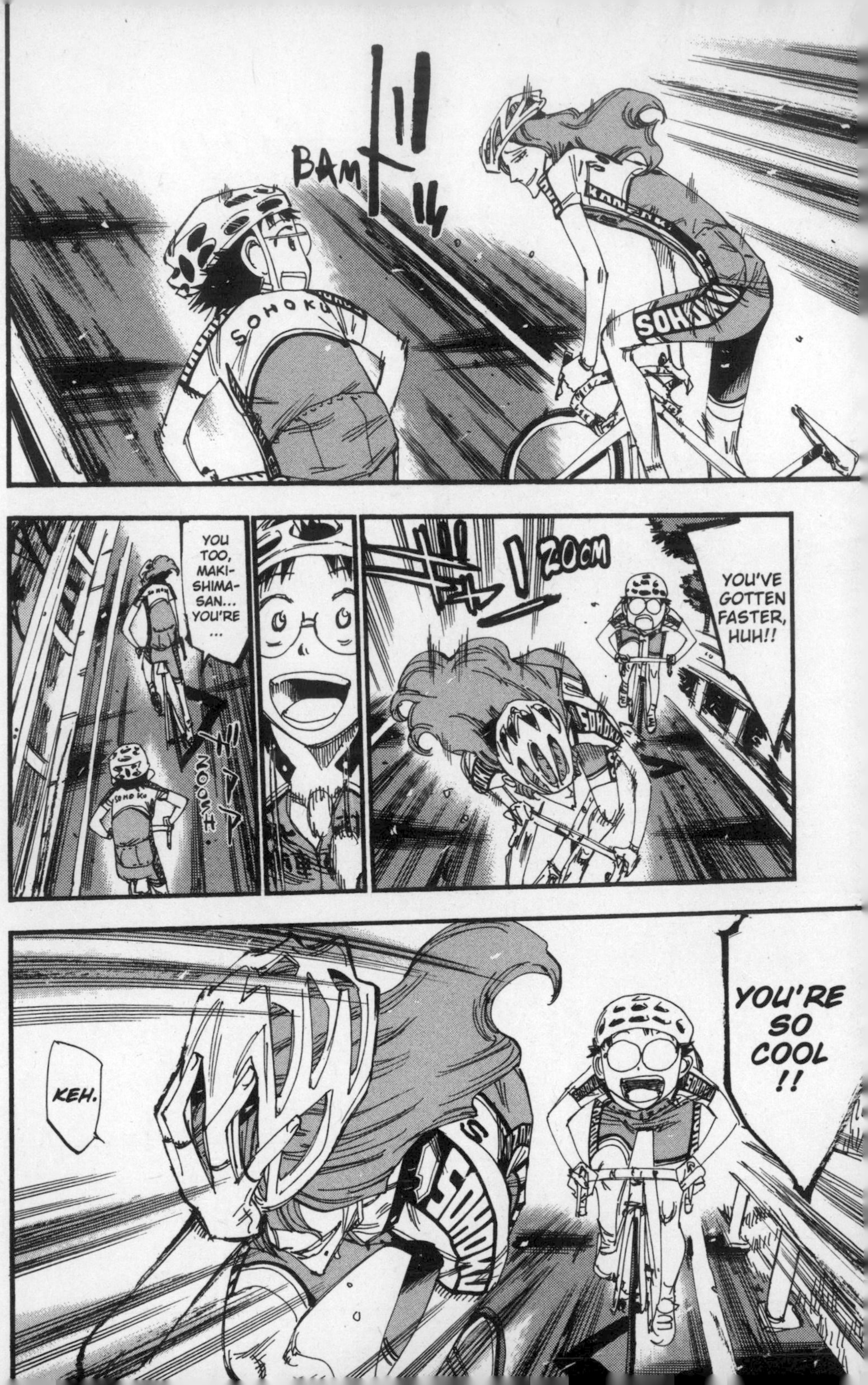
BAM
YOU'VE GOTTEN FASTER, HUH!!
ZOOM
YOU TOO, MAKI-SHIMA-SAN... YOU'RE ...
ZOOOSH
YOU'RE SO COOL !!
KEH.

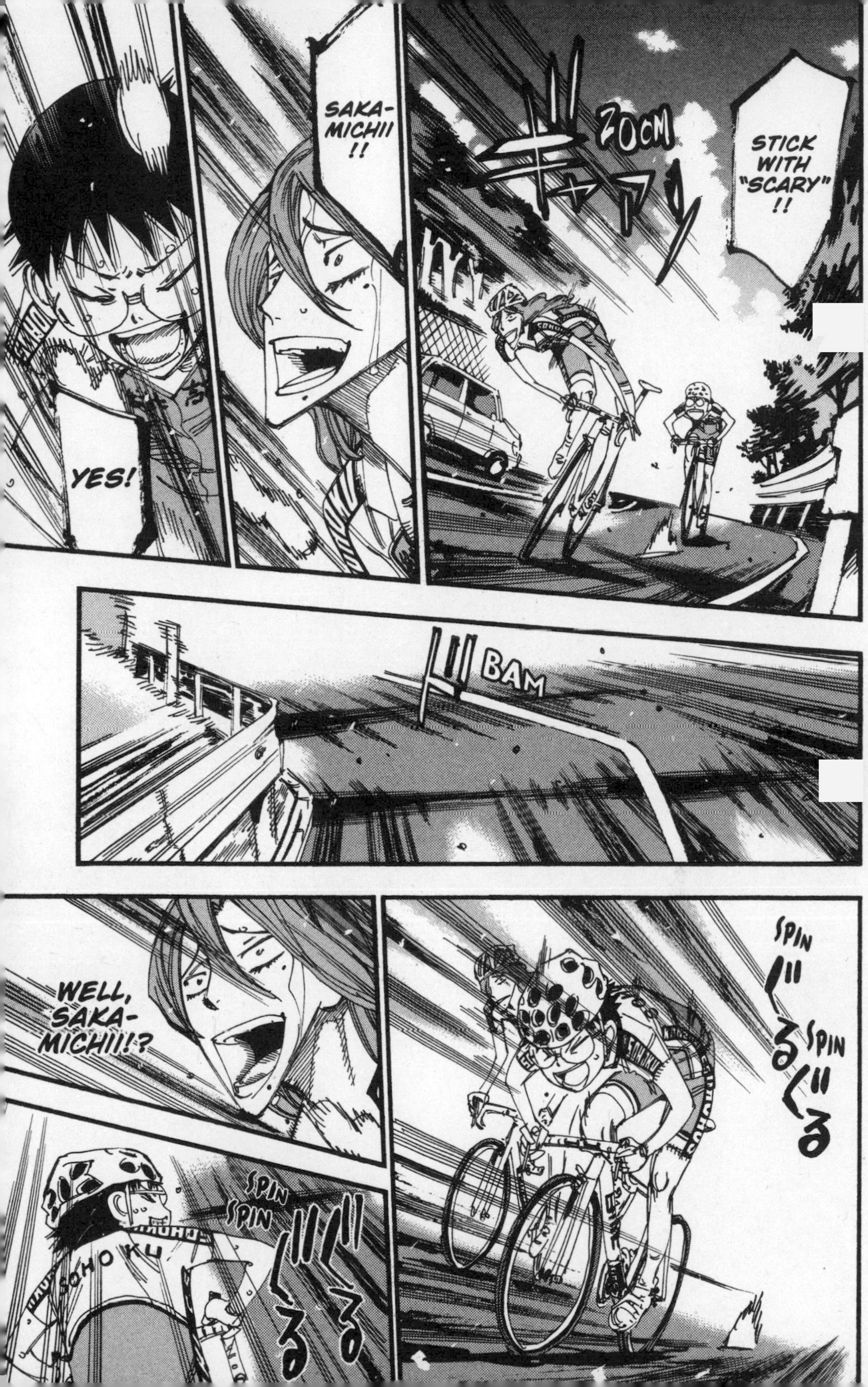
STICK WITH "SCARY" !!
ZOOM
SAKA-MICHI! !!
YES!
BAM
SPIN
SPIN
WELL, SAKA-MICHI!!?
SPIN
SPIN

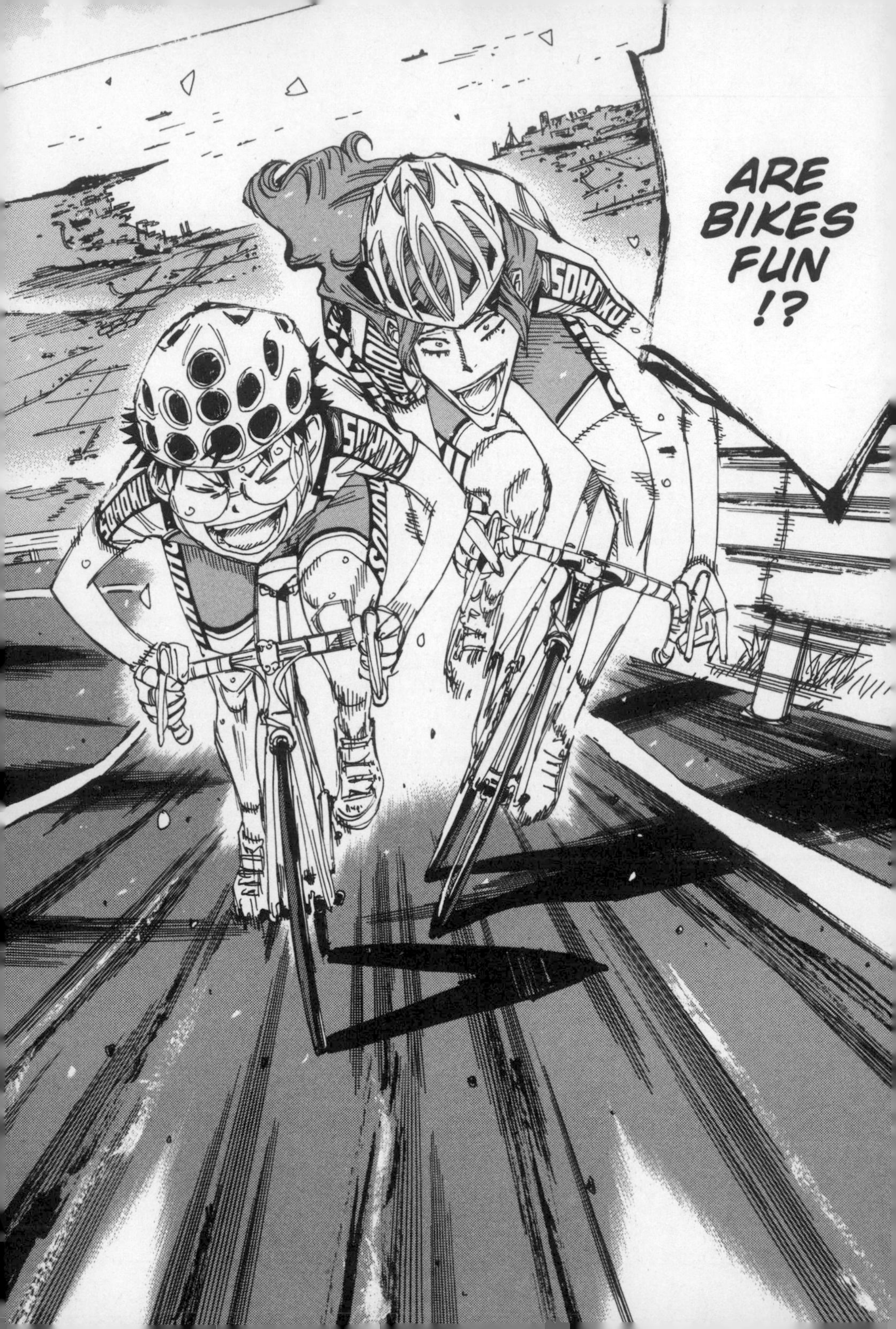
ARE BIKES FUN !?

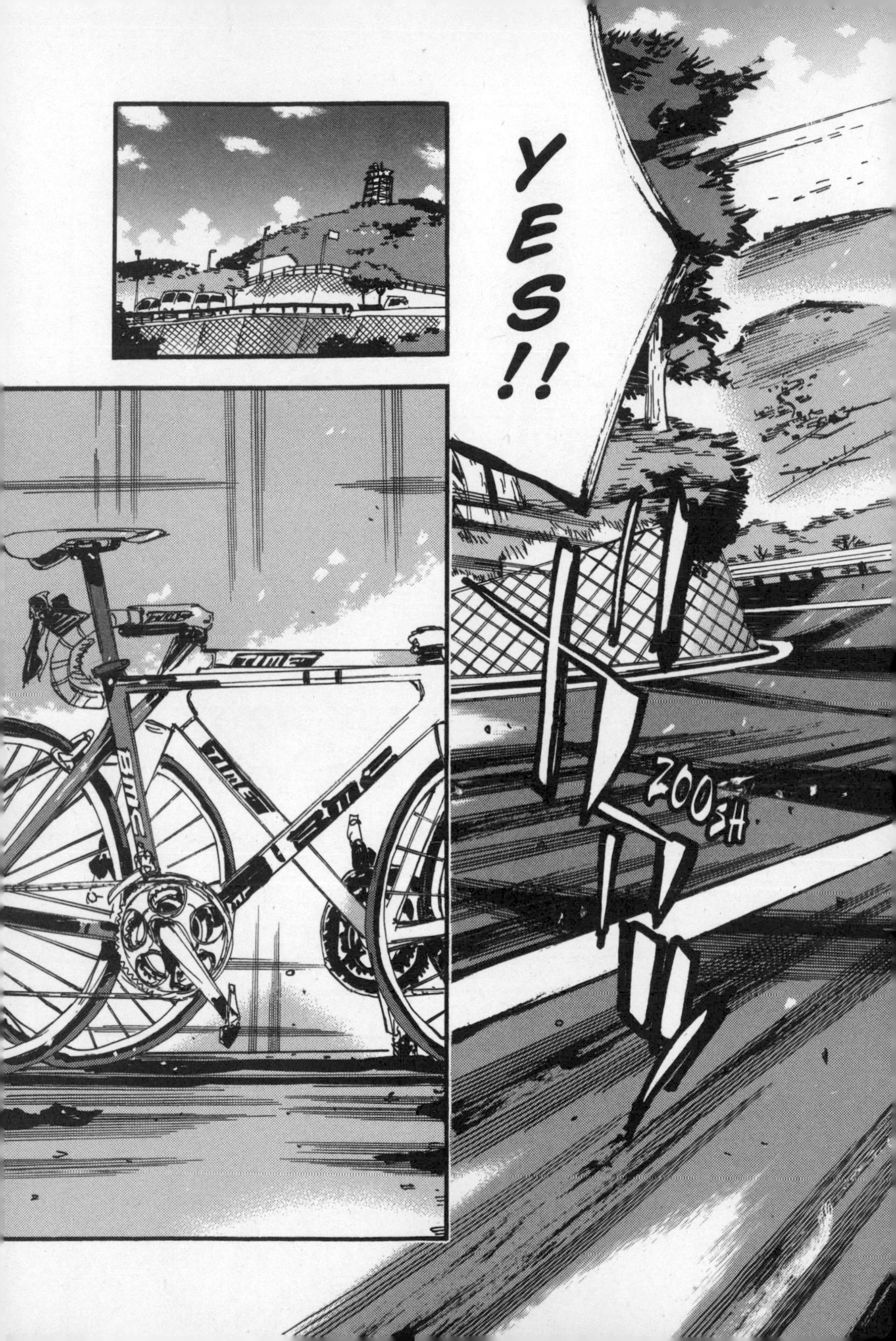
YES!!
ZOOSH
TIME
BMC

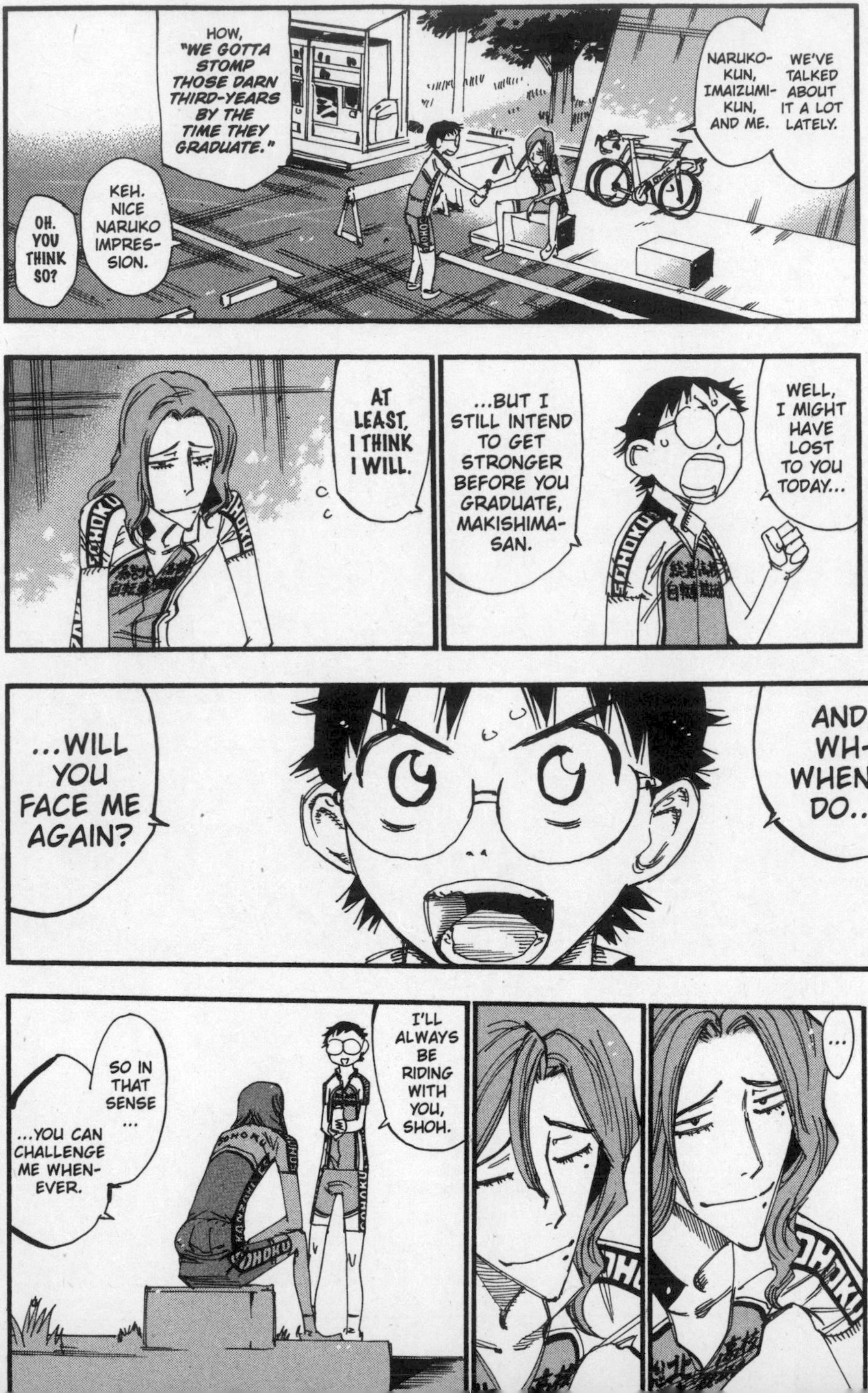
NARUKO-KUN, IMAIZUMI-KUN, AND ME. WE'VE TALKED ABOUT IT A LOT LATELY.
HOW, "WE GOTTA STOMP THOSE DARN THIRD-YEARS BY THE TIME THEY GRADUATE."
KEH. NICE NARUKO IMPRES-SION.
OH. YOU THINK SO?
WELL, I MIGHT HAVE LOST TO YOU TODAY...
...BUT I STILL INTEND TO GET STRONGER BEFORE YOU GRADUATE, MAKISHIMA-SAN.
AT LEAST, I THINK I WILL.
AND, WH-WHEN I DO...
...WILL YOU FACE ME AGAIN?
...
I'LL ALWAYS BE RIDING WITH YOU, SHOH.
SO IN THAT SENSE...
...YOU CAN CHALLENGE ME WHEN-EVER.

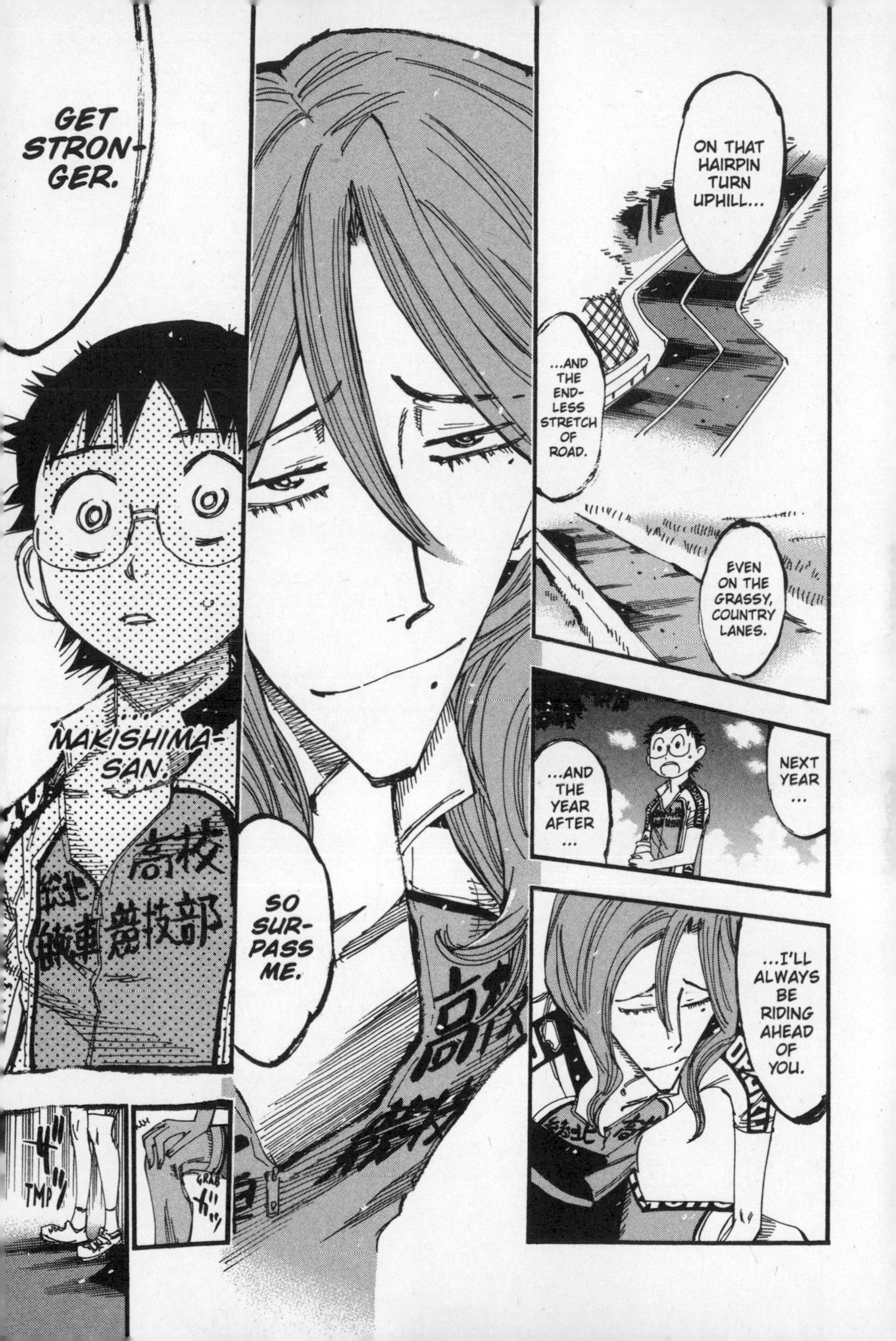
ON THAT HAIRPIN TURN UPHILL...
...AND THE ENDLESS STRETCH OF ROAD.
EVEN ON THE GRASSY, COUNTRY LANES.
NEXT YEAR...
...AND THE YEAR AFTER...
...I'LL ALWAYS BE RIDING AHEAD OF YOU.
GET STRONGER.
SO SURPASS ME.
...MAKISHIMA-SAN.
GRAB
TMP

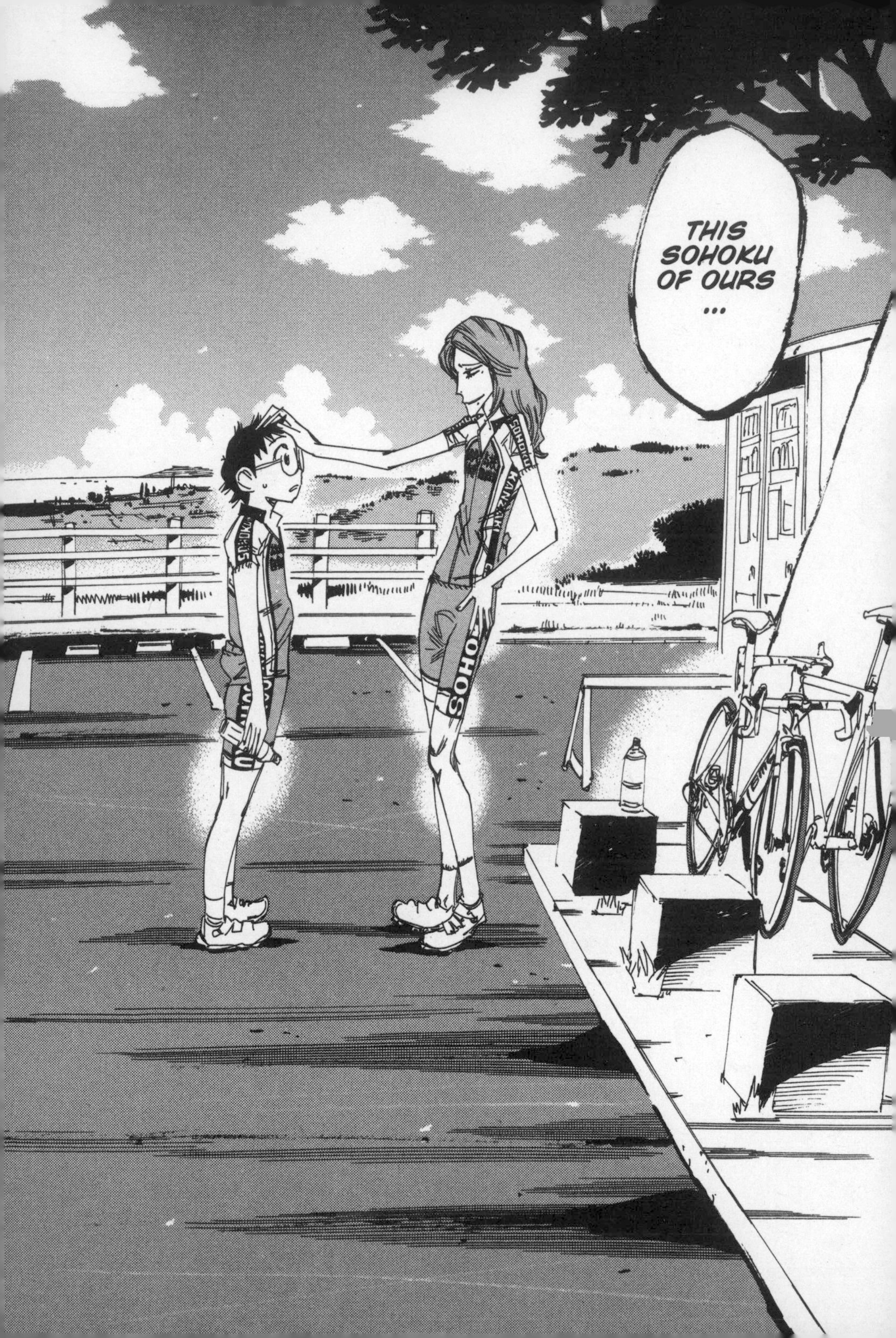
THIS SOHOKU OF OURS ...

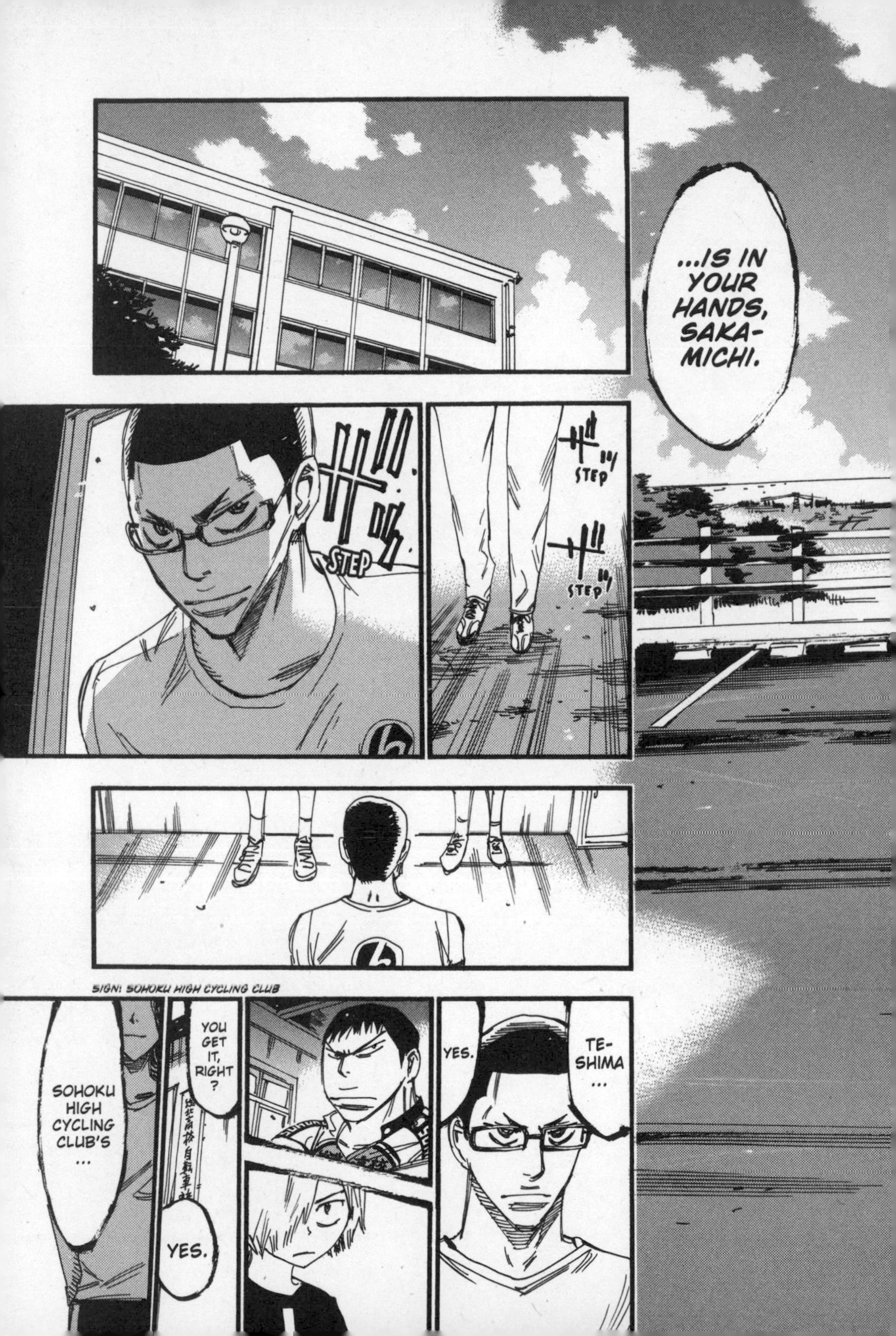
...IS IN YOUR HANDS, SAKA-MICHI.
STEP
STEP
STEP
SIGN: SOHOKU HIGH CYCLING CLUB
TE-SHIMA ...
YES.
YOU GET IT, RIGHT?
YES.
SOHOKU HIGH CYCLING CLUB'S ...

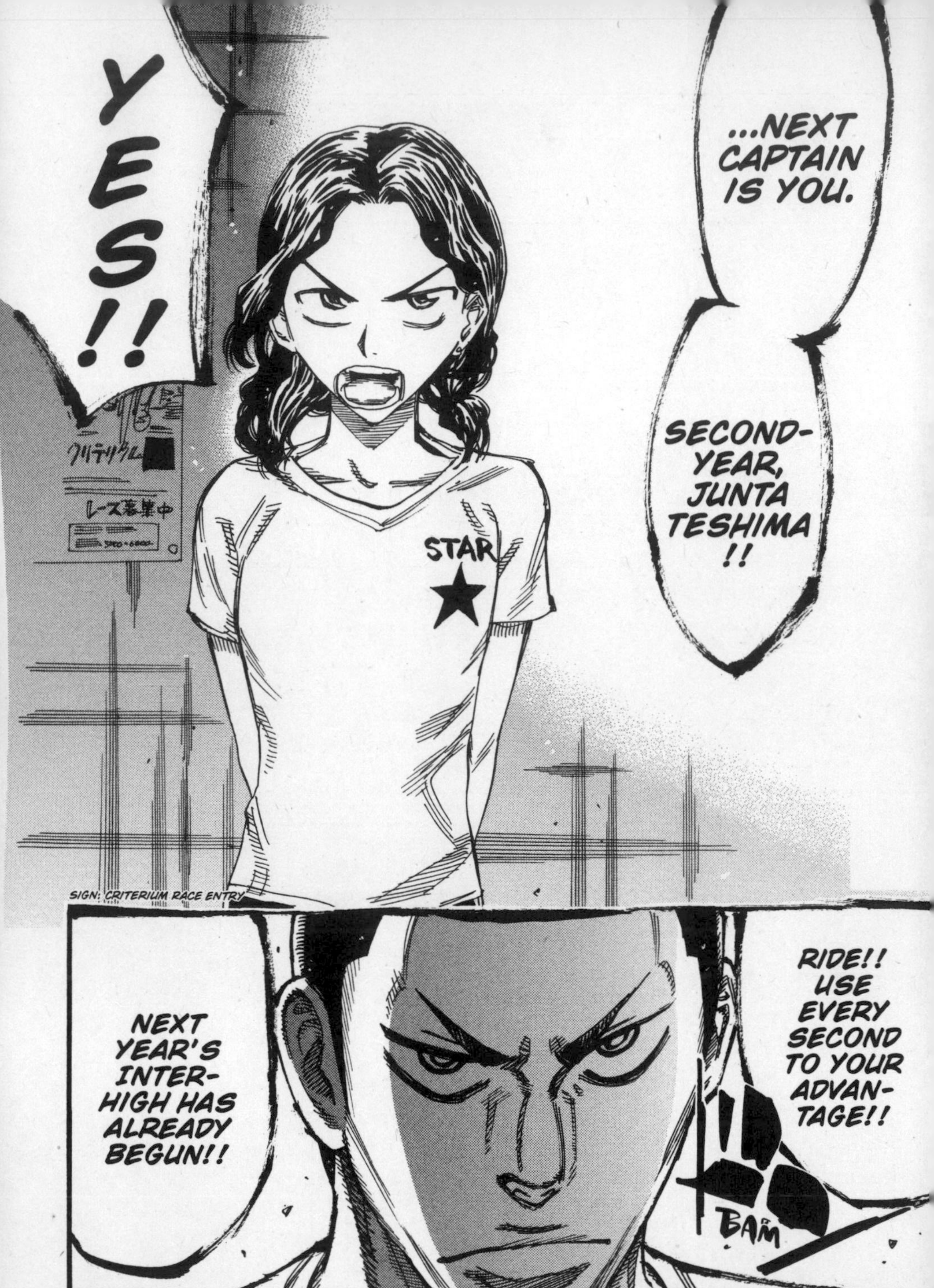
...NEXT CAPTAIN IS YOU.
SECOND-YEAR, JUNTA TESHIMA!!
YES!!
SIGN: CRITERIUM RACE ENTRY
RIDE!! USE EVERY SECOND TO YOUR ADVANTAGE!!
BAM
NEXT YEAR'S INTER-HIGH HAS ALREADY BEGUN!!

RIDE.236 THE NEW SOHOKU

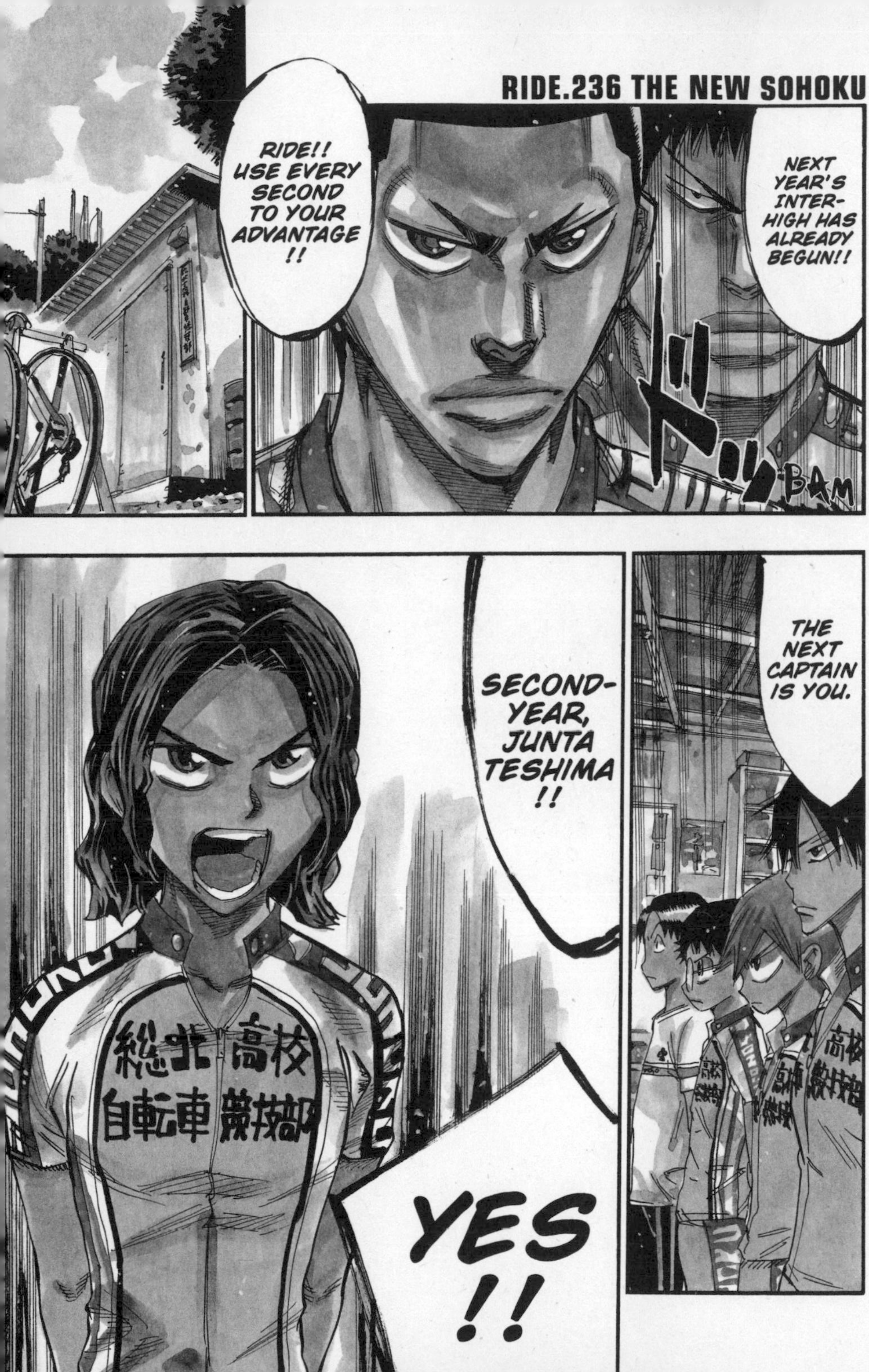
NEXT YEAR'S INTER-HIGH HAS ALREADY BEGUN!!
BAM
RIDE!! USE EVERY SECOND TO YOUR ADVANTAGE !!
THE NEXT CAPTAIN IS YOU.
SECOND-YEAR, JUNTA TESHIMA !!
YES !!
総北高校
自転車競技部

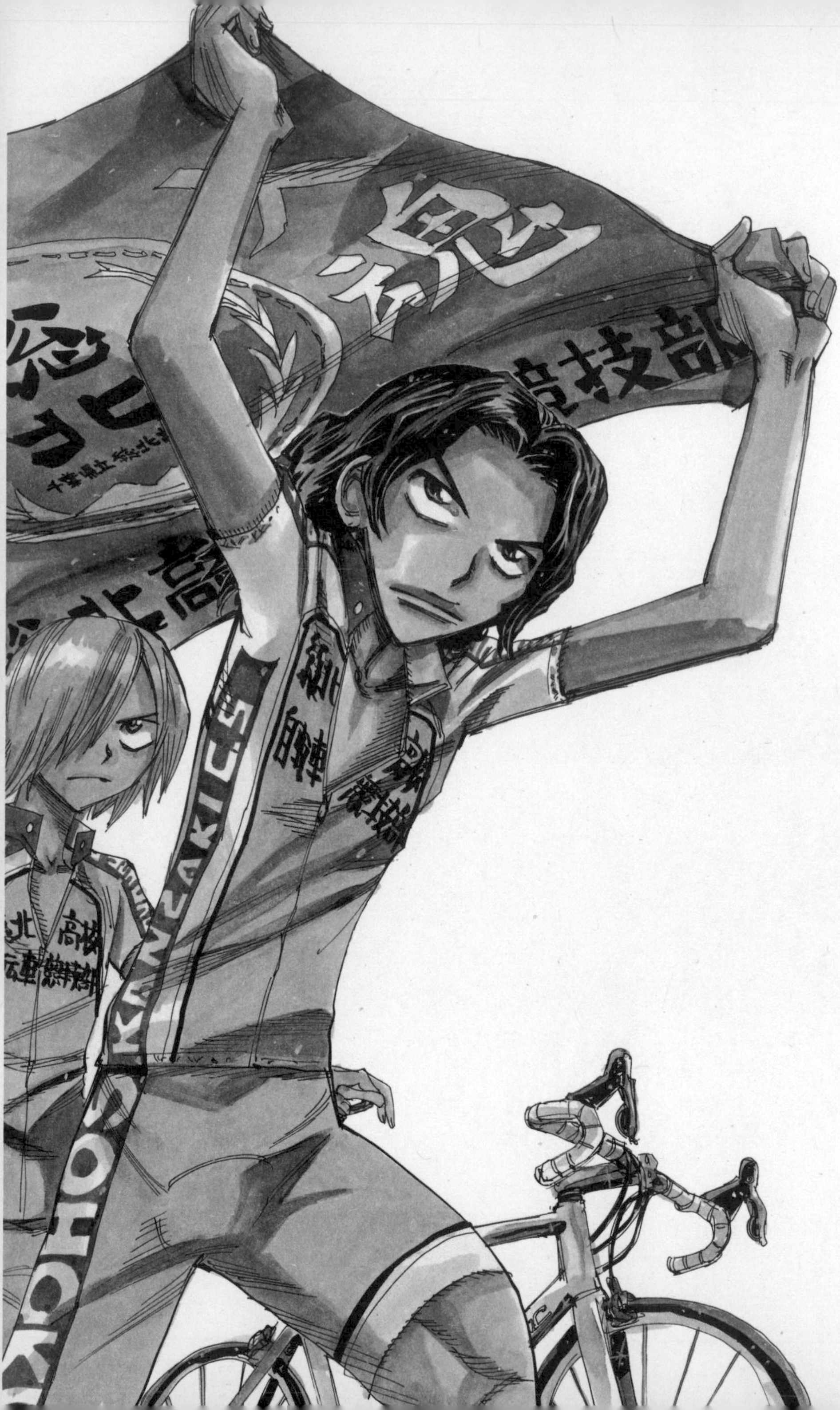

RIDE.236 THE NEW SOHOKU

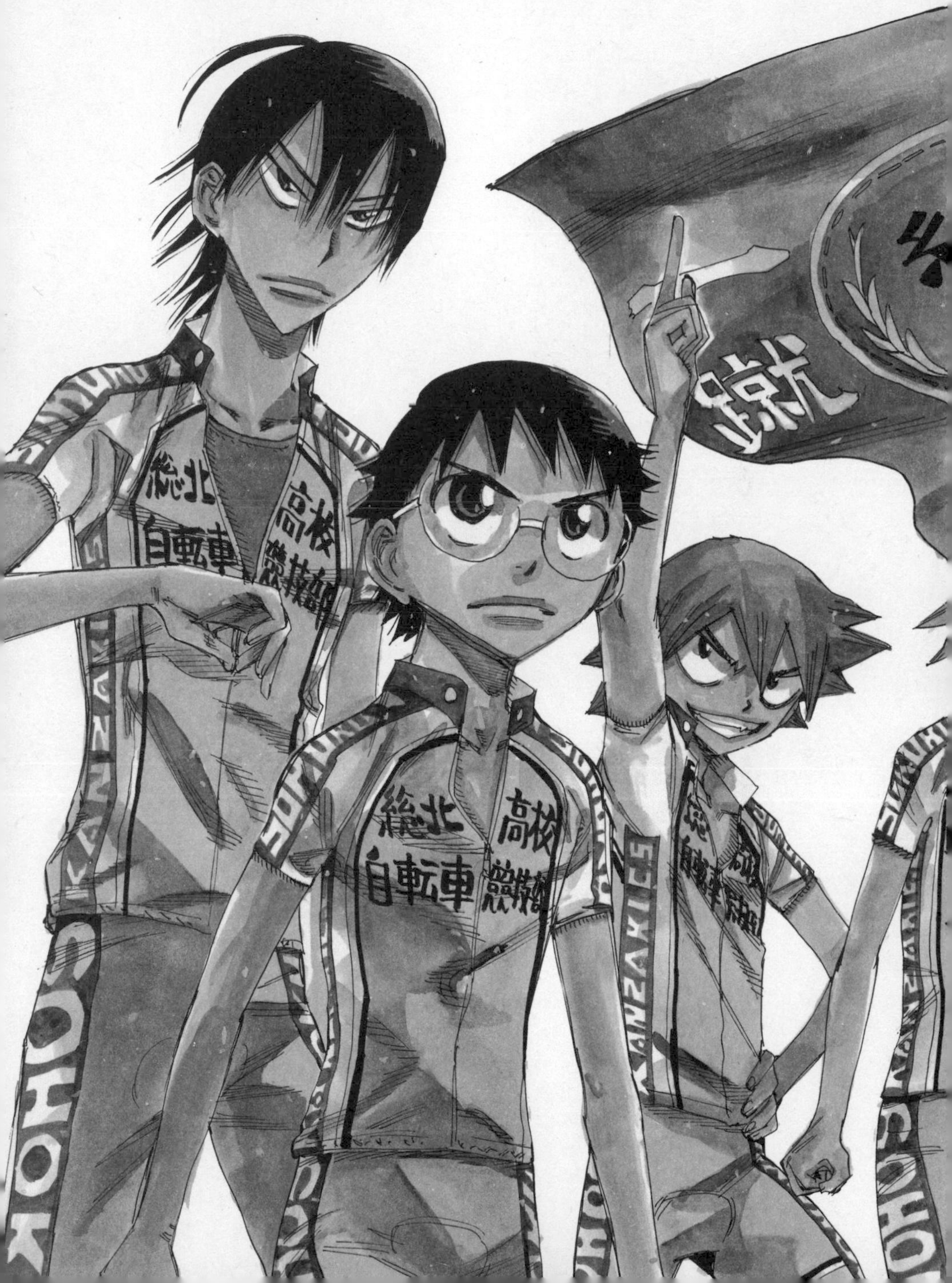
SOHOKU

So long, MAKISHIMA,

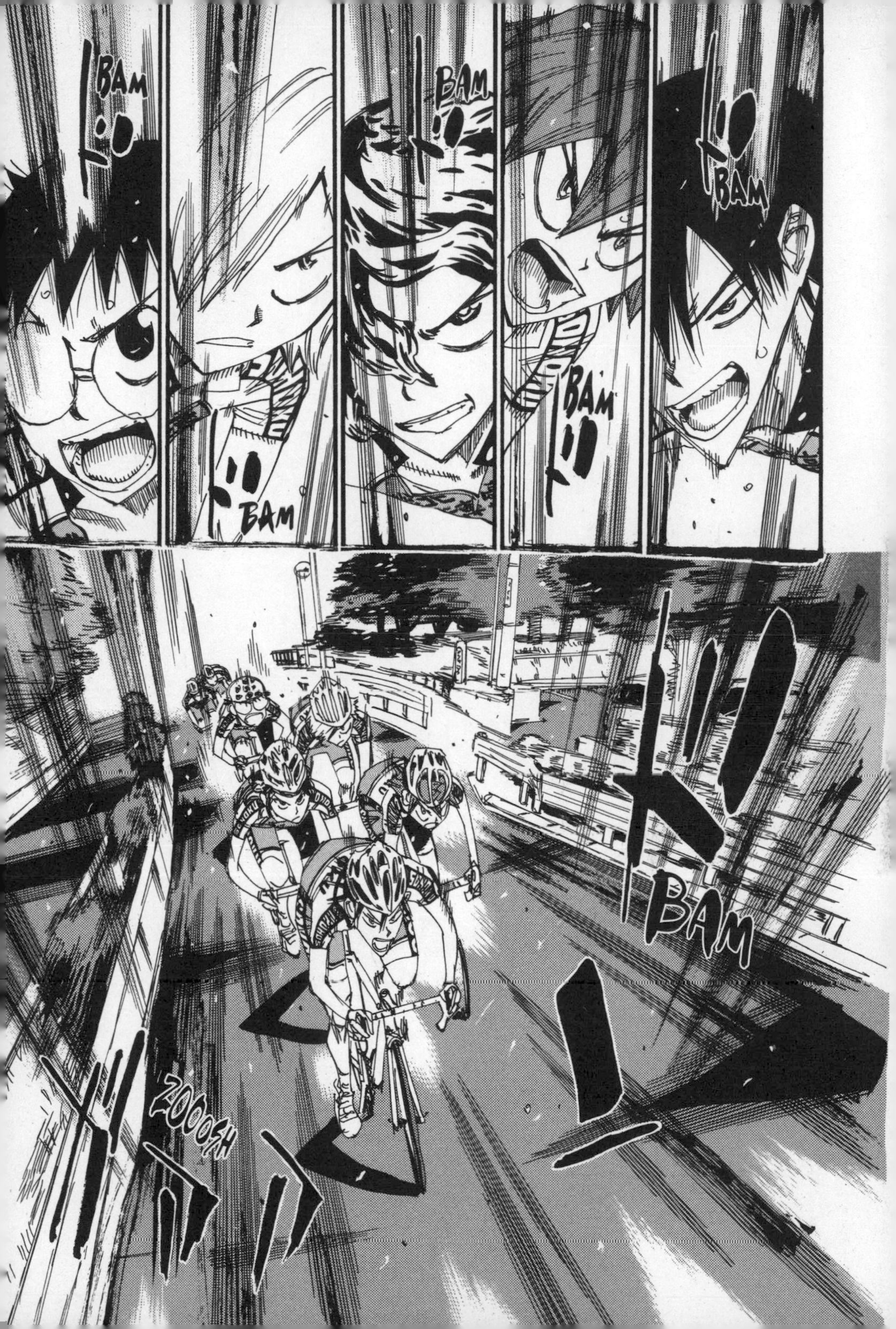
BAM
BAM
BAM
BAM
BAM
BAM
ZOOOSH

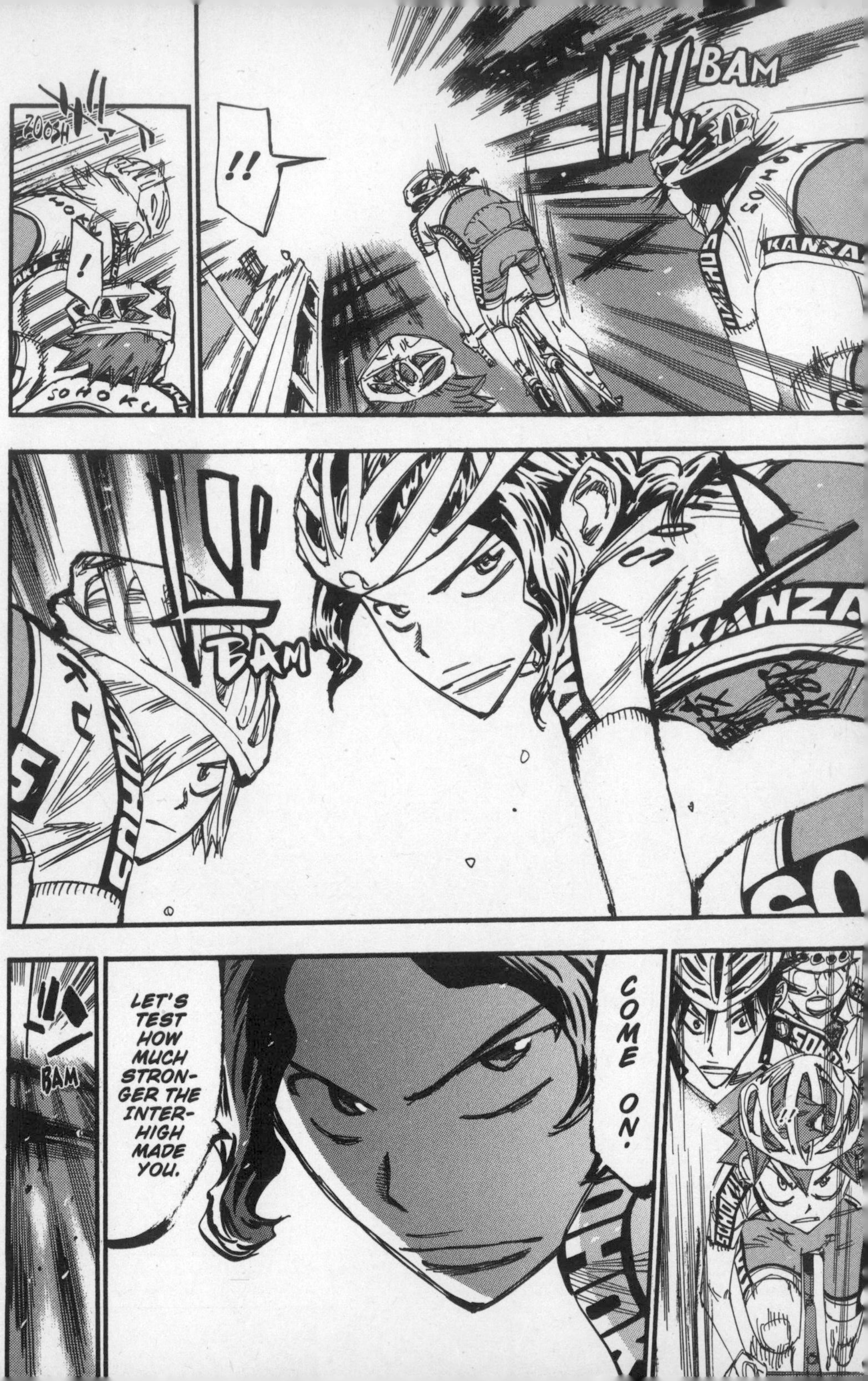
BAM
!!
ZOOSH
!
BAM
COME ON.
!!
LET'S TEST HOW MUCH STRONGER THE INTER-HIGH MADE YOU.
BAM

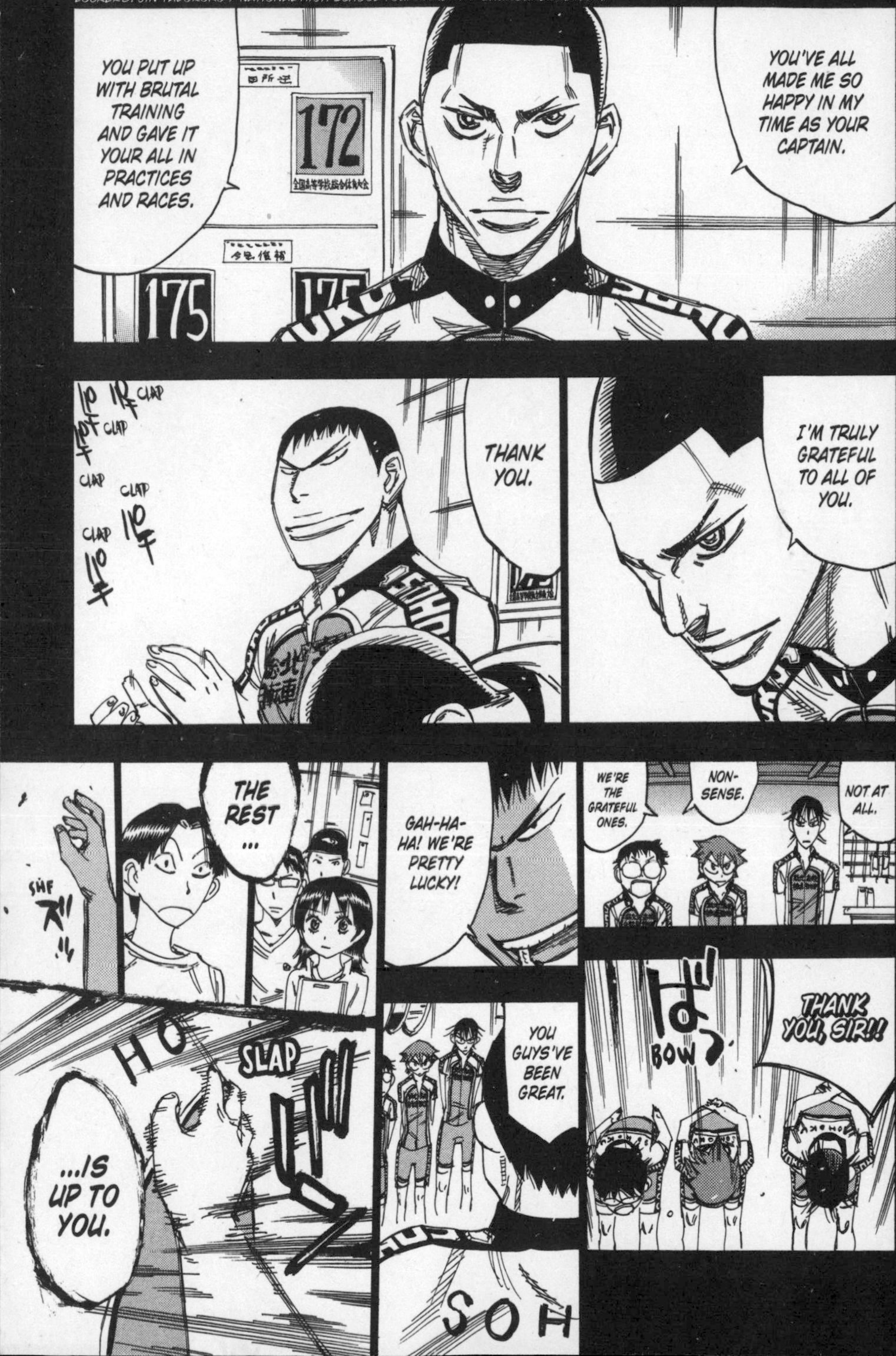
YOU'VE ALL MADE ME SO HAPPY IN MY TIME AS YOUR CAPTAIN.
YOU PUT UP WITH BRUTAL TRAINING AND GAVE IT YOUR ALL IN PRACTICES AND RACES.
172
175
175
I'M TRULY GRATEFUL TO ALL OF YOU.
THANK YOU.
CLAP
CLAP
CLAP
CLAP
CLAP
NOT AT ALL.
NON-SENSE.
WE'RE THE GRATEFUL ONES.
GAH-HA-HA! WE'RE PRETTY LUCKY!
THE REST...
SHF
THANK YOU, SIR!!
BOW
YOU GUYS'VE BEEN GREAT.
SOH
HO
SLAP
...IS UP TO YOU.

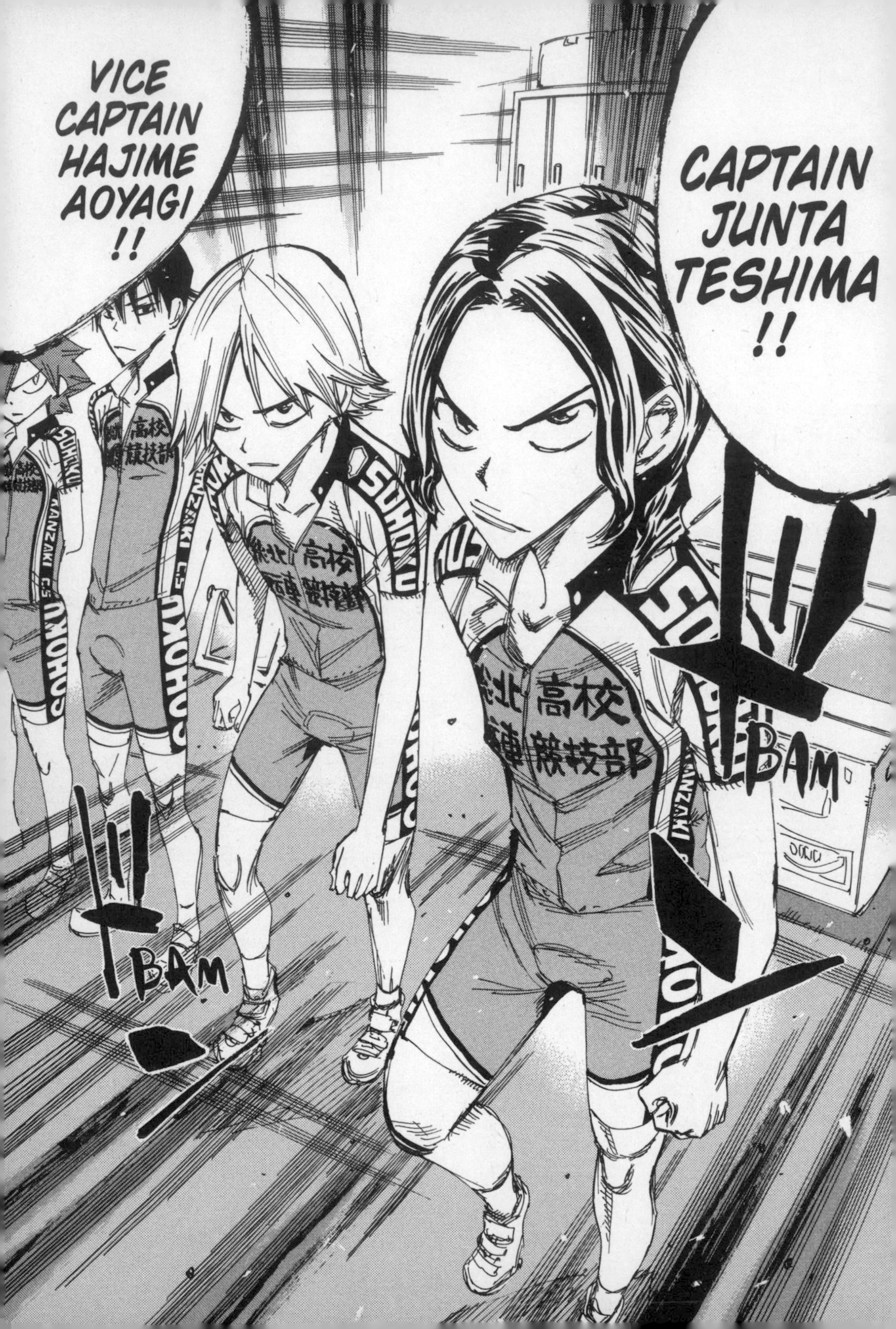
CAPTAIN JUNTA TESHIMA !!
BAM
VICE CAPTAIN HAJIME AOYAGI !!
BAM

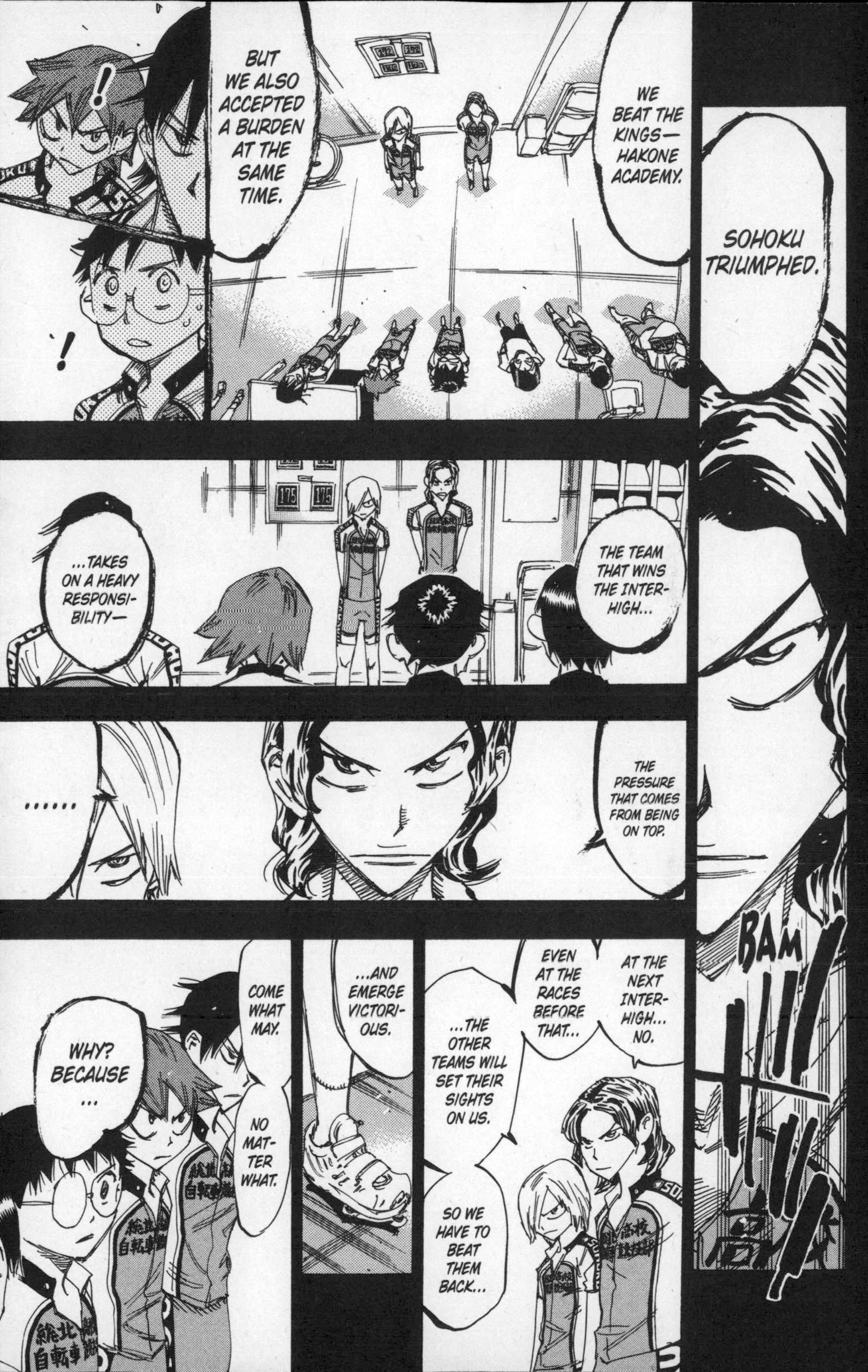
SOHOKU TRIUMPHED.
BAM
WE BEAT THE KINGS— HAKONE ACADEMY.
BUT WE ALSO ACCEPTED A BURDEN AT THE SAME TIME.
!
!
THE TEAM THAT WINS THE INTER-HIGH...
...TAKES ON A HEAVY RESPONSIBILITY—
THE PRESSURE THAT COMES FROM BEING ON TOP.
......
AT THE NEXT INTER-HIGH... NO.
EVEN AT THE RACES BEFORE THAT...
...THE OTHER TEAMS WILL SET THEIR SIGHTS ON US.
SO WE HAVE TO BEAT THEM BACK...
...AND EMERGE VICTORIOUS.
COME WHAT MAY.
NO MATTER WHAT.
WHY? BECAUSE ...

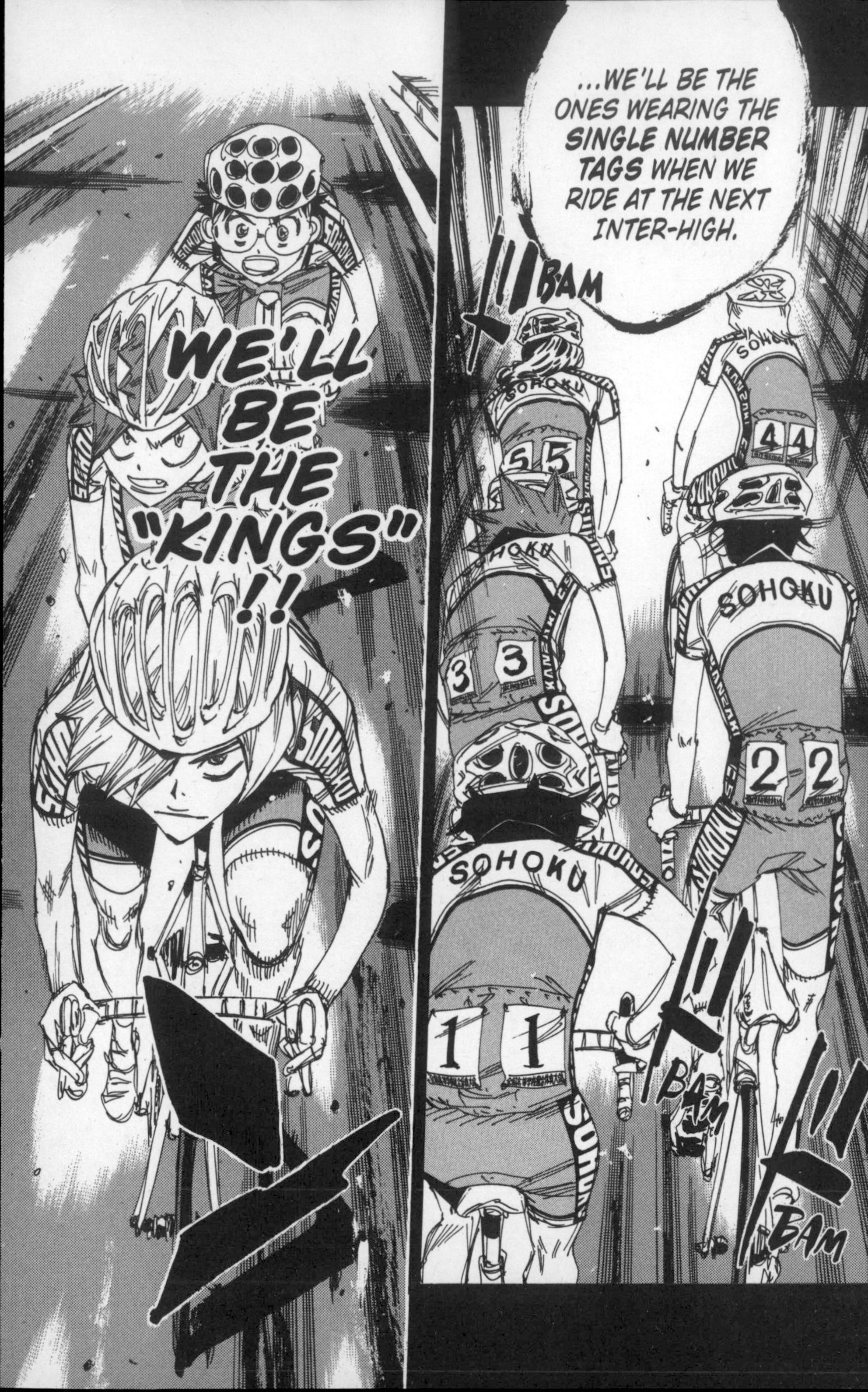
...WE'LL BE THE ONES WEARING THE SINGLE NUMBER TAGS WHEN WE RIDE AT THE NEXT INTER-HIGH.
BAM
BAM
BAM
WE'LL BE THE "KINGS"!!

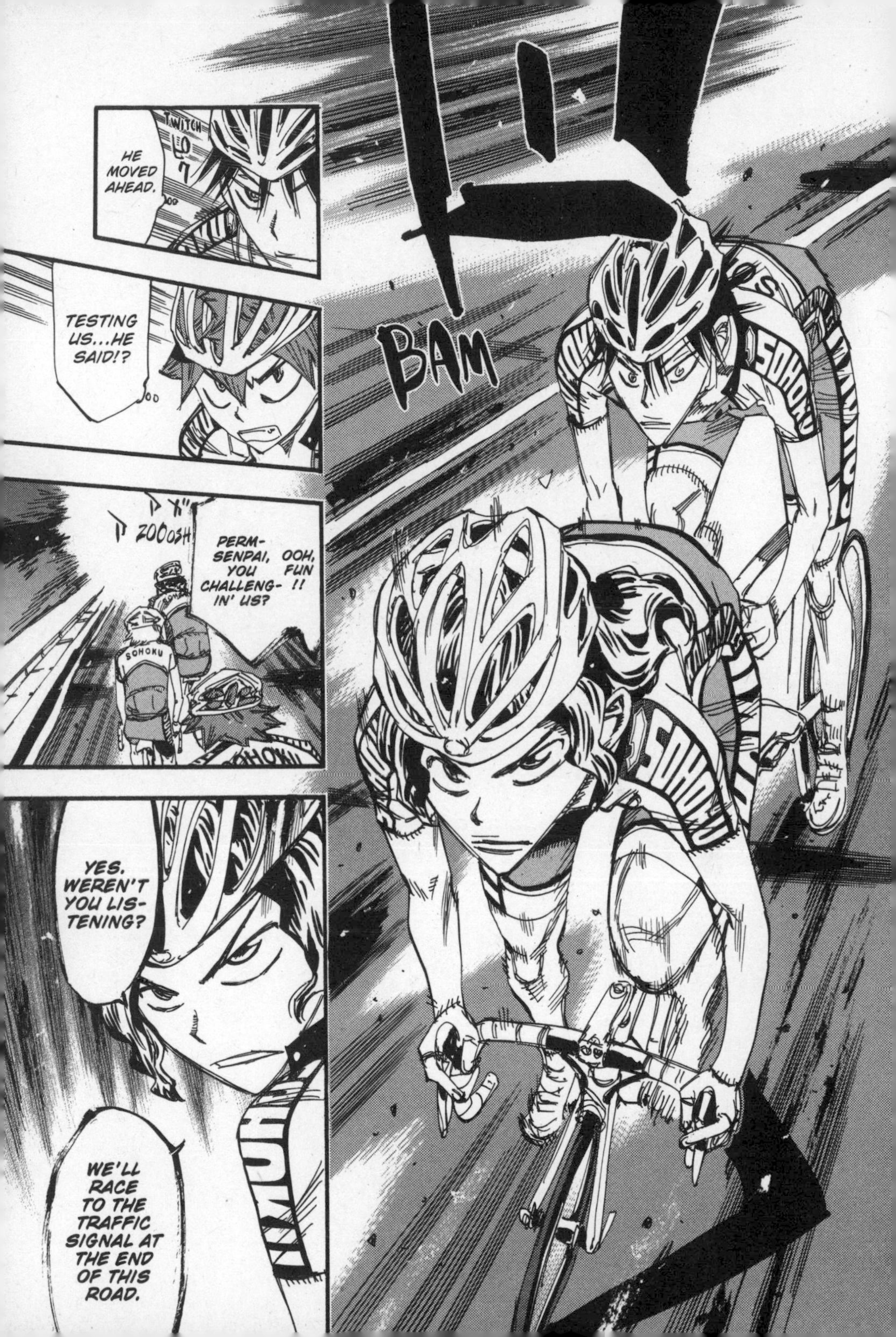
BAM
TWITCH
HE MOVED AHEAD.
TESTING US...HE SAID!?
ZOOOSH
OOH, FUN!!
PERM-SENPAI, YOU CHALLENGIN' US?
YES. WEREN'T YOU LISTENING?
WE'LL RACE TO THE TRAFFIC SIGNAL AT THE END OF THIS ROAD.

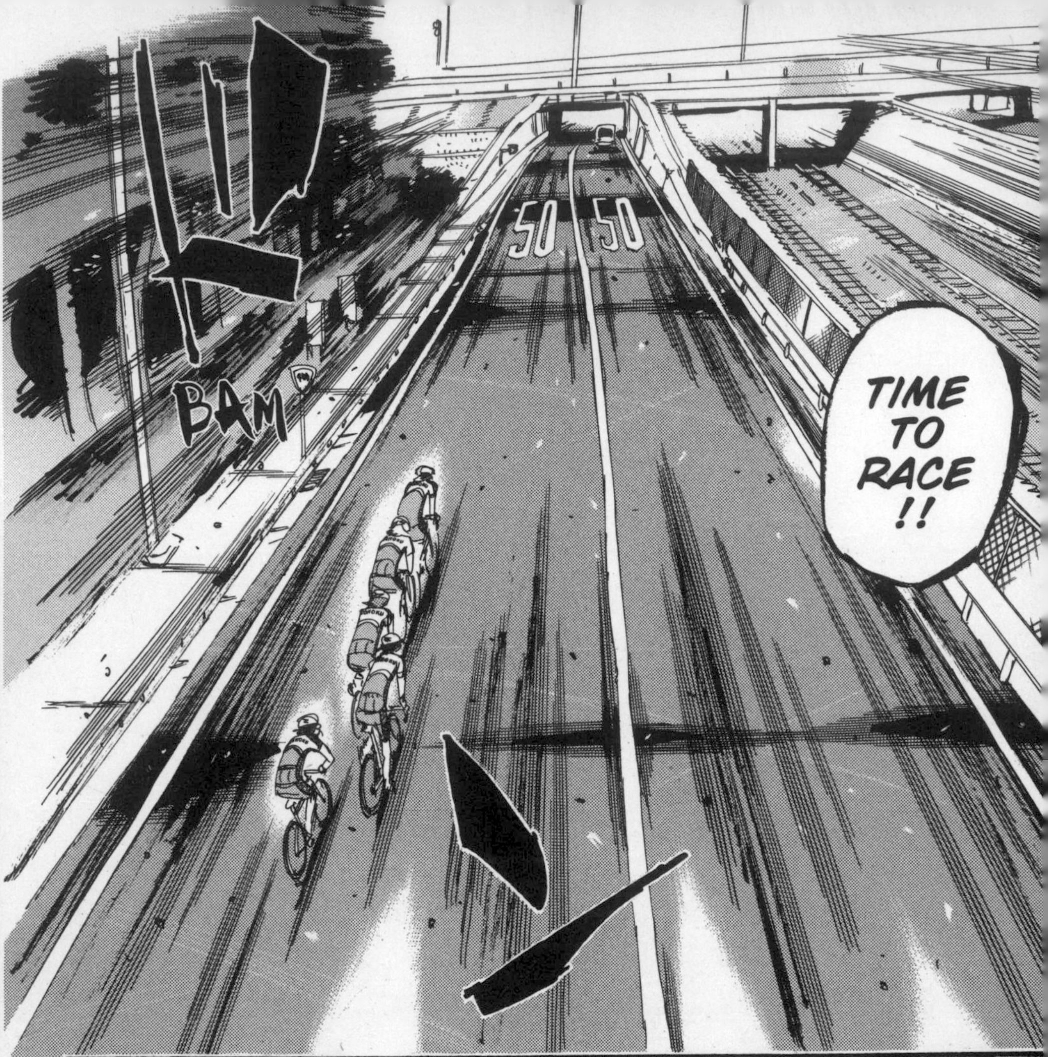
BAM
TIME TO RACE!!
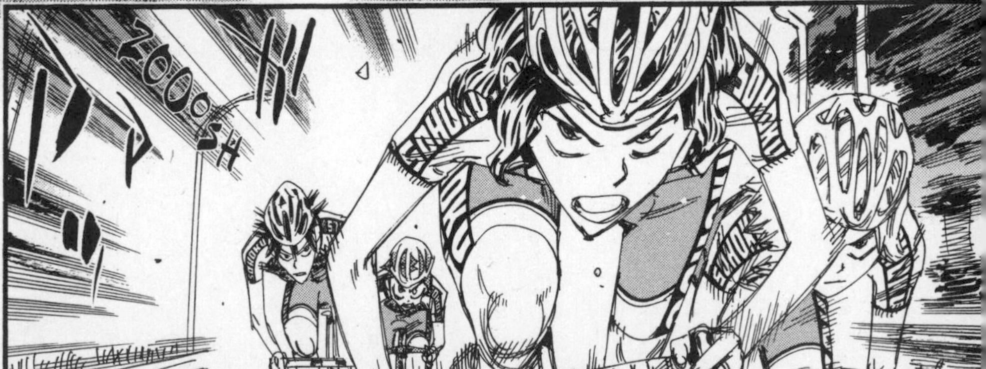
ZOOOSH

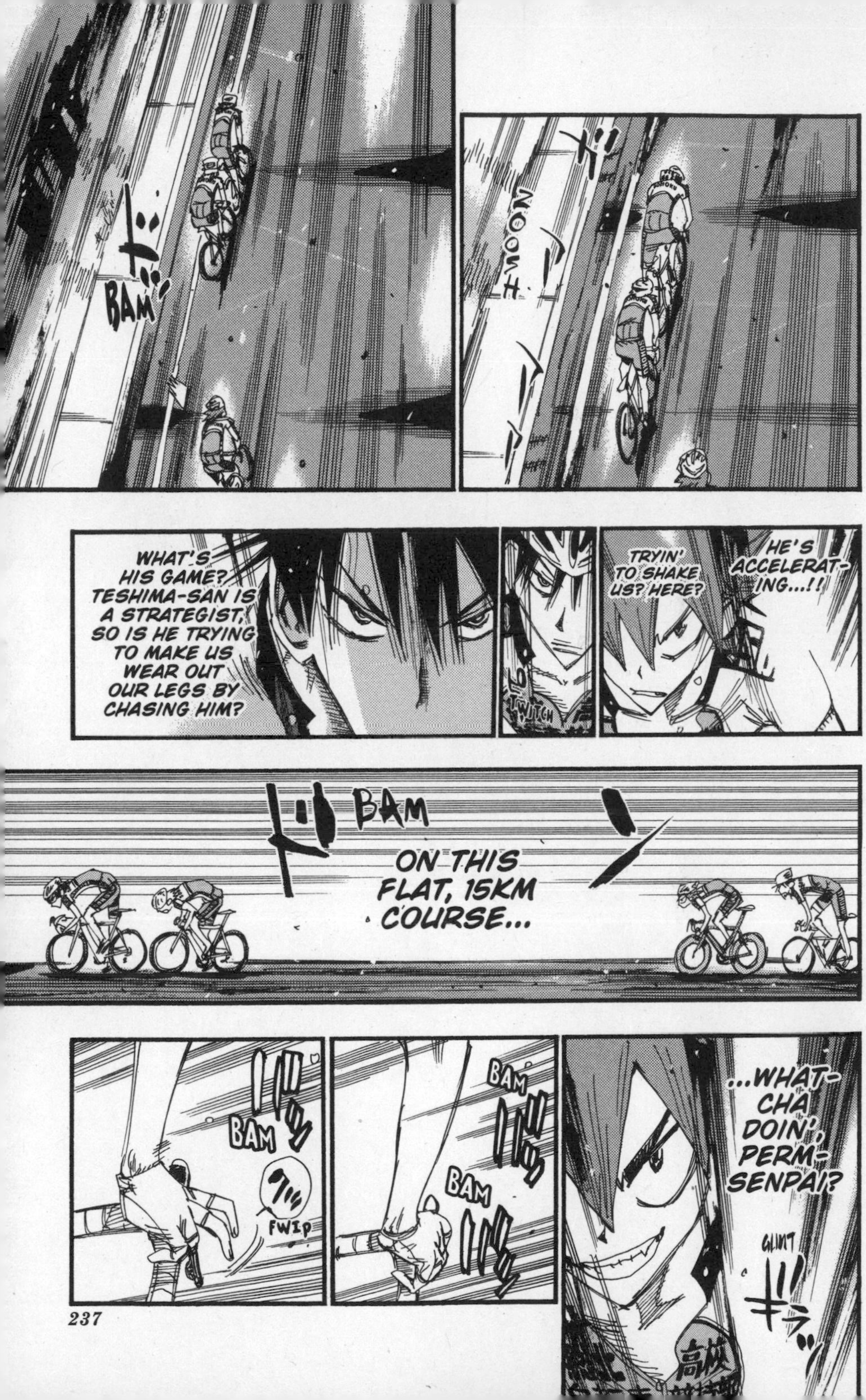
ZOOM
BAM
WHAT'S HIS GAME? TESHIMA-SAN IS A STRATEGIST, SO IS HE TRYING TO MAKE US WEAR OUT OUR LEGS BY CHASING HIM?
HE'S ACCELERATING...!!
TRYIN' TO SHAKE US? HERE?
TWITCH
BAM
ON THIS FLAT, 15KM COURSE...
...WHATCHA DOIN', PERM-SENPAI?
GLINT
BAM
BAM
BAM
FWIP

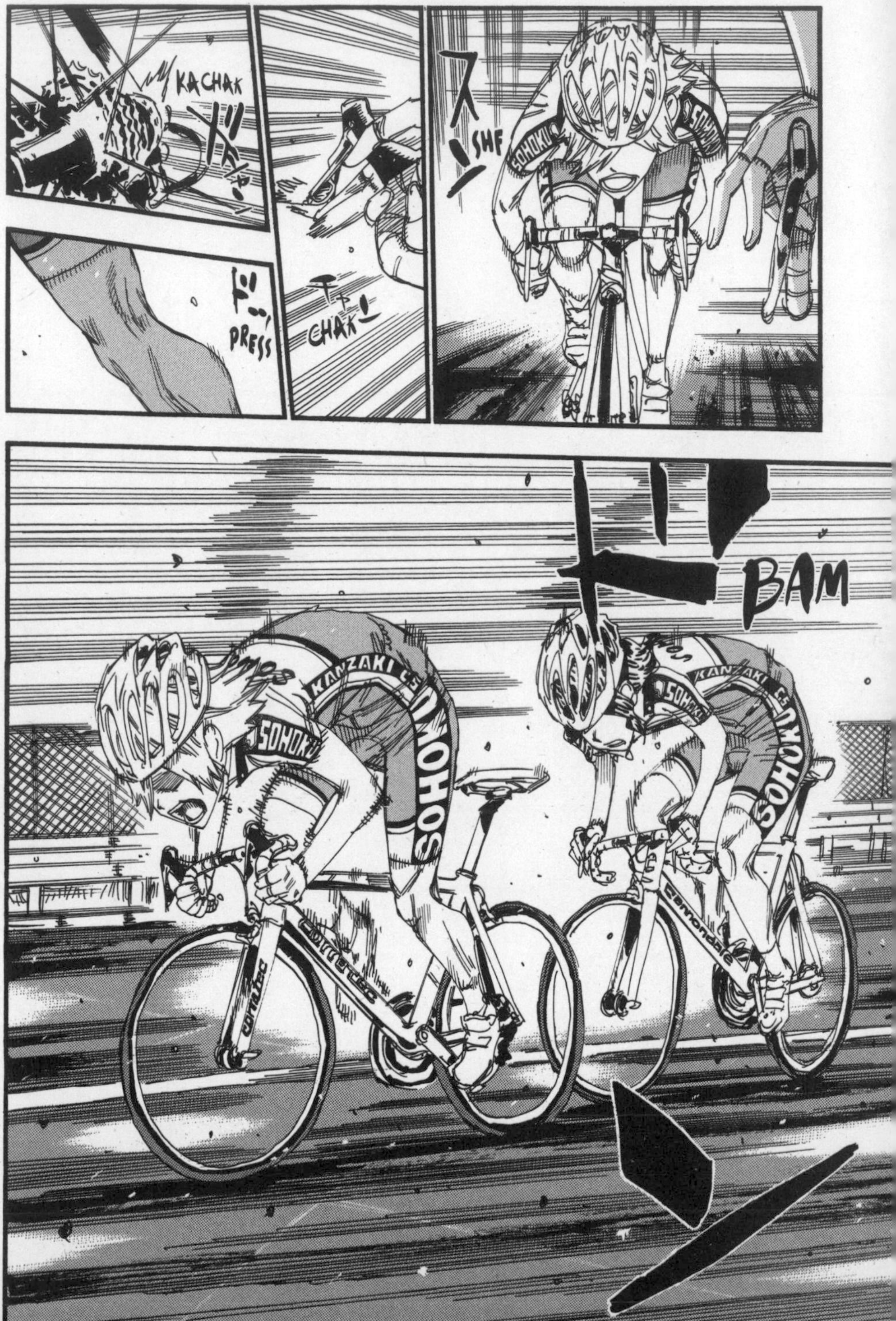
SHF
CHAK
KACHAK
PRESS
BAM

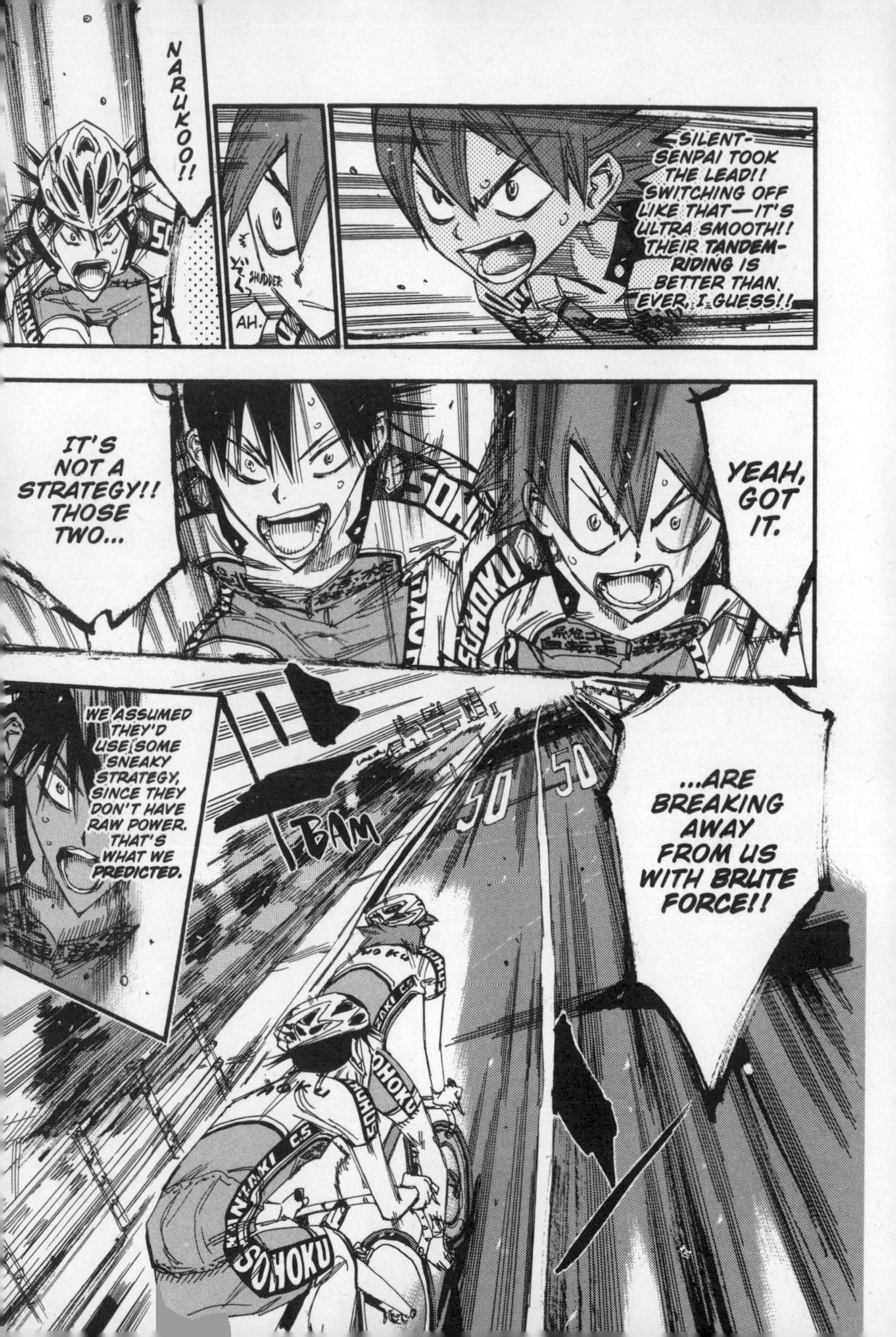
SILENT-SENPAI TOOK THE LEAD!! SWITCHING OFF LIKE THAT—IT'S ULTRA SMOOTH!! THEIR TANDEM-RIDING IS BETTER THAN EVER, I GUESS!!
SHUDDER
AH.
NARUKOOO!!
YEAH, GOT IT.
IT'S NOT A STRATEGY!! THOSE TWO...
...ARE BREAKING AWAY FROM US WITH BRUTE FORCE!!
BAM
WE ASSUMED THEY'D USE SOME SNEAKY STRATEGY, SINCE THEY DON'T HAVE RAW POWER. THAT'S WHAT WE PREDICTED.

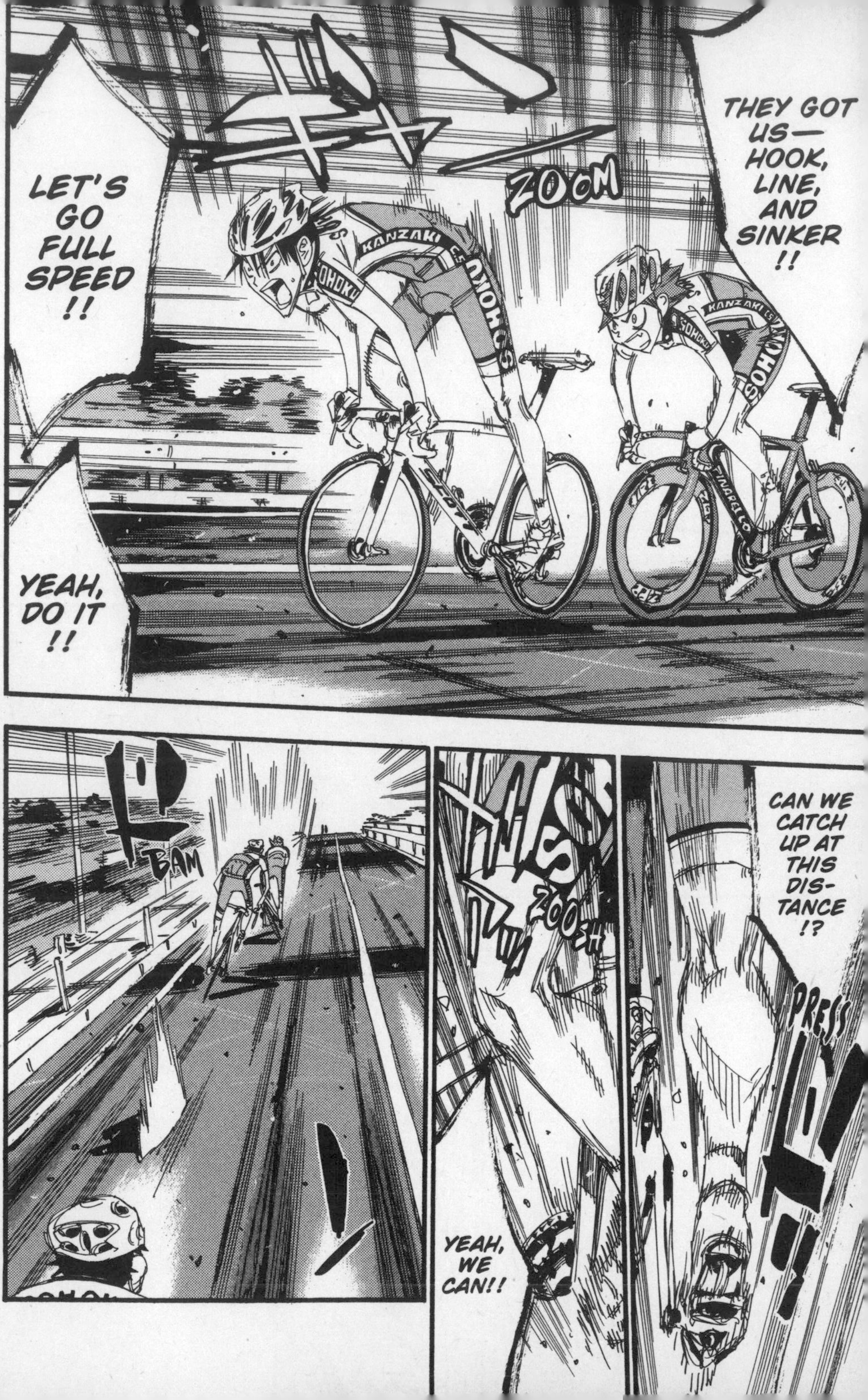
THEY GOT US— HOOK, LINE, AND SINKER!!
ZOOM
LET'S GO FULL SPEED!!
YEAH, DO IT!!
CAN WE CATCH UP AT THIS DIS-TANCE!?
PRESS
ZOOSH
YEAH, WE CAN!!
BAM

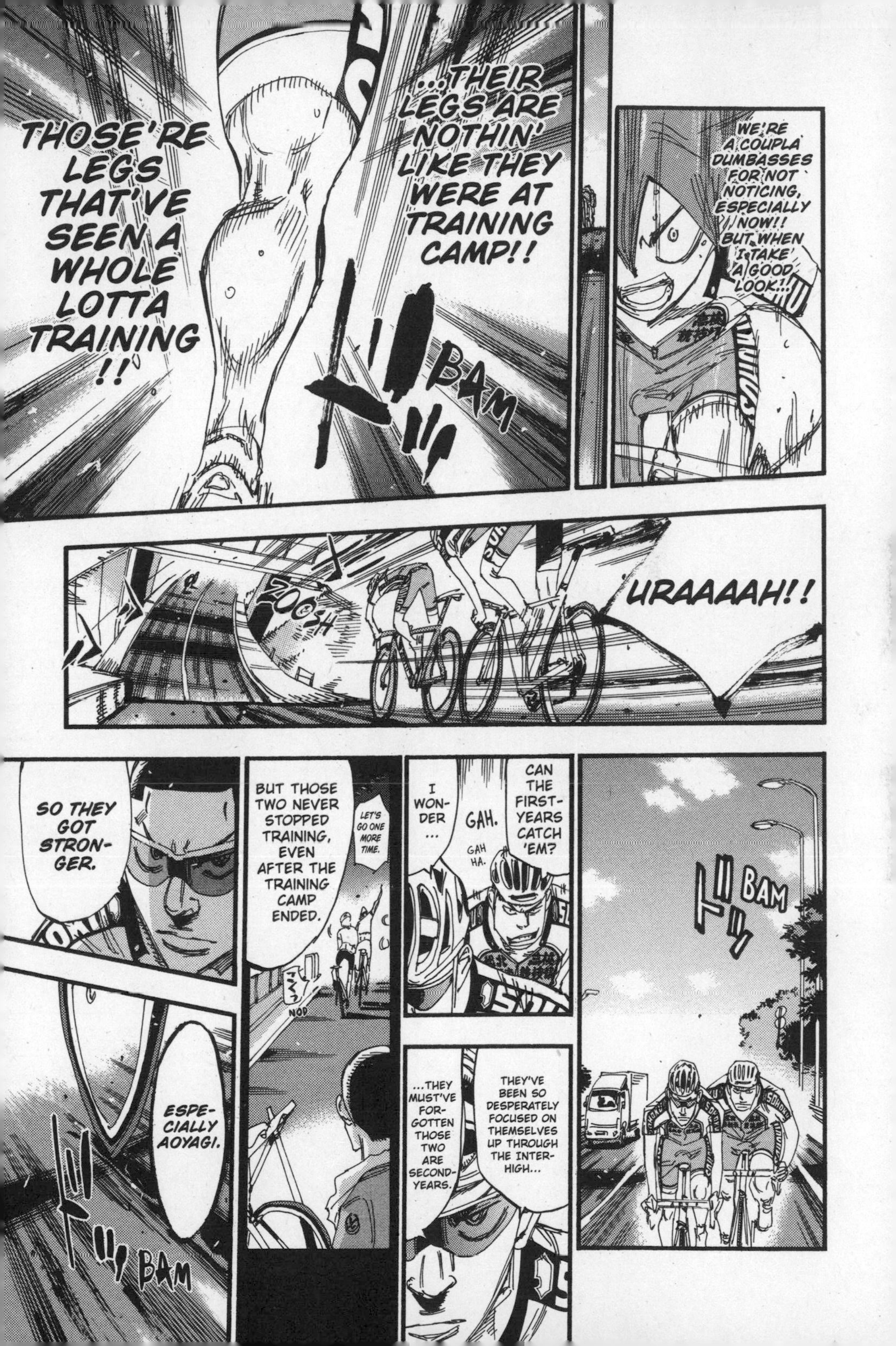
WE'RE A COUPLA DUMBASSES FOR NOT NOTICING, ESPECIALLY NOW!! BUT WHEN I TAKE A GOOD LOOK...!!
...THEIR LEGS ARE NOTHIN' LIKE THEY WERE AT TRAINING CAMP!!
THOSE'RE LEGS THAT'VE SEEN A WHOLE LOTTA TRAINING!!
BAM
URAAAAH!!
ZOOSH
BAM
CAN THE FIRST-YEARS CATCH 'EM?
I WONDER...
GAH.
GAH HA.
THEY'VE BEEN SO DESPERATELY FOCUSED ON THEMSELVES UP THROUGH THE INTER-HIGH...
...THEY MUST'VE FORGOTTEN THOSE TWO ARE SECOND-YEARS.
BUT THOSE TWO NEVER STOPPED TRAINING, EVEN AFTER THE TRAINING CAMP ENDED.
LET'S GO ONE MORE TIME.
NOD
SO THEY GOT STRONGER.
ESPE-CIALLY AOYAGI.
BAM

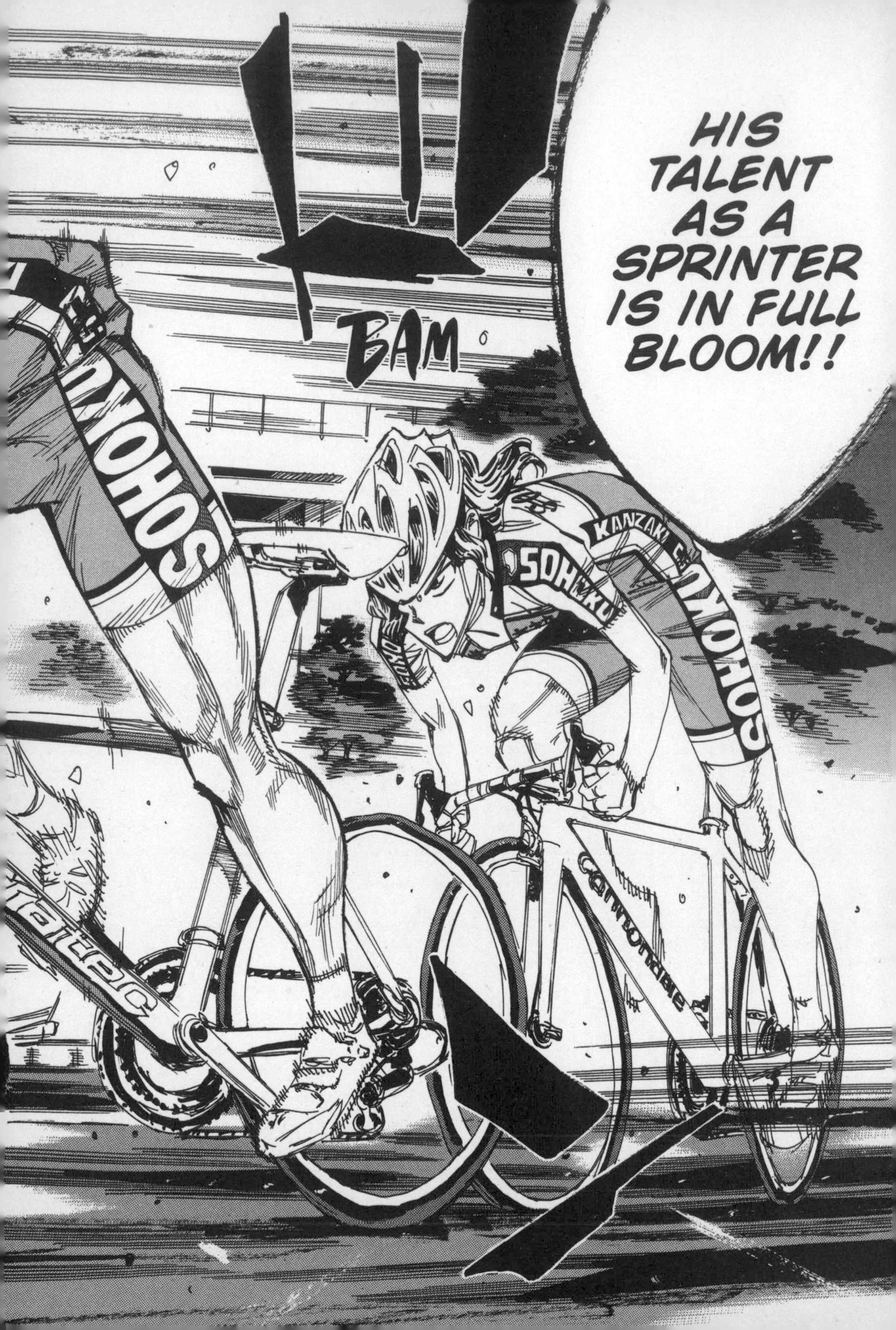
HIS TALENT AS A SPRINTER IS IN FULL BLOOM!!
BAM

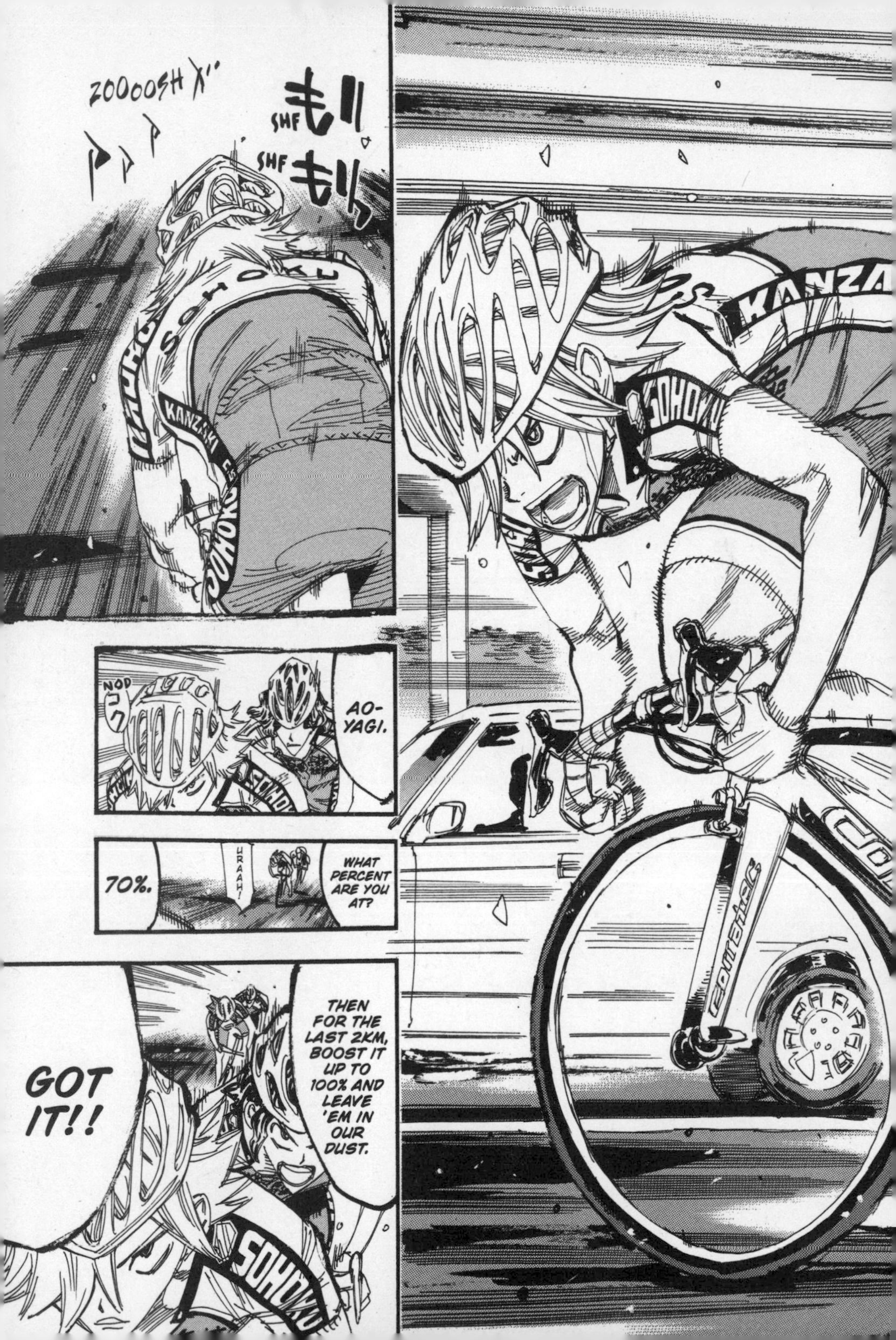
ZOOOOSH
SHF
SHF
NOD
AO-YAGI.
WHAT PERCENT ARE YOU AT?
URAAH!
70%.
THEN FOR THE LAST 2KM, BOOST IT UP TO 100% AND LEAVE 'EM IN OUR DUST.
GOT IT!!

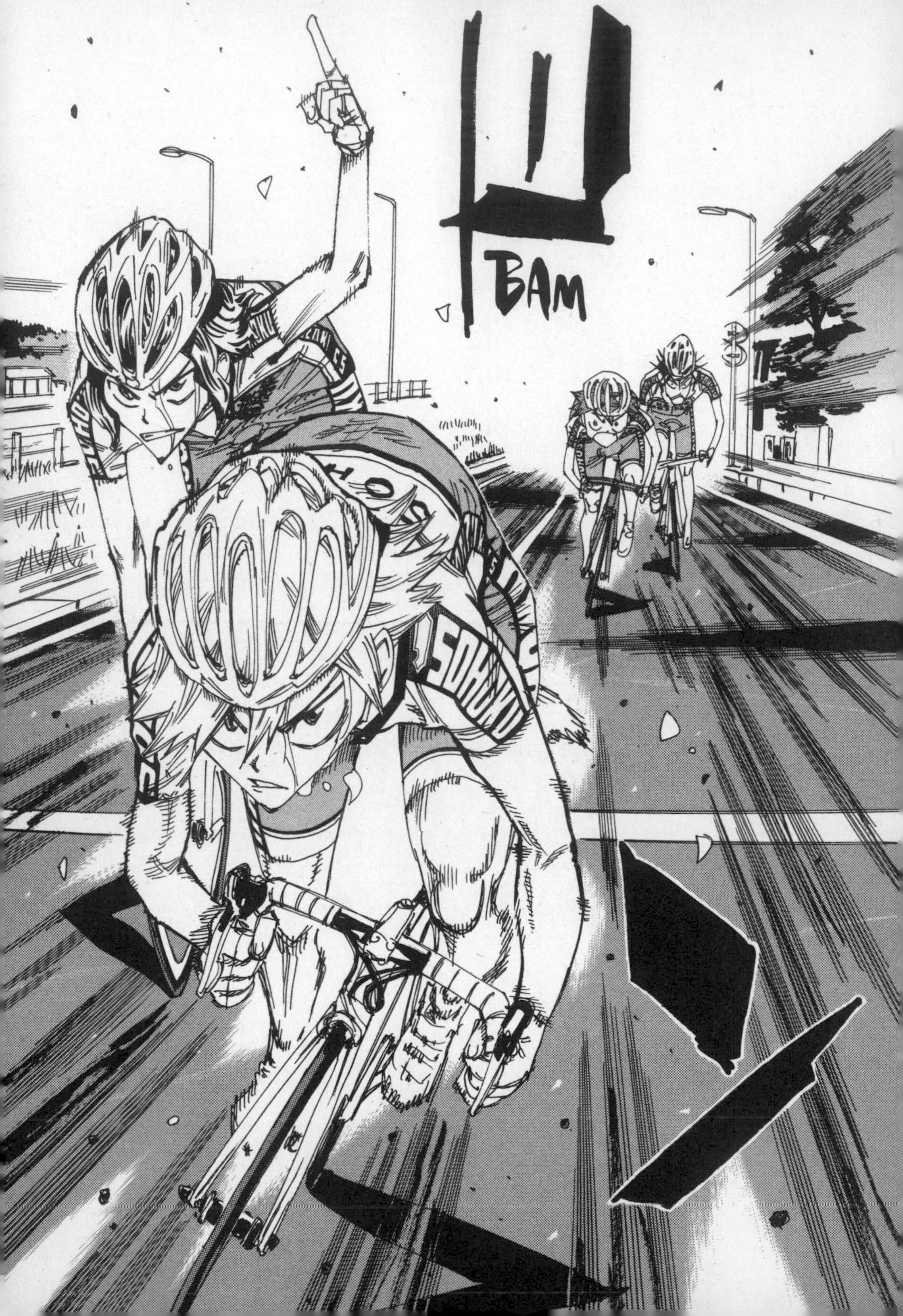
BAM
SOHOKU

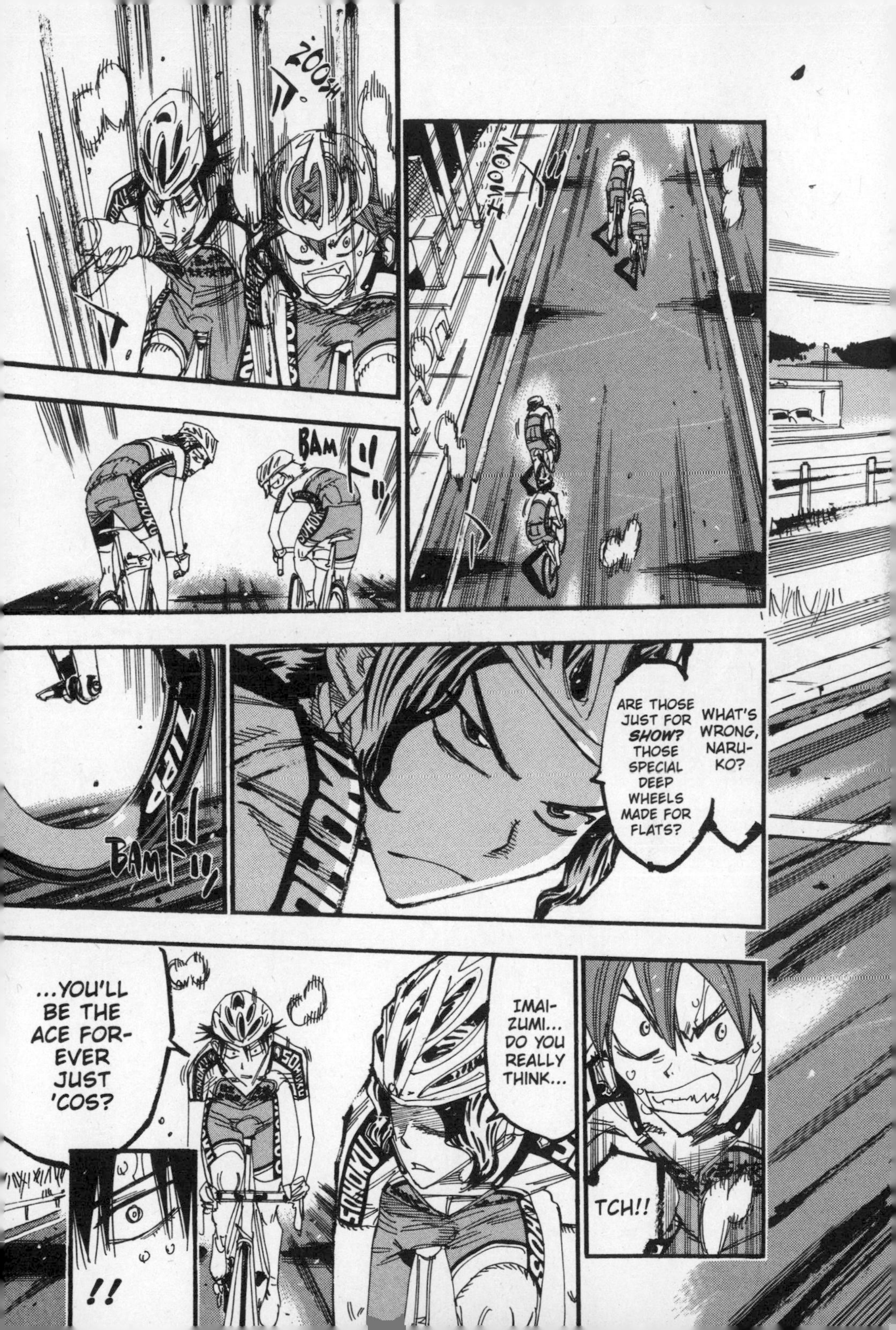
ZOOSH
BAM
WHAT'S WRONG, NARUKO?
ARE THOSE JUST FOR **SHOW?** THOSE SPECIAL DEEP WHEELS MADE FOR FLATS?
BAM
TCH!!
IMAI-ZUMI... DO YOU REALLY THINK...
...YOU'LL BE THE ACE FOR-EVER JUST 'COS?
!!

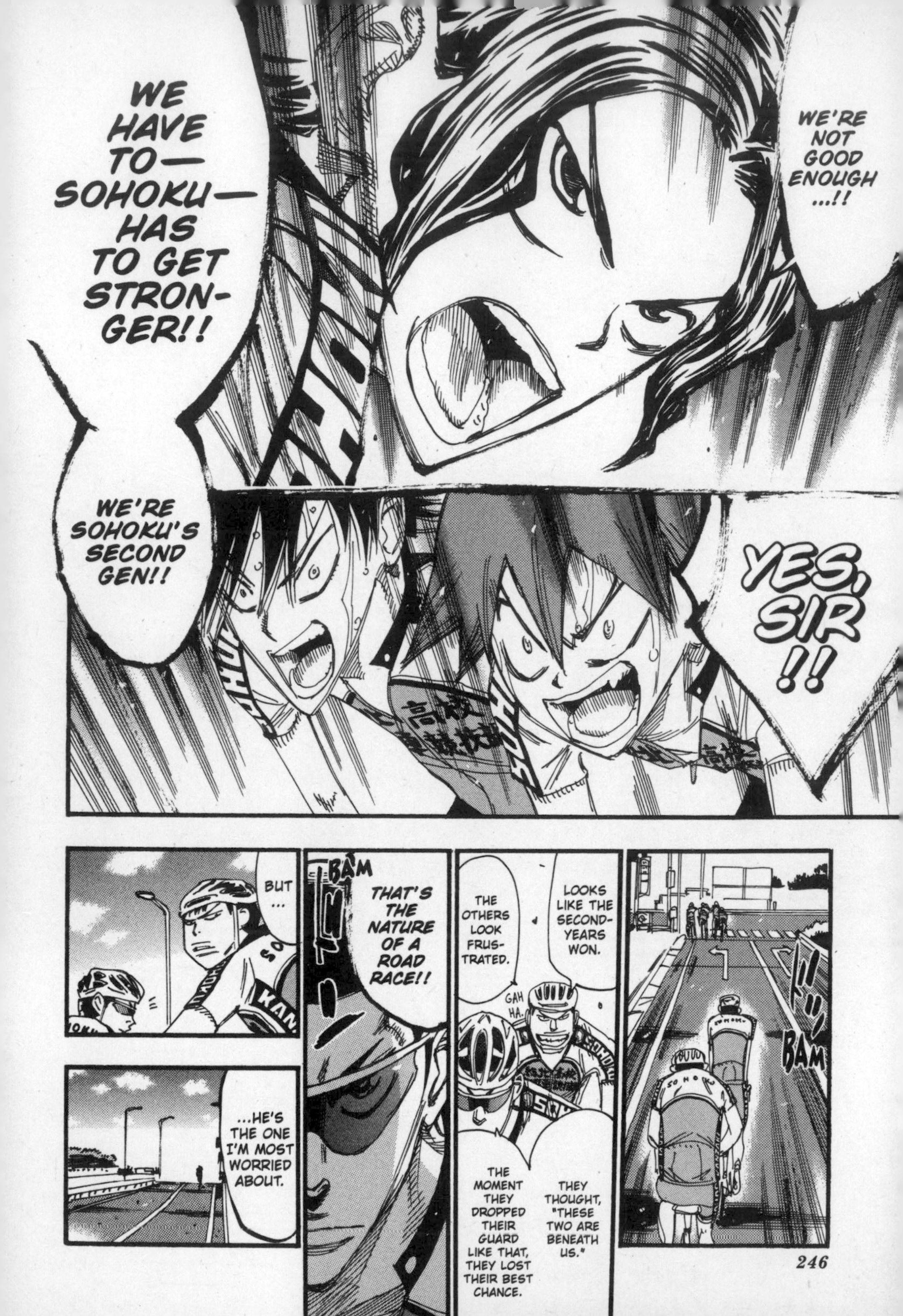

WE'RE NOT GOOD ENOUGH...!!
WE HAVE TO— SOHOKU— HAS TO GET STRONGER!!
WE'RE SOHOKU'S SECOND GEN!!
YES, SIR!!
BAM
LOOKS LIKE THE SECOND-YEARS WON.
THE OTHERS LOOK FRUSTRATED.
GAH HA.
THEY THOUGHT, "THESE TWO ARE BENEATH US."
THE MOMENT THEY DROPPED THEIR GUARD LIKE THAT, THEY LOST THEIR BEST CHANCE.
BAM
THAT'S THE NATURE OF A ROAD RACE!!
BUT...
...HE'S THE ONE I'M MOST WORRIED ABOUT.

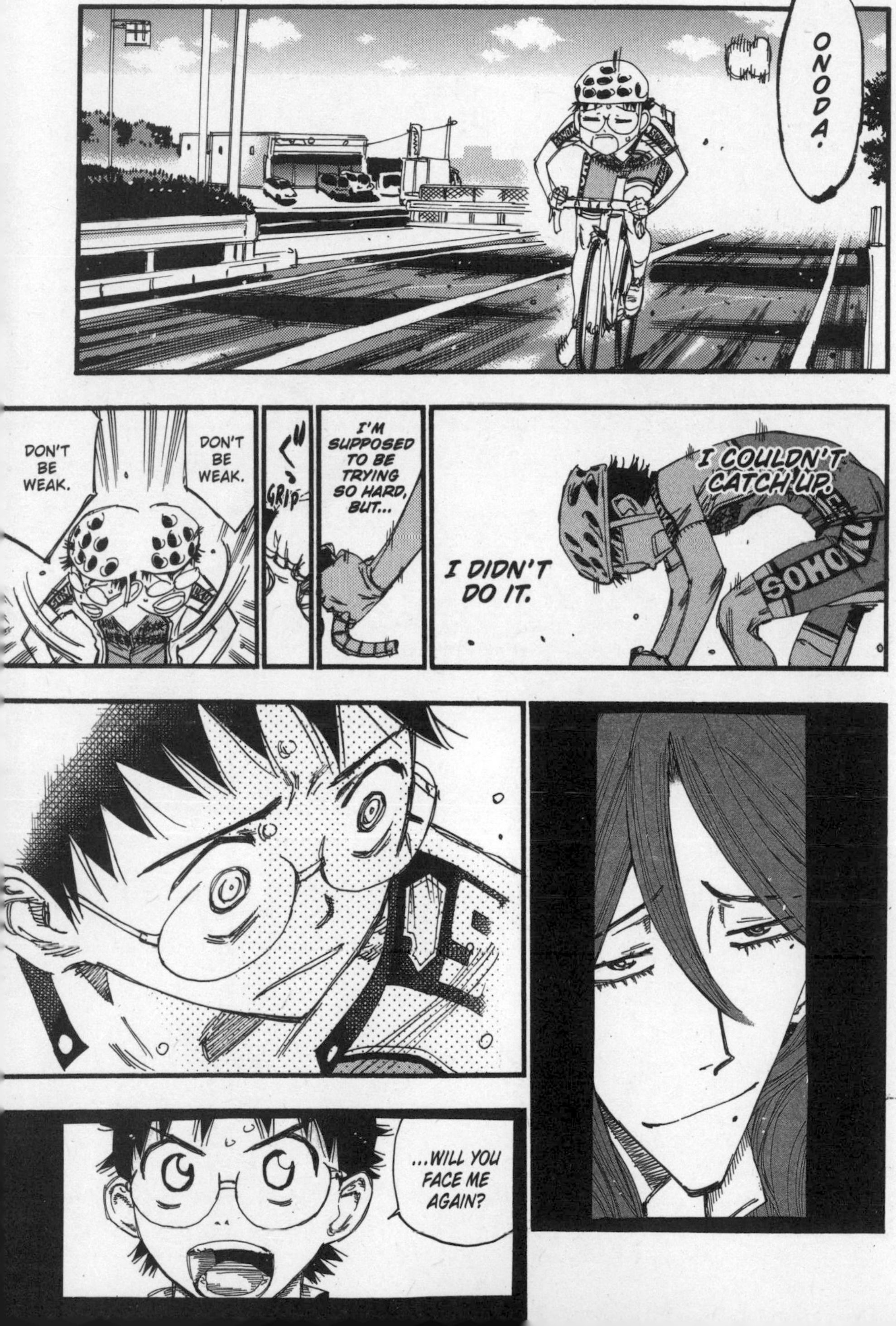
ONODA.
I COULDN'T CATCH UP.
I DIDN'T DO IT.
I'M SUPPOSED TO BE TRYING SO HARD, BUT...
GRIP
DON'T BE WEAK.
DON'T BE WEAK.
...WILL YOU FACE ME AGAIN?

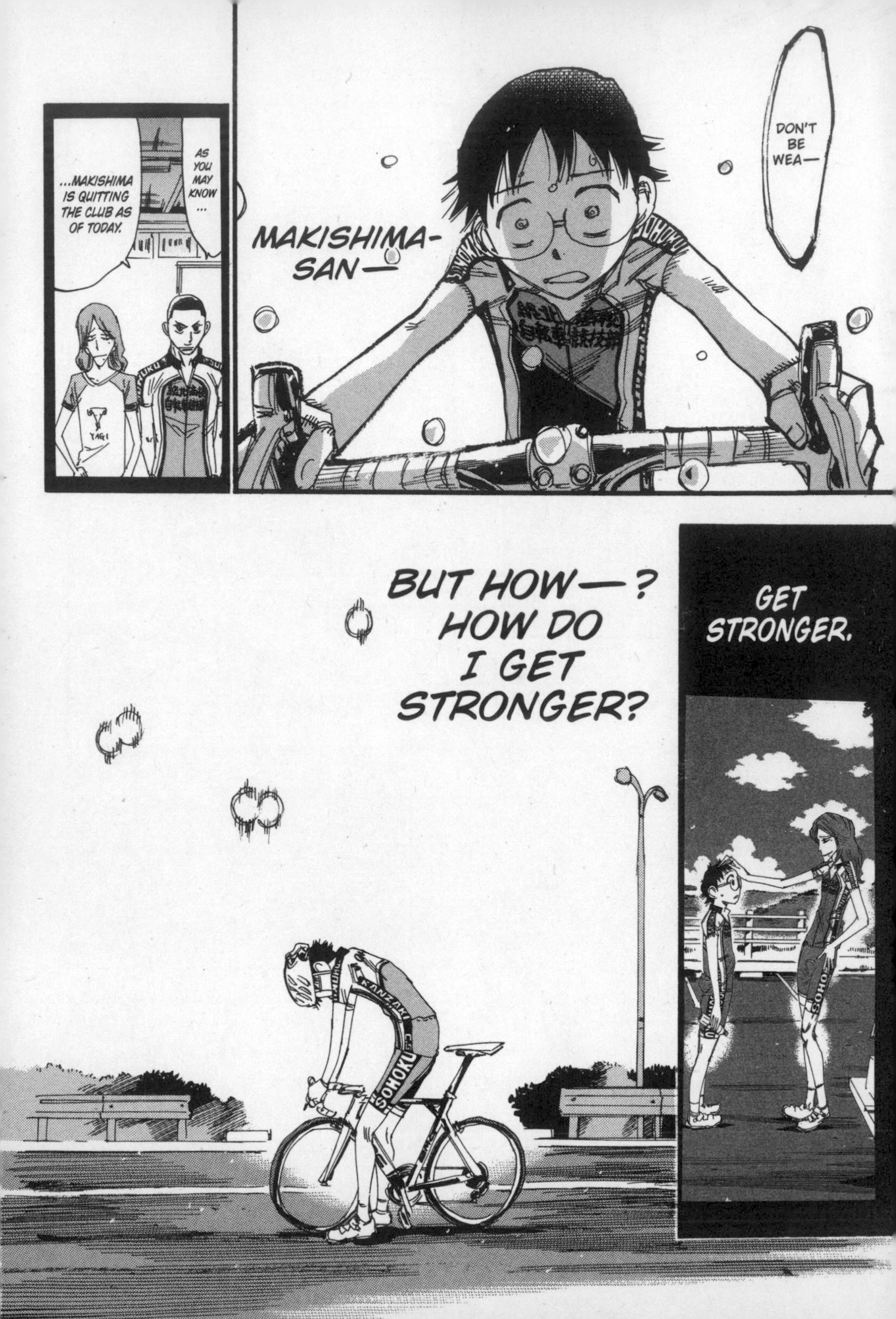
DON'T BE WEA—
MAKISHIMA-SAN—
AS YOU MAY KNOW ...
...MAKISHIMA IS QUITTING THE CLUB AS OF TODAY.
GET STRONGER.
BUT HOW—? HOW DO I GET STRONGER?

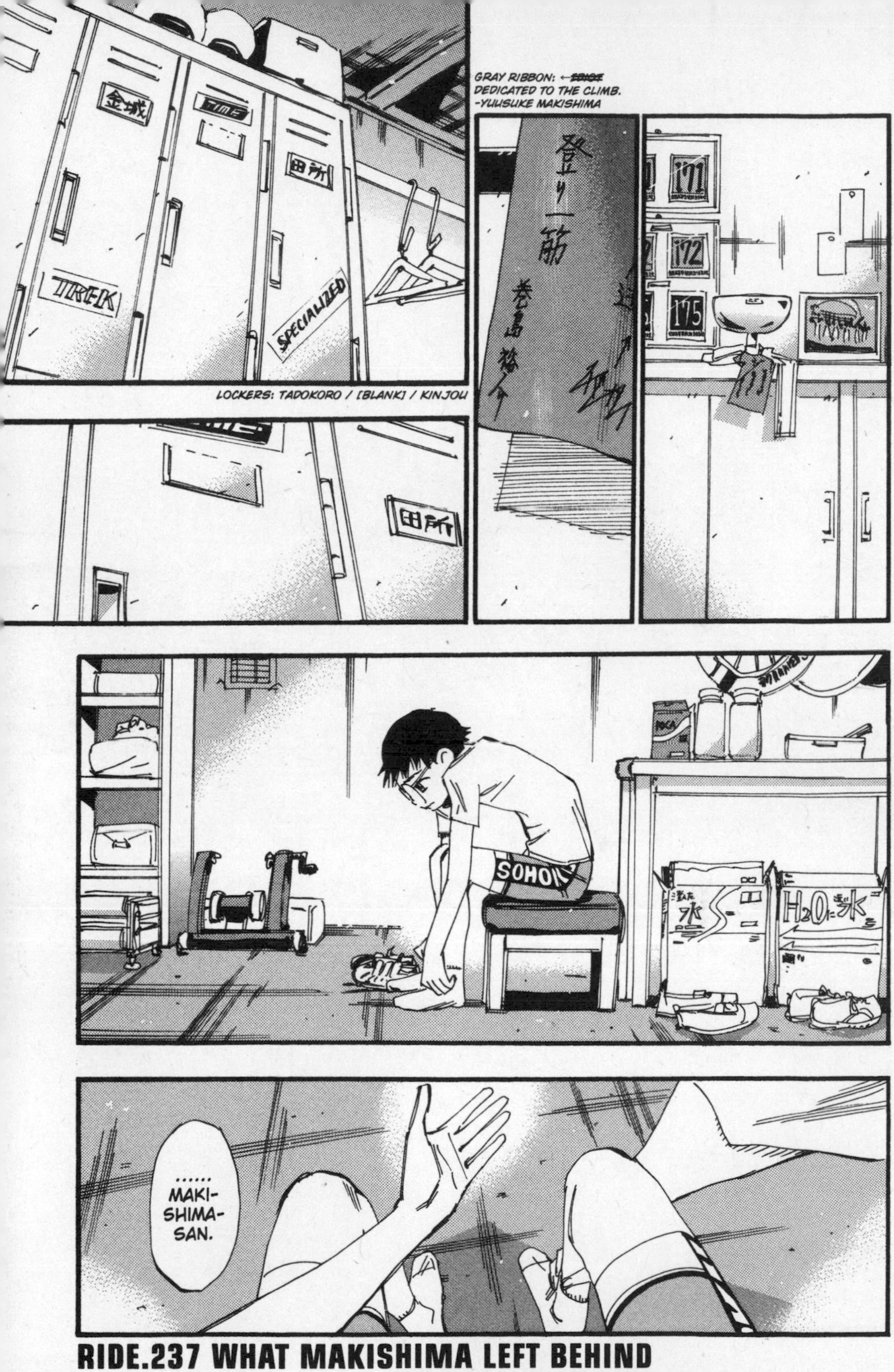
GRAY RIBBON: ←
DEDICATED TO THE CLIMB.
-YUUSUKE MAKISHIMA
LOCKERS: TADOKORO / [BLANK] / KINJOU
TREK
SPECIALIZED
SOHOKU
......MAKI-SHIMA-SAN.

RIDE.237 WHAT MAKISHIMA LEFT BEHIND

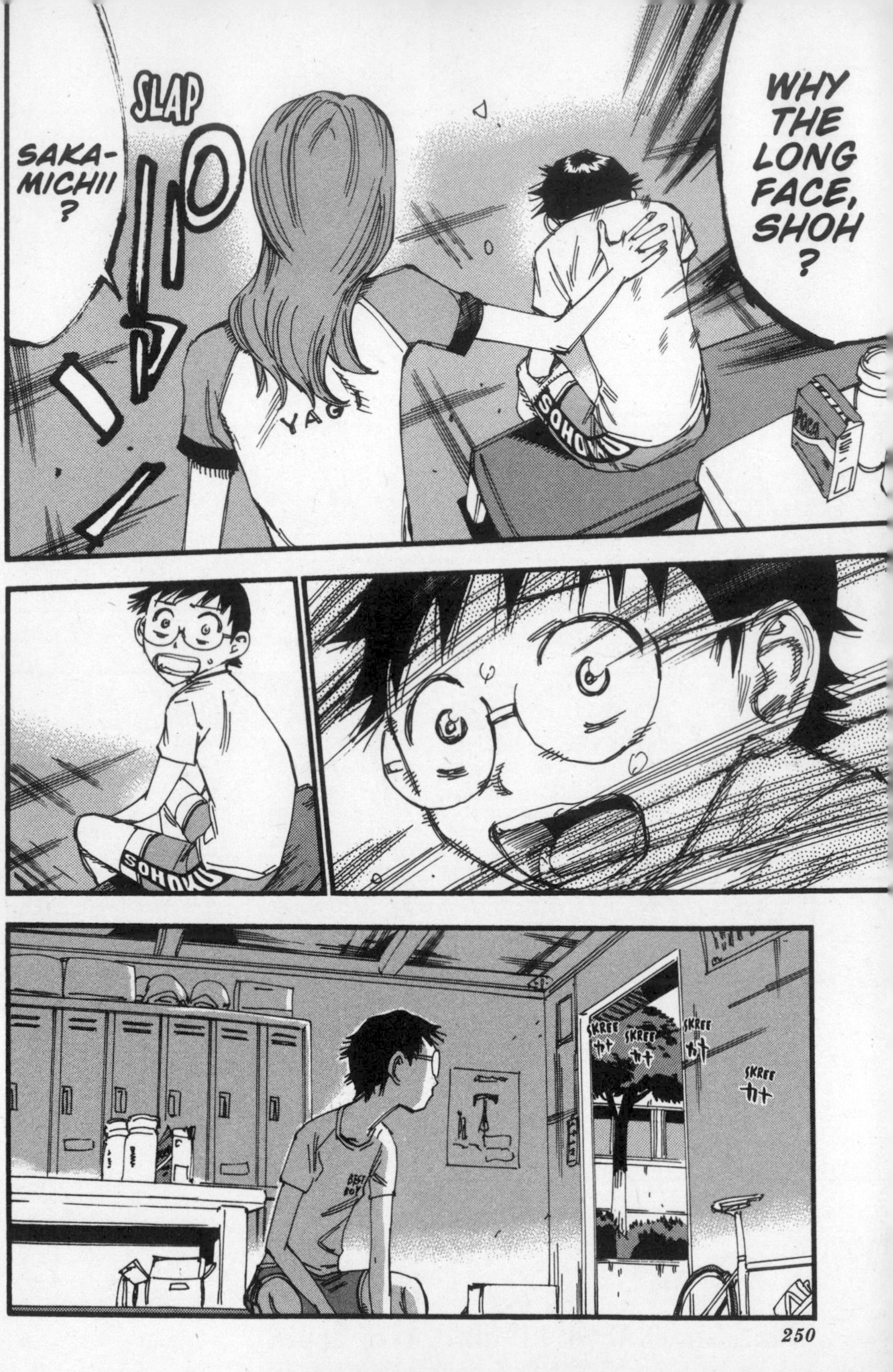
WHY THE LONG FACE, SHOH?
SLAP
SAKA-MICHII?
SKREE
SKREE
SKREE
SKREE

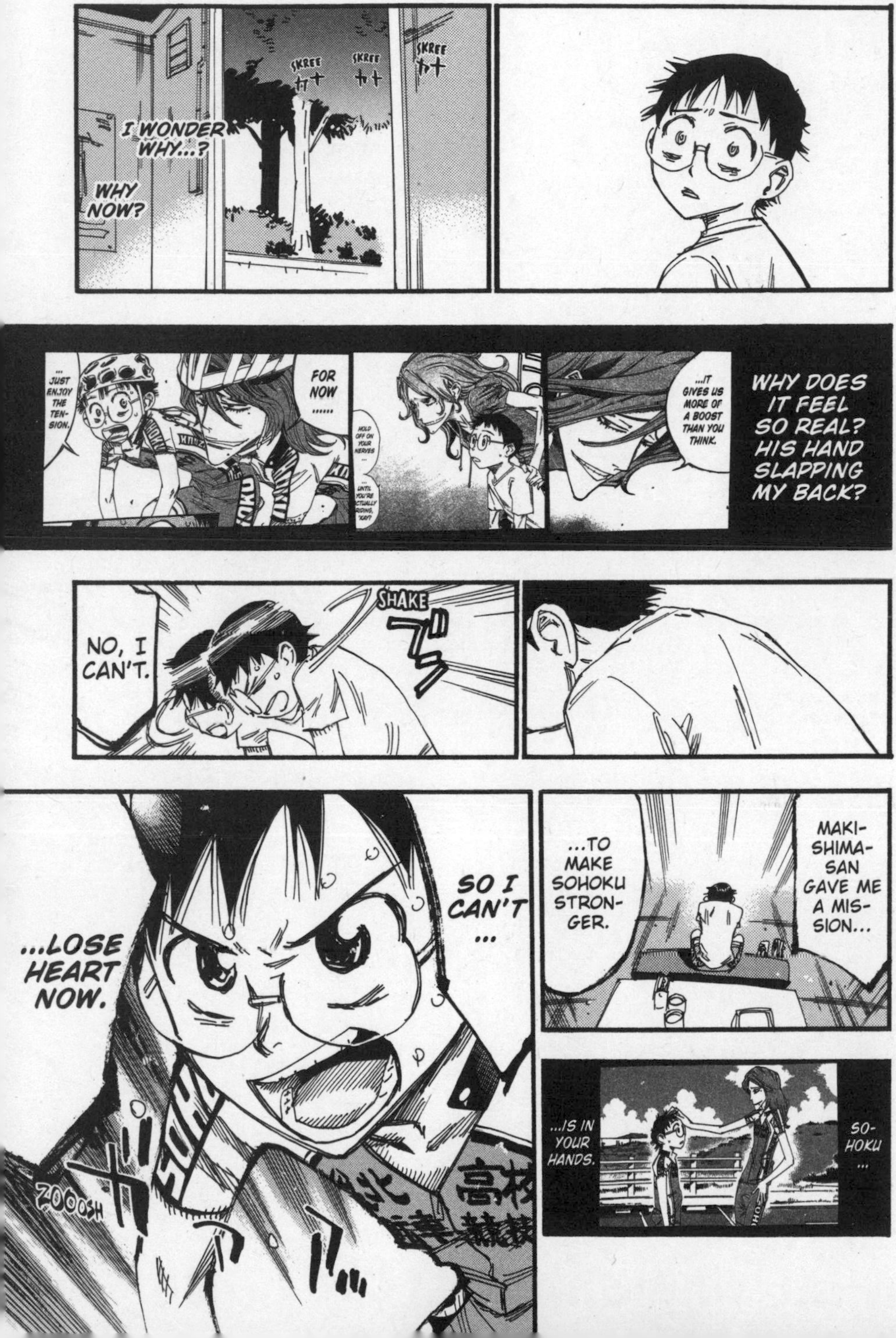
SKREE
SKREE
SKREE
I WONDER WHY...?
WHY NOW?
WHY DOES IT FEEL SO REAL? HIS HAND SLAPPING MY BACK?
...IT GIVES US MORE OF A BOOST THAN YOU THINK.
HOLD OFF ON YOUR NERVES...
UNTIL YOU'RE ACTUALLY RIDING, 'KAY?
FOR NOW ......
...JUST ENJOY THE TENSION.
SHAKE
NO, I CAN'T.
MAKI-SHIMA-SAN GAVE ME A MIS-SION...
...TO MAKE SOHOKU STRON-GER.
SO-HOKU ...
...IS IN YOUR HANDS.
SO I CAN'T ...
...LOSE HEART NOW.
ZOOOSH

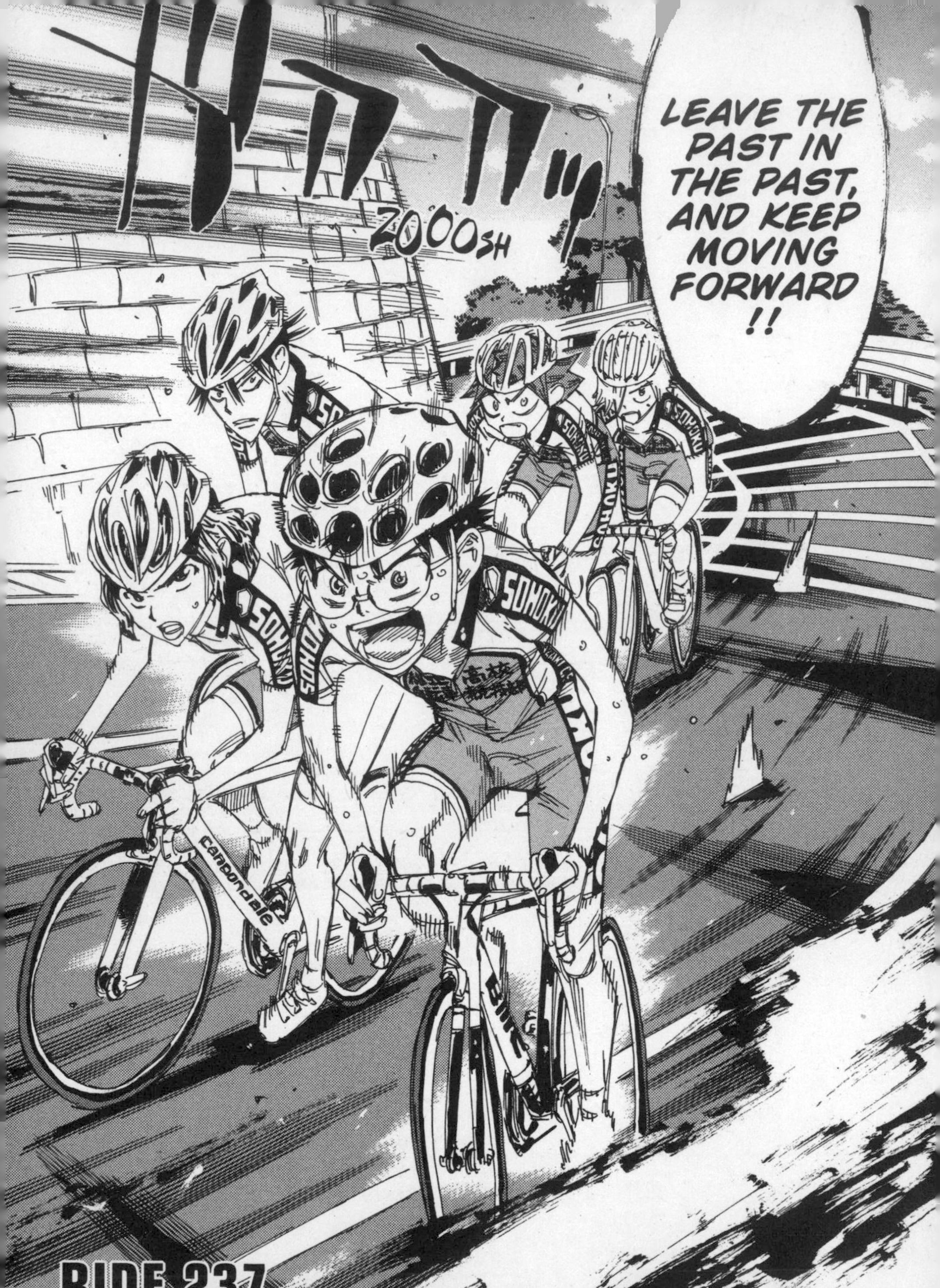
ZOOOSH
LEAVE THE PAST IN THE PAST, AND KEEP MOVING FORWARD !!

RIDE.237
WHAT MAKISHIMA LEFT BEHIND

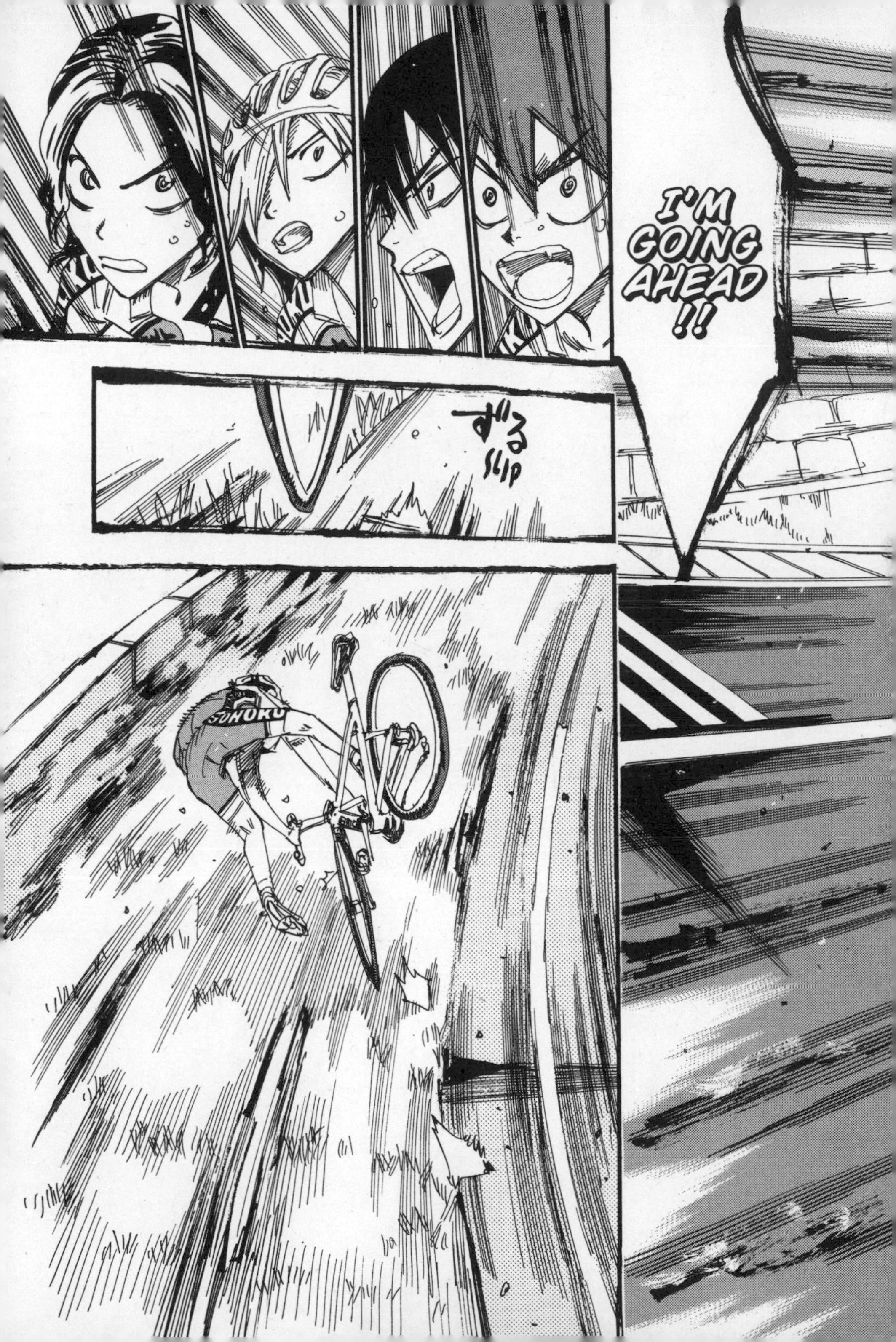
I'M GOING AHEAD !!
ずる
SLIP
SOHOKU

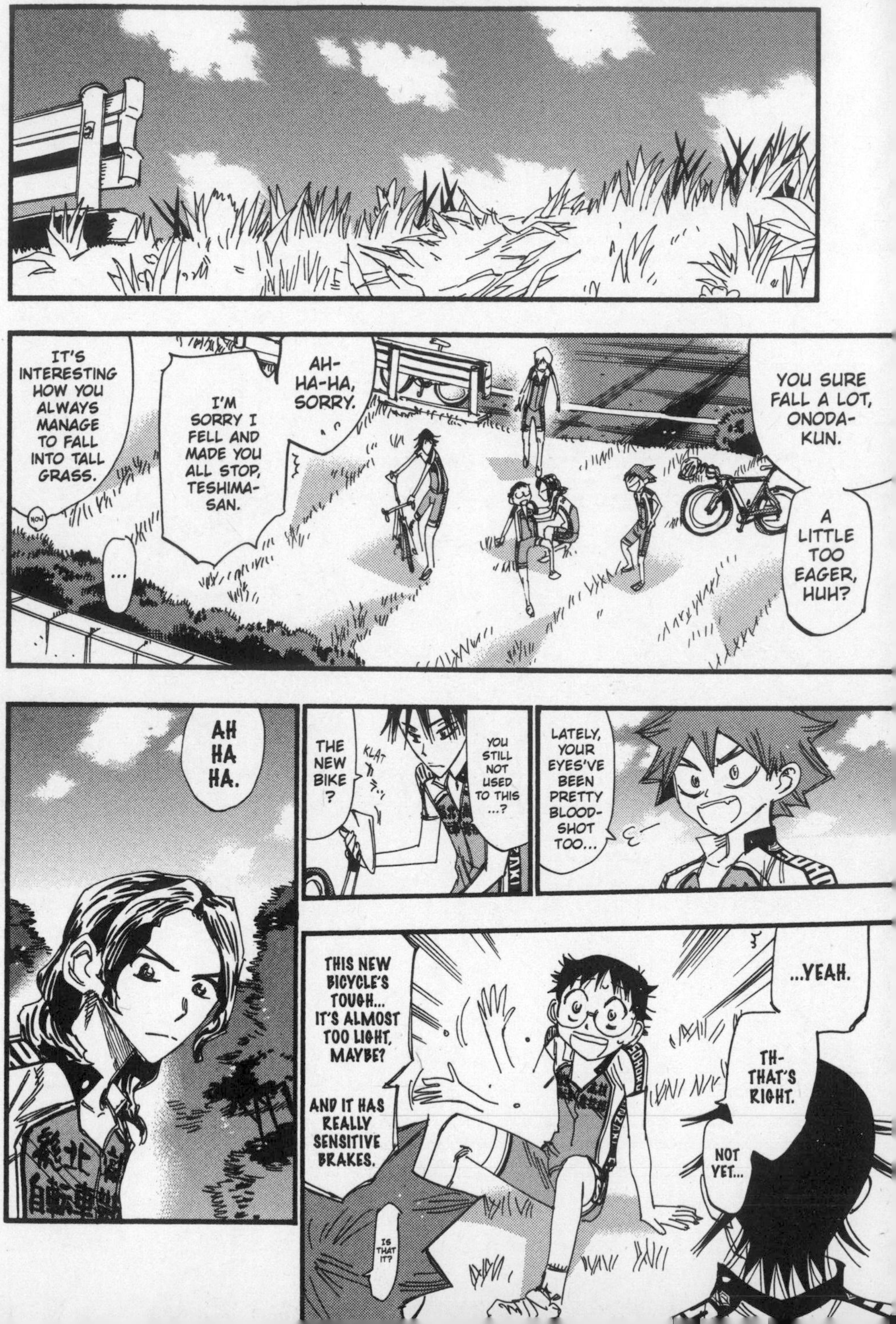
YOU SURE FALL A LOT, ONODA-KUN.
A LITTLE TOO EAGER, HUH?
AH-HA-HA, SORRY.
I'M SORRY I FELL AND MADE YOU ALL STOP, TESHIMA-SAN.
IT'S INTERESTING HOW YOU ALWAYS MANAGE TO FALL INTO TALL GRASS.
NOW
...
LATELY, YOUR EYES'VE BEEN PRETTY BLOOD-SHOT TOO...
YOU STILL NOT USED TO THIS ...?
KLAT
THE NEW BIKE ?
...YEAH.
TH-THAT'S RIGHT.
NOT YET...
THIS NEW BICYCLE'S TOUGH... IT'S ALMOST TOO LIGHT, MAYBE?
AND IT HAS REALLY SENSITIVE BRAKES.
IS THAT IT?
AH HA HA.

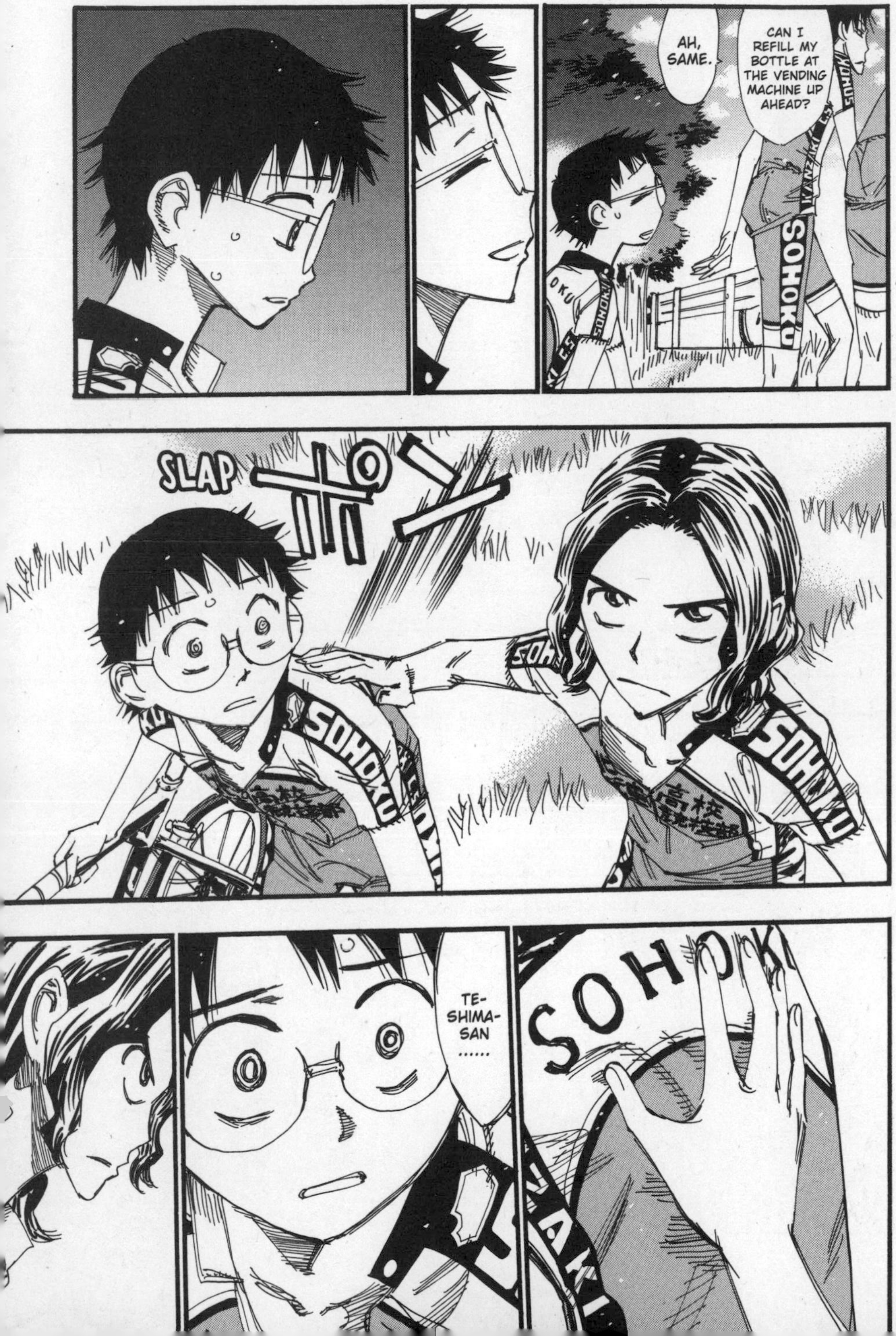
CAN I REFILL MY BOTTLE AT THE VENDING MACHINE UP AHEAD?
AH, SAME.
SOHOKU
SLAP
SOHOKU
TE-SHIMA-SAN ......

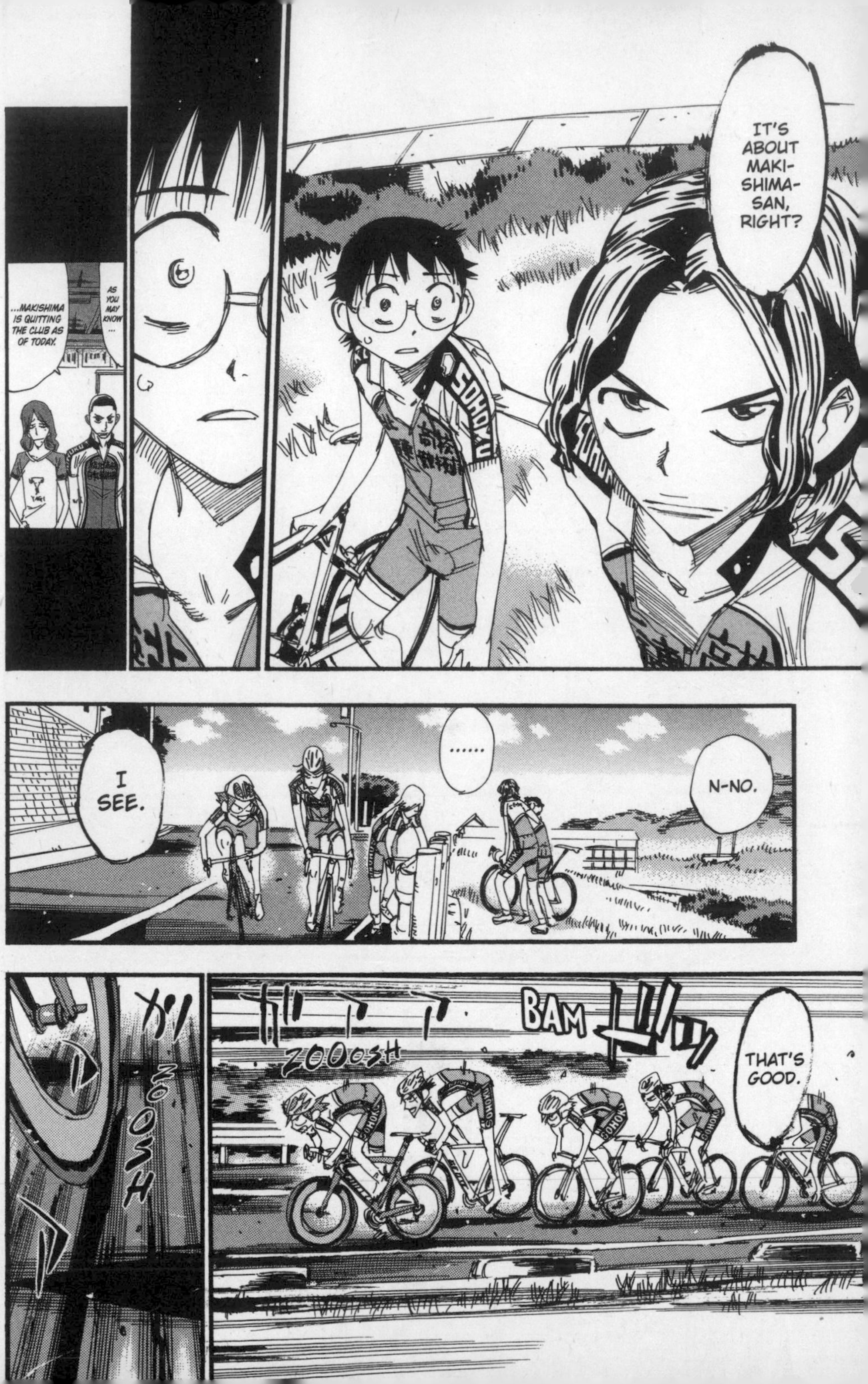
IT'S ABOUT MAKI-SHIMA-SAN, RIGHT?
AS YOU MAY KNOW ...
...MAKISHIMA IS QUITTING THE CLUB AS OF TODAY.
N-NO.
......
I SEE.
BAM
THAT'S GOOD.
ZOOOSH
ZOOOSH

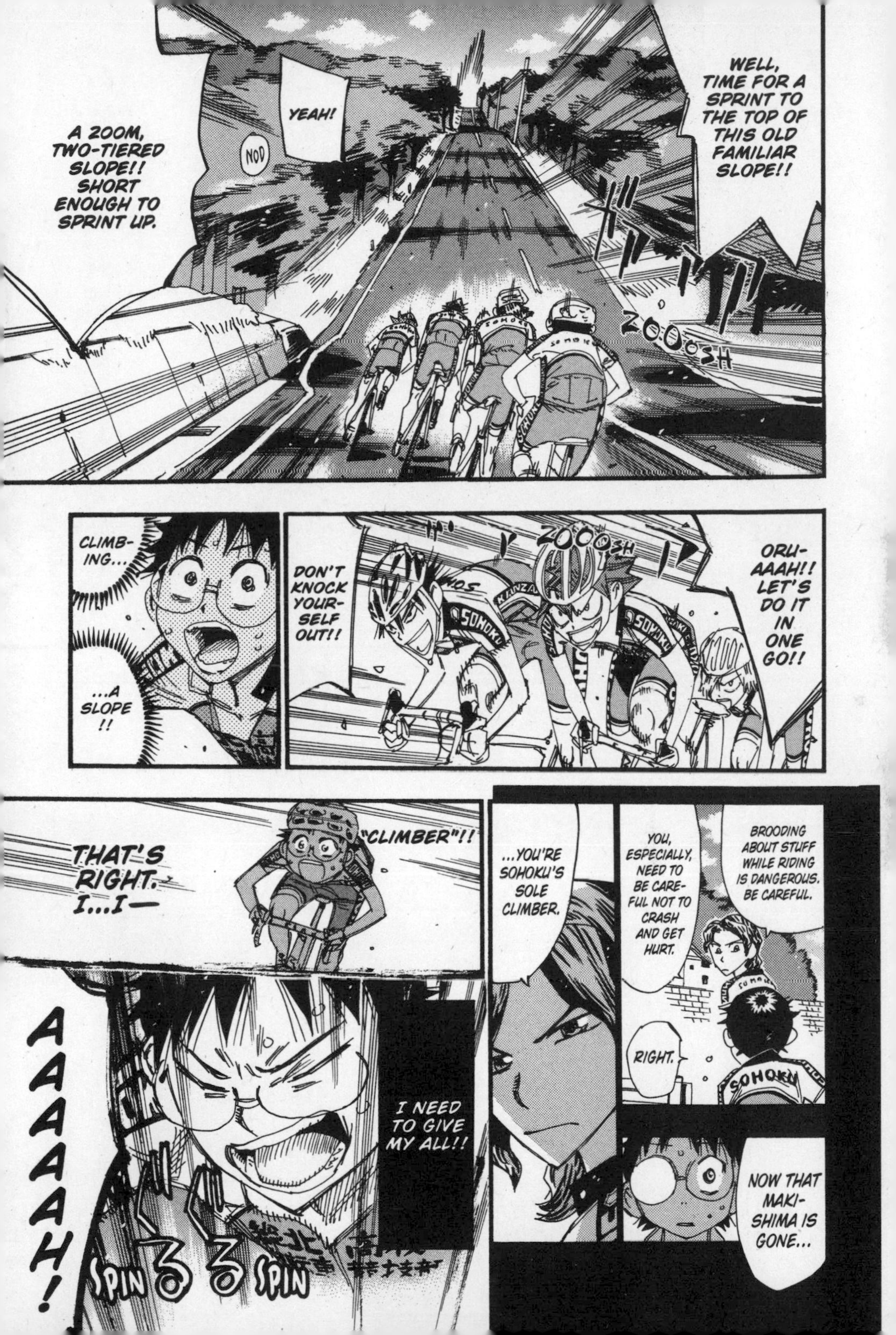
WELL, TIME FOR A SPRINT TO THE TOP OF THIS OLD FAMILIAR SLOPE!!
ZOOOSH
YEAH!
NOD
A ZOOM, TWO-TIERED SLOPE!! SHORT ENOUGH TO SPRINT UP.
ORU-AAAH!! LET'S DO IT IN ONE GO!!
ZOOOSH
DON'T KNOCK YOURSELF OUT!!
CLIMBING...
...A SLOPE!!
BROODING ABOUT STUFF WHILE RIDING IS DANGEROUS. BE CAREFUL.
YOU, ESPECIALLY, NEED TO BE CAREFUL NOT TO CRASH AND GET HURT.
RIGHT.
NOW THAT MAKISHIMA IS GONE...
...YOU'RE SOHOKU'S SOLE CLIMBER.
"CLIMBER"!!
THAT'S RIGHT. I...I—
I NEED TO GIVE MY ALL!!
AAAAAAH!
SPIN SPIN

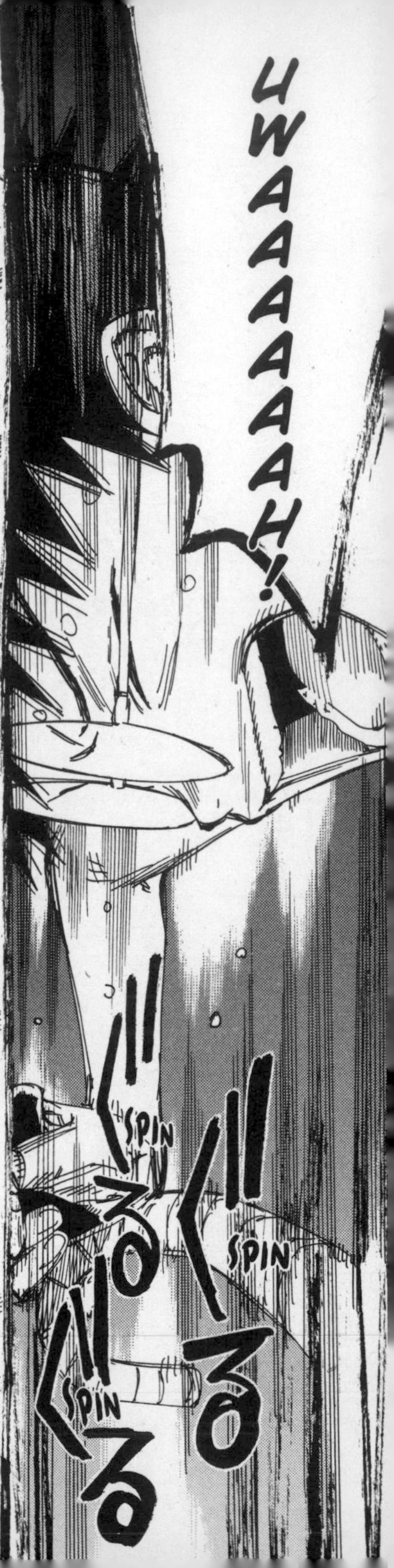
UWAAAAAAH!
SPIN
SPIN
SPIN
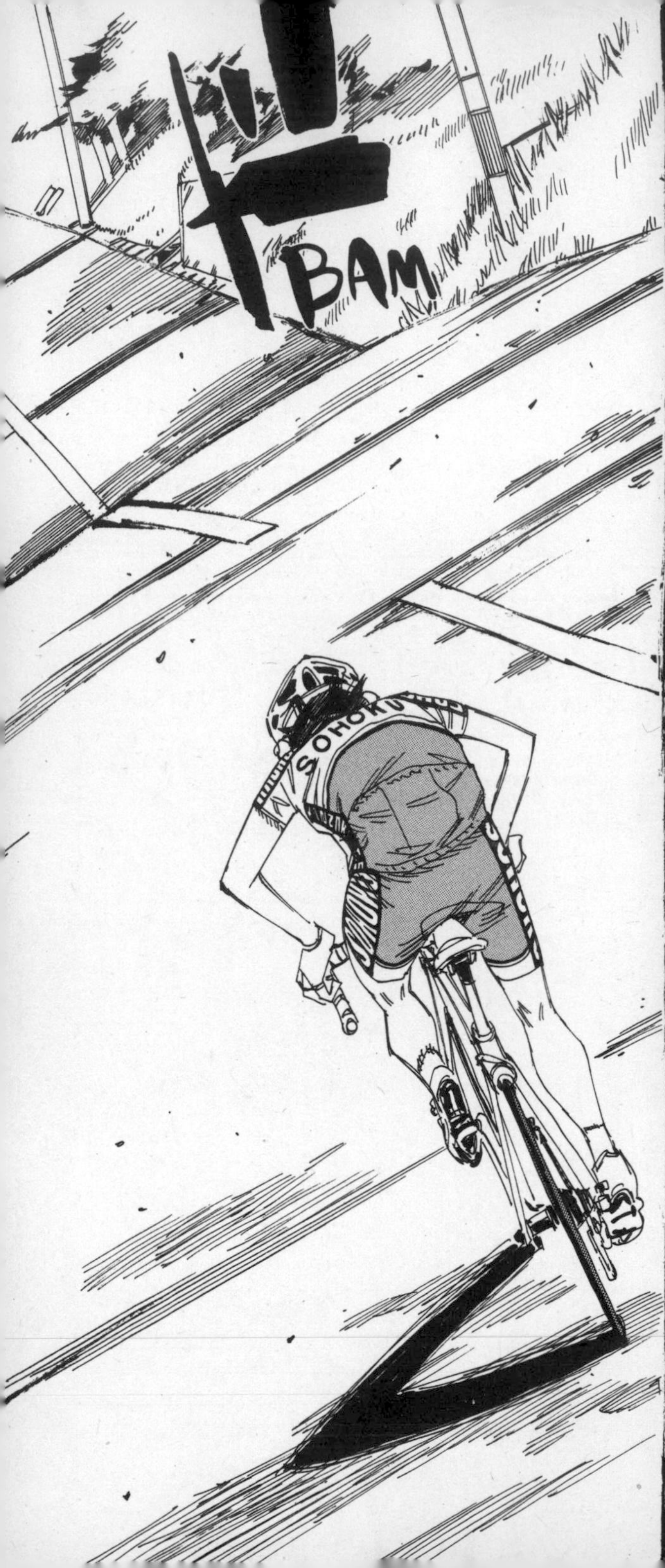
BAM
SOHOKU

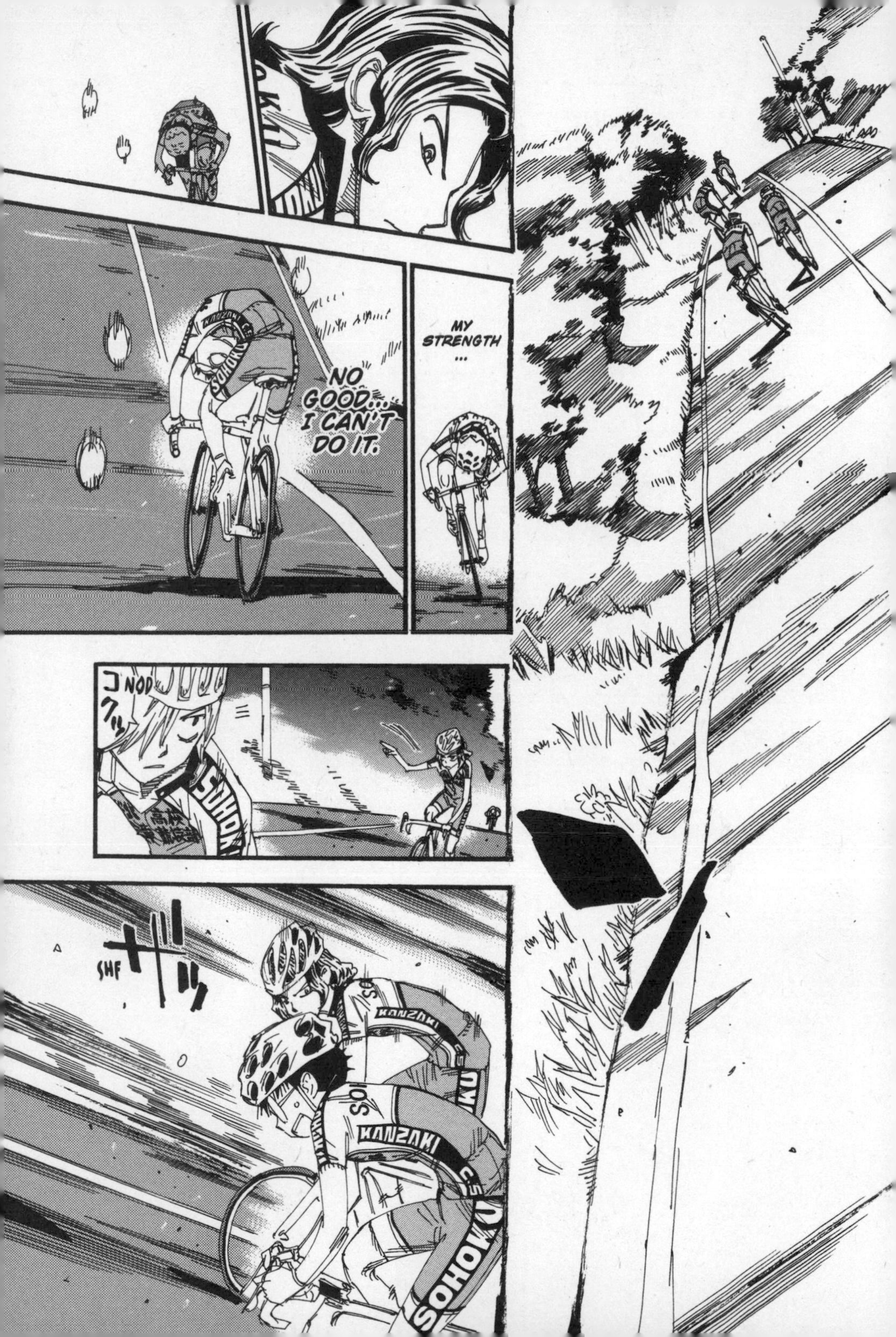
MY STRENGTH...
NO GOOD... I CAN'T DO IT.
NOD
SHF

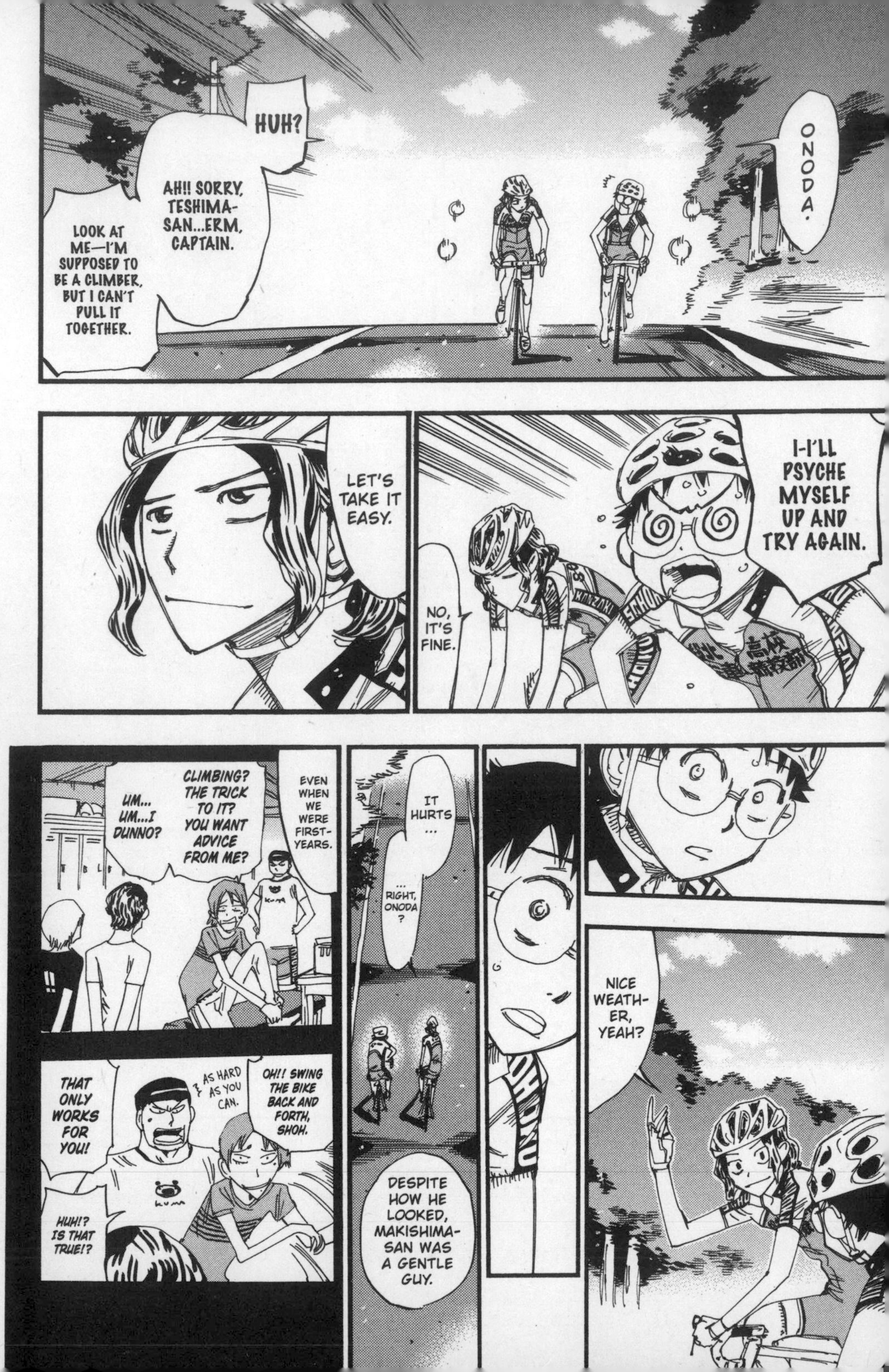
ONODA.
HUH?
AH!! SORRY, TESHIMA-SAN...ERM, CAPTAIN.
LOOK AT ME—I'M SUPPOSED TO BE A CLIMBER, BUT I CAN'T PULL IT TOGETHER.
I-I'LL PSYCHE MYSELF UP AND TRY AGAIN.
NO, IT'S FINE.
LET'S TAKE IT EASY.
NICE WEATHER, YEAH?
IT HURTS...
...RIGHT, ONODA?
DESPITE HOW HE LOOKED, MAKISHIMA-SAN WAS A GENTLE GUY.
EVEN WHEN WE WERE FIRST-YEARS.
CLIMBING? THE TRICK TO IT? YOU WANT ADVICE FROM ME?
UM... UM...I DUNNO?
OH!! SWING THE BIKE BACK AND FORTH, SHOH.
AS HARD AS YOU CAN.
THAT ONLY WORKS FOR YOU!
HUH!? IS THAT TRUE!?

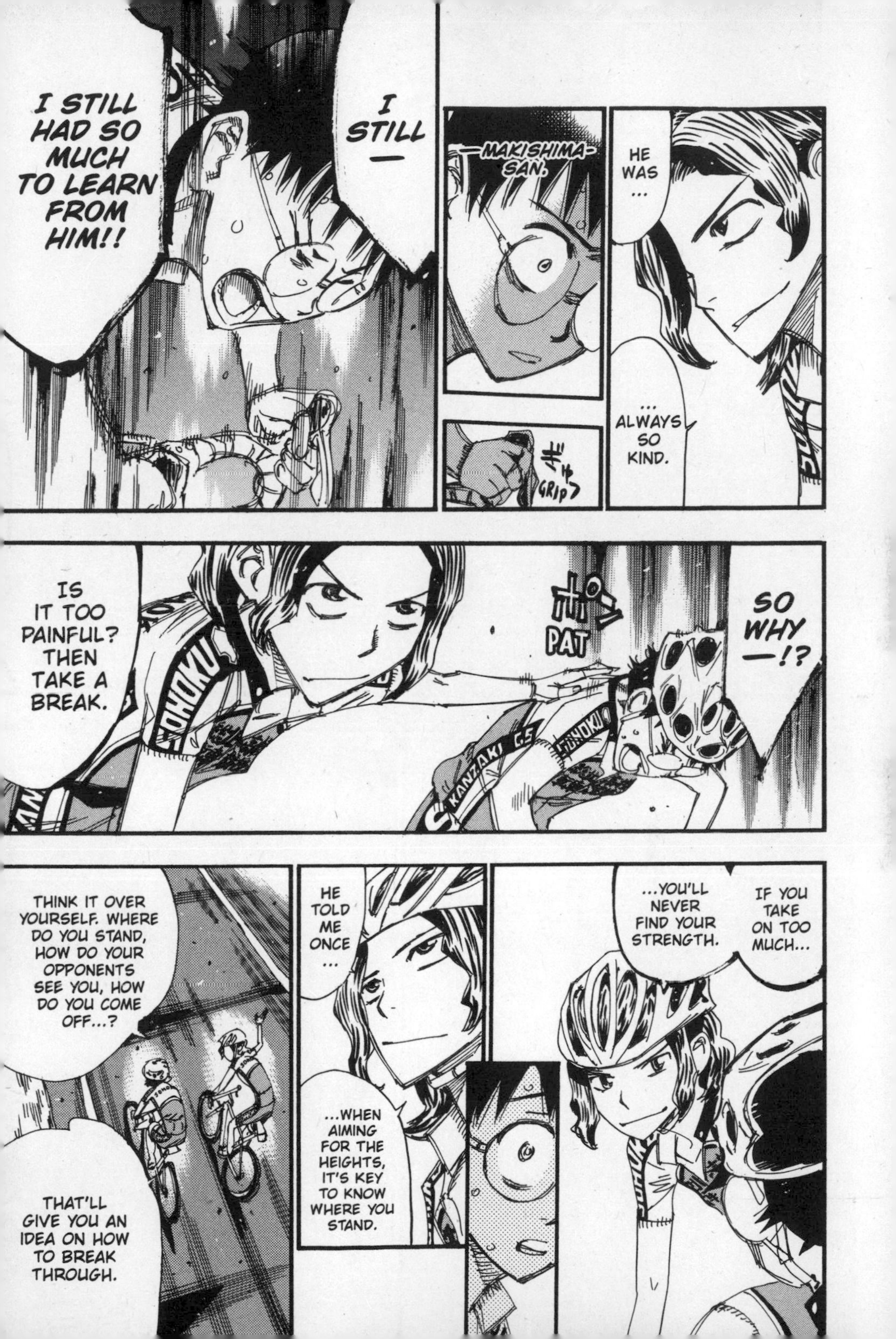
HE WAS ...
... ALWAYS SO KIND.
—MAKISHIMA-SAN.
GRIP
I STILL —
I STILL HAD SO MUCH TO LEARN FROM HIM!!
SO WHY—!?
PAT
IS IT TOO PAINFUL? THEN TAKE A BREAK.
IF YOU TAKE ON TOO MUCH...
...YOU'LL NEVER FIND YOUR STRENGTH.
HE TOLD ME ONCE ...
...WHEN AIMING FOR THE HEIGHTS, IT'S KEY TO KNOW WHERE YOU STAND.
THINK IT OVER YOURSELF. WHERE DO YOU STAND, HOW DO YOUR OPPONENTS SEE YOU, HOW DO YOU COME OFF...?
THAT'LL GIVE YOU AN IDEA ON HOW TO BREAK THROUGH.

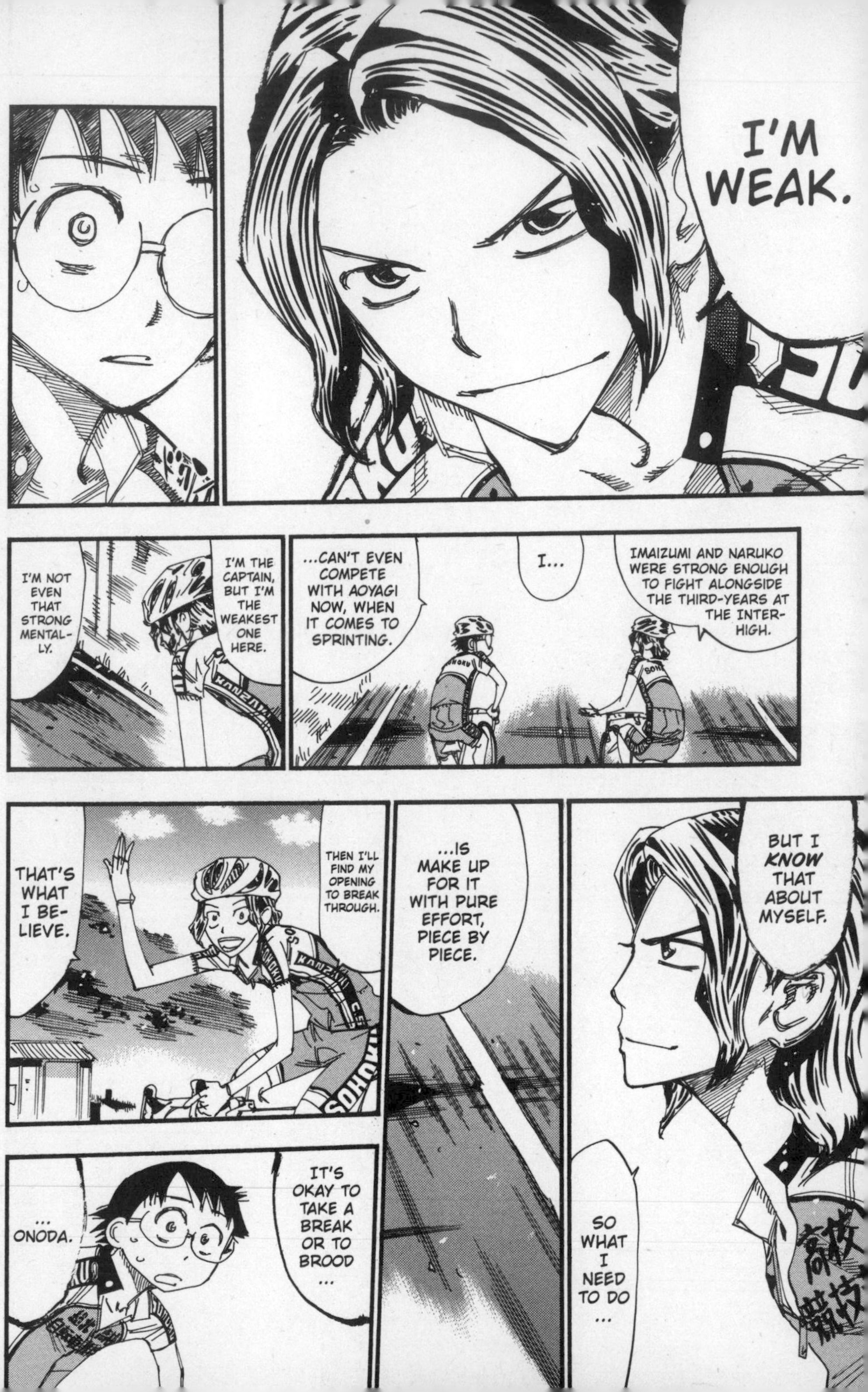
I'M WEAK.
IMAIZUMI AND NARUKO WERE STRONG ENOUGH TO FIGHT ALONGSIDE THE THIRD-YEARS AT THE INTER-HIGH.
I...
...CAN'T EVEN COMPETE WITH AOYAGI NOW, WHEN IT COMES TO SPRINTING.
I'M THE CAPTAIN, BUT I'M THE WEAKEST ONE HERE.
I'M NOT EVEN THAT STRONG MENTAL-LY.
BUT I *KNOW* THAT ABOUT MYSELF.
SO WHAT I NEED TO DO ...
...IS MAKE UP FOR IT WITH PURE EFFORT, PIECE BY PIECE.
THEN I'LL FIND MY OPENING TO BREAK THROUGH.
THAT'S WHAT I BE-LIEVE.
IT'S OKAY TO TAKE A BREAK OR TO BROOD ...
... ONODA.

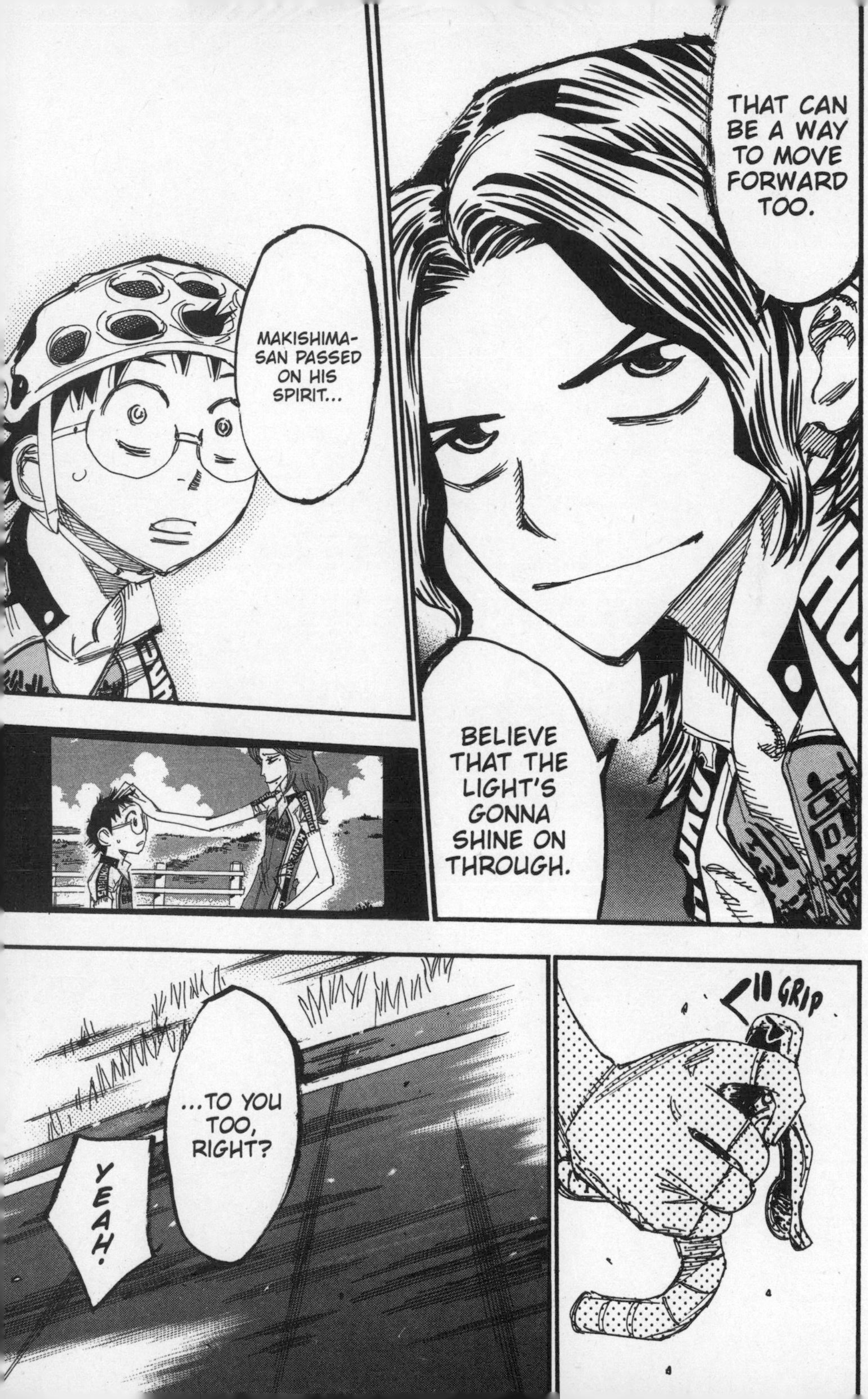
THAT CAN BE A WAY TO MOVE FORWARD TOO.
BELIEVE THAT THE LIGHT'S GONNA SHINE ON THROUGH.
MAKISHIMA-SAN PASSED ON HIS SPIRIT...
GRIP
...TO YOU TOO, RIGHT?
YEAH!

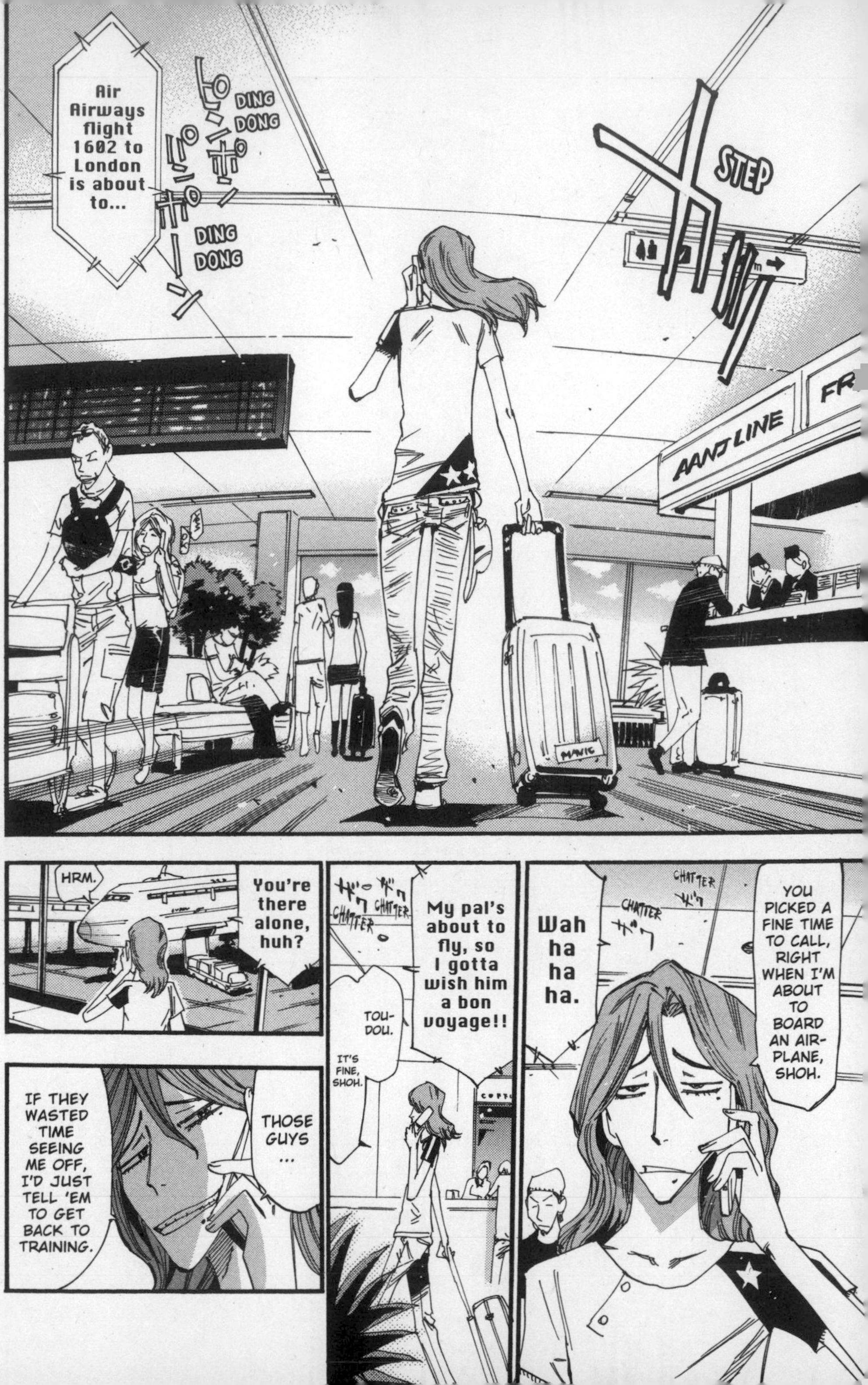

Air Airways flight 1602 to London is about to...
DING DONG
DING DONG
STEP
AANJ LINE
CHATTER
YOU PICKED A FINE TIME TO CALL, RIGHT WHEN I'M ABOUT TO BOARD AN AIRPLANE, SHOH.
CHATTER
Wah ha ha ha.
CHATTER
CHATTER
My pal's about to fly, so I gotta wish him a bon voyage!!
TOU-DOU.
IT'S FINE, SHOH.
HRM.
You're there alone, huh?
THOSE GUYS...
IF THEY WASTED TIME SEEING ME OFF, I'D JUST TELL 'EM TO GET BACK TO TRAINING.

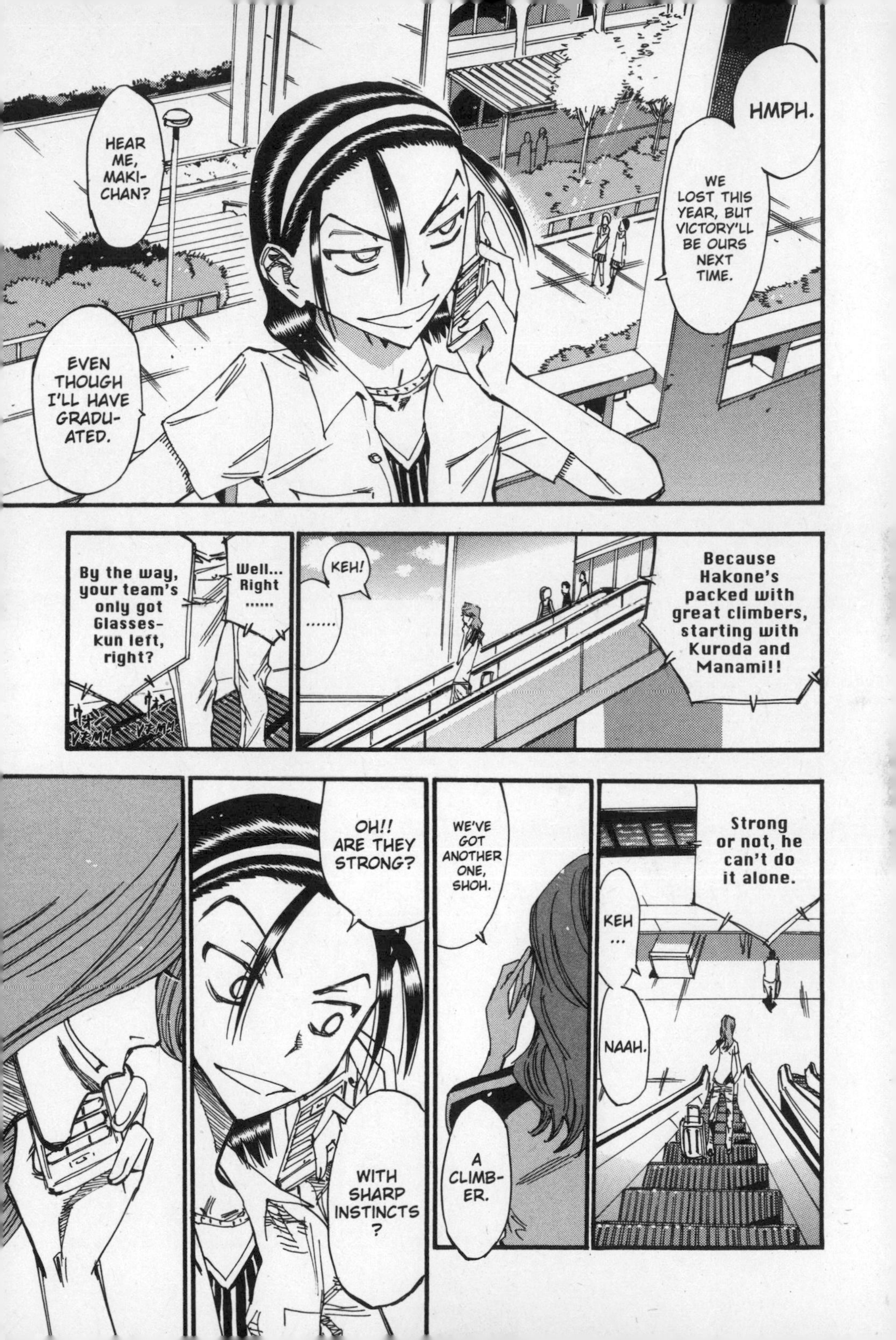
HMPH.
WE LOST THIS YEAR, BUT VICTORY'LL BE OURS NEXT TIME.
HEAR ME, MAKI-CHAN?
EVEN THOUGH I'LL HAVE GRADU-ATED.
Because Hakone's packed with great climbers, starting with Kuroda and Manami!!
KEH!
......
Well... Right ......
By the way, your team's only got Glasses-kun left, right?
VRMM VRMM
Strong or not, he can't do it alone.
KEH ...
NAAH.
WE'VE GOT ANOTHER ONE, SHOH.
A CLIMB-ER.
OH!! ARE THEY STRONG?
WITH SHARP INSTINCTS?

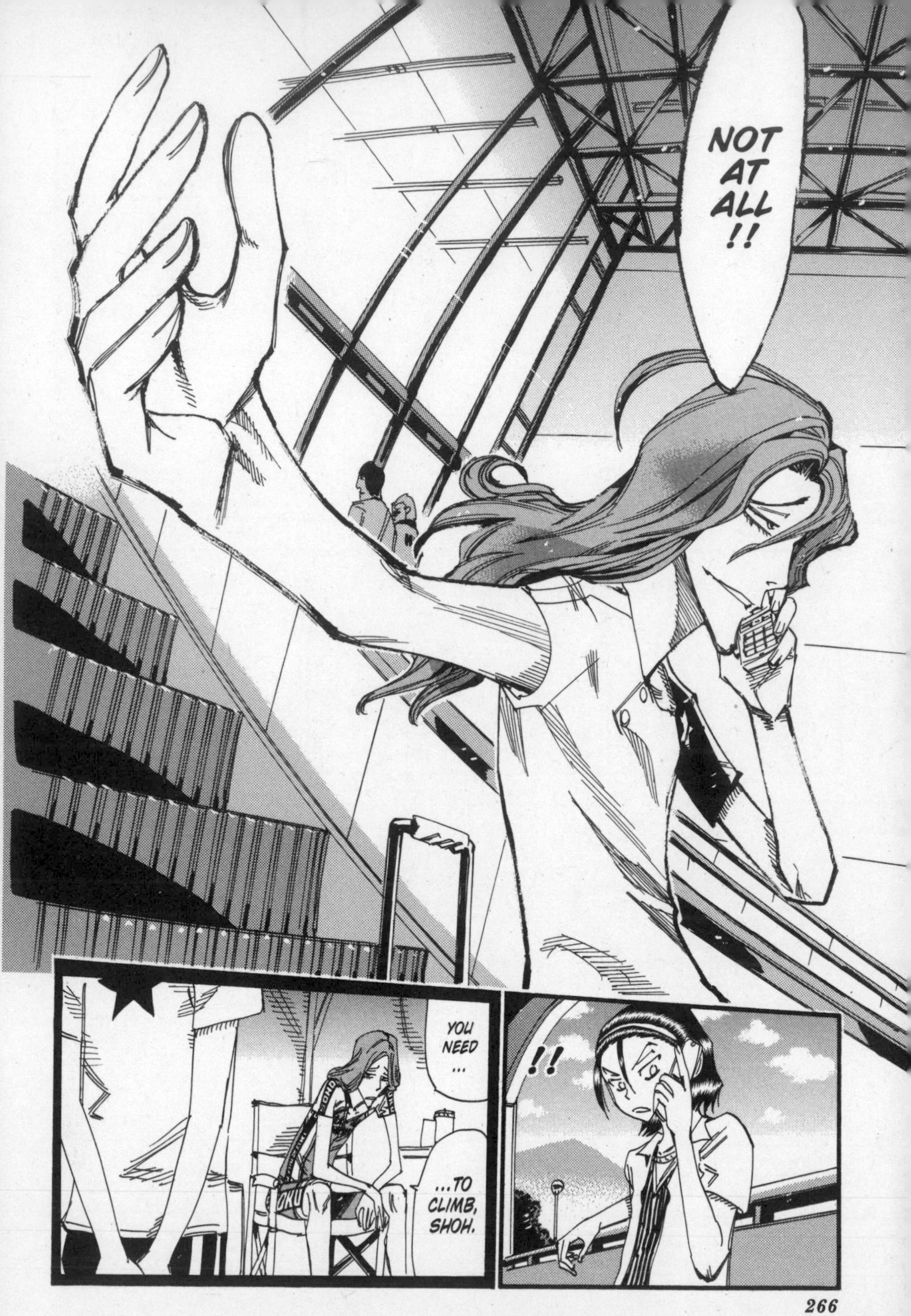
NOT AT ALL!!
!!
YOU NEED...
...TO CLIMB, SHOH.

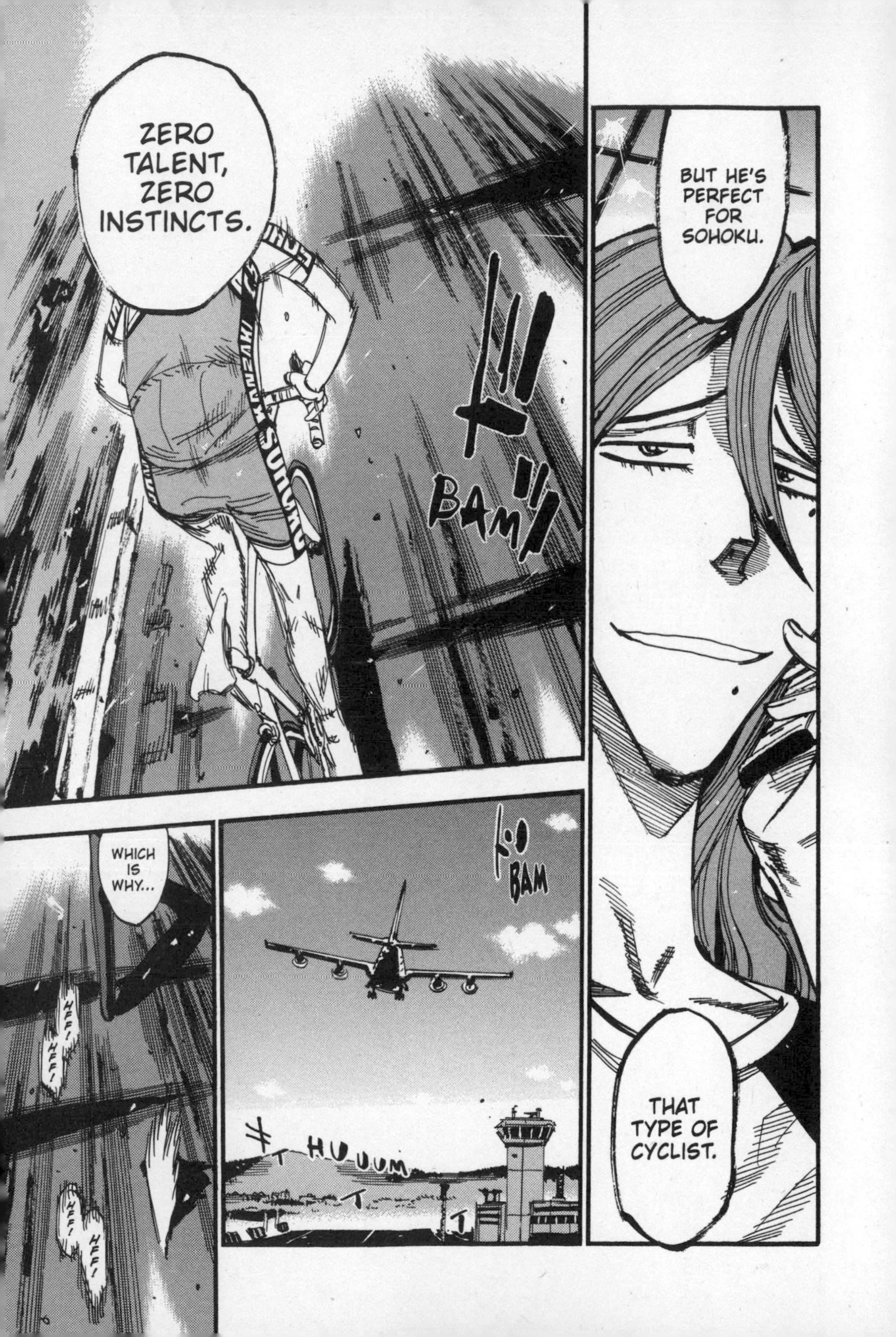

ZERO TALENT, ZERO INSTINCTS.
BAM
BUT HE'S PERFECT FOR SOHOKU.
THAT TYPE OF CYCLIST.
BAM
HUUUM
WHICH IS WHY...
HFF HFF
HFF HFF

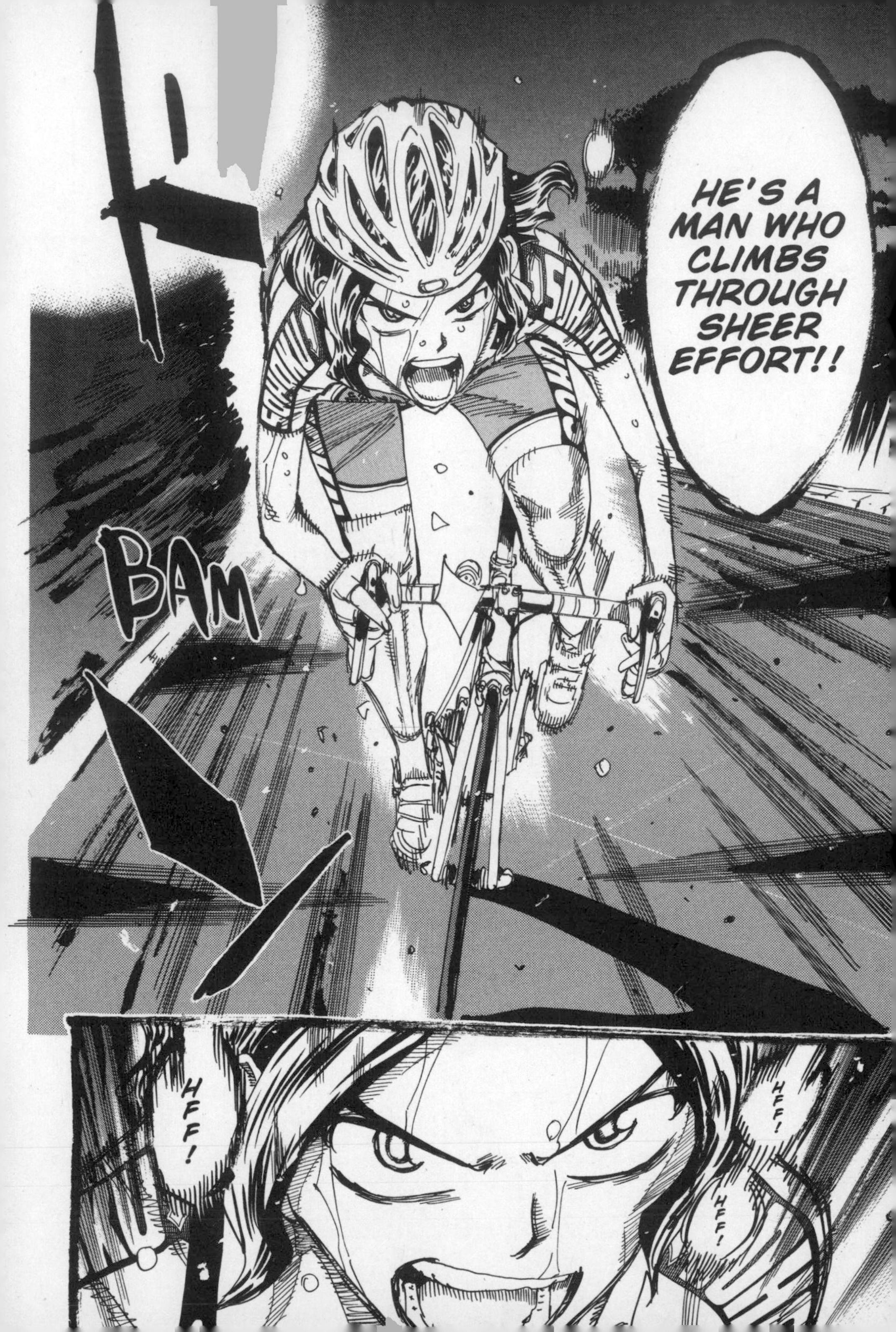
HE'S A MAN WHO CLIMBS THROUGH SHEER EFFORT!!
BAM
HFF!
HFF!
HFF!

RIDE.238 THE FIRE IN HIS HEART

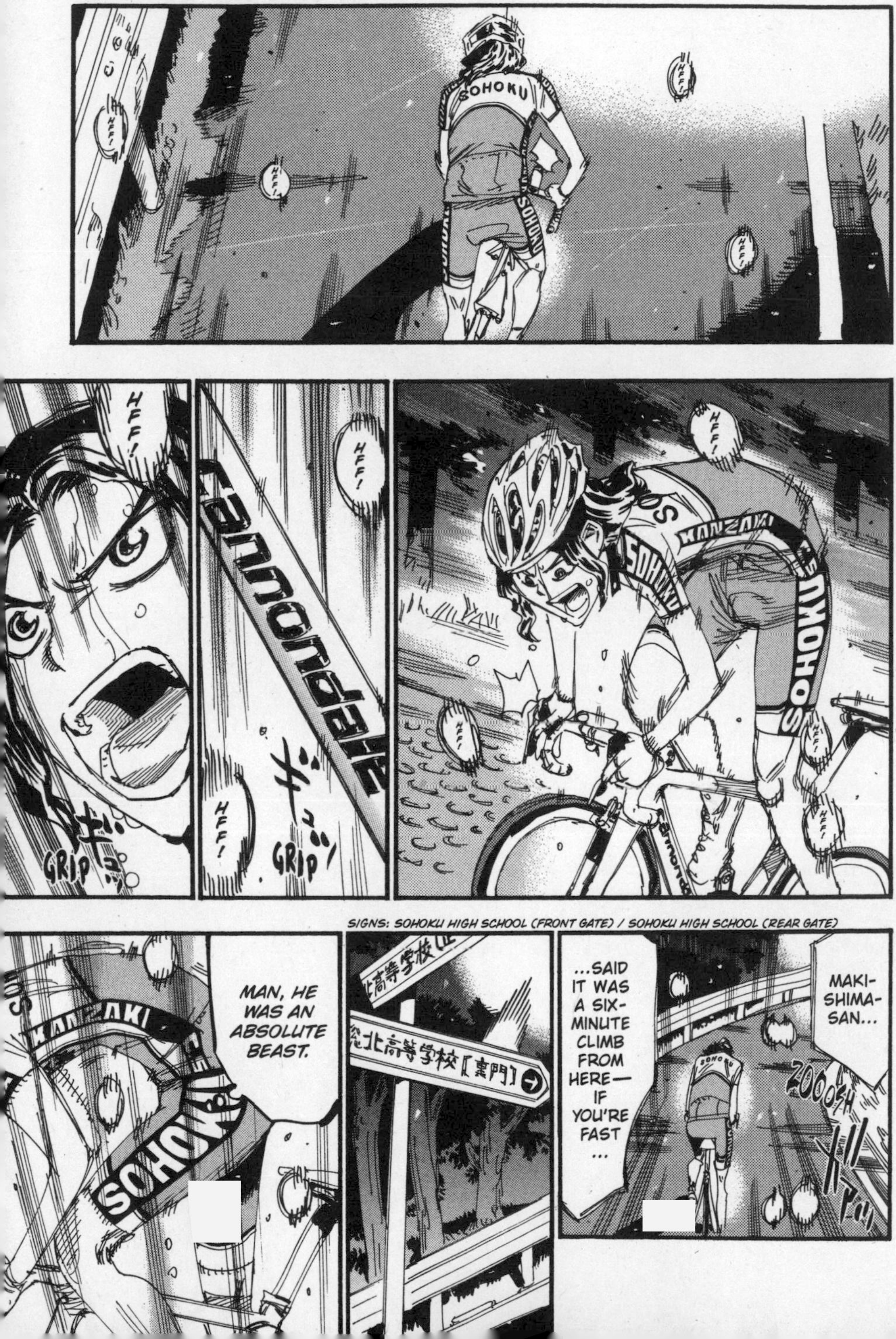
HFF!
HFF!
HFF!
HFF!
HFF!
HFF!
HFF!
HFF!
GRIP
HFF!
HFF!
GRIP
SIGNS: SOHOKU HIGH SCHOOL (FRONT GATE) / SOHOKU HIGH SCHOOL (REAR GATE)
MAKI-SHIMA-SAN...
...SAID IT WAS A SIX-MINUTE CLIMB FROM HERE— IF YOU'RE FAST...
ZOOOSH
総北高等学校〔裏門〕
MAN, HE WAS AN ABSOLUTE BEAST.

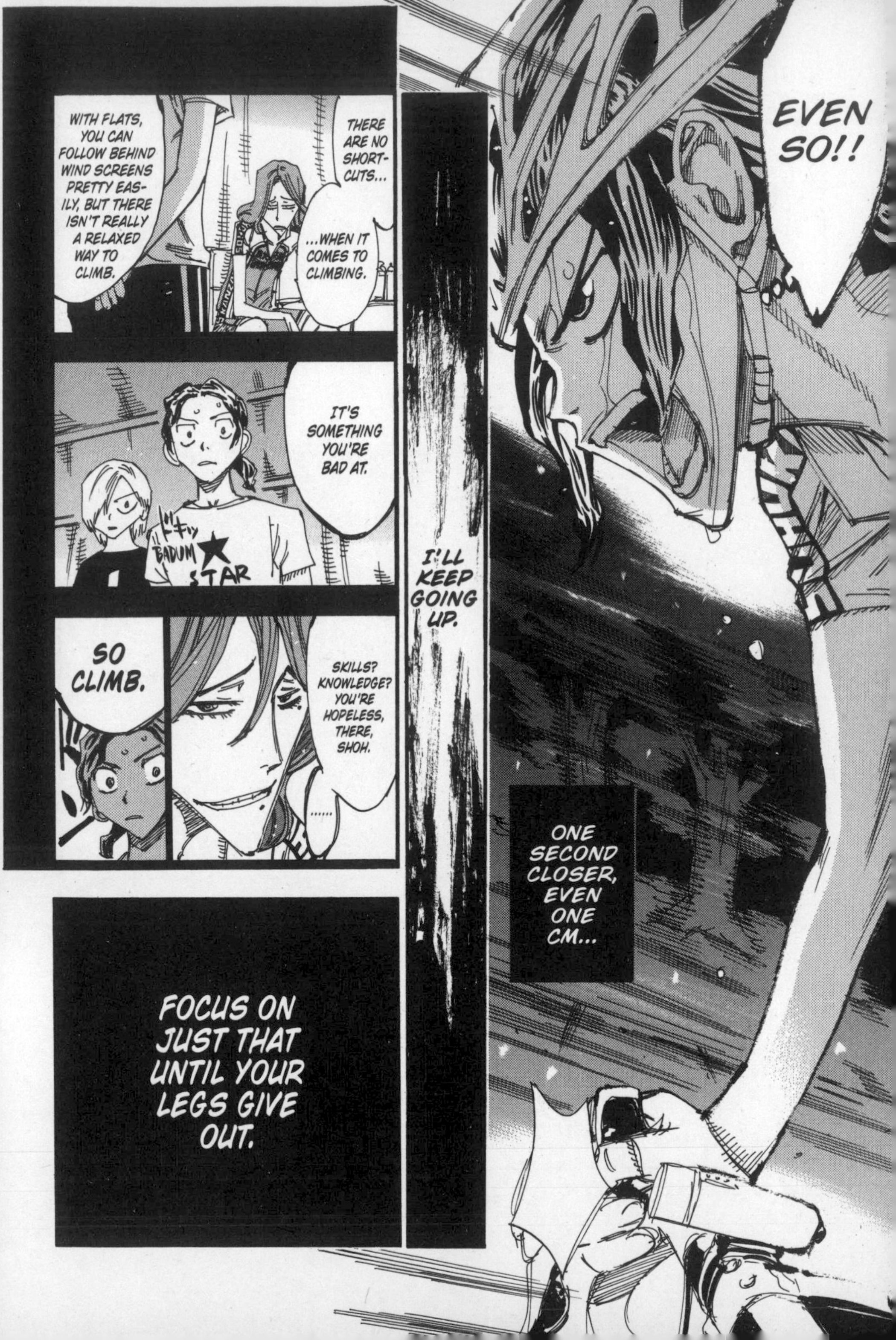
EVEN SO!!
ONE SECOND CLOSER, EVEN ONE CM...
I'LL KEEP GOING UP.
THERE ARE NO SHORT-CUTS...
...WHEN IT COMES TO CLIMBING.
WITH FLATS, YOU CAN FOLLOW BEHIND WIND SCREENS PRETTY EAS-ILY, BUT THERE ISN'T REALLY A RELAXED WAY TO CLIMB.
IT'S SOMETHING YOU'RE BAD AT.
BADUM
STAR
SKILLS? KNOWLEDGE? YOU'RE HOPELESS, THERE, SHOH.
......
SO CLIMB.
FOCUS ON JUST THAT UNTIL YOUR LEGS GIVE OUT.

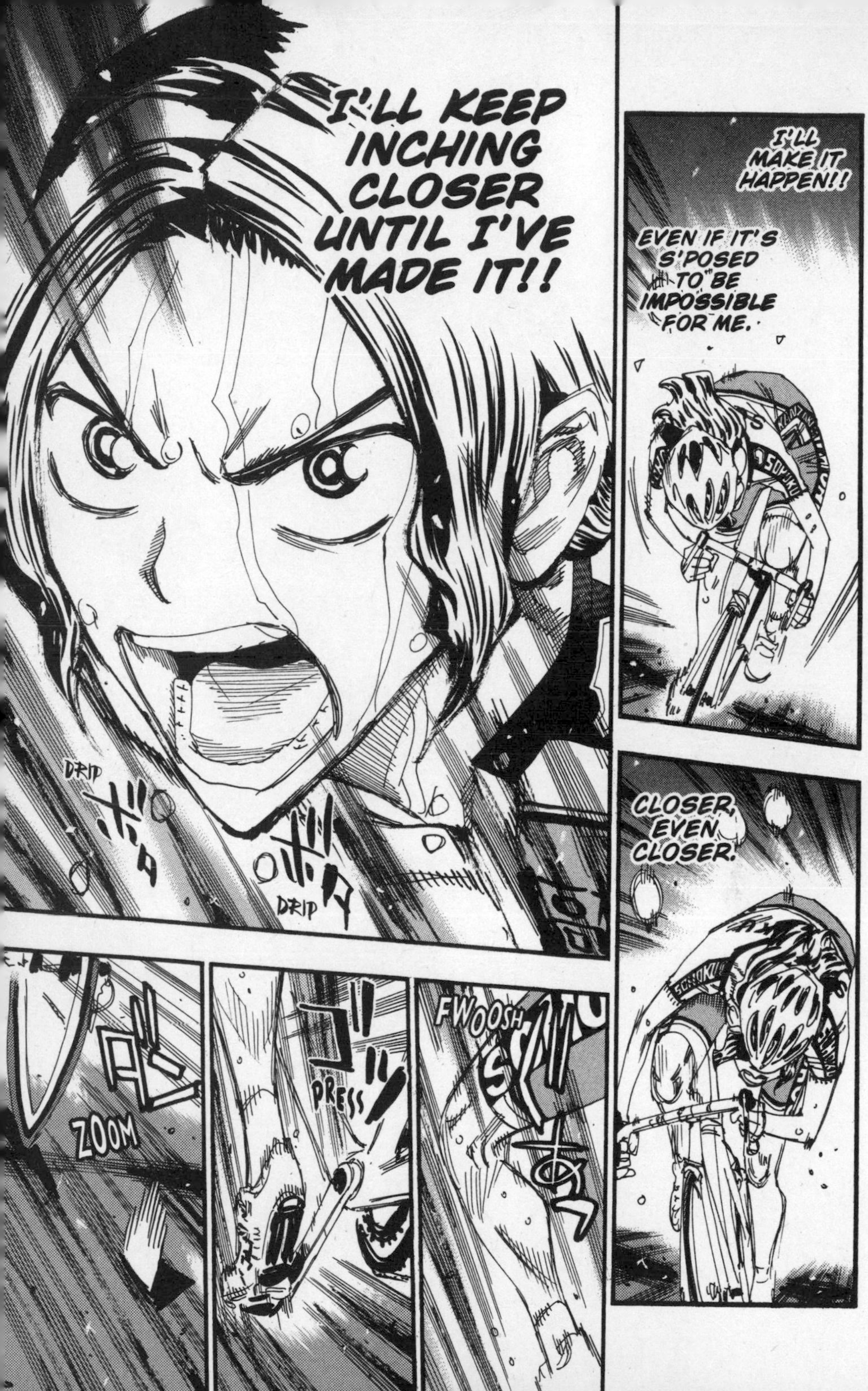
I'LL MAKE IT HAPPEN!!
EVEN IF IT'S S'POSED TO BE IMPOSSIBLE FOR ME.
I'LL KEEP INCHING CLOSER UNTIL I'VE MADE IT!!
DRIP
DRIP
CLOSER, EVEN CLOSER.
FWOOSH
PRESS
ZOOM

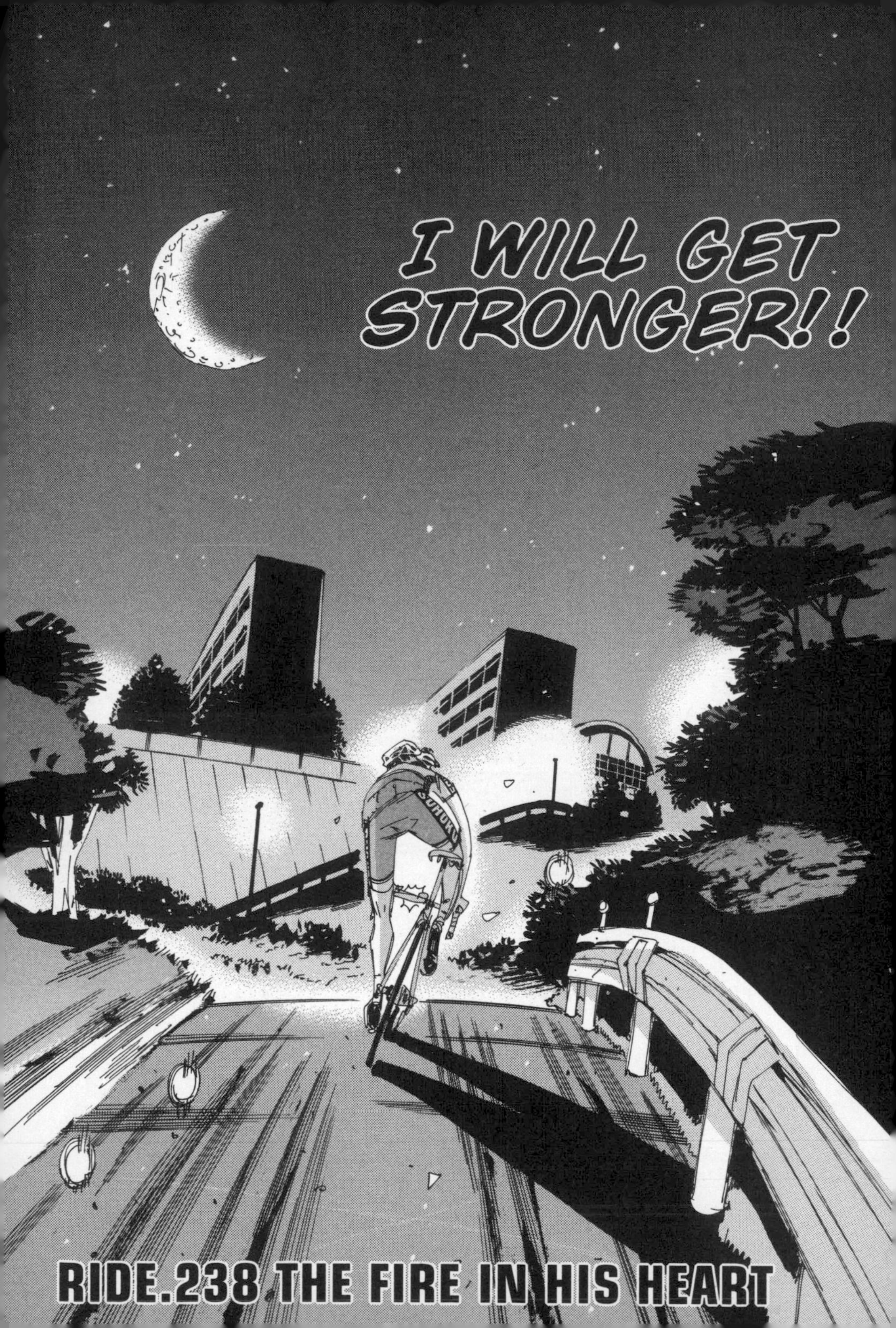
I WILL GET STRONGER!!
SOHOKU
RIDE.238 THE FIRE IN HIS HEART

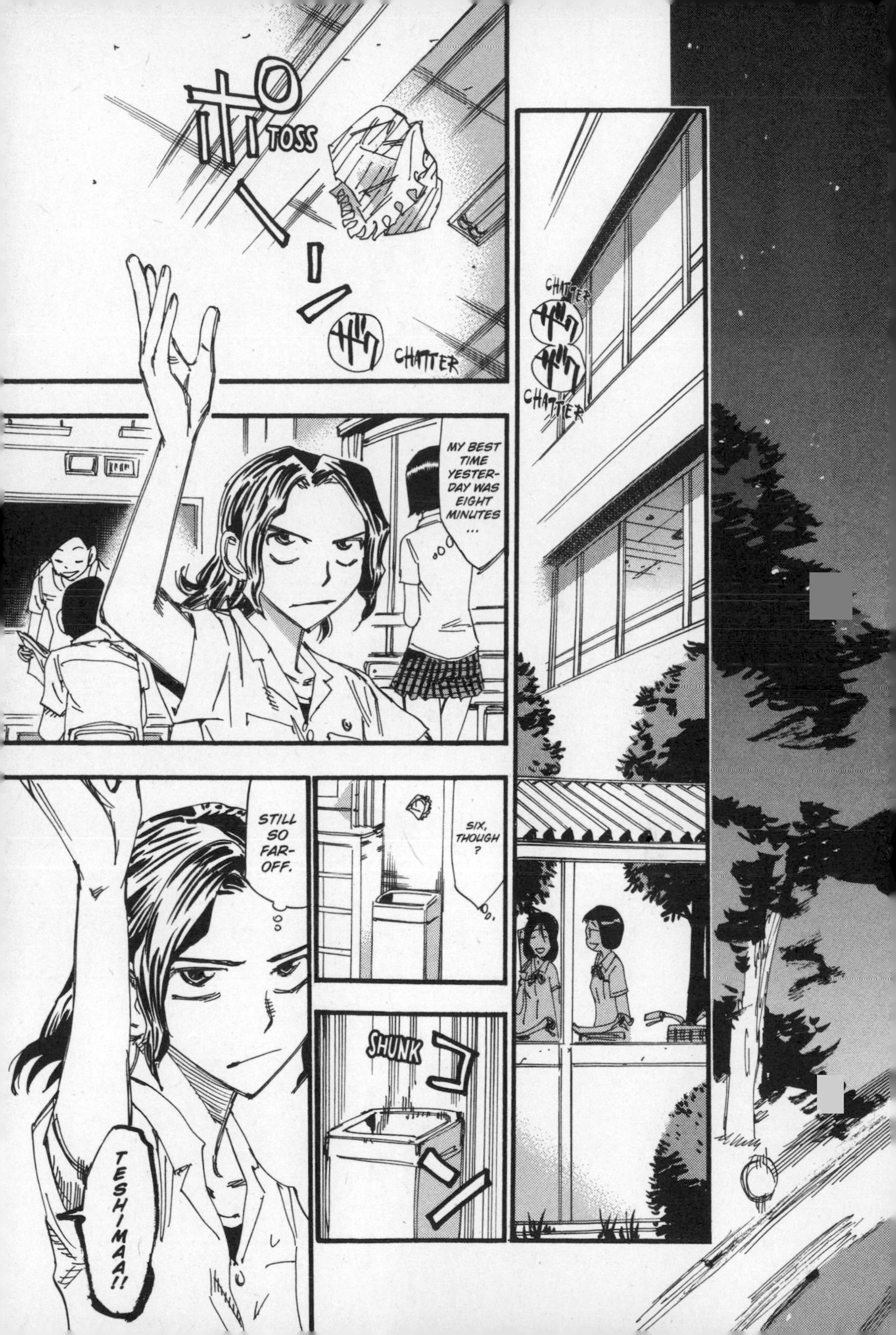
CHATTER
CHATTER
TOSS
CHATTER
MY BEST TIME YESTERDAY WAS EIGHT MINUTES...
SIX, THOUGH?
SHUNK
STILL SO FAR-OFF.
TESHIMAA!!

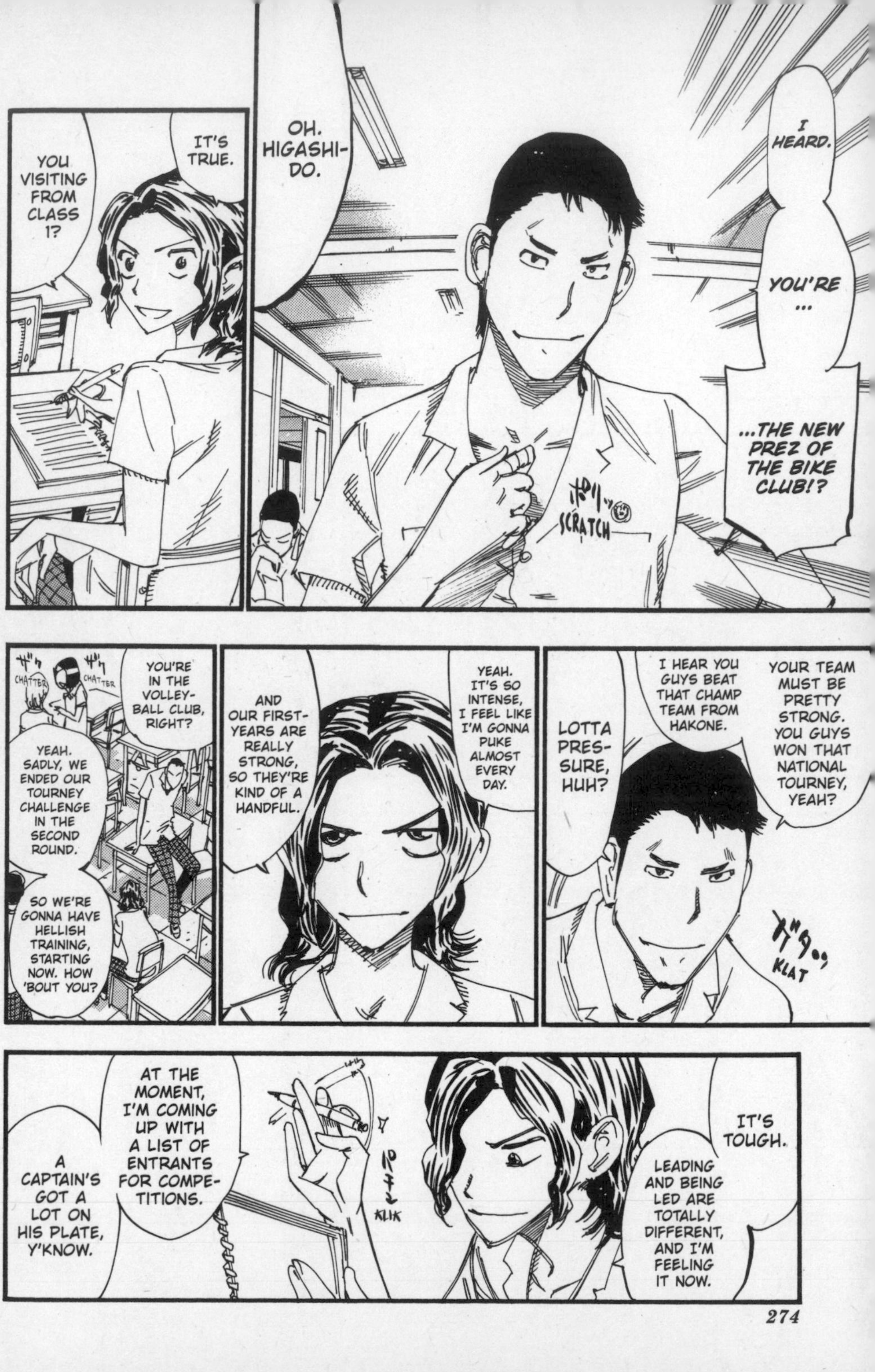
I HEARD.
YOU'RE...
...THE NEW PREZ OF THE BIKE CLUB!?
SCRATCH
OH. HIGASHIDO.
IT'S TRUE.
YOU VISITING FROM CLASS 1?
YOUR TEAM MUST BE PRETTY STRONG. YOU GUYS WON THAT NATIONAL TOURNEY, YEAH?
I HEAR YOU GUYS BEAT THAT CHAMP TEAM FROM HAKONE.
LOTTA PRESSURE, HUH?
KLAT
YEAH. IT'S SO INTENSE, I FEEL LIKE I'M GONNA PUKE ALMOST EVERY DAY.
AND OUR FIRST-YEARS ARE REALLY STRONG, SO THEY'RE KIND OF A HANDFUL.
CHATTER
CHATTER
YOU'RE IN THE VOLLEYBALL CLUB, RIGHT?
YEAH. SADLY, WE ENDED OUR TOURNEY CHALLENGE IN THE SECOND ROUND.
SO WE'RE GONNA HAVE HELLISH TRAINING, STARTING NOW. HOW 'BOUT YOU?
IT'S TOUGH.
LEADING AND BEING LED ARE TOTALLY DIFFERENT, AND I'M FEELING IT NOW.
KLIK
AT THE MOMENT, I'M COMING UP WITH A LIST OF ENTRANTS FOR COMPETITIONS.
A CAPTAIN'S GOT A LOT ON HIS PLATE, Y'KNOW.

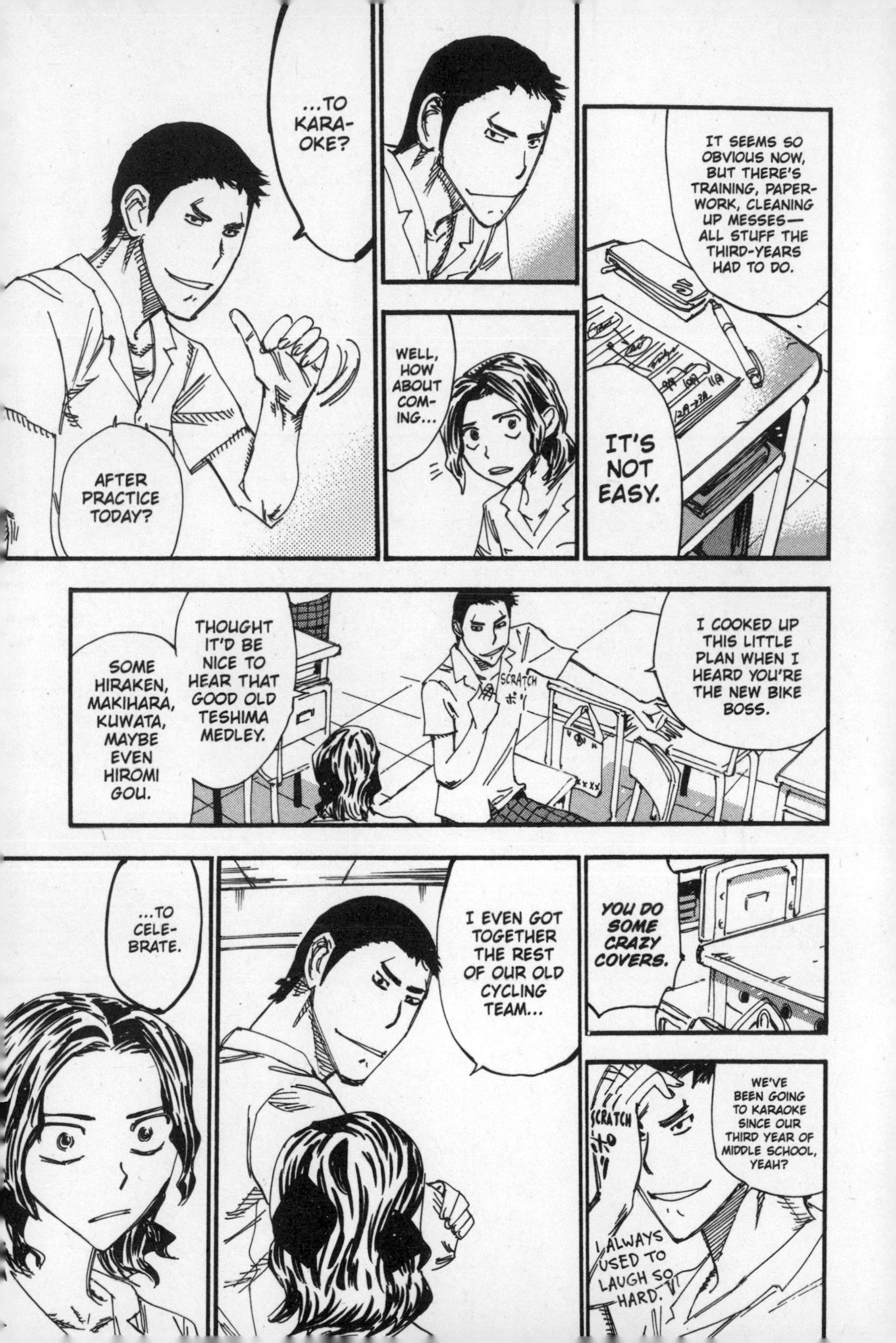
IT SEEMS SO OBVIOUS NOW, BUT THERE'S TRAINING, PAPERWORK, CLEANING UP MESSES—ALL STUFF THE THIRD-YEARS HAD TO DO.
IT'S NOT EASY.
WELL, HOW ABOUT COMING...
...TO KARAOKE?
AFTER PRACTICE TODAY?
I COOKED UP THIS LITTLE PLAN WHEN I HEARD YOU'RE THE NEW BIKE BOSS.
SCRATCH
THOUGHT IT'D BE NICE TO HEAR THAT GOOD OLD TESHIMA MEDLEY.
SOME HIRAKEN, MAKIHARA, KUWATA, MAYBE EVEN HIROMI GOU.
YOU DO SOME CRAZY COVERS.
WE'VE BEEN GOING TO KARAOKE SINCE OUR THIRD YEAR OF MIDDLE SCHOOL, YEAH?
SCRATCH
I ALWAYS USED TO LAUGH SO HARD.
I EVEN GOT TOGETHER THE REST OF OUR OLD CYCLING TEAM...
...TO CELEBRATE.

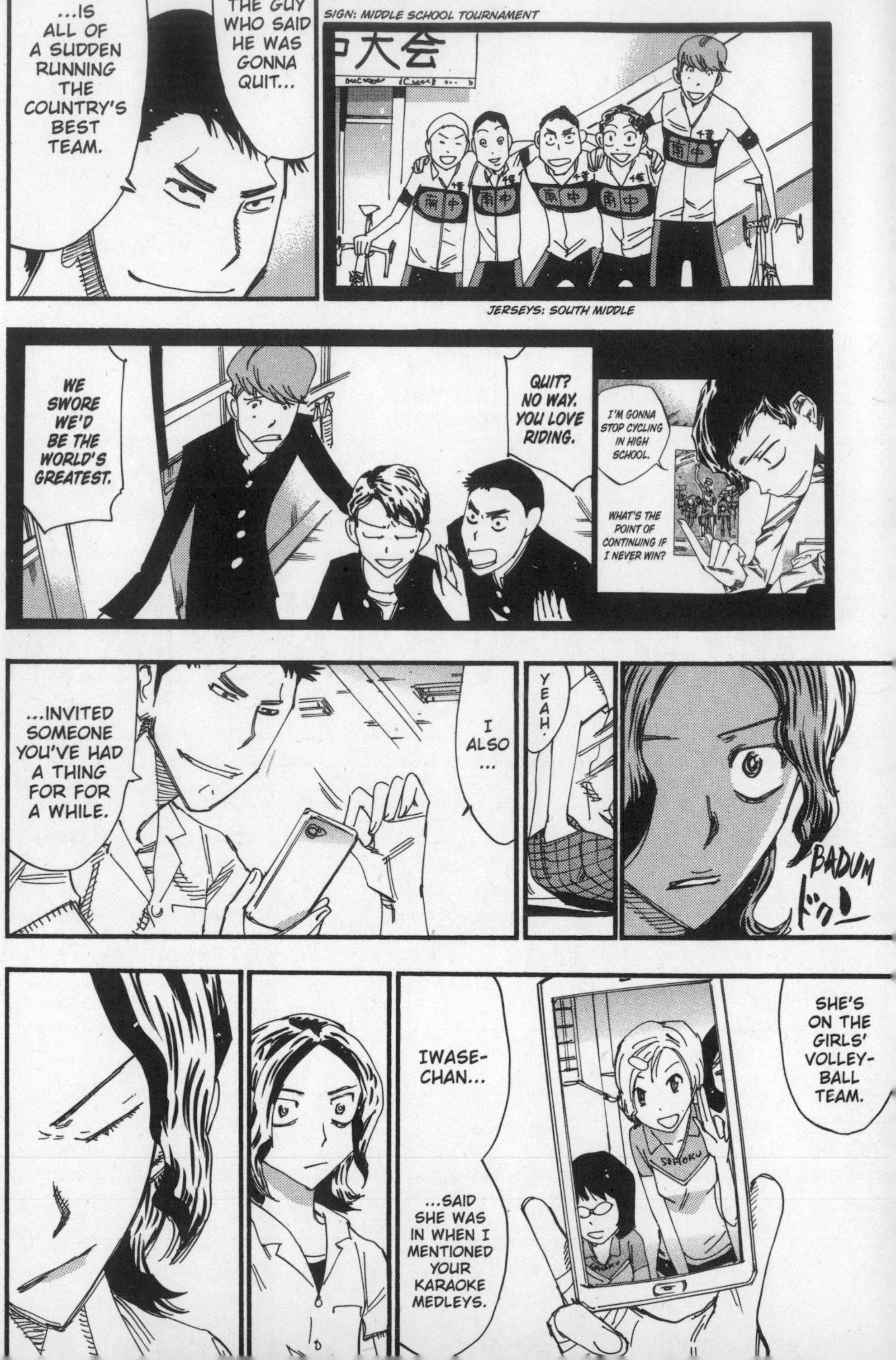
SIGN: MIDDLE SCHOOL TOURNAMENT
JERSEYS: SOUTH MIDDLE
THE GUY WHO SAID HE WAS GONNA QUIT...
...IS ALL OF A SUDDEN RUNNING THE COUNTRY'S BEST TEAM.
I'M GONNA STOP CYCLING IN HIGH SCHOOL.
WHAT'S THE POINT OF CONTINUING IF I NEVER WIN?
QUIT? NO WAY. YOU LOVE RIDING.
WE SWORE WE'D BE THE WORLD'S GREATEST.
BADUM
YEAH.
I ALSO...
...INVITED SOMEONE YOU'VE HAD A THING FOR FOR A WHILE.
SHE'S ON THE GIRLS' VOLLEY-BALL TEAM.
IWASE-CHAN...
...SAID SHE WAS IN WHEN I MENTIONED YOUR KARAOKE MEDLEYS.

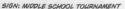

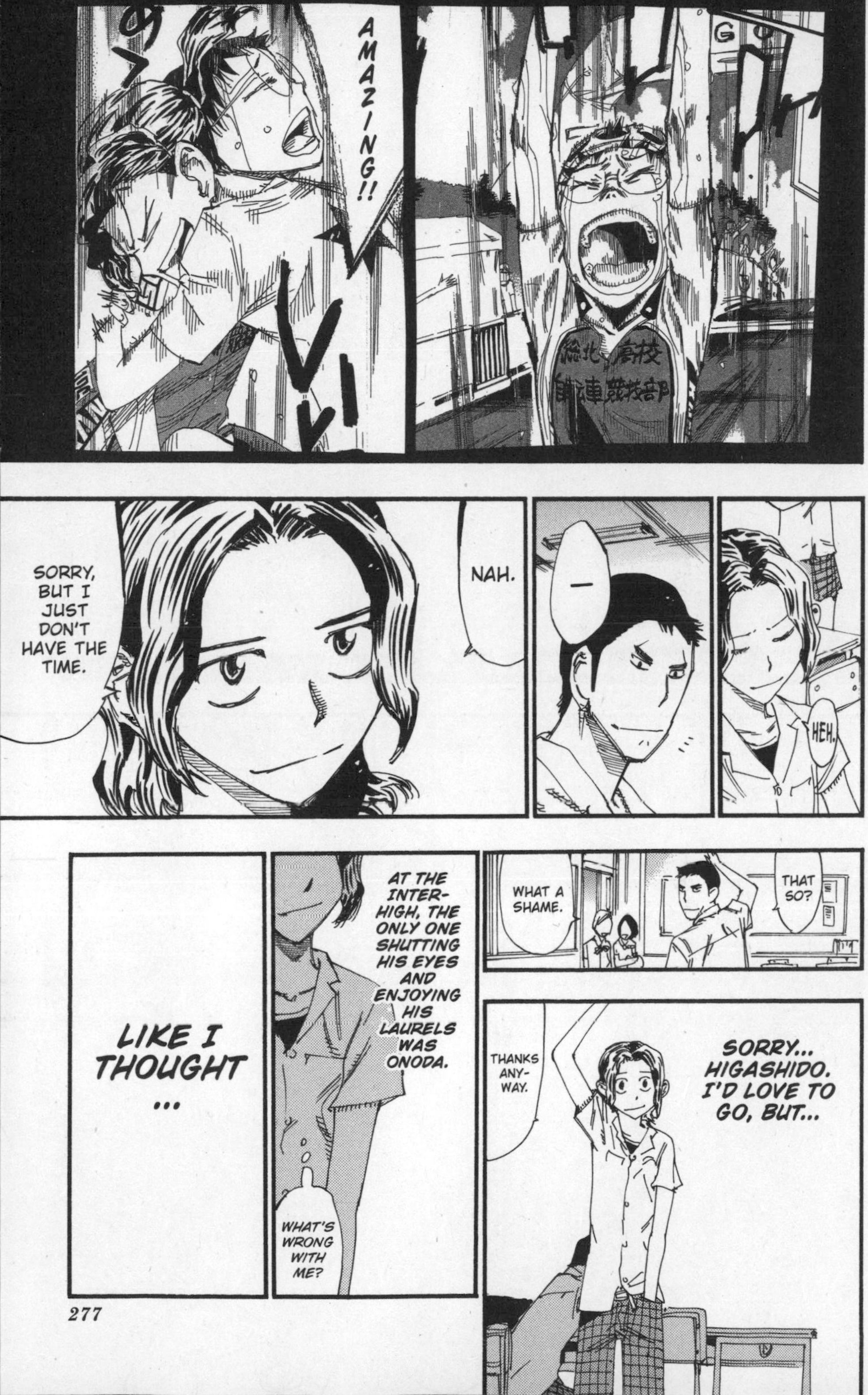
AMAZING!!
HEH.
—
NAH.
SORRY, BUT I JUST DON'T HAVE THE TIME.
THAT SO?
WHAT A SHAME.
SORRY... HIGASHIDO. I'D LOVE TO GO, BUT...
THANKS ANYWAY.
AT THE INTER-HIGH, THE ONLY ONE SHUTTING HIS EYES AND ENJOYING HIS LAURELS WAS ONODA.
WHAT'S WRONG WITH ME?
LIKE I THOUGHT...

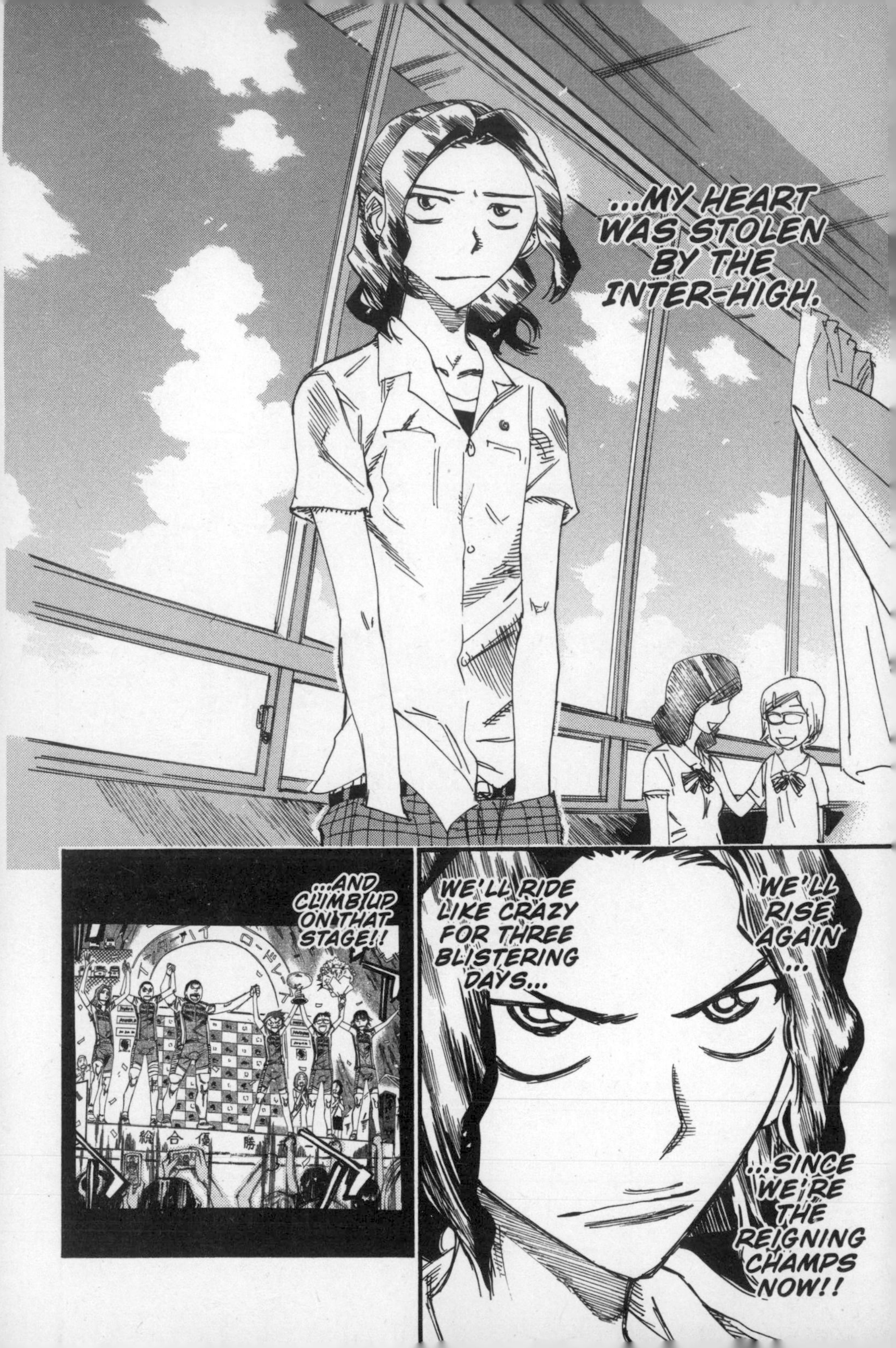
...MY HEART WAS STOLEN BY THE INTER-HIGH.
WE'LL RISE AGAIN...
...SINCE WE'RE THE REIGNING CHAMPS NOW!!
WE'LL RIDE LIKE CRAZY FOR THREE BLISTERING DAYS...
...AND CLIMB UP ON THAT STAGE!!

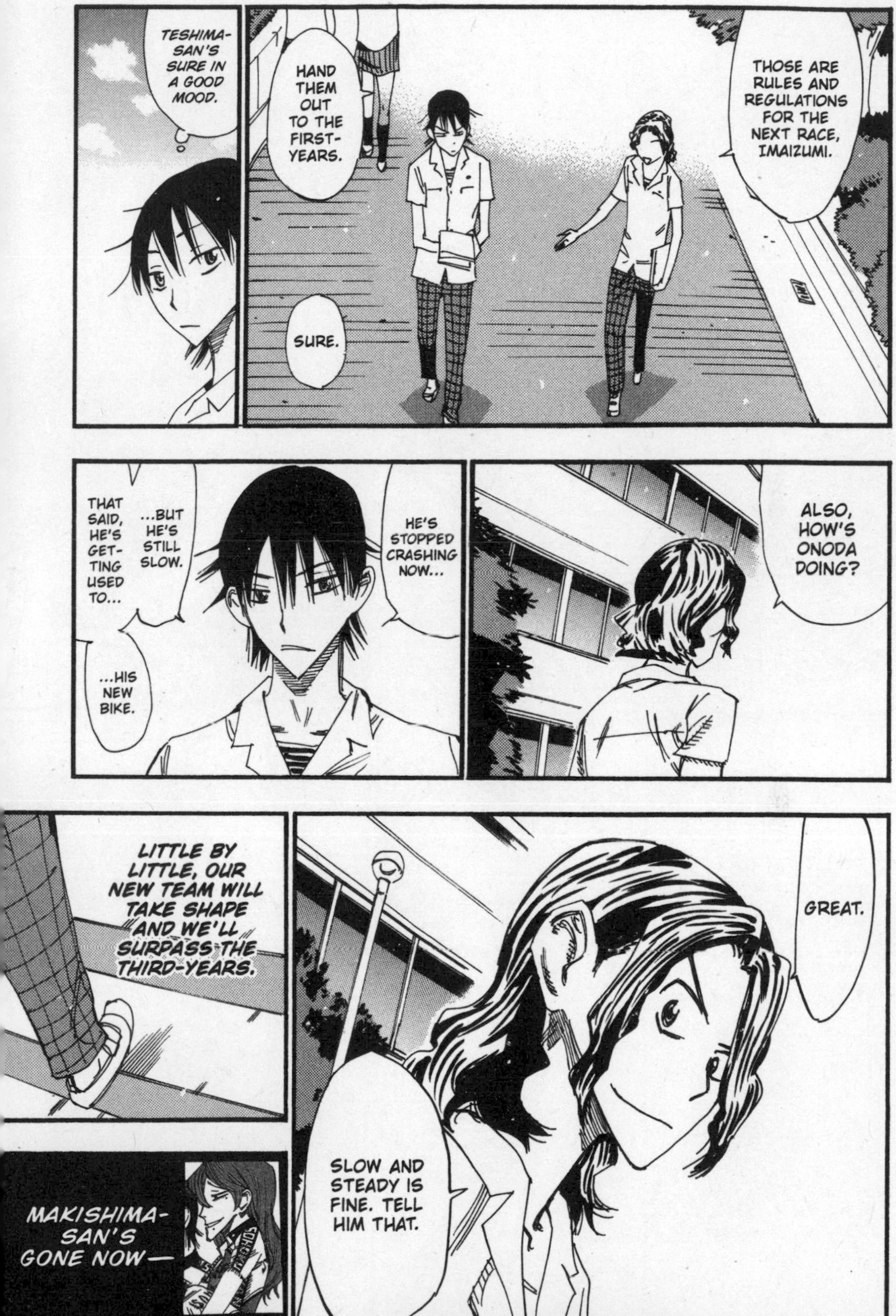
THOSE ARE RULES AND REGULATIONS FOR THE NEXT RACE, IMAIZUMI.
HAND THEM OUT TO THE FIRST-YEARS.
SURE.
TESHIMA-SAN'S SURE IN A GOOD MOOD.
ALSO, HOW'S ONODA DOING?
HE'S STOPPED CRASHING NOW...
...BUT HE'S STILL SLOW.
THAT SAID, HE'S GETTING USED TO...
...HIS NEW BIKE.
GREAT.
SLOW AND STEADY IS FINE. TELL HIM THAT.
LITTLE BY LITTLE, OUR NEW TEAM WILL TAKE SHAPE AND WE'LL SURPASS THE THIRD-YEARS.
MAKISHIMA-SAN'S GONE NOW—

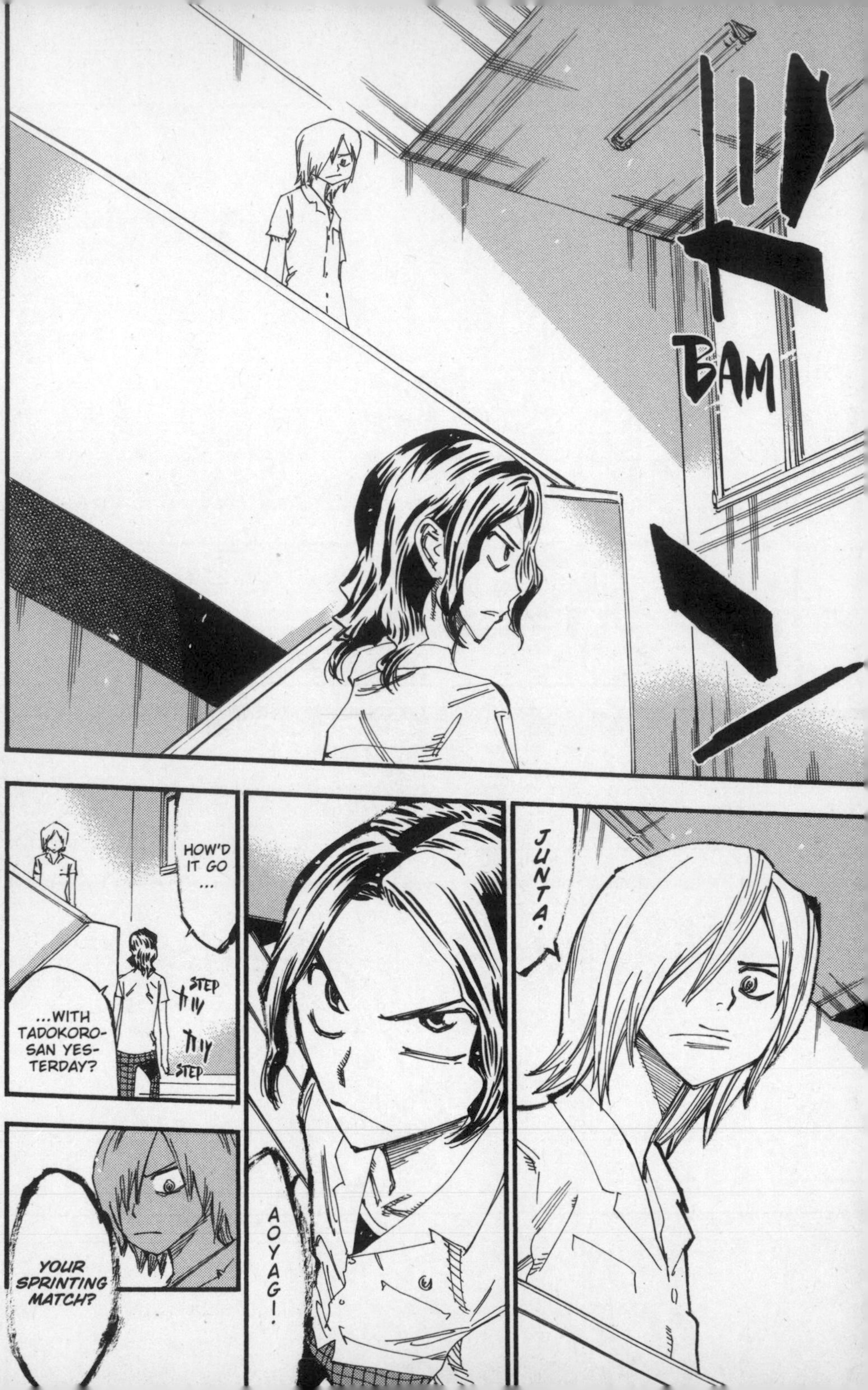
BAM
JUNTA.
AOYAGI!
HOW'D IT GO ...
...WITH TADOKORO-SAN YES-TERDAY?
STEP
STEP
YOUR SPRINTING MATCH?

WITH 200M TO GO, I ATTACKED.

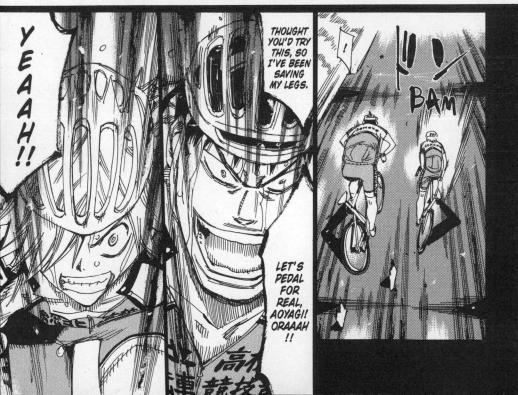

YEAAH!!

THOUGHT YOU'D TRY THIS, SO I'VE BEEN SAVING MY LEGS.

LET'S PEDAL FOR REAL, AOYAGI! ORAAAH!!

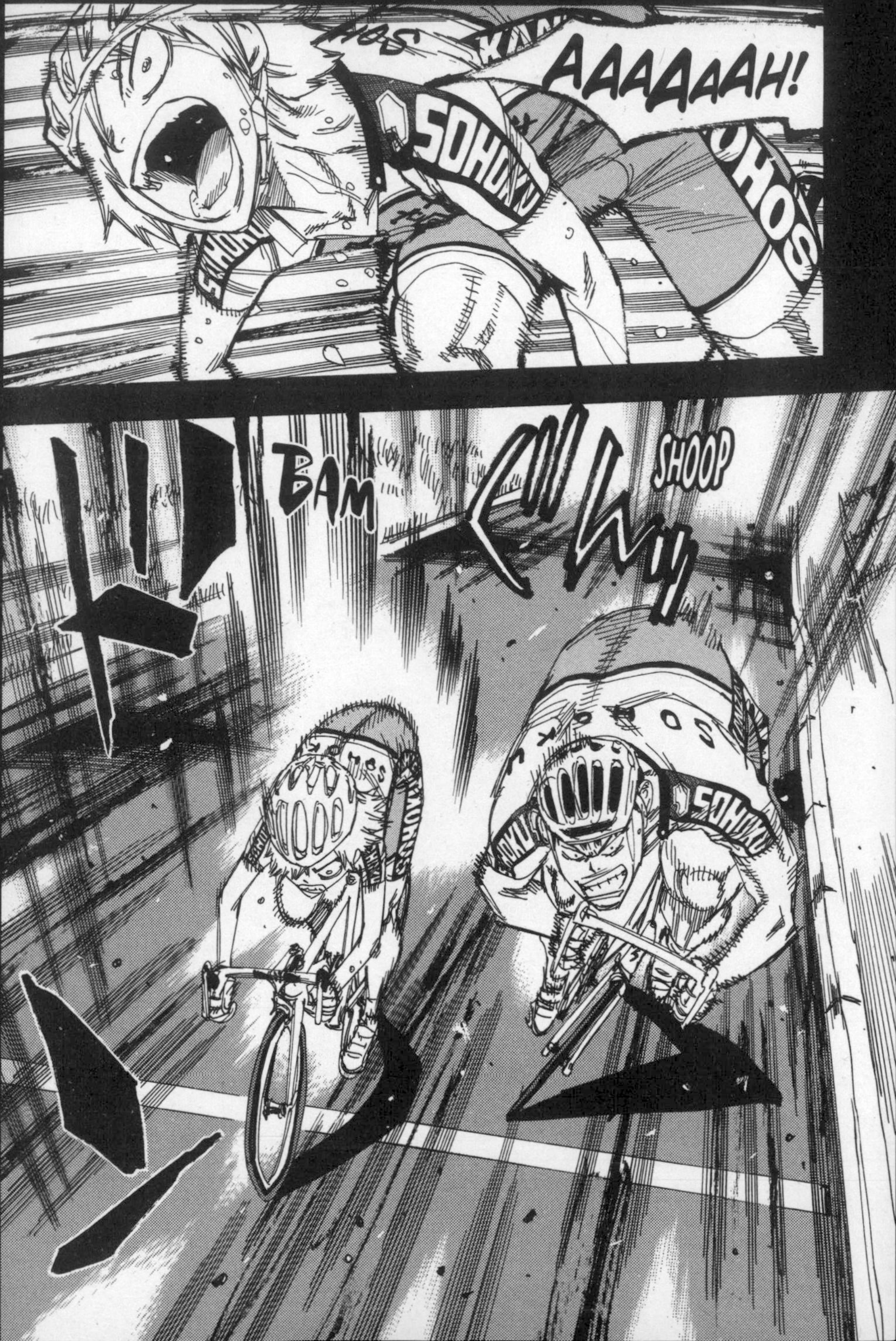
AAAAAAH!
BAM
SHOOP

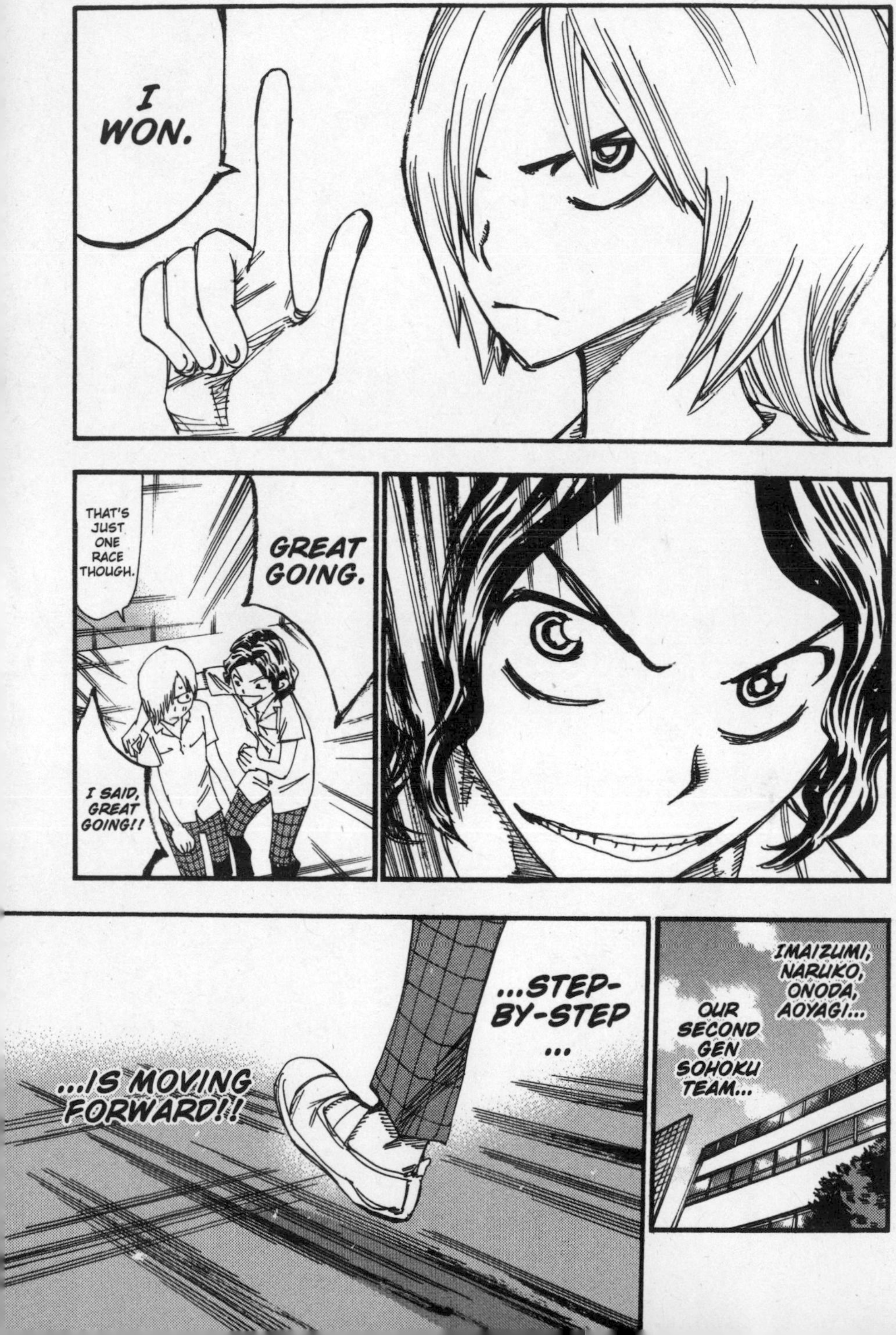
I WON.
GREAT GOING.
THAT'S JUST ONE RACE THOUGH.
I SAID, GREAT GOING!!
IMAIZUMI, NARUKO, ONODA, AOYAGI...
OUR SECOND GEN SOHOKU TEAM...
...STEP-BY-STEP...
...IS MOVING FORWARD!!

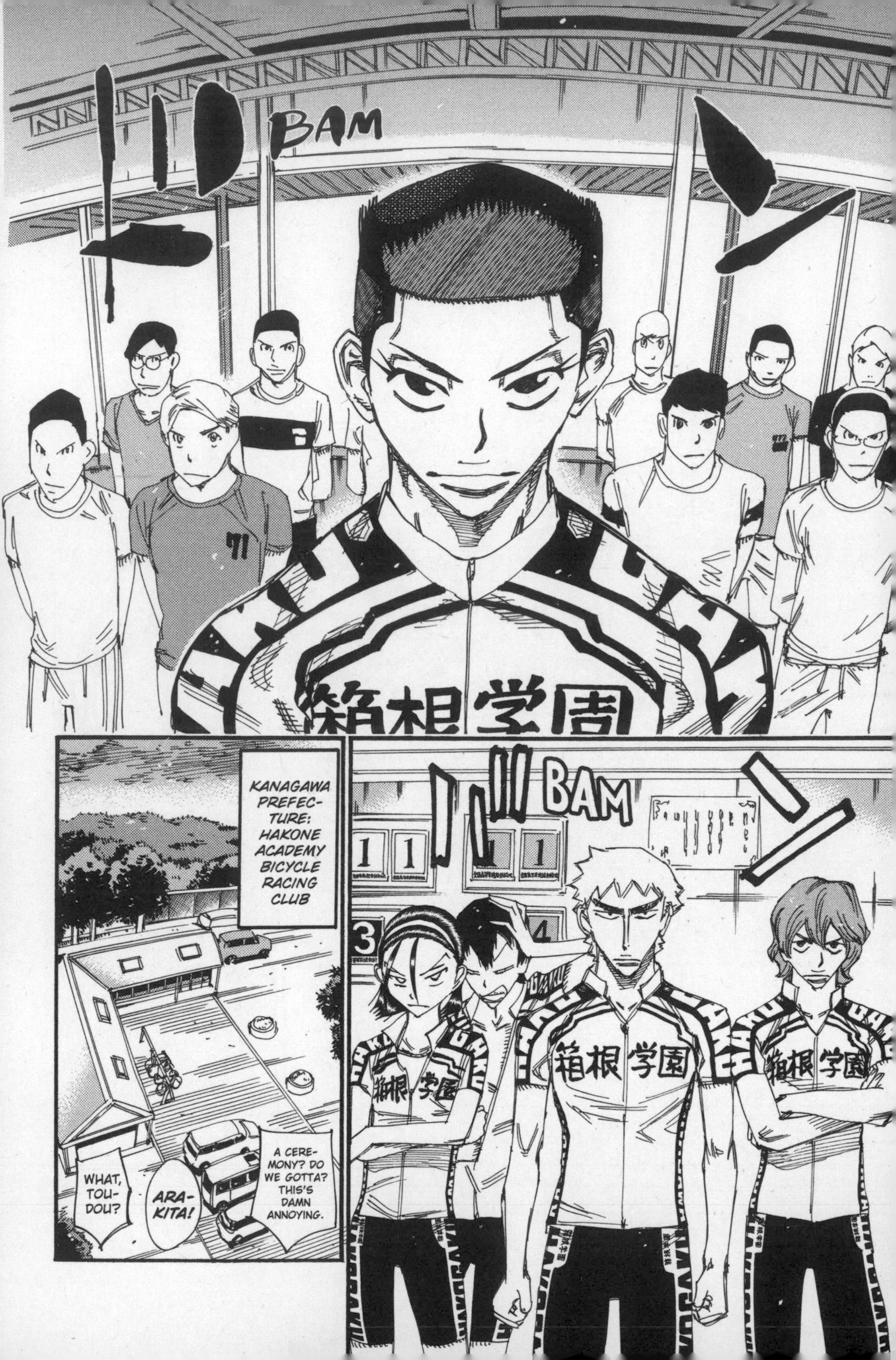
BAM
箱根学園
BAM
箱根学園
KANAGAWA PREFECTURE: HAKONE ACADEMY BICYCLE RACING CLUB
A CEREMONY? DO WE GOTTA? THIS'S DAMN ANNOYING.
ARAKITA!
WHAT, TOUDOU?

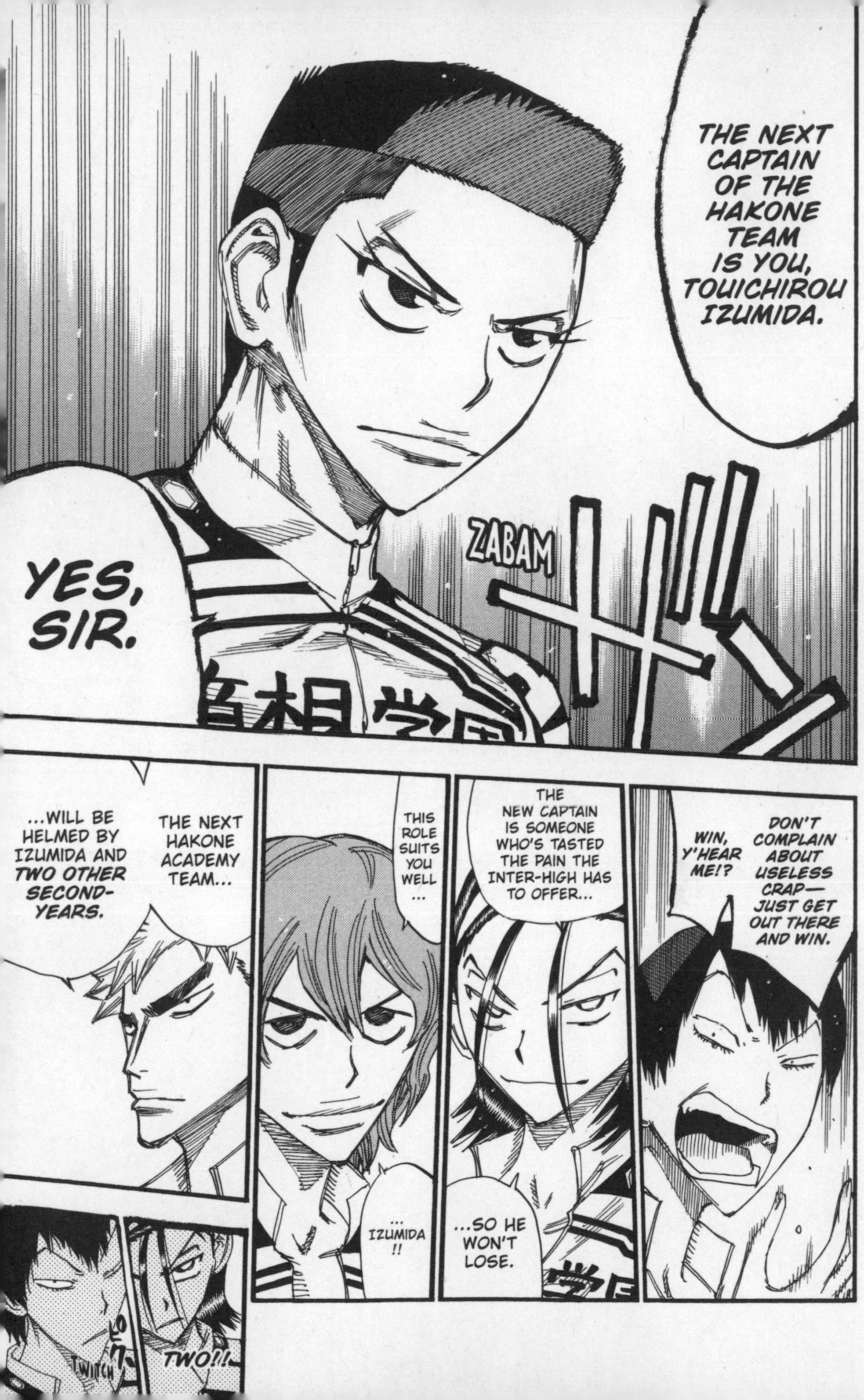
THE NEXT CAPTAIN OF THE HAKONE TEAM IS YOU, TOUICHIROU IZUMIDA.
ZABAM
YES, SIR.
DON'T COMPLAIN ABOUT USELESS CRAP— JUST GET OUT THERE AND WIN.
WIN, Y'HEAR ME!?
THE NEW CAPTAIN IS SOMEONE WHO'S TASTED THE PAIN THE INTER-HIGH HAS TO OFFER...
...SO HE WON'T LOSE.
THIS ROLE SUITS YOU WELL ...
... IZUMIDA !!
THE NEXT HAKONE ACADEMY TEAM...
...WILL BE HELMED BY IZUMIDA AND TWO OTHER SECOND-YEARS.
TWO!!
TWITCH

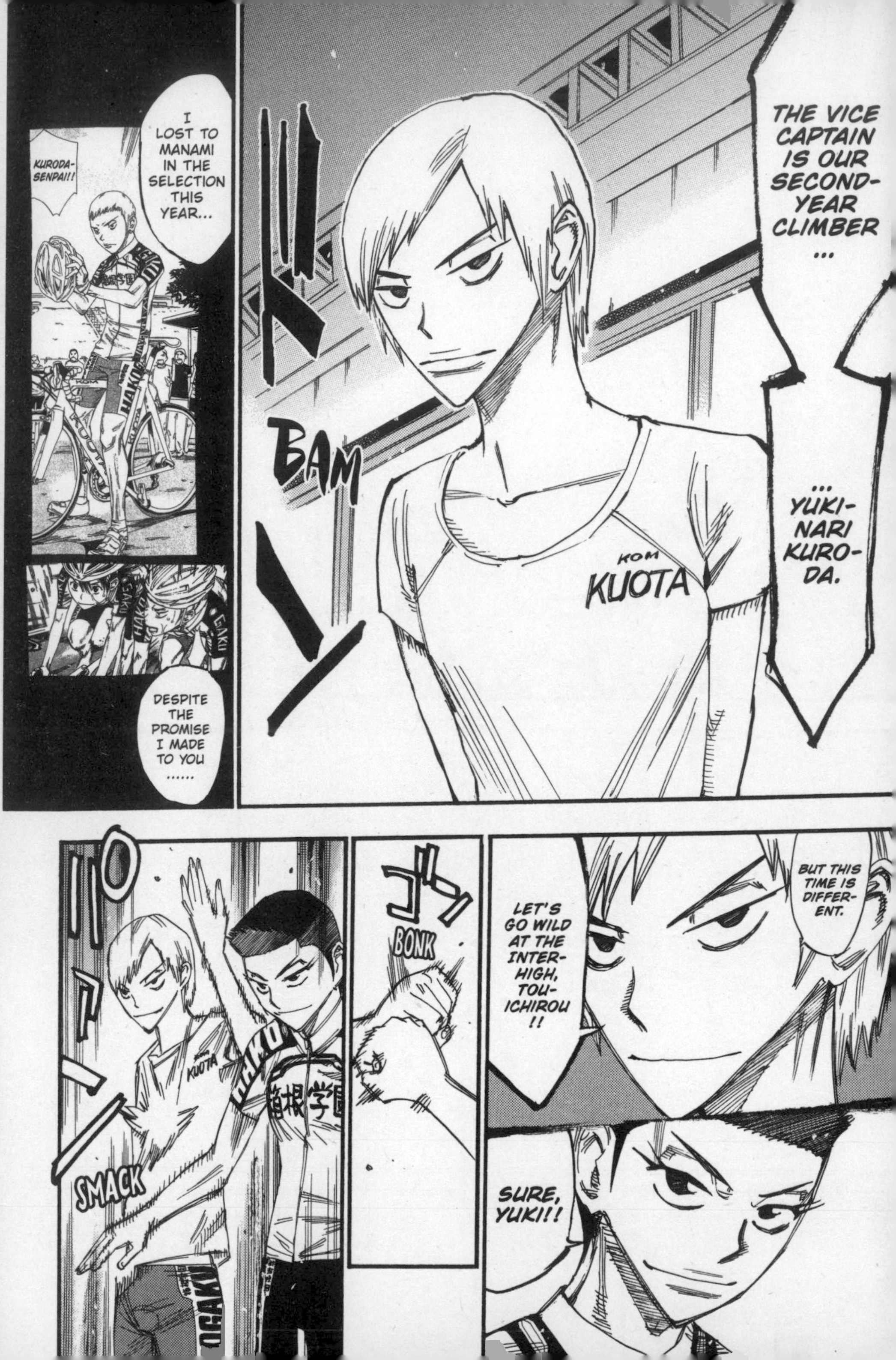
THE VICE CAPTAIN IS OUR SECOND-YEAR CLIMBER...
BAM
...YUKINARI KURODA.
KOM KUOTA
I LOST TO MANAMI IN THE SELECTION THIS YEAR...
KURODA-SENPAI!!
DESPITE THE PROMISE I MADE TO YOU......
BUT THIS TIME IS DIFFERENT.
LET'S GO WILD AT THE INTER-HIGH, TOUICHIROU!!
SURE, YUKI!!
BONK
SMACK

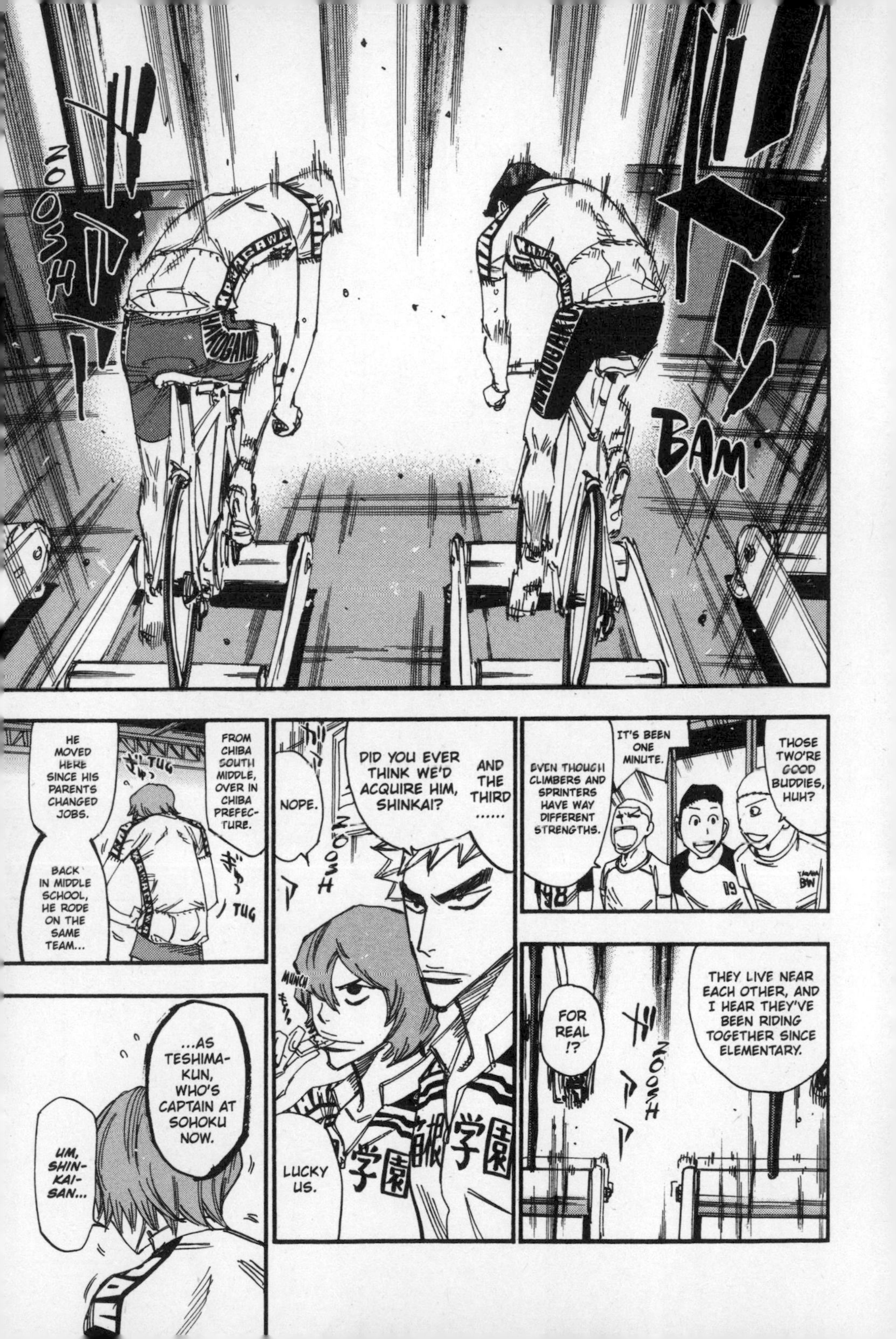
BAM
ZOOSH
THOSE TWO'RE GOOD BUDDIES, HUH?
IT'S BEEN ONE MINUTE.
EVEN THOUGH CLIMBERS AND SPRINTERS HAVE WAY DIFFERENT STRENGTHS.
THEY LIVE NEAR EACH OTHER, AND I HEAR THEY'VE BEEN RIDING TOGETHER SINCE ELEMENTARY.
ZOOSH
FOR REAL!?
AND THE THIRD……
DID YOU EVER THINK WE'D ACQUIRE HIM, SHINKAI?
NOPE.
ZOOSH
MUNCH
LUCKY US.
FROM CHIBA SOUTH MIDDLE, OVER IN CHIBA PREFECTURE.
HE MOVED HERE SINCE HIS PARENTS CHANGED JOBS.
TUG
TUG
BACK IN MIDDLE SCHOOL, HE RODE ON THE SAME TEAM...
...AS TESHIMA-KUN, WHO'S CAPTAIN AT SOHOKU NOW.
UM, SHINKAI-SAN...

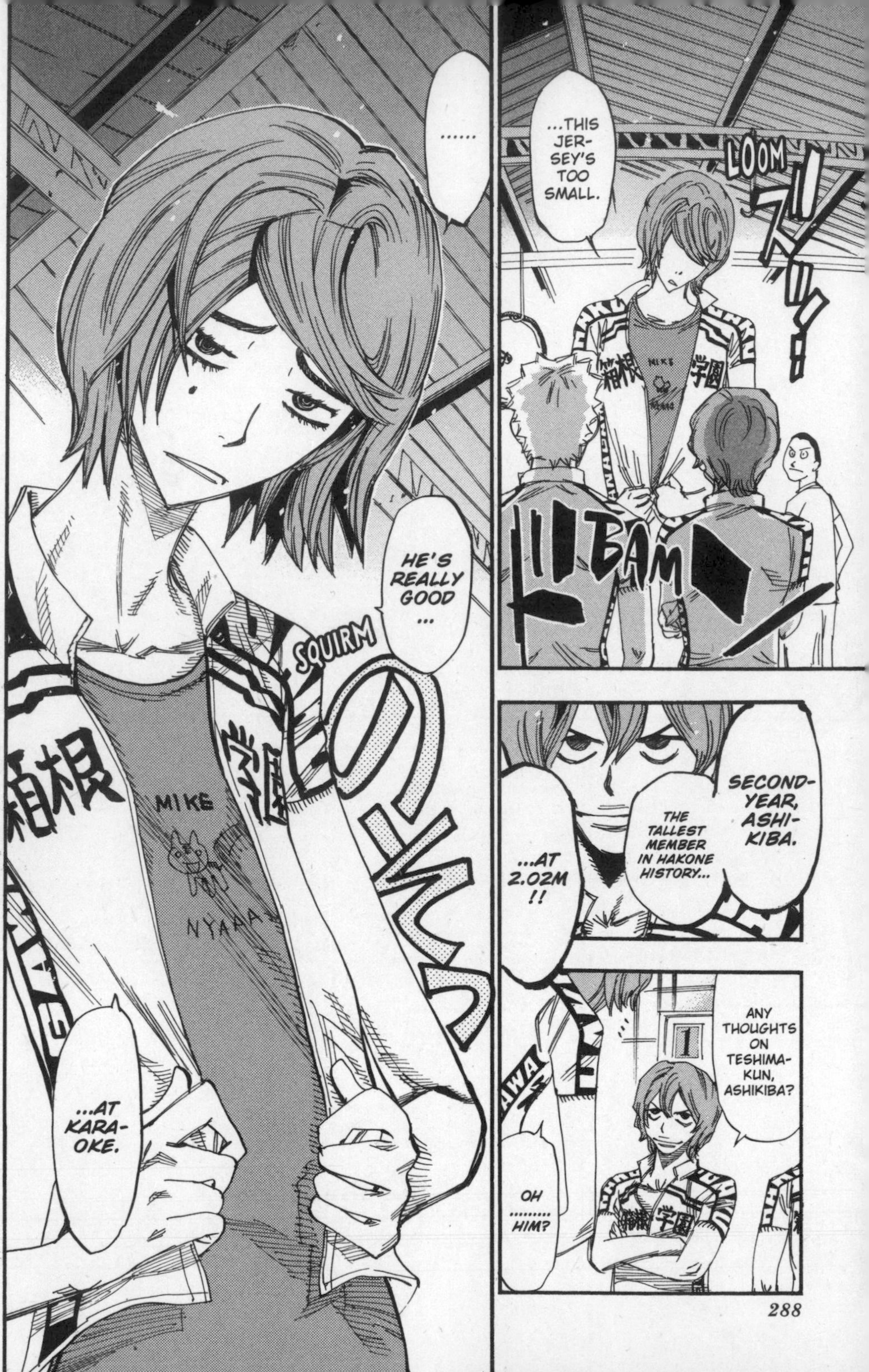
...THIS JER-SEY'S TOO SMALL.
LOOM
MIKE
BAM
SECOND-YEAR, ASHI-KIBA.
THE TALLEST MEMBER IN HAKONE HISTORY...
...AT 2.02M !!
ANY THOUGHTS ON TESHIMA-KUN, ASHIKIBA?
OH .... HIM?
......
HE'S REALLY GOOD ...
SQUIRM
MIKE
NYAAA
...AT KARA-OKE.

RIDE.239 THE THIRD MAN

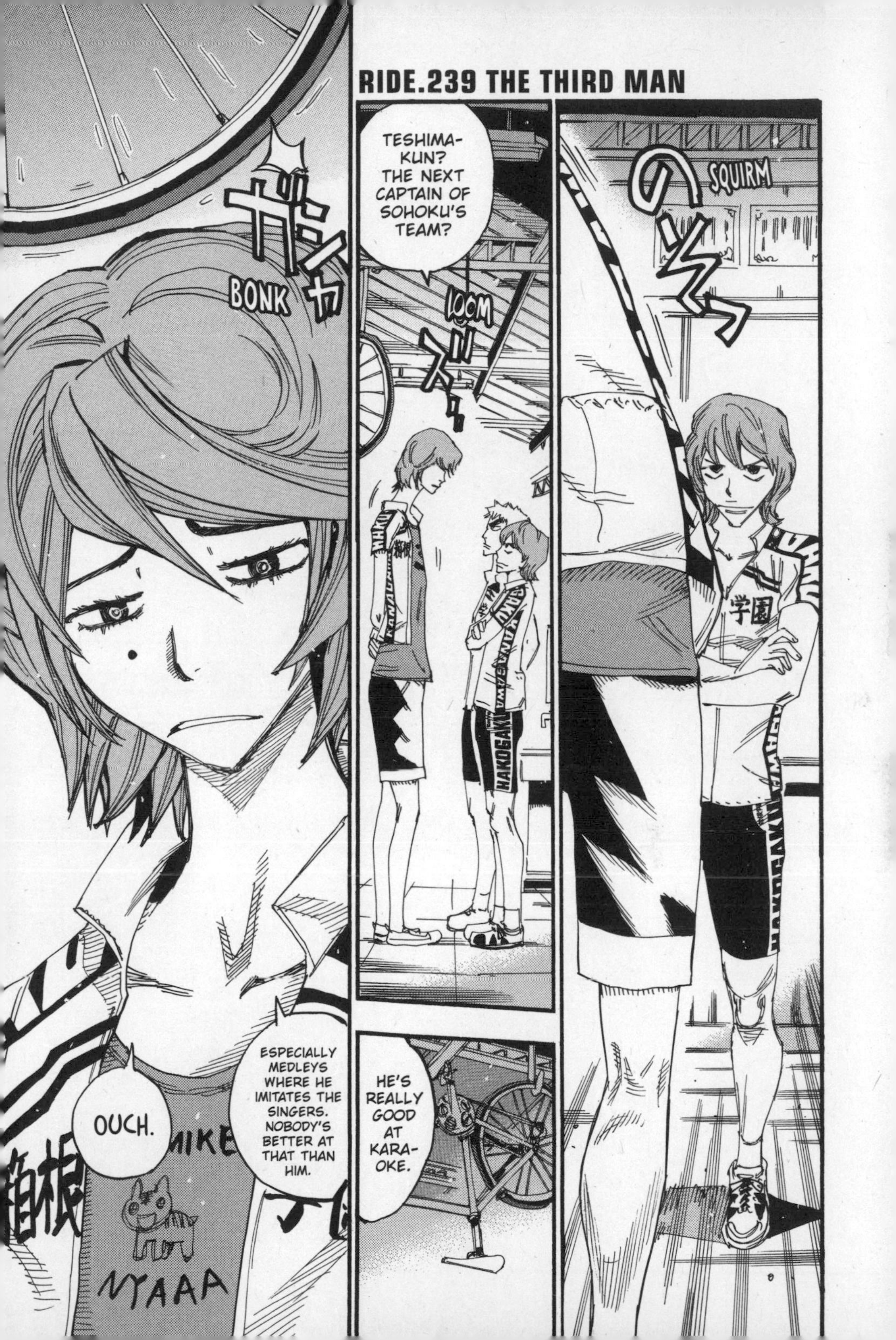
SQUIRM
TESHIMA-KUN? THE NEXT CAPTAIN OF SOHOKU'S TEAM?
LOOM
HE'S REALLY GOOD AT KARAOKE.
ESPECIALLY MEDLEYS WHERE HE IMITATES THE SINGERS. NOBODY'S BETTER AT THAT THAN HIM.
BONK
OUCH.
NYAAA

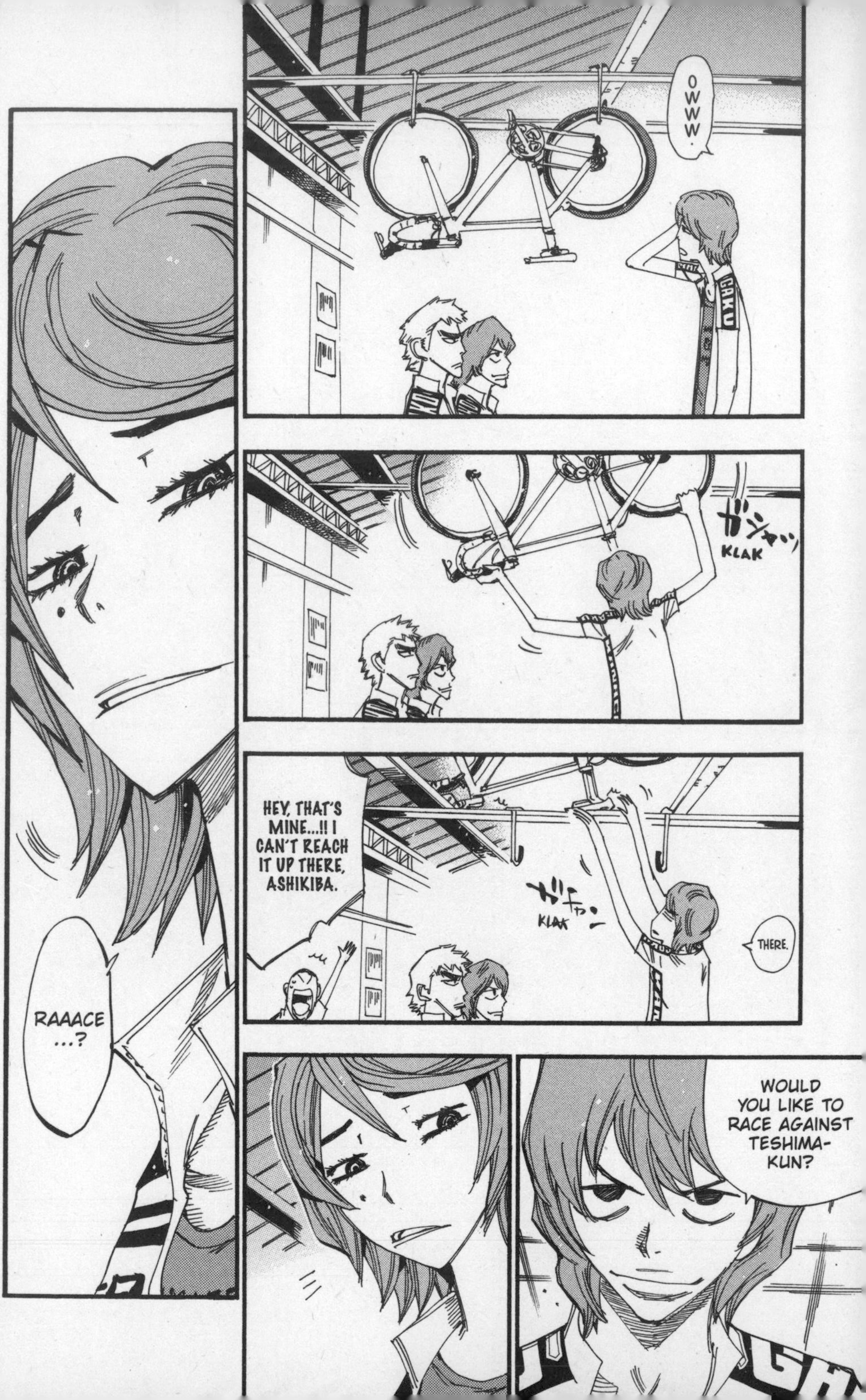
OWWW.
ガシャッ
KLAK
HEY, THAT'S MINE...!! I CAN'T REACH IT UP THERE, ASHIKIBA.
KLAK
THERE.
WOULD YOU LIKE TO RACE AGAINST TESHIMA-KUN?
RAAACE ...?

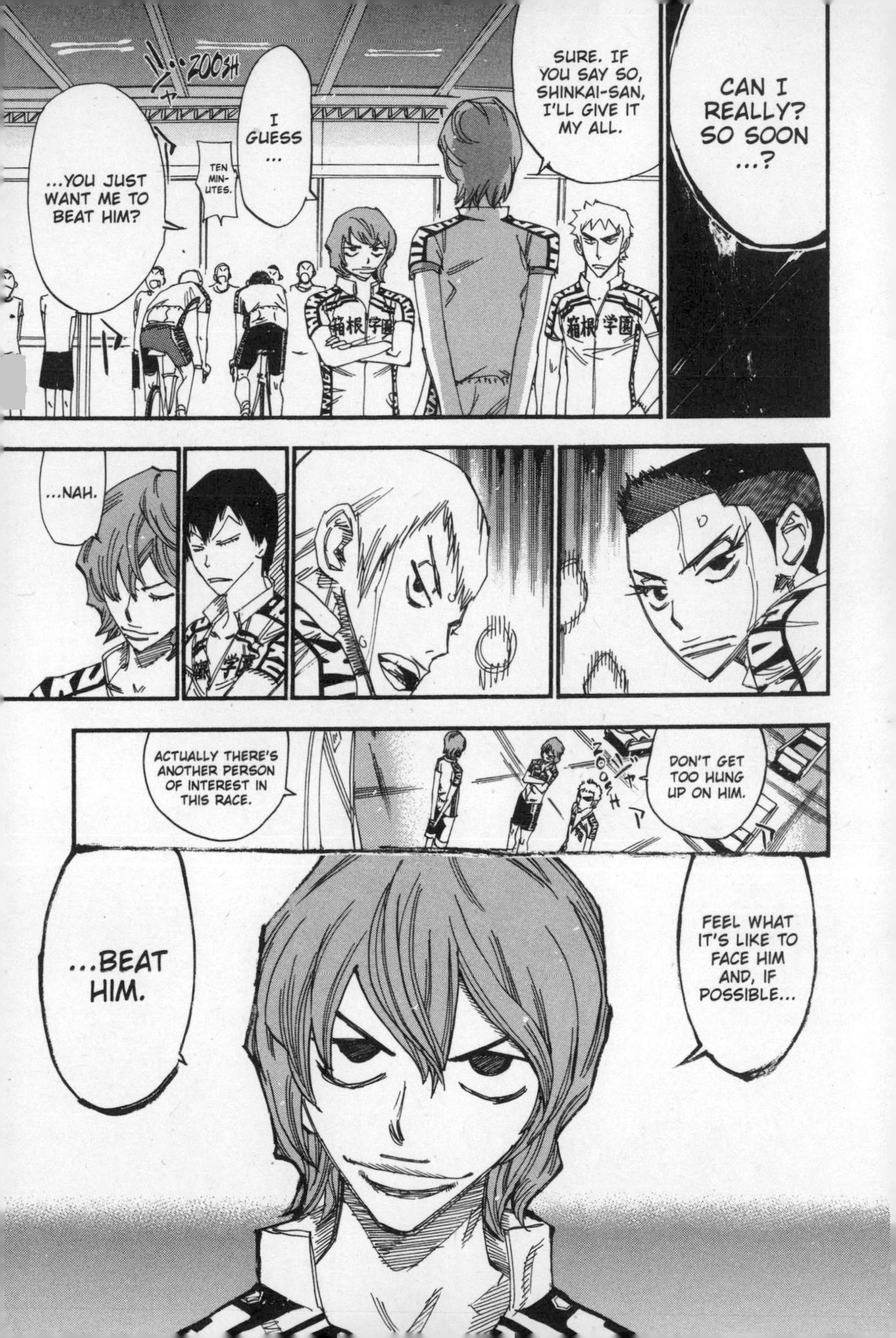
ZOOSH
...YOU JUST WANT ME TO BEAT HIM?
I GUESS ...
TEN MINUTES.
SURE. IF YOU SAY SO, SHINKAI-SAN, I'LL GIVE IT MY ALL.
CAN I REALLY? SO SOON ...?
...NAH.
ACTUALLY THERE'S ANOTHER PERSON OF INTEREST IN THIS RACE.
ZOOSH
DON'T GET TOO HUNG UP ON HIM.
FEEL WHAT IT'S LIKE TO FACE HIM AND, IF POSSIBLE...
...BEAT HIM.

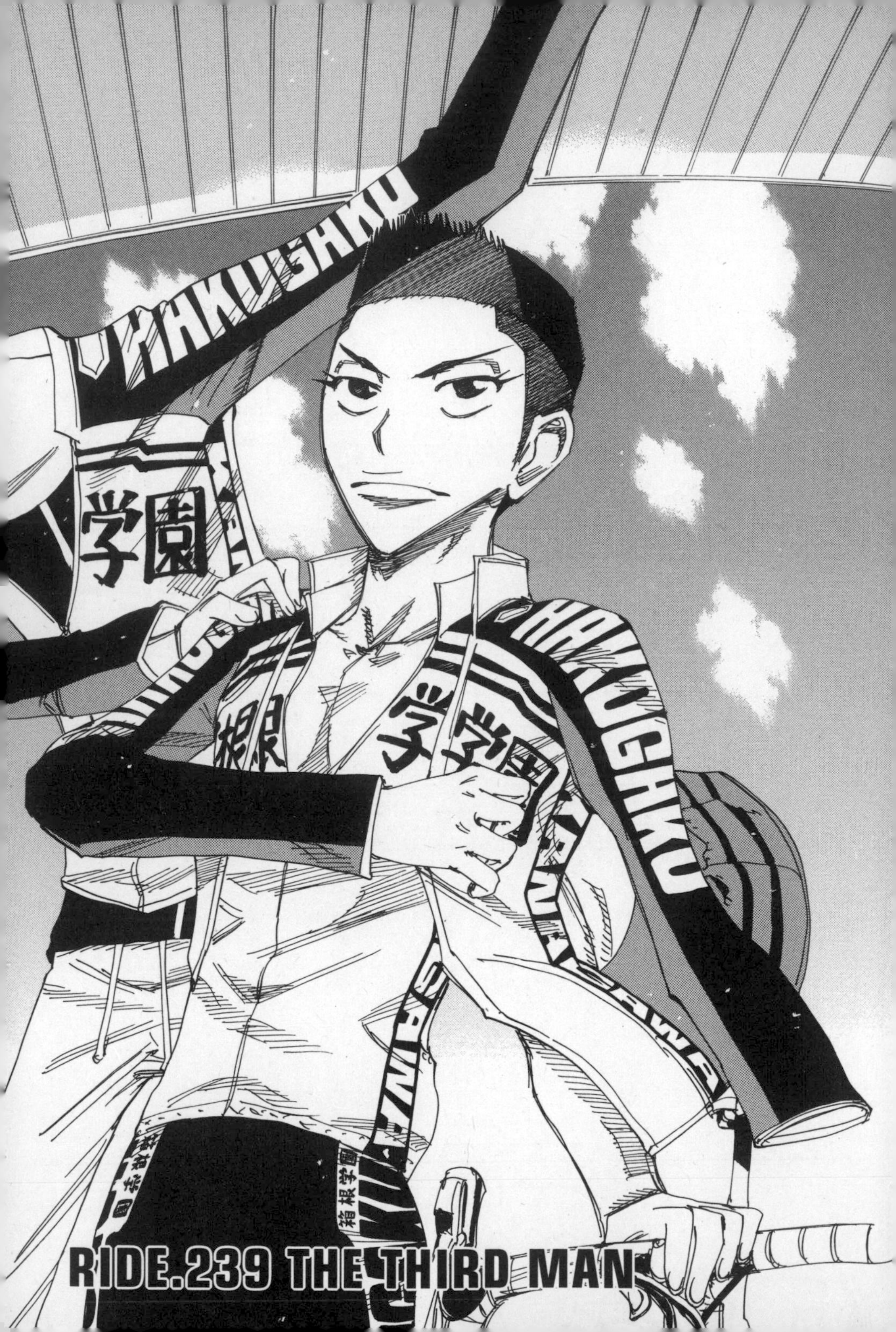

RIDE.239 THE THIRD MAN

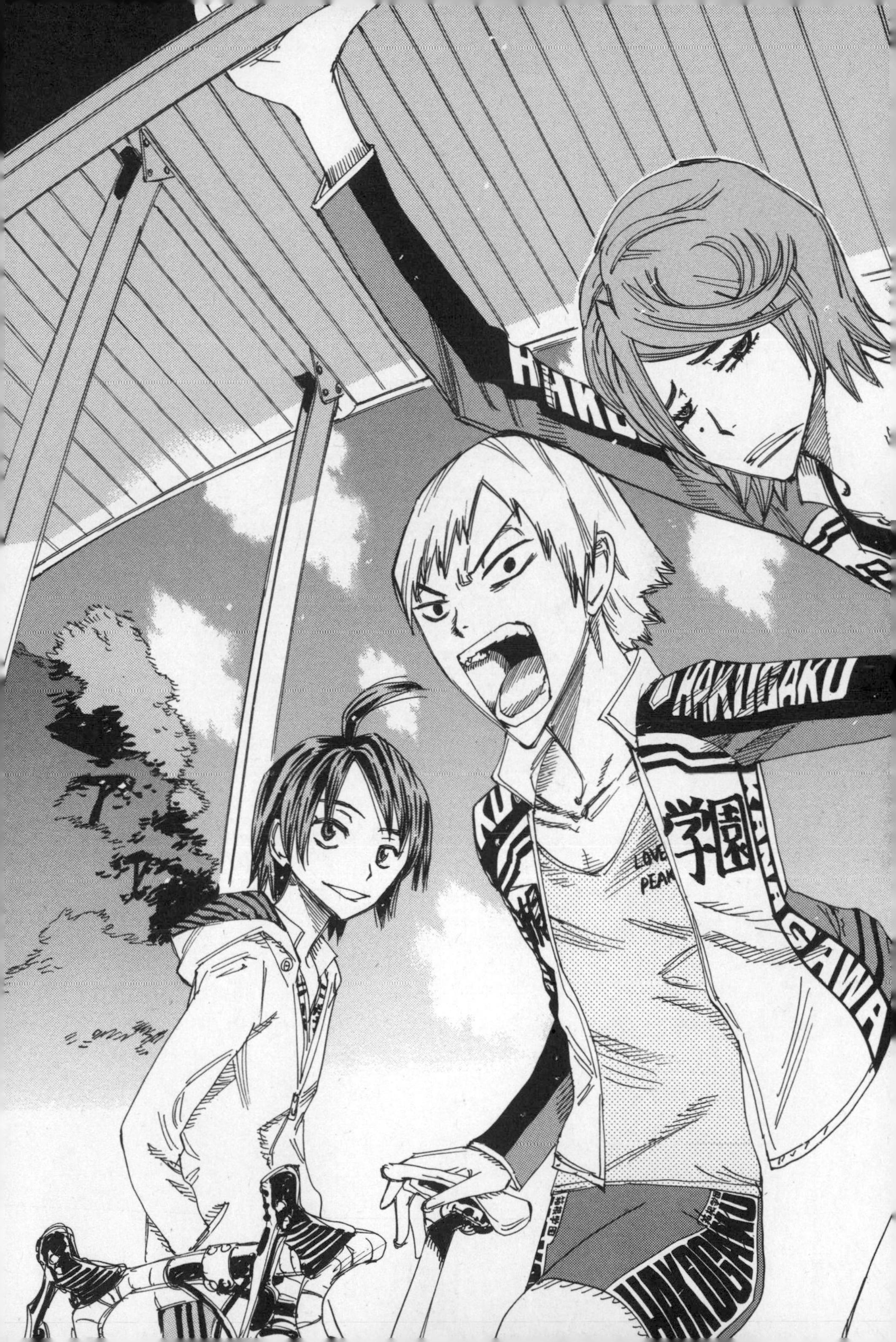
学園

SIGN: MEETING IN PROGRESS, DO NOT ENTER

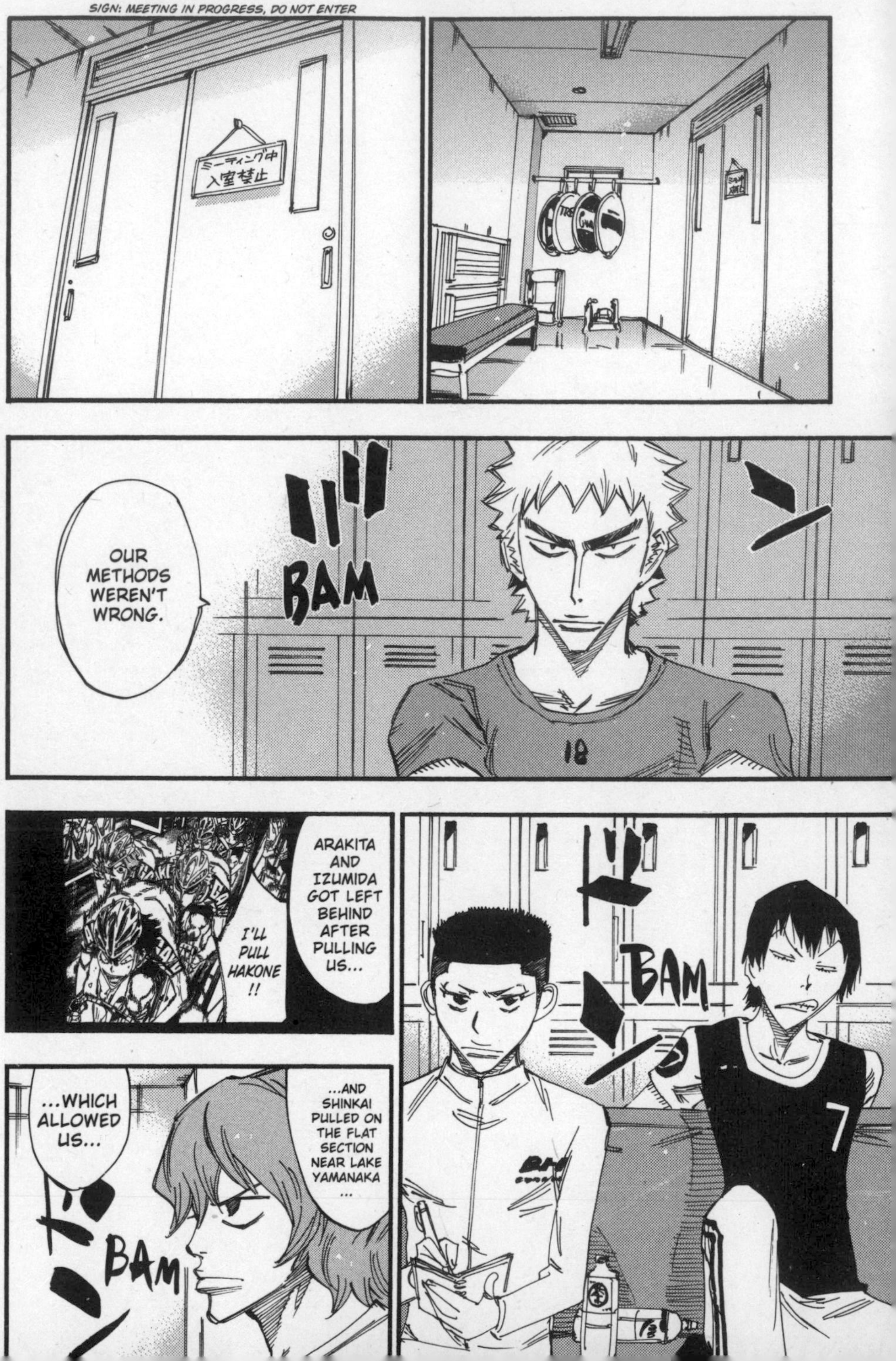
ミーティング中
入室禁止
BAM
OUR METHODS WEREN'T WRONG.
BAM
ARAKITA AND IZUMIDA GOT LEFT BEHIND AFTER PULLING US...
I'LL PULL HAKONE!!
...AND SHINKAI PULLED ON THE FLAT SECTION NEAR LAKE YAMANAKA...
...WHICH ALLOWED US...
BAM

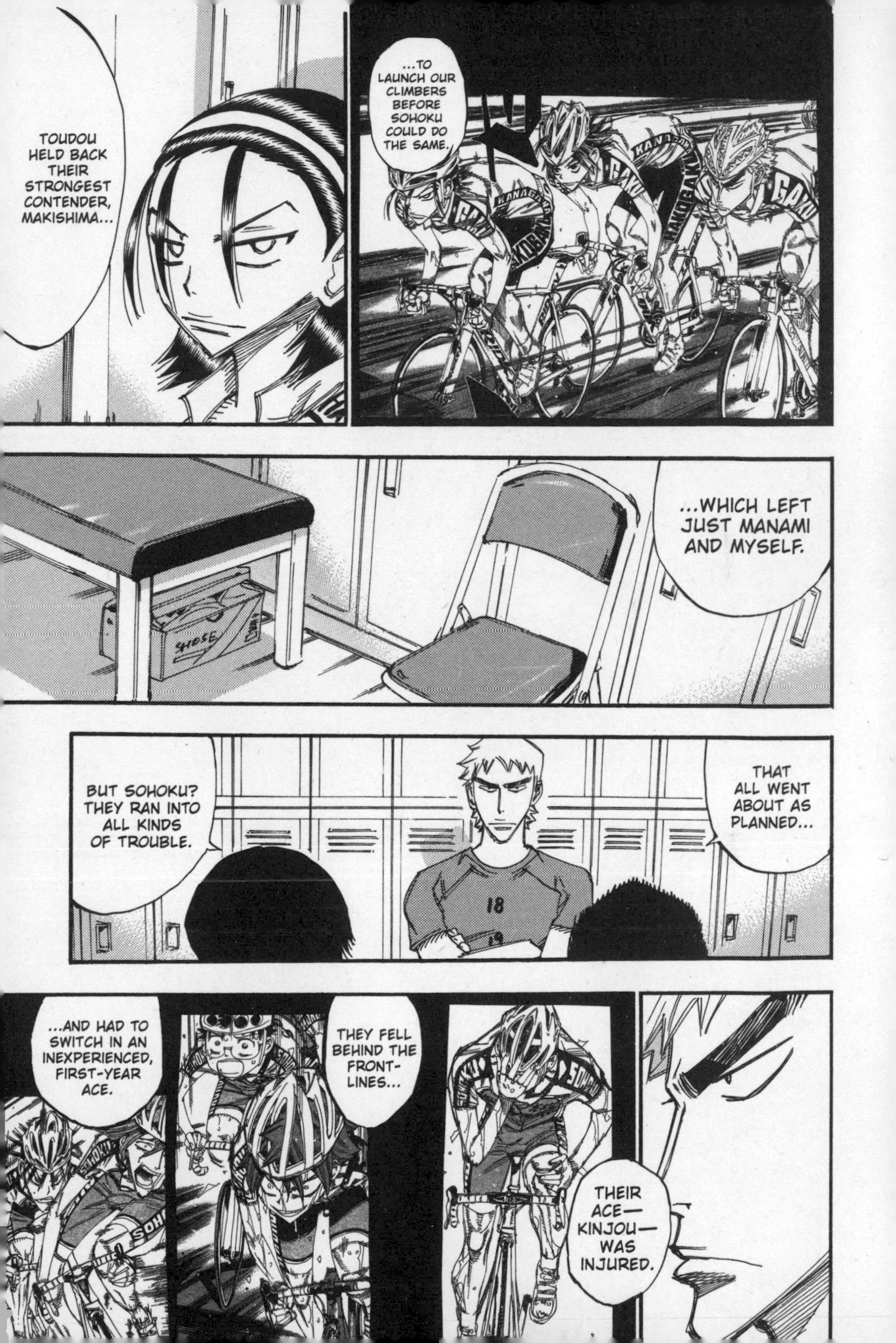
...TO LAUNCH OUR CLIMBERS BEFORE SOHOKU COULD DO THE SAME.
TOUDOU HELD BACK THEIR STRONGEST CONTENDER, MAKISHIMA...
...WHICH LEFT JUST MANAMI AND MYSELF.
THAT ALL WENT ABOUT AS PLANNED...
BUT SOHOKU? THEY RAN INTO ALL KINDS OF TROUBLE.
THEIR ACE—KINJOU—WAS INJURED.
THEY FELL BEHIND THE FRONT-LINES...
...AND HAD TO SWITCH IN AN INEXPERIENCED, FIRST-YEAR ACE.

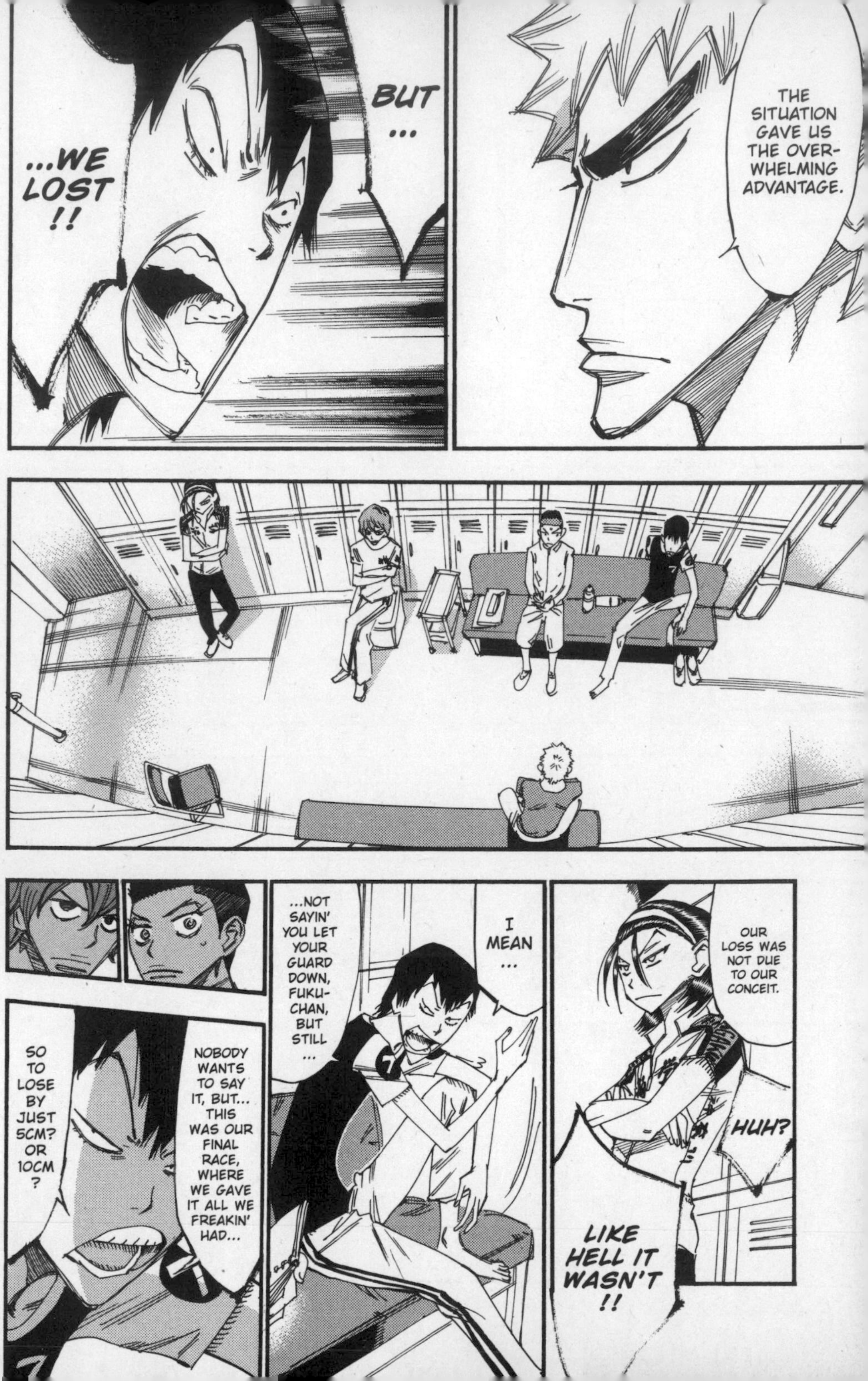
THE SITUATION GAVE US THE OVER-WHELMING ADVANTAGE.
BUT...
...WE LOST!!
OUR LOSS WAS NOT DUE TO OUR CONCEIT.
HUH?
LIKE HELL IT WASN'T!!
I MEAN...
...NOT SAYIN' YOU LET YOUR GUARD DOWN, FUKU-CHAN, BUT STILL...
NOBODY WANTS TO SAY IT, BUT... THIS WAS OUR FINAL RACE, WHERE WE GAVE IT ALL WE FREAKIN' HAD...
SO TO LOSE BY JUST 5CM? OR 10CM?

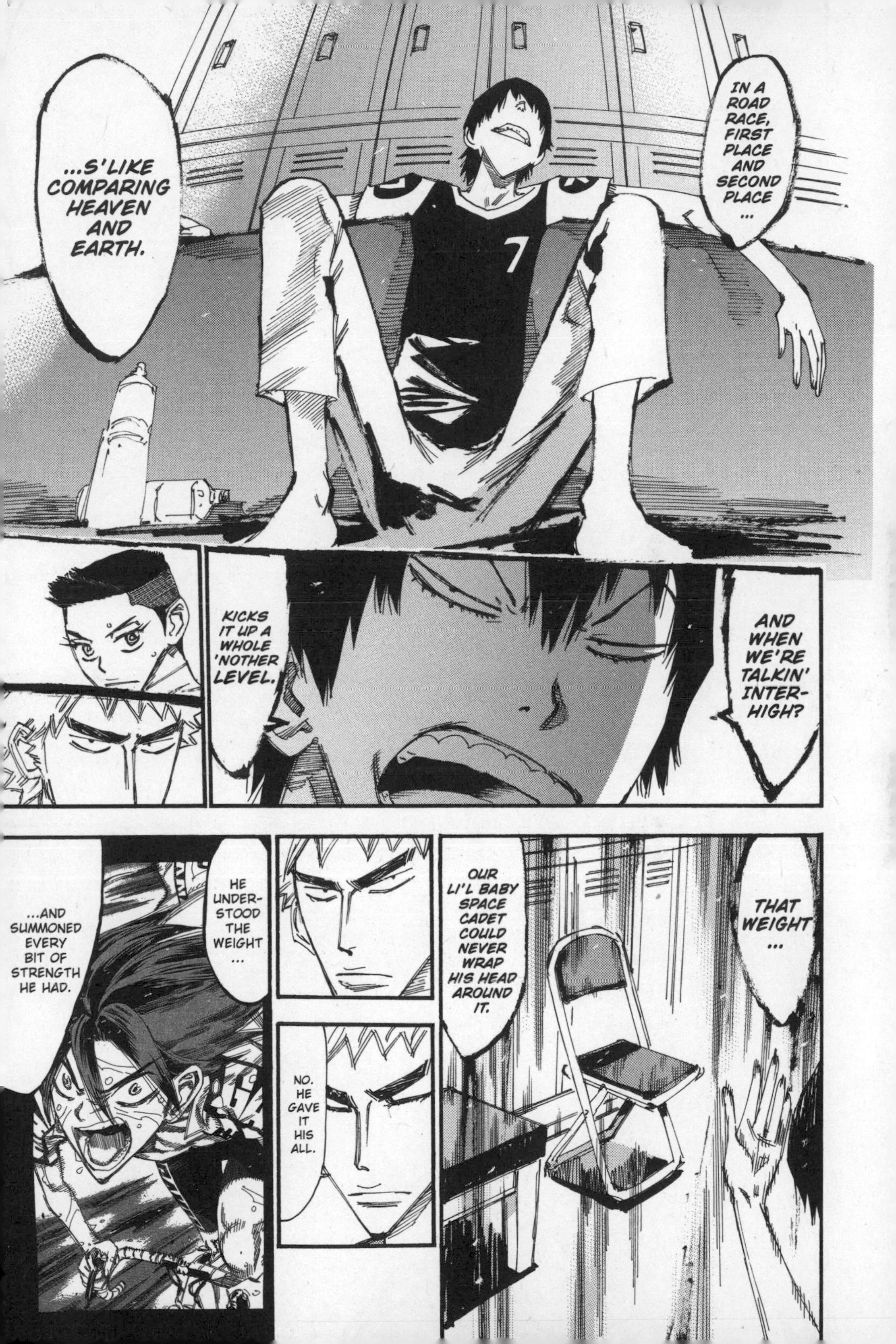
IN A ROAD RACE, FIRST PLACE AND SECOND PLACE ...
...S'LIKE COMPARING HEAVEN AND EARTH.
AND WHEN WE'RE TALKIN' INTER-HIGH?
KICKS IT UP A WHOLE 'NOTHER LEVEL.
THAT WEIGHT ...
OUR LI'L BABY SPACE CADET COULD NEVER WRAP HIS HEAD AROUND IT.
NO. HE GAVE IT HIS ALL.
HE UNDER-STOOD THE WEIGHT ...
...AND SUMMONED EVERY BIT OF STRENGTH HE HAD.

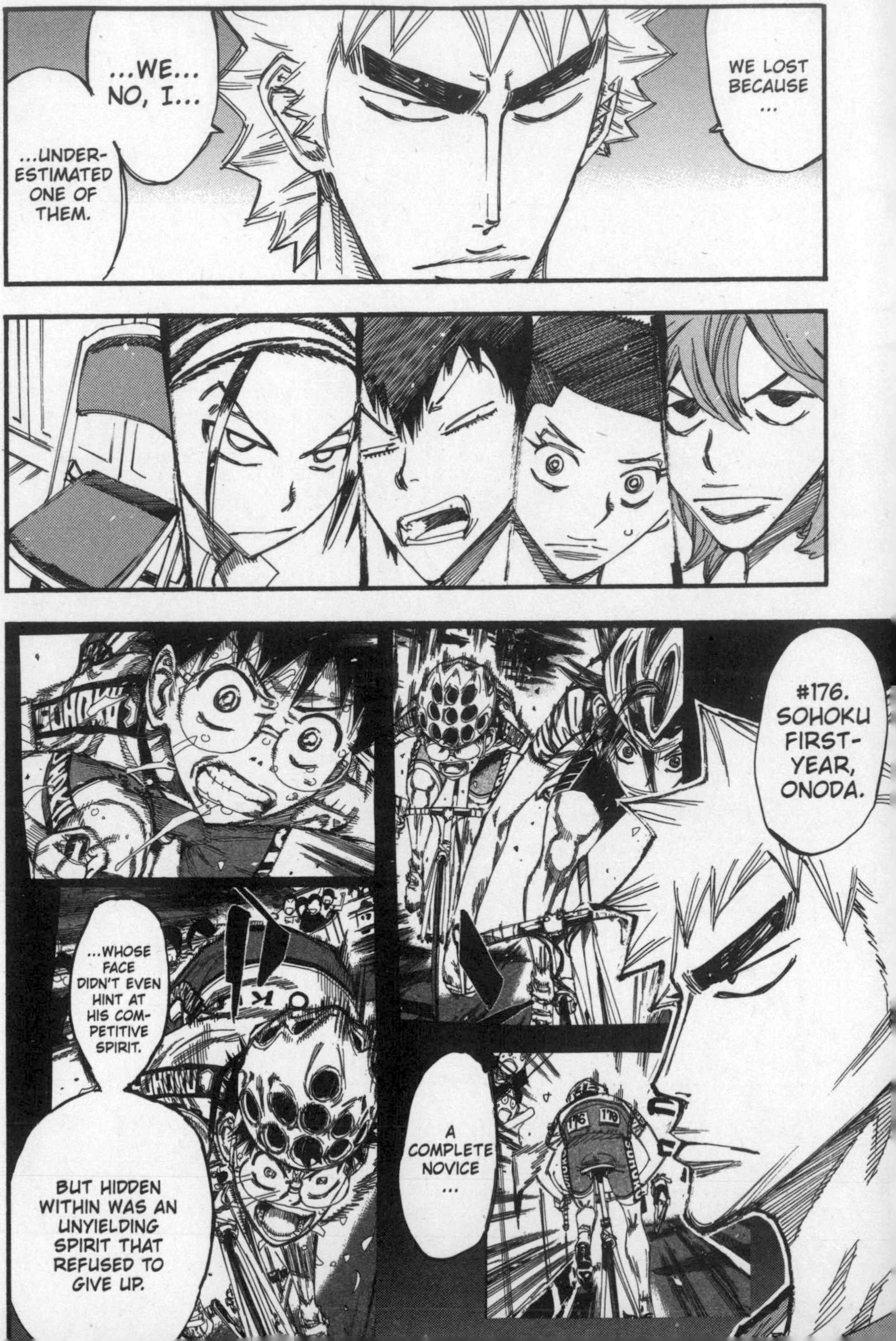
WE LOST BECAUSE ...
...WE... NO, I...
...UNDER-ESTIMATED ONE OF THEM.
#176. SOHOKU FIRST-YEAR, ONODA.
A COMPLETE NOVICE ...
...WHOSE FACE DIDN'T EVEN HINT AT HIS COMPETITIVE SPIRIT.
BUT HIDDEN WITHIN WAS AN UNYIELDING SPIRIT THAT REFUSED TO GIVE UP.

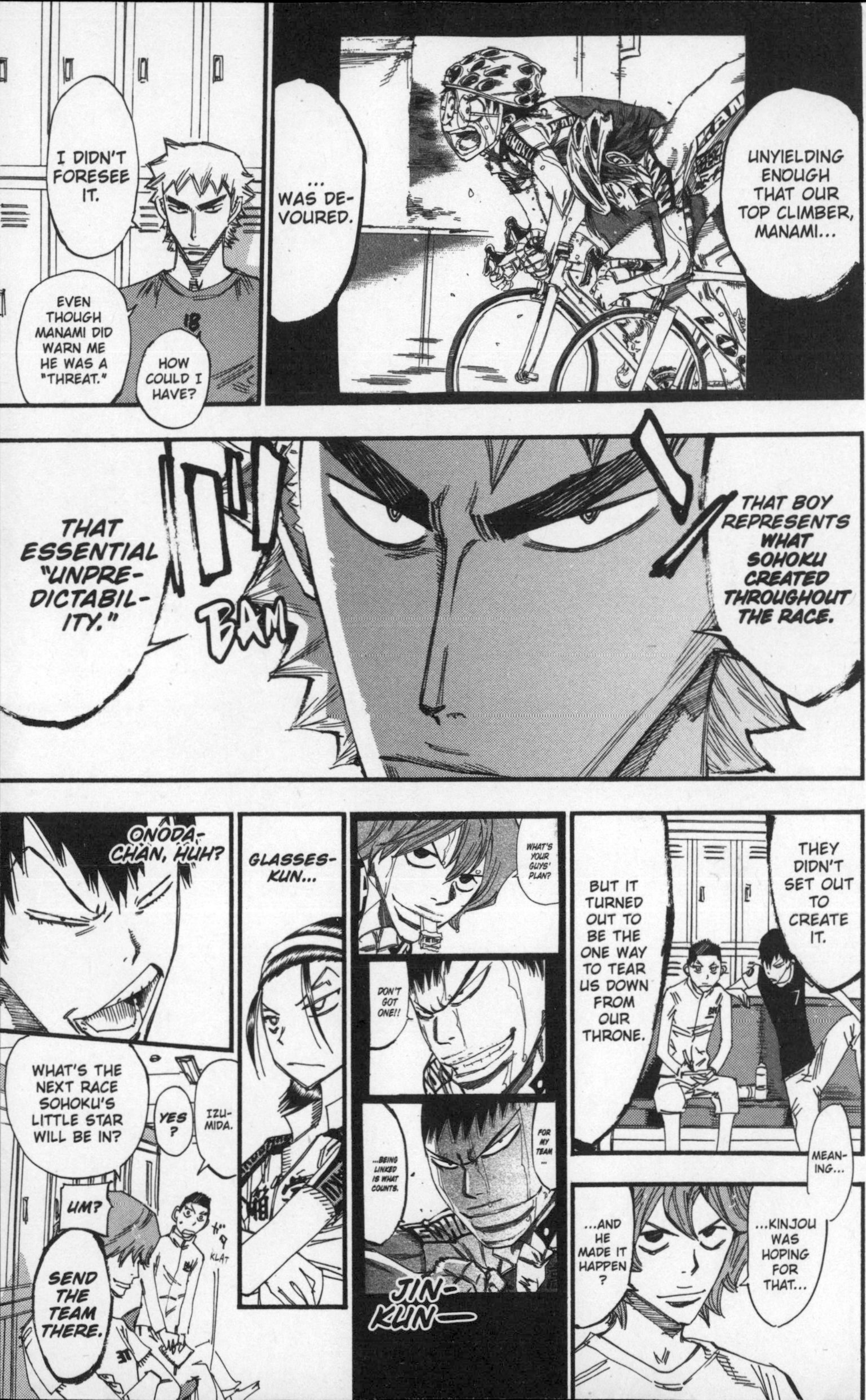
UNYIELDING ENOUGH THAT OUR TOP CLIMBER, MANAMI...
...WAS DE-VOURED.
I DIDN'T FORESEE IT.
EVEN THOUGH MANAMI DID WARN ME HE WAS A "THREAT."
HOW COULD I HAVE?
THAT BOY REPRESENTS WHAT SOHOKU CREATED THROUGHOUT THE RACE.
THAT ESSENTIAL "UNPRE-DICTABIL-ITY."
BAM
THEY DIDN'T SET OUT TO CREATE IT.
BUT IT TURNED OUT TO BE THE ONE WAY TO TEAR US DOWN FROM OUR THRONE.
MEANING...
...KINJOU WAS HOPING FOR THAT...
...AND HE MADE IT HAPPEN?
WHAT'S YOUR GUYS' PLAN?
DON'T GOT ONE!!
FOR MY TEAM...
...BEING LINKED IS WHAT COUNTS.
JIN-KUN—
GLASSES-KUN...
ONODA-CHAN, HUH?
IZU-MIDA.
YES?
WHAT'S THE NEXT RACE SOHOKU'S LITTLE STAR WILL BE IN?
UM?
KLAT
SEND THE TEAM THERE.

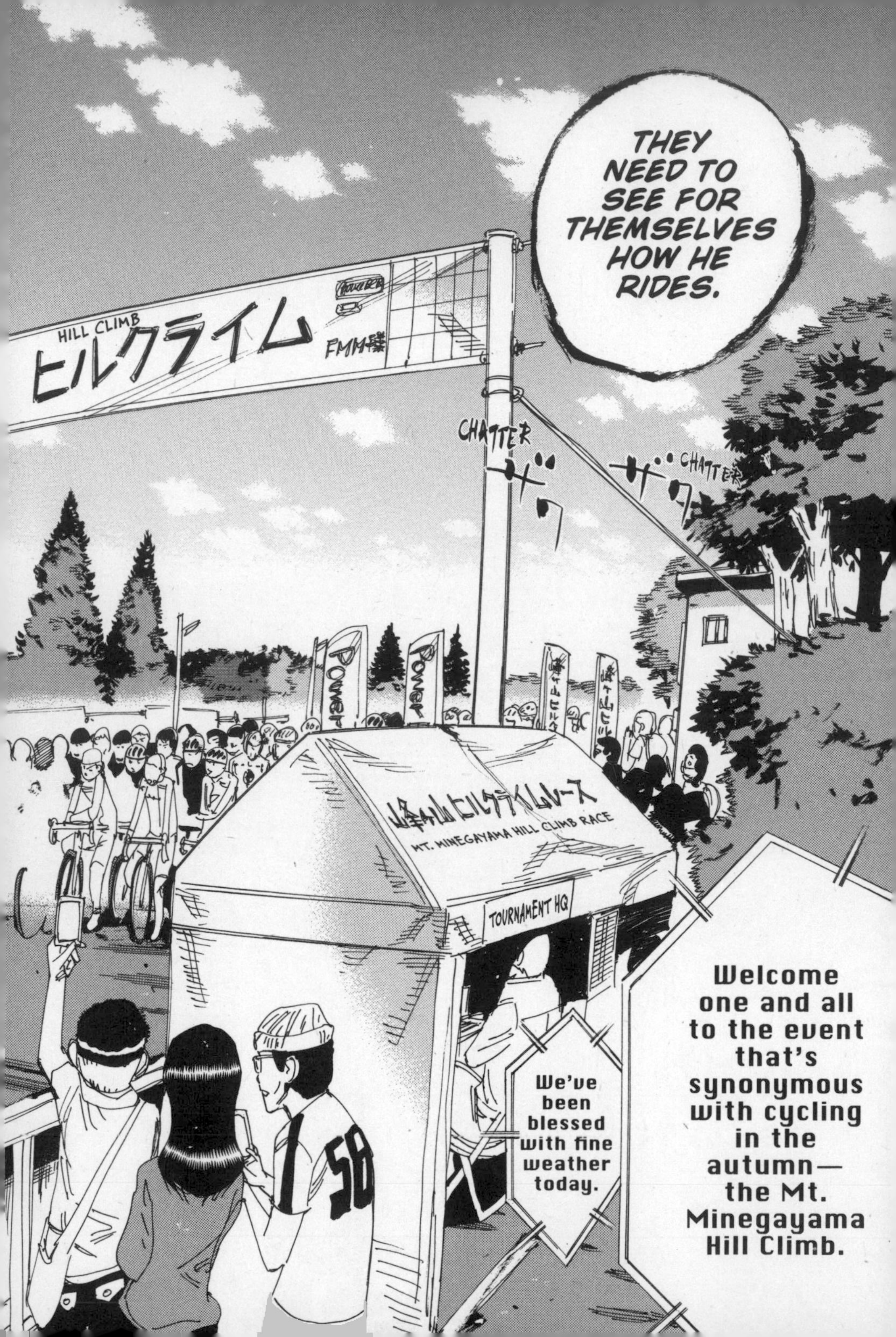
THEY NEED TO SEE FOR THEMSELVES HOW HE RIDES.
HILL CLIMB
ヒルクライム
CHATTER
ザワ
ザワ
CHATTER
峰ヶ山ヒルクライムレース
MT. MINEGAYAMA HILL CLIMB RACE
TOURNAMENT HQ
Welcome one and all to the event that's synonymous with cycling in the autumn—the Mt. Minegayama Hill Climb.
We've been blessed with fine weather today.

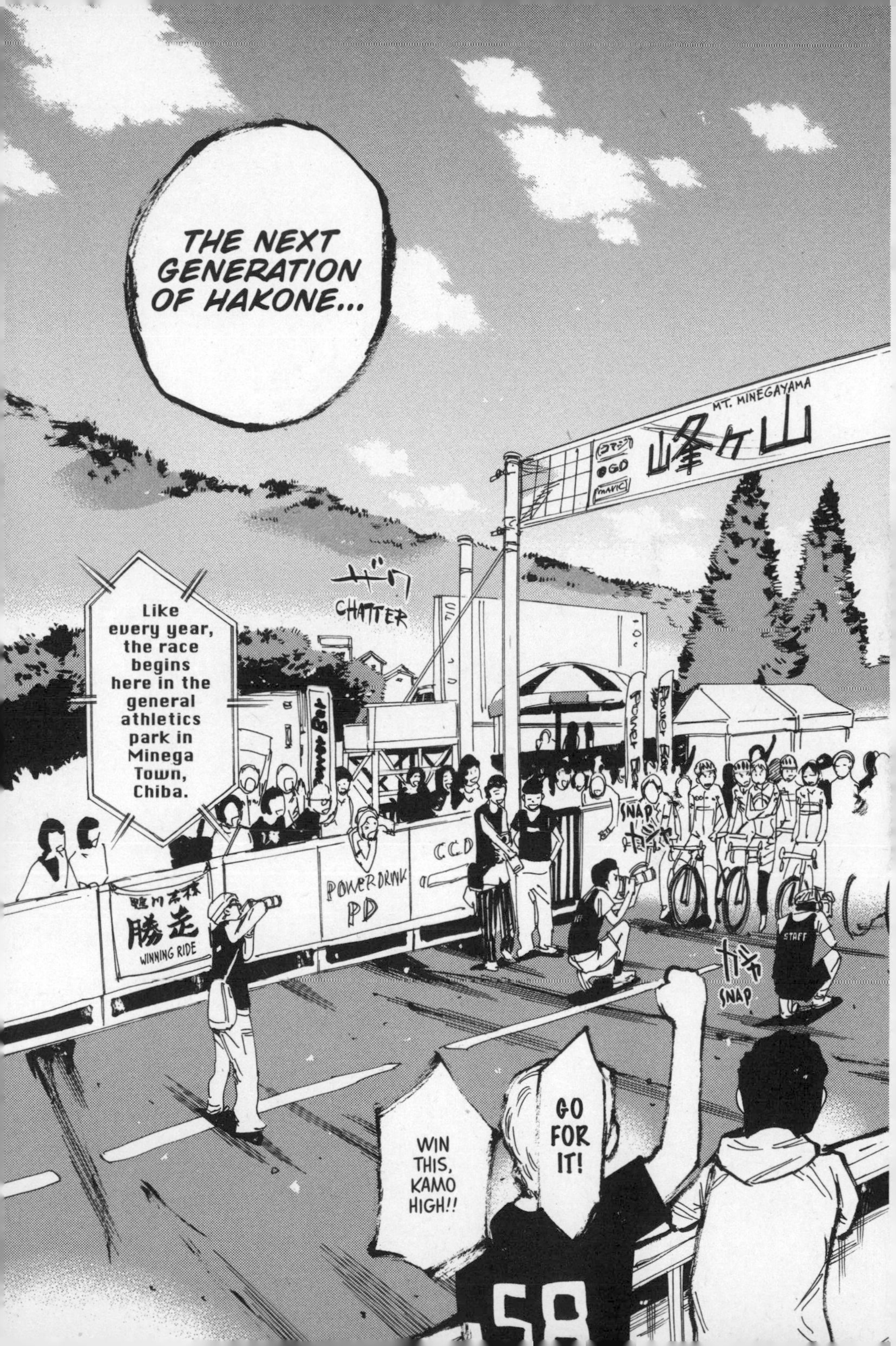
THE NEXT GENERATION OF HAKONE...
MT. MINEGAYAMA
峰ヶ山
ザワ
CHATTER
Like every year, the race begins here in the general athletics park in Minega Town, Chiba.
POWER DRINK PD
勝走
WINNING RIDE
SNAP
SNAP
STAFF
GO FOR IT!
WIN THIS, KAMO HIGH!!

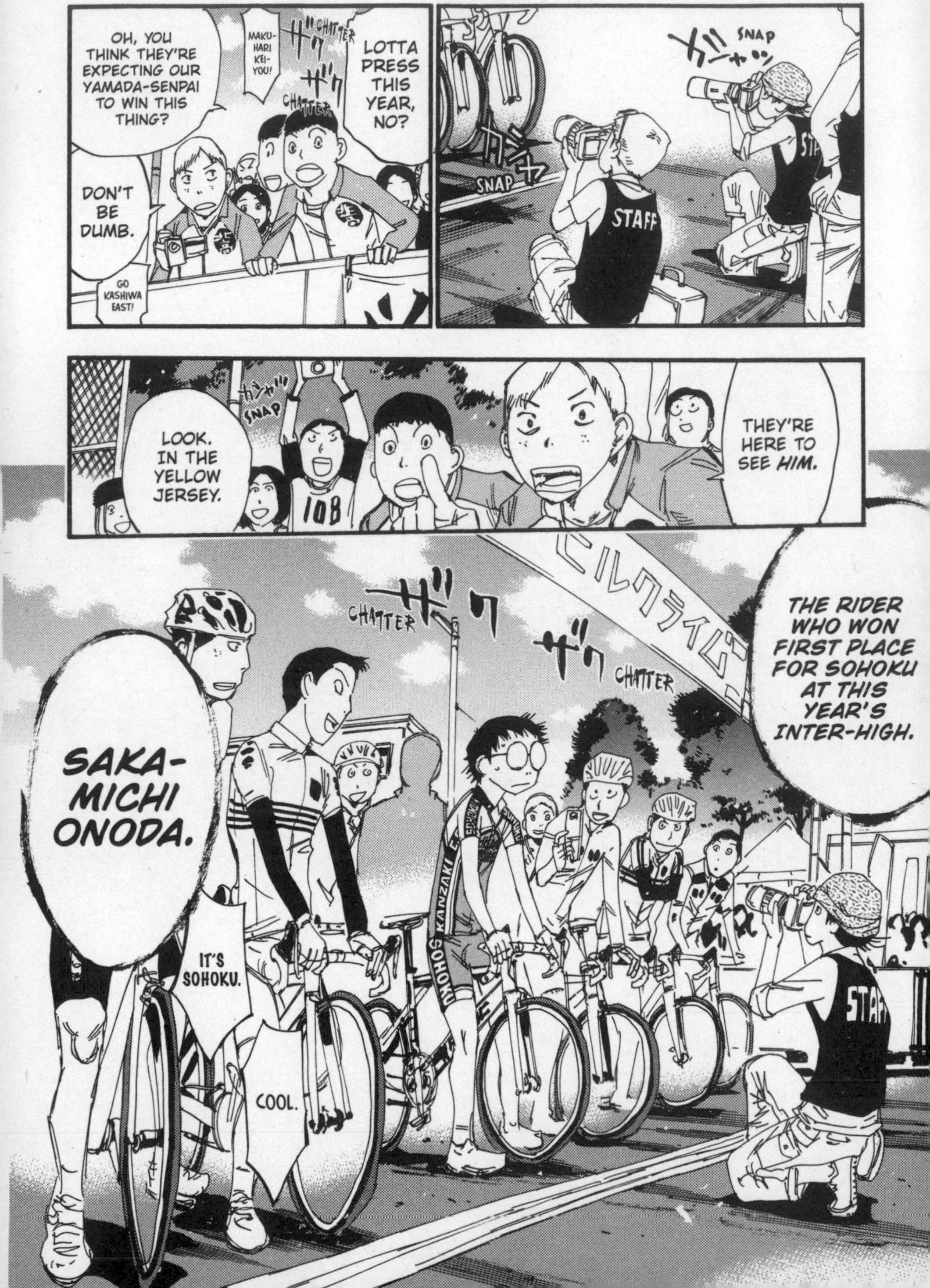
SNAP
SNAP
LOTTA PRESS THIS YEAR, NO?
CHATTER
CHATTER
MAKU-HARI KEI-YOU!
OH, YOU THINK THEY'RE EXPECTING OUR YAMADA-SENPAI TO WIN THIS THING?
DON'T BE DUMB.
GO KASHIWA EAST!
THEY'RE HERE TO SEE *HIM*.
SNAP
LOOK. IN THE YELLOW JERSEY.
THE RIDER WHO WON FIRST PLACE FOR SOHOKU AT THIS YEAR'S INTER-HIGH.
CHATTER
CHATTER
SAKA-MICHI ONODA.
IT'S SOHOKU.
COOL.

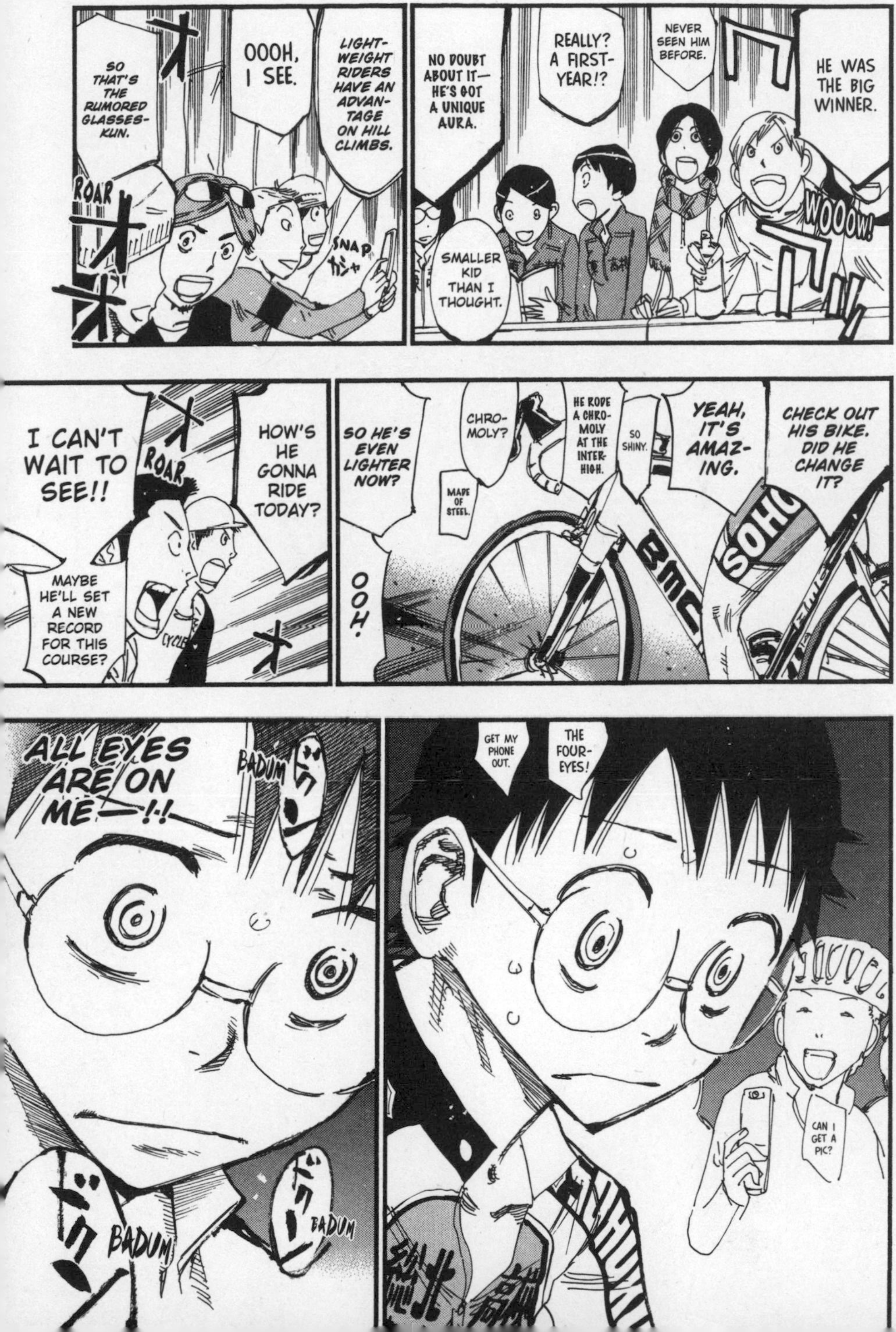
HE WAS THE BIG WINNER.
NEVER SEEN HIM BEFORE.
REALLY? A FIRST-YEAR!?
NO DOUBT ABOUT IT—HE'S GOT A UNIQUE AURA.
WOOOW!
SMALLER KID THAN I THOUGHT.
LIGHT-WEIGHT RIDERS HAVE AN ADVANTAGE ON HILL CLIMBS.
OOOH, I SEE.
SO THAT'S THE RUMORED GLASSES-KUN.
ROAR
SNAP
CHECK OUT HIS BIKE. DID HE CHANGE IT?
YEAH, IT'S AMAZING.
SO SHINY.
HE RODE A CHROMOLY AT THE INTER-HIGH.
CHROMOLY?
MADE OF STEEL.
SO HE'S EVEN LIGHTER NOW?
OOH.
HOW'S HE GONNA RIDE TODAY?
ROAR
I CAN'T WAIT TO SEE!!
MAYBE HE'LL SET A NEW RECORD FOR THIS COURSE?
THE FOUR-EYES!
GET MY PHONE OUT.
CAN I GET A PIC?
ALL EYES ARE ON ME—!!
BADUM
BADUM
BADUM

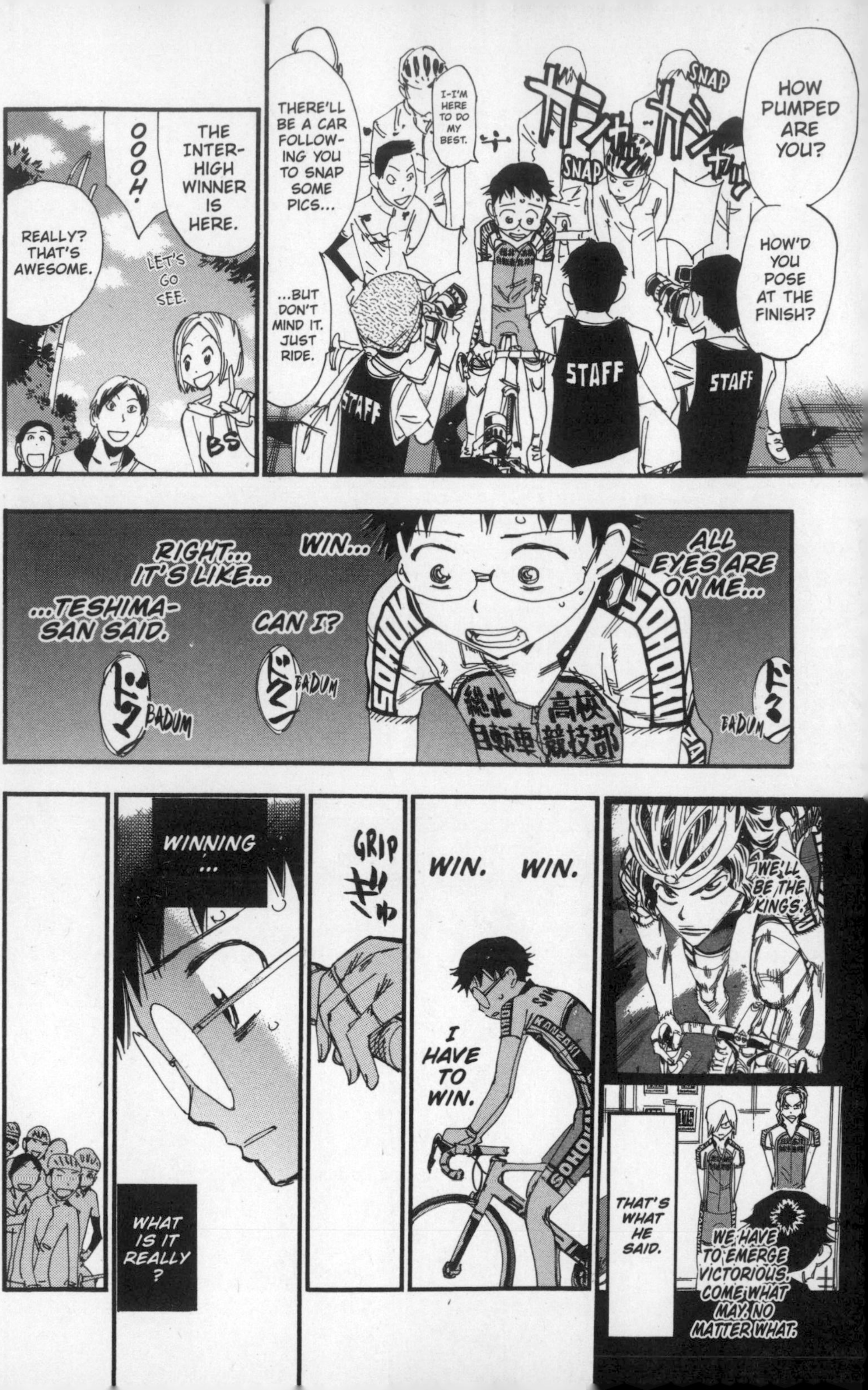
HOW PUMPED ARE YOU?
SNAP
SNAP
HOW'D YOU POSE AT THE FINISH?
I-I'M HERE TO DO MY BEST.
THERE'LL BE A CAR FOLLOWING YOU TO SNAP SOME PICS...
...BUT DON'T MIND IT. JUST RIDE.
STAFF
STAFF
STAFF
THE INTER-HIGH WINNER IS HERE.
OOOH!
REALLY? THAT'S AWESOME.
LET'S GO SEE.
ALL EYES ARE ON ME...
BADUM
WIN...
CAN I?
BADUM
RIGHT... IT'S LIKE...
...TESHIMA-SAN SAID.
BADUM
WE'LL BE THE KINGS.
THAT'S WHAT HE SAID.
WE HAVE TO EMERGE VICTORIOUS, COME WHAT MAY. NO MATTER WHAT.
WIN. WIN.
I HAVE TO WIN.
GRIP
WINNING...
WHAT IS IT REALLY?

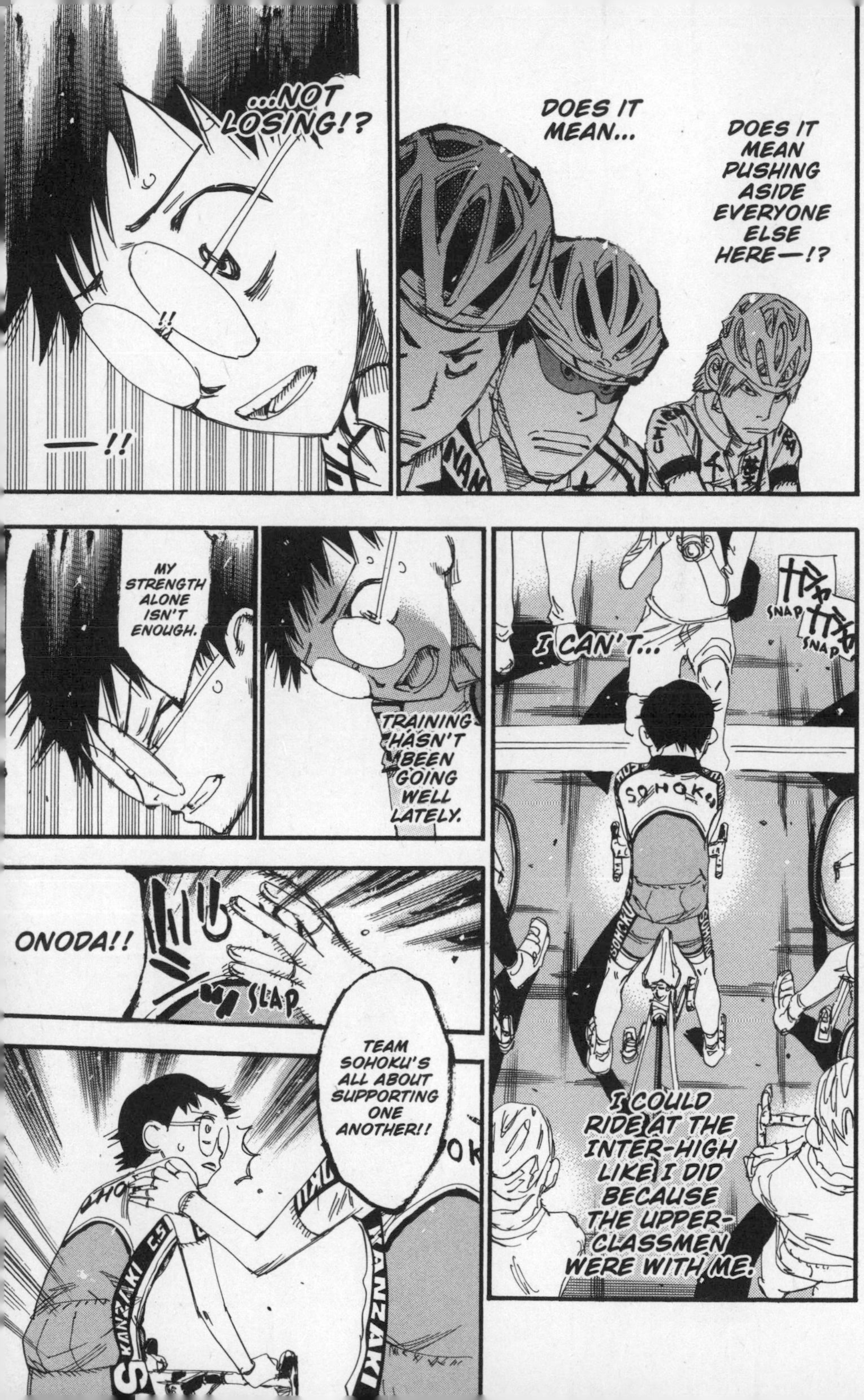
DOES IT MEAN...
DOES IT MEAN PUSHING ASIDE EVERYONE ELSE HERE—!?
...NOT LOSING!?
—!!
I CAN'T...
SNAP
SNAP
I COULD RIDE AT THE INTER-HIGH LIKE I DID BECAUSE THE UPPER-CLASSMEN WERE WITH ME.
TRAINING HASN'T BEEN GOING WELL LATELY.
MY STRENGTH ALONE ISN'T ENOUGH.
ONODA!!
SLAP
TEAM SOHOKU'S ALL ABOUT SUPPORTING ONE ANOTHER!!

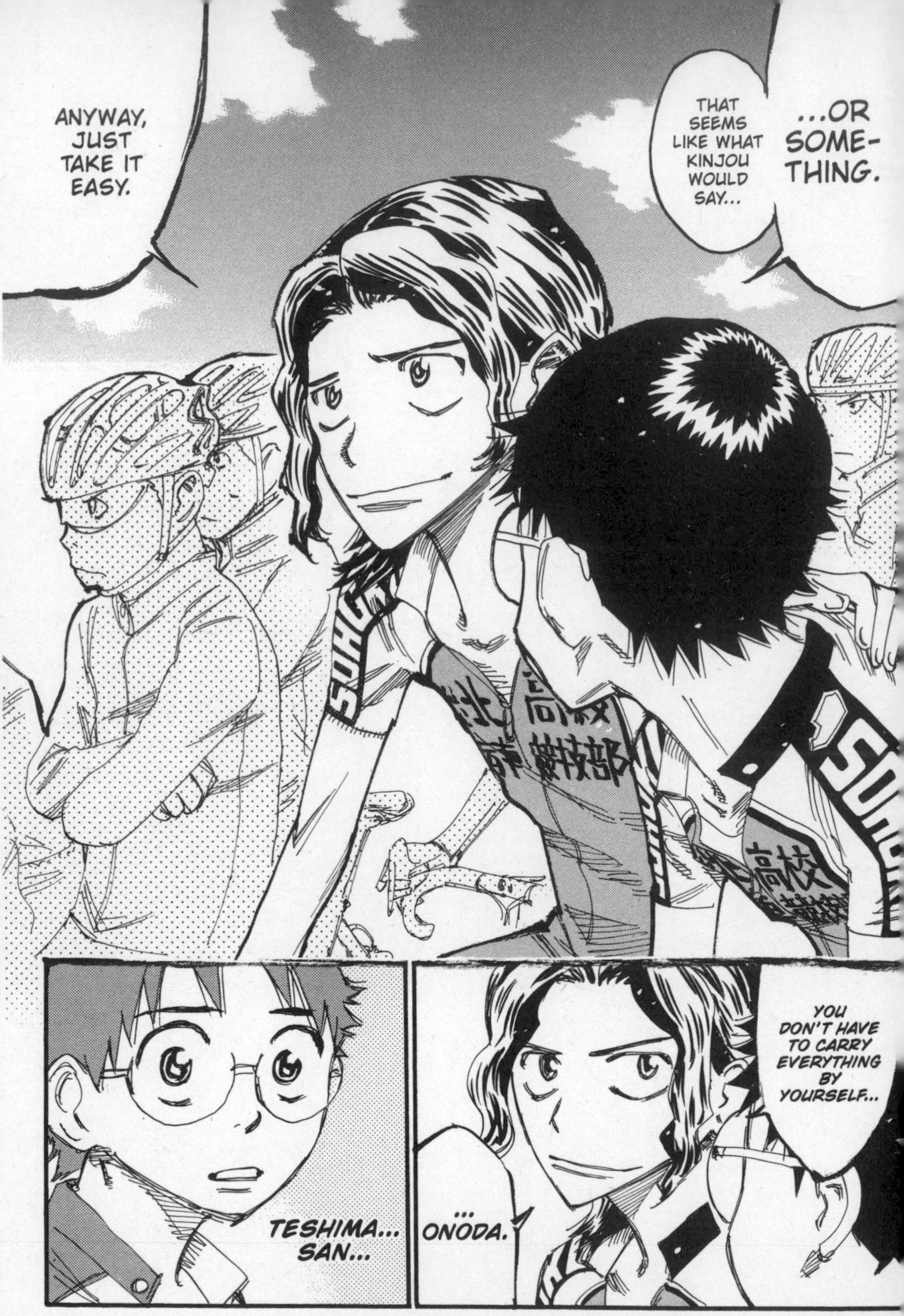
THAT SEEMS LIKE WHAT KINJOU WOULD SAY...
...OR SOMETHING.
ANYWAY, JUST TAKE IT EASY.
YOU DON'T HAVE TO CARRY EVERYTHING BY YOURSELF...
...ONODA.
TESHIMA... SAN...

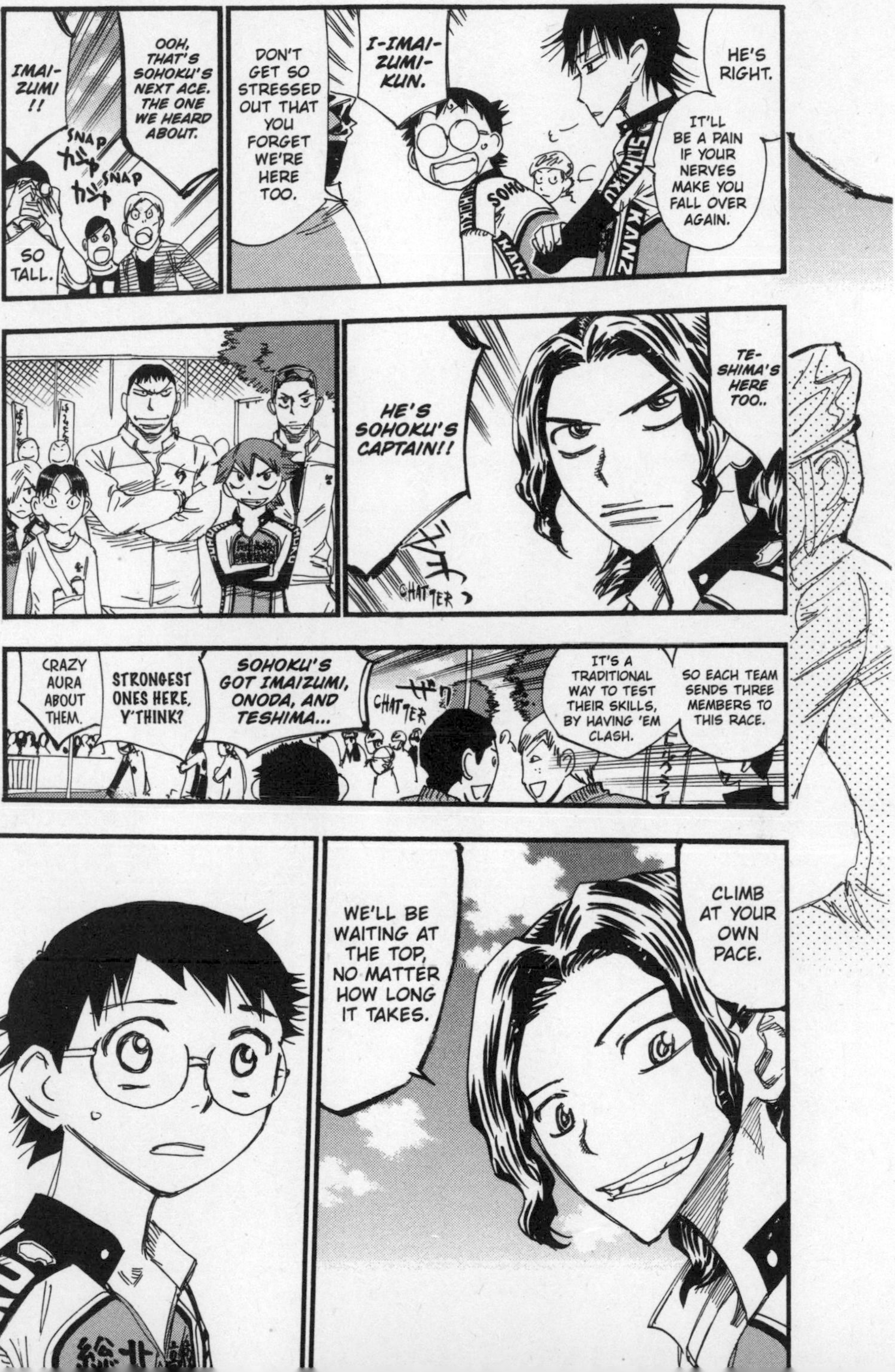
HE'S RIGHT.
IT'LL BE A PAIN IF YOUR NERVES MAKE YOU FALL OVER AGAIN.
I-IMAI-ZUMI-KUN.
DON'T GET SO STRESSED OUT THAT YOU FORGET WE'RE HERE TOO.
OOH, THAT'S SOHOKU'S NEXT ACE. THE ONE WE HEARD ABOUT.
IMAI-ZUMI!!
SNAP
SNAP
SO TALL.
TE-SHIMA'S HERE TOO..
HE'S SOHOKU'S CAPTAIN!!
CHATTER
SO EACH TEAM SENDS THREE MEMBERS TO THIS RACE.
IT'S A TRADITIONAL WAY TO TEST THEIR SKILLS, BY HAVING 'EM CLASH.
CHATTER
SOHOKU'S GOT IMAIZUMI, ONODA, AND TESHIMA...
STRONGEST ONES HERE, Y'THINK?
CRAZY AURA ABOUT THEM.
CLIMB AT YOUR OWN PACE.
WE'LL BE WAITING AT THE TOP, NO MATTER HOW LONG IT TAKES.

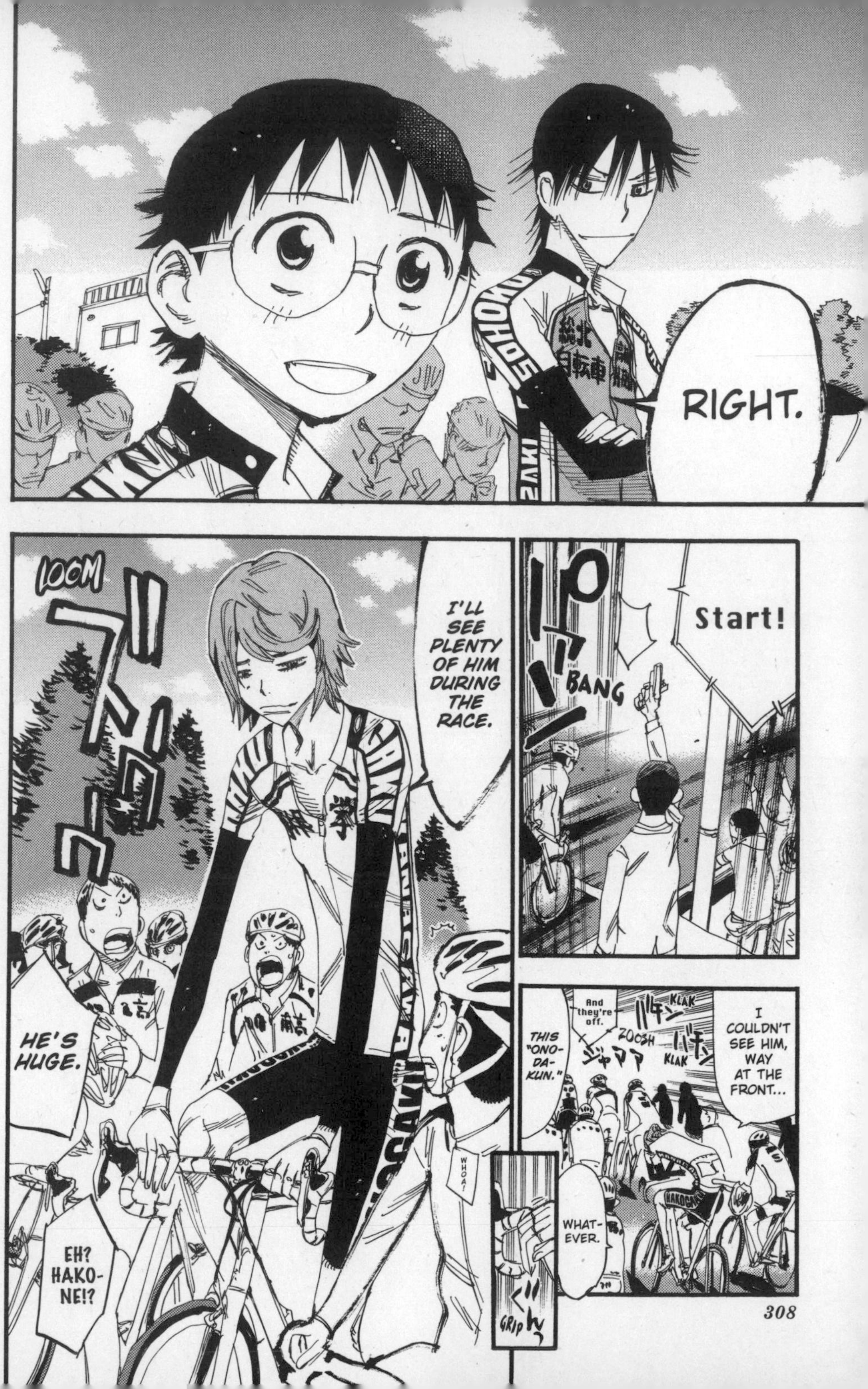
RIGHT.
Start!
BANG
I COULDN'T SEE HIM, WAY AT THE FRONT...
And they're off.
KLAK
ZOOSH
KLAK
THIS "ONODA-KUN."
WHOA!
WHATEVER.
GRIP
I'LL SEE PLENTY OF HIM DURING THE RACE.
HE'S HUGE.
EH? HAKONE!?

RIDE.240 METRONOME

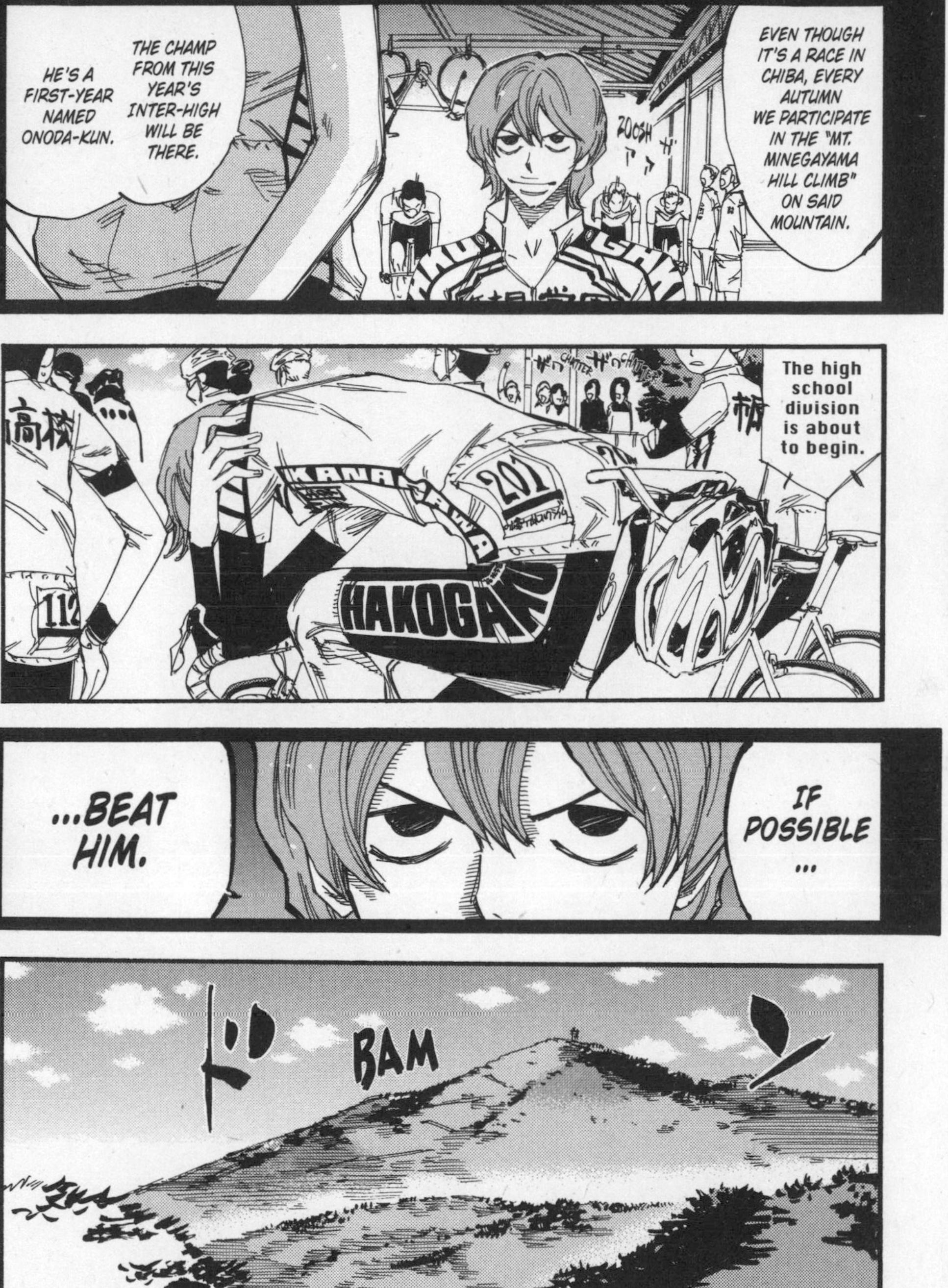
EVEN THOUGH IT'S A RACE IN CHIBA, EVERY AUTUMN WE PARTICIPATE IN THE "MT. MINEGAYAMA HILL CLIMB" ON SAID MOUNTAIN.
ZOOSH
THE CHAMP FROM THIS YEAR'S INTER-HIGH WILL BE THERE.
HE'S A FIRST-YEAR NAMED ONODA-KUN.
The high school division is about to begin.
CHATTER
CHATTER
IF POSSIBLE...
...BEAT HIM.
BAM

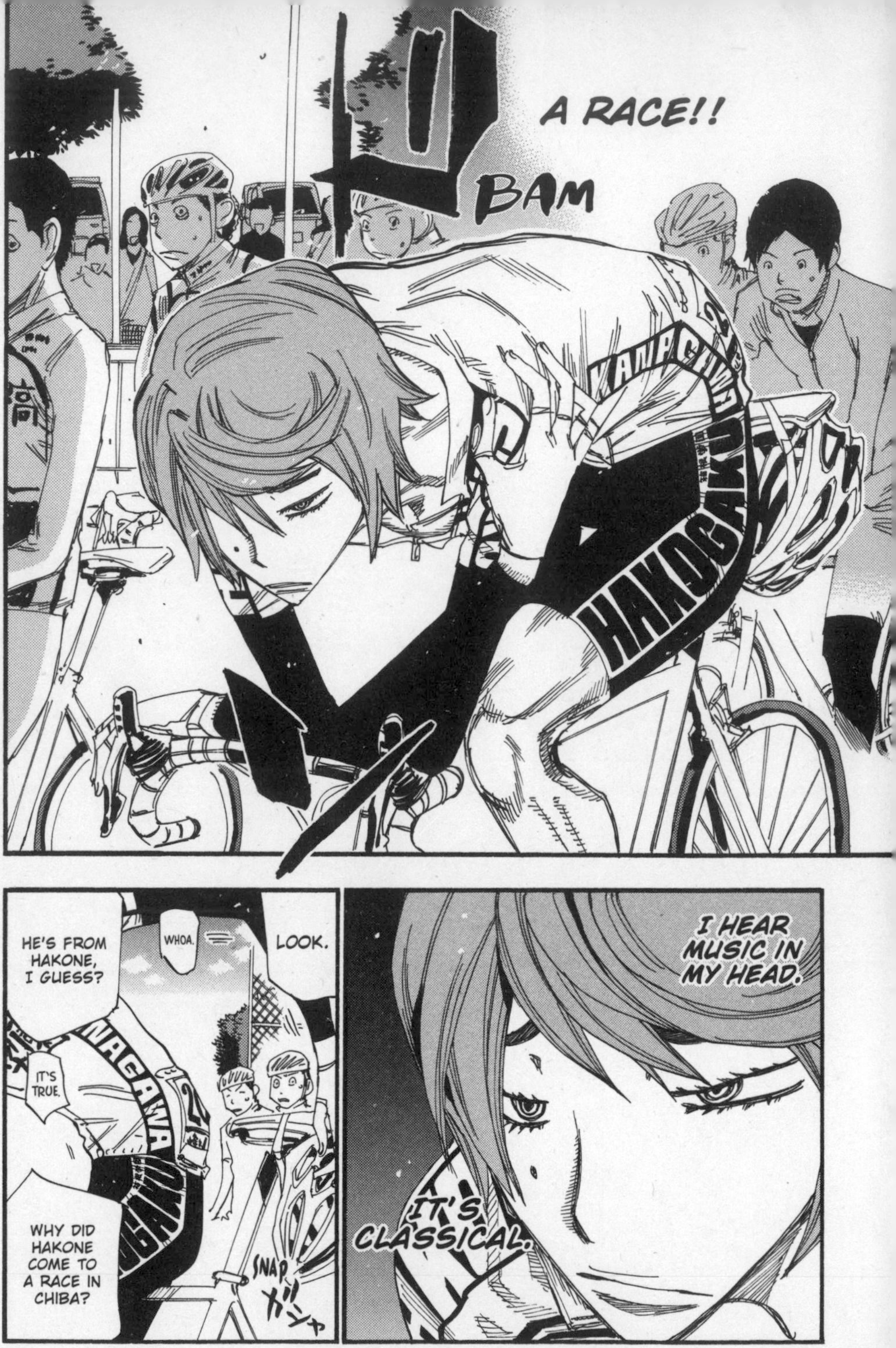
A RACE!!
BAM
I HEAR MUSIC IN MY HEAD.
IT'S CLASSICAL.
LOOK.
WHOA.
HE'S FROM HAKONE, I GUESS?
IT'S TRUE.
WHY DID HAKONE COME TO A RACE IN CHIBA?
SNAP

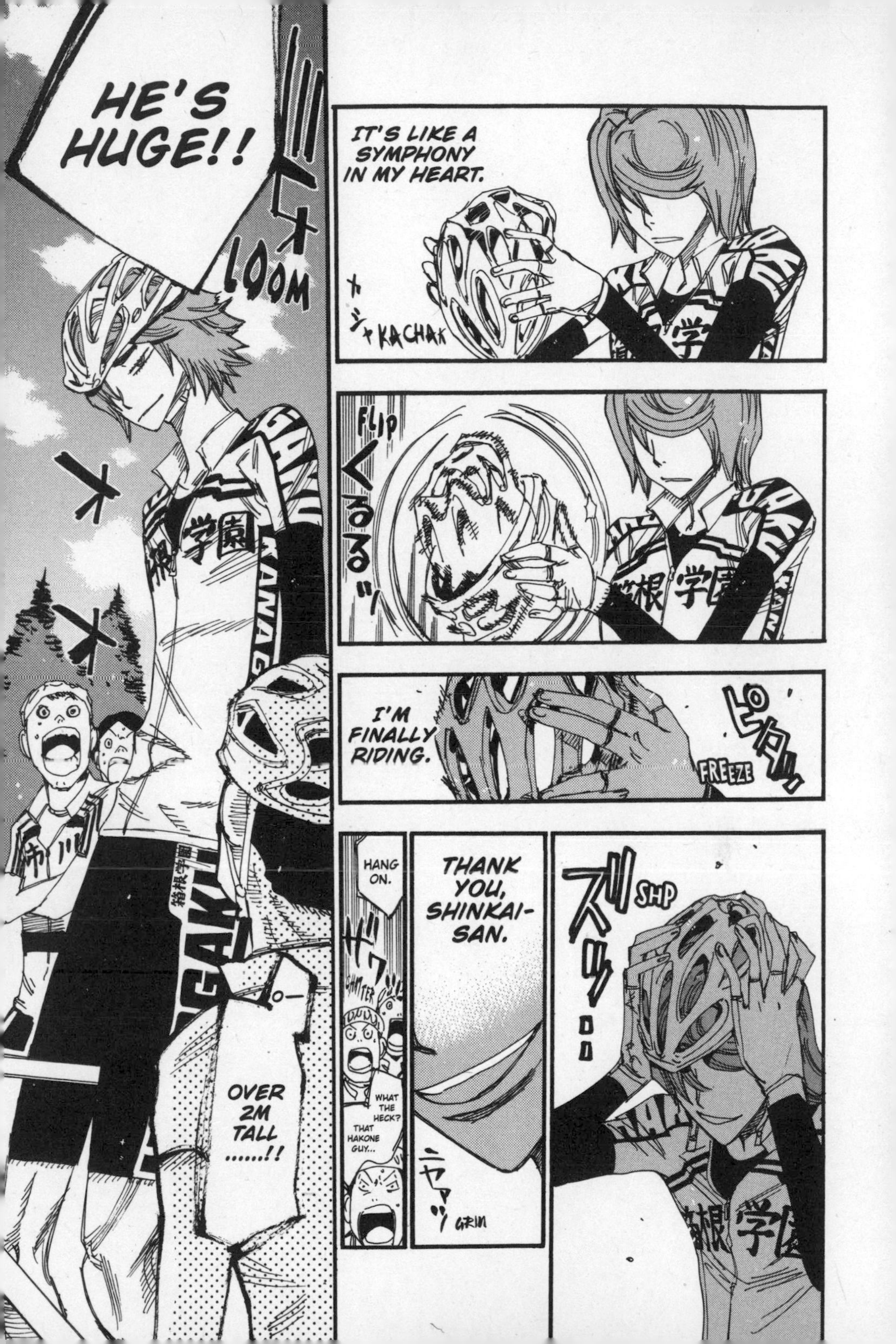
IT'S LIKE A SYMPHONY IN MY HEART.
KACHAK
FLIP
I'M FINALLY RIDING.
FREEZE
SHP
THANK YOU, SHINKAI-SAN.
GRIN
HANG ON.
CHATTER
WHAT THE HECK?
THAT HAKONE GUY...
HE'S HUGE!!
LOOM
OVER 2M TALL ......!!

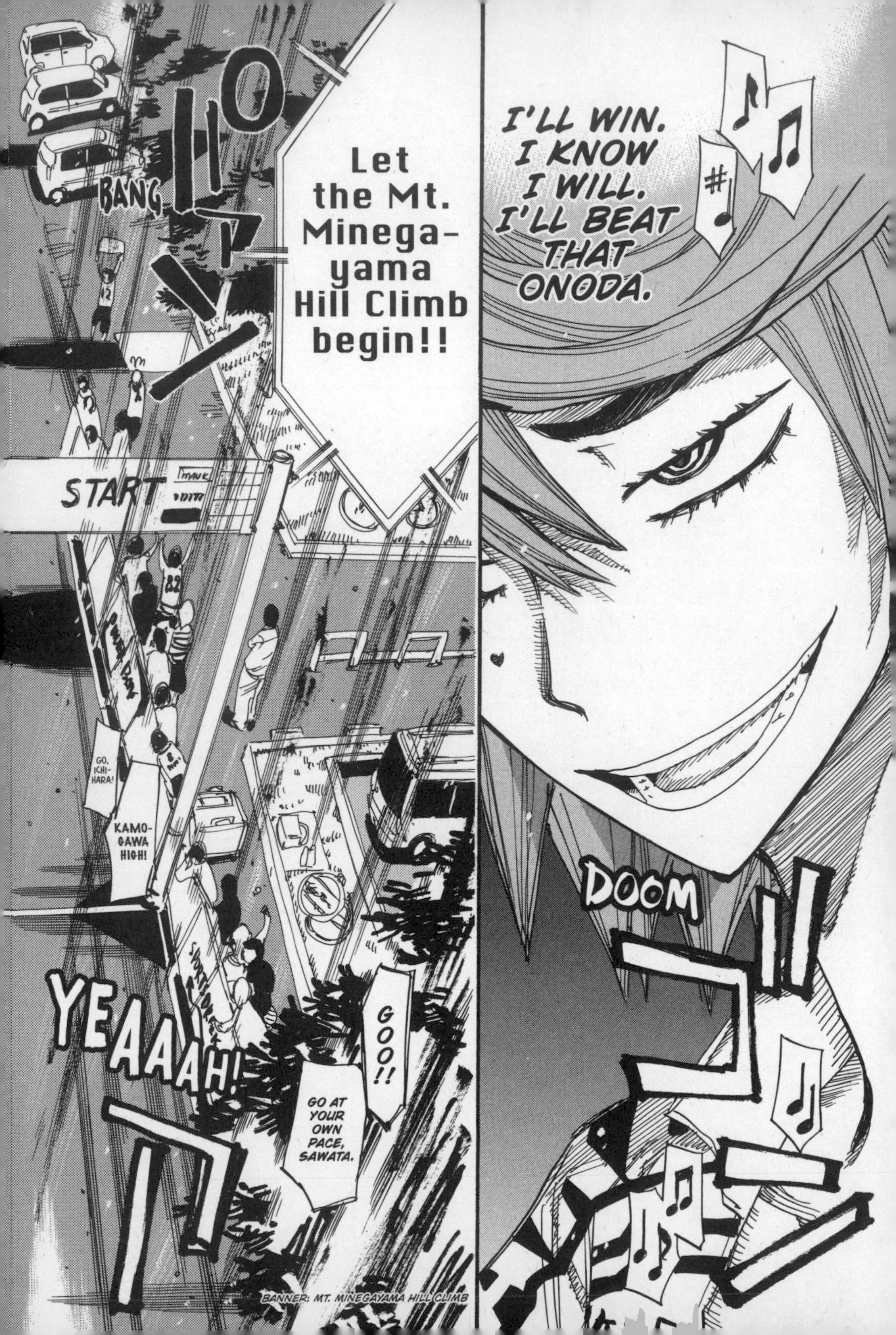
I'LL WIN. I KNOW I WILL. I'LL BEAT THAT ONODA.
DOOM
Let the Mt. Minega-yama Hill Climb begin!!
BANG
START
GO, ICHI-HARA!
KAMO-GAWA HIGH!
YEAAAH!
GOOO!!
GO AT YOUR OWN PACE, SAWATA.
BANNER: MT. MINEGAYAMA HILL CLIMB

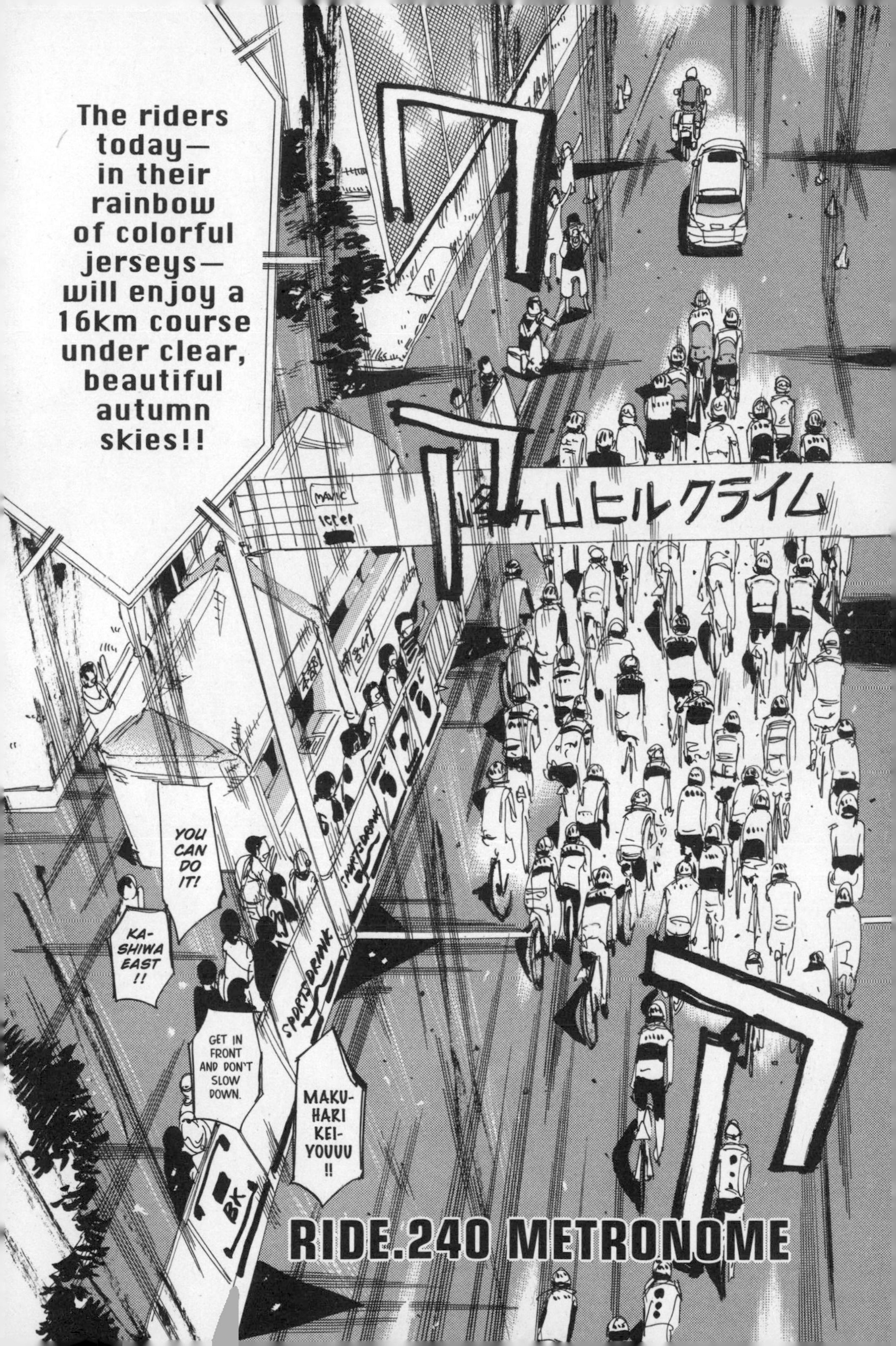
The riders today—in their rainbow of colorful jerseys—will enjoy a 16km course under clear, beautiful autumn skies!!
峰ヶ山ヒルクライム
MAVIC
MAKU-HARI KEI-YOUUU!!
GET IN FRONT AND DON'T SLOW DOWN.
YOU CAN DO IT!
KA-SHIWA EAST!!
SPORTS DRINK
SPORTS DRINK

RIDE.240 METRONOME

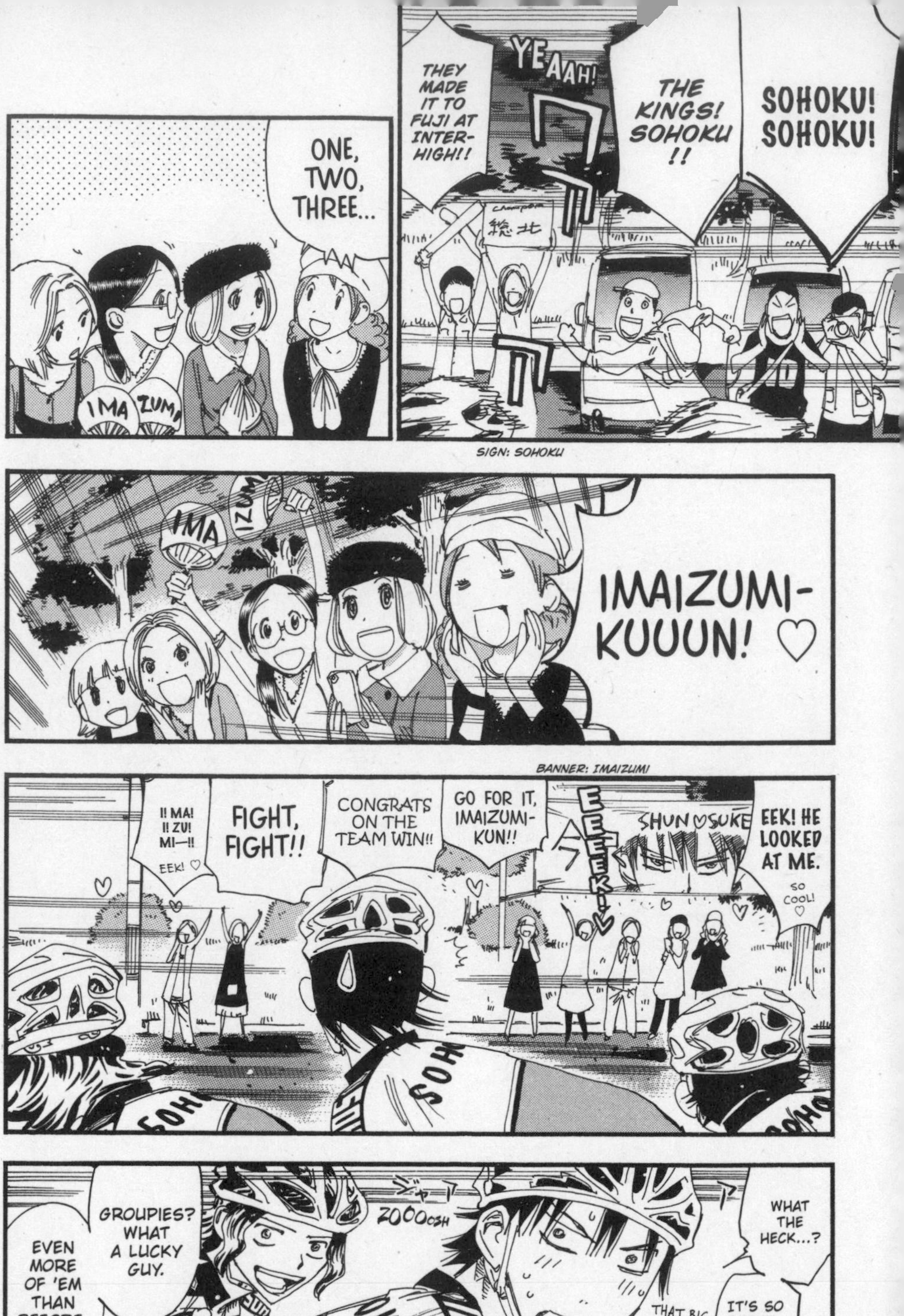
SOHOKU! SOHOKU!
THE KINGS! SOHOKU!!
YEAAAH!
THEY MADE IT TO FUJI AT INTER-HIGH!!
SIGN: SOHOKU
ONE, TWO, THREE...
IMA ZUMI
IMA ZUM
IMAIZUMI-KUUUN! ♡
BANNER: IMAIZUMI
EEK! HE LOOKED AT ME.
SO COOL! ♡
SHUN♡SUKE
EEEEEK!
GO FOR IT, IMAIZUMI-KUN!!
CONGRATS ON THE TEAM WIN!!
FIGHT, FIGHT!!
!! MA! !! ZU! MI—!!
EEK! ♡
WHAT THE HECK...?
IT'S SO EMBAR-RASSING...
THAT BIG BANNER...
ZOOOOSH
GROUPIES? WHAT A LUCKY GUY.
EVEN MORE OF 'EM THAN BEFORE, HUH?

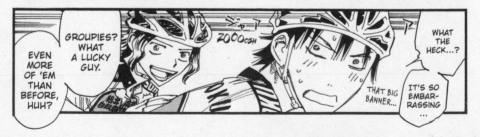

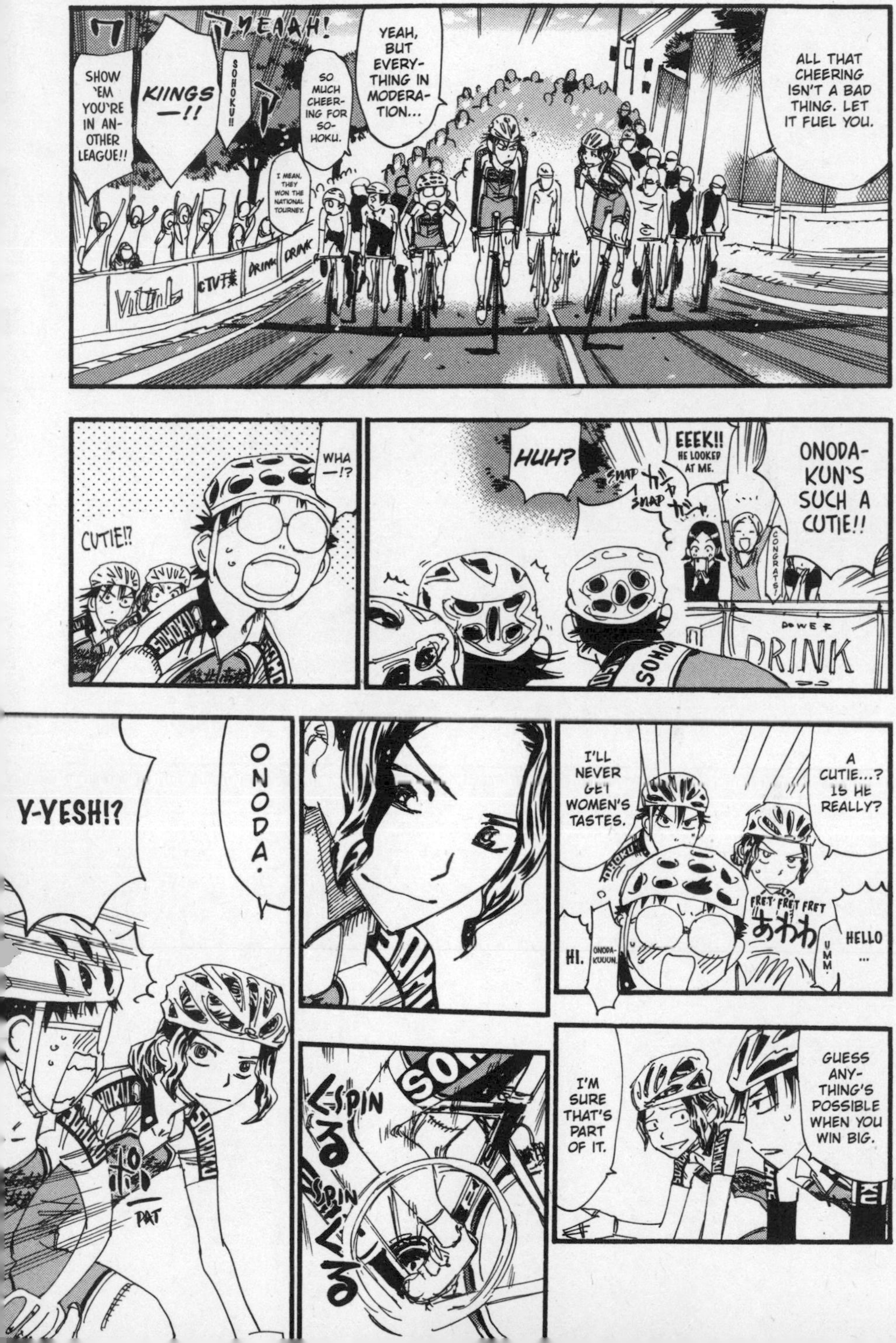
ALL THAT CHEERING ISN'T A BAD THING. LET IT FUEL YOU.
YEAH, BUT EVERYTHING IN MODERATION...
SO MUCH CHEERING FOR SO-HOKU.
I MEAN, THEY WON THE NATIONAL TOURNEY.
YEAAAH!
SOHOKU!!
KIINGS—!!
SHOW 'EM YOU'RE IN AN-OTHER LEAGUE!!
DRINK
DRINK
ONODA-KUN'S SUCH A CUTIE!!
CONGRATS!
EEEK!! HE LOOKED AT ME.
SNAP
SNAP
HUH?
POWER DRINK
WHA—!?
CUTIE!?
A CUTIE...? IS HE REALLY?
I'LL NEVER GET WOMEN'S TASTES.
HELLO...
UMM.
FRET FRET FRET
ONODA-KUUUN.
HI.
GUESS ANY-THING'S POSSIBLE WHEN YOU WIN BIG.
I'M SURE THAT'S PART OF IT.
SPIN
SPIN
ONODA.
Y-YESH!?
PAT

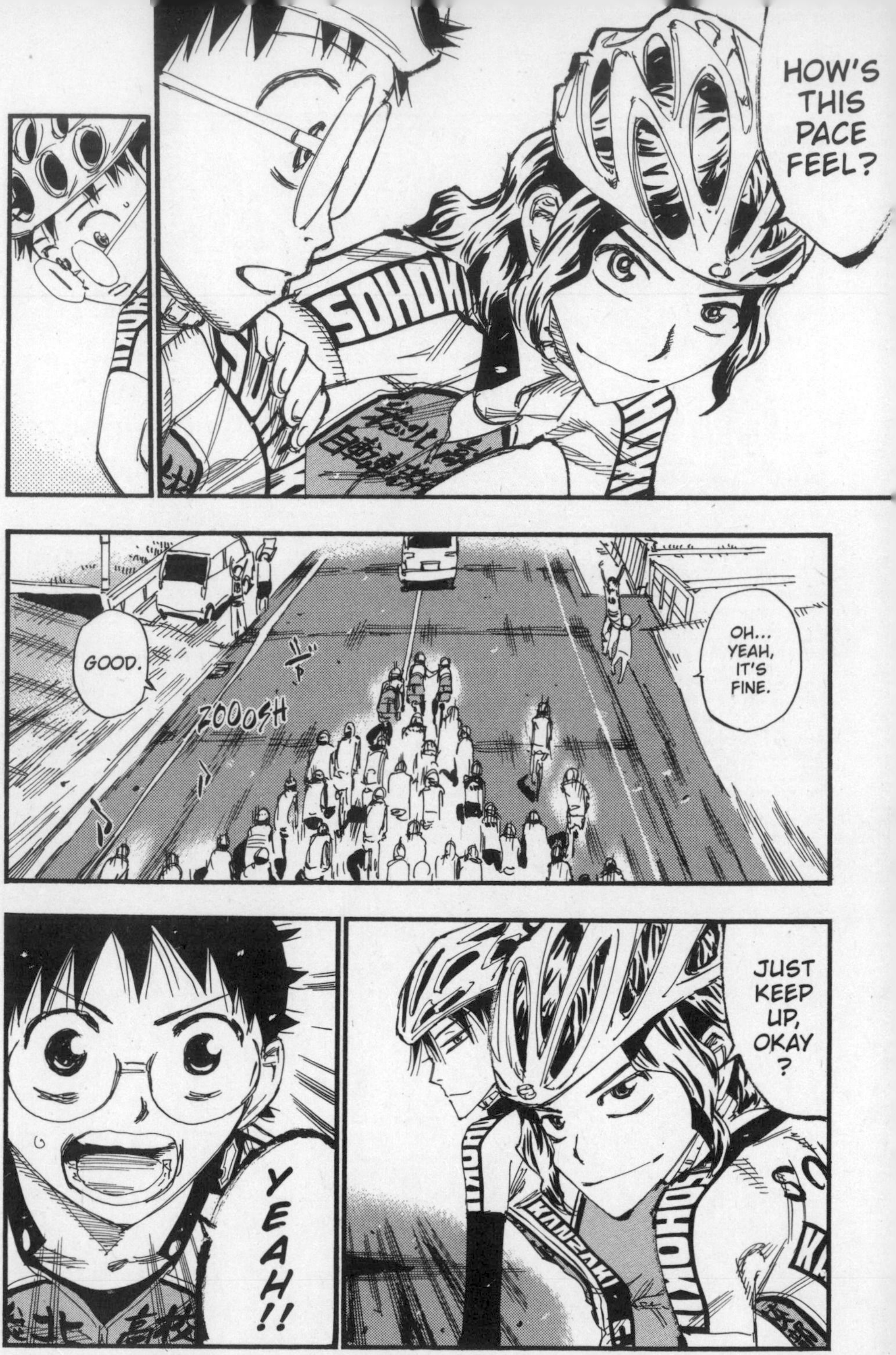
HOW'S THIS PACE FEEL?
OH... YEAH, IT'S FINE.
GOOD.
ZOOOSH
JUST KEEP UP, OKAY?
YEAH!!

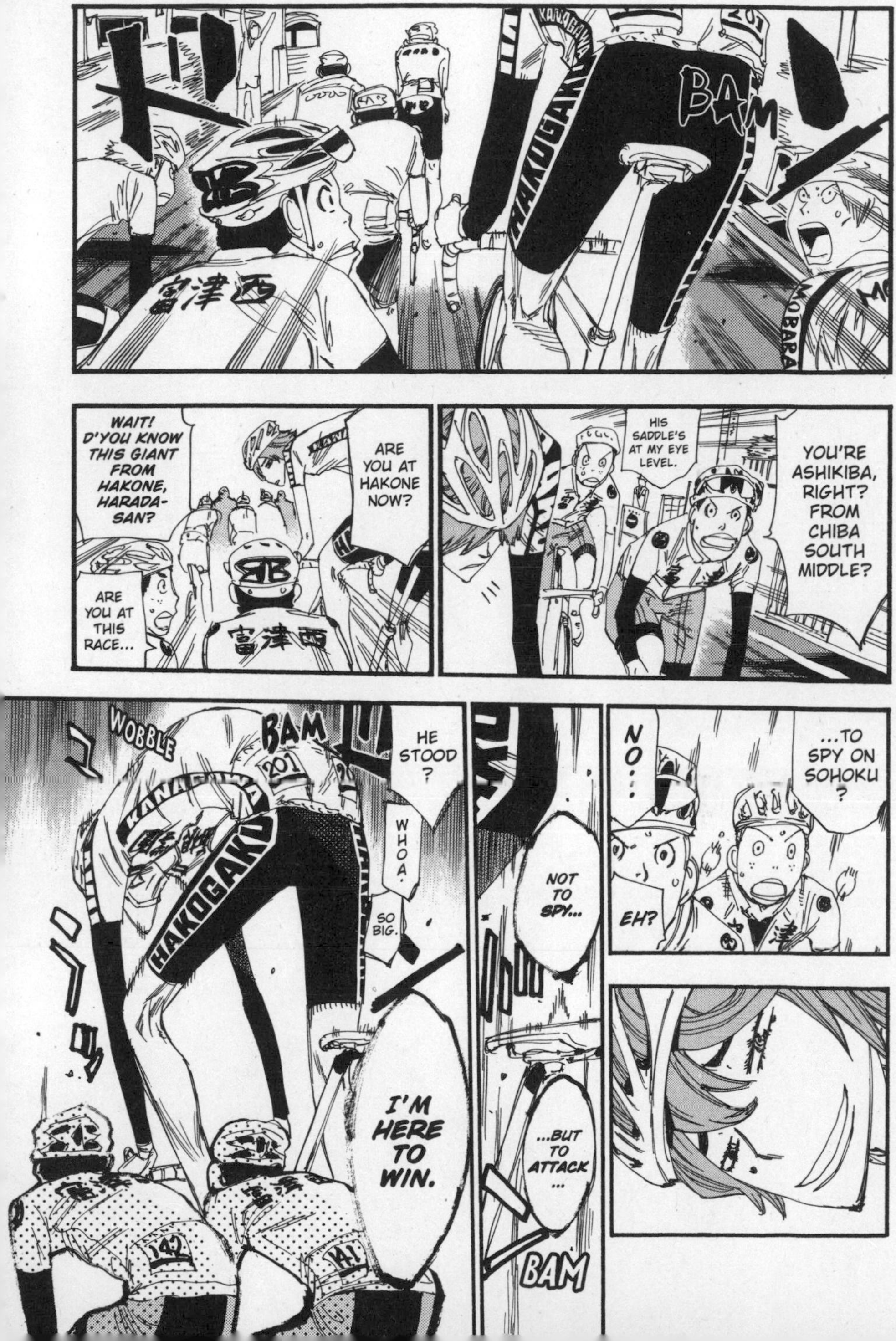
BAM
YOU'RE ASHIKIBA, RIGHT? FROM CHIBA SOUTH MIDDLE?
HIS SADDLE'S AT MY EYE LEVEL.
ARE YOU AT HAKONE NOW?
WAIT! D'YOU KNOW THIS GIANT FROM HAKONE, HARADA-SAN?
ARE YOU AT THIS RACE...
...TO SPY ON SOHOKU?
NO...
EH?
NOT TO SPY...
...BUT TO ATTACK...
BAM
HE STOOD?
WHOA.
SO BIG.
BAM
WOBBLE
I'M HERE TO WIN.

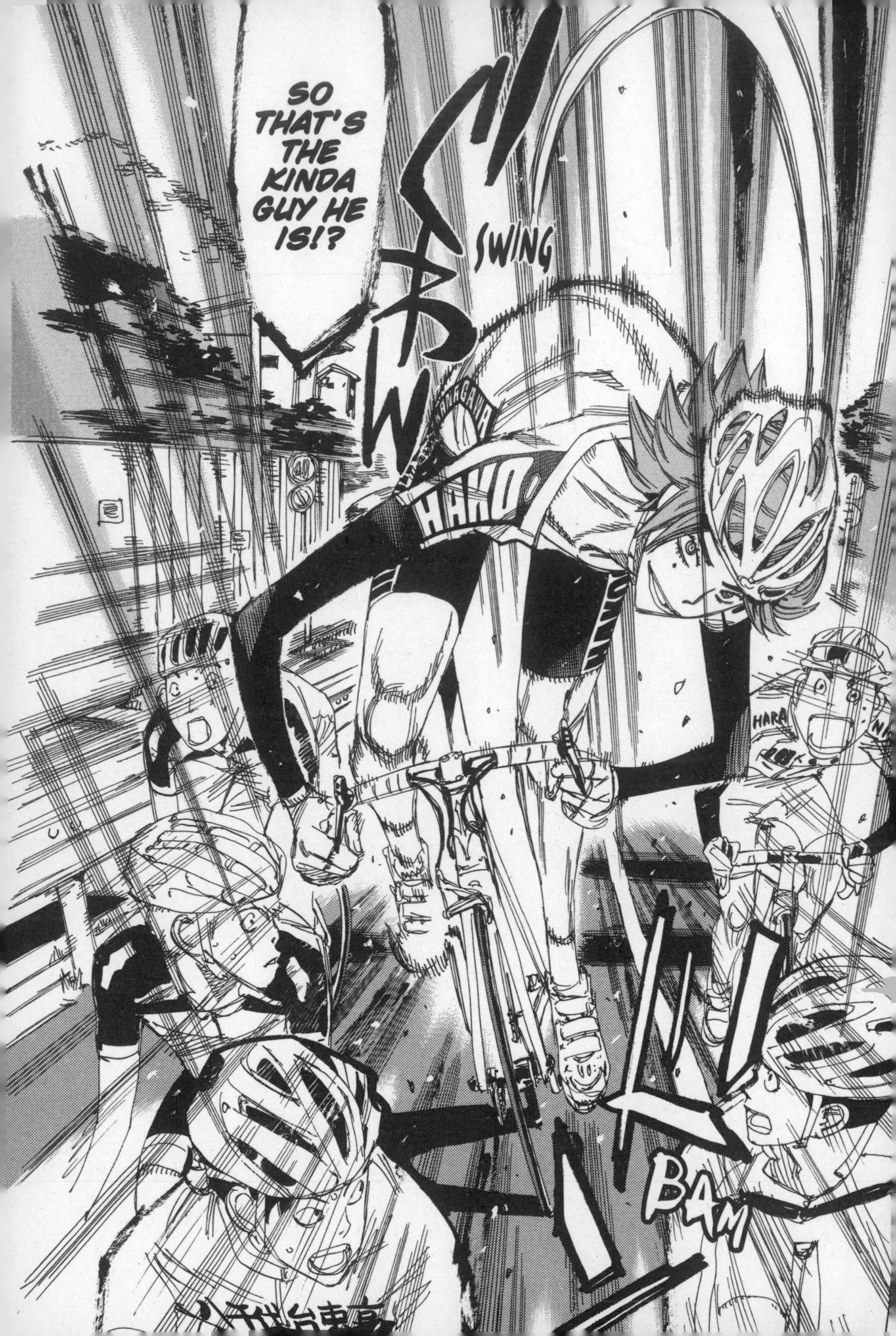
SO THAT'S THE KINDA GUY HE IS!?
SWING
BAM

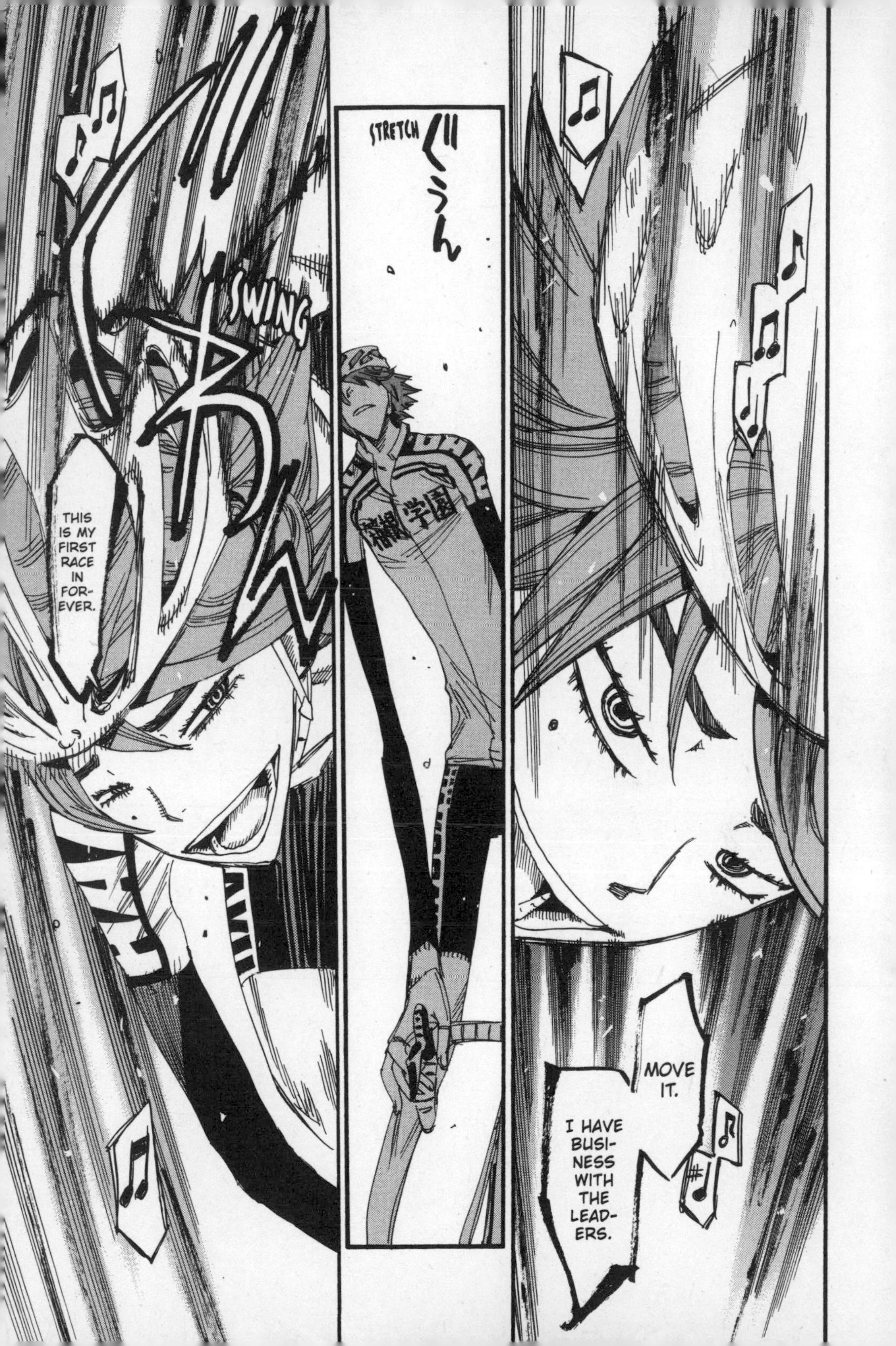
MOVE IT.
I HAVE BUSINESS WITH THE LEADERS.
STRETCH
ぐうん
SWING
THIS IS MY FIRST RACE IN FOREVER.

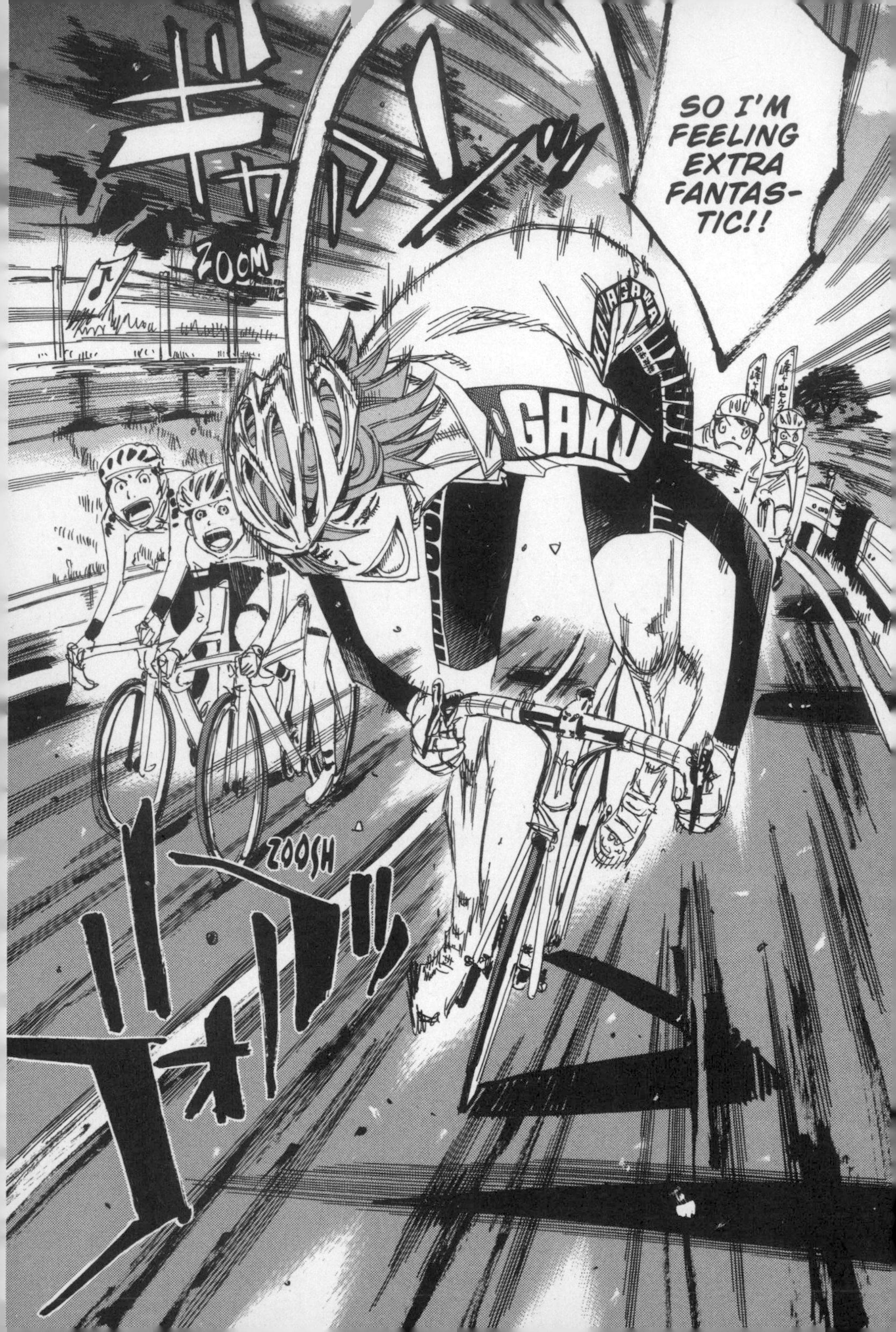
SO I'M FEELING EXTRA FANTAS-TIC!!
ZOOM
GAKU
ZOOSH

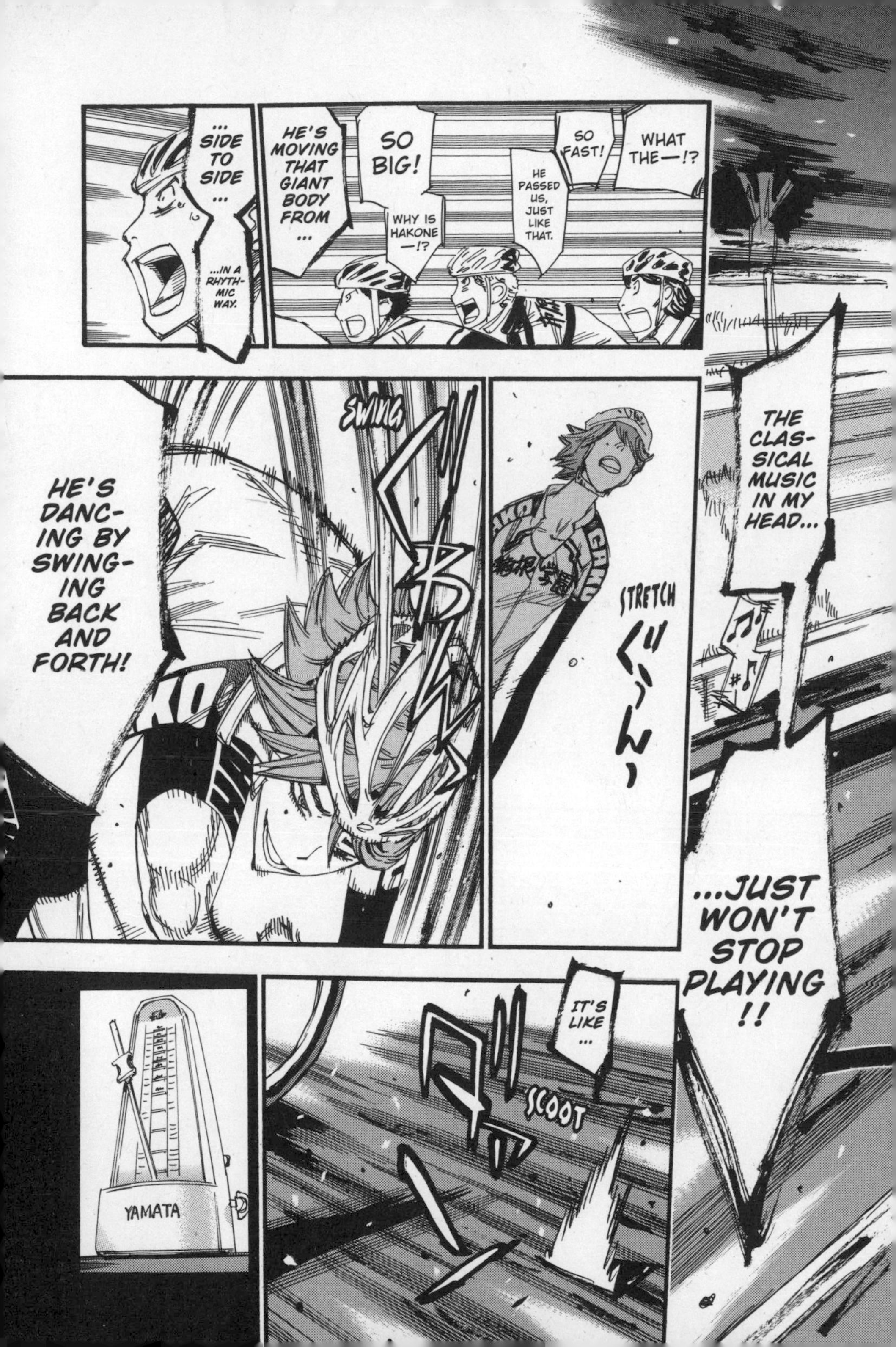
WHAT THE—!?
SO FAST!
HE PASSED US, JUST LIKE THAT.
SO BIG!
WHY IS HAKONE—!?
HE'S MOVING THAT GIANT BODY FROM ...
... SIDE TO SIDE ...
...IN A RHYTHMIC WAY.
THE CLASSICAL MUSIC IN MY HEAD...
STRETCH
SWING
HE'S DANCING BY SWINGING BACK AND FORTH!
...JUST WON'T STOP PLAYING!!
IT'S LIKE ...
SCOOT
YAMATA

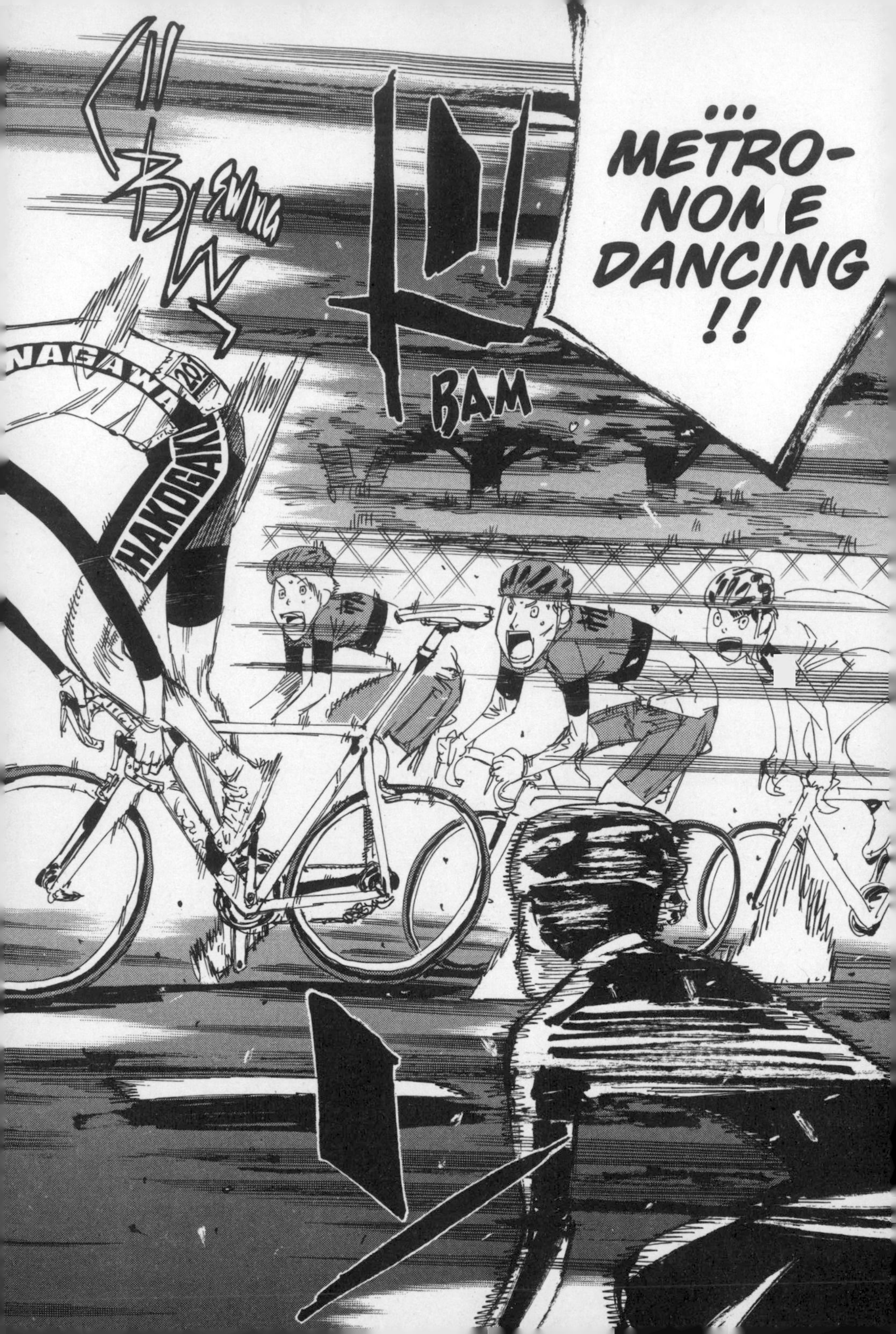
...METRO-
NOME
DANCING
!!
SWING
BAM
NAGAWA
20
HAKOGAKU

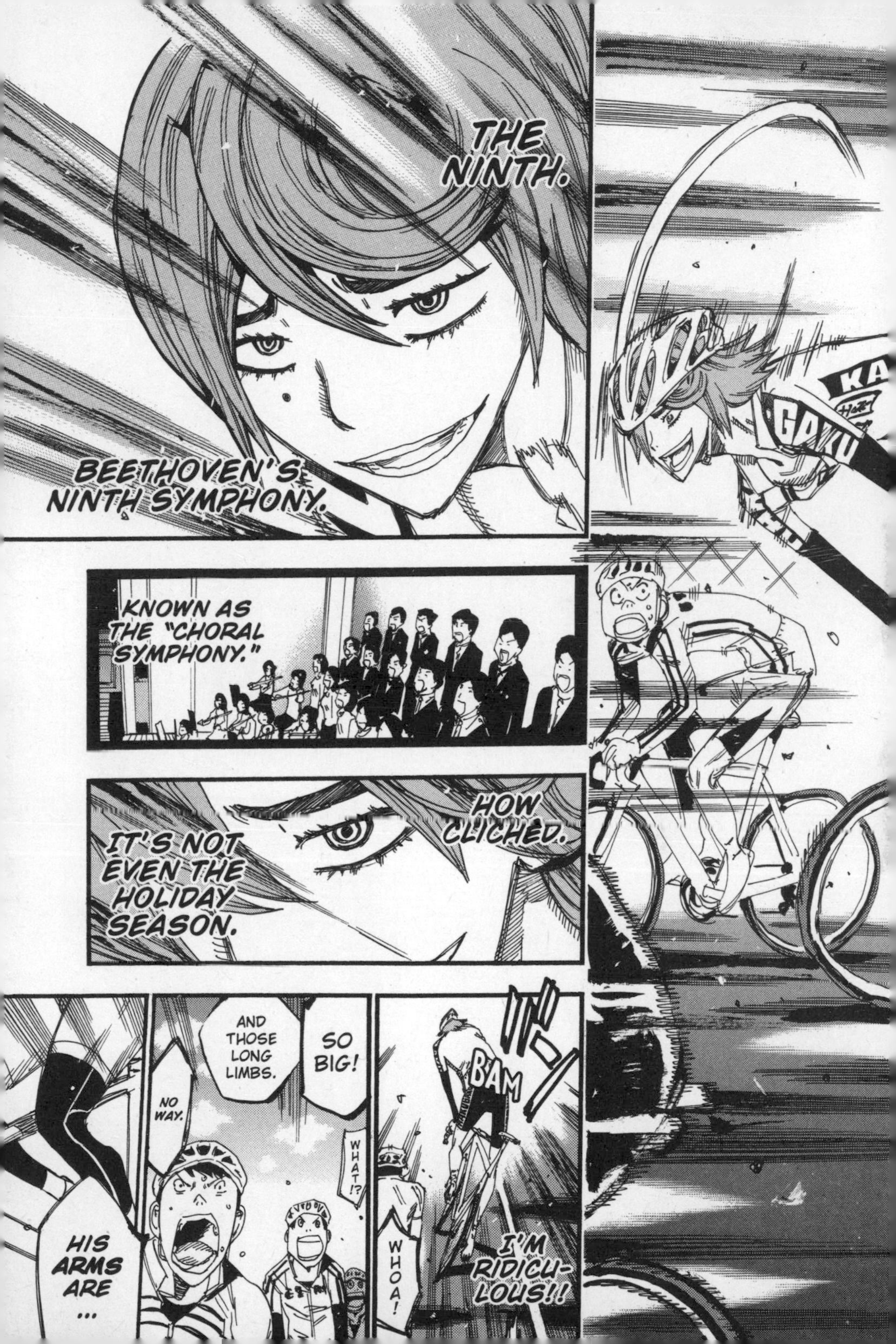
THE NINTH.
BEETHOVEN'S NINTH SYMPHONY.
KNOWN AS THE "CHORAL SYMPHONY."
HOW CLICHED.
IT'S NOT EVEN THE HOLIDAY SEASON.
BAM
WHAT!?
WHOA!
I'M RIDICULOUS!!
SO BIG!
AND THOSE LONG LIMBS.
NO WAY.
HIS ARMS ARE ...

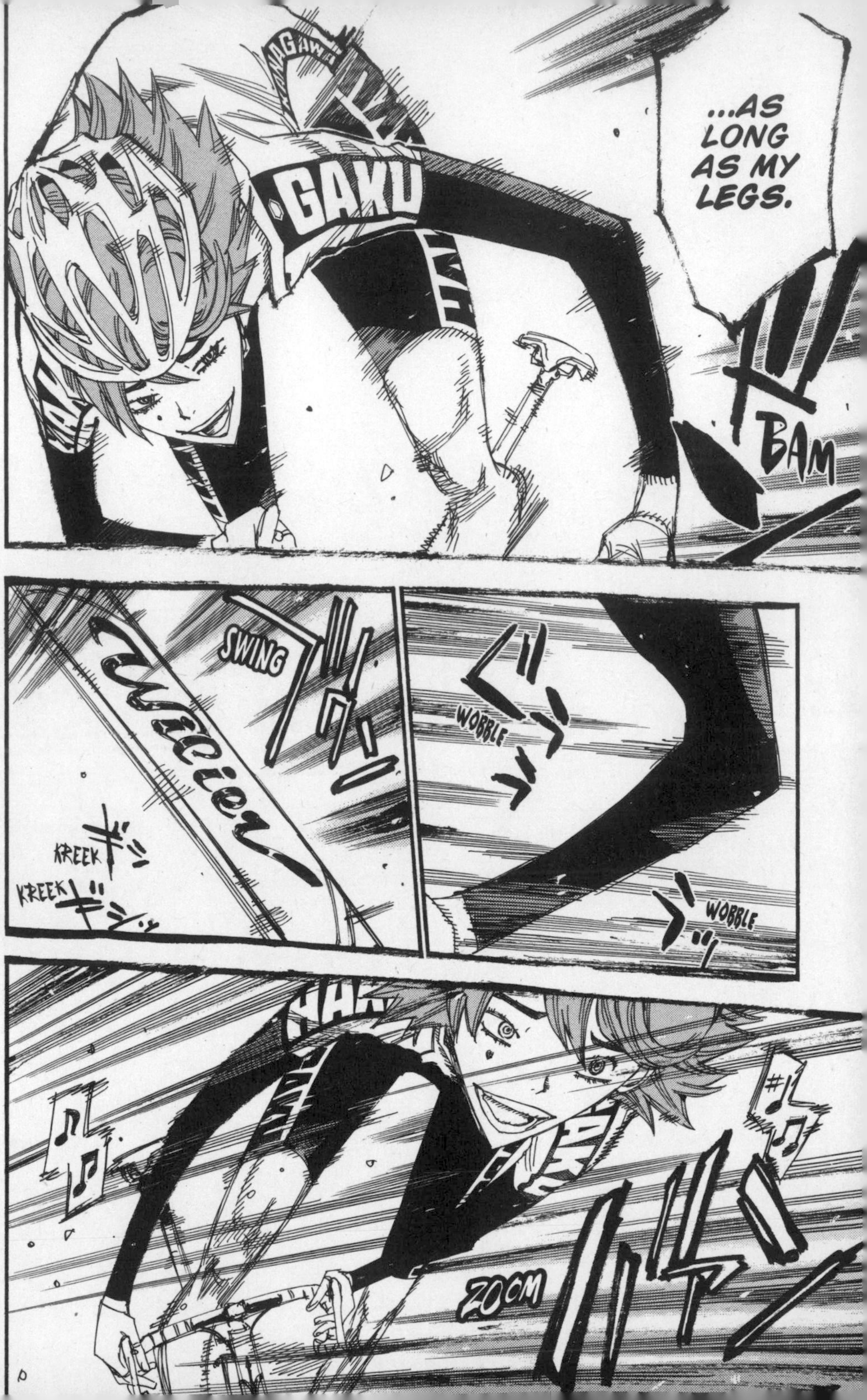

...AS LONG AS MY LEGS.
BAM
WOBBLE
WOBBLE
SWING
KREEK
KREEK
ZOOM

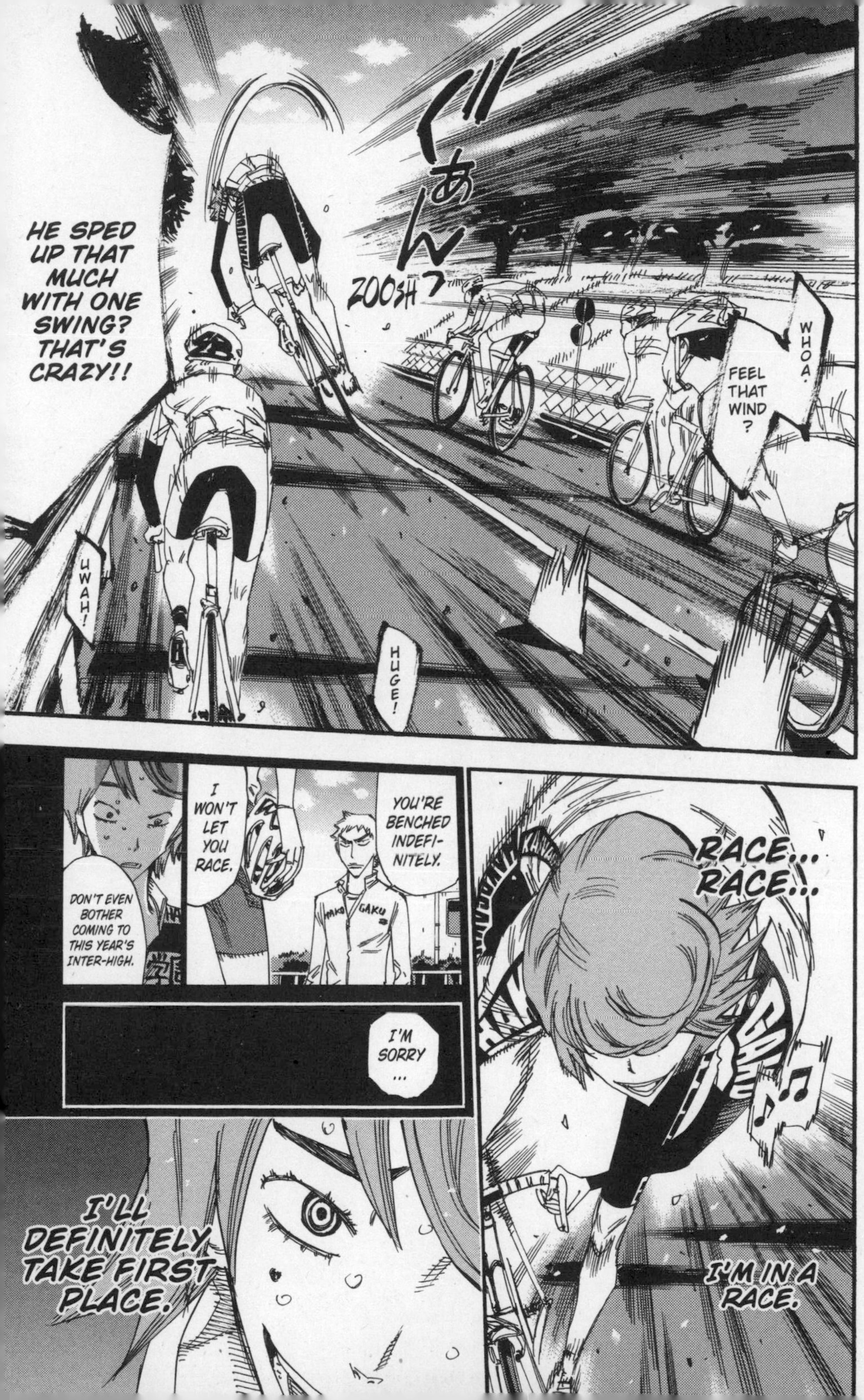

WHOA. FEEL THAT WIND?
ぐあんっ
ZOOSH
HUGE!
UWAH!
HE SPED UP THAT MUCH WITH ONE SWING? THAT'S CRAZY!!
RACE... RACE...
I'M IN A RACE.
YOU'RE BENCHED INDEFINITELY.
I WON'T LET YOU RACE.
DON'T EVEN BOTHER COMING TO THIS YEAR'S INTER-HIGH.
I'M SORRY...
I'LL DEFINITELY TAKE FIRST PLACE.

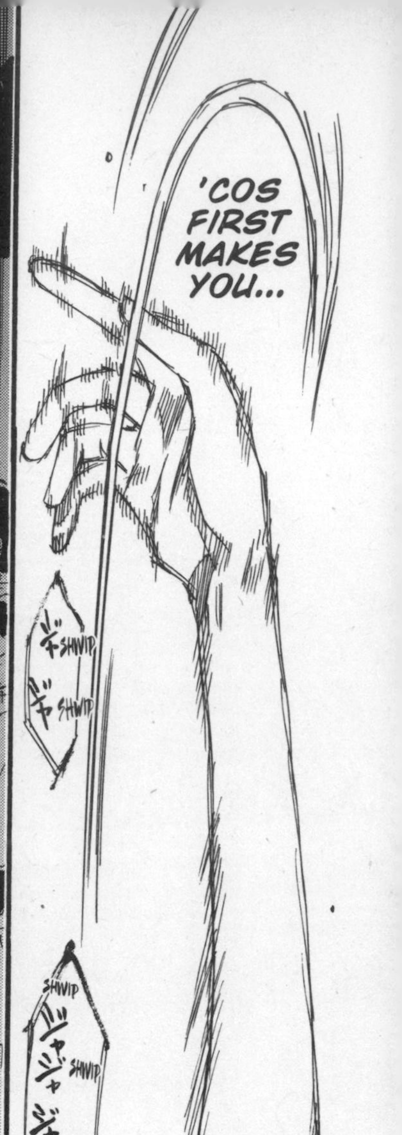
'COS FIRST MAKES YOU...
SHWIP
SHWIP
SHWIP
SHWIP
SHWOOP
SHWIP
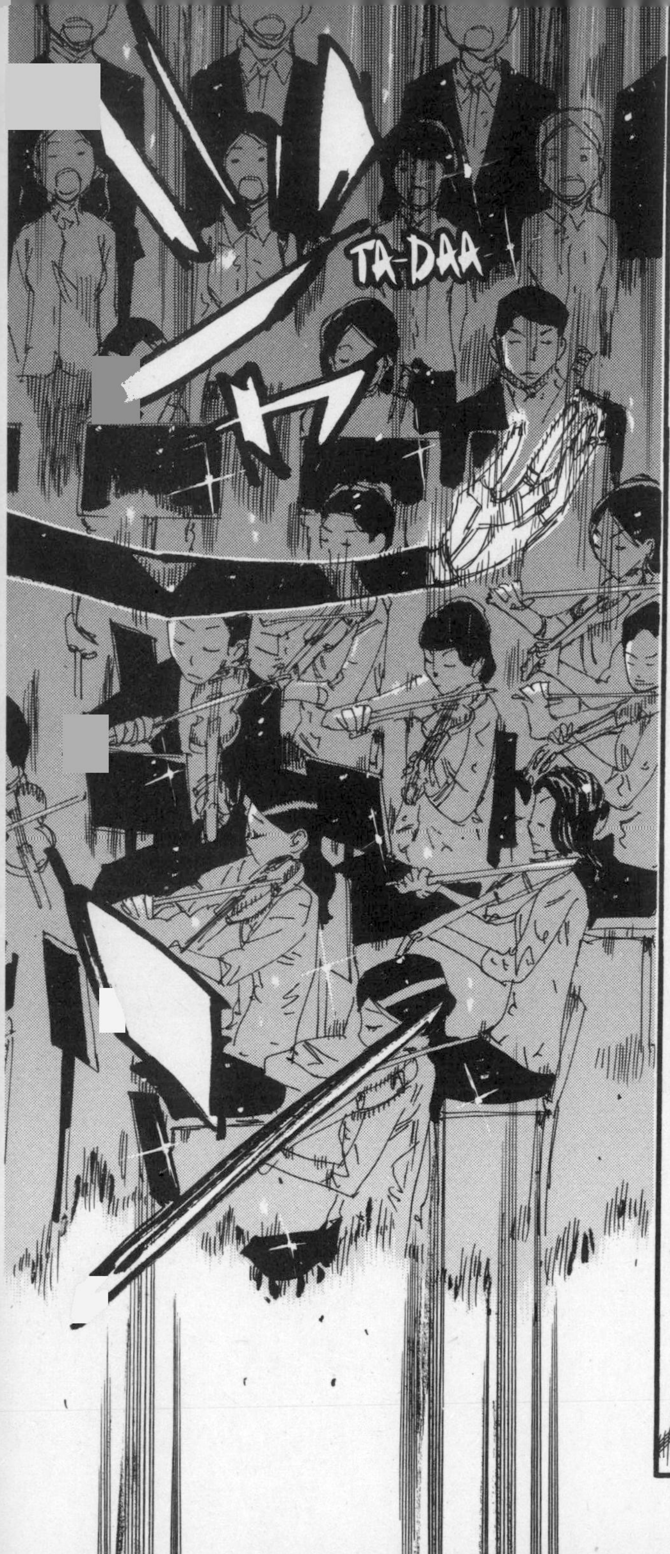
TA-DAA

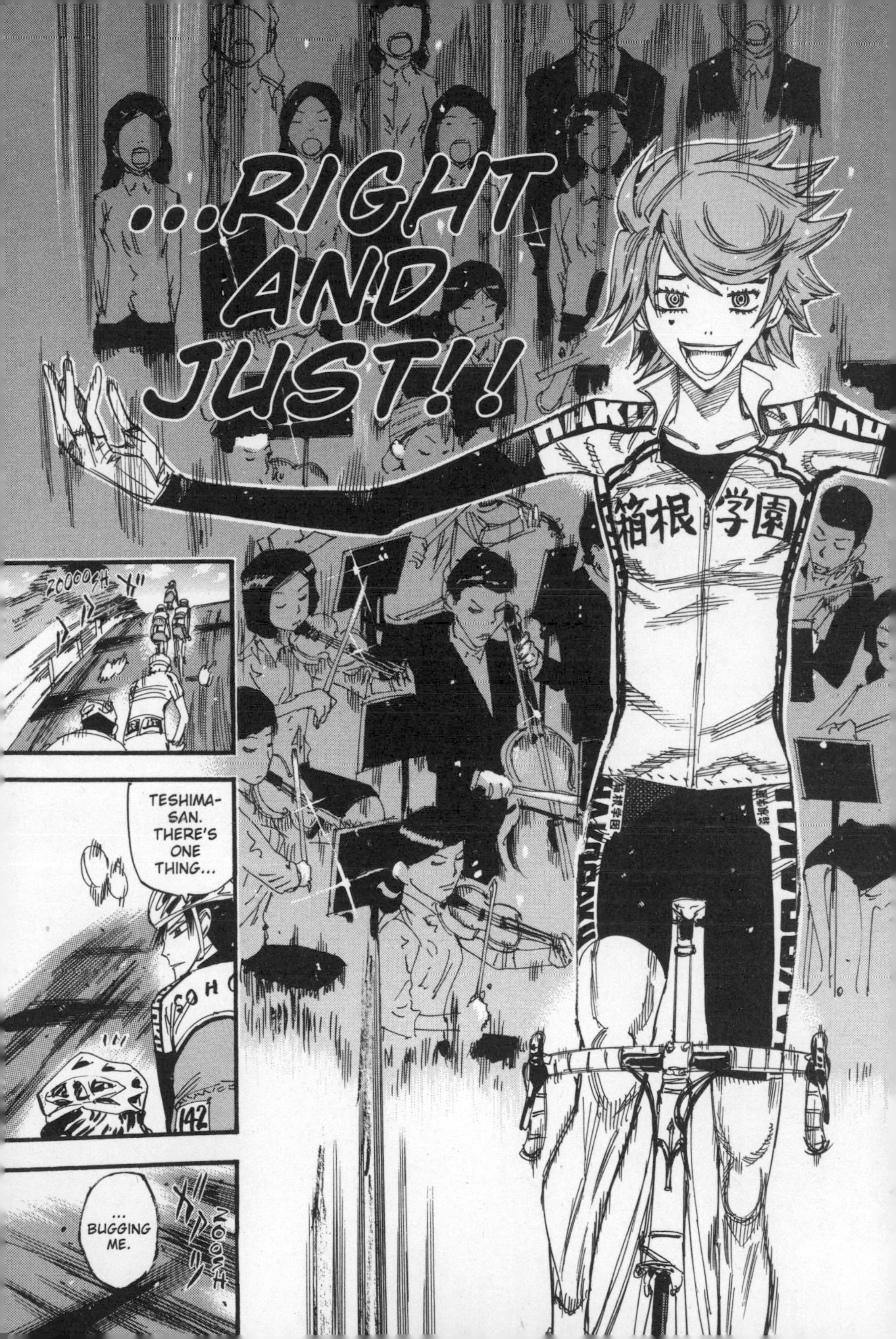
...RIGHT AND JUST!!
ZOOOOSH
TESHIMA-SAN. THERE'S ONE THING...
...BUGGING ME.
ZOOOSH

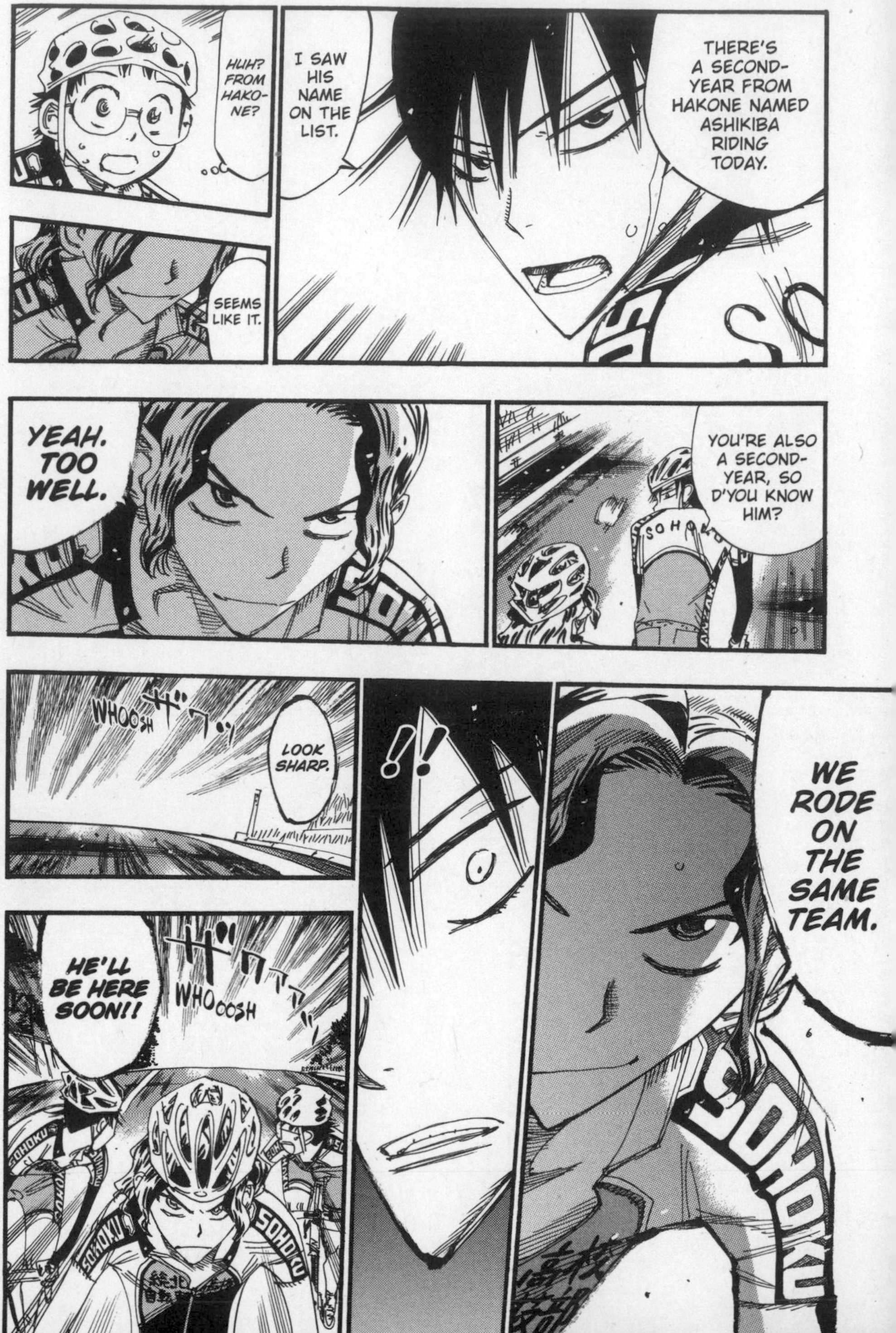
THERE'S A SECOND-YEAR FROM HAKONE NAMED ASHIKIBA RIDING TODAY.
I SAW HIS NAME ON THE LIST.
HUH? FROM HAKONE?
SEEMS LIKE IT.
YOU'RE ALSO A SECOND-YEAR, SO D'YOU KNOW HIM?
YEAH. TOO WELL.
WE RODE ON THE SAME TEAM.
!!
LOOK SHARP.
WHOOSH
WHOOOSH
HE'LL BE HERE SOON!!

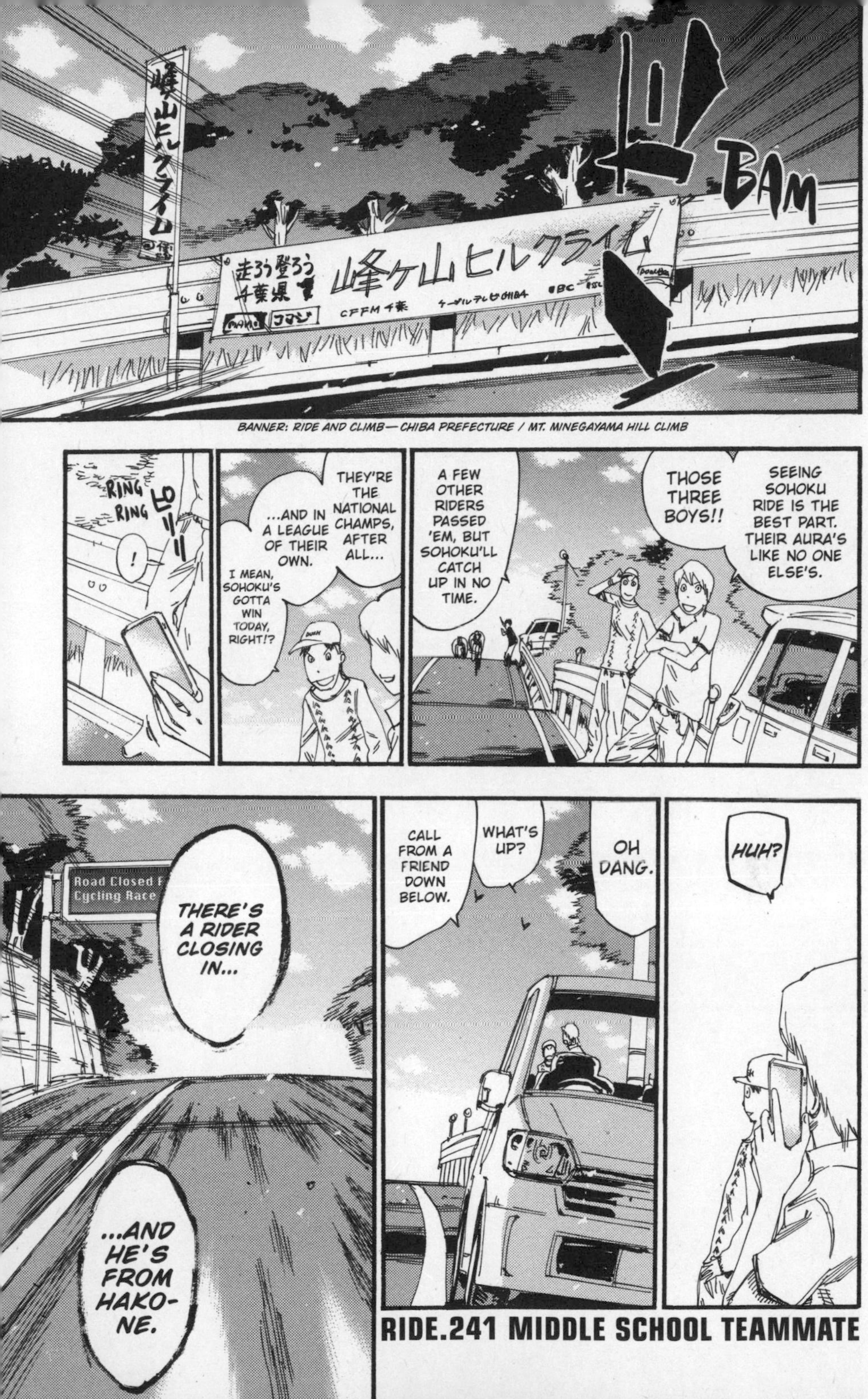
BAM
峰ケ山ヒルクライム
走ろう登ろう千葉県
峰ケ山ヒルクライム
BANNER: RIDE AND CLIMB—CHIBA PREFECTURE / MT. MINEGAYAMA HILL CLIMB
SEEING SOHOKU RIDE IS THE BEST PART. THEIR AURA'S LIKE NO ONE ELSE'S.
THOSE THREE BOYS!!
A FEW OTHER RIDERS PASSED 'EM, BUT SOHOKU'LL CATCH UP IN NO TIME.
THEY'RE THE NATIONAL CHAMPS, AFTER ALL...
...AND IN A LEAGUE OF THEIR OWN.
I MEAN, SOHOKU'S GOTTA WIN TODAY, RIGHT!?
RING RING
ピリリ
!
HUH?
OH DANG.
WHAT'S UP?
CALL FROM A FRIEND DOWN BELOW.
Road Closed F
Cycling Race
THERE'S A RIDER CLOSING IN...
...AND HE'S FROM HAKO-NE.
RIDE.241 MIDDLE SCHOOL TEAMMATE

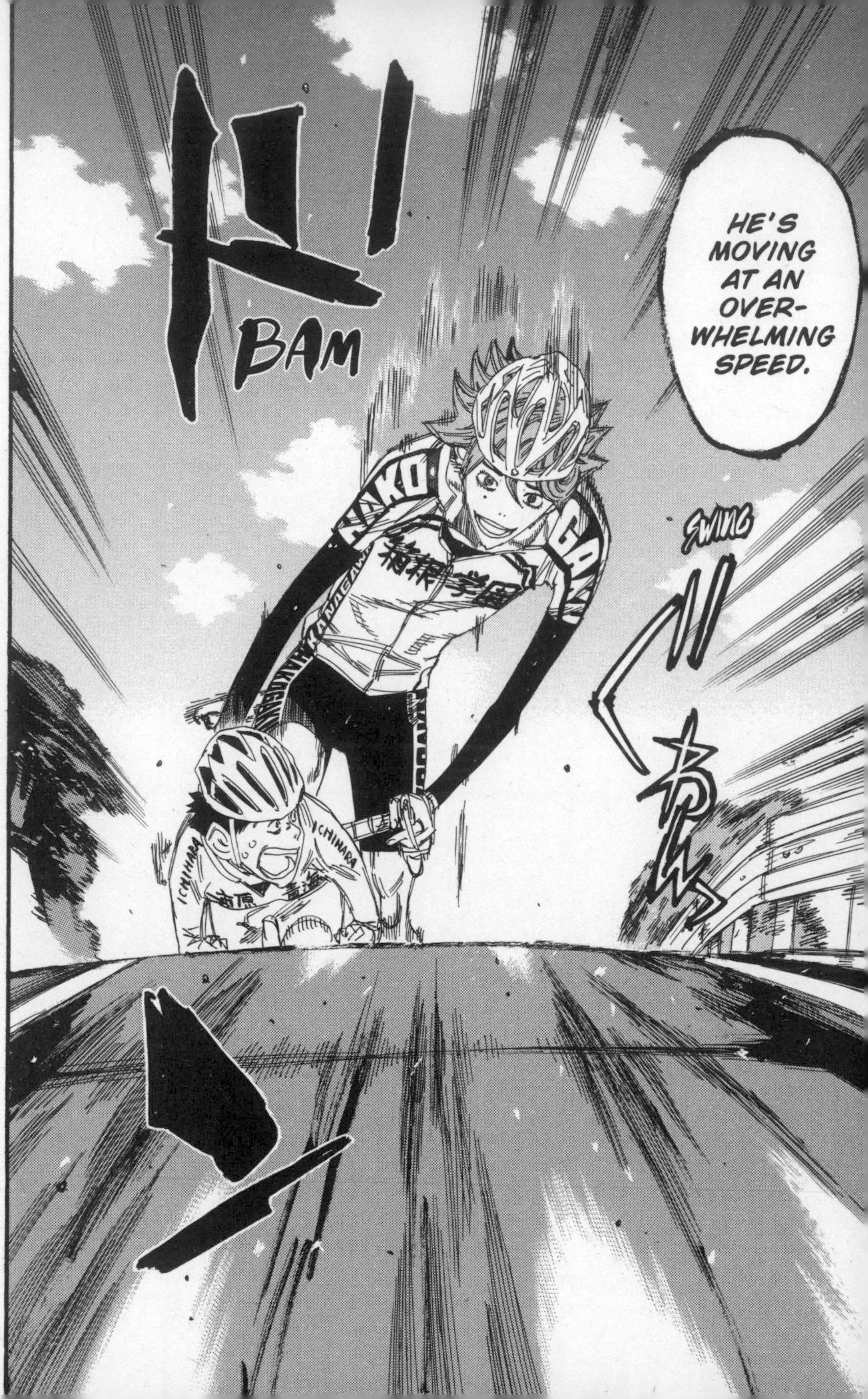
HE'S MOVING AT AN OVER-WHELMING SPEED.
BAM
SWING

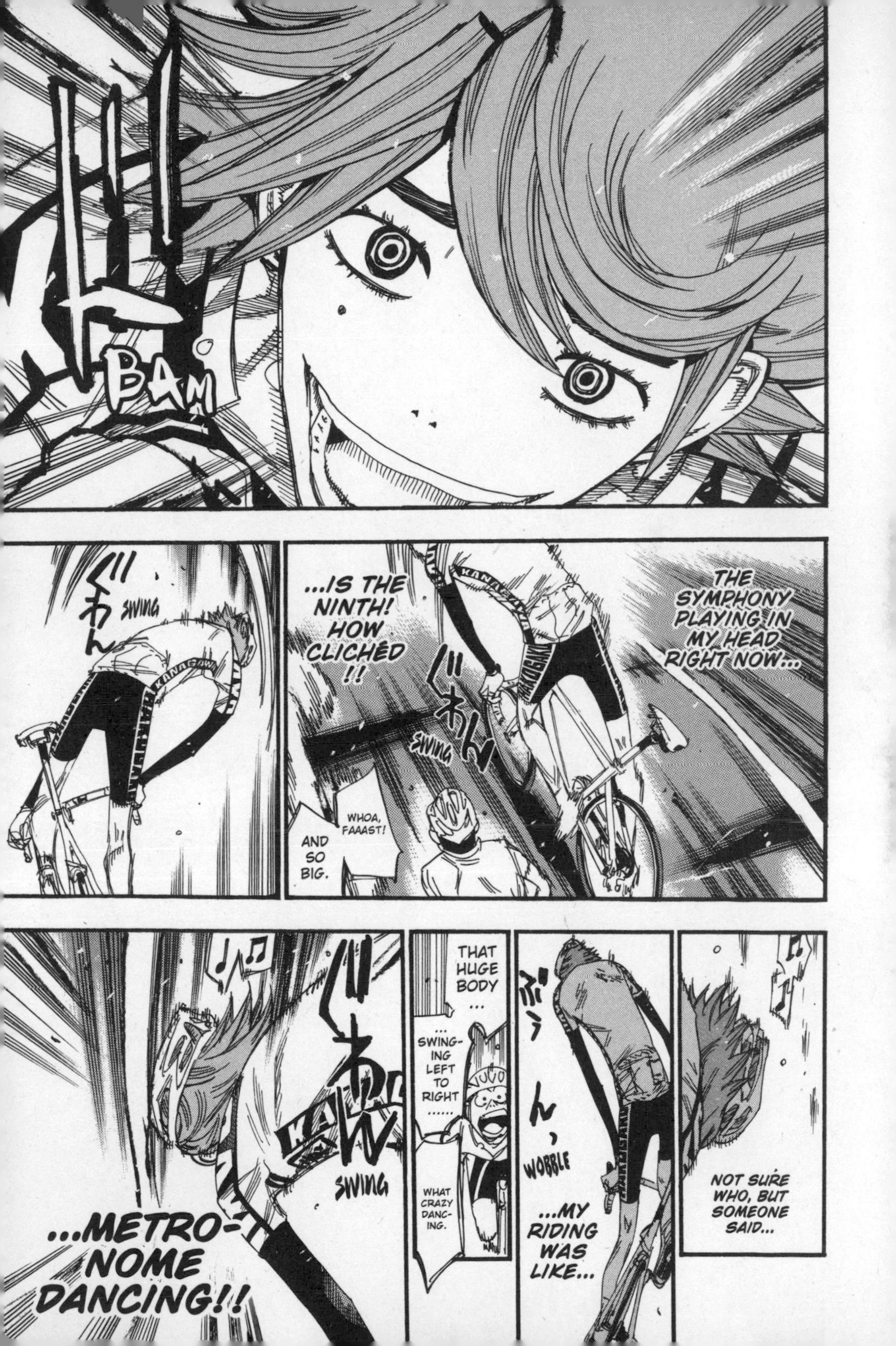
BAM
THE SYMPHONY PLAYING IN MY HEAD RIGHT NOW...
...IS THE NINTH! HOW CLICHÉD!!
ぐわん
SWING
WHOA, FAAAST!
AND SO BIG.
ぐわん
SWING
NOT SURE WHO, BUT SOMEONE SAID...
ぶぅん
WOBBLE
...MY RIDING WAS LIKE...
THAT HUGE BODY...
...SWINGING LEFT TO RIGHT......
WHAT CRAZY DANCING.
ぐわん
SWING
...METRO-NOME DANCING!!

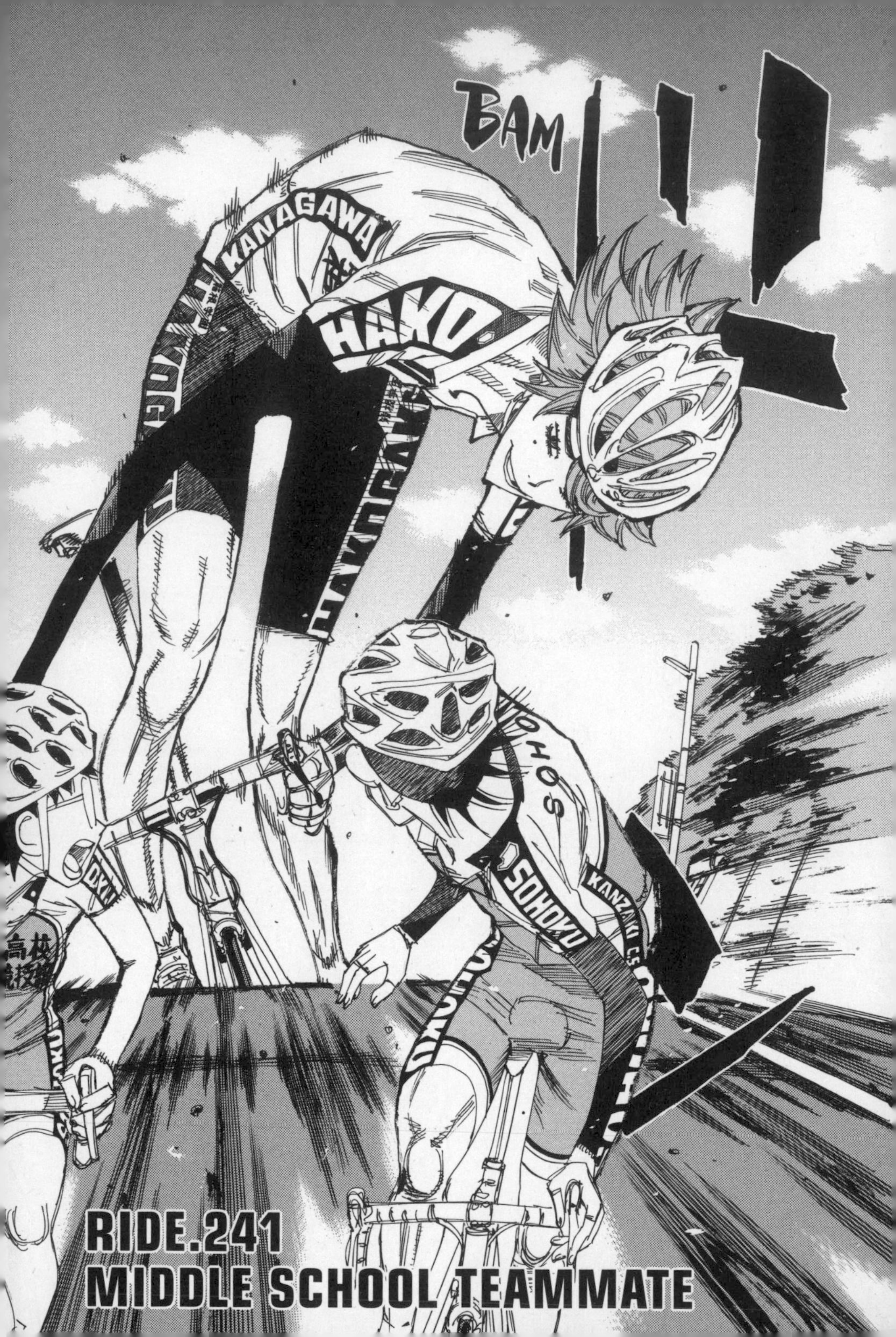
BAM
RIDE.241
MIDDLE SCHOOL TEAMMATE

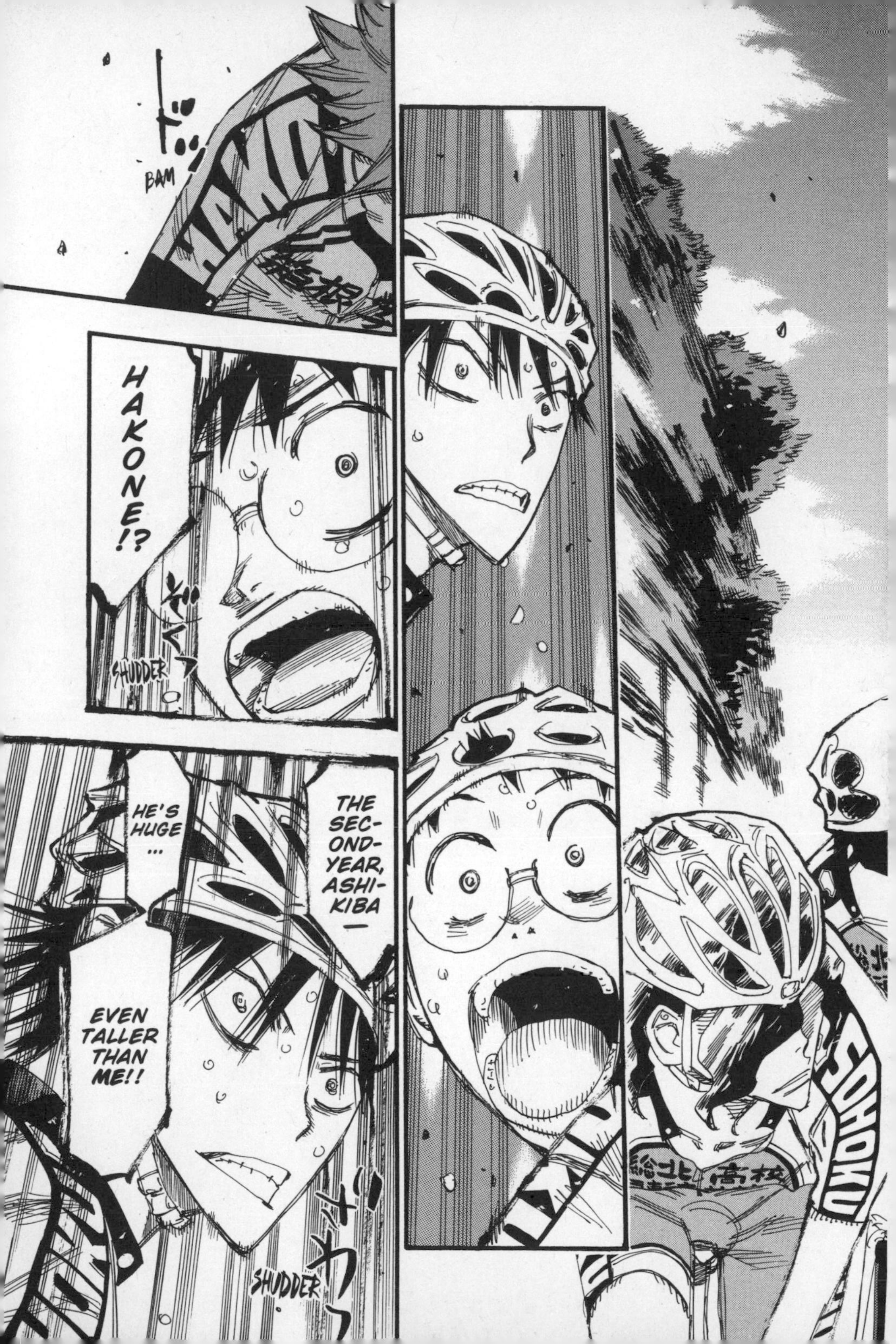

BAM
HAKONE!?
SHUDDER
THE SECOND-YEAR, ASHIKIBA—
HE'S HUGE...
EVEN TALLER THAN ME!!
SHUDDER

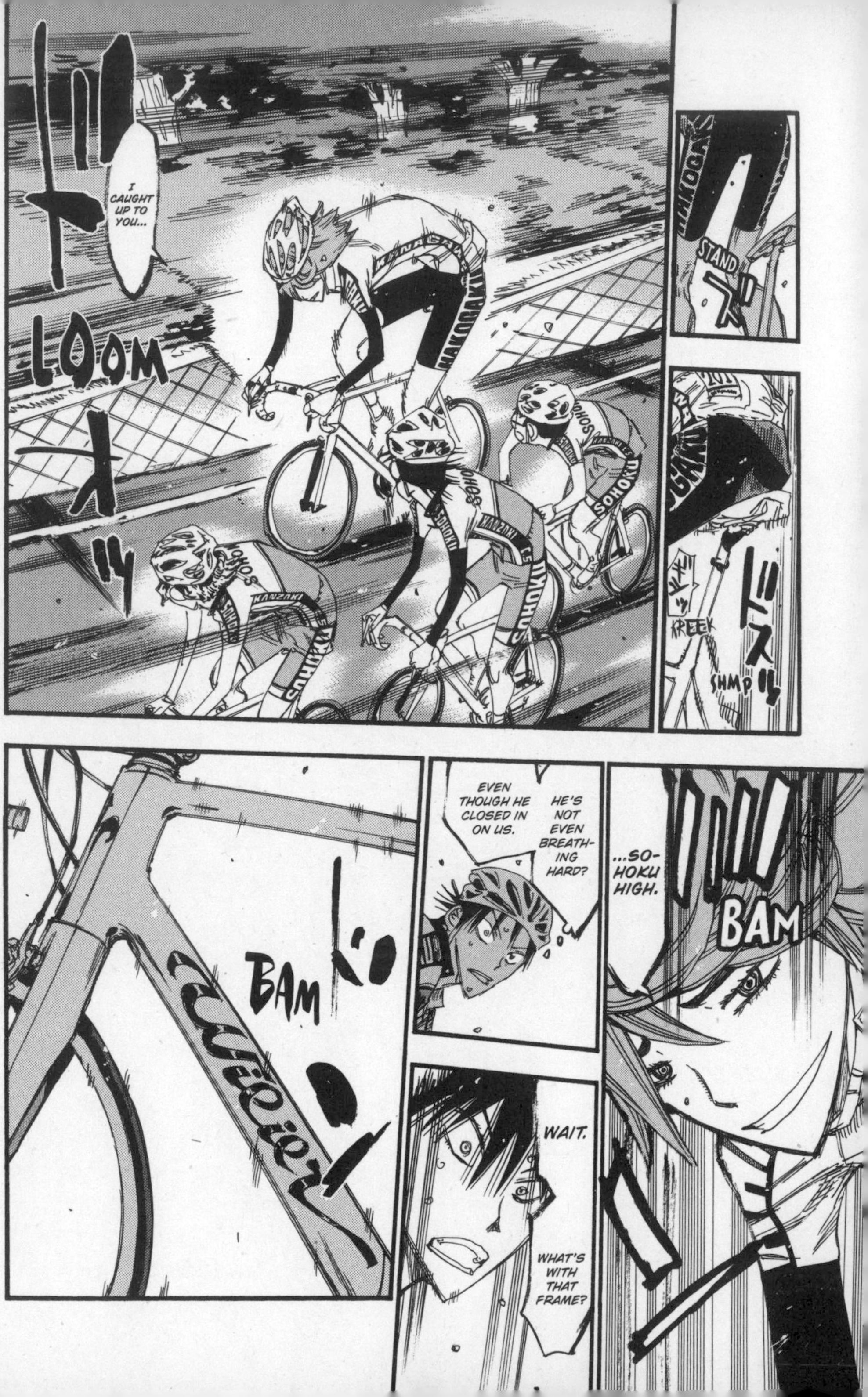
STAND
KREEK
SHMP
I CAUGHT UP TO YOU...
LOOM
...SO-HOKU HIGH.
BAM
HE'S NOT EVEN BREATHING HARD?
EVEN THOUGH HE CLOSED IN ON US.
WAIT.
WHAT'S WITH THAT FRAME?
BAM

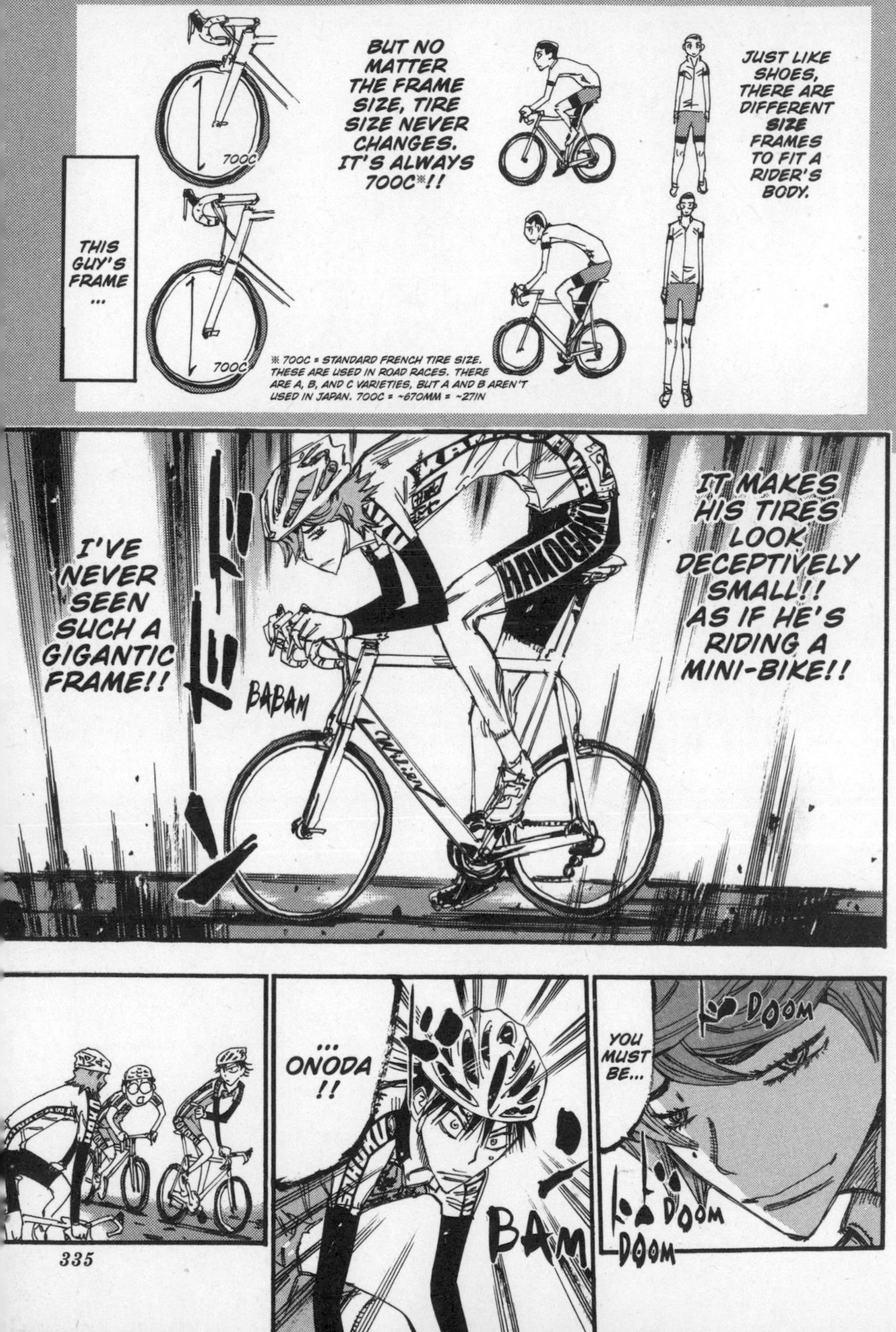
JUST LIKE SHOES, THERE ARE DIFFERENT SIZE FRAMES TO FIT A RIDER'S BODY.
BUT NO MATTER THE FRAME SIZE, TIRE SIZE NEVER CHANGES. IT'S ALWAYS 700C※!!
700C
700C
※ 700C = STANDARD FRENCH TIRE SIZE. THESE ARE USED IN ROAD RACES. THERE ARE A, B, AND C VARIETIES, BUT A AND B AREN'T USED IN JAPAN. 700C = ~670MM = ~27IN
THIS GUY'S FRAME ...
IT MAKES HIS TIRES LOOK DECEPTIVELY SMALL!! AS IF HE'S RIDING A MINI-BIKE!!
I'VE NEVER SEEN SUCH A GIGANTIC FRAME!!
BABAM
HAKOGAKU
DOOM
YOU MUST BE...
DOOM
DOOM
...ONODA!!
BAM

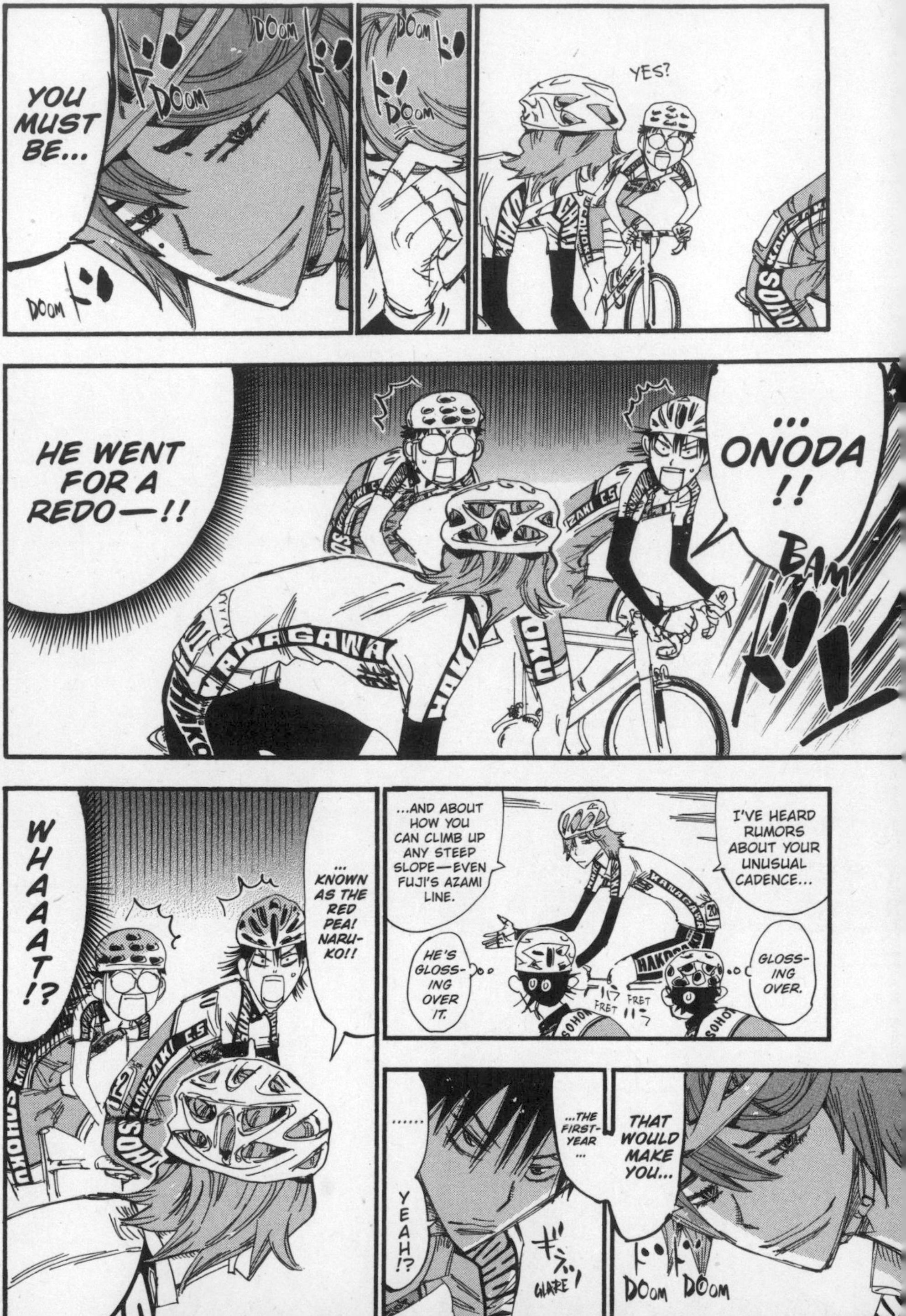
YES?
DOOM
DOOM
DOOM
DOOM
YOU MUST BE...
DOOM
DOOM
...ONODA!!
BAM
HE WENT FOR A REDO—!!
I'VE HEARD RUMORS ABOUT YOUR UNUSUAL CADENCE...
...AND ABOUT HOW YOU CAN CLIMB UP ANY STEEP SLOPE—EVEN FUJI'S AZAMI LINE.
GLOSSING OVER.
HE'S GLOSSING OVER IT.
FRET
FRET
THAT WOULD MAKE YOU...
...THE FIRST-YEAR...
......
YEAH!?
GLARE
DOOM
DOOM
...KNOWN AS THE RED PEA! NARUKO!!
WHAAAAT!?

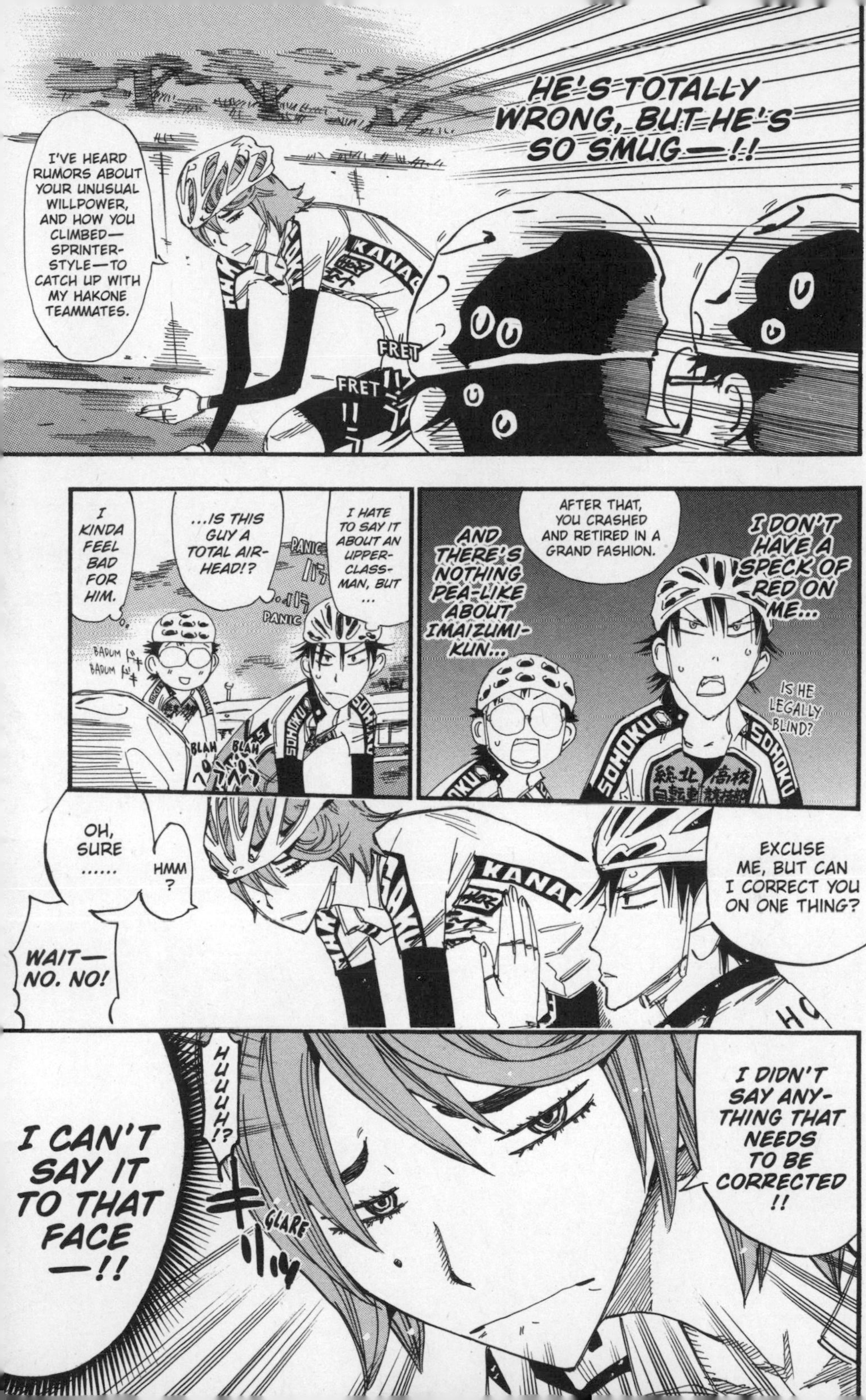
I'VE HEARD RUMORS ABOUT YOUR UNUSUAL WILLPOWER, AND HOW YOU CLIMBED—SPRINTER-STYLE—TO CATCH UP WITH MY HAKONE TEAMMATES.
FRET
FRET
HE'S TOTALLY WRONG, BUT HE'S SO SMUG—!!
AFTER THAT, YOU CRASHED AND RETIRED IN A GRAND FASHION.
I DON'T HAVE A SPECK OF RED ON ME...
AND THERE'S NOTHING PEA-LIKE ABOUT IMAIZUMI-KUN...
IS HE LEGALLY BLIND?
I HATE TO SAY IT ABOUT AN UPPER-CLASSMAN, BUT ...
PANIC
PANIC
...IS THIS GUY A TOTAL AIR-HEAD!?
I KINDA FEEL BAD FOR HIM.
BADUM
BADUM
BLAH
BLAH
EXCUSE ME, BUT CAN I CORRECT YOU ON ONE THING?
HMM ?
OH, SURE ......
WAIT— NO. NO!
I DIDN'T SAY ANYTHING THAT NEEDS TO BE CORRECTED !!
HUUUH!?
GLARE
I CAN'T SAY IT TO THAT FACE —!!

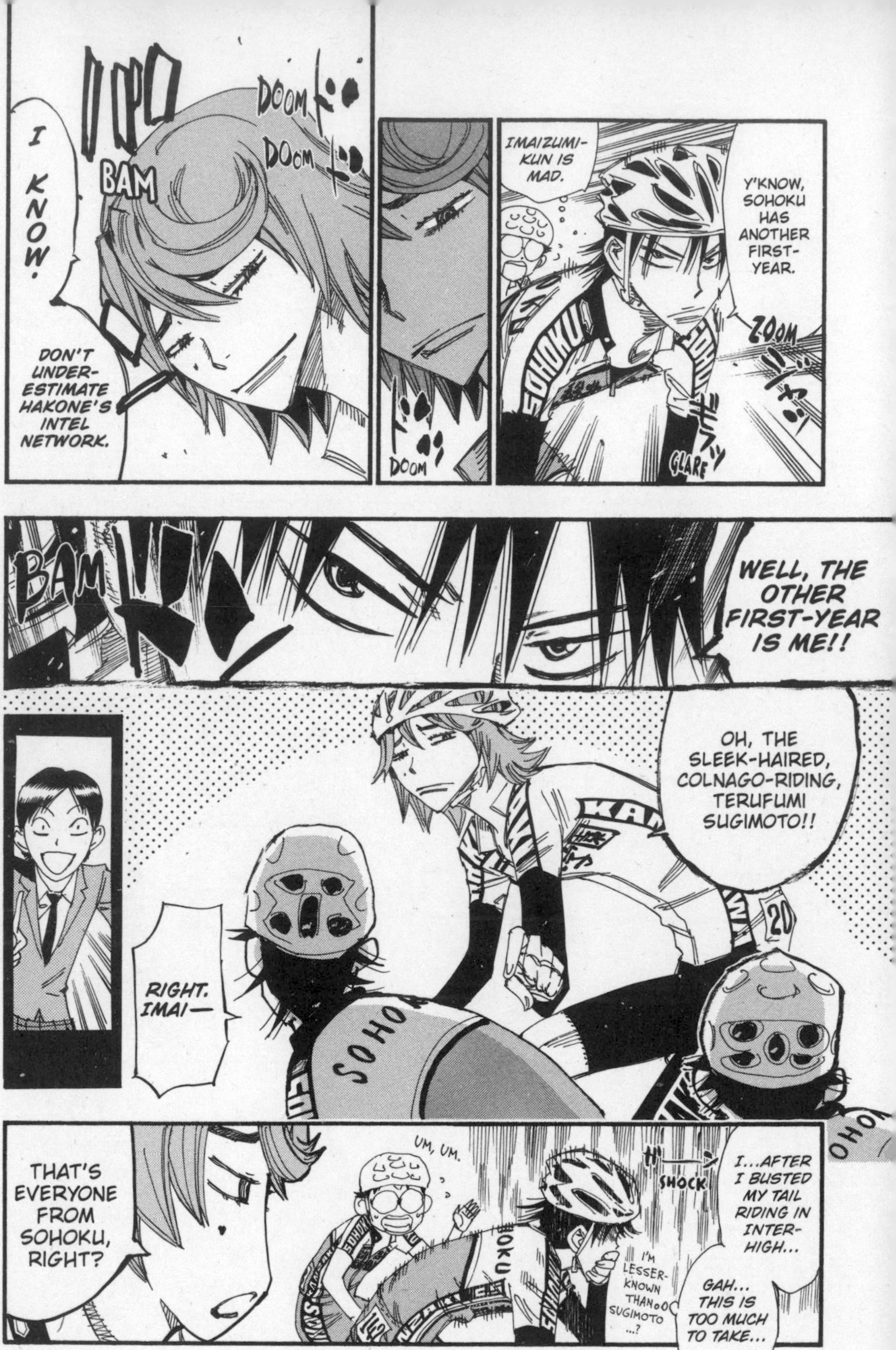
IMAIZUMI-KUN IS MAD.
Y'KNOW, SOHOKU HAS ANOTHER FIRST-YEAR.
ZOOM
GLARE
DOOM
DOOM
DOOM
BAM
I KNOW.
DON'T UNDER-ESTIMATE HAKONE'S INTEL NETWORK.
WELL, THE OTHER FIRST-YEAR IS ME!!
BAM
OH, THE SLEEK-HAIRED, COLNAGO-RIDING, TERUFUMI SUGIMOTO!!
RIGHT. IMAI—
I...AFTER I BUSTED MY TAIL RIDING IN INTER-HIGH...
GAH... THIS IS TOO MUCH TO TAKE...
SHOCK
I'M LESSER-KNOWN THAN SUGIMOTO ...?
UM, UM.
THAT'S EVERYONE FROM SOHOKU, RIGHT?

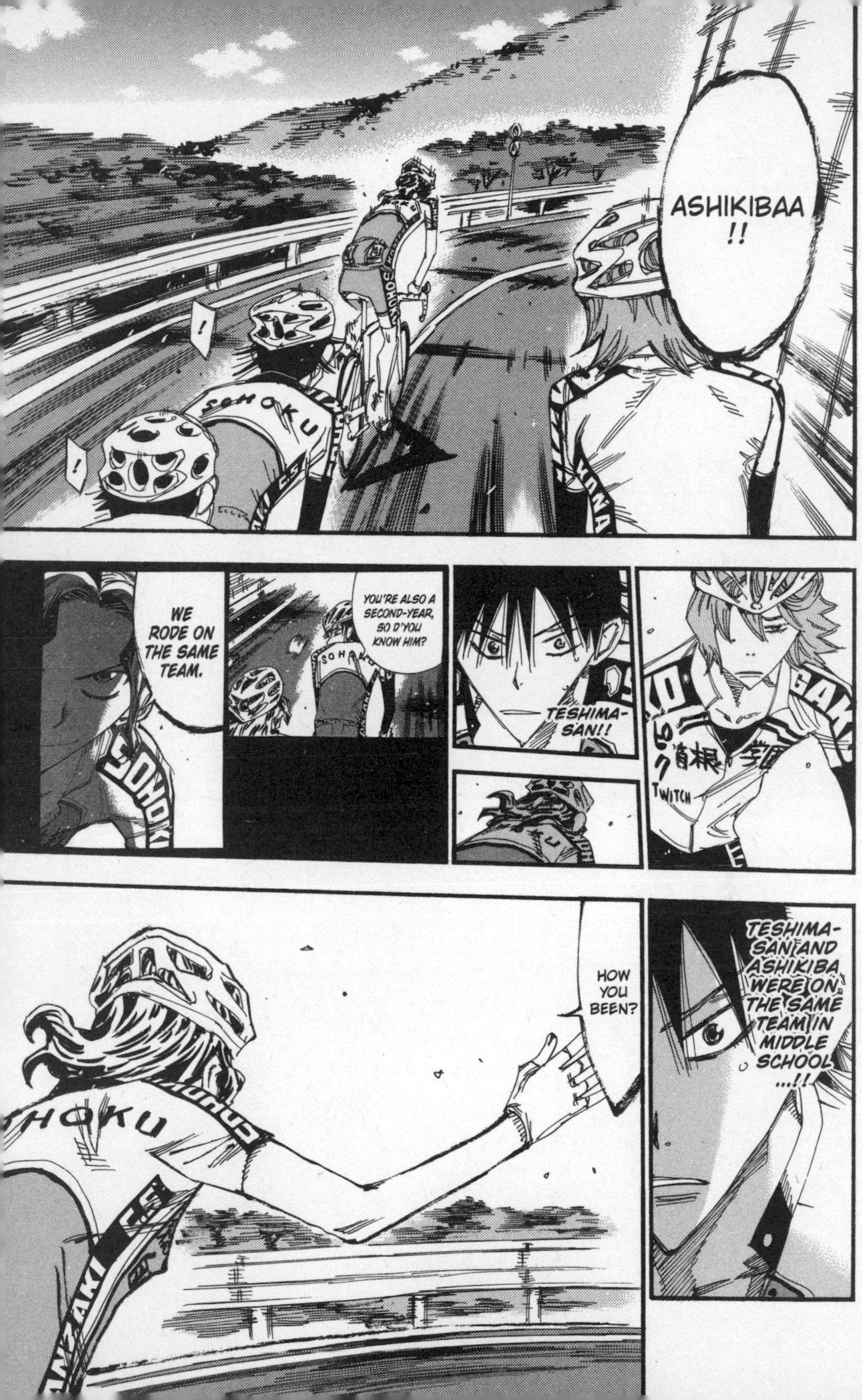
ASHIKIBAA !!
!
!
ピク
TWITCH
TESHIMA-SAN!!
YOU'RE ALSO A SECOND-YEAR, SO D'YOU KNOW HIM?
WE RODE ON THE SAME TEAM.
TESHIMA-SAN AND ASHIKIBA WERE ON THE SAME TEAM IN MIDDLE SCHOOL ...!!
HOW YOU BEEN?

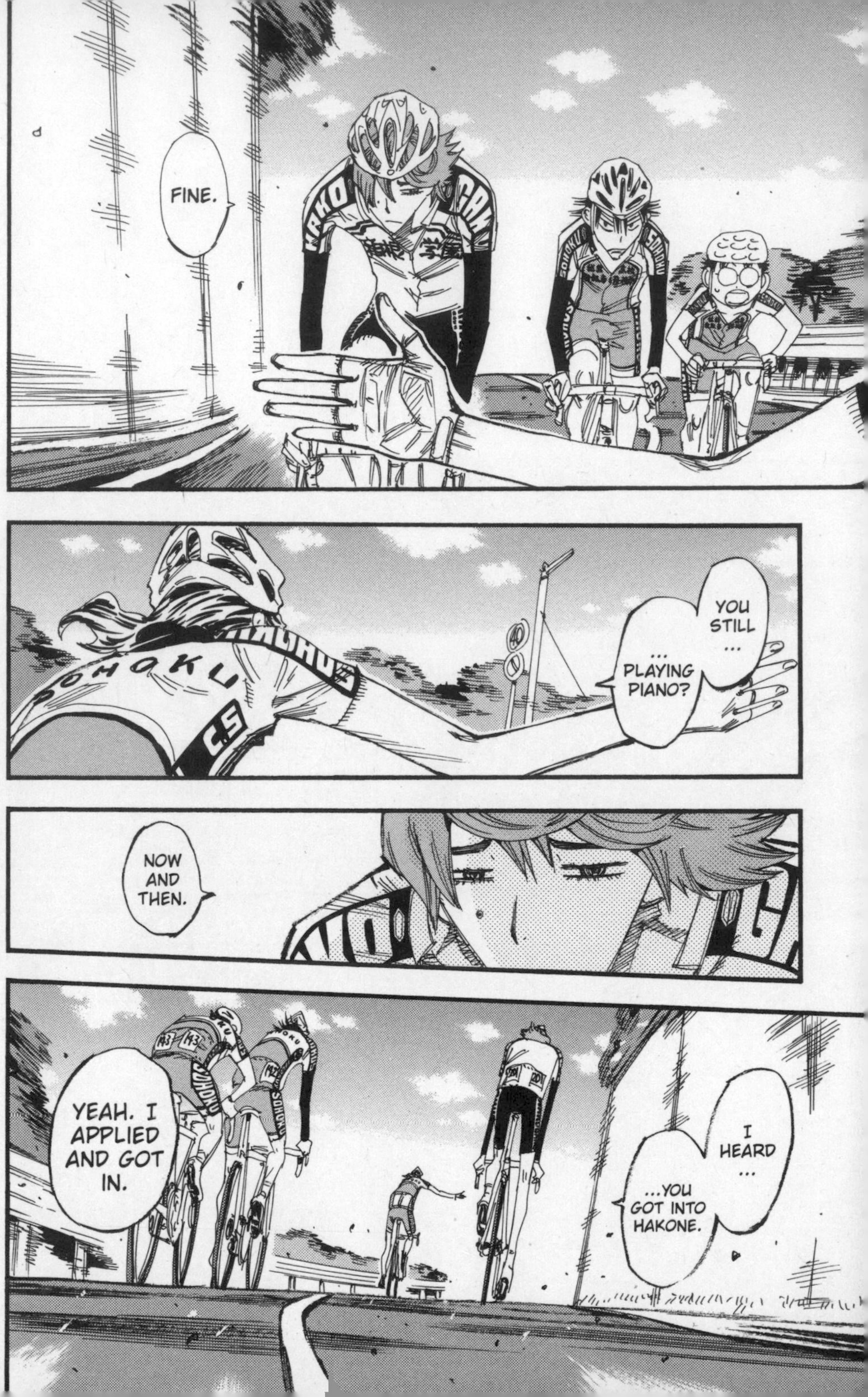
FINE.
YOU STILL... ...PLAYING PIANO?
NOW AND THEN.
I HEARD... ...YOU GOT INTO HAKONE.
YEAH. I APPLIED AND GOT IN.

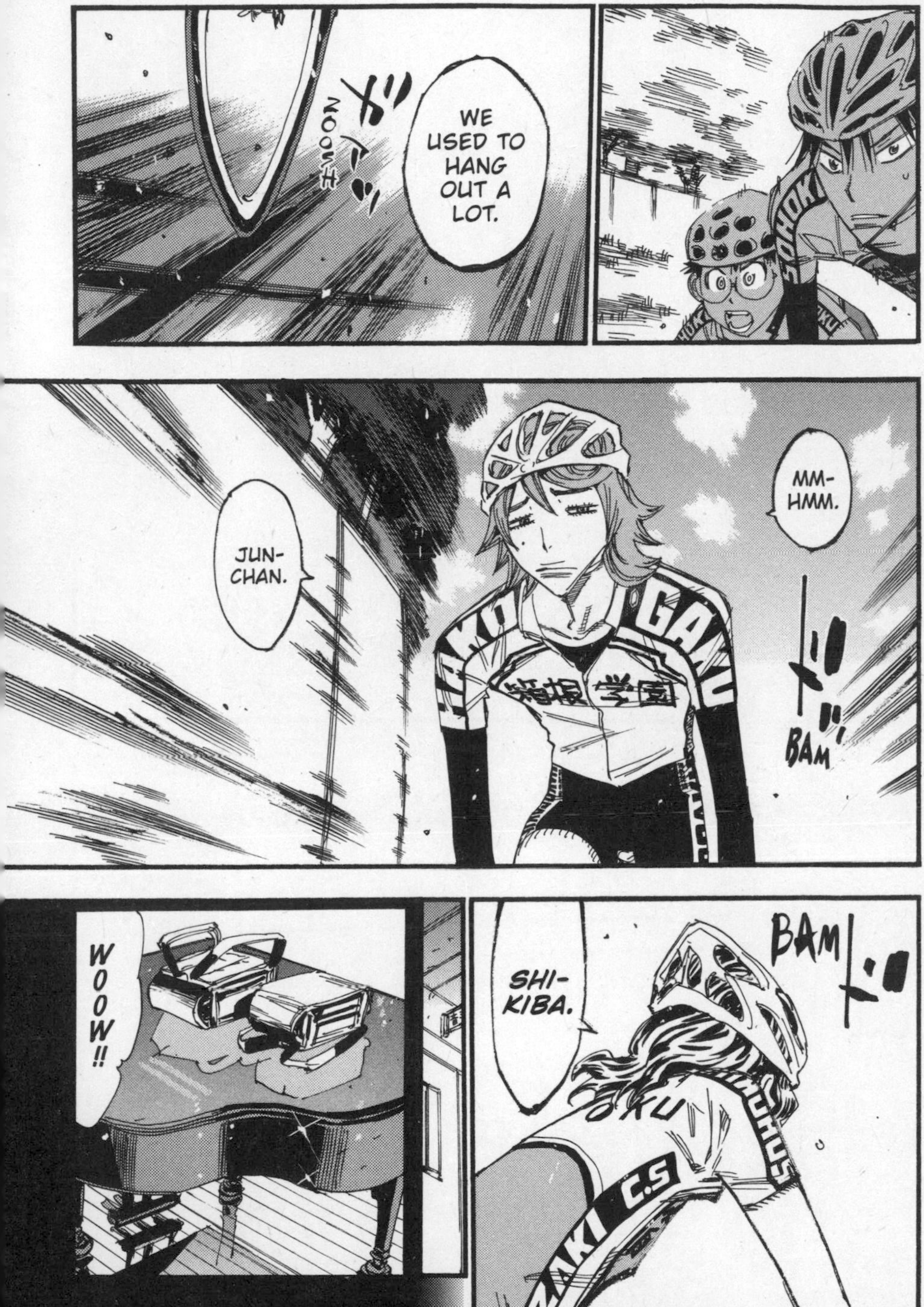
WE USED TO HANG OUT A LOT.
WHOOSH
MM-HMM.
BAM
JUN-CHAN.
BAM
SHI-KIBA.
WOOOW!!

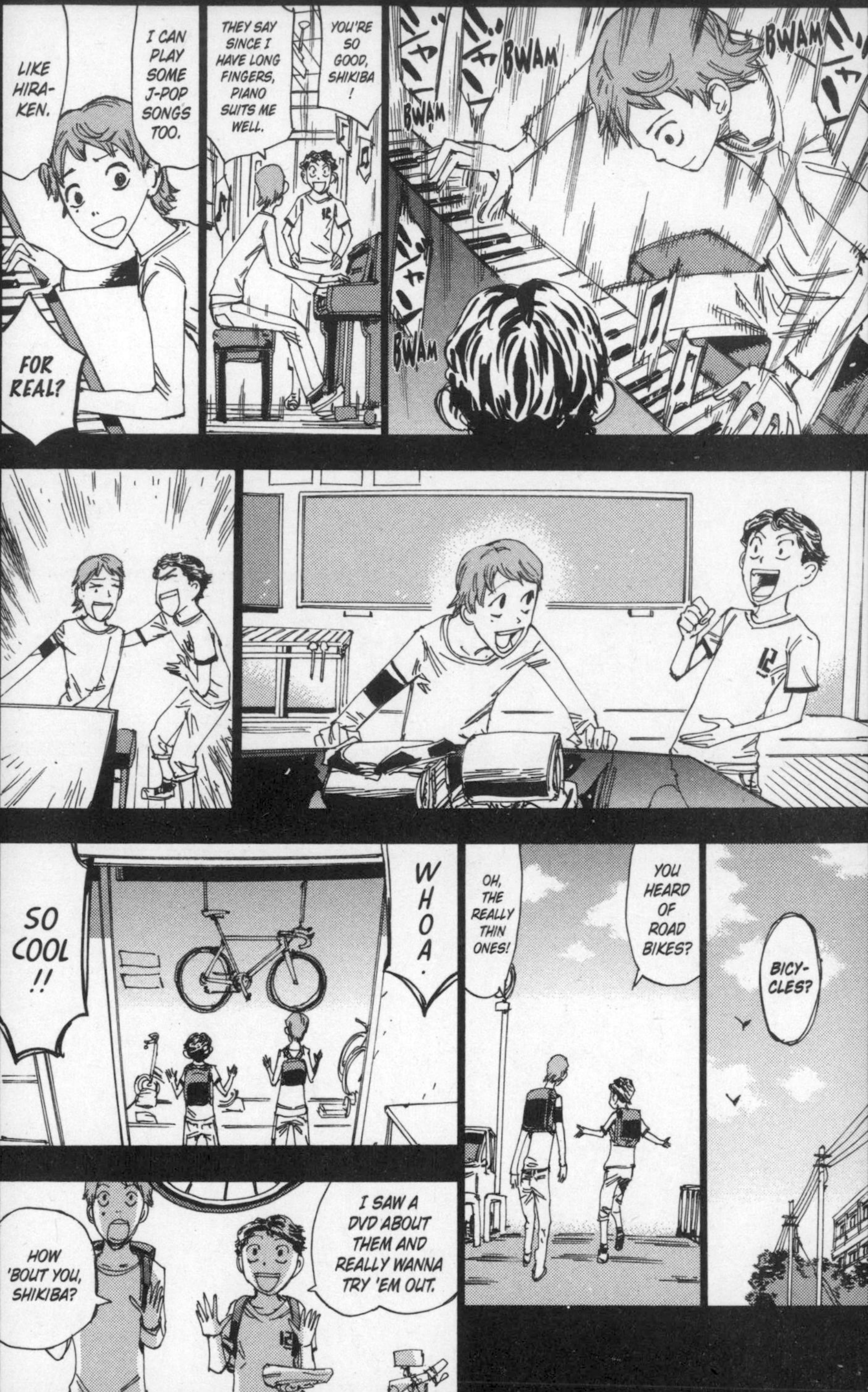
BWAM
BWAM
BWAM
BWAM
YOU'RE SO GOOD, SHIKIBA!
THEY SAY SINCE I HAVE LONG FINGERS, PIANO SUITS ME WELL.
I CAN PLAY SOME J-POP SONGS TOO.
LIKE HIRA-KEN.
FOR REAL?
BICY-CLES?
YOU HEARD OF ROAD BIKES?
OH, THE REALLY THIN ONES!
WHOA.
SO COOL!!
I SAW A DVD ABOUT THEM AND REALLY WANNA TRY 'EM OUT.
HOW 'BOUT YOU, SHIKIBA?

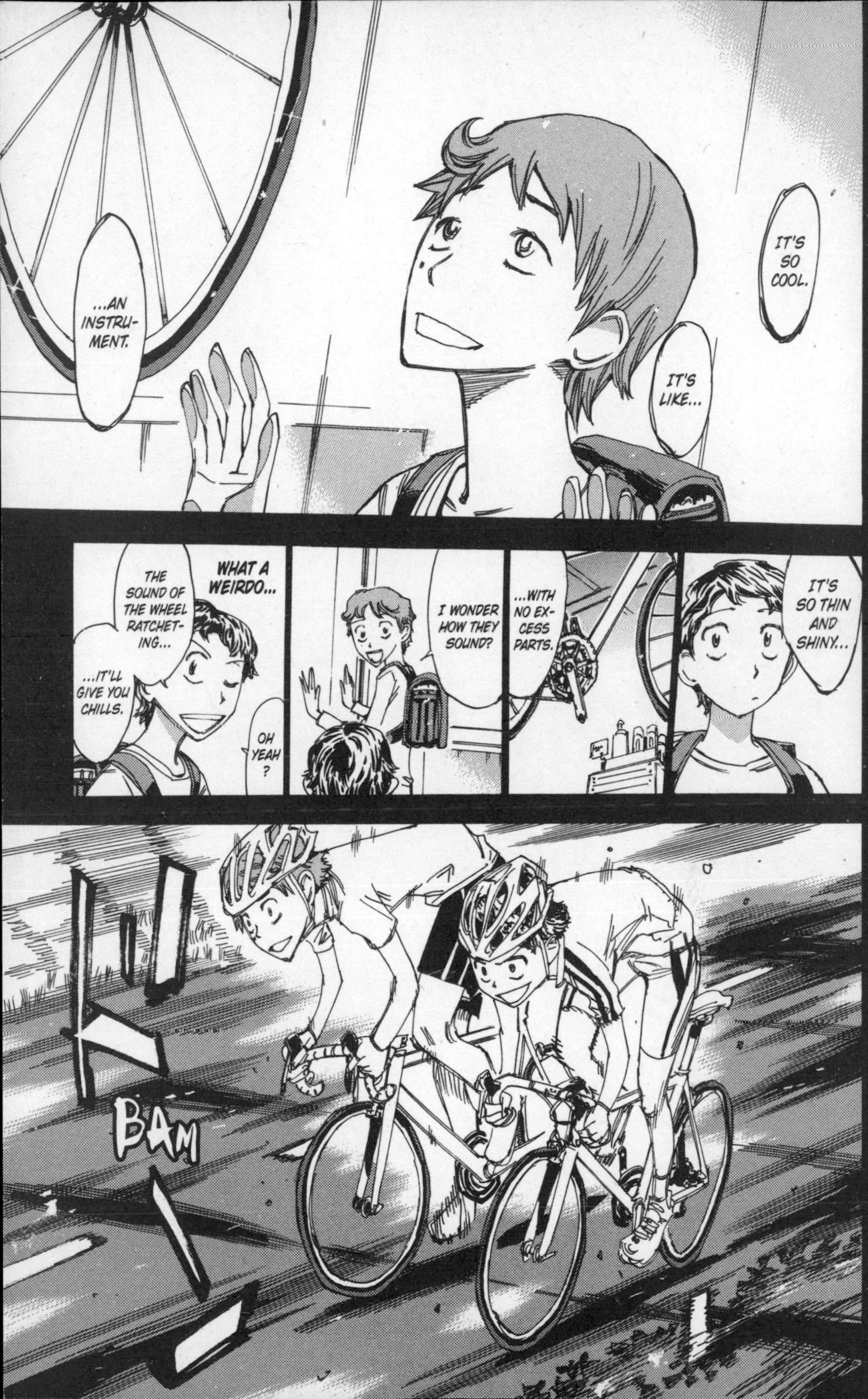
IT'S SO COOL.
IT'S LIKE...
...AN INSTRUMENT.
IT'S SO THIN AND SHINY...
...WITH NO EXCESS PARTS.
I WONDER HOW THEY SOUND?
OH YEAH?
WHAT A WEIRDO...
THE SOUND OF THE WHEEL RATCHETING...
...IT'LL GIVE YOU CHILLS.
BAM

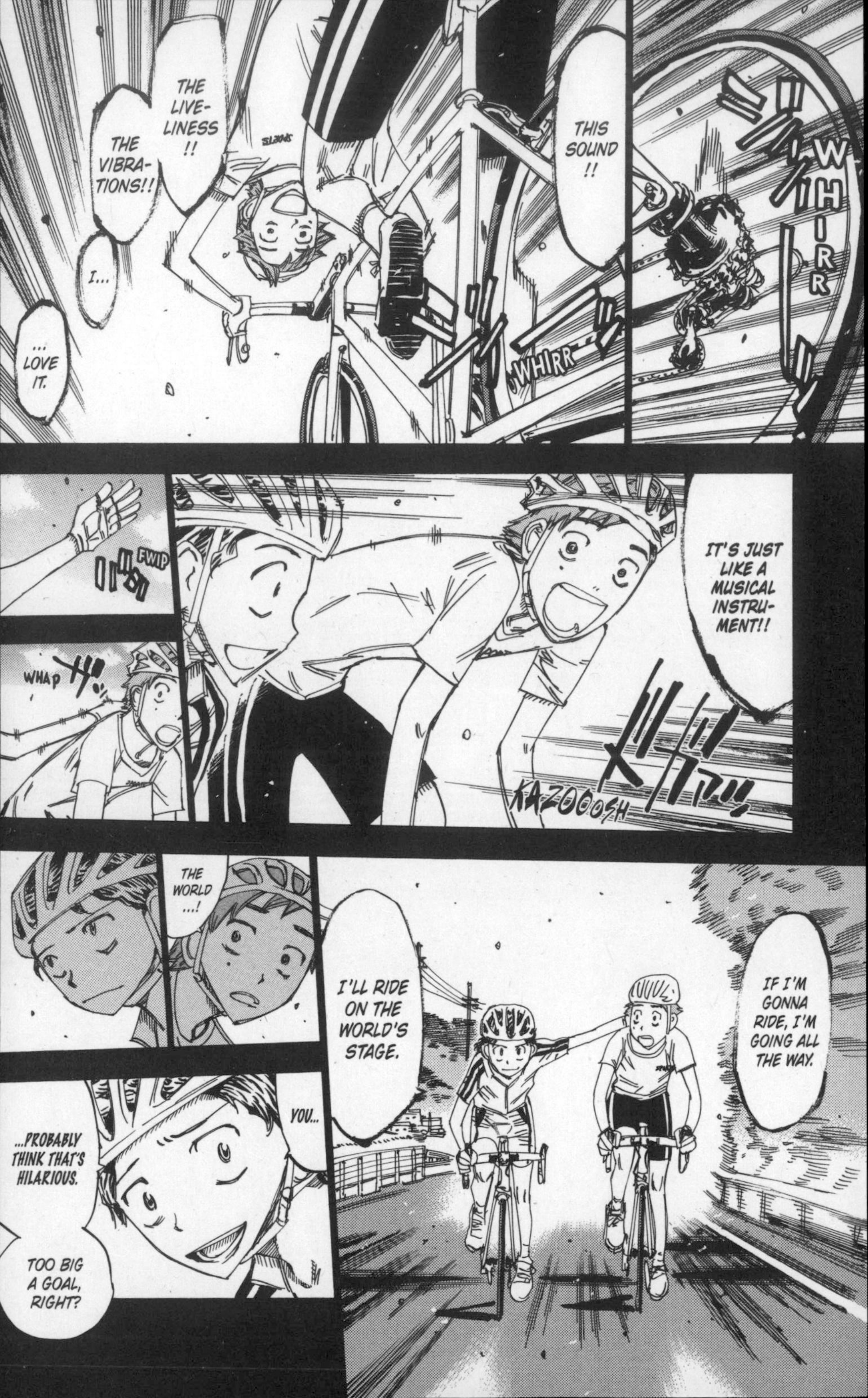
THIS SOUND!!
WHIRR
WHIRR
THE LIVE-LINESS!!
THE VIBRA-TIONS!!
I...
...LOVE IT.
IT'S JUST LIKE A MUSICAL INSTRU-MENT!!
KAZOOOSH
FWIP
WHAP
IF I'M GONNA RIDE, I'M GOING ALL THE WAY.
I'LL RIDE ON THE WORLD'S STAGE.
THE WORLD...!
YOU...
...PROBABLY THINK THAT'S HILARIOUS.
TOO BIG A GOAL, RIGHT?

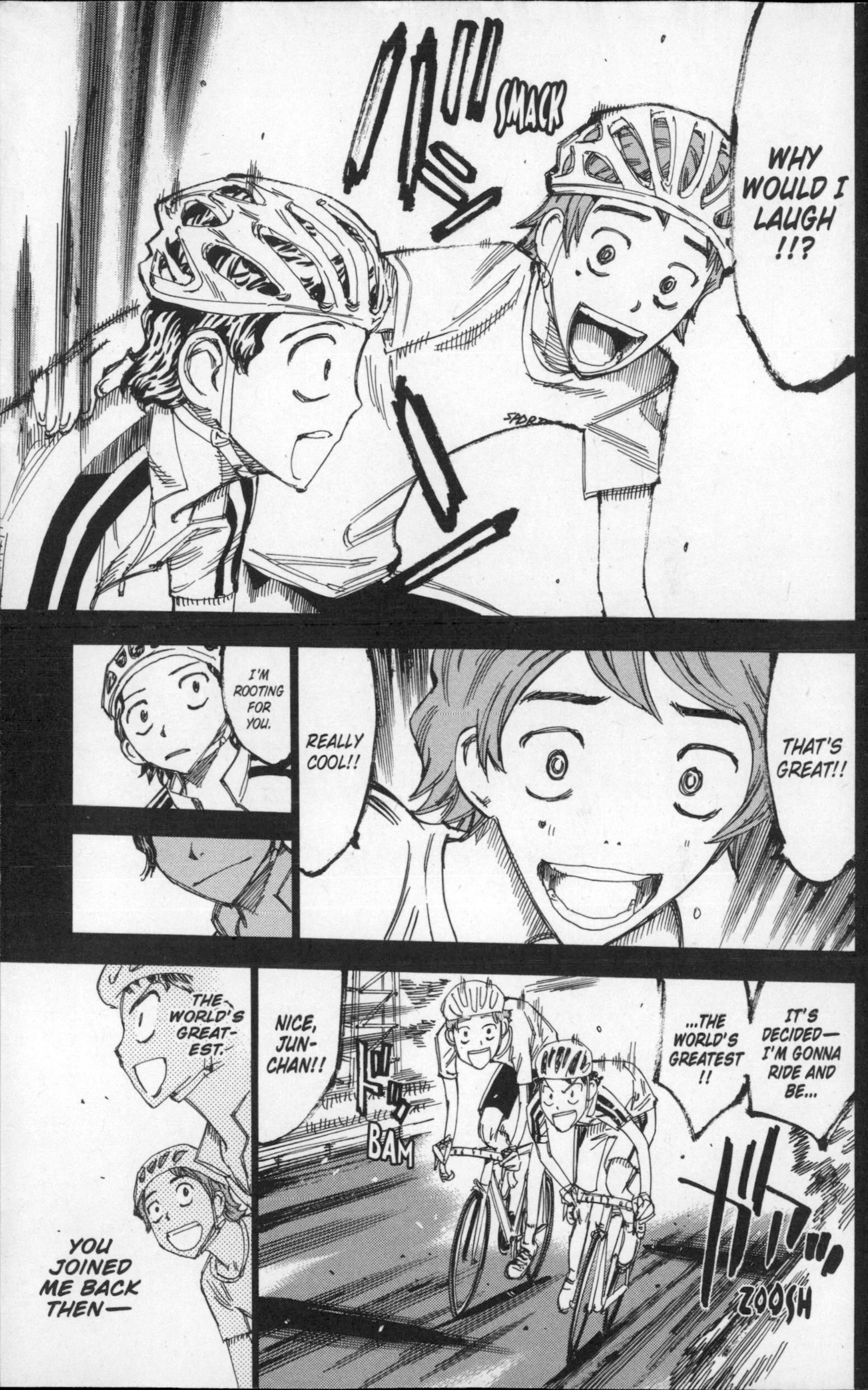
WHY WOULD I LAUGH!!?
SMACK
THAT'S GREAT!!
REALLY COOL!!
I'M ROOTING FOR YOU.
IT'S DECIDED—I'M GONNA RIDE AND BE...
...THE WORLD'S GREATEST!!
NICE, JUN-CHAN!!
BAM
ZOOSH
THE WORLD'S GREATEST.
YOU JOINED ME BACK THEN—

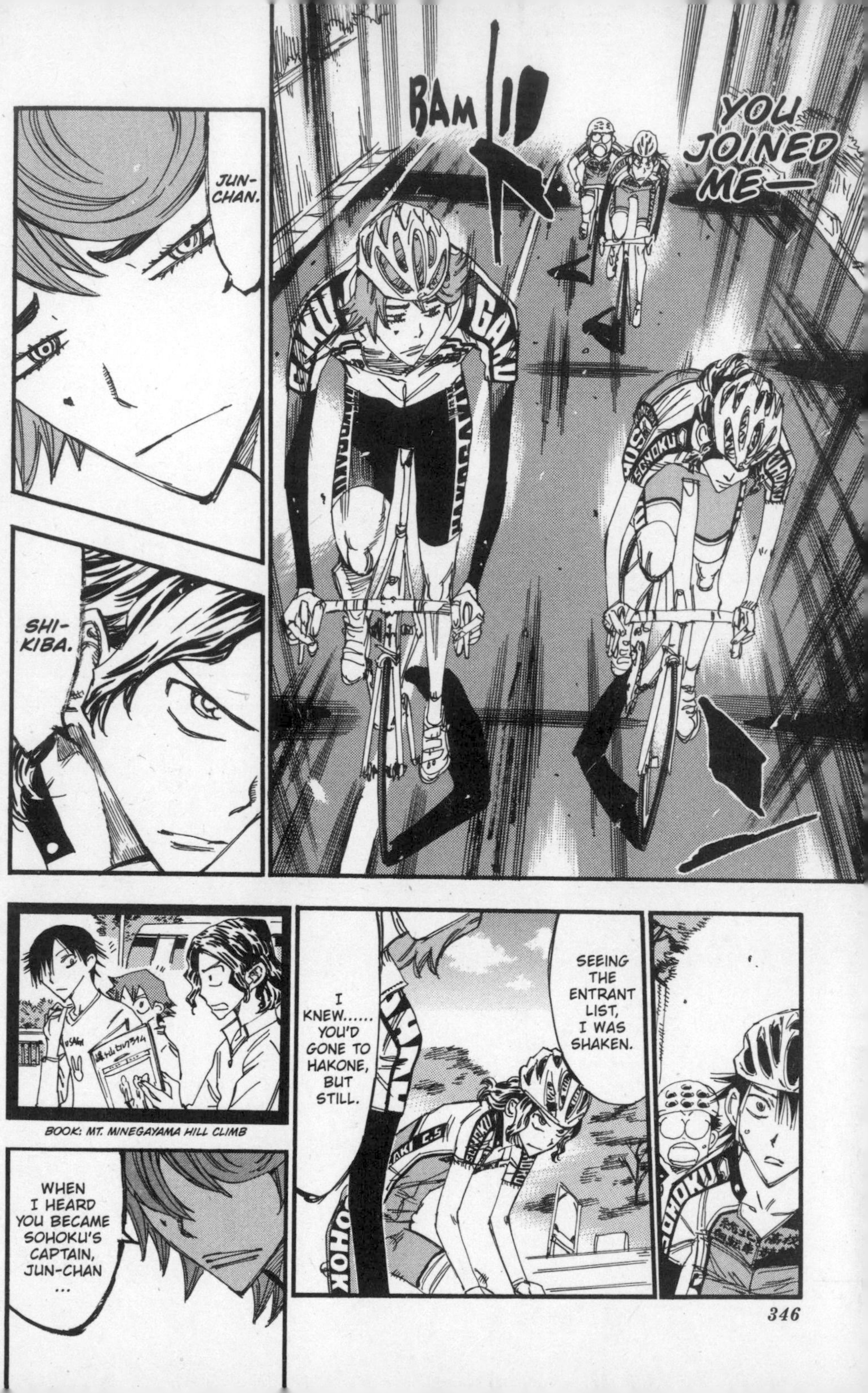
BAM
YOU JOINED ME—
JUN-CHAN.
SHI-KIBA.
SEEING THE ENTRANT LIST, I WAS SHAKEN.
I KNEW...... YOU'D GONE TO HAKONE, BUT STILL.
BOOK: MT. MINEGAYAMA HILL CLIMB
WHEN I HEARD YOU BECAME SOHOKU'S CAPTAIN, JUN-CHAN ...

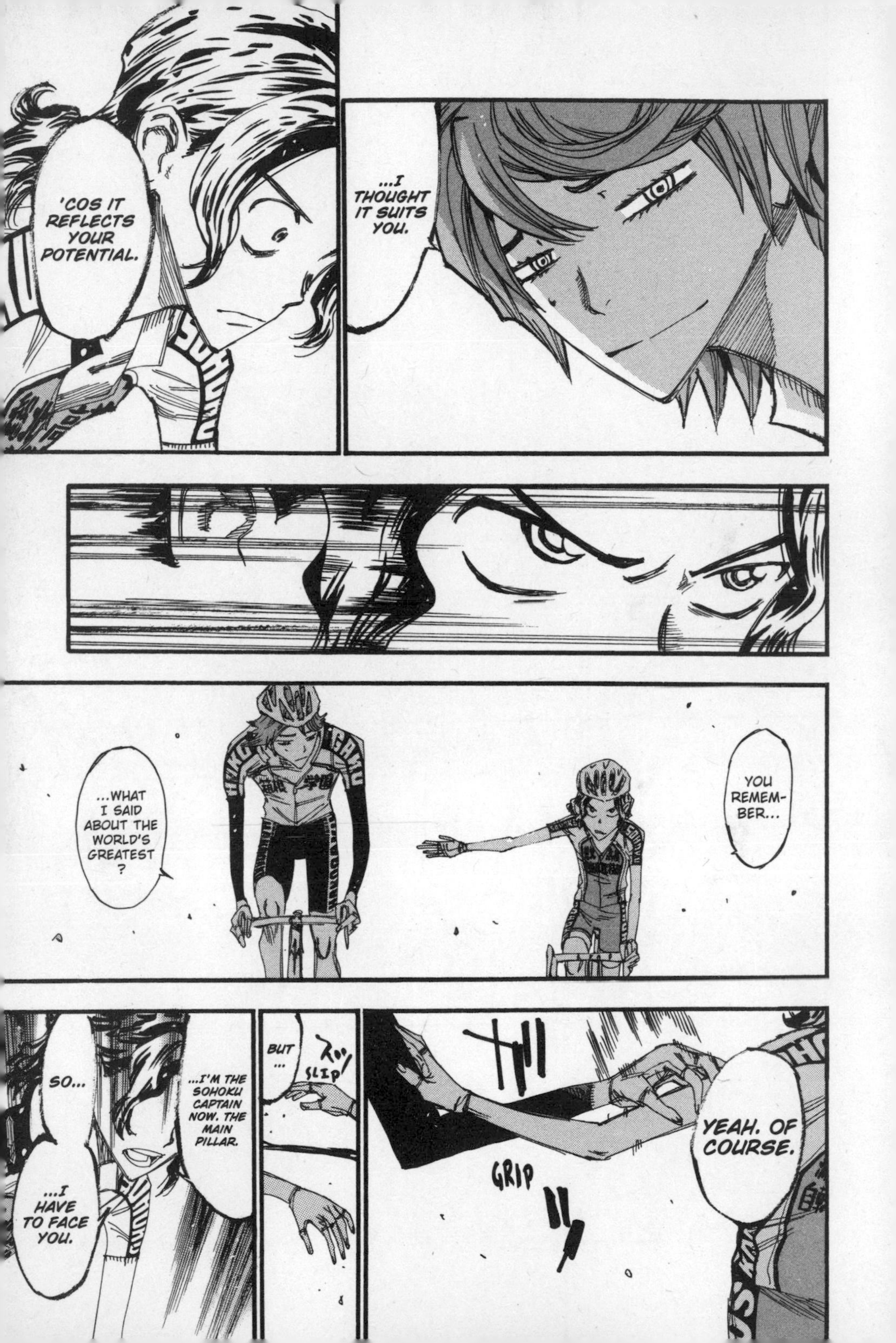
...I THOUGHT IT SUITS YOU.
'COS IT REFLECTS YOUR POTENTIAL.
YOU REMEMBER-BER...
...WHAT I SAID ABOUT THE WORLD'S GREATEST?
YEAH. OF COURSE.
GRIP
BUT...
SLIP
...I'M THE SOHOKU CAPTAIN NOW. THE MAIN PILLAR.
SO...
...I HAVE TO FACE YOU.

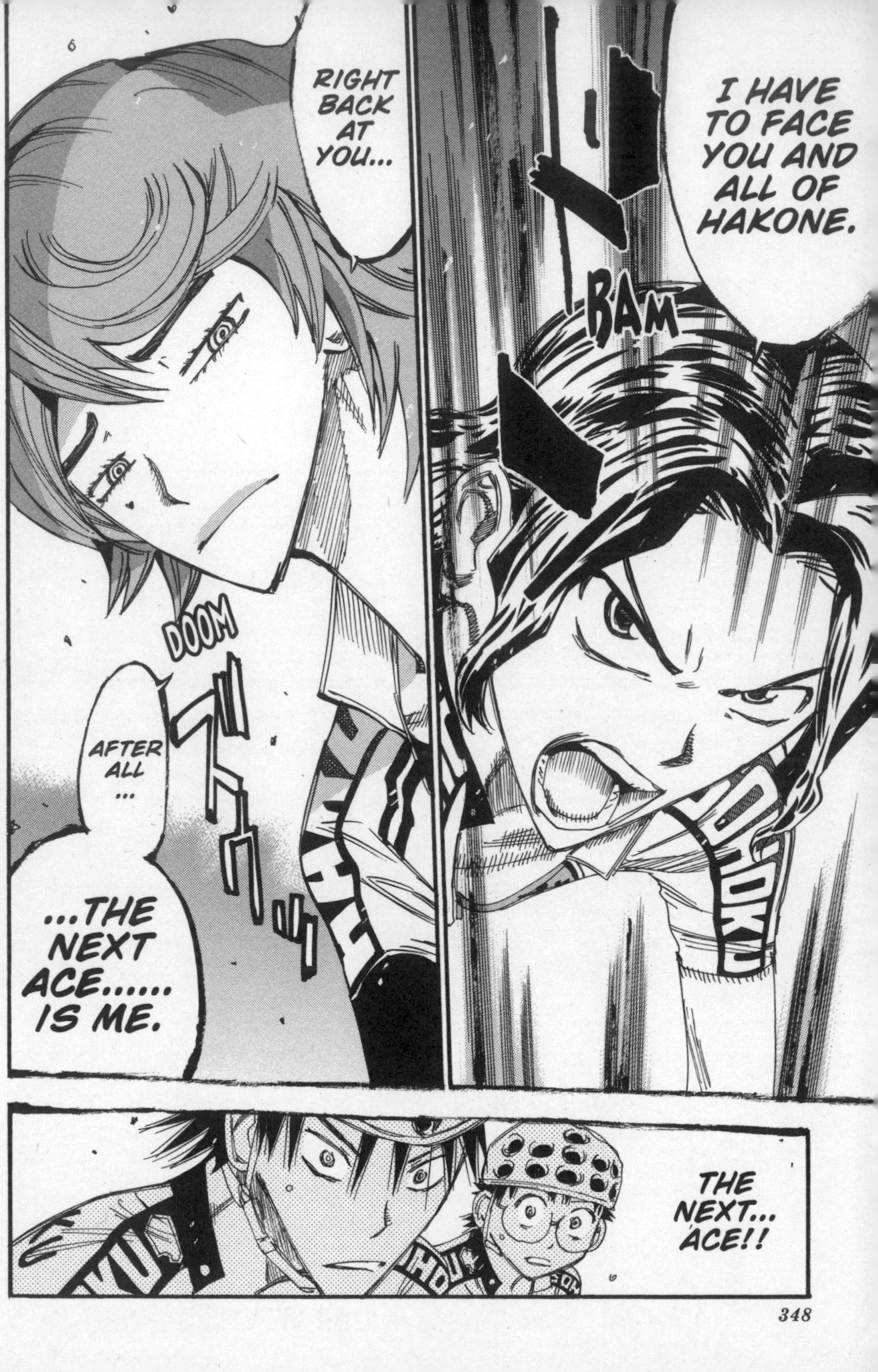
I HAVE TO FACE YOU AND ALL OF HAKONE.
BAM
RIGHT BACK AT YOU...
DOOM
AFTER ALL ...
...THE NEXT ACE...... IS ME.
THE NEXT... ACE!!

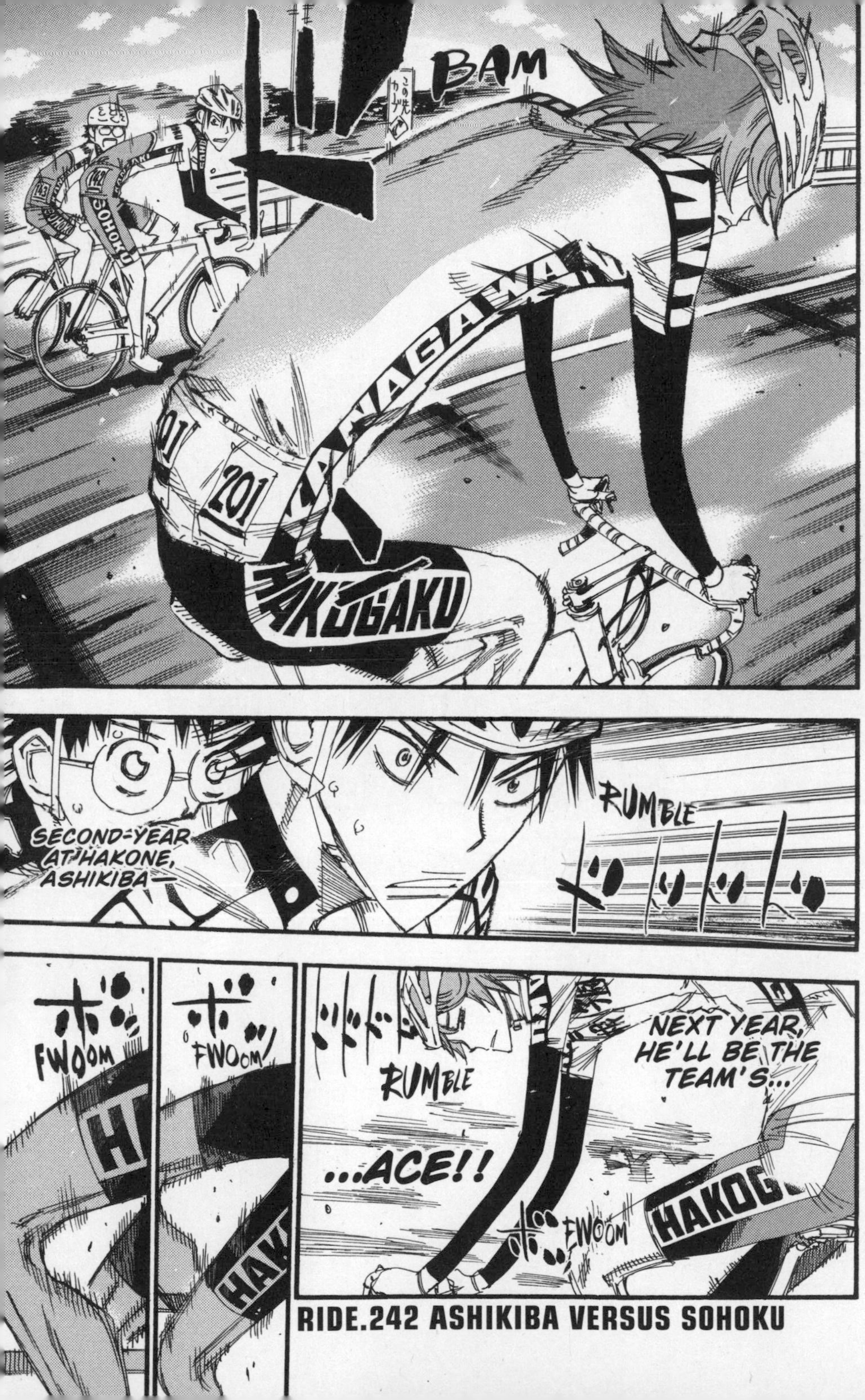
BAM
RUMBLE
SECOND-YEAR AT HAKONE, ASHIKIBA—
NEXT YEAR, HE'LL BE THE TEAM'S...
RUMBLE
...ACE!!
FWOOM
FWOOM
FWOOM

RIDE.242 ASHIKIBA VERSUS SOHOKU

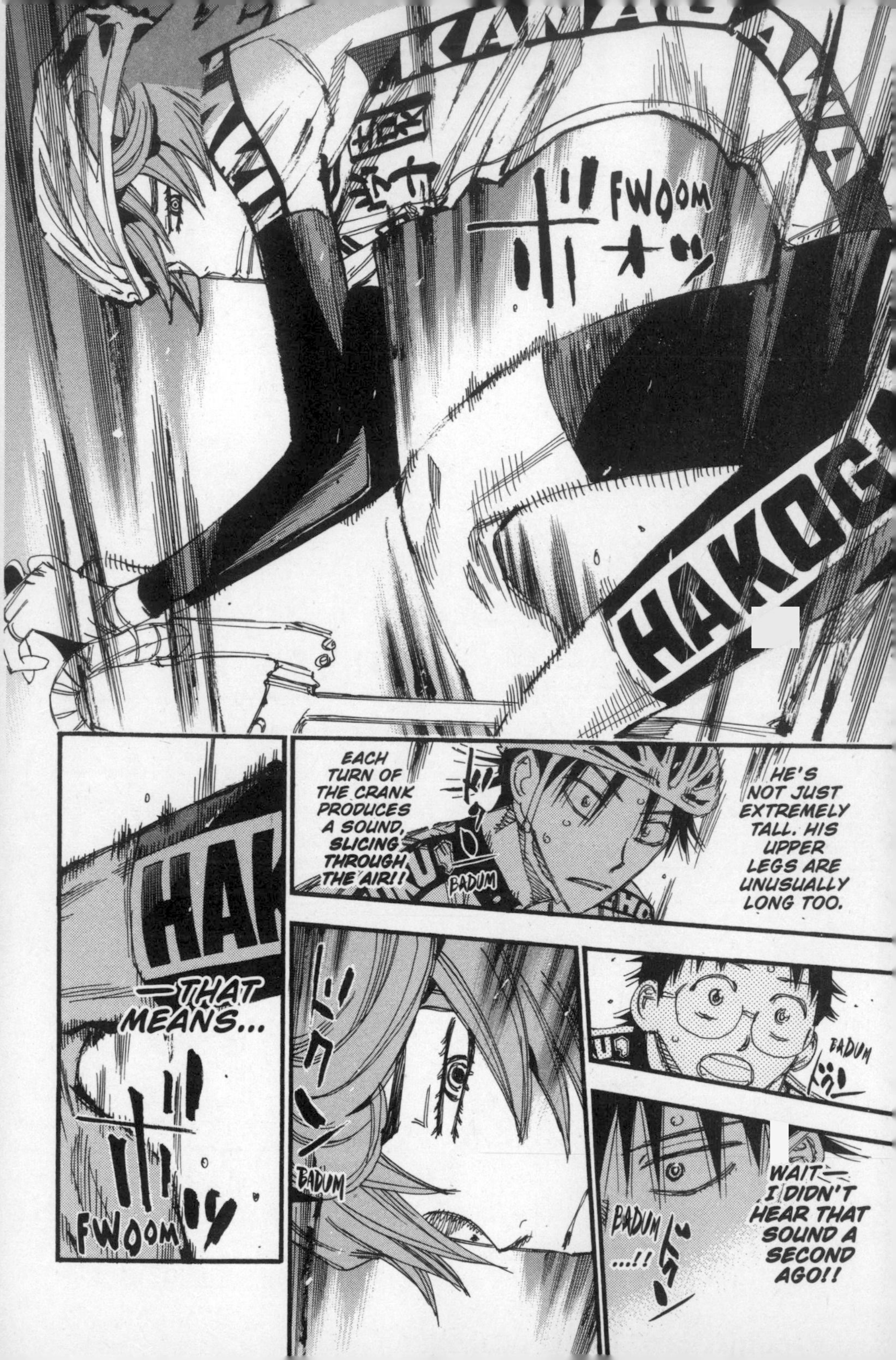
FWOOM
HE'S NOT JUST EXTREMELY TALL. HIS UPPER LEGS ARE UNUSUALLY LONG TOO.
EACH TURN OF THE CRANK PRODUCES A SOUND, SLICING THROUGH THE AIR!!
BADUM
BADUM
WAIT I DIDN'T HEAR THAT SOUND A SECOND AGO!!
BADUM
...!!
BADUM
—THAT MEANS...
FWOOM

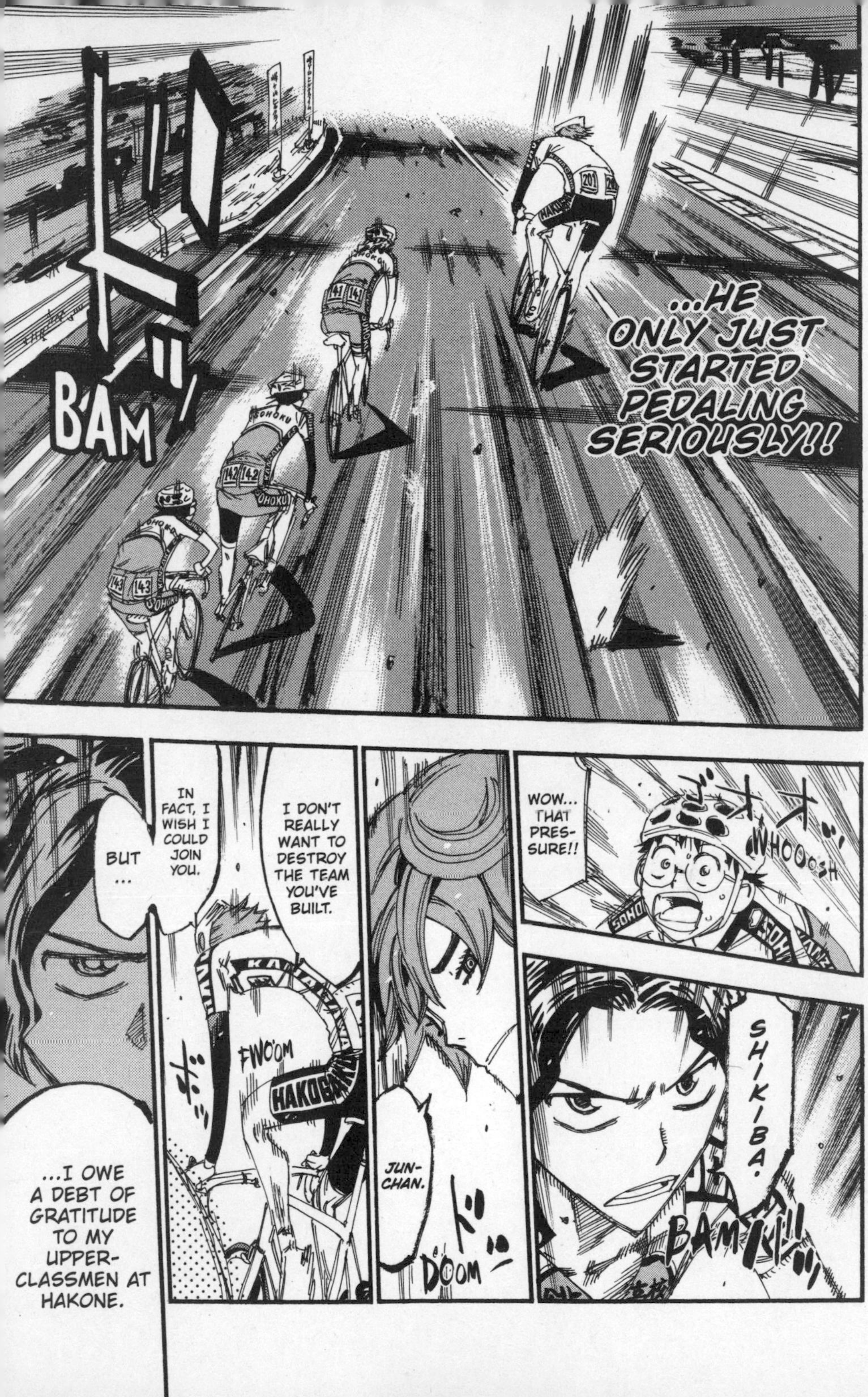
...HE ONLY JUST STARTED PEDALING SERIOUSLY!!
BAM
WOW... THAT PRESSURE!!
WHOOOSH
SHIKIBA.
BAM!!
JUN-CHAN.
DOOM
I DON'T REALLY WANT TO DESTROY THE TEAM YOU'VE BUILT.
IN FACT, I WISH I COULD JOIN YOU.
FWOOM
BUT...
...I OWE A DEBT OF GRATITUDE TO MY UPPERCLASSMEN AT HAKONE.

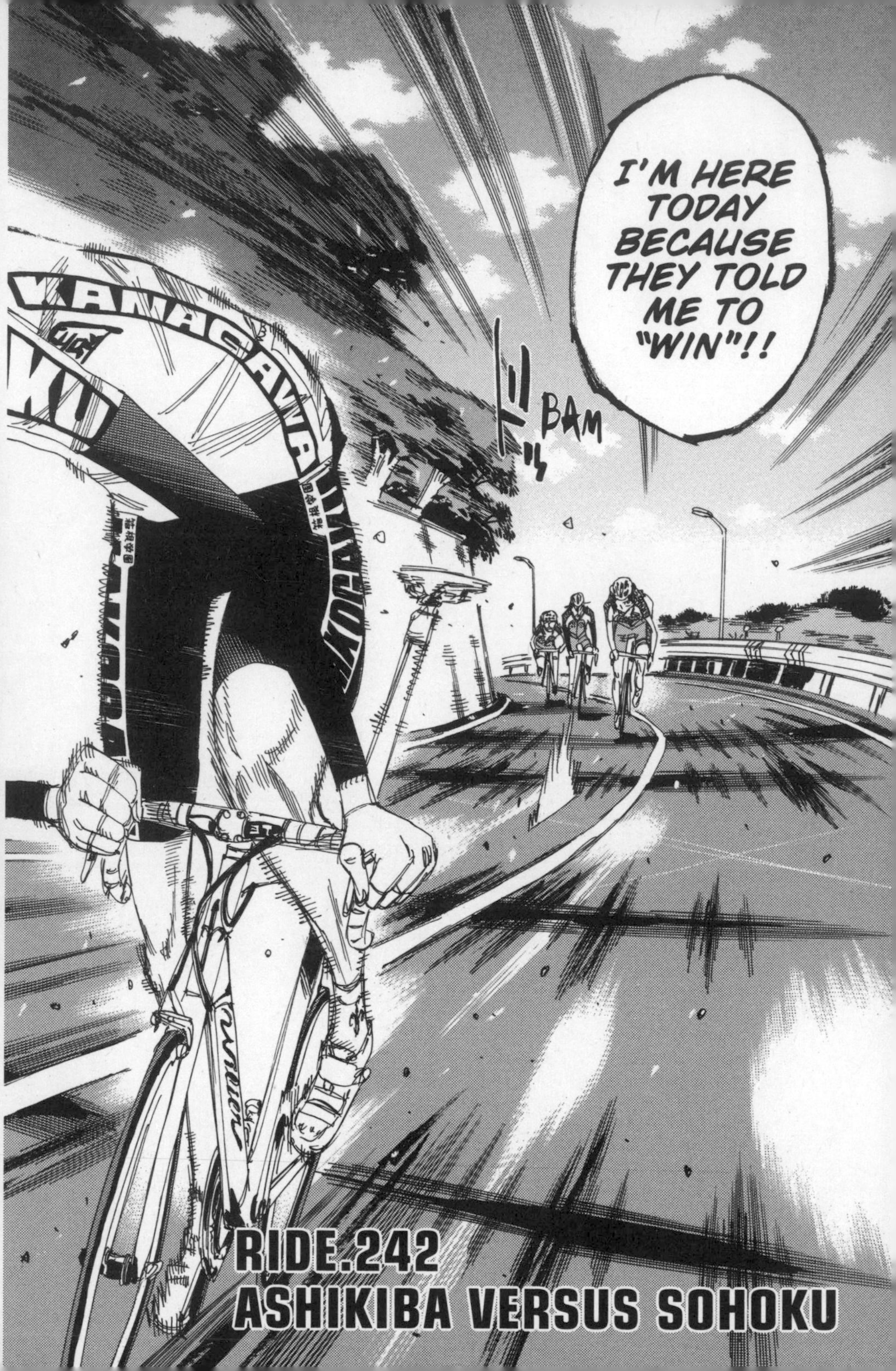
I'M HERE TODAY BECAUSE THEY TOLD ME TO "WIN"!!
BAM
RIDE.242
ASHIKIBA VERSUS SOHOKU

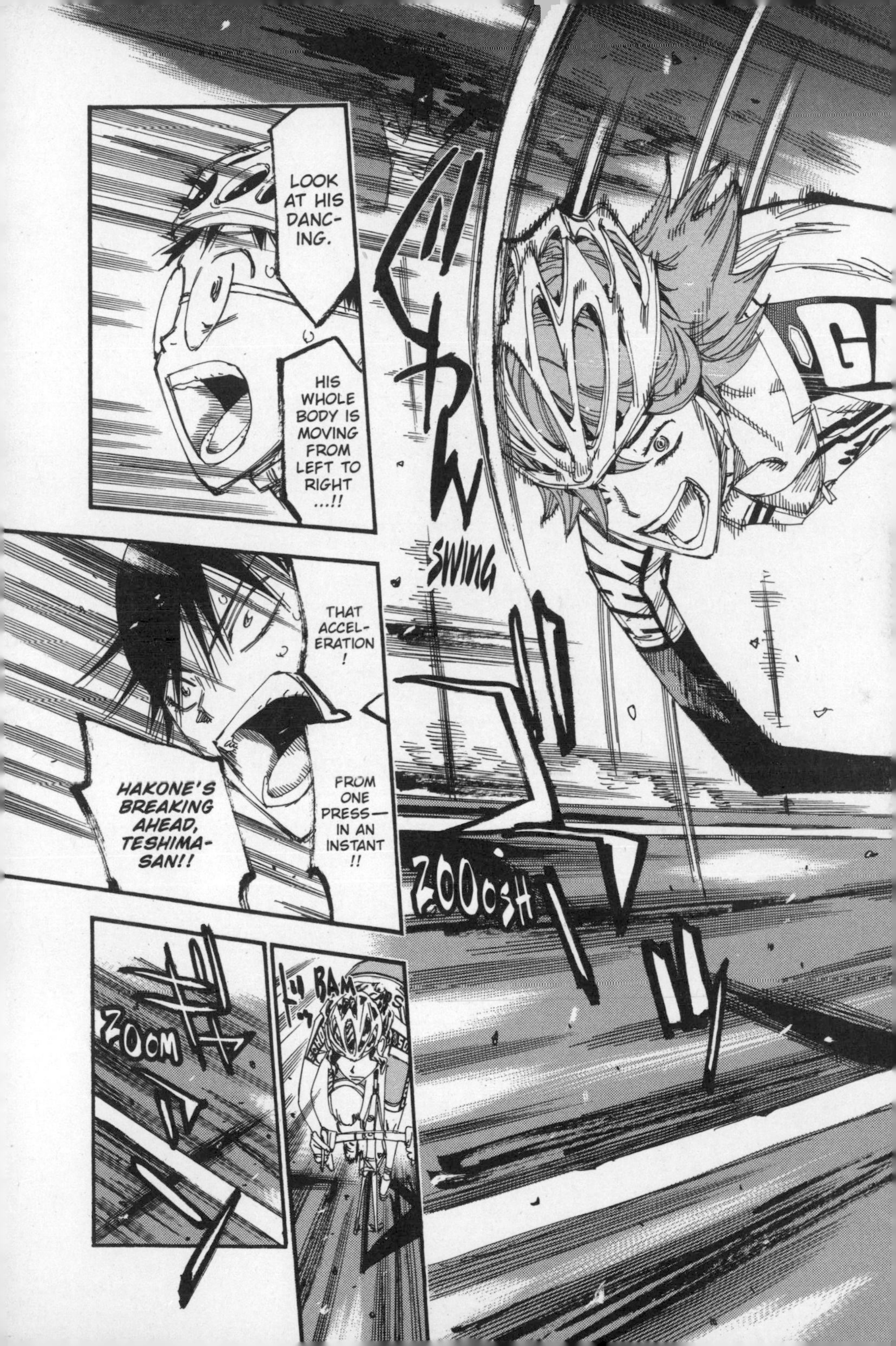
SWING
LOOK AT HIS DANC- ING.
HIS WHOLE BODY IS MOVING FROM LEFT TO RIGHT ...!!
THAT ACCEL- ERATION !
FROM ONE PRESS— IN AN INSTANT !!
HAKONE'S BREAKING AHEAD, TESHIMA- SAN!!
ZOOOSH
BAM
ZOOM

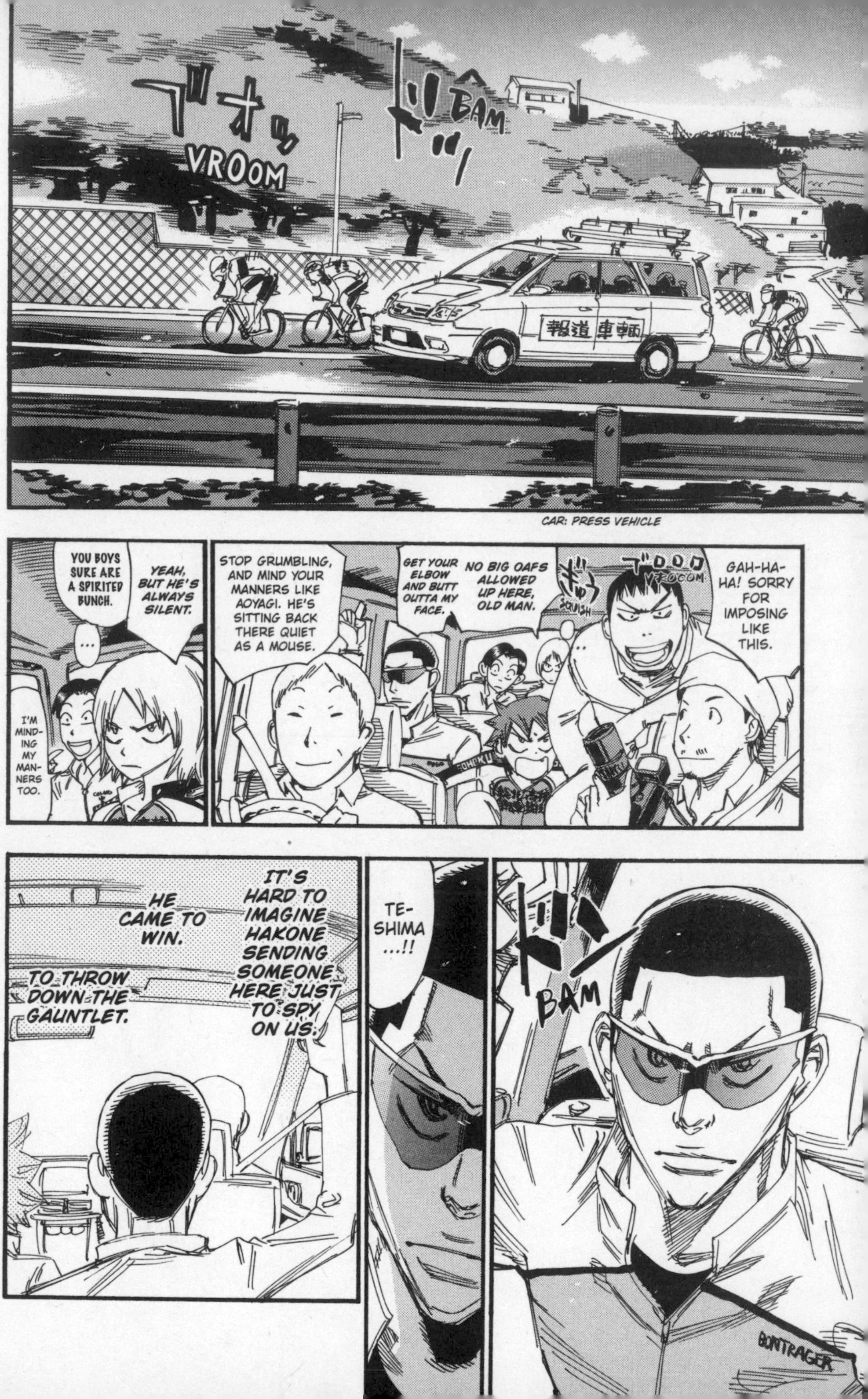
BAM
VROOM
CAR: PRESS VEHICLE
GAH-HA-HA! SORRY FOR IMPOSING LIKE THIS.
VROOOM
SQUISH
NO BIG OAFS ALLOWED UP HERE, OLD MAN.
GET YOUR ELBOW AND BUTT OUTTA MY FACE.
STOP GRUMBLING, AND MIND YOUR MANNERS LIKE AOYAGI. HE'S SITTING BACK THERE QUIET AS A MOUSE.
YEAH, BUT HE'S ALWAYS SILENT.
YOU BOYS SURE ARE A SPIRITED BUNCH.
...
I'M MINDING MY MANNERS TOO.
BAM
TE-SHIMA ...!!
IT'S HARD TO IMAGINE HAKONE SENDING SOMEONE HERE JUST TO SPY ON US.
HE CAME TO WIN.
TO THROW DOWN THE GAUNTLET.

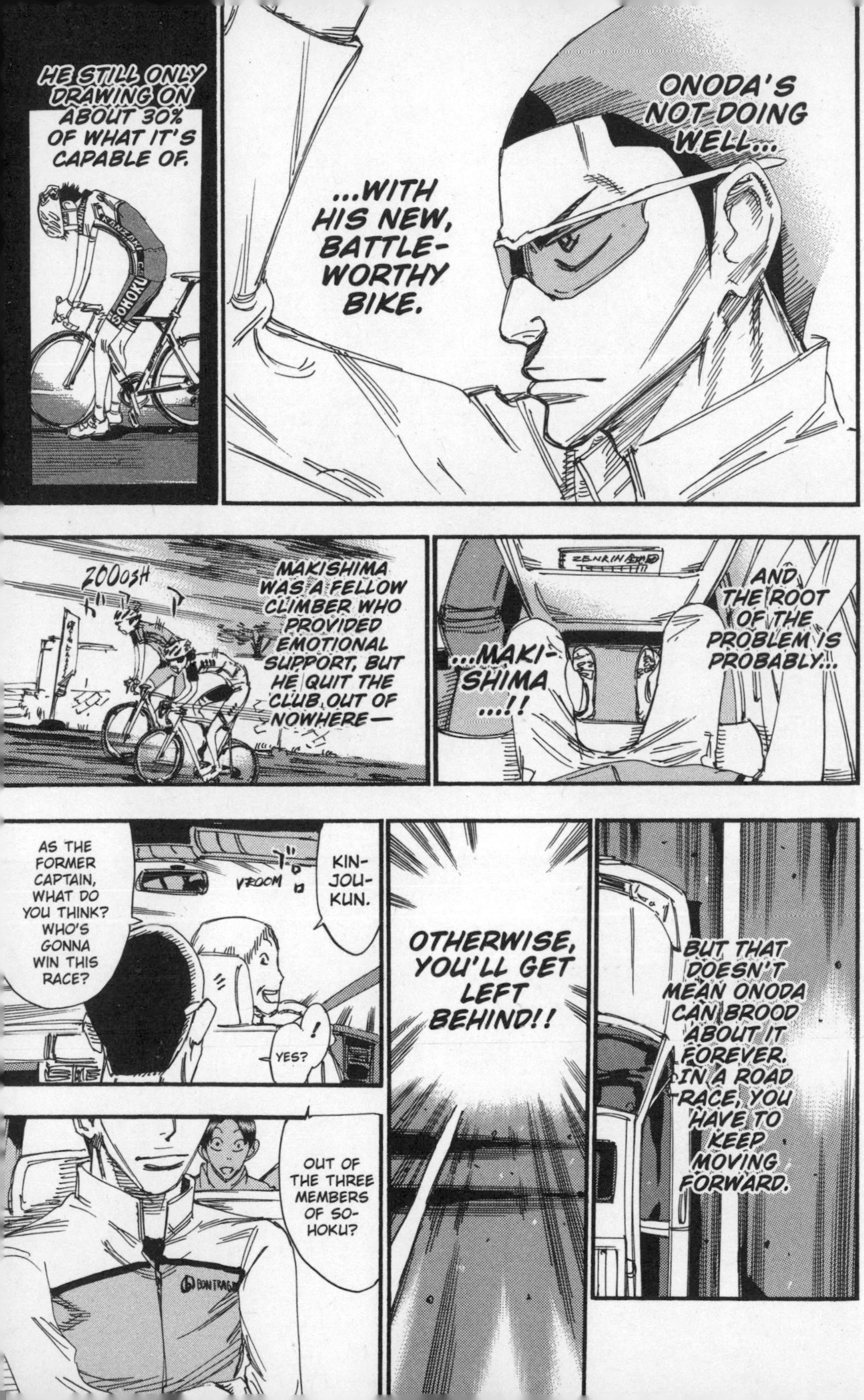
ONODA'S NOT DOING WELL...
...WITH HIS NEW, BATTLE-WORTHY BIKE.
HE STILL ONLY DRAWING ON ABOUT 30% OF WHAT IT'S CAPABLE OF.
AND THE ROOT OF THE PROBLEM IS PROBABLY...
...MAKI-SHIMA ...!!
MAKISHIMA WAS A FELLOW CLIMBER WHO PROVIDED EMOTIONAL SUPPORT, BUT HE QUIT THE CLUB OUT OF NOWHERE—
ZOOOSH
BUT THAT DOESN'T MEAN ONODA CAN BROOD ABOUT IT FOREVER. IN A ROAD RACE, YOU HAVE TO KEEP MOVING FORWARD.
OTHERWISE, YOU'LL GET LEFT BEHIND!!
KIN-JOU-KUN.
VROOM
AS THE FORMER CAPTAIN, WHAT DO YOU THINK? WHO'S GONNA WIN THIS RACE?
!
YES?
OUT OF THE THREE MEMBERS OF SO-HOKU?

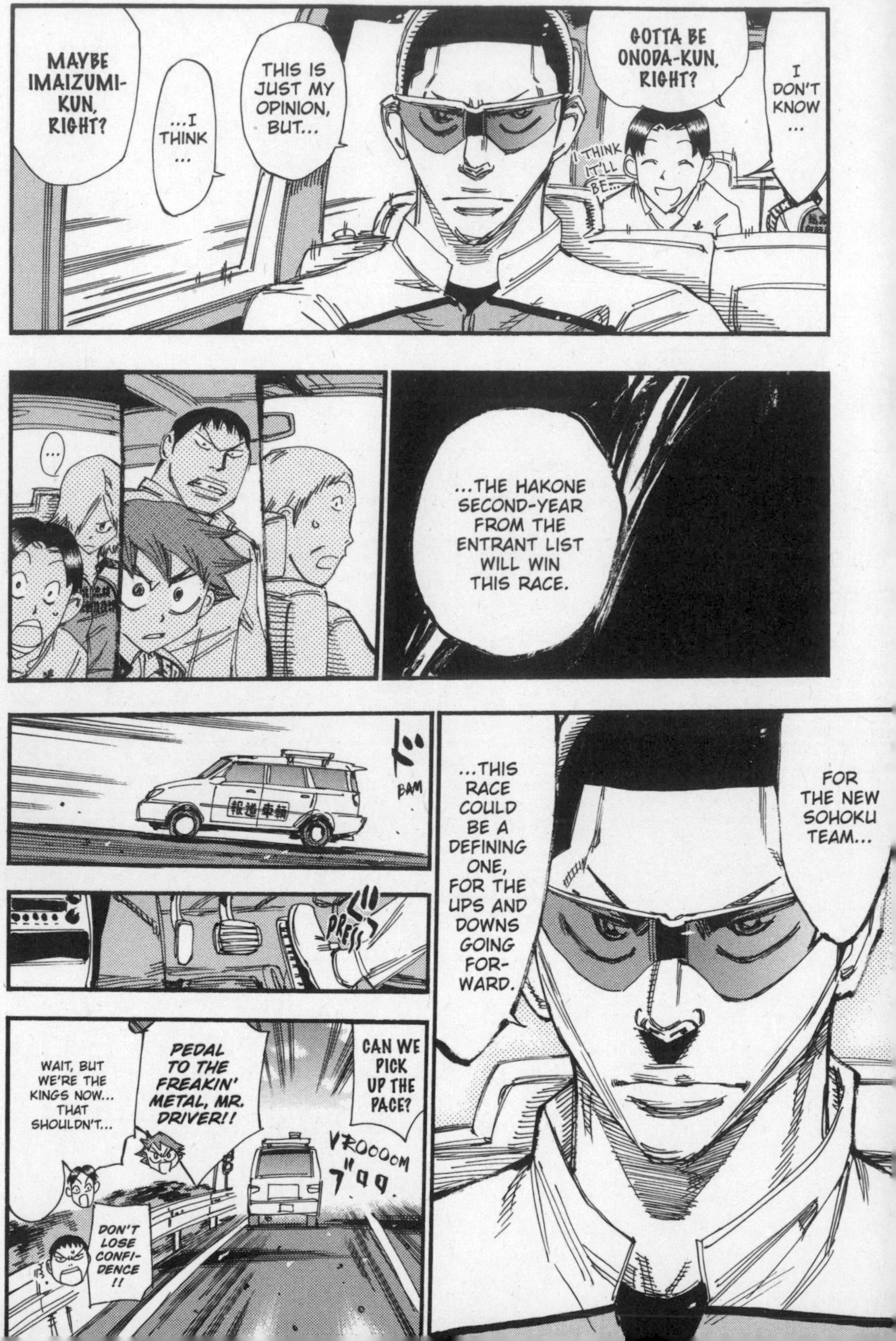
I DON'T KNOW ...
GOTTA BE ONODA-KUN, RIGHT?
I THINK IT'LL BE...
THIS IS JUST MY OPINION, BUT...
...I THINK ...
MAYBE IMAIZUMI-KUN, RIGHT?
...THE HAKONE SECOND-YEAR FROM THE ENTRANT LIST WILL WIN THIS RACE.
...
FOR THE NEW SOHOKU TEAM...
...THIS RACE COULD BE A DEFINING ONE, FOR THE UPS AND DOWNS GOING FORWARD.
ド
BAM
PRESS
CAN WE PICK UP THE PACE?
PEDAL TO THE FREAKIN' METAL, MR. DRIVER!!
WAIT, BUT WE'RE THE KINGS NOW... THAT SHOULDN'T...
VROOOOM
DON'T LOSE CONFIDENCE!!

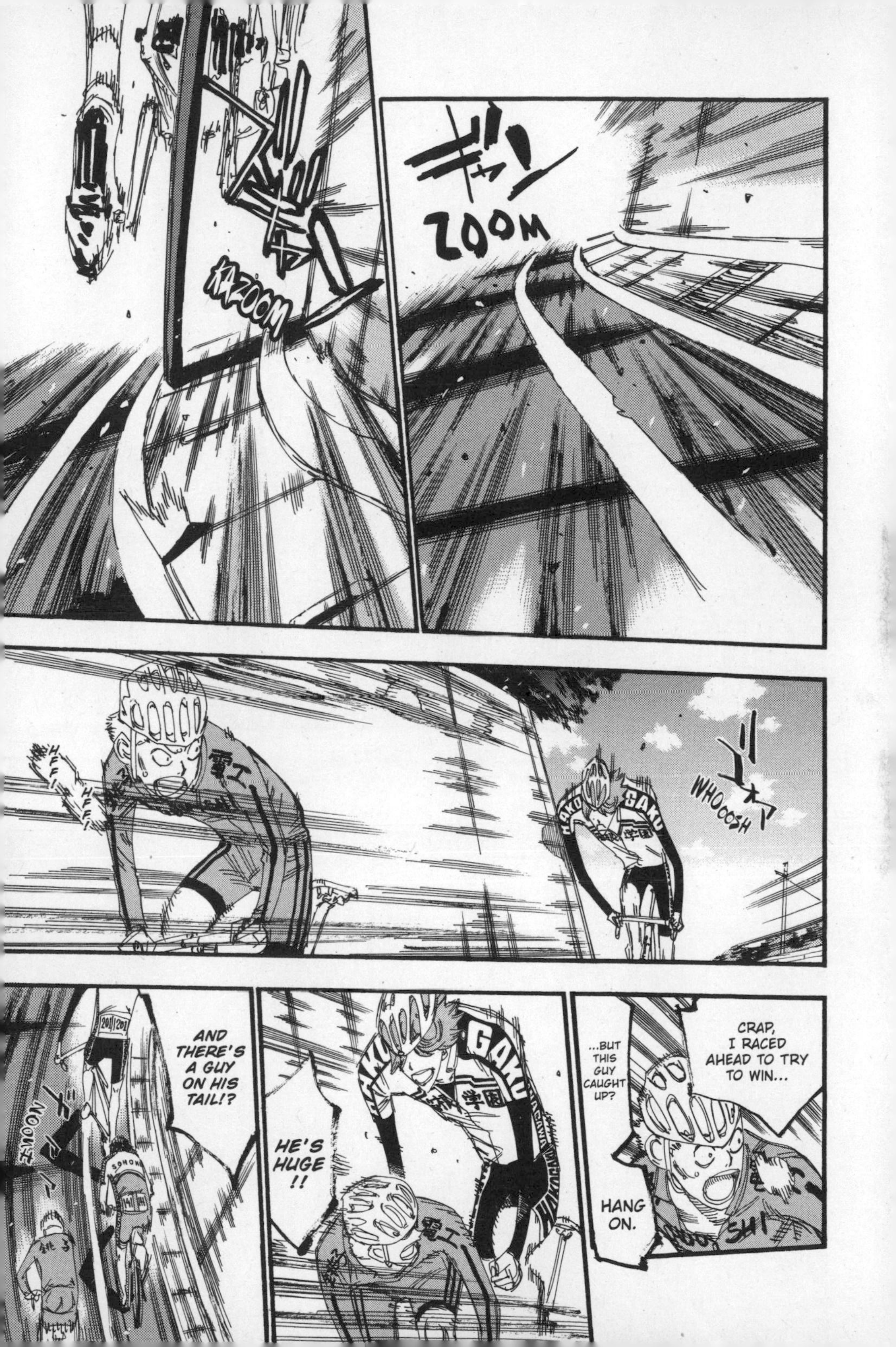
ZOOM
KAZOOM
WHOOOSH
HFF! HFF!
CRAP, I RACED AHEAD TO TRY TO WIN...
...BUT THIS GUY CAUGHT UP?
HANG ON.
HE'S HUGE!!
AND THERE'S A GUY ON HIS TAIL!?

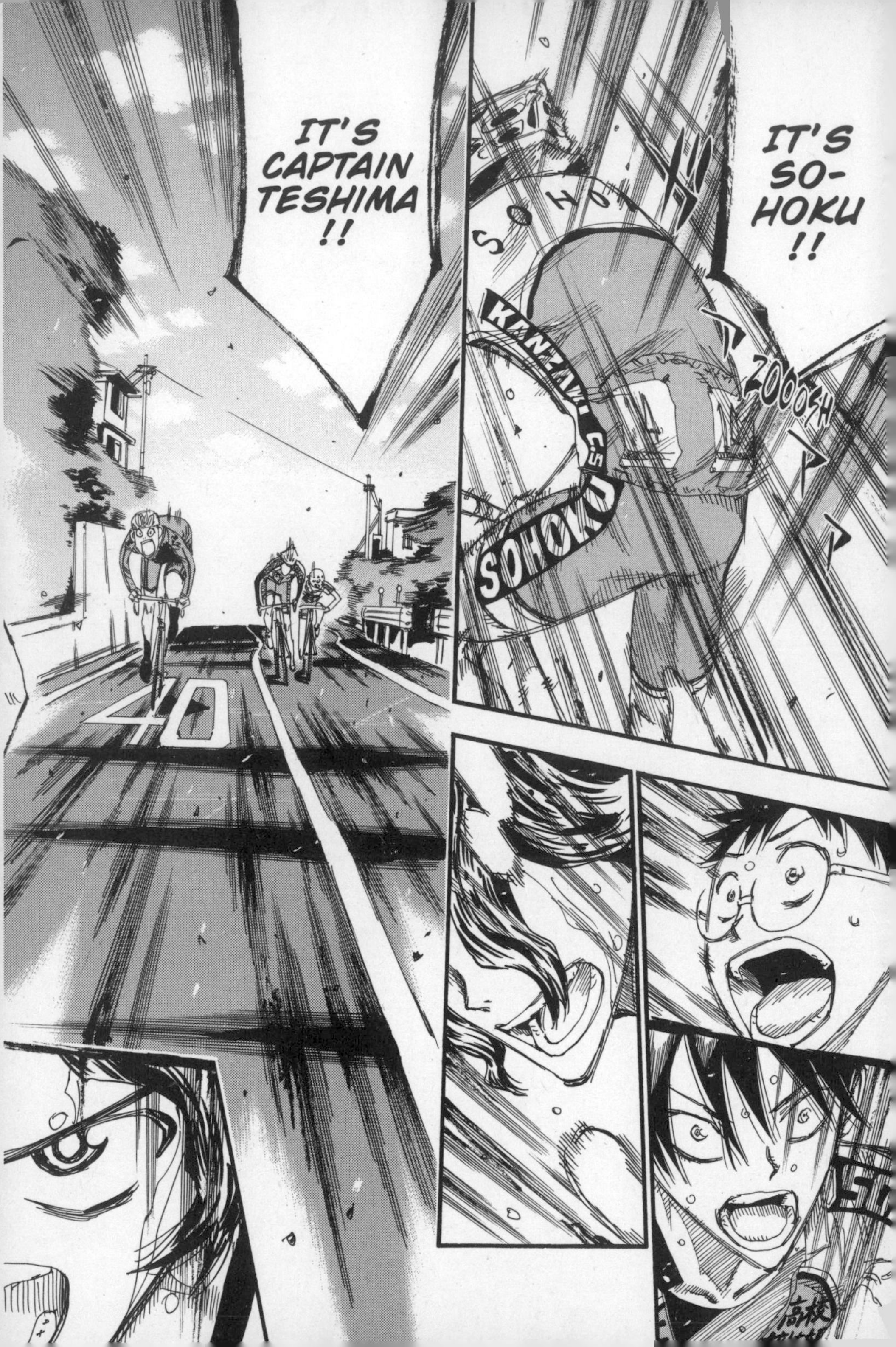
IT'S SO-HOKU!!
ZOOOSH
SOHOKU
IT'S CAPTAIN TESHIMA!!
40

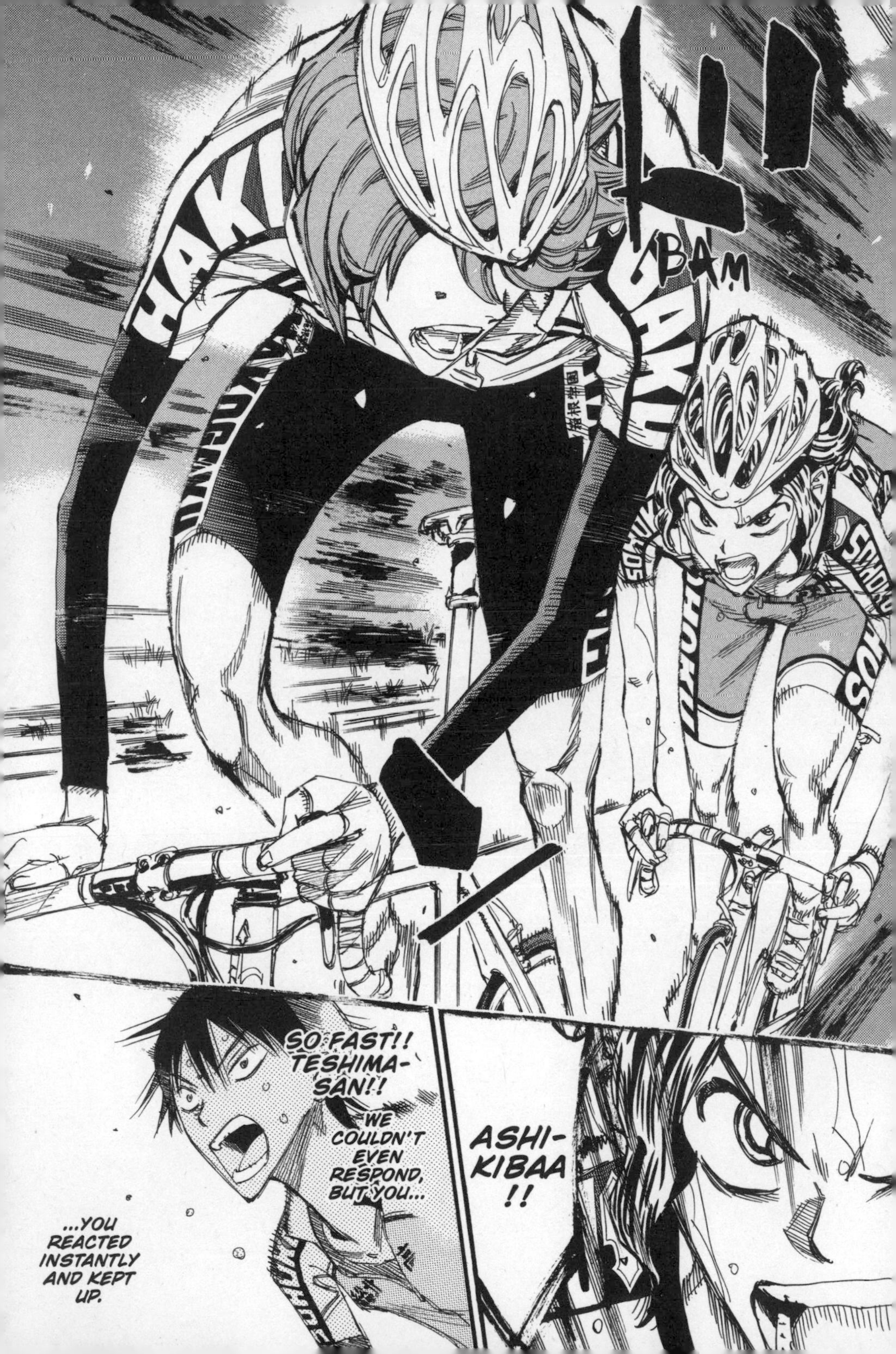
!!
BAM
ASHI-KIBAA!!
SO FAST!! TESHIMA-SAN!!
WE COULDN'T EVEN RESPOND, BUT YOU...
...YOU REACTED INSTANTLY AND KEPT UP.

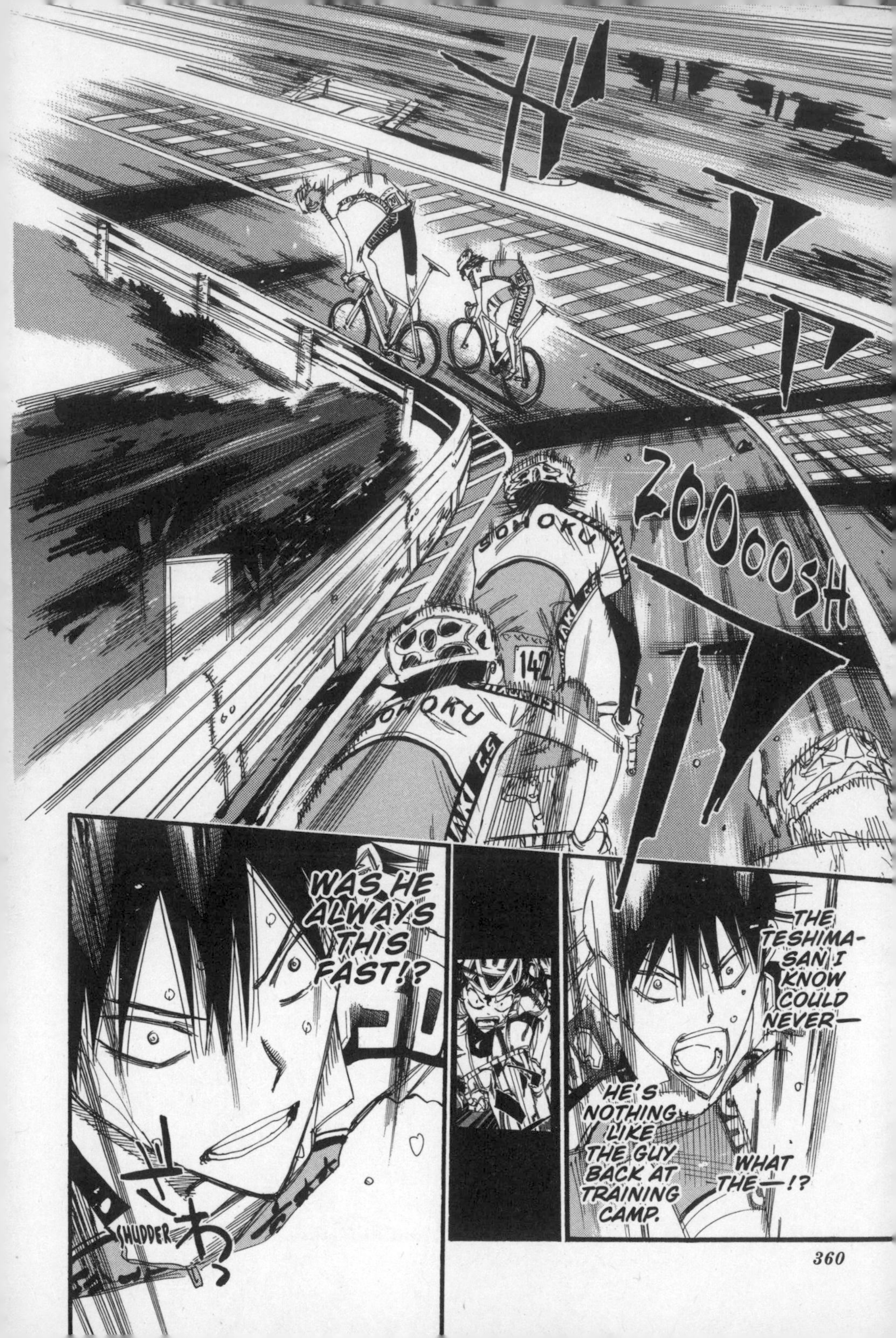
ZOOOOSH
THE TESHIMA-SAN I KNOW COULD NEVER—
WHAT THE—!?
HE'S NOTHING LIKE THE GUY BACK AT TRAINING CAMP.
WAS HE ALWAYS THIS FAST!?
SHUDDER

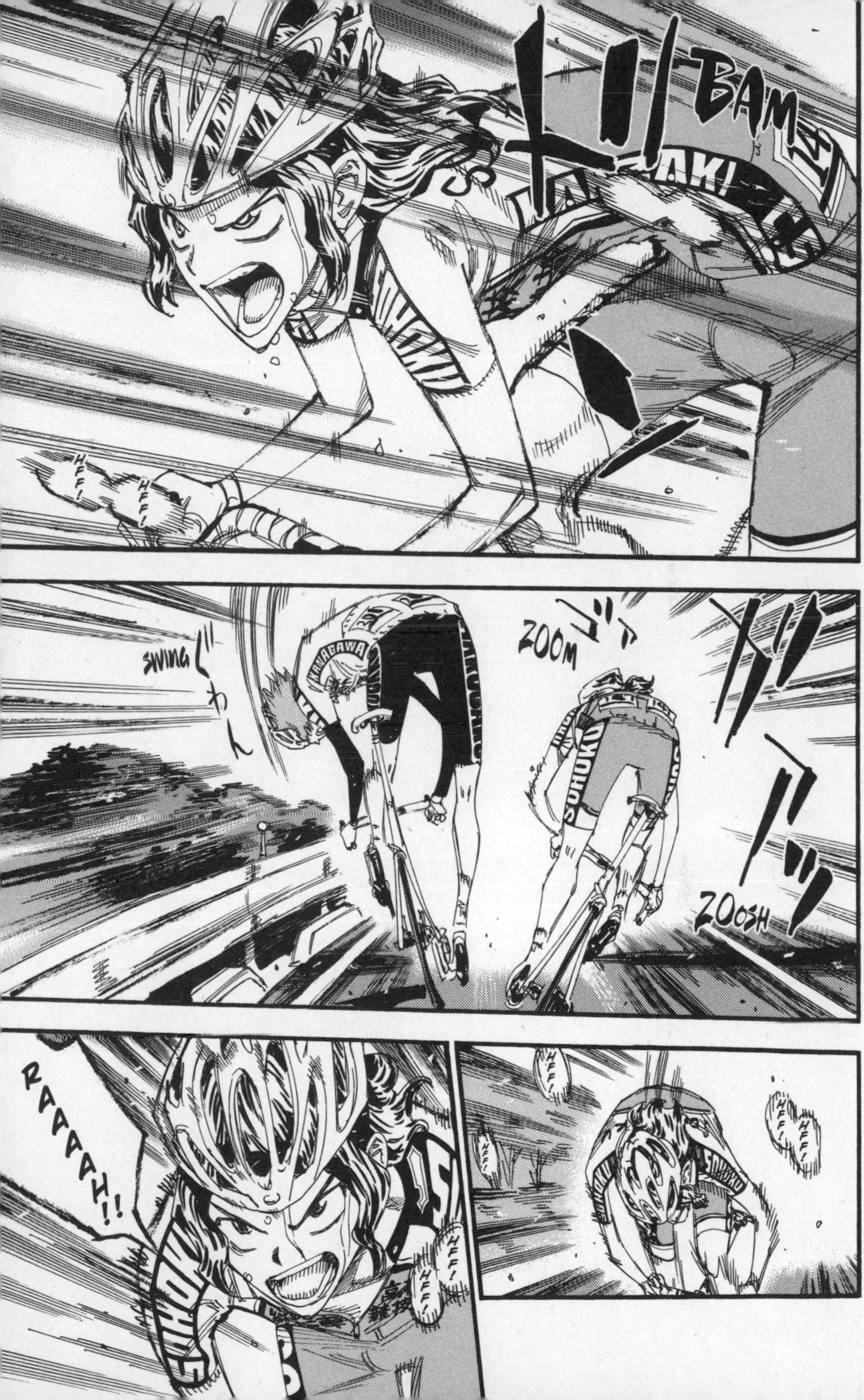
BAM
HFF!
HFF!
SWING
ZOOM
ZOOSH!
HFF!
HFF!
HFF!
HFF!
RAAAAH!!
HFF!
HFF!

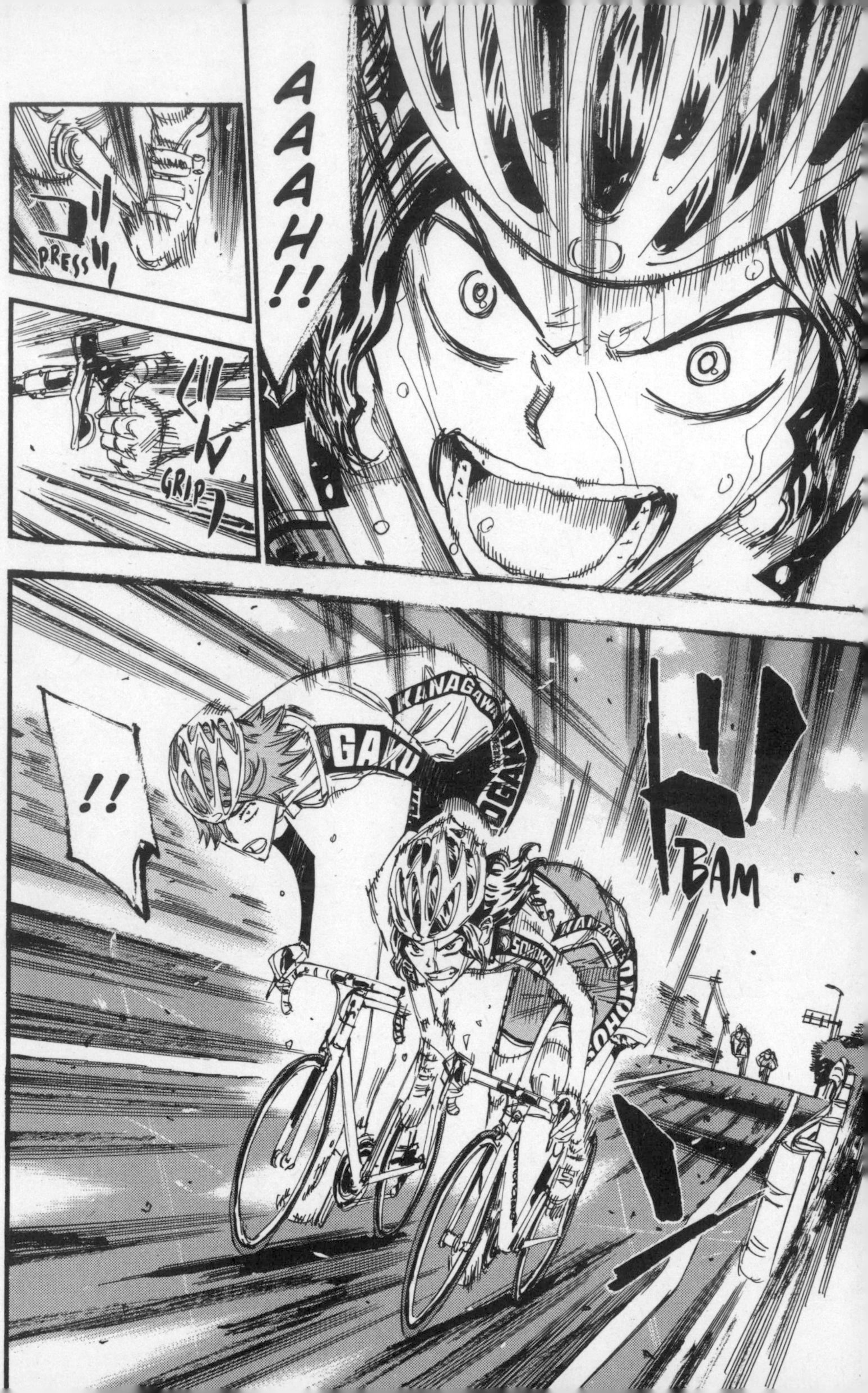
AAAAH!!
PRESS
GRIP
BAM
!!
KANAGAWA
GAKU
SOHOKU

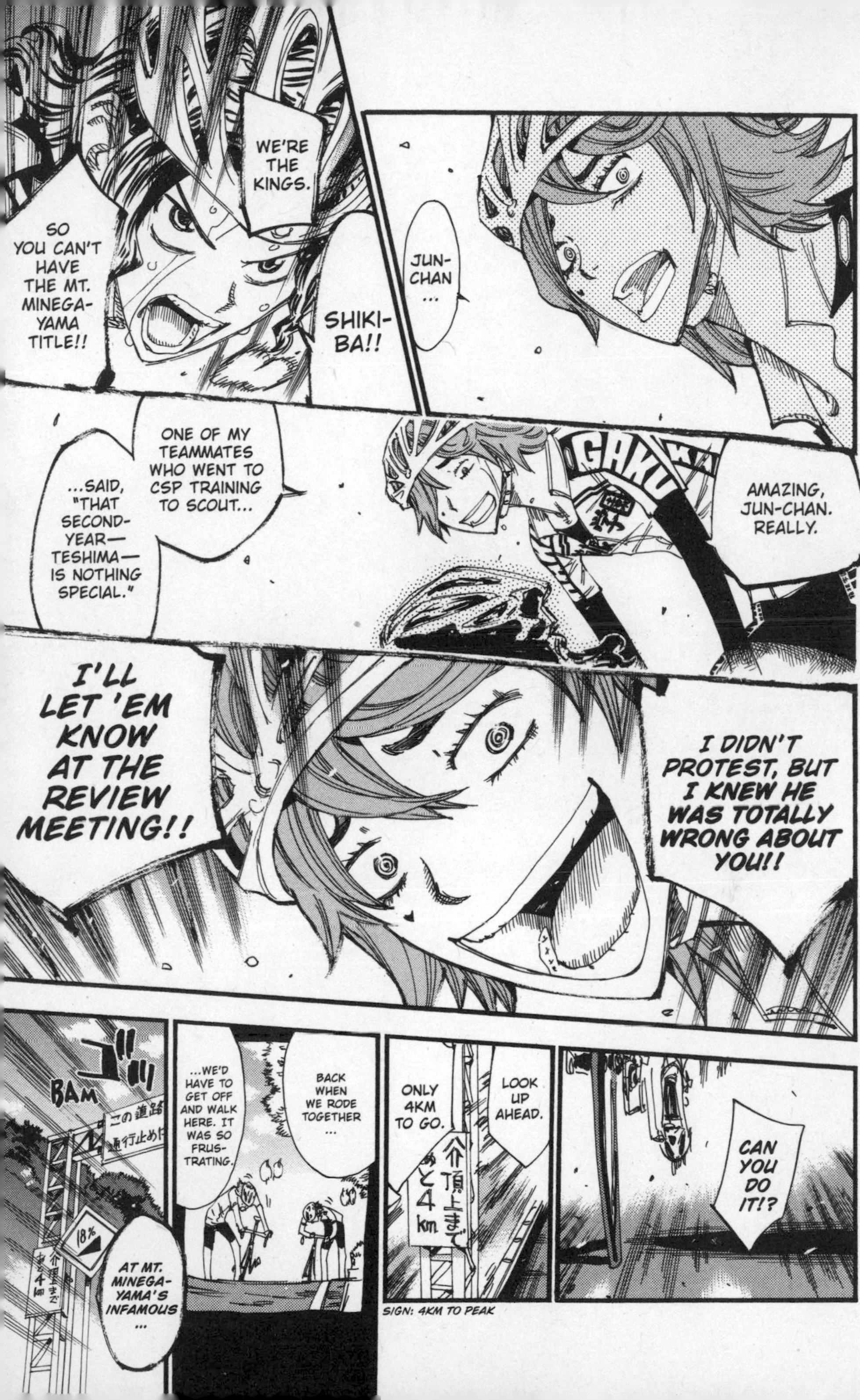
JUN-CHAN...
SHIKI-BA!!
WE'RE THE KINGS.
SO YOU CAN'T HAVE THE MT. MINEGA-YAMA TITLE!!
AMAZING, JUN-CHAN. REALLY.
ONE OF MY TEAMMATES WHO WENT TO CSP TRAINING TO SCOUT...
...SAID, "THAT SECOND-YEAR—TESHIMA—IS NOTHING SPECIAL."
I DIDN'T PROTEST, BUT I KNEW HE WAS TOTALLY WRONG ABOUT YOU!!
I'LL LET 'EM KNOW AT THE REVIEW MEETING!!
CAN YOU DO IT!?
LOOK UP AHEAD.
ONLY 4KM TO GO.
BACK WHEN WE RODE TOGETHER...
AT MT. MINEGAYAMA'S INFAMOUS...
...WE'D HAVE TO GET OFF AND WALK HERE. IT WAS SO FRUS-TRATING.
BAM
18%
SIGN: 4KM TO PEAK

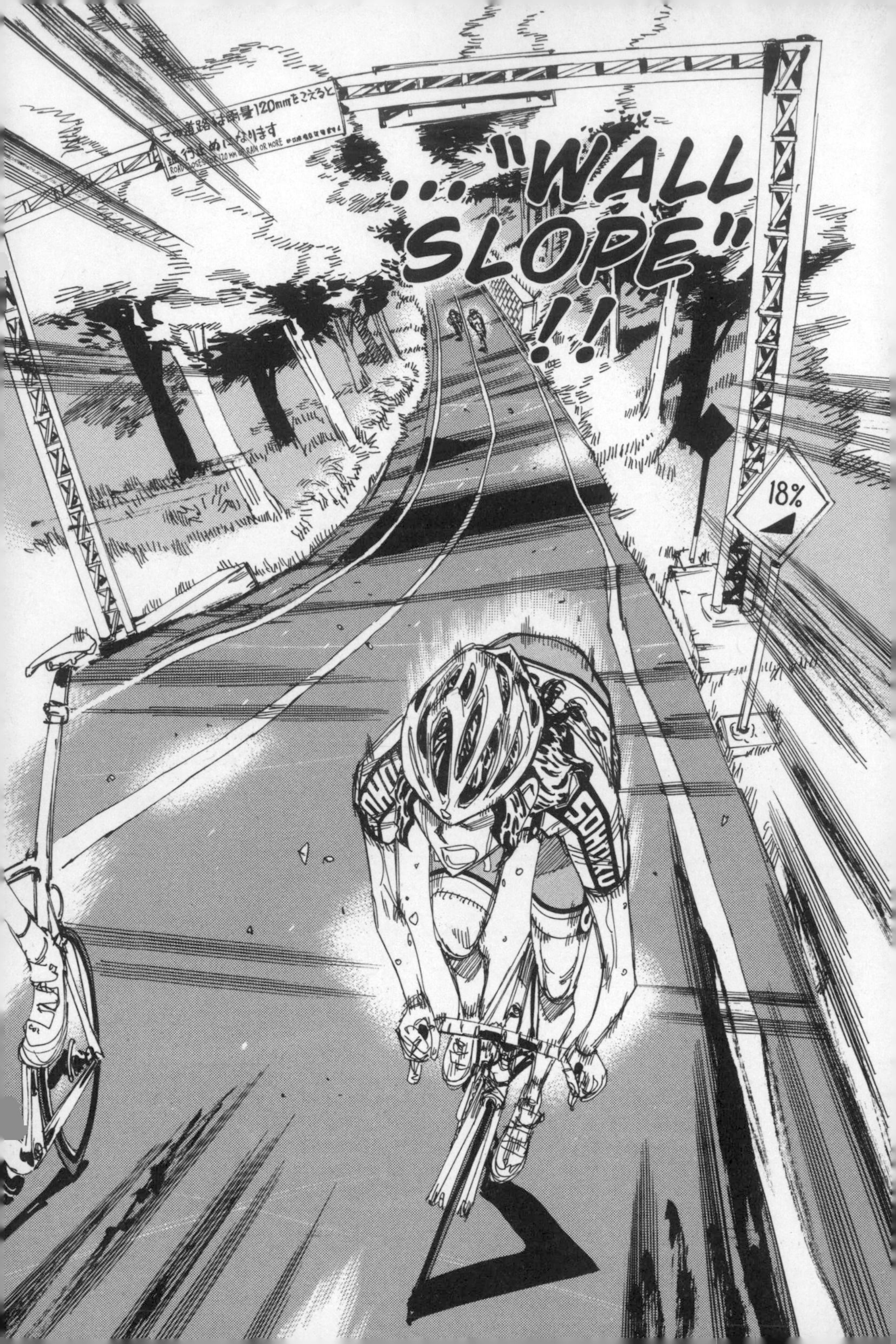
..."WALL SLOPE"!!
18%

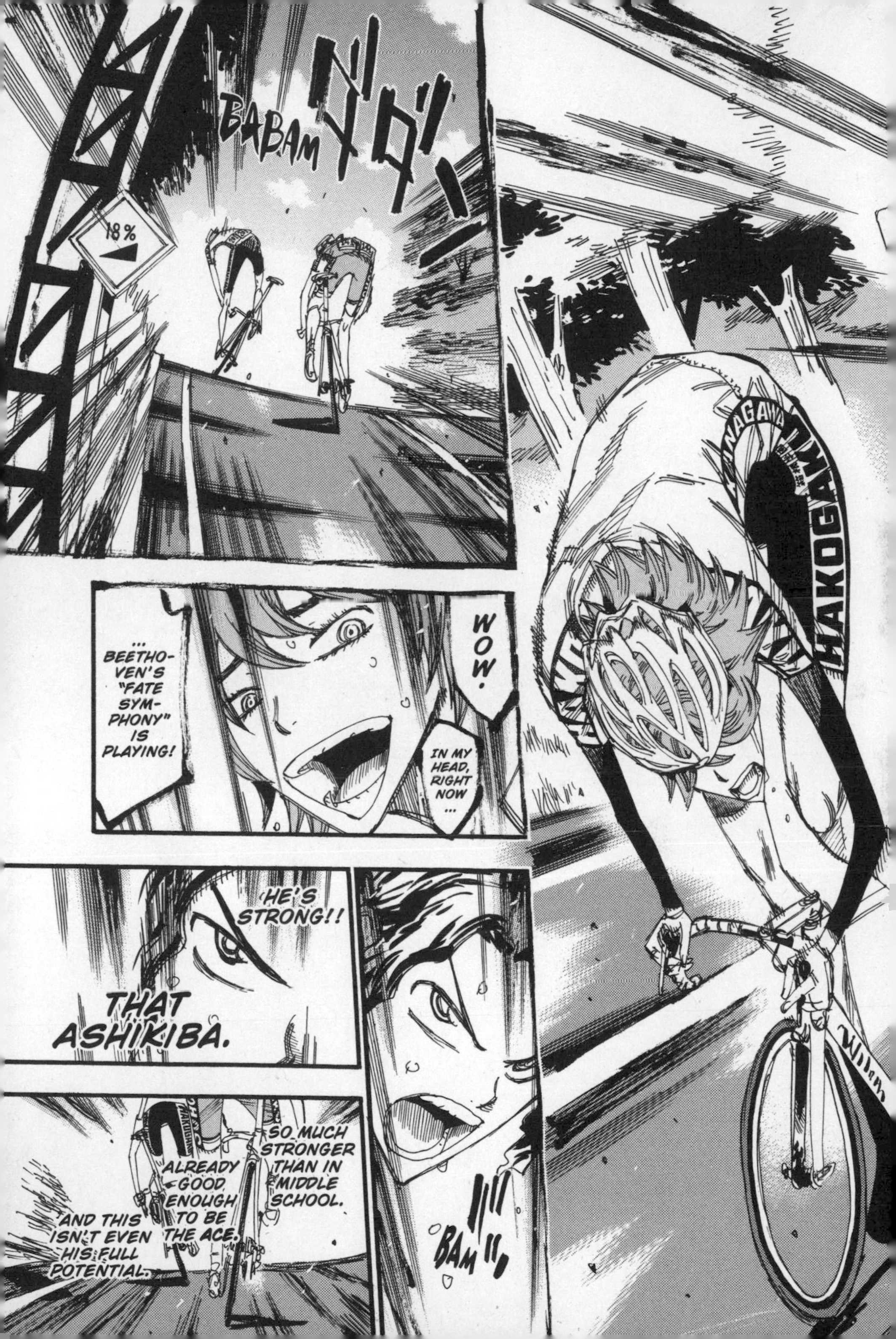
BABAM
18%
WOW.
IN MY HEAD, RIGHT NOW...
...BEETHOVEN'S "FATE SYMPHONY" IS PLAYING!
BAM
HE'S STRONG!!
THAT ASHIKIBA.
SO MUCH STRONGER THAN IN MIDDLE SCHOOL.
ALREADY GOOD ENOUGH TO BE THE ACE.
AND THIS ISN'T EVEN HIS FULL POTENTIAL.

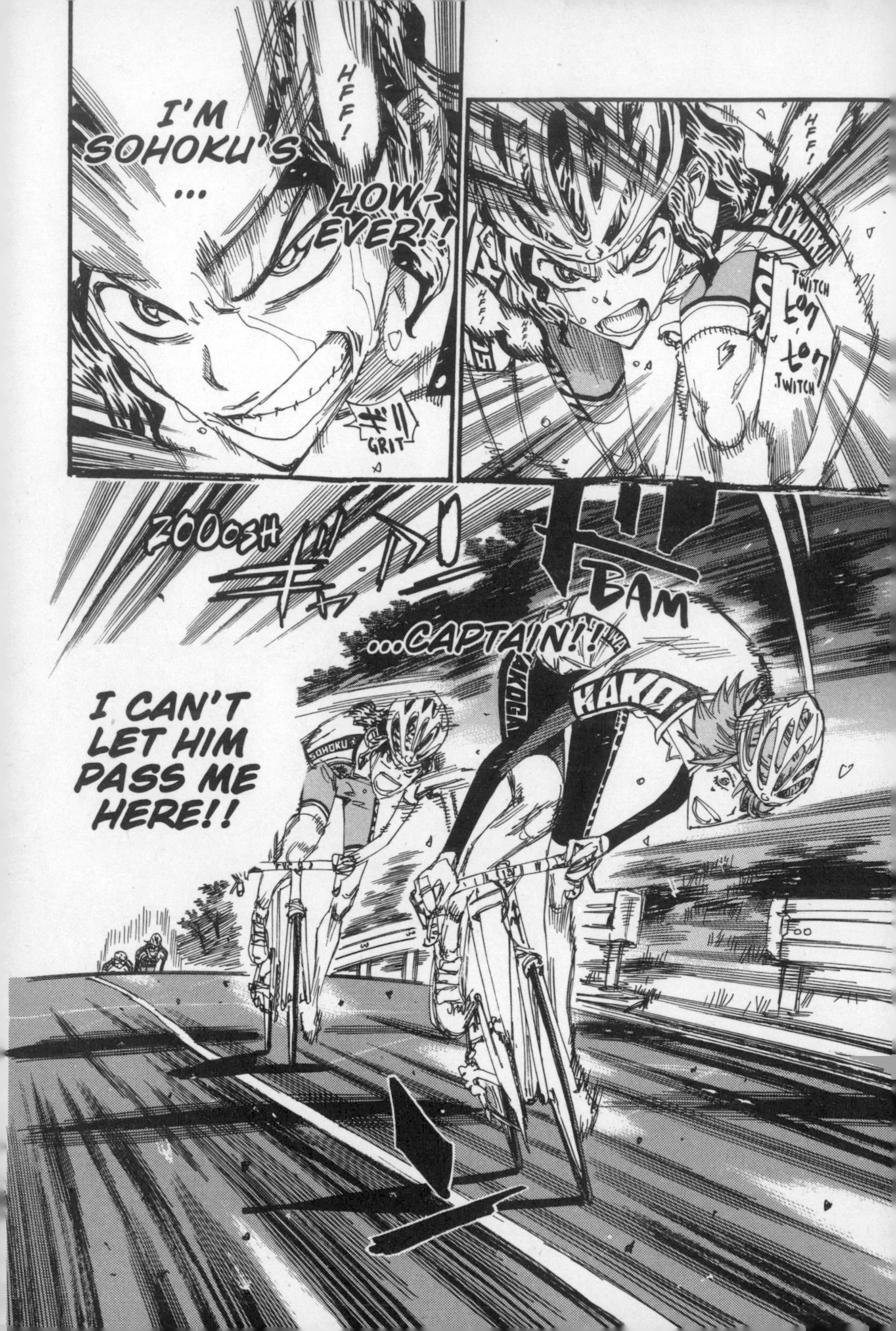
HFF!
HFF!
TWITCH
TWITCH
HFF!
I'M SOHOKU'S ...
HOW-EVER!!
GRIT
BAM
...CAPTAIN!!
ZOOOSH
I CAN'T LET HIM PASS ME HERE!!

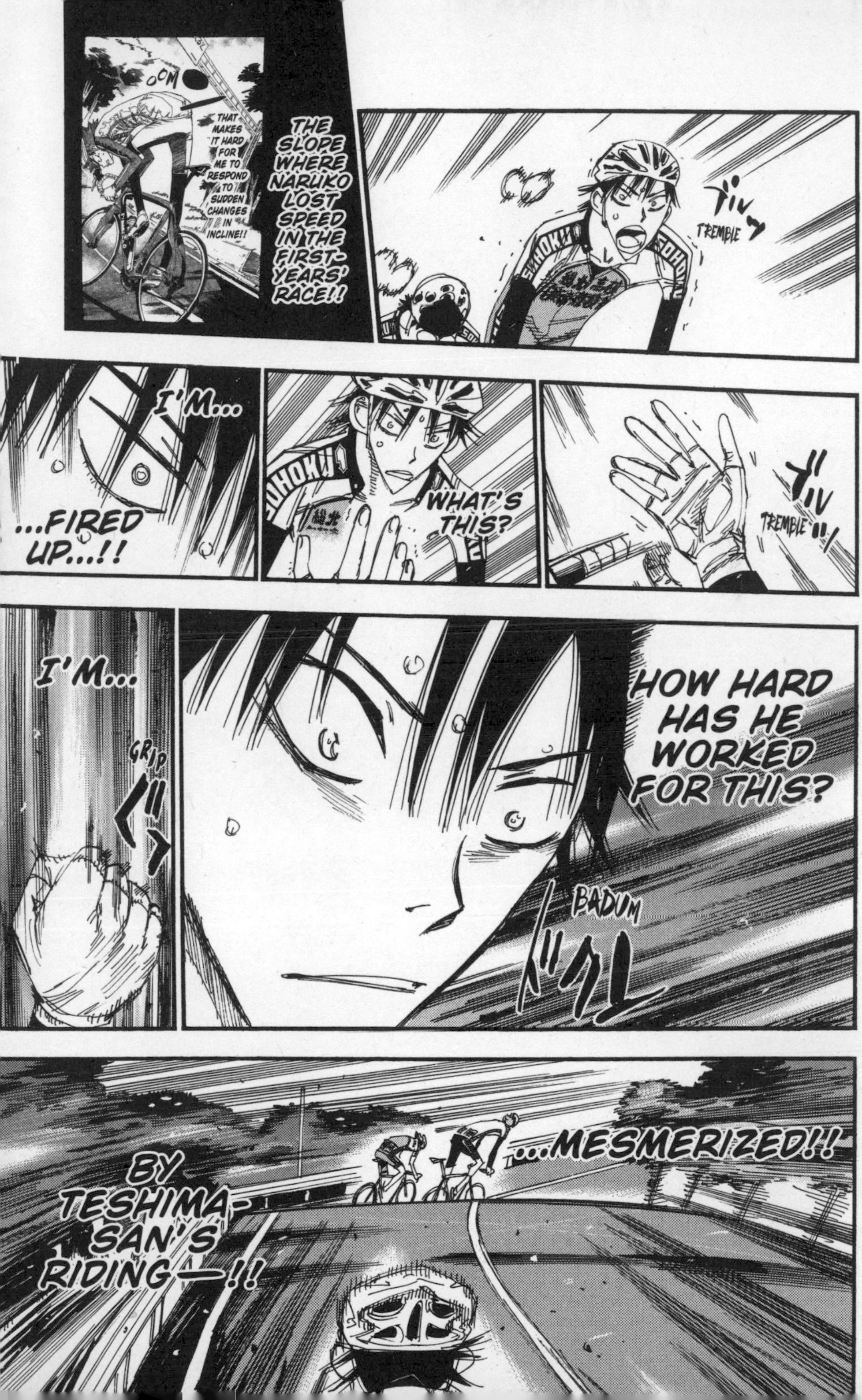
TREMBLE
THE SLOPE WHERE NARUKO LOST SPEED IN THE FIRST-YEARS' RACE!!
OOM
THAT MAKES IT HARD FOR ME TO RESPOND TO SUDDEN CHANGES IN INCLINE!!
TREMBLE
WHAT'S THIS?
I'M...
...FIRED UP...!!
HOW HARD HAS HE WORKED FOR THIS?
BADUM
I'M...
GRIP
...MESMERIZED!!
BY TESHIMA-SAN'S RIDING—!!

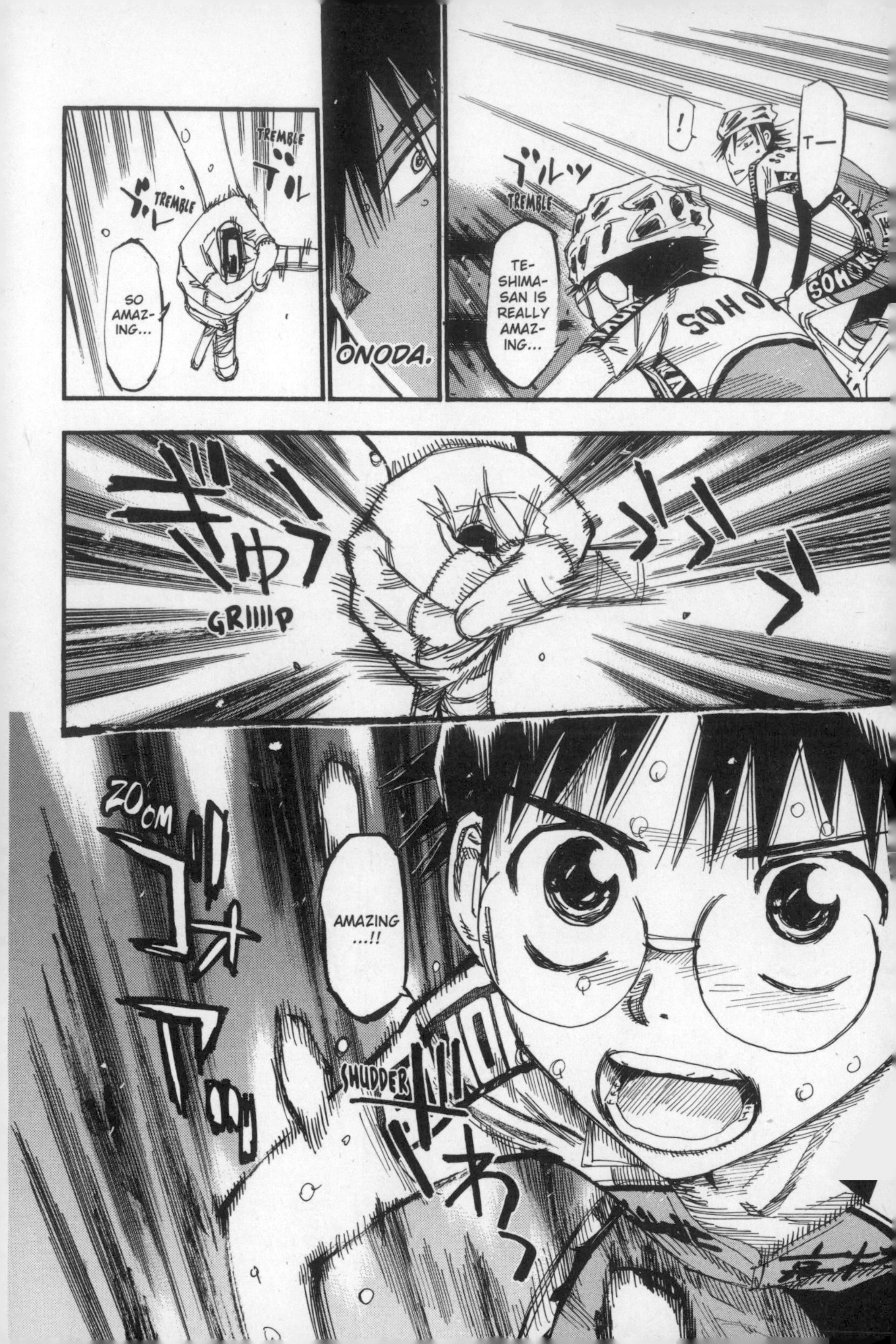
!
T—
ブルッ
TREMBLE
TE-SHIMA-SAN IS REALLY AMAZ-ING...
ONODA.
TREMBLE
ブル
TREMBLE
SO AMAZ-ING...
ぎゅっ
GRIIIIP
SHUDDER
AMAZING ...!!
ZOOM

RIDE.243 TESHIMA'S SPIRITED RIDE

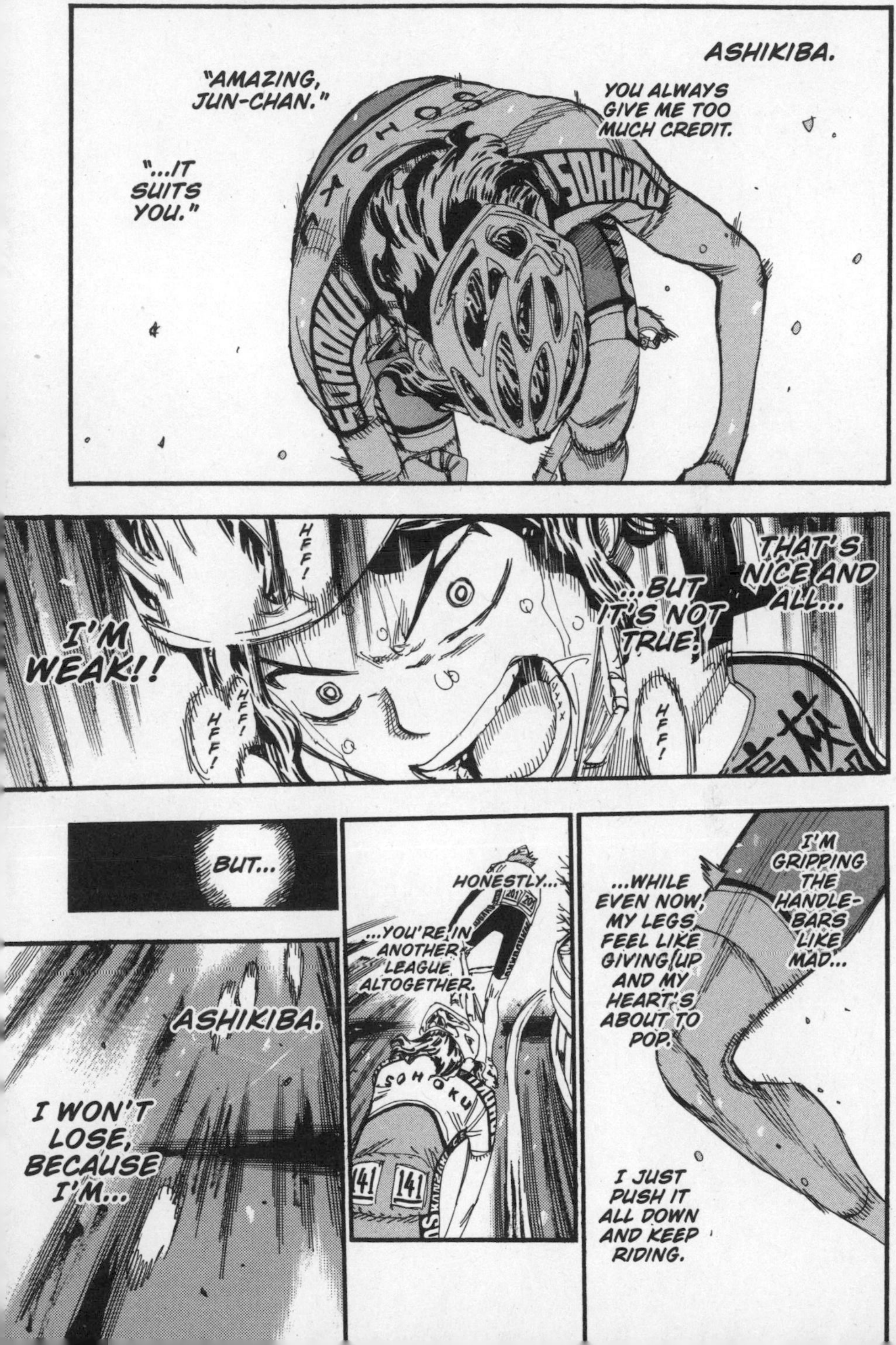
ASHIKIBA.
YOU ALWAYS GIVE ME TOO MUCH CREDIT.
"AMAZING, JUN-CHAN."
"...IT SUITS YOU."
THAT'S NICE AND ALL...
...BUT IT'S NOT TRUE!
HFF!
I'M WEAK!!
HFF! HFF!
HFF!
I'M GRIPPING THE HANDLE-BARS LIKE MAD...
...WHILE EVEN NOW, MY LEGS FEEL LIKE GIVING UP AND MY HEART'S ABOUT TO POP.
I JUST PUSH IT ALL DOWN AND KEEP RIDING.
HONESTLY...
...YOU'RE IN ANOTHER LEAGUE ALTOGETHER.
BUT...
ASHIKIBA.
I WON'T LOSE, BECAUSE I'M...

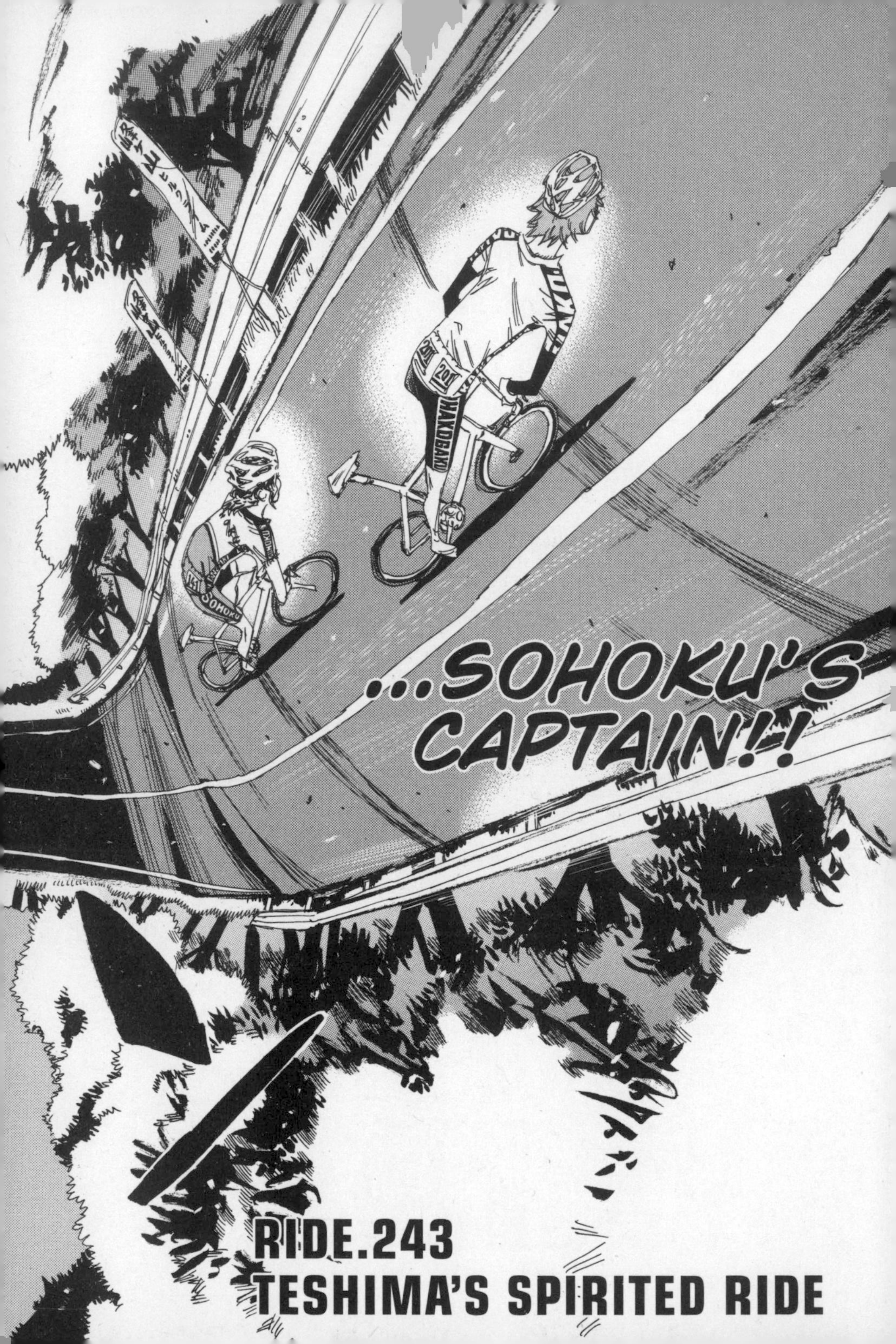
...SOHOKU'S CAPTAIN!!

RIDE.243
TESHIMA'S SPIRITED RIDE

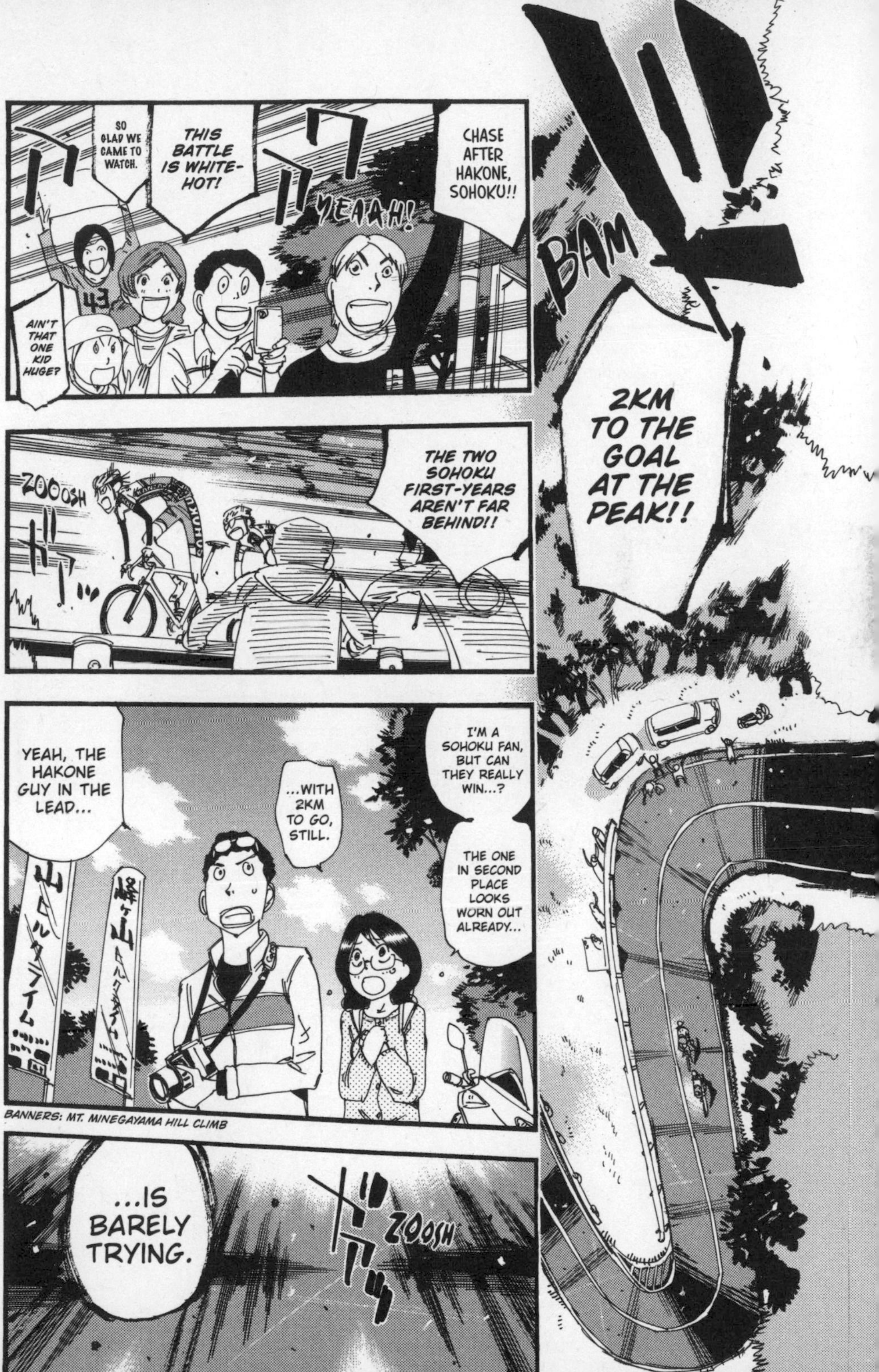
BAM
2KM TO THE GOAL AT THE PEAK!!
CHASE AFTER HAKONE, SOHOKU!!
YEAAAH!
THIS BATTLE IS WHITE-HOT!
SO GLAD WE CAME TO WATCH.
AIN'T THAT ONE KID HUGE?
ZOOOSH
THE TWO SOHOKU FIRST-YEARS AREN'T FAR BEHIND!!
I'M A SOHOKU FAN, BUT CAN THEY REALLY WIN...?
THE ONE IN SECOND PLACE LOOKS WORN OUT ALREADY...
...WITH 2KM TO GO, STILL.
YEAH, THE HAKONE GUY IN THE LEAD...
...IS BARELY TRYING.
ZOOSH
BANNERS: MT. MINEGAYAMA HILL CLIMB

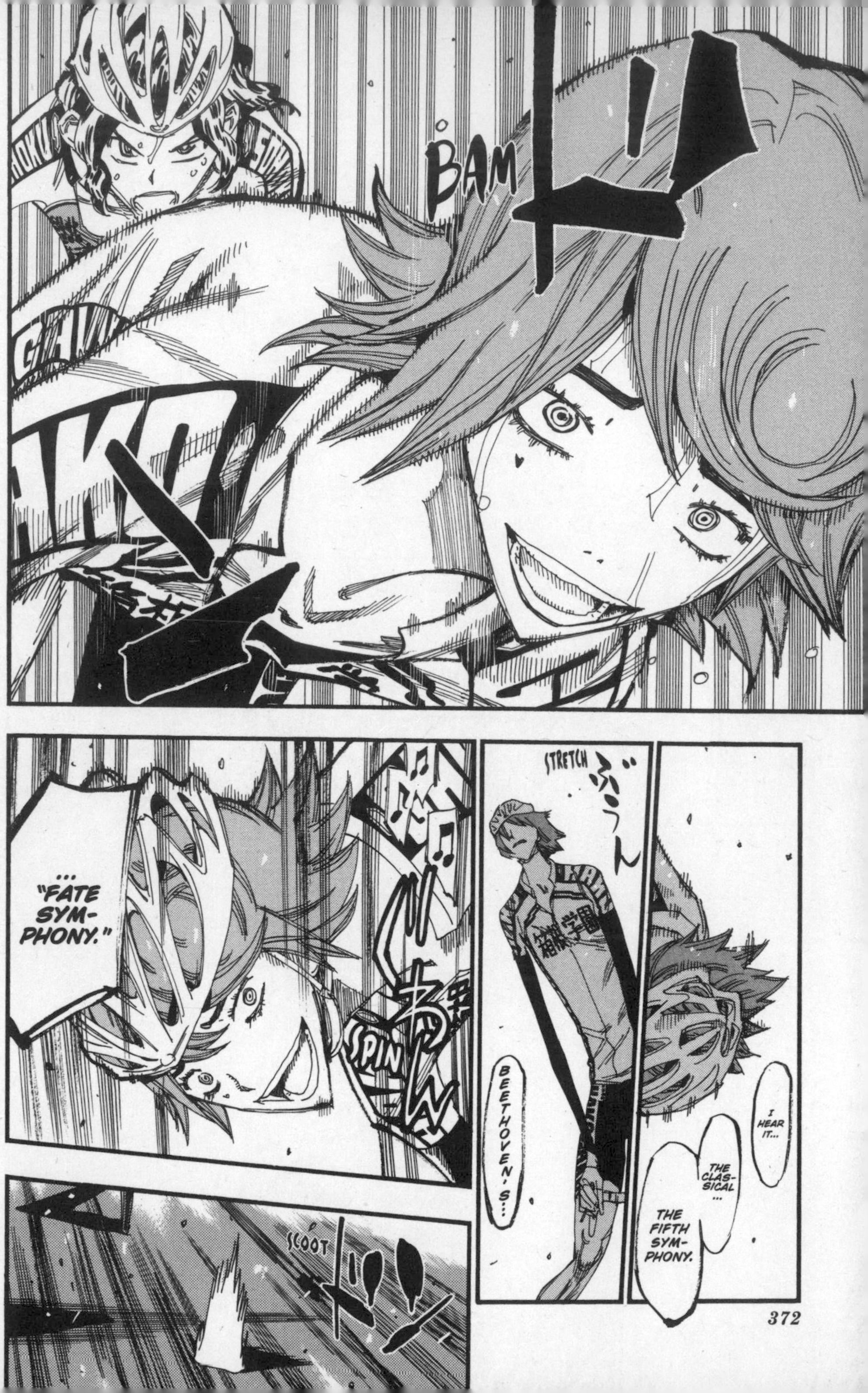
BAM
I HEAR IT...
THE CLASSICAL...
THE FIFTH SYMPHONY.
STRETCH
BEETHOVEN'S...
..."FATE SYMPHONY."
SPIN
SCOOT

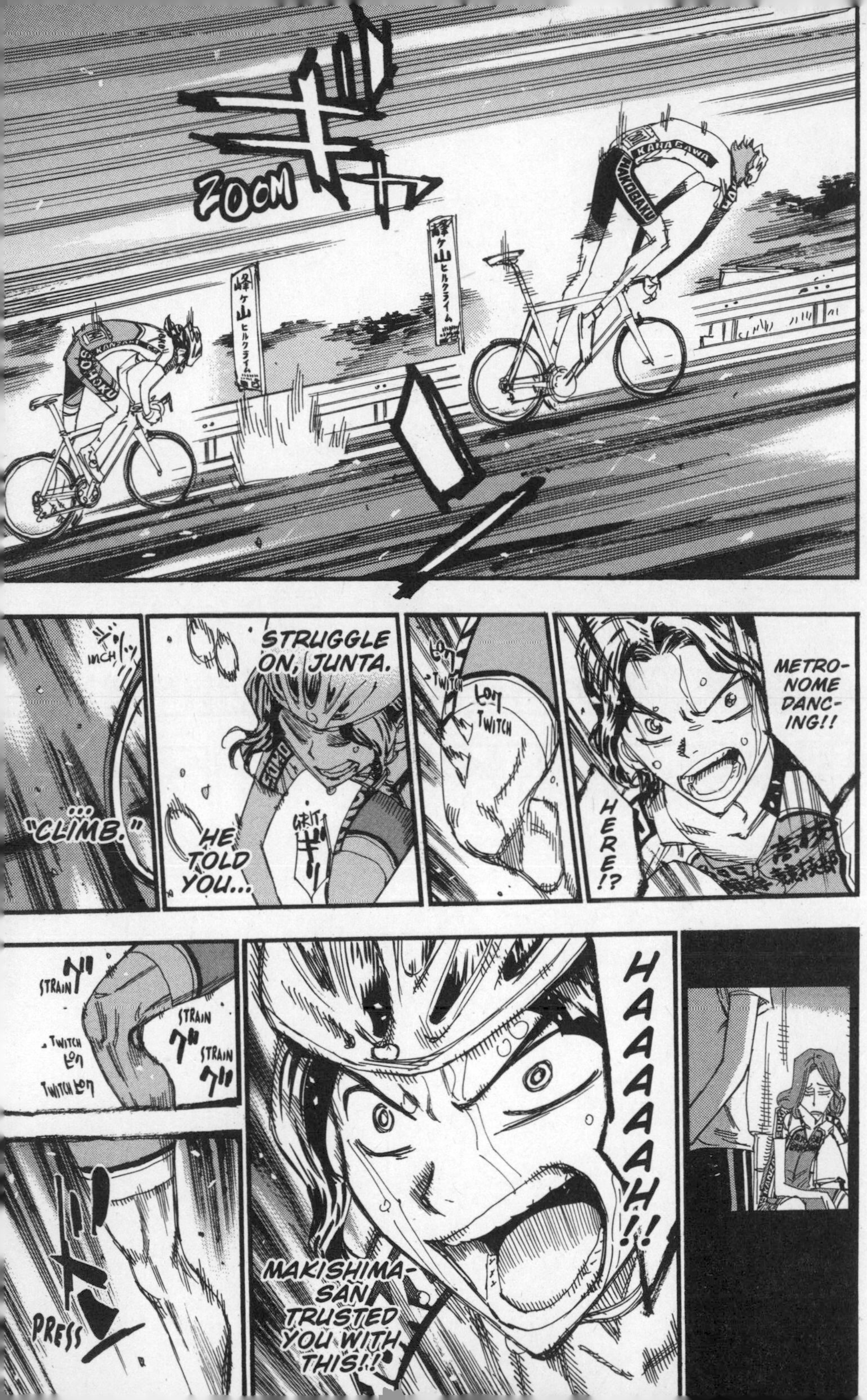
ZOOM
METRO-NOME DANCING!!
HERE!?
TWITCH
TWITCH
STRUGGLE ON, JUNTA.
HE TOLD YOU...
GRIT
INCH
..."CLIMB."
HAAAAAAH!!
MAKISHIMA-SAN TRUSTED YOU WITH THIS!!
STRAIN
STRAIN
STRAIN
TWITCH
TWITCH
PRESS

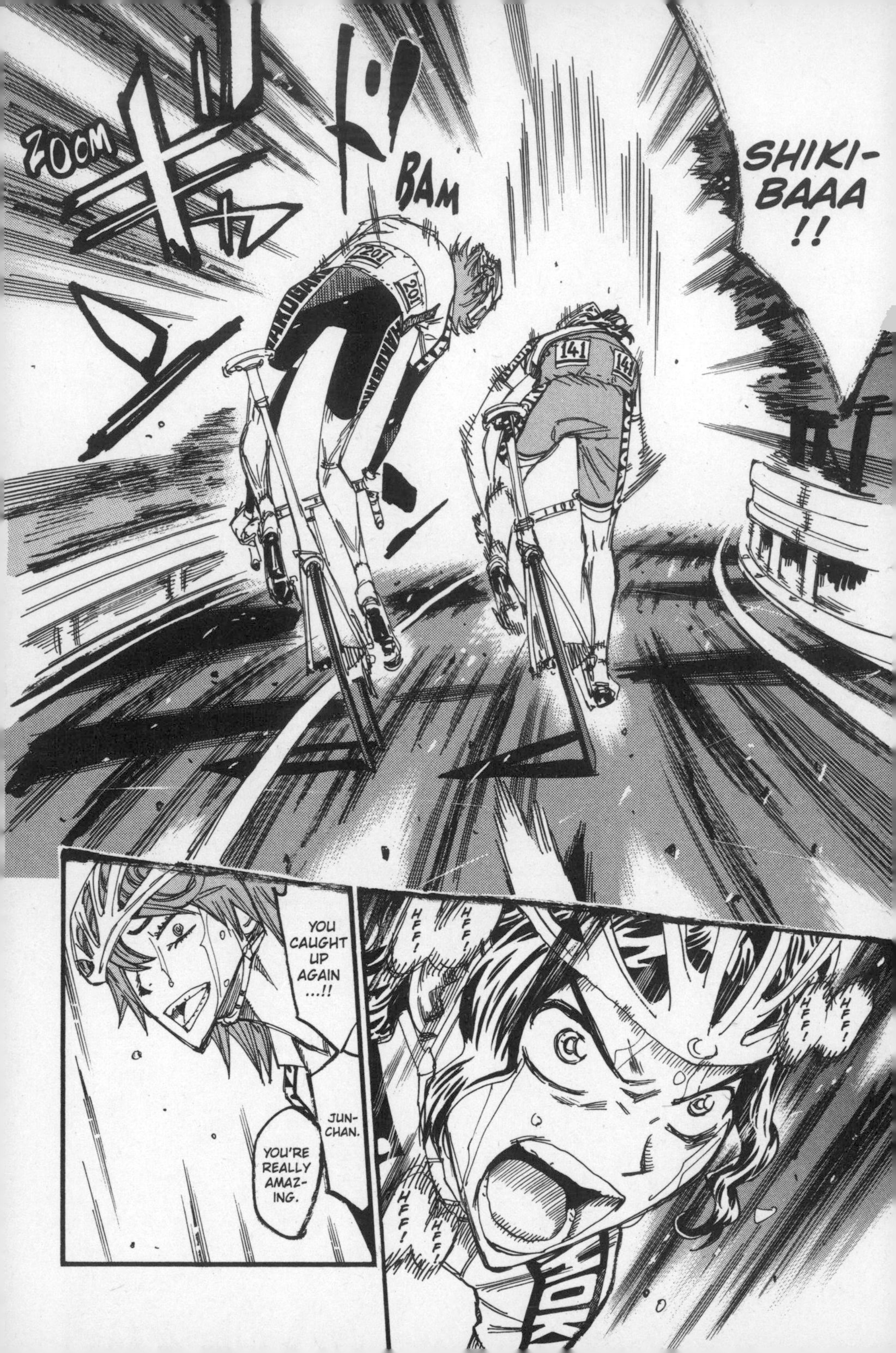
SHIKI-BAAA!!
BAM
ZOOM
HFF! HFF!
HFF! HFF!
HFF! HFF!
YOU CAUGHT UP AGAIN ...!!
JUN-CHAN.
YOU'RE REALLY AMAZ-ING.

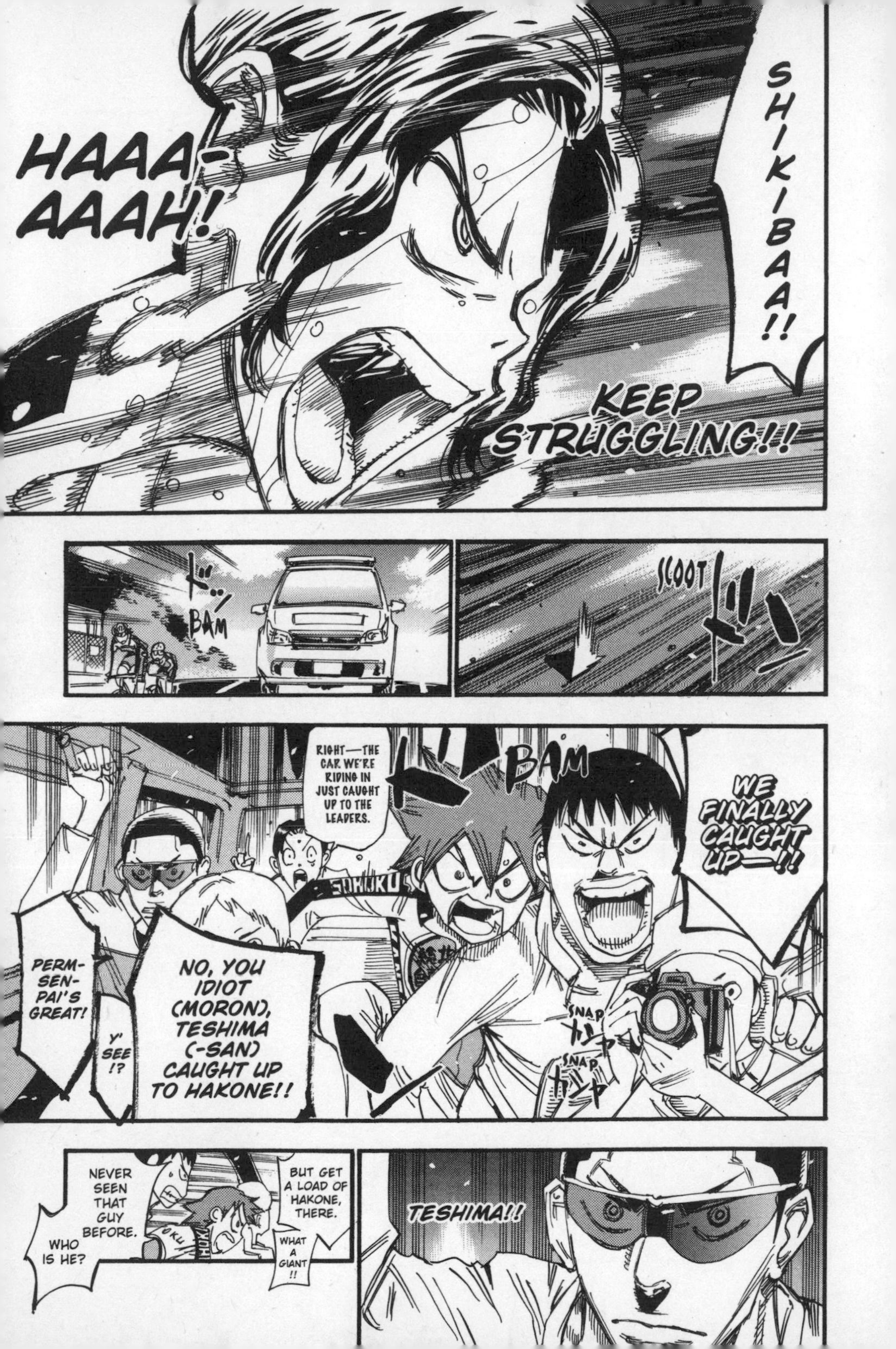
SHIKIBAAA!!
KEEP STRUGGLING!!
HAAAA-AAAH!
SCOOT
BAM
WE FINALLY CAUGHT UP—!!
BAM
RIGHT—THE CAR WE'RE RIDING IN JUST CAUGHT UP TO THE LEADERS.
NO, YOU IDIOT (MORON), TESHIMA (-SAN) CAUGHT UP TO HAKONE!!
Y' SEE!?
PERM-SEN-PAI'S GREAT!
SNAP
SNAP
TESHIMA!!
BUT GET A LOAD OF HAKONE, THERE.
WHAT A GIANT!!
NEVER SEEN THAT GUY BEFORE.
WHO IS HE?

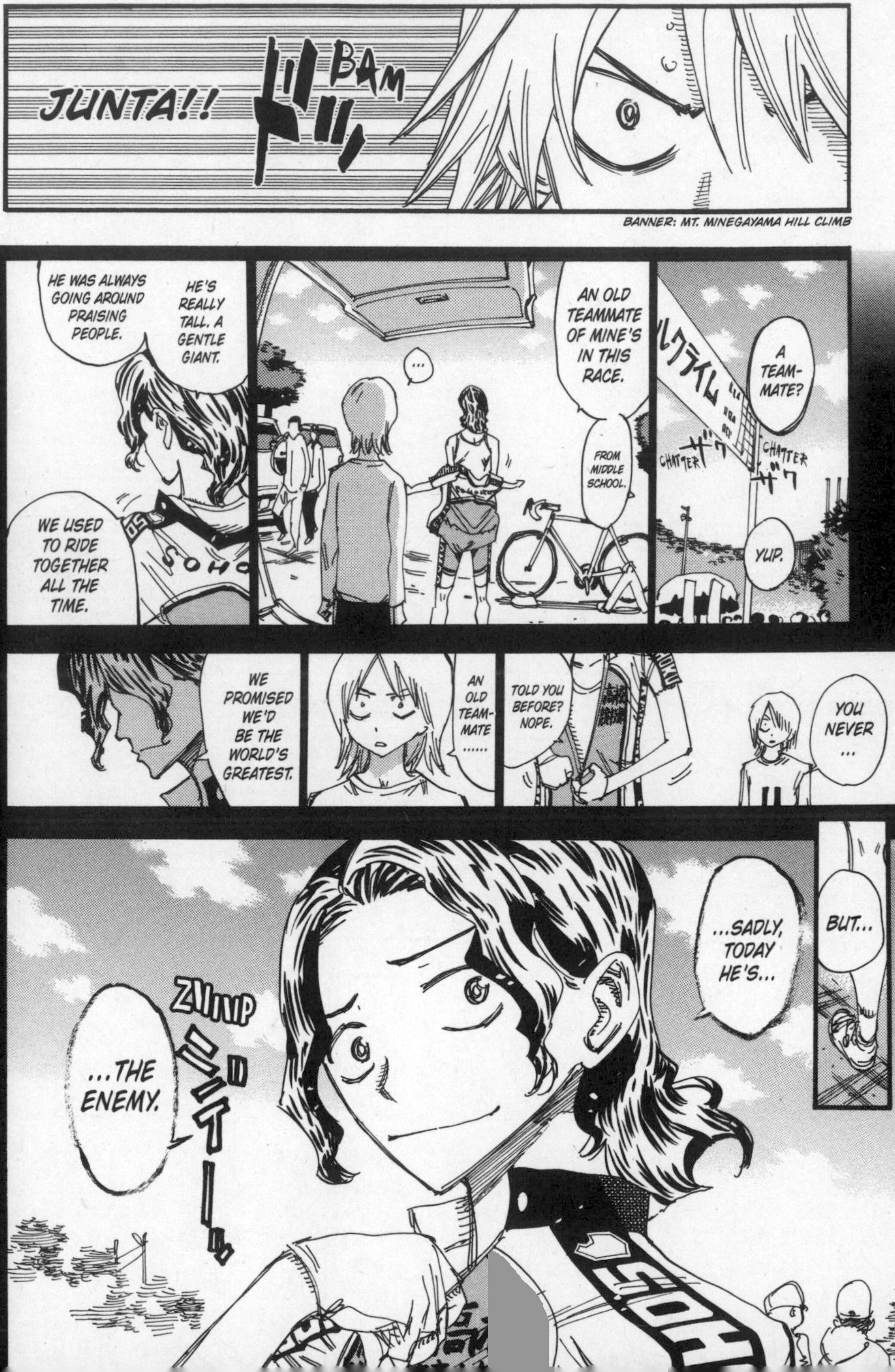
JUNTA!!
BAM
BANNER: MT. MINEGAYAMA HILL CLIMB
A TEAMMATE?
CHATTER
CHATTER
YUP.
AN OLD TEAMMATE OF MINE'S IN THIS RACE.
FROM MIDDLE SCHOOL.
...
HE'S REALLY TALL. A GENTLE GIANT.
HE WAS ALWAYS GOING AROUND PRAISING PEOPLE.
WE USED TO RIDE TOGETHER ALL THE TIME.
YOU NEVER ...
TOLD YOU BEFORE? NOPE.
AN OLD TEAMMATE ......
WE PROMISED WE'D BE THE WORLD'S GREATEST.
BUT...
...SADLY, TODAY HE'S...
...THE ENEMY.
ZIIIP

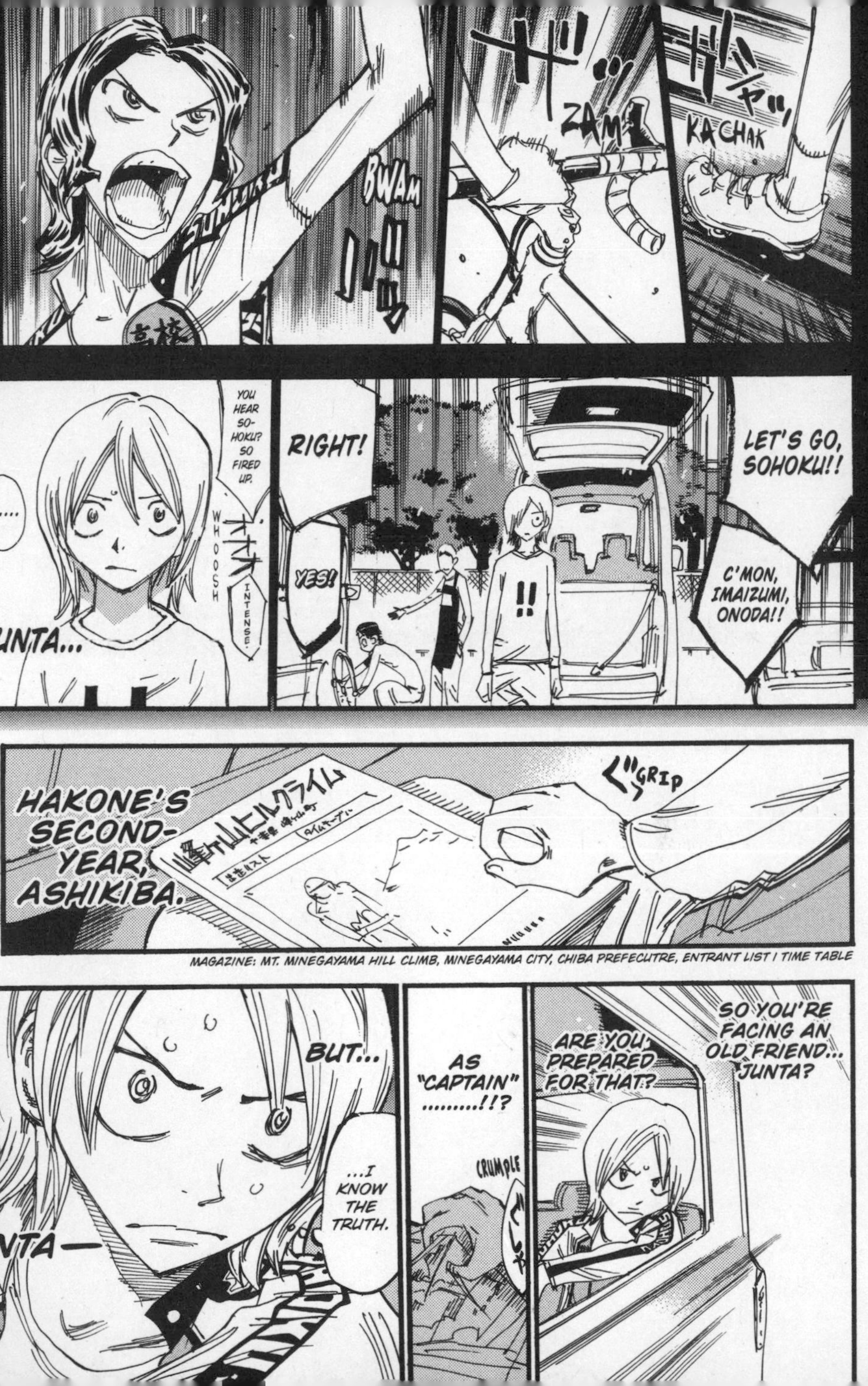
KACHAK
ZAM
BWAM
LET'S GO, SOHOKU!!
C'MON, IMAIZUMI, ONODA!!
RIGHT!
YES!
YOU HEAR SO-HOKU? SO FIRED UP.
WHOOSH
INTENSE.
......
JUNTA...
GRIP
HAKONE'S SECOND-YEAR, ASHIKIBA.
SO YOU'RE FACING AN OLD FRIEND... JUNTA?
ARE YOU PREPARED FOR THAT?
CRUMPLE
AS "CAPTAIN" ....!!?
BUT...
...I KNOW THE TRUTH.
JUNTA—

MAGAZINE: MT. MINEGAYAMA HILL CLIMB, MINEGAYAMA CITY, CHIBA PREFECUTRE, ENTRANT LIST I TIME TABLE

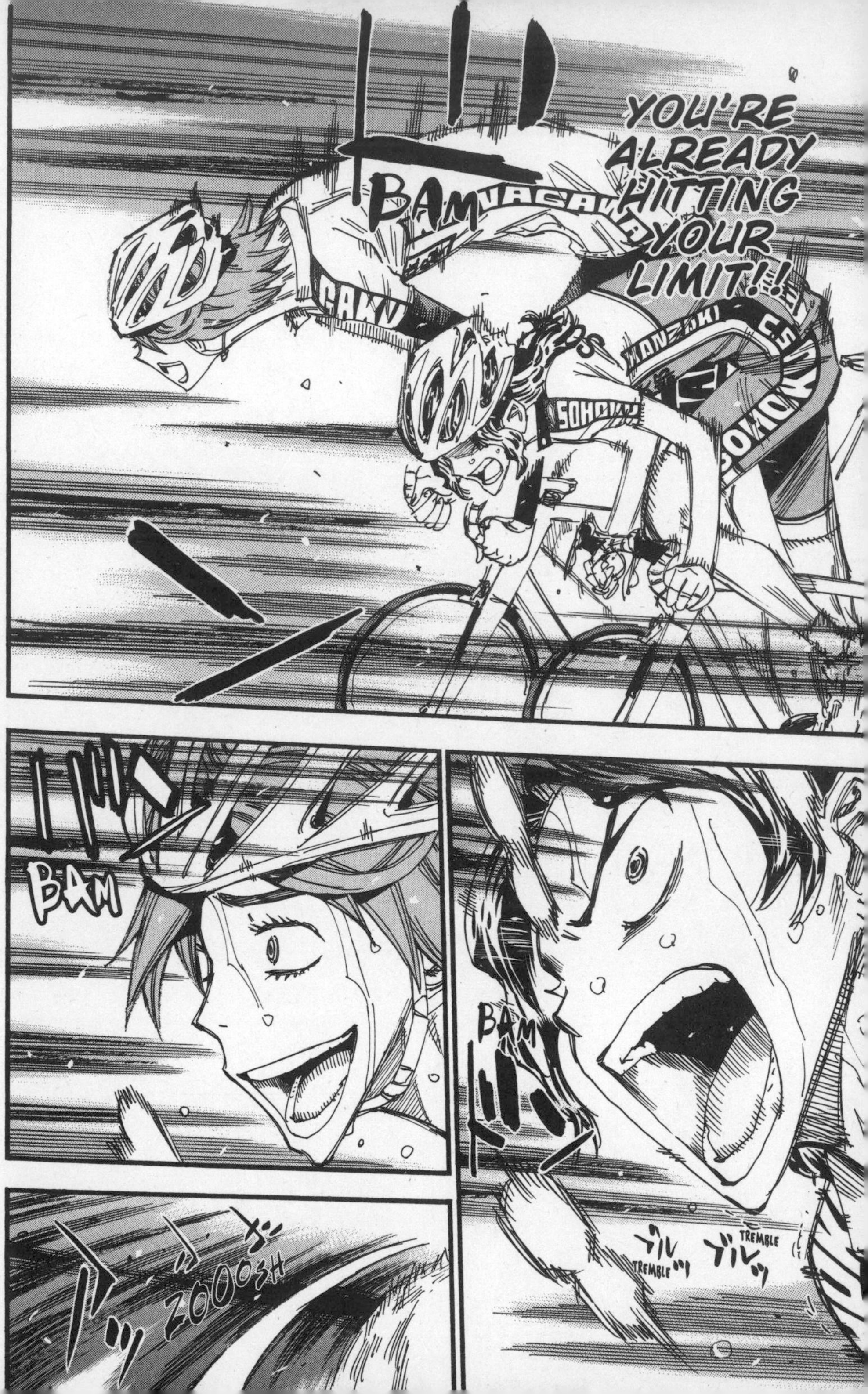
YOU'RE ALREADY HITTING YOUR LIMIT!!
BAM
BAM
BAM
TREMBLE TREMBLE
ZOOOSH

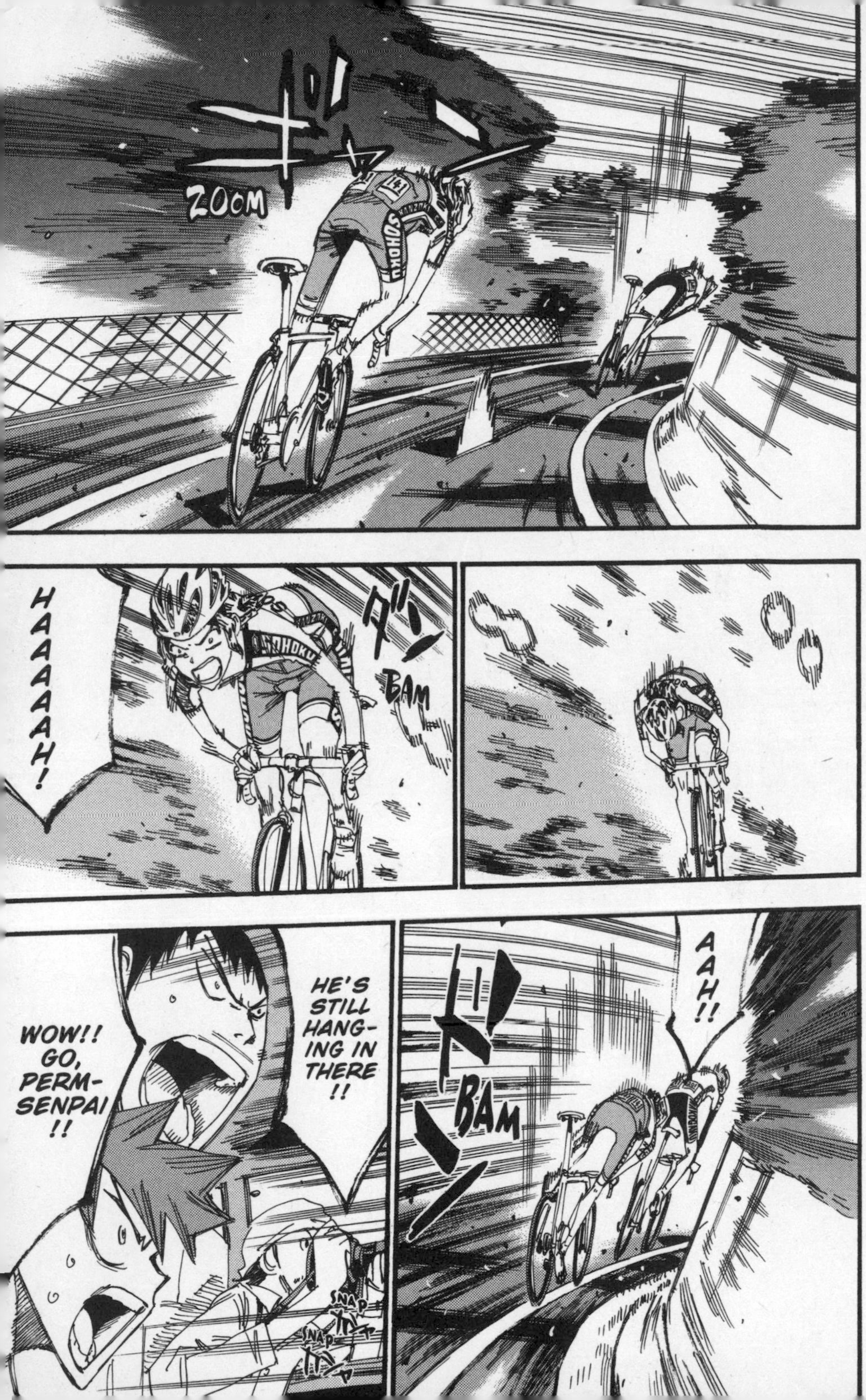
ZOOM
HAAAAAAH!
BAM
AAH!!
BAM
HE'S STILL HANG-ING IN THERE!!
WOW!! GO, PERM-SENPAI!!
SNAP
SNAP

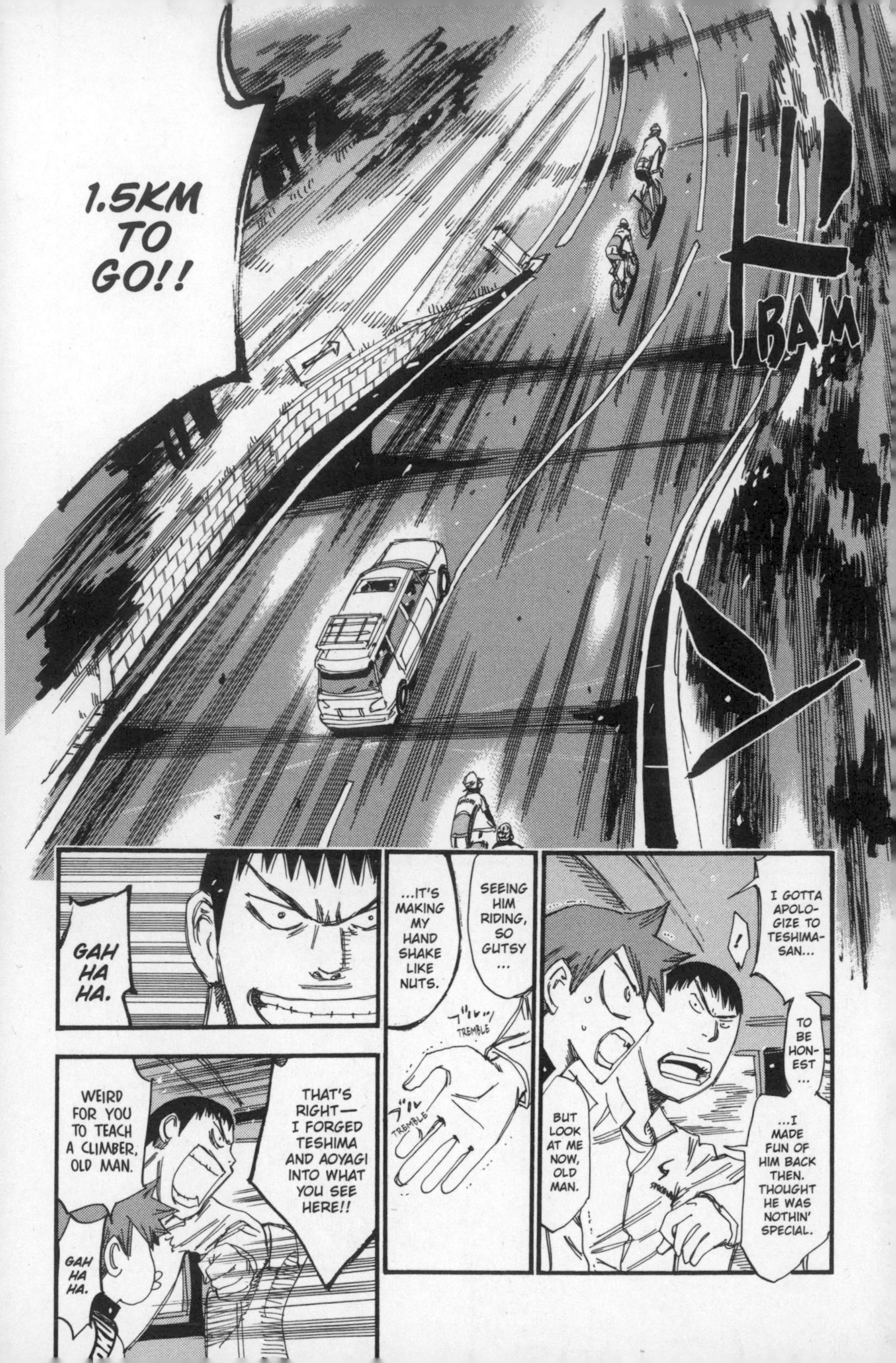
1.5KM TO GO!!
BAM
I GOTTA APOLOGIZE TO TESHIMA-SAN...
!
TO BE HONEST...
...I MADE FUN OF HIM BACK THEN. THOUGHT HE WAS NOTHIN' SPECIAL.
BUT LOOK AT ME NOW, OLD MAN.
SEEING HIM RIDING, SO GUTSY...
...IT'S MAKING MY HAND SHAKE LIKE NUTS.
TREMBLE
TREMBLE
GAH HA HA.
THAT'S RIGHT— I FORGED TESHIMA AND AOYAGI INTO WHAT YOU SEE HERE!!
WEIRD FOR YOU TO TEACH A CLIMBER, OLD MAN.
GAH HA HA.

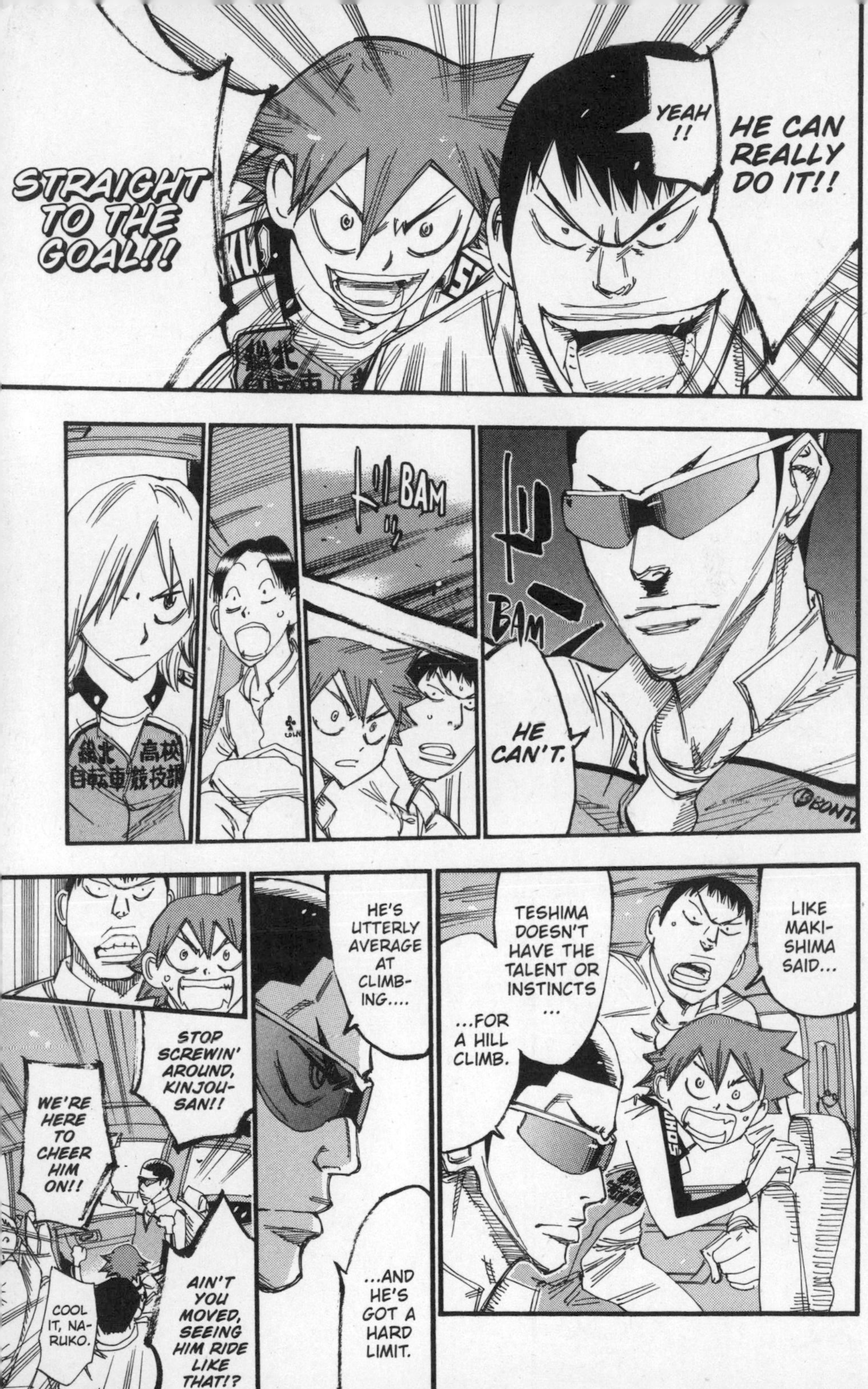
HE CAN REALLY DO IT!!
YEAH!!
STRAIGHT TO THE GOAL!!
BAM
HE CAN'T.
BAM
LIKE MAKI-SHIMA SAID...
TESHIMA DOESN'T HAVE THE TALENT OR INSTINCTS...
...FOR A HILL CLIMB.
HE'S UTTERLY AVERAGE AT CLIMB-ING....
...AND HE'S GOT A HARD LIMIT.
STOP SCREWIN' AROUND, KINJOU-SAN!!
WE'RE HERE TO CHEER HIM ON!!
AIN'T YOU MOVED, SEEING HIM RIDE LIKE THAT!?
COOL IT, NA-RUKO.

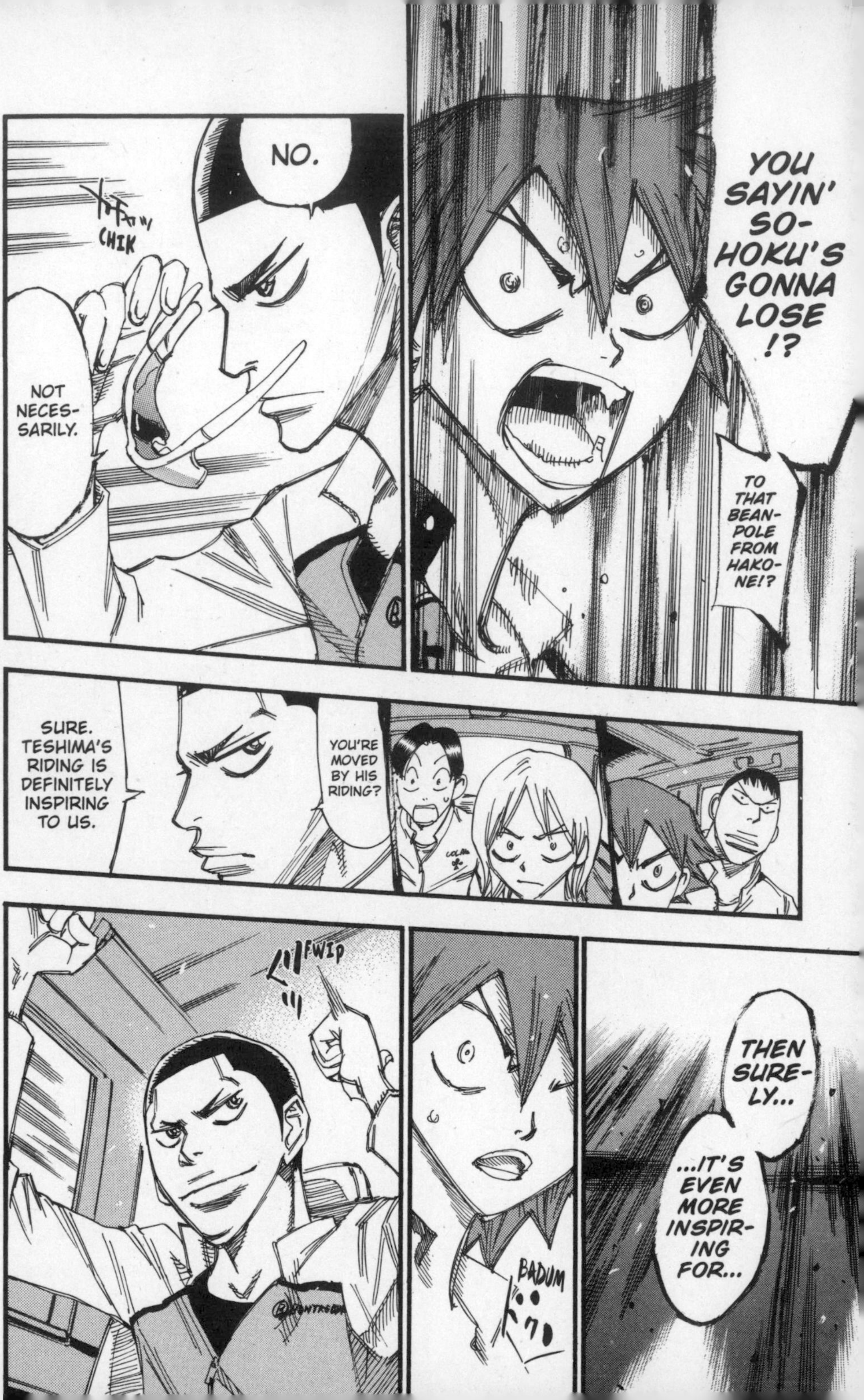
YOU SAYIN' SO-HOKU'S GONNA LOSE !?
TO THAT BEAN-POLE FROM HAKO-NE!?
NO.
CHIK
NOT NECES-SARILY.
YOU'RE MOVED BY HIS RIDING?
SURE. TESHIMA'S RIDING IS DEFINITELY INSPIRING TO US.
THEN SURE-LY...
...IT'S EVEN MORE INSPIR-ING FOR...
BADUM
FWIP

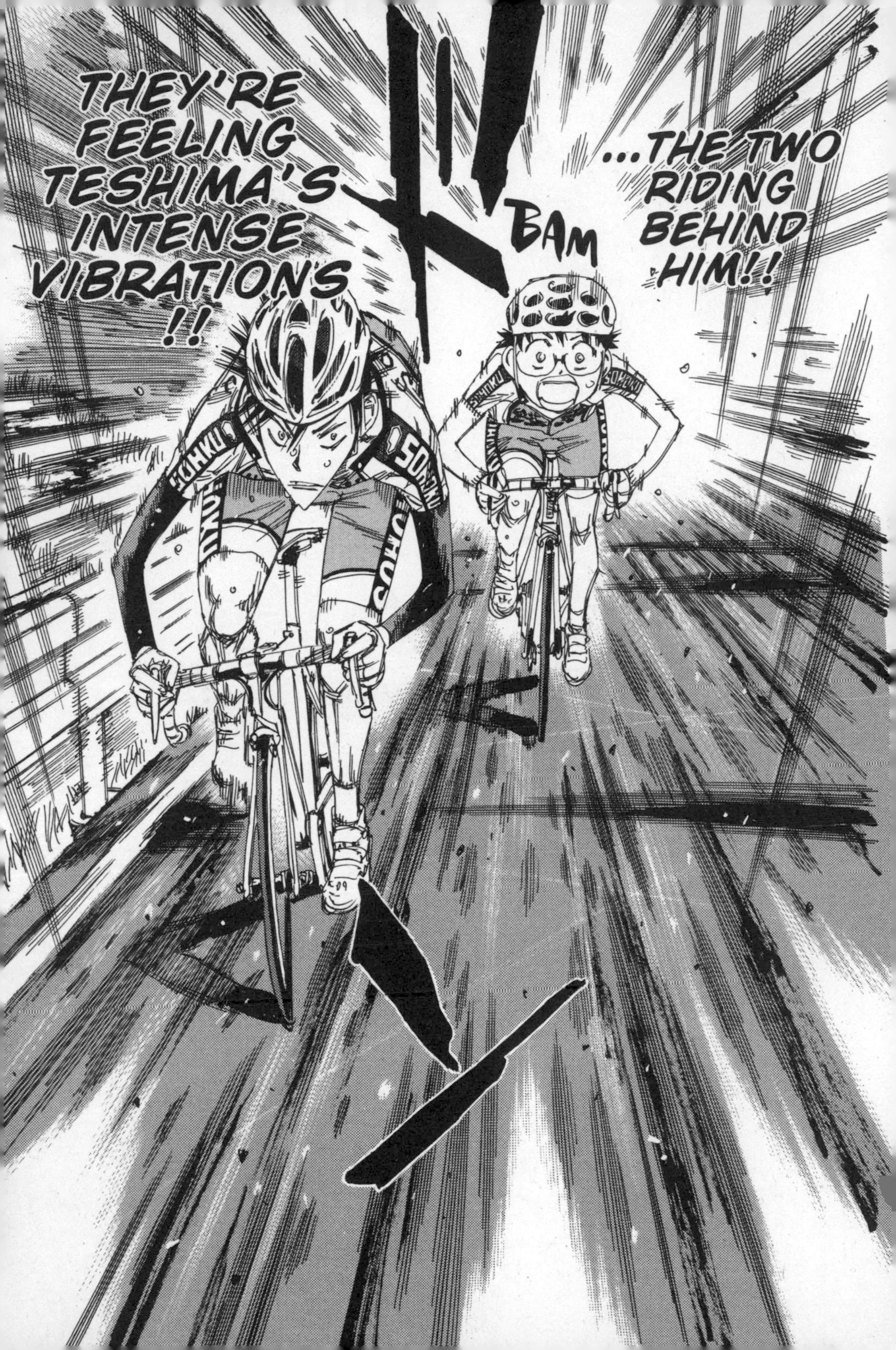
...THE TWO RIDING BEHIND HIM!!
BAM
THEY'RE FEELING TESHIMA'S INTENSE VIBRATIONS!!

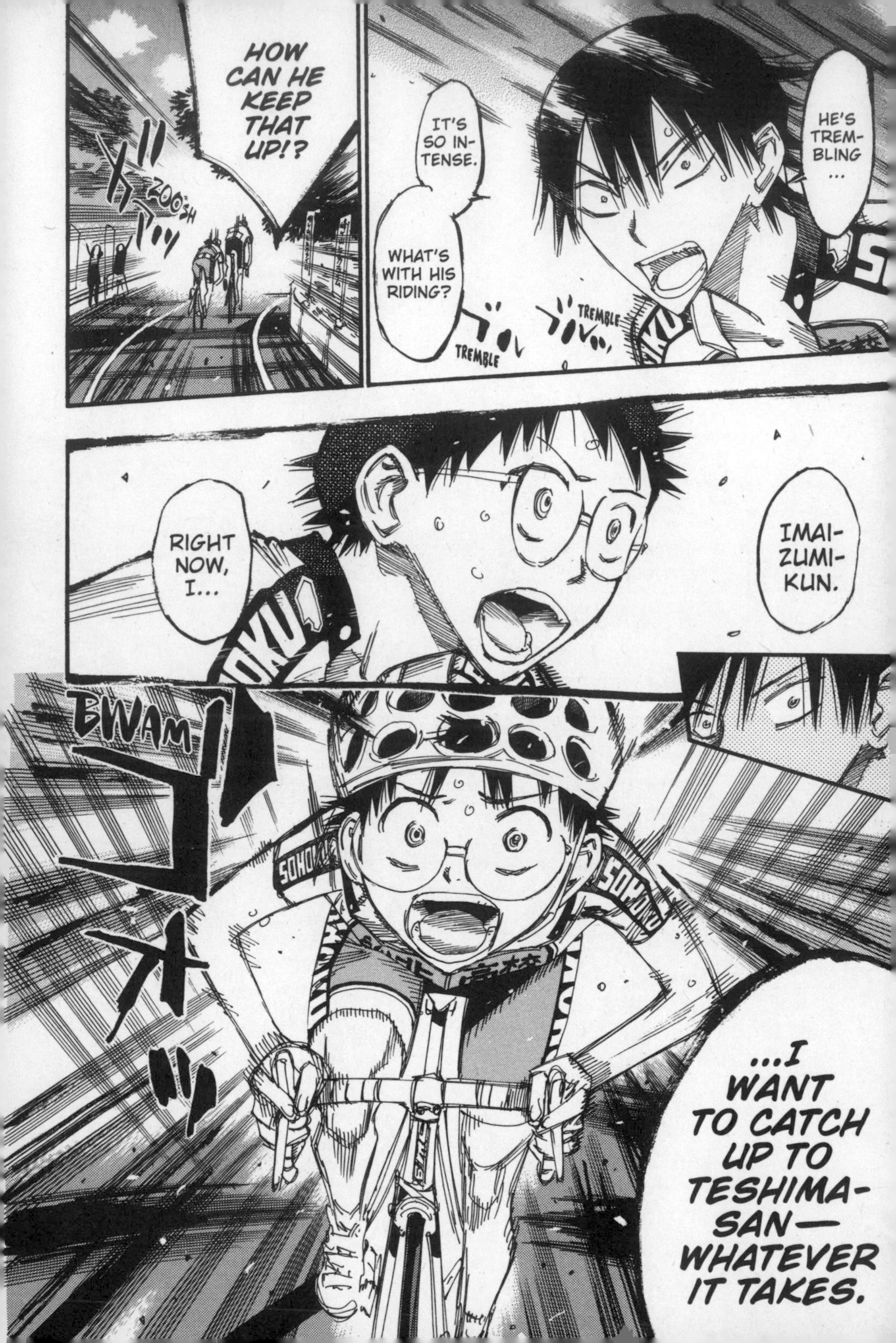
HE'S TREMBLING...
IT'S SO INTENSE.
WHAT'S WITH HIS RIDING?
TREMBLE
TREMBLE
HOW CAN HE KEEP THAT UP!?
ZOOSH
IMAIZUMI-KUN.
RIGHT NOW, I...
BWAM
...I WANT TO CATCH UP TO TESHIMA-SAN—WHATEVER IT TAKES.

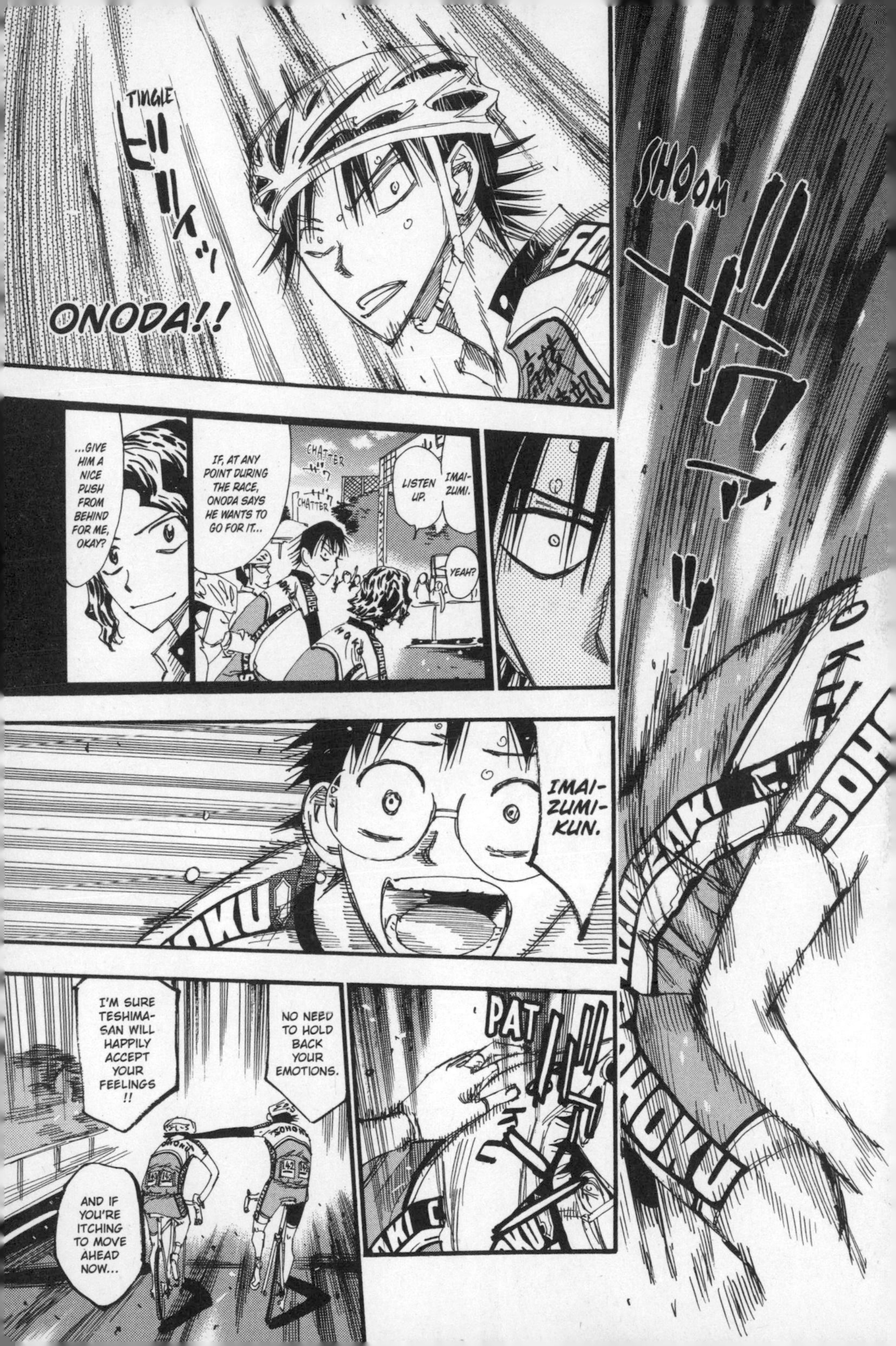
SHOOM
TINGLE
ONODA!!
IMAI-ZUMI.
LISTEN UP.
YEAH?
CHATTER
CHATTER
IF, AT ANY POINT DURING THE RACE, ONODA SAYS HE WANTS TO GO FOR IT...
...GIVE HIM A NICE PUSH FROM BEHIND FOR ME, OKAY?
IMAI-ZUMI-KUN.
PAT
NO NEED TO HOLD BACK YOUR EMOTIONS.
I'M SURE TESHIMA-SAN WILL HAPPILY ACCEPT YOUR FEELINGS!!
AND IF YOU'RE ITCHING TO MOVE AHEAD NOW...

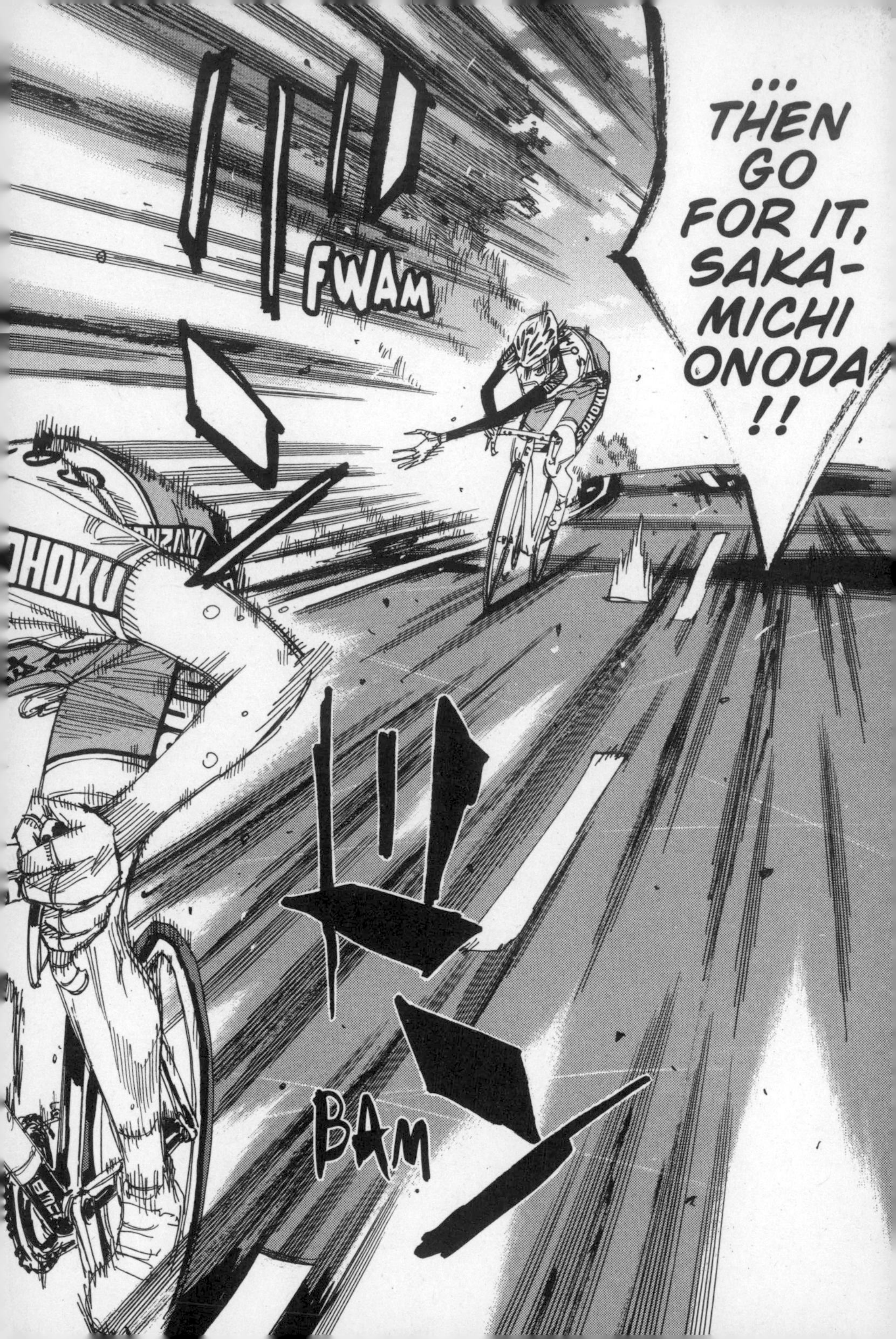
...THEN GO FOR IT, SAKAMICHI ONODA!!
FWAM
SOHOKU
BAM

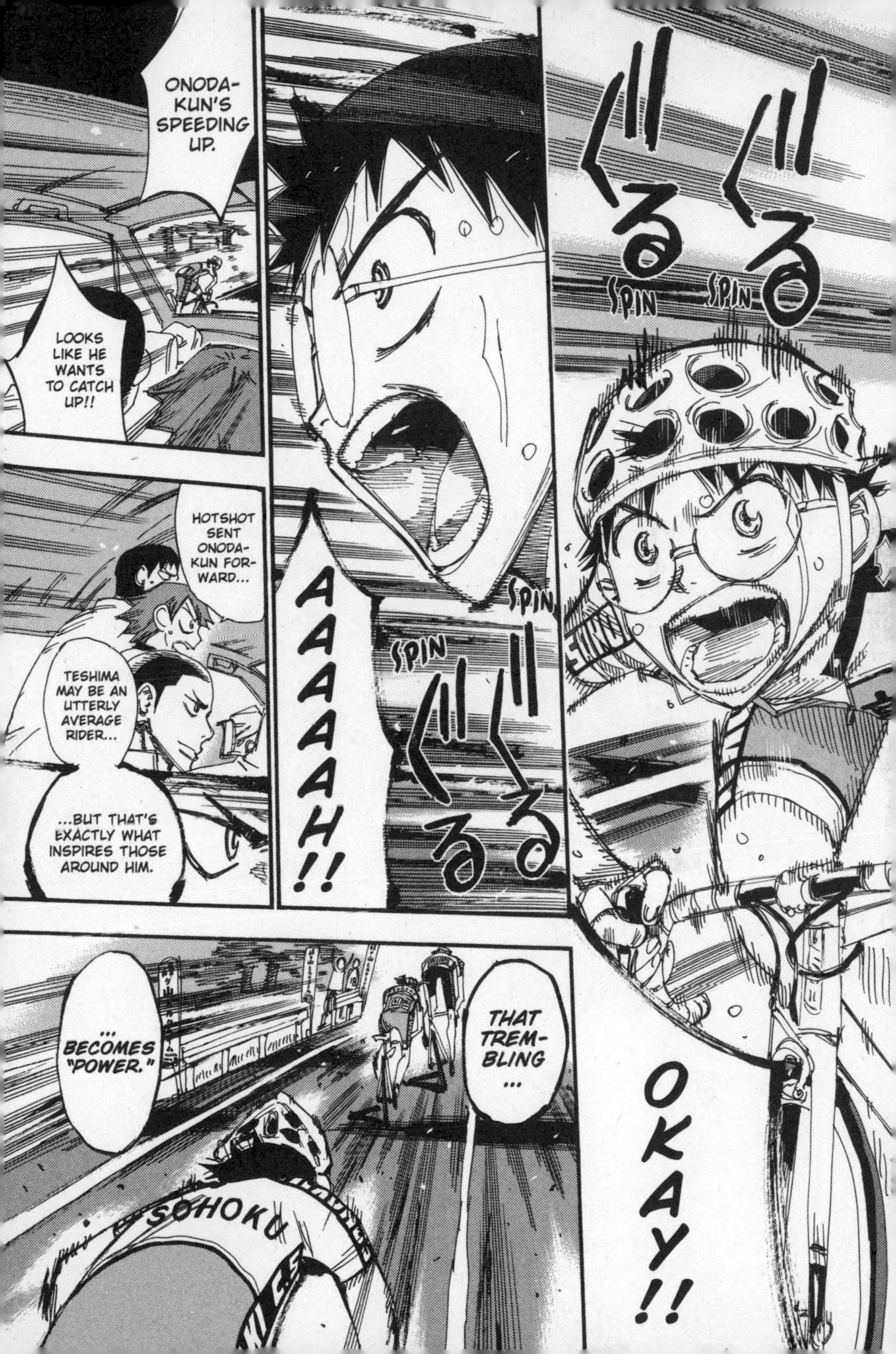
ぐるぐる
SPIN SPIN
OKAY!!
AAAAAH!!
ぐるぐる
SPIN SPIN
ONODA-KUN'S SPEEDING UP.
LOOKS LIKE HE WANTS TO CATCH UP!!
HOTSHOT SENT ONODA-KUN FORWARD...
TESHIMA MAY BE AN UTTERLY AVERAGE RIDER...
...BUT THAT'S EXACTLY WHAT INSPIRES THOSE AROUND HIM.
THAT TREMBLING...
...BECOMES "POWER."
SOHOKU

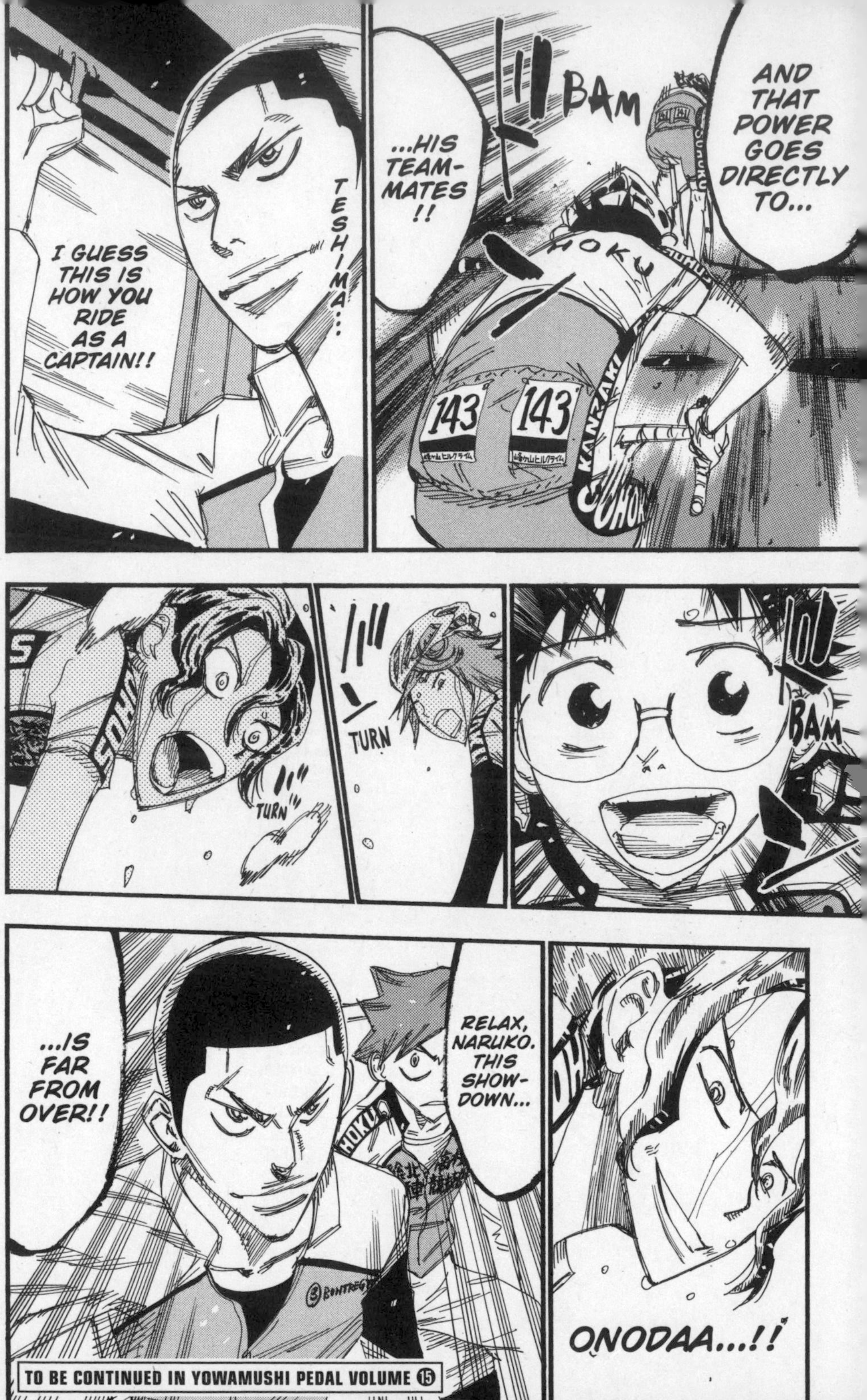
AND THAT POWER GOES DIRECTLY TO...
BAM
...HIS TEAMMATES!!
TESHIMA...
I GUESS THIS IS HOW YOU RIDE AS A CAPTAIN!!
BAM
TURN
TURN
ONODAA...!!
RELAX, NARUKO. THIS SHOWDOWN...
...IS FAR FROM OVER!!
TO BE CONTINUED IN YOWAMUSHI PEDAL VOLUME 15

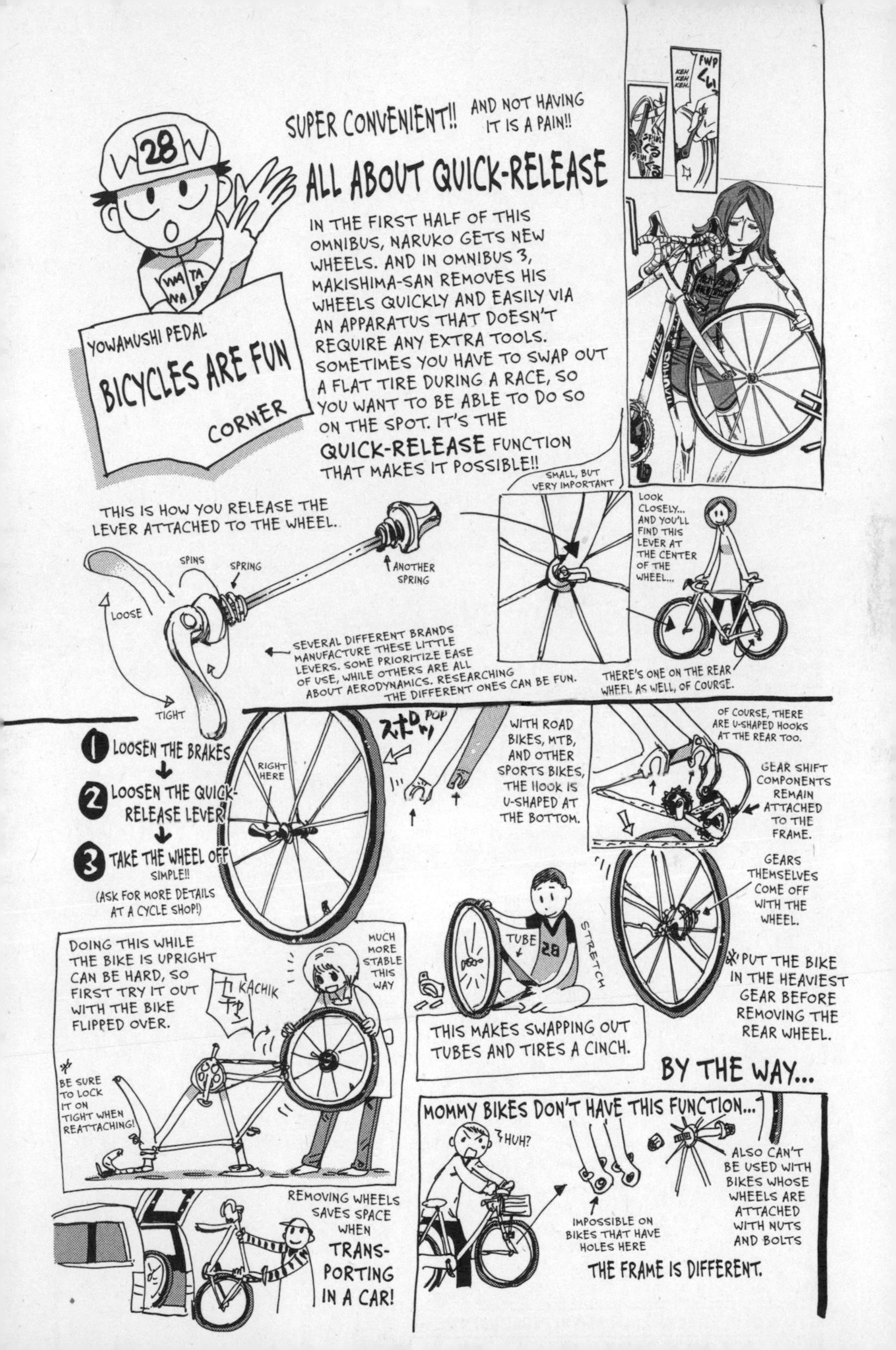
SUPER CONVENIENT!!
AND NOT HAVING IT IS A PAIN!!
ALL ABOUT QUICK-RELEASE
YOWAMUSHI PEDAL
BICYCLES ARE FUN
CORNER
IN THE FIRST HALF OF THIS OMNIBUS, NARUKO GETS NEW WHEELS. AND IN OMNIBUS 3, MAKISHIMA-SAN REMOVES HIS WHEELS QUICKLY AND EASILY VIA AN APPARATUS THAT DOESN'T REQUIRE ANY EXTRA TOOLS. SOMETIMES YOU HAVE TO SWAP OUT A FLAT TIRE DURING A RACE, SO YOU WANT TO BE ABLE TO DO SO ON THE SPOT. IT'S THE QUICK-RELEASE FUNCTION THAT MAKES IT POSSIBLE!!
KEH KEH KEH.
FWP
SPIN
SMALL, BUT VERY IMPORTANT
THIS IS HOW YOU RELEASE THE LEVER ATTACHED TO THE WHEEL.
SPINS
SPRING
ANOTHER SPRING
LOOSE
TIGHT
SEVERAL DIFFERENT BRANDS MANUFACTURE THESE LITTLE LEVERS. SOME PRIORITIZE EASE OF USE, WHILE OTHERS ARE ALL ABOUT AERODYNAMICS. RESEARCHING THE DIFFERENT ONES CAN BE FUN.
LOOK CLOSELY... AND YOU'LL FIND THIS LEVER AT THE CENTER OF THE WHEEL...
THERE'S ONE ON THE REAR WHEEL AS WELL, OF COURSE.
1 LOOSEN THE BRAKES
2 LOOSEN THE QUICK-RELEASE LEVER
3 TAKE THE WHEEL OFF
SIMPLE!!
(ASK FOR MORE DETAILS AT A CYCLE SHOP!)
RIGHT HERE
POP
WITH ROAD BIKES, MTB, AND OTHER SPORTS BIKES, THE HOOK IS U-SHAPED AT THE BOTTOM.
OF COURSE, THERE ARE U-SHAPED HOOKS AT THE REAR TOO.
GEAR SHIFT COMPONENTS REMAIN ATTACHED TO THE FRAME.
GEARS THEMSELVES COME OFF WITH THE WHEEL.
※PUT THE BIKE IN THE HEAVIEST GEAR BEFORE REMOVING THE REAR WHEEL.
DOING THIS WHILE THE BIKE IS UPRIGHT CAN BE HARD, SO FIRST TRY IT OUT WITH THE BIKE FLIPPED OVER.
MUCH MORE STABLE THIS WAY
KACHIK
※BE SURE TO LOCK IT ON TIGHT WHEN REATTACHING!
TUBE
STRETCH
THIS MAKES SWAPPING OUT TUBES AND TIRES A CINCH.
REMOVING WHEELS SAVES SPACE WHEN TRANSPORTING IN A CAR!
BY THE WAY...
MOMMY BIKES DON'T HAVE THIS FUNCTION...
HUH?
IMPOSSIBLE ON BIKES THAT HAVE HOLES HERE
ALSO CAN'T BE USED WITH BIKES WHOSE WHEELS ARE ATTACHED WITH NUTS AND BOLTS
THE FRAME IS DIFFERENT.

Translation Notes

Common Honorifics

-*san*: The Japanese equivalent of Mr./Mrs./Miss. If a situation calls for politeness, this is the fail-safe honorific.

-*kun*: Used most often when referring to boys, this indicates affection or familiarity. Occasionally used by older men among their peers, but it may also be used by anyone referring to a person of lower standing.

-*chan*: An affectionate honorific indicating familiarity used mostly in reference to girls; also used in reference to cute persons or animals of either gender.

-*senpai*: A suffix used to address upperclassmen or more experienced co-workers.

-*shi*: A more formal version of *san* common to written Japanese, it's the default honorific used in newspapers.

no honorific: Indicates familiarity or closeness; if used without permission or reason, addressing someone in this manner would constitute an insult.

A kilometer is approximately .6 of a mile.

PAGE 78
Peloton: A cycling term for the "pack," or the main group of riders in a race.

PAGE 138
Chiba: A prefecture in the Kantou region of Japan. Chiba has both long stretches of mountains and large areas of flat plains and is known for having mild summers and winters.

PAGE 161
Seiza: A kneeling position that demonstrates a certain level of either remorse or formality in Japan. Naruko, Imaizumi, and Onoda are depicted sitting in this position during this scene. This panel is meant to be comedic, since Naruko and Imaizumi are also being scolded by Onoda's mother even though they have nothing to do with the situation.

Naruko's explanation of his name is an explanation of the meaning of the Chinese characters (or *kanji*) he uses to write his name.

PAGE 168
Akiba: Popular nickname for Akihabara District in Tokyo. Well-known as a cultural center for anything related to anime, manga, games, or electronics.

PAGE 170
Nendoroids: Plastic figurines made by the Good Smile Company. Nendoroids are well-known for depicting manga, anime, or video game characters with large heads and small bodies to give them cuter appearances.

PAGE 207
Nobunaga Otadokoro: A pun on Tadokoro's name. Nobunaga Oda was a Japanese warlord during the Sengoku period in the sixteenth century. He is most famous for conquering most of Honshu and is often referred to as one of Japan's "unifiers" alongside Hideyoshi Toyotomi and Ieyasu Tokugawa.

PAGE 275
Hiraken, Makihara, Kuwata, Hiromi Gou: These names are references to various Japanese musicians that were popular in the 1990s.

PAGE 363
CSP: Stands for "Cycling Sports Center." The CSP was the location of the 1,000km-long training camp for Sohoku High.

PAGE 389
MTB: Stands for "mountain bike." Used as an abbreviation among cyclists.

YOWAMUSHI PEDAL  VOLUME 15

Read on for a sneak
peek of Volume 15!

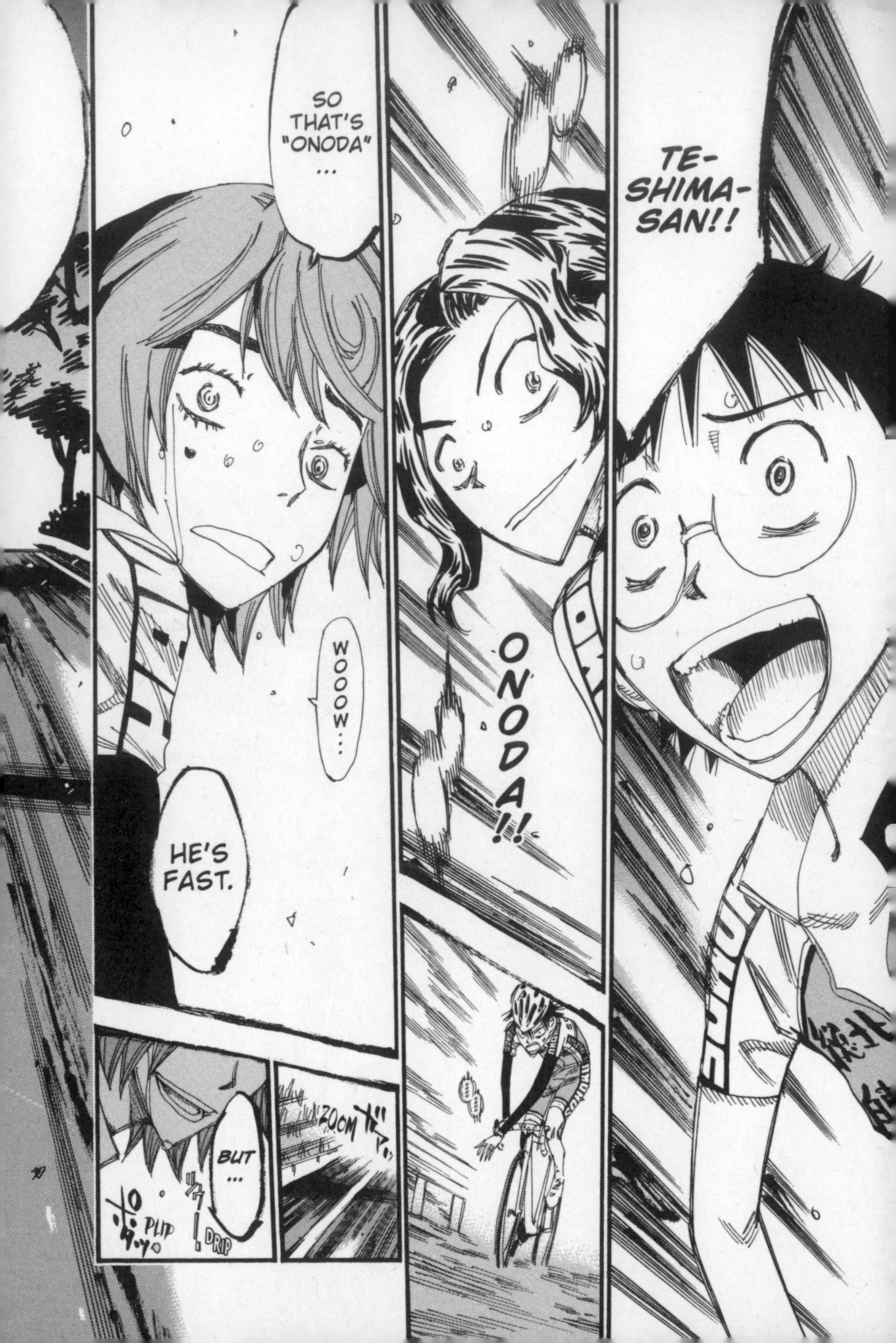
TE-SHIMA-SAN!!
ONODA!!
SO THAT'S "ONODA"...
WOOOW...
HE'S FAST.
ZOOM
BUT...
PLIP
DRIP

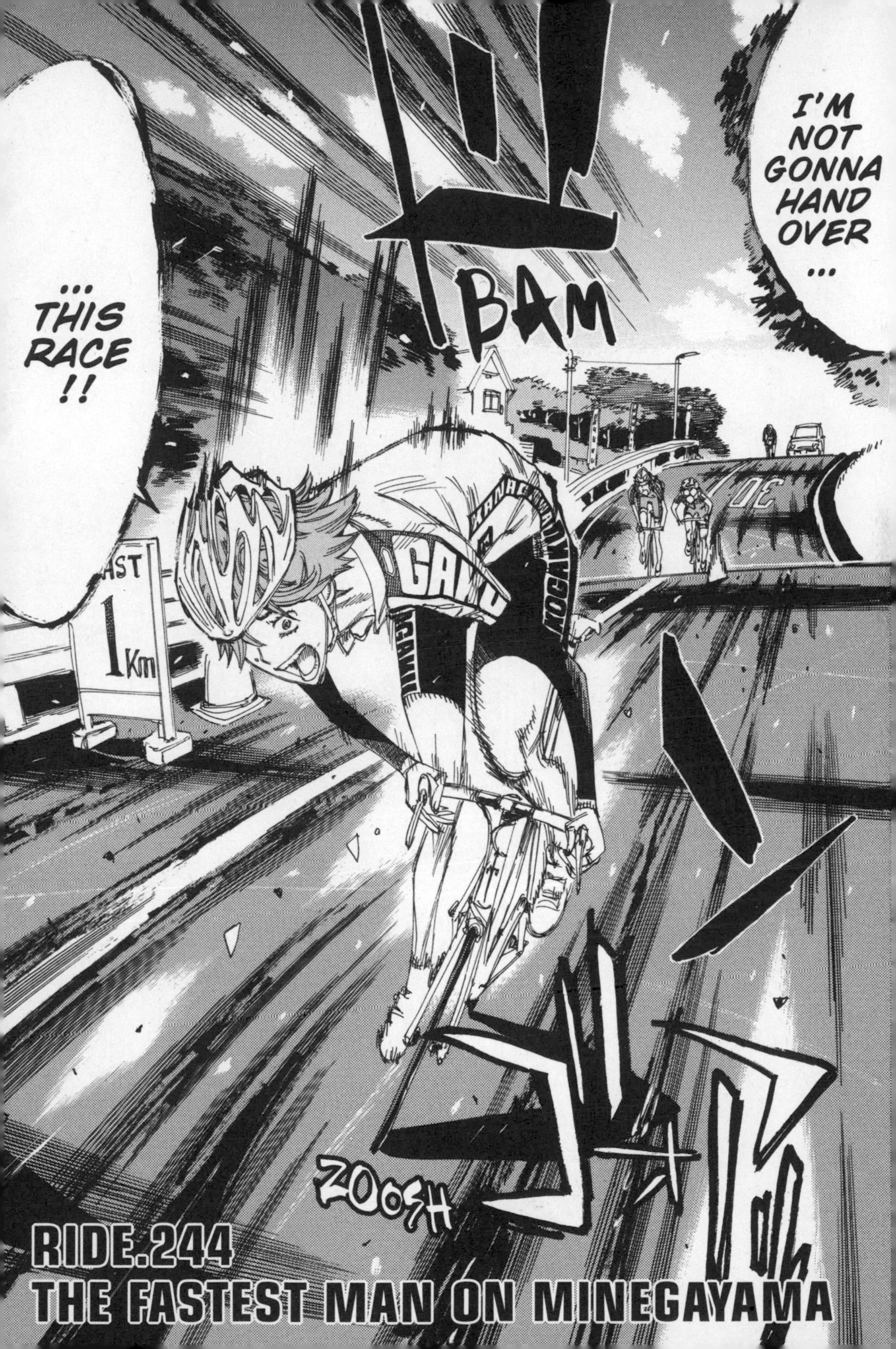
I'M NOT GONNA HAND OVER...
...THIS RACE!!
BAM
1Km
ZOOSH

RIDE.244
THE FASTEST MAN ON MINEGAYAMA

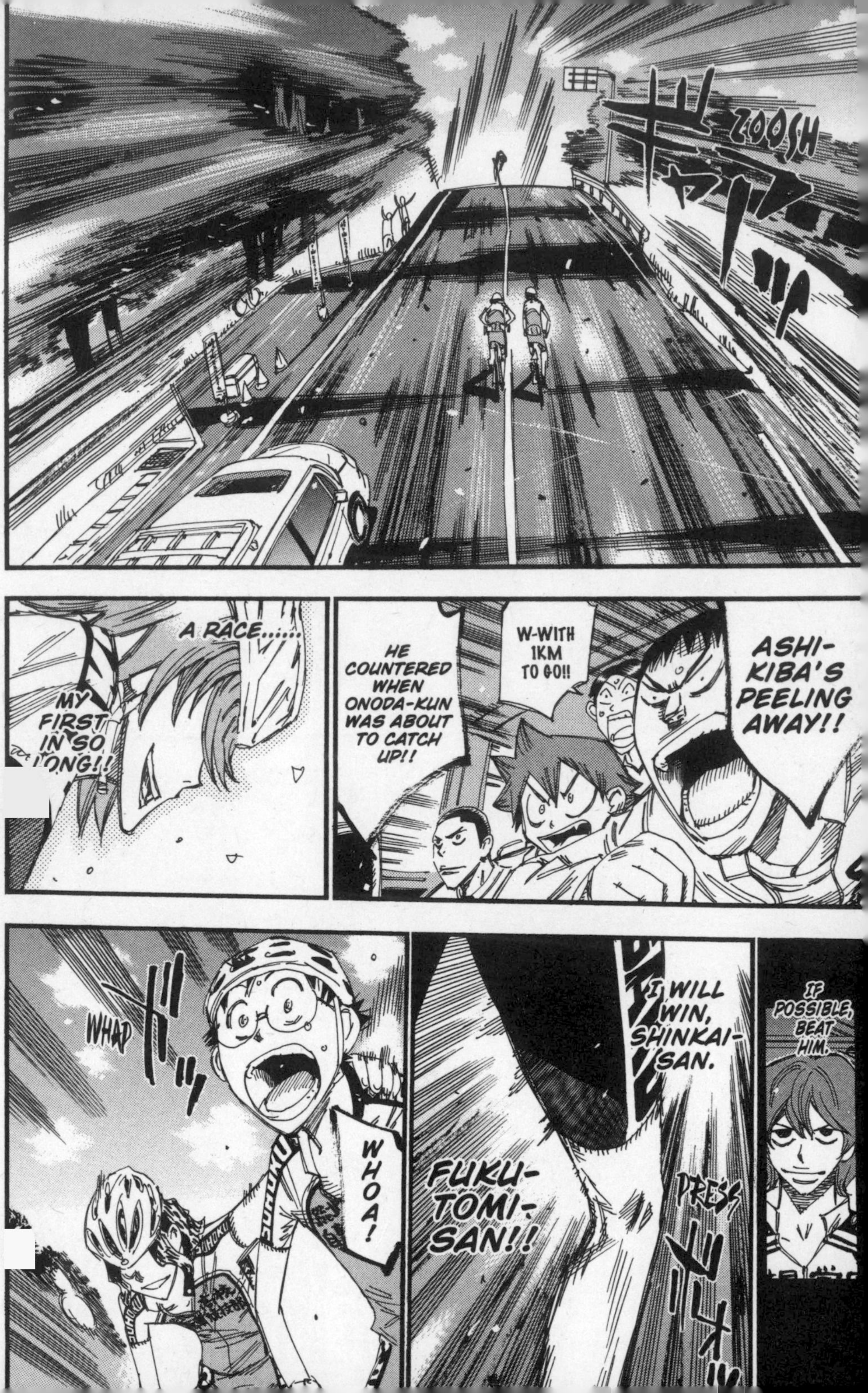
ZOOSH
ASHI-KIBA'S PEELING AWAY!!
W-WITH 1KM TO GO!!
HE COUNTERED WHEN ONODA-KUN WAS ABOUT TO CATCH UP!!
A RACE......
MY FIRST IN SO LONG!!
IF POSSIBLE, BEAT HIM.
I WILL WIN, SHINKAI-SAN.
FUKU-TOMI-SAN!!
PRESS
WHAP
WHOA!

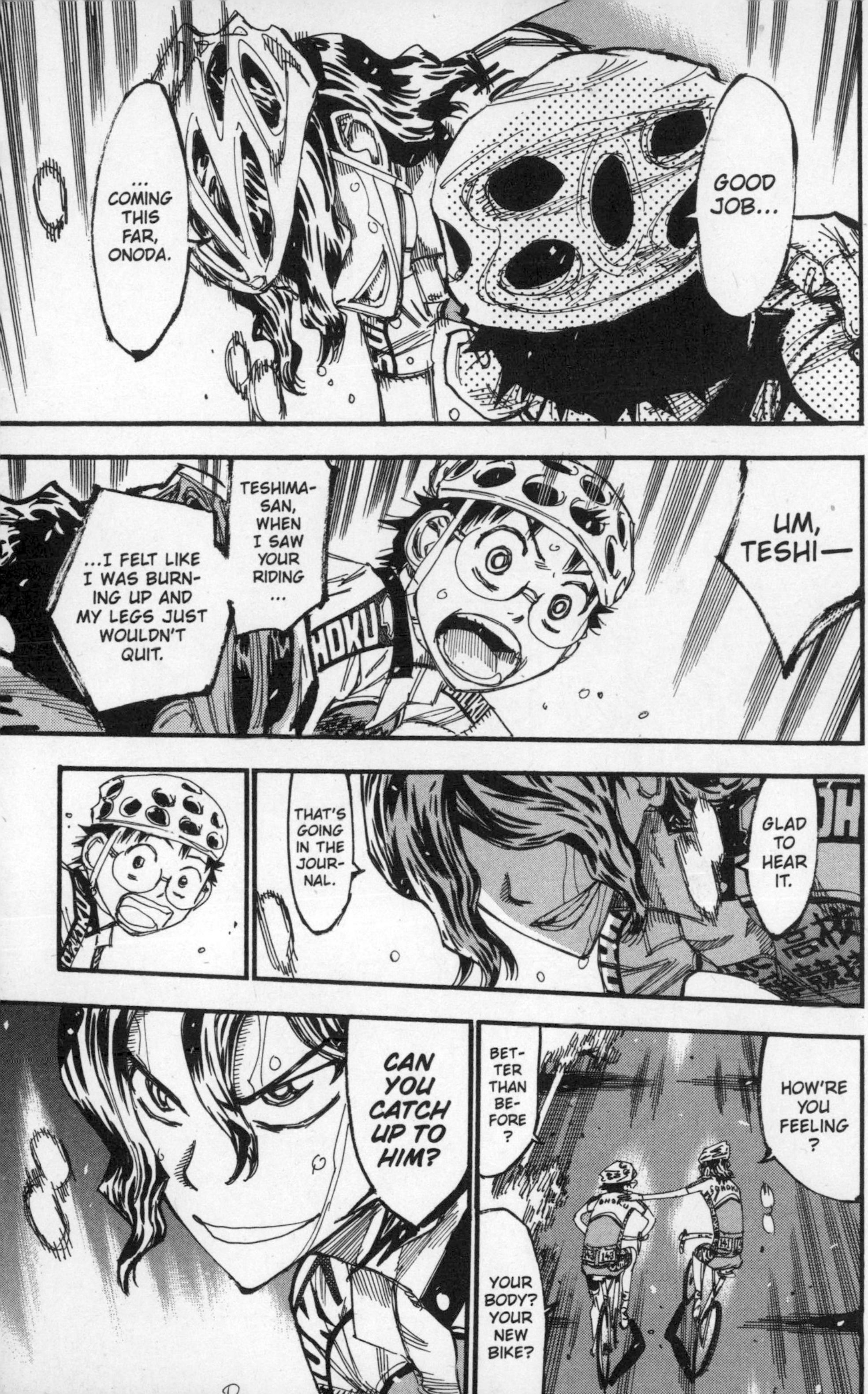
GOOD JOB...
...COMING THIS FAR, ONODA.
UM, TESHI—
TESHIMA-SAN, WHEN I SAW YOUR RIDING...
...I FELT LIKE I WAS BURNING UP AND MY LEGS JUST WOULDN'T QUIT.
GLAD TO HEAR IT.
THAT'S GOING IN THE JOURNAL.
HOW'RE YOU FEELING?
BETTER THAN BEFORE?
YOUR BODY? YOUR NEW BIKE?
CAN YOU CATCH UP TO HIM?

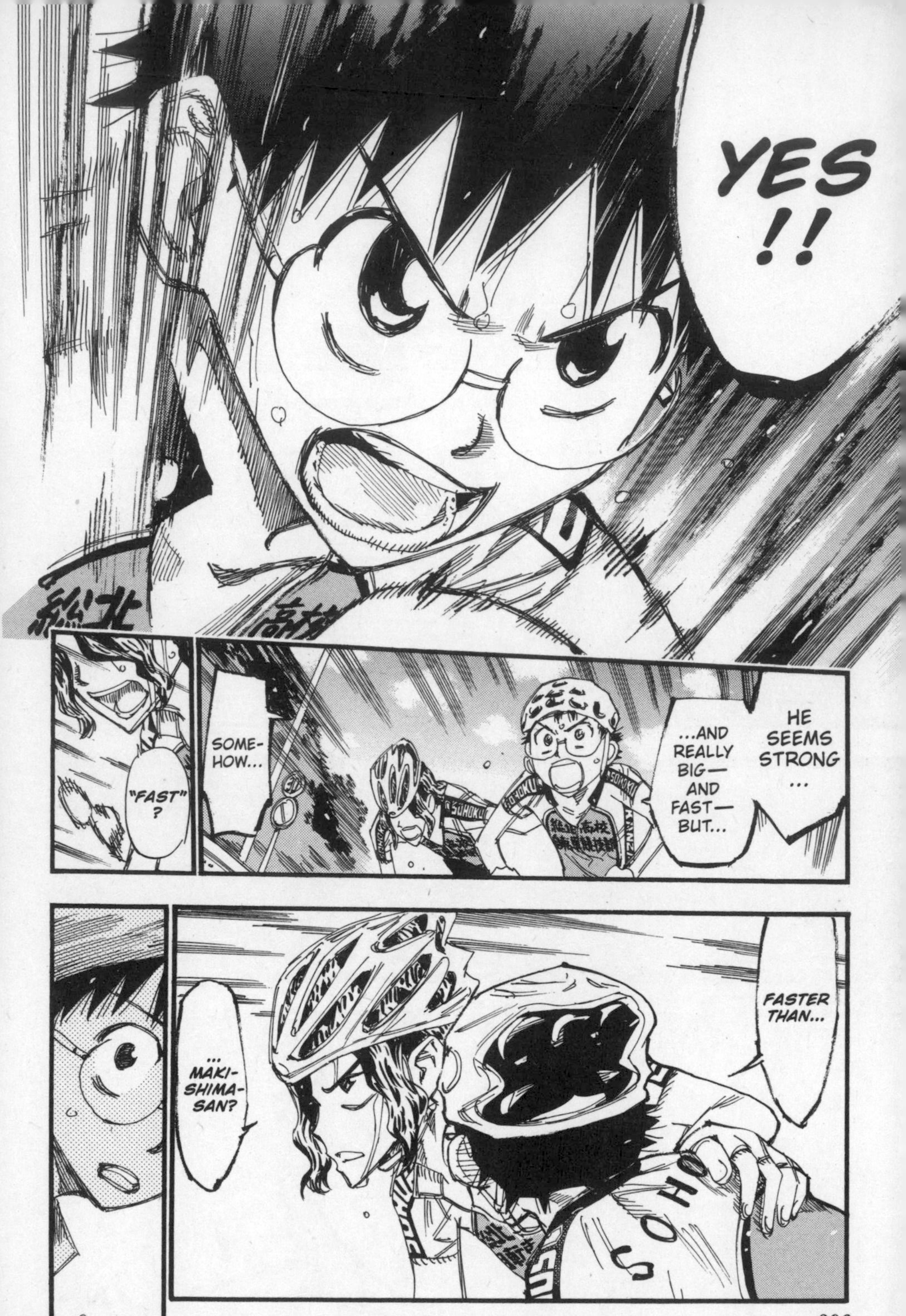
YES!!
HE SEEMS STRONG...
...AND REALLY BIG—AND FAST—BUT...
SOME-HOW...
"FAST"?
FASTER THAN...
...MAKI-SHIMA-SAN?

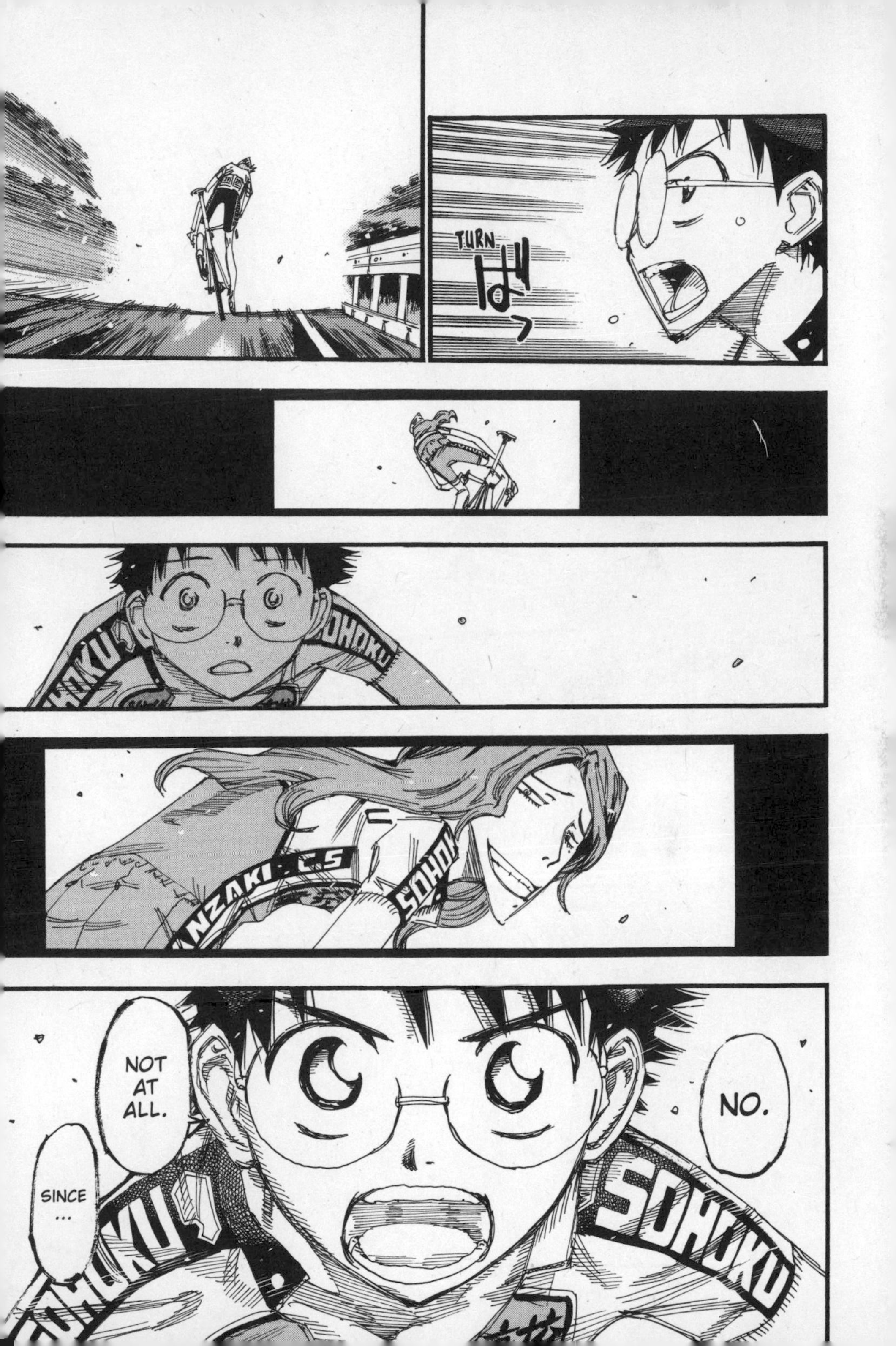
TURN
NO.
NOT AT ALL.
SINCE ...

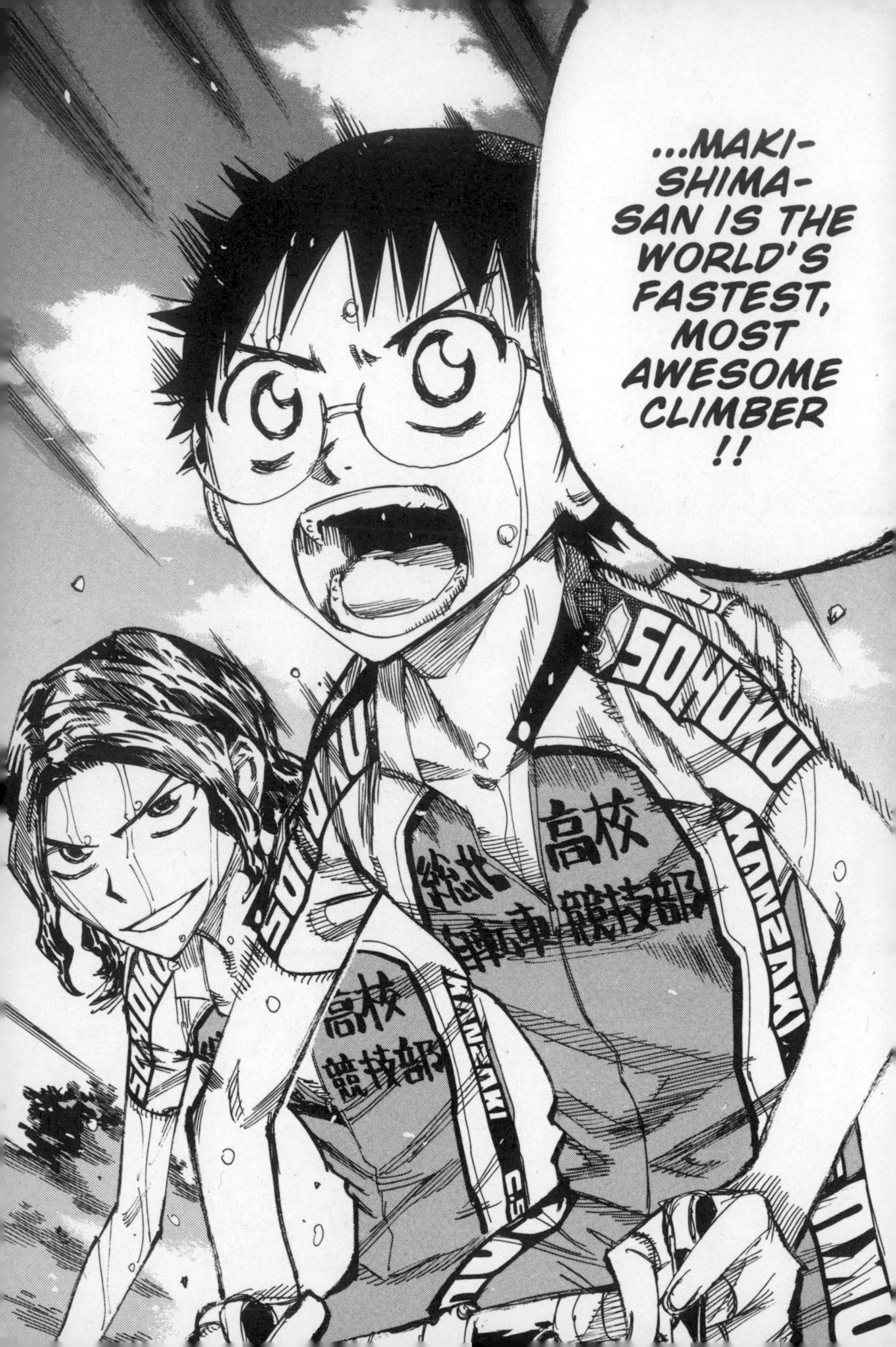
...MAKI-SHIMA-SAN IS THE WORLD'S FASTEST, MOST AWESOME CLIMBER!!
SOHOKU
高校
総北
自転車競技部
KANZAKI

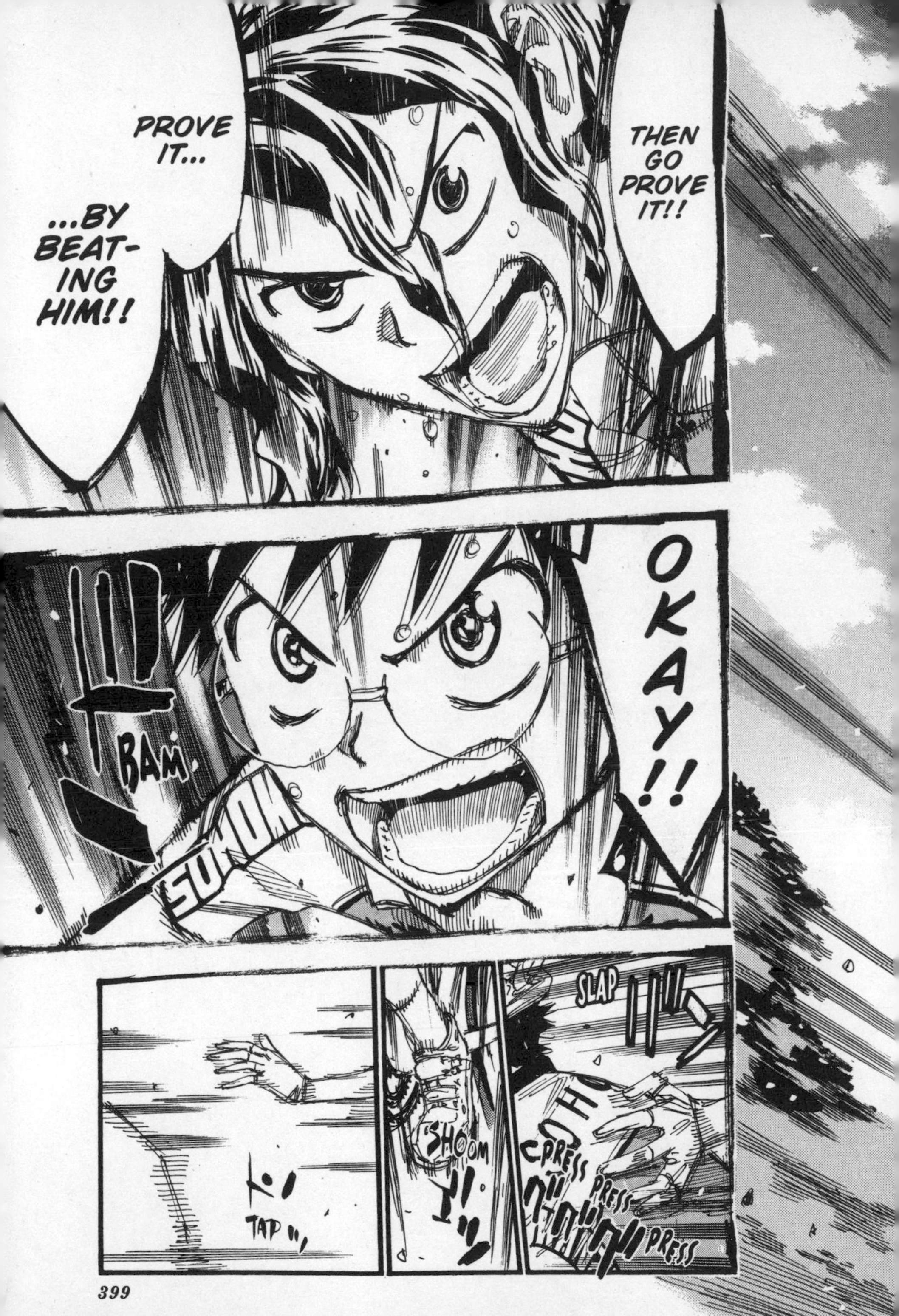
THEN GO PROVE IT!!
PROVE IT...
...BY BEAT-ING HIM!!
OKAY!!
BAM
SLAP
PRESS
PRESS
PRESS
SHOOM
TAP

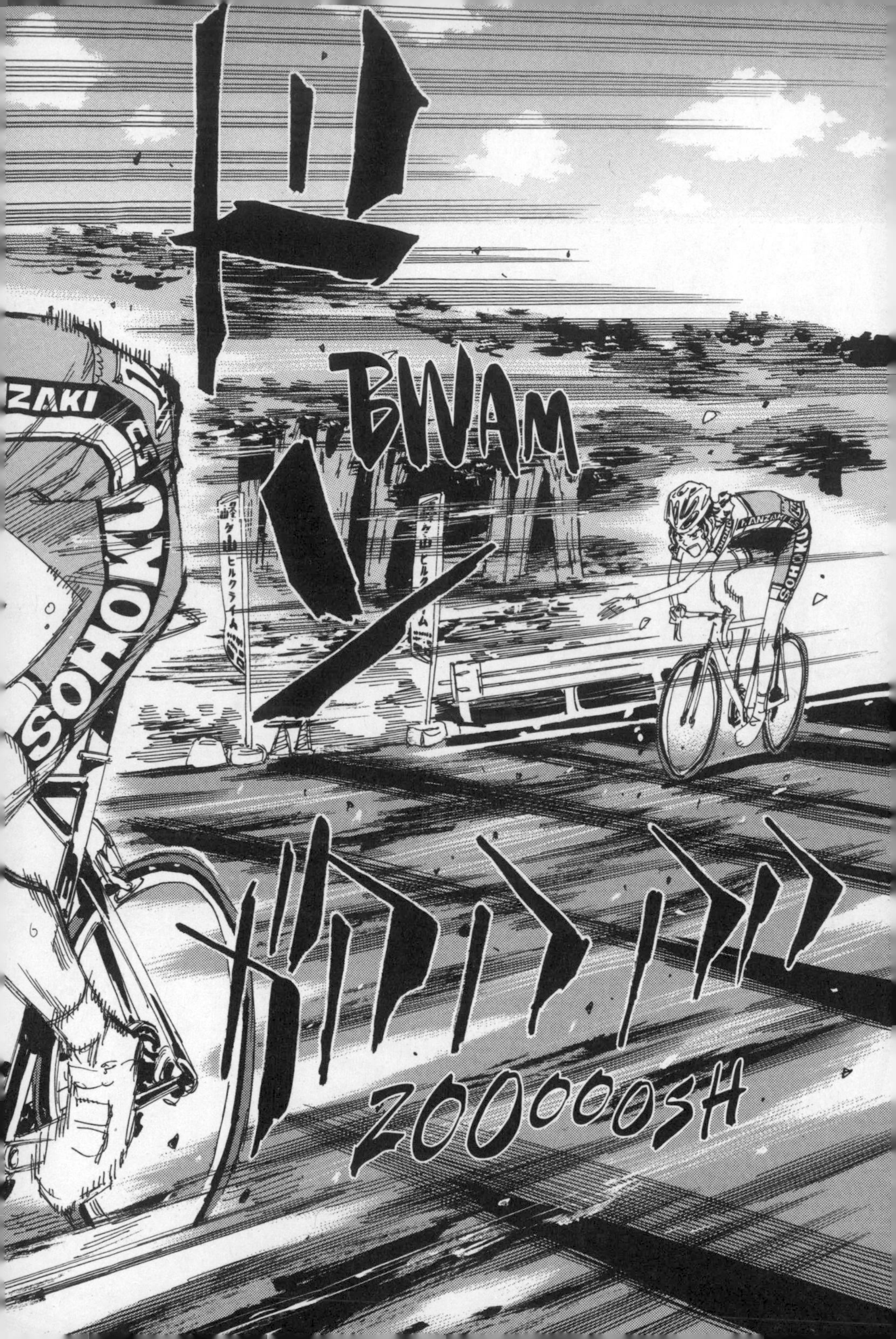
BWAM
ZOOOOOSH

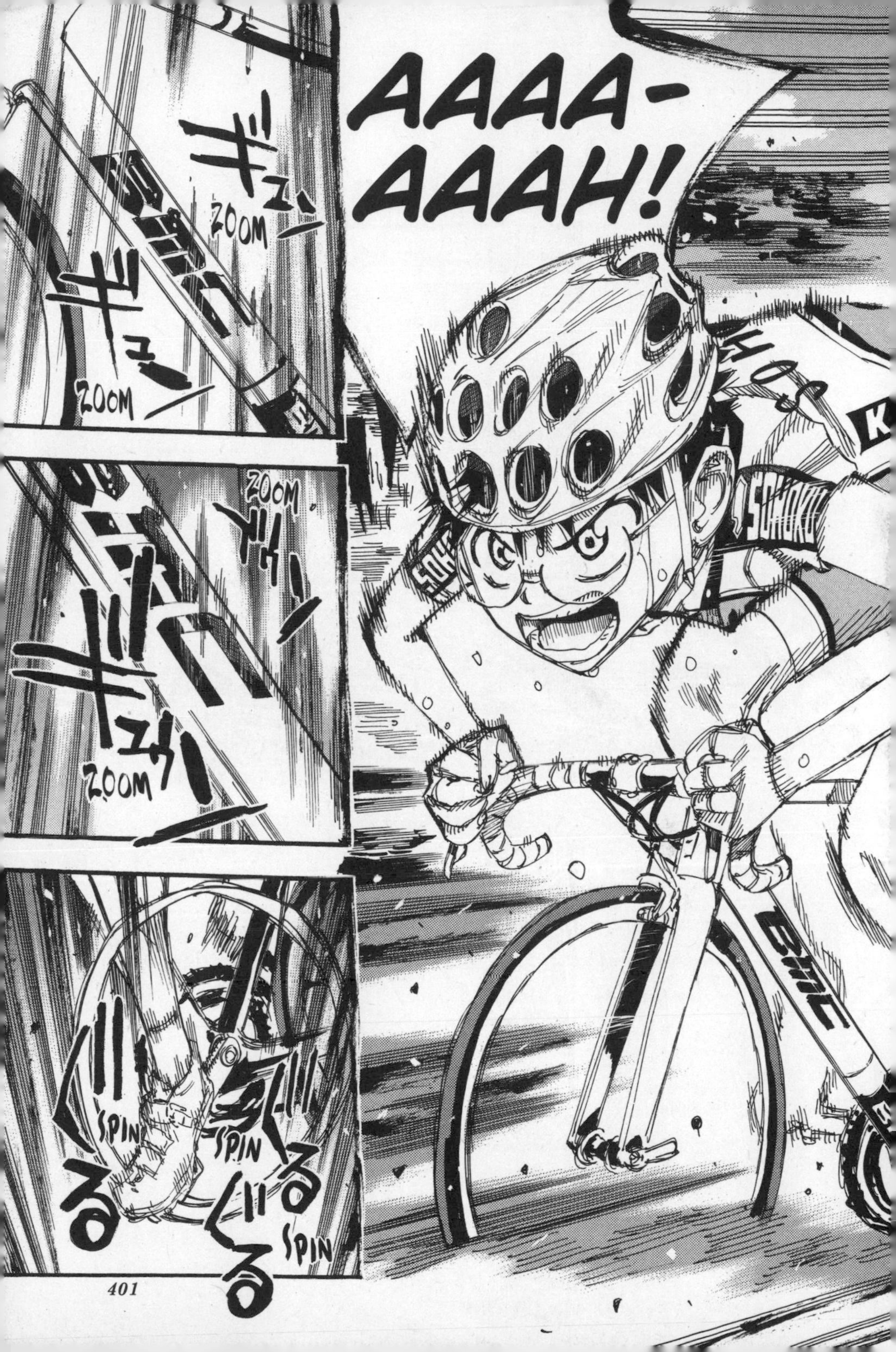
AAAA-AAAAH!
ZOOM
ZOOM
ZOOM
ZOOM
SPIN
SPIN
SPIN

YOWAMUSHI PEDAL 14

WATARU WATANABE

Translation: Caleb D. Cook

Lettering: Lys Blakeslee, Rachel J. Pierce

YOWAMUSHI PEDAL Volume 27, 28
© 2013 Wataru Watanabe
All rights reserved.
First published in Japan in 2013 by Akita Publishing Co., Ltd., Tokyo.
English translation rights arranged with Akita Publishing Co., Ltd. through Tuttle-Mori Agency, Inc., Tokyo.

English translation © 2020 by Yen Press, LLC

Yen Press
150 West 30th Street, 19th Floor
New York, NY 10001

Visit us at yenpress.com
facebook.com/yenpress
twitter.com/yenpress
yenpress.tumblr.com

First Yen Press Edition: April 2020

Yen Press is an imprint of Yen Press, LLC.
The Yen Press name and logo are trademarks of Yen Press, LLC.

Library of Congress Control Number: 2015960124

ISBNs: 978-1-9753-0794-3 (paperback)
       978-1-9753-0795-0 (ebook)

10 9 8 7 6 5 4 3 2 1

WOR

Printed in the United States of America